The Treasury of Precious Instructions: Essential Teachings of the Eight Practice Lineages of Tibet

Volume 12: Shangpa Kagyu
Part 2

The Tsadra Foundation Series

published by Snow Lion, an imprint of Shambhala Publications

Tsadra Foundation is a U.S.-based nonprofit organization that contributes to the ongoing development of wisdom and compassion in Western minds by advancing the combined study and practice of Tibetan Buddhism.

Taking its inspiration from the nineteenth-century nonsectarian Tibetan Buddhist scholar and meditation master Jamgön Kongtrul Lodrö Taye, Tsadra Foundation is named after his hermitage in eastern Tibet, Tsadra Rinchen Drak. The Foundation's various program areas reflect his values of excellence in both scholarship and contemplative practice, and the recognition of their mutual complementarity.

Tsadra Foundation envisions a flourishing community of Western contemplatives and scholar-practitioners who are fully trained in the traditions of Tibetan Buddhism. It is our conviction that, grounded in wisdom and compassion, these individuals will actively enrich the world through their openness and excellence.

This publication is a part of Tsadra Foundation's Translation Program, which aims to make authentic and authoritative texts from the Tibetan traditions available in English. The Foundation is honored to present the work of its fellows and grantees, individuals of confirmed contemplative and intellectual integrity; however, their views do not necessarily reflect those of the Foundation.

Tsadra Foundation is delighted to collaborate with Shambhala Publications in making these important texts available in the English language.

Shangpa Kagyu

The Tradition of Khyungpo Naljor
Part 2

THE TREASURY OF PRECIOUS INSTRUCTIONS:
ESSENTIAL TEACHINGS OF THE EIGHT PRACTICE
LINEAGES OF TIBET
VOLUME 12

Compiled by Jamgön Kongtrul Lodrö Taye

TRANSLATED BY
Sarah Harding

SNOW LION

Snow Lion
An imprint of Shambhala Publications, Inc.
2129 13th Street
Boulder, Colorado 80302
www.shambhala.com

Cover art: Detail from thangka "The Shangpa Kagyu Practice Lineage of Tibetan Buddhism." Collection Eric Colombel. Photo: Rafael Ortet, 2018. © Eric Colombel, New York.

9 8 7 6 5 4 3 2 1

First Edition
Printed in the United States of America

Shambhala Publications makes every effort to print on acid-free, recycled paper. For more information please visit www.shambhala.com.
Snow Lion is distributed worldwide by Penguin Random House, Inc., and its subsidiaries.

LIBRARY OF CONGRESS CATALOGING-IN-PUBLICATION DATA
Names: Kong-sprul Blo-gros-mtha'-yas, 1813–1899, author. | Harding, Sarah, 1951– translator.
Title: Shangpa kagyu. / compiled by Jamgön Kongtrul Lodrö Taye; translated by Sarah Harding.
Description: Boulder: Snow Lion, an imprint of Shambhala Publications, Inc., 2022. | Series: The treasury of precious instructions: essential teachings of the eight practice lineages of Tibet | Includes bibliographical references and index.
Identifiers: LCCN 2021020395 | ISBN 9781611809640 (hardcover, part one)
ISBN 9781645472117 (hardcover, part two)
Subjects: LCSH: Shangs-pa (Sect)—Early works to 1800. | Shangs-pa (Sect)—Rituals—Texts. | Shangs-pa (Sect)—Prayers and devotions. | Spiritual life—Śaṅs-pa (Sect) | Buddhist literature, Tibetan—Translations into English. | Buddhist literature, Sanskrit—Translations into English.
Classification: LCC BQ7680.4 .K65 2022 | DDC 294.3/923—dc23
LC record available at https://lccn.loc.gov/2021020395

Contents

Six-Armed Mahākāla

Foreword

In his vast work *The Treasury of Precious Instructions* (*gDams ngag rin po che'i mdzod*), Jamgön Kongtrul Lodrö Taye, that most eminent of Tibetan Buddhist masters, collected together all the empowerments, instructions, and practices of the eight great chariots of the practice lineages. Not only that, but he himself received the complete transmissions for all the practices, accomplished them including the retreats, and preserved them in his own mind stream. He then passed on the transmissions to his own students and all who requested them.

The Treasury of Precious Instructions exemplifies how Jamgön Kongtrul Lodrö Taye's whole life was dedicated to teaching and spreading the dharma, whether it be sutra or mantra, *kama* or *terma*, old or new translation school, free of sectarian bias. Without his supreme efforts, many traditions of Tibetan Buddhism would have been lost.

The teachings of the Buddha have now spread throughout the Western world, and there is a growing need for major texts to be translated into English so that Western dharma students and scholars have access to these essential teachings. I was, therefore, delighted to hear that having successfully published a translation in ten volumes of Jamgön Kongtrul Lodrö Taye's *Treasury of Knowledge* (*Shes bya kun khyab mdzod*), the Tsadra Foundation has embarked on a second major project, the translation of *The Treasury of Precious Instructions*, and I would like to express my gratitude to them.

May their work be of benefit to countless sentient beings.

His Holiness the Seventeenth Karmapa, Ogyen Trinley Dorje
Bodhgaya
February 21, 2016

Foreword

WITHOUT THE TEACHING and guidance of my guru Tai Situ Rinpoche, I would not have an opportunity to serve this great lineage. The Shangpa lineage was founded by Khyungpo Naljor and based primarily on the teachings of the wisdom ḍākinī Niguma. Khyungpo Naljor traveled to India seven times, studying with one hundred fifty learned and accomplished gurus and bringing the teachings from India back to Tibet. He sought out a teacher who had met Vajradhara face to face and was directed to Niguma, whom he found in the charnel ground of Sosadvīpa.

After an initially "testy" introduction by Niguma, Khyungpo Naljor received many of the empowerments and teachings that became the Shangpa Kagyu lineage practices. Niguma ordered Khyungpo Naljor to restrict her teachings' transmission to a single disciple for seven generations. Since then, the Shangpa Kagyu teachings have spread throughout all the lineages from India to Tibet, then to China, and now globally. Niguma's teachings are practiced by all the different masters and schools of Tibetan Buddhism.

In the sixteenth century, the great master Tāranātha revived the teachings of the Shangpa Kagyu lineage. Later, in the nineteenth century, Jamgön Kongtrul collected and preserved these precious teachings and practices. Then, in the twentieth century, the first Kalu Rinpoche—an incarnation of Jamgön Kongtrul—spread the Shangpa Kagyu teachings and practices around the world.

Many thanks to the Tsadra Foundation for supporting and funding this translation. Much gratitude also to Lama Sarah Harding for her translation of these practice texts and for the many other translations she has done. Lama Sarah was one of the first women to complete the three-year retreat, and her combined translation and practice experience is invaluable here

May Six-Armed Mahākāla protect those doing these practices.

Kyapje Kalu Rinpoche
May 1, 2021

Series Introduction

The *Treasury of Precious Instructions* (*gDams ngag rin po che'i mdzod*) is the fourth of the five great treasuries compiled or composed by Jamgön Kongtrul Lodrö Taye (1813–1900), also known as Karma Ngawang Yönten Gyatso, among many other names. Kongtrul was one of the greatest Buddhist masters of Tibet. His accomplishments were so vast and varied that it is impossible to do them justice here. The reader is referred to an excellent short biography in the introduction to the first translated volume of another of his great works, *The Treasury of Knowledge*, or the lengthy *Autobiography of Jamgön Kongtrul*. Even if his achievements had consisted solely of his literary output represented in these five treasuries, it would be difficult to comprehend his level of scholarship.

Unlike *The Treasury of Knowledge*, which is Kongtrul's own composition, his other four treasuries may be considered anthologies. Kongtrul's stated mission was to collect and preserve without bias the teachings and practices of all the lineages of Tibetan Buddhism, particularly those that were in danger of disappearing. The English publication of *The Treasury of Knowledge* in ten volumes and the forthcoming translations of this *Treasury of Precious Instructions* in some eighteen volumes can attest to the success of his endeavor, perhaps even beyond what he had imagined.

The Treasury of Precious Instructions is, in some ways, the epitome of Kongtrul's intention. He first conceived of the project around 1870, as always in close consultation with his spiritual friend and mentor Jamyang Khyentse Wangpo (1820–1892). The two of them, along with other great masters, such as Chokgyur Dechen Lingpa, Mipam Gyatso, and Ponlop Loter Wangpo, were active in an eclectic trend in which the preservation of the texts of Tibetan Buddhism was paramount.[1] It was with Khyentse's encouragement and collaboration that Kongtrul had created *The Treasury of Knowledge*—his incredible summation of all that was to be known—and compiled the anthologies of *The Treasury of Kagyu Mantra* and *The Treasury of Precious Hidden Teachings*. This next treasury expanded the scope by aiming to collect in one place the most important instructions of *all* the main practice lineages.

Kongtrul employed a scheme for organizing the vast array of teachings that flourished, or floundered, in Tibet during his time into the Eight Great Chariots of the practice lineages (*sgrub brgyud shing rta chen po brgyad*), or eight lineages that are vehicles of attainment. He based this on a much earlier text by Sherap Özer (Skt. Prajñāraśmi, 1518–1584).[2] The structure and contents of that early text indicate that the seeds of the so-called nonsectarian movement (*ris med*) of the nineteenth century in eastern Tibet had already been planted and just needed cultivation. The organizing principle of the scheme was to trace the lineages of the instructions for religious practice that had come into Tibet from India. This came down to eight "charioteers"—individuals who could be identified as the conduits between India and Tibet and who were therefore the sources of the practice lineages, all equally valid in terms of origin and comparable in terms of practice. This scheme of eight practice lineages became a kind of paradigm for the nonsectarian approach championed by Kongtrul and his colleagues.[3]

The Treasury of Precious Instructions implements this scheme in a tangible way by collecting the crucial texts and organizing them around those eight lineages. These may be summarized as follows:

1. The Nyingma tradition derives from the transmissions of Padmasambhava and Vimalamitra during the eighth century, along with the former's illustrious twenty-five disciples (*rje 'bangs nyer lnga*) headed by the sovereign Trisong Detsen.
2. The Kadam tradition derives from Atiśa (982–1054) and his Tibetan disciples headed by Dromtön Gyalwai Jungne (1004–1063).
3. The Sakya tradition, emphasizing the system known as the "Path with Its Result," derives from Virūpa, Ḍombi Heruka, and other mahāsiddhas, and passes through Gayadhara and his Tibetan disciple Drokmi Lotsāwa Śākya Yeshe (992–1072).
4. The Marpa Kagyu tradition derives from the Indian masters Saraha, Tilopa, Nāropa, and Maitrīpa, along with the Tibetan Marpa Chökyi Lodrö (1000?–1081?).
5. The Shangpa Kagyu tradition derives from the Ḍākinī Niguma

and her Tibetan disciple Khyungpo Naljor Tsultrim Gönpo of Shang.

6. Pacification and Severance derive from Pa Dampa Sangye (d. 1117) and his Tibetan successor, Machik Lapkyi Drönma (ca. 1055–1143).
7. The Six-Branch Yoga of the *Kālacakra Tantra* derives from Somanātha and his Tibetan disciple Gyijo Lotsāwa Dawai Özer during the eleventh century and was maintained preeminently through the lineages associated with Zhalu and Jonang.
8. The Approach and Attainment of the Three Vajras derives from the revelations of the deity Vajrayoginī, compiled by the Tibetan master Orgyenpa Rinchen Pal (1230–1309) during his travels in Oḍḍiyāna.

The very structure of *The Treasury* thus stands as a statement of the nonsectarian approach. With all these teachings gathered together and set side by side—and each one authenticated by its identification with a direct lineage traced back to the source of Buddhism (India)—maintaining a sectarian attitude would be next to impossible. Or at least that must have been Kongtrul's hope. In explaining his purpose for the collection, he states:

> Generally speaking, in each of the eight great mainstream lineages of accomplishment there exists such a profound and vast range of authentic sources from the Sutra and Tantra traditions, and such limitless cycles of scriptures and pith instructions, that no one could compile everything.[4]

Nevertheless, he made a good start in *The Treasury of Precious Instructions*, which he kept expanding over the years until at least 1887. The woodblocks for the original printing—carved at Palpung Monastery, where Kongtrul resided in his nearby retreat center—took up ten volumes. An edition of this is currently available in twelve volumes as the Kundeling printing, published in 1971–1972.[5] With the addition of several missing texts, an expanded and altered version was published in eighteen volumes in 1979–1981 by Dilgo Khyentse Rinpoche. Finally, in 1999 the most complete version became available in the edition published by Shechen Monastery, which is the basis for the current translations.[6] The structure of this enhanced edition, of course, still centers on the eight lineages, as follows:

1. Nyingma ("Ancient Tradition"), volumes 1 and 2;
2. Kadampa ("Transmitted Precepts and Instructions Lineage"), volumes 3 and 4;
3. Sakya, or Lamdre ("Path with Its Result"), volumes 5 and 6;
4. Marpa Kagyu ("Precept Lineage of Marpa"), volumes 7 through 10;
5. Shangpa Kagyu ("Precept Lineage of Shang"), volumes 11 and 12;
6. Zhije ("Pacification"), volume 13, and Chöd ("Severance"), volume 14;
7. Jordruk ("Six Yogas [of Kālacakra]"), volume 15; and
8. Dorje Sumgyi Nyendrup ("Approach and Attainment of Three Vajras," also called after its founder "Orgyenpa"), volume 15.

Volumes 16 and 17 are devoted to various other cycles of instruction. Volume 18 mainly consists of the *One Hundred and Eight Teaching Manuals of Jonang*, a prototype and inspiration for Kongtrul's eclectic anthology, and also includes his catalog to the whole *Treasury*.

Translator's Introduction

The Shangpa tradition takes its name from the area where a monastery was established (ca. 1021) by the Tibetan who is considered the founder, the "charioteer," of the order. This was the great adept, or mahāsiddha, Khyungpo Naljor Tsultrim Gönpo (978–1128? or 1050–1140?), whose dates have not yet been satisfactorily resolved.[1] In his *Shangpa Dharma Directory*, Kongtrul states:

> The one carrying the name of Great Shangpa Master, Great Adept Khyungpo Naljor, attended innumerable learned and accomplished gurus of India and Tibet. In particular, in the south and west and all over India he received countless instructions from one hundred and fifty learned and accomplished gurus. Of those, there were thirteen specially exalted gurus, four root gurus, and the incomparable pair of ḍākinīs of timeless awareness. When he had all of their inestimable explanations and dharma practices, he established a seat at Zhangzhong Monastery in Shang in [Tsang] Yeru. Thus he became known by the name Great Lama Shangpa. The dharma cycles taught by him carry the name Shangpa Dharma, and the lineage of those who uphold them is also renowned as the Glorious Shangpa Precept Lineage (Shangpa Kagyu).
>
> What that great adept Khyungpo Naljor received earlier and later in India and Tibet, and what he taught to his disciples—that entirety of innumerable dharma teachings—these days cannot be listed even by name. That guru had six capable spiritual heirs and eighty thousand [disciples who became] spiritual mentors, and more who established the theory and practice and spread the dharma. However, other than a few special vital points

> of the esoteric instructions on practice, we don't see the [whole] precept tradition of the lineage. Only a very rough outline can be gleaned from the great adept Khyungpo's own life story.[2]

That biography and those of his successors seem indeed to be the earliest sources and the bases of all later accounts. We learn that Khyungpo Naljor, "the yogin of the Garuḍa clan," first trained in Bön and Nyingma traditions in Tibet. He is said to have mastered those teachings and even attracted hundreds of disciples. Still not satisfied, he ventured to Nepal and India with loads of gold and studied with many gurus. In particular, he went in search of a teacher who had heard the actual words from the Buddha. He was directed to a certain Niguma, who had met Buddha Vajradhara face to face and would often feast with a host of women in the charnel ground of Sosadvīpa. He went there to meet the ḍākinī in person, or in vision, and after passing the test of some scary experiences and verbal abuse, he received multiple times most of the instructions featured in the Shangpa tradition and wrote them down. Tāranātha writes:

> The great accomplished master Khyungpo Neljor, who was endowed with five culminations, received many Sanskrit texts that were well known throughout the sublime land of India. In particular, in the evening of the fifteenth day of the month of Vaiśākha, as the pale moon rose, Niguma conferred the Great Empowerment of the Illusory Body upon him in an emanated maṇḍala; and at dawn in a dream he received the *Six Doctrines* all at once. Later he received them from her twice in person, so that he actually received them on three occasions.[3]

His other main female guru was Sukhasiddhi, who showed him special kindness, not nearly so fierce as the dark, bone-wearing Niguma. Her story and source texts are given later in this volume. These two became his preeminent gurus and are considered the deep source of the tradition.

Khyungpo Naljor received many spiritual practices and classic text transmissions from other adepts of India, often in duplicate and triplicate form. The practice of Five Tantras all at once, a transmission received primarily from Vajrāsana, figures prominently in his life, as he was able to reach the culmination of each of these important tantras and manifest them in the five chakras of his body. His disciple Mokchokpa even saw him in the company of these deities, and so he earned the epithet Endowed with Five Culminations (*mthar thug lnga ldan*).

In addition, he received many more teachings covering a wide range of topics. Kongtrul reports that as part of his training in India he learned everything in the three areas of exegesis (*bshad pa*), debate (*rtsod pa*), and accomplishment (*sgrub pa*).[4] Unfortunately, only the latter endured: mainly the five cycles from Niguma, Sukhasiddhi, Vajrāsana, Maitrīpa, and Rāhula, along with miscellaneous esoteric instructions.

Due to that specialized concentration on those aspects of Khyungpo Naljor's vast knowledge that did survive, the Shangpa tradition became a practice-makes-perfect lineage. Khyungpo returned to Tibet to disseminate the teachings, establishing his monastic seat at Zhangzhong Dorjeden in the Shang region of western Tsang.[5] He is also said to have founded some one hundred and eight (of course) other monasteries over a three-year period. Clearly, in the early years the Shangpa was an independent tradition with its own lineage and set of teachings. That emphasis on meditation obviated the need to establish monastic colleges (*bshad grwa*) to propagate philosophical studies. Indeed, to this day the emphasis is on retreat facilities (*sgrub grwa*), perhaps more so than in any other tradition. For that and other reasons, those practice centers and the independence of the lineage diminished over time. The Shangpa Kagyu was partly subsumed under other more successful orders, especially the Kagyu, Jonang, and Gelukpa establishments. But it should be noted that in the common moniker Shangpa Kagyu, *Kagyu* literally means "precept (*bka'*) lineage (*brgyud*)" and does not indicate that the Shangpa is somehow a subsect of the Marpa Kagyu, in the same sense that the four great and eight later Kagyu traditions that branched off from Gampopa's disciples are so considered. Nevertheless, the Shangpa establishment has had many close ties and advocates within the Kagyu, particularly the Karma Kagyu, as well as "crossover" lamas who figure prominently in both, such as Jamgön Kongtrul himself.

The Five Golden Dharmas of the Glorious Shangpa (*Shangs pa gser chos lnga*) are at the heart of the tradition. They earned that name because of the enormous amount of gold that Khyungpo Naljor offered to receive them. These will be introduced individually in the following translations. Usually they are diagrammed in the mnemonic device of a living tree:

The roots are Niguma's Six Dharmas (*rtsa ba ni gu chos drug*).
The trunk is Amulet Mahāmudrā (*sdong po phyag chen ga'u ma*).

The branches are the Three Integrations on the Path (*yal kha lam khyer rnam gsum*).
The flowers are the White and Red Khecarīs (*me tog mkha' spyod dkar dmar*).
The fruit is Immortal and Infallible (*'bras bu 'chi med 'chugs med*).

Shangpa Lineages

From the very start, the Shangpa lineage was marked as autonomous and somewhat exclusive on account of Ḍākinī Niguma's command seal that Khyungpo Naljor restrict her teachings to being heard by a single disciple and that it continue in that one-to-one fashion until the seventh generation. This is known as the aural or hearing lineage (*snyan brgyud*). Khyungpo Naljor is reputed to have had hundreds or perhaps thousands of disciples. His six main Tibetan disciples were Meu Tönpa, Yorpo Gyamoche, Ngultön Rinwang, Latöpa Könchok Khar, Zhangom Chöseng, and Mokchokpa Rinchen Tsöndru.[6] Only the last of these received the complete esoteric precepts of Niguma. Mokchokpa founded the monastery of Mokchok, and it was here that the tulku lineage continued to propagate the Shangpa teachings until about 1940.[7] In this sealed lineage, Niguma and Buddha Vajradhara are counted retroactively, creating the magnificent seven as follows:

1. Great Vajradhara
2. Niguma, Ḍākinī of Timeless Awareness
3. Khedrup Khyungpo Naljor (978/1050–1128/1140?)[8]
4. Mokchokpa Rinchen Tsöndru (1110–1170)
5. Öntön Kyergangpa Chökyi Senge (1154/1143–1217)
6. Sangye Nyentön Chökyi Sherap (Rigongpa) (1175–1255)
7. Sangye Tönpa Tsöndru Senge (1207–1278)

These became known as the Seven Jewels of the Glorious Shangpa. Some, such as Lochen Gyurme Dechen (1540–1615), a prominent lineage holder, have wondered what happened to Niguma's own declared teacher Lavapa of the East, or the importance of Atiśa Dipaṃkara in the lineage.[9] And the Sukhasiddhi lineage differs slightly, passing as it does from Vajradhara to the female buddha Nairātmya to Sukhasiddhi to Āryadeva before getting to Khyungpo Naljor.[10] This would make Sangye Tönpa the ninth. Be that as it may, it is he who spread the teachings without restriction in the thirteenth century. "Then," says Kongtrul, "the world of Jambudvīpa and its surrounding lands were filled with his adept disciples."[11] Tāranātha elaborates in the "Supplementary Historical Anecdotes" for *The One Hundred and Eight Teaching Manuals of Jonang*, translated by Gyurme Dorje:

> Drogon [Sangye] Tonpa had an inestimable number of disciples whom he favored with the oral instructions of Pacification, Severance, and those of Jowojé Atiśa, Nāropā, and so forth; and with the oral instructions of Maitrīpā, Rāhula, Vajrāsanapāda, and the others that constitute the sacred doctrines of the Shangpa. Although there were an infinite number who obtained from him a portion of the oral instructions of Nigumā and Sukhasiddhi, there were three on whom he bestowed the maturational empowerments and liberating path along with the ancillaries in their entirety—namely, the master Ayi Sengé, Khedrub Shangton, and Khedrub Zhonu Drub. Although there are an inestimable number of different lineage transmissions that derived from the last two, the symbolic meanings were never differentiated because they are contained in the Ḍākinī [Nigumā's] *Inventory* [*Clarifying the Six Doctrines*]. Since they were without contrived views, they arrived at the summit of all lineages of attainment.[12]

Khedrup Shangtön (1234–1309) founded the Jakchung Pal and the Jakpa Kagyupa. Khedrup Chöje Zhönu Drup (d. 1319) established Nyangme Samding and the Nyangme Samding transmission. These represent two major transmissions, often referred to in shorthand simply as "Jak-Sam" (*'jag bsam*). Jak became famous as the seat of the important Shangpa authors Jakchen Gyaltsen Bum (1261–1334) and his nephew Jakchen Jampa Pal (1310–1391). This last was one of the teachers of Je Tsongkhapa (1357–1419), whence the Shangpa teachings entered the Gelukpa school.[13]

The succession in this long lineage continued from Sangye Tönpa and, beginning with Khedrup Shangtön, became known as the Later Seven Jewels:

1. Khedrup Tsangma Shangtön (1234–1309)
2. Khyungpo Tsultrim Gönpo (fl. 13th century)
3. Jadral Ritrö Rechen Sangye Senge (fl. 14th century)
4. Shangkarwa Rinchen Gyaltsen (1353–1434)
5. Nyame Kunlung Sangye Palzang (1398–1465)

6. Drupchen Namkha Gyaltsen (fl. 14th–15th centuries)
7. Gyagom Lekpa Gyaltsen (fl. 15th–16th centuries)
(And thence to Kunga Drolchok, 1507–1566)

The lineages continued unbroken, and it is said of the succession of Shangpa gurus that it consists exclusively of great adepts. Their stories can be found in the first volume of the eleven-volume *Shangpa Texts* (partially translated in Riggs, *Like an Illusion*), and in brief versions in volume 12 of this *Treasury* (partially translated in Zangpo, *Timeless Rapture*), as well as iterations in many Tibetan histories.

In general, there were twenty-five lineages upholding Niguma's Six Dharmas diverging from these masters, which are known as the long lineages (*ring brgyud*). Twenty-four were consolidated into a single one by Jakchen Jampa Pal and Samdingpa Zhönu Drup. The twenty-fifth is the lineage that was held by the iron-bridge builder, the great adept Tangtong Gyalpo, who received this long lineage from Jangsem Jinpa Zangpo via Muchen Gyaltsen Palzang, a disciple of Tsangma Shangtön. Thus they all came to be subsumed under two transmissions.[14] Tangtong Gyalpo also received profound instructions on the practices in visionary experiences of Ḍākinī Niguma herself. This is known as a short or direct lineage (*nye brgyud*). The lineage that has come down from Tangtong Gyalpo is known as the Iron Bridge tradition (*lcags zam lugs*) or Tang tradition (*thang lugs*) and figures prominently in the Shangpa tradition as a whole.[15]

Similar circumstances were experienced by the great master at the Jonang Monastery, Venerable Kunga Drolchok (1507–1566), who reportedly transmitted the teachings of the twenty-five lineages over one hundred times as well as receiving the direct transmission in visionary encounters with Niguma. In his formulation of one hundred and eight guidebooks of Jonang (*jo nang khrid brgya*), six of them relate directly to the Shangpa Kagyu, while the majority are of Sakya and Kagyu provenance. The name Jonang in this case reflects the setting in which the anthology was eventually composed and its later transmission through Kunga Drolchok's reincarnation Tāranātha and the later Shangpa Kagyu succession. The details are extensively recorded in volume 18 of *The Treasury* and expertly translated by the late Gyurme Dorje as part of this series, so more comment here is not needed. Jonang Tāranātha, and hence his self-proclaimed reincarnation, Jamgön Kongtrul, are direct recipients of this line. Most of the contributions in volumes 11 and 12 are by these two great masters, who displayed a special affinity with the Shangpa teachings.

These, then, are considered the main lineages of the Shangpa Kagyu. Though he is often neglected in the histories, perhaps more needs to be included concerning the prolific Bodong Chokle Namgyal (1376–1451), who also received direct transmission from the two ḍākinīs Niguma and Sukhasiddhi at the age of sixteen. In his *Catalog of The Treasury of Precious Instructions*, Jamgön Kongtrul relates this story and the specific succession that resulted.[16] The texts concerning many of the traditional Shangpa practices can be found in Bodongpa's massive *Compendium of Suchness*.[17]

Two Shangpa Volumes in *The Treasury of Precious Instructions*

The volume translated here, volume 12, is the second of the two volumes containing the teachings and rituals of the Shangpa tradition, doubling the number contained in volume 8 of the original Palpung woodblock and Kundeling editions. Though the texts collected here are exemplary of the Shangpa practices, they still constitute only a fraction. Many more are contained in the eleven volumes edited by Kalu Rinpoche (called *Shangpa Texts* in this book) and in various other collections and miscellaneous texts. Nevertheless, the texts in these two volumes probably represent the most utilized in modern times. This is not necessarily because Kongtrul knew which ones would become popular but simply because they are here in his collection, preserved and accessible.[18]

In his catalog to the original edition of *The Treasury*, Kongtrul specifically mentioned that the Shangpa tradition was one of the precarious ones:

> The continuity of the teaching of Shangpa, Pacification, Approach and Accomplishment of the Three Vajras, and some others are extremely rare and nearly going extinct.

It should be noted that because *The Treasury of Precious Instructions* has gone through several iterations over time, the detailed catalog that Jamgön Kongtrul wrote to describe the logic of its contents no longer applies very well to the Shechen edition translated here. Kongtrul's original plan for each of the eight lineages was to present them in a threefold scheme: source texts, empowerments, and instructions. However, the material has now been divided up over two volumes in a way that is not particularly transparent. So it may be helpful to give a rough overview of the contents of both volumes, which will also serve as a very brief survey of the main Shangpa practice traditions. Individual introductions will appear in each section.

Volume 11

The texts in the first volume focus on the Niguma lineage and major Shangpa tantric deity practices. The first section presents the source texts, such as the Vajra Lines (*rdo rje tshig rkang*) attributed to Niguma, that cover the earliest versions of the Five Golden Dharmas. Some are attributed to Niguma, and in others Khyungpo Naljor takes credit, but in all cases it was he who wrote them down, so deciding whom to credit is somewhat random. The source texts on the practice of the celestial goddesses White and Red Khecarīs are by Atiśa and Lama Rāhula, respectively, and the cryptic esoteric instruction on Immortal Body is attributed to Virūpa. These are followed by two ritual liturgies for the preliminaries and main practices of the Five Golden Dharmas added by Jamgön Kongtrul to facilitate their enactment.

The next section contains the preeminent yidam practice, that of the Five Tantras (*rgyud sde lnga*). Any account of Khyungpo Naljor, such as the one above by Tāranātha, describes him as the one who achieved the culmination of these five important tantras of the new dissemination (*gsar ma*) of Buddhism in Tibet—Cakrasaṃvara, Mahāmāya, Hevajra, Guhyasamāja, and Yamāntaka. These practices involve the full array of deities as they appeared in the separate source tantras. The section also contains three lineage supplications.

The next section covers the Five-Deity Cakrasaṃvara (*bde mchog lha lnga*)—Cakrasaṃvara and Vajravārāhī (counted as one) surrounded by the four ḍākinīs. It follows a similar pattern, presenting the ritual liturgies and descriptions for the practice and empowerment, accompanied by Tāranātha's excellent commentary.

Next is, again, the Principal Deities of the Five Tantras (*rgyud sde lnga gtso bsdus*), but this time the practice involves only the principal deity couples rather than the full complement of deities in each of their mandalas. These two—the Five Tantras' Deities in two versions and the Five-Deity Cakrasaṃvara—together constitute the tantric basis of the Shangpa tradition, and receiving one or both of their empowerments is considered essential for further practice.

The last section, nearly half the book, had nowhere else to go in this new arrangement and so ended up here. This comprises two texts by Losal Tenkyong consisting of "permissions," a type of empowerment, for almost all the Shangpa practices. The ten permissions (*bka' bcu*) in the first text are two for the Five-Deity Cakrasaṃvara (although only one is presented), the Five Tantras' Deities, the important Great Empowerment of Illusory Body, and the individual empowerments for the Six Dharmas. The second text of six subsequent permissions (*bka' phyi ma*) covers the other four Golden Dharmas as well as some lesser-known Shangpa practices.

Volume 12

There are forty texts in this large volume that attempts to include everything else. It begins with Jonang Tāranātha's lengthy classic commentary (*Thang brdal ma*) and its supplement (*Ma mo'i lhan thabs*) expounding the Six Dharmas of Niguma. A short text on Niguma's yogic exercises by Tāranātha is also included.

The next section contains five brief texts comprising some of Tangtong Gyalpo's versions of the Five Golden Dharmas from his *Collection of Essentials* (*gnad yig snying po kun 'dus*): the Six Dharmas, Mahāmudrā, the Three Integrations, and Immortal Body and Mind; as well as guidance in the Shangpa protector Six-Armed Mahākāla.

A section of two texts, Kongtrul's own composition on the practice of all Six Dharmas in a Single Sitting and Tāranātha's manual on Mahāmudrā, represent the twofold approach of method and wisdom, respectively, that is so prevalent in all Kagyu lineages. (Most of the foregoing have been previously translated by me in *Four Tibetan Lineages.*)[19]

The two celestial goddesses, manifestations of Vajrayoginī, are White Khecarī and Red Khecarī. They are practiced together in the first text in this section by Kongtrul. This is followed by Atiśa's well-known praise of White Khecarī, also called simply Vajrayoginī. Then two practices of Consciousness Transference (*'pho ba*) based on the goddesses are authored by Lochen Gyurme Dechen (white) and Rāhulagupta (red).

Ḍākinī Sukhasiddhi's cycle of teachings is presented next. A collection including her history, Indian source text, secret sādhana, and empowerment are the ancient Indian sources. Kongtrul adds the lineage prayer and practice instruction for the Six Dharmas of Sukhasiddhi. Then there are instructions that the lineage-holder Sangye Nyentön received directly from the ḍākinī.

Three lineage supplications for the Six Dharmas of Niguma are next, seemingly out of place. In fact, they were already out of place in the Kundeling printing, as attested by its editor.

The next section presents the important Shangpa practice of Four Deities Combined Practice (*lha bzhi dril grub*). This involves visualizing oneself as Cakrasaṃvara with the Buddha Vajradhara couple above one's head, surrounded by Six-Armed Mahākāla, Vajrayoginī, Avalokiteśvara, and Green Tārā. The practice text and its commentary are by Jamgön Kongtrul.

The next section contains prayers, biographical supplications, and aspirations of lineage holders. The lengthy collection of spiritual songs (*mgur mtsho*) of the Shangpa masters collected by Kongtrul has been given its own section. It is also employed as liturgy, but it stands alone as a collection of great poetry.[20]

The empowerment and torma rituals for the Five Ḍākinīs (*mkha' 'gro sde lnga*) present another important Shangpa practice.

The rest of the volume, some two hundred pages, is taken up by eight texts devoted to the Swift-Acting Awareness Protector, Six-Armed Mahākāla (*phyag drug pa*), and his retinue. All of these texts should require authentic transmission.

Acknowledgments

Kyapje Kalu Rinpoche (1905–1989) was the initial inspiration for rendering Jamgön Kongtrul's *Treasury of Knowledge* into English, and that inspiration is still at work here in *The Treasury of Precious Instructions*. I am most grateful that Rinpoche's aspirations will reach fulfillment through the continual support of Eric Colombel and everyone at Tsadra Foundation. I am also deeply thankful for my fellow translators and all those who have gone before who advance the field and make the work that much easier. It is truly a group effort. In particular, for this volume, it was a tremendous help to check my work against previous drafts of some of the practices for three-year retreats translated by Ngawang Zangpo, who also had access to the comments of Bokar Rinpoche. As usual, Lama Tenpa Gyaltsen helped with difficult passages, though I had only one week with him between pandemics. I would like to thank L. S. Summer for her constant support with Sanskrit and the creation of the index, and her friendship. Many thanks to Nikko Odiseos and the crew at Shambhala Publications, including editors Anna Wolcott Johnson, John Golebiewski, Tucker Foley, and Emily Wichland.

Technical Note

The anthology of Tibetan texts translated here is the twelfth volume (*na*) of the Shechen edition of *The Treasury of Precious Instructions* (*gDams ngag rin po che'i mdzod*). It is the second of two volumes devoted to the Shangpa Kagyu. Page numbers in curly brackets { } throughout the texts indicate the Arabic page numbers of the Shechen edition. (Cross-references found in the endnotes to the texts in this volume refer to these bracketed numbers.) The Kundeling edition was also consulted. Most of these texts are also contained in the *Shangpa Texts*—that is, *Indian Source Texts of the Five Dharma Cycles of Glorious Shangpa* (*dPal ldan shangs pa'i chos skor rnam lnga'i rgya gzhung*), edited by Karma Rangjung Kunkhyap (Kalu Rinpoche), based on the Palpung edition. Generous use was made of this source, as well as texts in the collected works of individual authors, particularly those of Tāranātha. In comparing editions, however, it was not practical to cite every mistake or variance in words, so only the most significant have been mentioned in the endnotes, where variant translations or enhanced explanations of certain passages are provided.

Throughout this book, any text found in square brackets [ ] has been added by the translator. Section headings, however, were occasionally added without brackets, and most of the separate outlines were provided.

With a few exceptions, Tibetan and Sanskrit technical terms have been rendered into English to the best of my ability. However, a given term cannot always be translated in the same way every time it occurs. Wherever similarity in context and meaning permits it, I have tried to maintain consistency in translation.

In the main body of the translations, names of persons, gods, spirits, and places that originated in India have been rendered into Sanskrit. Reconstructed Sanskrit is indicated on first instance and in the endnotes with an asterisk (*). Tibetan names of persons, gods, spirits, and places that originated in Tibet appear in the phonetic system that has been developed for *The Treasury of Precious Instructions* by the translators of Tsadra Foundation. This includes the use of the umlauted ö (as heard in the English *push* and *pull*). A final *e* in Tibetan words is pronounced as *ay* (thus *rinpoche* is pronounced *rin po chay*). In the endnotes and bibliographies, Tibetan words are transliterated according to the extended Wylie system, with the modification that the initial root letter (rather than the first letter) is capitalized in proper names and text titles to help recognition.

In the case of Sanskrit terms and names, the traditional system of transliteration using diacritics, universally accepted in academic circles, has been employed. Every attempt has been made to apply these rules. However, in the case of the mantras, there is so much variation that I have had to rely on rendering them as they appear in the consulted editions based on the Tibetan system of transliteration from Sanskrit to Tibetan, with the exception of universally accepted renditions. The scribes who create the Tibetan texts may be forgiven if their Sanskrit grammar was not perfect, as may I.

If a Tibetan or Sanskrit term has entered common English usage and appears in *Merriam-Webster's Collegiate Dictionary*, then it is treated as an English word.

In the bibliography and endnotes, the various references from classical Indian works in the Kangyur and Tengyur are identified whenever possible according to the numbers in the Tohoku catalog (Toh.) of the Derge edition of these collections: *A Complete Catalogue of the Tibetan Buddhist Canons (bKaḥ-ḥgyur and bsTan-ḥgyur)*, published by Tohoku Imperial University. Citations and references from various Tibetan masters are often located in their respective collected works (*gsung 'bum*) or as autonomous texts that most often may be located in the indispensable digital library at the Buddhist Digital Resource Center (BDRC, formerly TBRC) using their catalog numbers.

The majority of the texts in this volume are liturgical practices, commentaries, rituals, or a combination of these. Wherever the Tibetan is written in metered verse, the translation follows roughly the same line breaks to give a sense of its rhythm. However, it is nearly impossible to replicate in English the repetitive, exact meters of the monosyllabic Tibetan, which lends itself so well to chanting.

In these translations, the term *yogin* refers inclusively to any practitioner, but when it is specifically a male, then *yogi* is used; when specifically a female, then it is *yoginī*. "The mind of awakening" or "awakening mind" translates the Tibetan rendering (*byang chub kyi sems*) of the Sanskrit *bodhicitta*, but when the term refers specifically to the generative fluids, whether actual or visualized, then the euphemistic *bodhicitta* is retained.

Special mention must be made concerning the liturgical texts for conferring empowerment. There are directions to the ritual preceptor, which usually appear in small font in the Tibetan text. These will be flush left. Then there is the actual liturgy that the preceptor is meant to recite aloud as instruction for the benefit of the recipients. These will be indented once. Finally, there are sections that the recipients are meant to chant or repeat after the preceptor, and these will be indented twice and in quotation marks. There are many parts that reference previous liturgy or well-known prayers, indicated only by the first few words and then "et cetera" (*la sogs pa*). Including all of these would make this long book much too long, so I have followed the Tibetan example with "etc." In any case, most of these practices, and particularly the empowerments, require years of study, practice, and permissions, during which such knowledge as would be needed to fill in the blanks (as it were) is gained. At least it should require some effort.

Tāranātha's Commentaries on the Six Dharmas of Niguma

Introduction

Venerable Tāranātha of Jonang was the author of the first three texts in this second volume of Shangpa teachings. These are commentaries and supplements for the practice of the Six Dharmas of Niguma. Tāranātha (1575–1634), also known as Drolwai Gönpo, was a true polymath, the author of countless works on history, grammar, philosophy, epistemology, tantric ritual, and meditation, among other subjects. He figures prominently in many schools and lineages as either protagonist or antagonist. He holds a special place in the Shangpa Kagyu, and it would seem that the Shangpa Kagyu held a special place for him.

Born in Karak into the clan of the great translator Ra Lotsāwa Dorje Drak, Tāranātha, while still a toddler, was declared to be an incarnation of Kunga Drolchok (1507–1566), also an important figure in the Shangpa lineage who is best known for his collection *The One Hundred and Eight Teaching Manuals of Jonang*. At about four years old he was brought to Kunga Drolchok's seat of Cholung Jangtse Monastery, where he was formally recognized and where he studied with Drolchok's disciples Jampa Lhundrup (d.u.), Doring Kunga Gyaltsen (d.u.), and others. At fourteen, he met the Indian adept Buddhaguptanātha, who became one of his main teachers, as well as other Indian adepts, who taught him Sanskrit grammar and led to his translation work. He was officially enthroned as holder of the monastic seat at Jomonang Monastery in 1598. There he became concerned about the continuity and correct interpretation of the special teachings on the *Kālacakra Tantra* that had been retranslated by Dolpopa Sherap Gyaltsen (1292–1361) and had become the central doctrine at Jomonang. Tāranātha set about defending and propagating the views of "extrinsic" or "qualified emptiness" (*gzhan stong*), which he felt held the definitive meaning of the dharma. This eventually led to quite a bit of trouble, including the confiscation by the Gelukpa rulers of his later residence at Takten Dam-chö Ling, which had been completed in 1615.[1] Tāranātha's vast collection of writings had been housed there, but they were suppressed and not reprinted for centuries, until a much later master, Losal Tenkyong, was able to restart the printery and publish his works.[2]

Tāranātha's successors, particularly Kunga Rinchen Gyatso and Yeshe Gyatso, carried on the many lines of teachings that were eventually inherited by Jamgön Kongtrul Lodrö Taye, who considered himself the incarnation of Tāranātha and hence Kunga Drolchok as well. Kongtrul continued the work of collection and preservation begun by Drolchok, and enhanced and commented on much of Tāranātha's work.

This line of Shangpa teachings, known as the Jonang transmission, is highly valued in the tradition, as can be seen by the predominance of texts by or based on Tāranātha in the two Shangpa volumes of *The Treasury of Precious Instructions*. In his autobiography (p. 217), Kongtrul also records granting the transmission of all eighteen volumes of *Tāranātha's Collected Works* in 1885–1886. These transmissions continued from Kongtrul to the present day, where Shangpa lineage holders such as Kyapje Kalu Rinpoche (1905–1989) and his incarnation, yangsi Kalu Rinpoche (b. 1990), carry it forward.

Displaying the Profound Meaning: A Guidebook on the Profound Path of Niguma's Six Dharmas, known for short simply as *Tangdalma*, is Tāranātha's exhaustive commentary on the Six Yogas of Niguma. It is aptly subtitled, in part, *The One Sufficient Reading* as it is here that one finds the most thorough and authoritative descriptions one needs for actual practice in the living tradition of Niguma's Six Dharmas. In Kongtrul's autobiography, he reports that Tāranātha had a visionary experience of Niguma in which she granted him permission to compose *Tangdalma*.[3] This kind of permission is considered the best assurance of a composition's authenticity. The source of the transmission is, of course, the Indian ḍākinī Niguma herself, who by her own account received the teachings from the adept Lavapa of the East. She, in turn, bestowed them on the Tibetan adept Khyungpo Naljor, who wrote them down and brought them back to Tibet. Most of these source texts can be found in volume 11 of *The Treasury*, while some are also in the Peking Tengyur.[4] Liturgies for initiation, meditation, and supplications are also in volume 11. These commentaries ended up in volume 12 when the original volume of Shangpa texts was expanded into the two volumes of the Shechen edition.

Tangdalma is written as a guide for teachers, or perhaps even as a guide for Tāranātha himself, when explaining the complex process of visualization of each of the six main subjects—Fierce Inner Heat (*gtum mo*), Illusory Body (*sgyu lus*), Dream practice (*rmi lam*), Lucid Clarity (*'od gsal*), Transference of Consciousness (*'pho ba*), and practice for the Intermediate State (*bar do*)—each of which has myriad subdivisions. These Six Dharmas, which have a parallel in the six dharmas of Niguma's brother Nāropa and of Sukhasiddhi, are based in the tantras and known as completion-phase practices; the second of the two phases of creation and completion that constitute the essence of tantric practice. They involve meditations and exercises based on the subtle energetic body of channels, chakras, winds, and vital drops in the path of methods, as well as meditations to recognize illusion, or emptiness. As Niguma stated in her *Vajra Lines of the Six Dharmas*, "One's own body is the means, with three channels and four chakras."

The text here is divided into "teaching sessions" (*chos thun*), fifty-six in all, or sixty-seven if one adds some that were left out, according to Tāranātha's own calculations. The number is, of course, flexible and may or may not correspond exactly to what he calls "rounds of visualization" (*dmigs skor*). This method of organizing an exposition, which is incredibly helpful for teachers and students alike and yet is quite rare in Tibetan literature, was also employed in Tāranātha's well-known commentary on the stages of the path, known for short as the *Three Types of Person* (*sKyes bu gsum*).[5] This was based on the prototype of this genre by Atiśa, but has been adopted by the Shangpa lineage as its own basic guidebook. That text contains sixty-four contemplative sessions. Put together, in a mere one hundred and twenty or so sessions, an instructor could guide students through the entire path of Niguma's Six Dharmas. Tāranātha's Shangpa preliminaries text is in volume 3 of *The Treasury*, among the many other gradual path (*lam rim*) and mind training (*blo byong*) texts of the Kadampa tradition.

Because of the length and complexity of the subject matter, Tāranātha's structural outline with corresponding teaching sessions has been extracted and presented first as a reference.

In *A Supplement to the Source Guide on the Profound Path of Niguma's Six Dharmas*, Tāranātha elaborates on some specialized practices associated with the Six Dharmas to fill out *Tangdalma*. There are six parts that seem as if they were originally six separate texts that he may have put together later. The first is instruction on how to practice the Six Dharmas in a Single Sitting, or, literally, on a single seat. Single-sitting instructions (*stan thog gcig ma*) are fairly common as an "easier" way to practice, and in this tradition they are even mentioned in the earliest sources. Jamgön Kongtrul's version based on this and other sources constitutes chapter 9 of this volume, where he elaborates so much that he is forced to make single-sitting instructions for each of the Six Dharmas separately. Tāranātha's instructions here remain comparatively simple.

The second part, called "sealed visualizations," contains eight subjects that one might need to enhance practice. Some are in addition to what was explained in *Tangdalma*, some were purposely left out of that source, and some pertain to solving problems that might come up in practice. These all have an esoteric nature and are therefore "sealed" or restricted.

The last four sections are summaries of four commentaries from important authors in the Shangpa lineage. *Jeweled Light Garland* by Mokchokpa Rinchen Tsöndru (1110–1170) employs the framework of the three bodies—fully ripened, habitual, and mental—pertaining to waking life, dreaming, and the intermediate state respectively. More esoteric instructions are presented in brief. In *Stainless Light Garland of the Path* by Sangye Tönpa Tsöndru Senge (1207–1278), Tāranātha briefly discusses some of the visualizations for the first four of the Six Dharmas, which are considered the main ones. Tāranātha gives the author of *Ocean of Experiential Qualities* also as Sangye Tönpa. This contains instructions for those who feel they just can't practice and so should focus on Illusory Body, Dream, and Lucid Clarity practices. Tāranātha spends considerable time discussing these three texts in terms of whether Niguma's command seal of restricting these teachings to a single individual for seven generations was broken before its time of the seventh "jewel," Sangye Tönpa, apparently to refute some allegations of that nature. Then he lambastes those who mix up or misrepresent texts in the Shangpa tradition, particularly taking aim at the second Dalai Lama, Gendun Gyatso.

Illusory Body in a Single Sitting is mentioned in the original notes by Khyungpo Naljor that record and clarify Niguma's *Vajra Lines of the Six Dharmas*, where it is categorized as being for those of lowest capability. Here Tāranātha mainly covers how to organize the session, rather than any new material on Illusory Body. Though he doesn't gloss a particular text on the subject, he recommends one by Jakpa Gyaltsen Bum (1261–1334) for further information.

Niguma's Yogic Exercises, Root and Commentary, is Tāranātha's explanation of eighteen physical yogic exercises (*'khrul 'khor*) that enhance the completion-phase practices based on the subtle body. The "root" here seems to pertain to the first two verses that are written in that arcane style of many of Niguma's vajra lines, although these have not been specifically located. The antecedents are the brief instructions on the subtle body that are attributed to Niguma, which are in the Peking Tengyur and the *Shangpa Texts*.[6] However, those and others mentioned by Kongtrul in *The Beryl Key* as Niguma's "minor visualizations," fall into his category of teachings that lack a continuous transmission (*lung rgyun*) and sometimes even an extant text.[7] Tāranātha unravels the cryptic verses and lays out a transparent outline of them. As mentioned in a previous translation of the Tengyur texts, they seem to roughly correspond to Tāranātha's fifth through eighteenth yogic exercises in this commentary. The eighteenth, which is subdivided into nine exercises for dispelling specific afflictive emotions, gives rise to the alternate enumeration of twenty-five exercises of Niguma. Tāranātha explains that the original texts attributed to Niguma are very difficult to interpret, and gives this as the reason for the composition, which is also probably why it is Tāranātha's text that is in use to the present day. However, the ancient texts do provide visualizations that accompany the exercises and that are not available here. Although a very helpful illustrated version of Tāranātha's text has been circulated in modern three-year retreats, there is really no way to clearly describe physical motions in words, any more than the forms of kung fu or the āsanas of hatha yoga. The text is simply a reminder of what a teacher must demonstrate in person.

1. *Tangdalma*: Displaying the Profound Meaning

A Guidebook on the Profound Path of Niguma's Six Dharmas, the One Sufficient Reading[1]

Tāranātha

Outline

I. Preliminaries
  A. Common preliminaries
    1. Going for refuge (session 1)
    2. Arousing the mind of awakening (session 2)
  B. Uncommon preliminaries
    1. The purifying *A* of inner space (session 3)
    2. The inner space that dispels sickness and spirits (session 4)
    3. The special inner space of three signs (session 5)
II. Main practice instructions
  A. Naturally blazing bliss-warmth, the path of methods
    1. Preliminary (session 6)
    2. The main practice of inner heat
      a. Eating the food of inner heat (session 7)
        i. Extensive visualization
        ii. Intermediate visualization for eating the food of inner heat
        iii. Brief visualization
      b. Wearing the clothes of inner heat (session 8)
      c. Spreading the seat (session 9)
      d. Riding the wind horse (session 10)
    3. Concluding practice guide
      a. Taking the empowerment of existence (session 11)
      b. Naturally liberating obstructions (session 12)

B. Illusory body, naturally liberated desire and anger
  1. Relying on the friendship of a holy guru
    a. Integrating devotion to the guru (session 13)
    b. Integrating the unreal nature of whatever appears (session 14)
  2. Guidance without interruption by other words for the average
    a. Meditating on one's body as the empty appearance of the deity's form (session 15)
    b. Integrating whatever appears as illusory body (session 16)
  3. Developing meditative absorption in a single sitting for those of the lowest capabilities
    a. Making the six kinds of migrators arise as illusion (session 17)
    b. Integrating sickness and spirits as illusion (session 18)
    c. The sixfold set of qualities that develop
    d. The natural arising of illusion free of attachment
C. Dream, naturally purified double delusion
  1. Recognizing dreams
    a. Instruction on the vital points of the four empowerments of drops if self-recognized (session 19)
    b. Relying on the nine unerring vital points if not recognized
      i. Extensive vital visualization of recognizing without concepts (session 20)
      ii. Short basic visualization (session 21)
      iii. Integration of concepts (session 22)
  2. Refining dreams
    a. Refining the mind through the body (session 23)
    b. Refining the body through the mind (session 24)
    c. Refining through Nairātmya (session 25)
    d. Refining through intentionality (session 26)
  3. Increasing dreams
    a. Increasing whatever is encountered
      i. Increasing subtle and coarse four elements (session 27)
      ii. Increasing subtle and coarse sentient beings (session 28)
    b. Increasing for whatever is to be tamed
      i. Taming with mundane beings (session 29)
      ii. Taming with transcendent beings (session 30)
  4. Emanating in dreams
    a. Emanating whatever is encountered
      i. Emanating as the subtle and coarse four elements (session 31)

3. Concluding practices
   a. General and specific sacred pledges
   b. Removing obstructions, the self-purification of faults and mistakes
   c. Enhancement practices that resolve doubt
   d. Identifying special perceptions
   e. Divisions of daytime and nighttime, experiences and realizations

E. Transference, buddhahood without meditation
1. Transference in the source texts
   a. Transference in the suchness of dharmakāya
   b. Transference in the union with the yidam (session 51)
   c. Transference in the blessings of the guru (session 52)
   d. Transference to the unerring celestial realm
2. Supplementary esoteric instructions
   a. Training (session 53)
   b. Application

F. Intermediate state, the victors' saṃbhogakāya
1. The natural arising of dharmakāya in the lucid clarity of the first intermediate state for the best
2. The natural arising of the victors' saṃbhogakāya for the average (session 54)
3. The natural arising of unrestricted nirmāṇakāya for the lesser (session 55)
4. General unerring vital points (session 56)

III. [Conclusion]
A. The extensive style wherein all the branches are presented in detail
B. The intermediate style that condenses them in general
C. The concise style that leaves no topic incomplete
D. The extremely concise style that condenses the vital points

namo guru

This is the guidebook on the profound path of Niguma's Six Dharmas called *Displaying the Profound Meaning*.

Father guru, I bow to you. I supplicate you. I take refuge in you. Grant your blessings.

Without a notion of separation
between guru and Vajradhara,
I bow at the feet of the guru
and live with our minds as one.

The Three Jewels, lords of the gods, the Buddha, the dharma, and the sangha,
took the guise of a mighty adept whose timeless awareness of melting bliss blazes in a hundred directions,
and whose acclaim fills the three regions without even leaving the dharmakāya,
equally serene in both existence and peace: to you I forever prostrate.

Though profound esoteric instructions are endless,
in these end-times, what will produce
confidence, signs of success, and experience
are the personal teachings of Ḍākinī Niguma.

These dharma cycles of Niguma, Ḍākinī of Timeless Awareness, generally summarize the intent of all Sutra and Tantra. {3} More specifically, they contain the most profound completion-phase practices drawn from the quintessential meaning of the Five Tantras. As is said:

> These tantras are known as the five culminations:
> Hevajra is the culmination of Fierce Inner Heat.
> Cakrasaṃvara is the culmination of karmamudrā.
> Guhyasamāja is the culmination of Illusory Body and Dream.
> Mahāmāya is the culmination of Lucid Clarity
> Vajrabhairava is the culmination of enlightened activity.

Moreover, the profound instructions from the lineage that began with the perfect Buddha, Great Vajradhara, until the present have not dried up, the flow of teachings from its river of blessings has not ebbed, the bridge of adepts in the lineage has not collapsed, the doors of rising experience and realization have not closed, and the dharma masters who hold the sealed precepts of the ḍākinī have not been compromised. This, then, is the indisputable esoteric instruction whose fame pervades everywhere.

She who dwells on the pure stages, who sees the actual face of Buddha Great Vajradhara, and hears his speech—Niguma, Ḍākinī of Timeless Awareness—made this pronouncement:

> In all of India, these dharmas are known only to myself and Master Lavapa. {4} Not only that, no one but you has ever received the entire dharma transmission in a single slumber.[2]

Thus she reassured the mighty adept Khyungpo Naljor, also known as Lotsāwa Tsultrim Gönpo. He was himself of a single essence with the five mandalas of timeless awareness: his body was Guhyasamāja, his speech was Mahāmāya, his mind was Hevajra, his qualities were Cakrasaṃvara, and his awakened activity was Vajrabhairava. That this was so had even been prophesied by the adept Amoghavajra.[3] Khyungpo Naljor is thus also known as Endowed with Five Culminations. That widely renowned person is the translator of this teaching. In contrast to the masters and translators of other doctrines, this one has the saṃbhogakāya ḍākinī of timeless awareness herself [as master] and the nirmāṇakāya great learned adept [Khyungpo Naljor as translator]. Furthermore, for seven generations beginning with Great Vajradhara, the lineage bore the command seal of an aural (or "heard") one-to-one lineage. It was prophesied that after [the seventh generation], this dharma would pervade everywhere over the land. And so it would actually come to pass.

It was Drogön Sangye Tönpa who finally lifted the command seal. He had three senior spiritual sons. The learned adept Zhönu Drup wrote the actual guidance manual and the learned adept Shangtön Tsultrim Gön gave teachings. The learned Venerable Gyaltsen Bum created a guidance manual [based on those], which was presented to the guru himself and verified. Master Nenyingpa, Ayi Senge, and nirmāṇakāya Rinchen Lodrö all came with teachings, which were written down by Serlingpa Tashi Pal. So there were serviceable, edited versions of all the visualizations, such as those of the Six Dharmas. {5} But in general, concerning this dharma system, the most helpful master in committing this aural tradition to writing was the learned and venerable Gyaltsen Bum himself, the single most prolific writer. The standard of authenticity in this tradition is the instructions of the aforementioned three learned adepts. The continuity of those instructions is completely contained in our own present dharma lineage. In addition, there were twenty-four different lineage traditions that diverged from the originals, all of which are also represented here.

At this point, there is no need for me to recount the extensive life stories, given the required reading transmissions for their extensive biographies. Nevertheless, it would be good to mention the appropriate major stories of the Seven Jewels [of the early one-to-one lineage].

The learned great adept Khyungpo Naljor received the spiritual quintessence of one hundred and fifty wise Indian masters, so he retained infinite doctrines of Sutra, Tantra, exegesis, and practice. Only a rough account of how these were taught to others is found in his biography. Of all those teachings, what remains extant these days is the original approach embellished slightly by auxiliary teachings. Thus what is widely known as the Dharma Cycle of Shangpa Kagyu consists of two sections: the dharma cycle produced by the learned adept Khyungpo himself and that which was disseminated later.

The first comprises the dharma cycles of Niguma, Sukhasiddhi, Vajrāsana, Maitrīpa, and Rāhula, along with other miscellaneous instructions. Alternatively, there is a classification into four: the cycle of maturing empowerments, the cycle of the liberating path, the cycle of the supportive scriptural transmissions, and the cycle of the command-guard protectors. Of those, the cycle of the liberating path that derived from Niguma, Ḍākinī of Timeless Awareness, includes what are known as the Five Golden Dharmas or Five Great Guides: {6} the roots are the Six Dharmas, the trunk is Amulet Mahāmudrā, the branches are the Three Integrations, the flowers are the Red and White Celestial Goddesses (Khecarī), and the fruit is the Immortal and Infallible state. Also there are any number of other instructions, such as the seven lesser guides, and so forth.

First, for the Six Dharmas, one should explain the initial preliminaries—the difficulty of finding the freedoms and endowments, death and impermanence, the shortcomings of cyclic existence, karmic cause and effect, the benefits of the Holy Dharma, the abiding nature of the fruition, and so forth—in accordance with the *Stages of Entering the Doctrine*[4] and other sources. Explain [these to the students] in an easily comprehensible style and have them meditate for a bit on these subjects.

The Actual Guidance

I. Preliminaries
A. Common Preliminaries

Teaching Session 1

1. Going for Refuge

The preceptor explains the general long or short style of refuge as appropriate. Regarding the visualization on this occasion, while there is certainly the custom of imparting the fourfold refuge in accordance with the general standard, that is for those who like elaboration. Of course, there is nothing wrong with that. However, our dharma tradition boasts a special profound method—*refuge rolled into one.* This possesses the certain blessings of an unbroken oral transmission, so this continual practice of the lineage masters is what is done. For this, sit on a comfortable seat in a secluded place, assume the standard physical posture, allow the mind to fall naturally, and carefully consider everything about yourself and others.

Think about this: "Why is it that I and all sentient beings throughout space have to experience the unbearable sufferings of cyclic existence without end? Alas, what is to be done?" {7} Now, when there is the need of a refuge that is capable of providing assured protection from all this, it is none other than an authentic holy guru who is the single embodied essence of all sources of refuge and Three Jewels. Therefore, think that no matter what, you must request refuge only from your root guru.

Imagine that everything in the region and building where you are staying is the pure realm. In the space before you, imagine a lion throne with a seat of lotus, sun, and moon, upon which your kind, holy root guru actually appears in real form, radiant and brilliant in an effulgence of light. The guru appears with a smiling countenance, pleased to see you. That guru is the unified epitome of all buddhas, all dharma, all sangha, all actual and lineage gurus, the whole pantheon of peaceful and wrathful deities, and all ḍākinīs and dharma protectors and guardians. Think, "Kind root guru, consider me." Then imagine that all sentient beings of the three realms—led by your actual parents of this life, hostile enemies and obstructors, and the local ground masters—completely surround you in all cardinal and intermediate directions. Imagine that they go for refuge along with you, saying:

> All sentient beings, my mothers, equal to the reaches of space,
> go for refuge in the precious guru, the unified essence of all
> refuges.

Repeat that as much as you can and think, "Until now, I and all sentient beings have lived in fear of the myriad sufferings of cyclic existence. Now, we ask you for refuge. We place our complete trust in you as our unfailing refuge. We have no other hope, no other protector, no other refuge. Please, out of compassion, grant us refuge." Supplicate in this way with constant intense yearning again and again. {8} At the end of the session, foster strong intentional devotion to that guru, the object of your refuge. This causes the guru to fill up with light and then melt and dissolve into you. Imagine that your mind is inseparable from the guru. Rest in equipoise for a while in that state. If there is to be a session break, dedicate the merit to awakening. This is one round of visualization.

Session 2

2. Arousing the Mind of Awakening

First complete taking refuge as it was explained before. Again have [the students] consider themselves and others, the environment and its inhabitants, and the sentient beings that pervade wherever space pervades as follows:

> Why is it? Wherever space pervades is also pervaded by sentient beings, each of whom has been my father, mother, and friend without exception. Not just once, but for innumerable lifetimes they became my parents. The desire they all have is for happiness, yet their experience is only that of suffering. How pitiful! Therefore, I must establish them in true happiness that is free of suffering. Ultimately I need to establish them in the state of perfect buddhahood once their twofold obscurations and habitual patterns are purified. There is no way to do that unless I myself attain buddhahood. And since buddhahood arises from meditating on the meaning of the Holy Dharma, I will now meditate on these profound Six Dharmas, the culmination of the profound path.

Say the following:

All sentient beings, equal to the reaches of space,
must attain the state of an all-knowing perfect buddha.
To that end, I will practice the profound path of Niguma's Six Dharmas.

Repeat those words slowly and with great emphasis while contemplating the meaning. {9} Spend the main part of the session meditating only on that practice repeatedly. At the end of every session, you must dedicate the virtue to awakening. This is the second round of visualization.

B. Uncommon Preliminaries

The Purifying *A* of Inner Space,
the inner space that dispels sickness and spirits,
the special inner space of three signs
this is divided into three headings.

Session 3

1. The Purifying *A* of Inner Space

This is the principal visualization. First repeat the taking of refuge and arousing of the awakening mind as it was explained before, seven times each. Again imagine above your head the complete fourfold seat or whatever seat is suitable, and visualize the actual form of the guru there. In connection with intense feelings of devotion, repeat:

Precious guru, unified essence of all buddhas of the three times:
for the sake of all sentient beings,
I pray to you to pacify all my sickness and spirits,
to purify all my negative acts and obscurations,
and for special meditative absorption to arise in my being.

Supplicate fervently and for a long time. In the end, the guru melts into light and dissolves into you. The description up to this point was for the preliminary practice of guru yoga required in this meditation.

Beyond that, [visualize that as the light] enters the top of your head and dissolves, it refines by way of getting rid of the brain, which has the nature of stupidity. It is said that the cranium becomes like a bone-mansion palace.

What that actually means is that this body that you have regarded as ordinary solid matter, while it retains its same shape above the neck, inside has become not only devoid of flesh, blood, and bone but you imagine even the external skin as a very soft, faint outline like [the skin of] a water bubble, white in color. {10} Within the head is a white, tetrahedral source of phenomena, empty inside, radiant, and clear like a crystal vase. [It stands upside down], with its sharp apex facing downward, touching the juncture of the throat. The broad side with its three vertices faces upward with one vertex level with the eyebrows and the other two vertices at the temples by the right and left ears, just touching the inside of the skin outline. Right in the center of that source of phenomena—not veering at all to the right, left, front, or rear—is a white letter *A* (ཨ) as the embodiment of your unborn, unembellished mind inseparable from the guru. It is radiant and clear, the intrinsic nature of light, and radiates extremely bright white light. It is taught that you should meditate on the height of the opening rim of the source of phenomena as level with the juncture of the "neck" of the *A* letter. In any case, the "head" of the *A* is definitely visualized as being higher than the rim of the source of phenomena.

First clarify that with concentrated effort, but afterward focus lightly on the letter and source of phenomena with your consciousness balanced between concentration and relaxation. After that, quietly recite short *A* twenty-one times. This causes a thick stream of white, radiant, shining elixir to fall from the *A*. In an instant it fills the source of phenomena to the brim and splashes over the opening on all [three] sides, all the time surging to the center of the body. You must imagine that it pushes out the negativities and obscurations accumulated since beginningless cyclic existence, as well as all temporary adverse conditions, sickness, spirits, obstacles, [corruption from] misappropriated funds and sale of images, contraventions and errors in sacred pledge, and so forth. Negative acts and obscurations don't actually have any color, but for the clarity of the visualization and because of the variety of special efficacious interdependent connections, those negativities, obscurations, and such take on a form like liquid smoke or liquid coal. {11} The very heavy streams that cannot flow out of the nine orifices break up—medium streams flow out from underneath the fingernails and toenails, while thin streams flow out from the tips of the hairs and pores. Imagine dark, winding streams exuding from the body. Imagine that at the borders of wherever the radiant and clear elixir reaches, any sickness, spirits, negative acts, and obscurations are unable to remain and are pushed down from above and out to the edges from the middle. All impure physical substances—such as the flesh, blood, and bones—also disperse, as if melted away, vanishing together with the negativities and obscurations, thereby purified. In this way, the inside of the body is washed. Again, the elixir flows out of the roots of your hairs and pores, cleansing the body's exterior. It becomes radiant clear white with just a faint outline of skin, like a polished crystal vase. Imagine that the body is filled with radiant clear elixir or else that it is made out of white rainbow light. The black ooze of sickness, spirits, negativities, and obscurations that passed outside falls far underground. Imagine that it too disappears. After you meditate vigorously with those visualizations, relax for a while to refresh yourself.

The above constitutes a single visualization. The guru yoga done at the start of the session is sufficient in itself—you needn't repeat it within that session. The main visualization should be repeated again and again. So, for example, in one session you could do the visualization a hundred times. Then if you can meditate that way in four to six sessions a day, signs will show quickly in a week or so. As this indicates, the speed with which the signs occur is connected with the degree of effort you put into it—whether best, middling, or least. In terms of contemplating the purification of negative actions and obscurations, {12} it is said that if you meditate on the body as unimpeded like a rainbow, then experiences of clarity will arise and awareness will be lucid. If you meditate on being filled with elixir, the body's vital energy will be excellent. If you meditate on the body as a pure crystal ball, lucid appearances will arise in dreams. This is the third round of visualization.

Session 4

2. The Inner Space That Dispels Sickness and Spirits

There are two parts: dispelling sickness and dispelling spirits. Although they each have many subdivisions of individual minor visualizations, generally they are just applications of the Purifying *A* of Inner Space and should be counted all together as the equivalent of one major visualization.

Now, for something like sicknesses of heat, visualize a white stream of elixir flowing from the *A*. It is soothing both to the touch and in its cooling potency. The stream falls to the site of the heat, whether it is in the torso or elsewhere. Imagine that in that place, a hole opens up and the heat sickness in the form of red ooze is pushed out through that opening. Similarly, for sicknesses of cold, a stream of red elixir with both warming properties of touch and potency falls to the cold sites, whether in the lower body or wherever. Think that all the sickness as white ooze issues forth from those places and passes outside. For sicknesses of the winds, yellow elixir, like ghee, with properties of refined nutrients, descends. Imagine that a blue or black ooze of sickness exudes from all parts of the body, or from the two lower orifices, or wherever a hole opens up. You can also think of the sickness exiting downward like swirling winds or billowing smoke. For sicknesses of the heart, imagine that a hole opens up at the heart level and the sickness leaves from there. All other sicknesses are dealt with following these examples.

Again, after you meditate on the main visualization of the Purifying *A* of Inner Space, imagine that elixir in the form of individual wrathful deities descends from the *A* like a fierce hailstorm. Innumerable hordes of small wrathful figures pack the inside of your body with no space between them. {13} Tongues of flame emanate, blazing downward and in all directions. Then a stream of molten bronze elixir descends. Frightening mantras, pounding weapons, burning mountains, and so forth drive out the bad spirits, who, without the power to remain inside your body, flee in the form of various embodied creatures. Imagine that, once outside, they are killed without any remainder. Wrathful deities needed as antidotes for particular spirits are described below in the section on taming (session 30). Those three emanations—wrathful deities, fire, and molten bronze—cannot be done at the same time, so do them consecutively. This is the fourth round of visualization.

Session 5

3. The Special Inner Space of Three Signs

The best signs of the purification of negativities and obscurations arise as actual phenomena after meditating on the Purifying *A* of Inner Space. Through this meditation alone, your body will become light when rising, consciousness will become clear, your character gentle, and your intellect tamed. Afflictions such as attachment and aggression will diminish; faith, compassion, wisdom, and other qualities will automatically increase. The intermediate signs will be experienced as part of the deluded appearances of waking life, while the lesser signs will arise similarly in clear dreaming: washing, flying in the sky, wearing white clothes, and so forth.

Through your meditation on the Inner Space That Dispels Sickness, the best sign of having expelled the sickness is that you are actually cured. The intermediate sign is to experience, and the least sign is to dream, that you have diarrhea and vomiting, pus and blood being expelled from your body, and so forth. After you meditate on the Inner Space That Dispels Spirits, the best signs of having dispelled the harm done by spirits are that dangers are actually pacified, joy and well-being arise in body and mind, and a positive attitude develops. {14} The intermediate experience and the least dream signs are of vanquishing vile creatures, being victorious over one's enemies, vermin leaving one's body, and so forth. Those three signs are the signs of purifying negativities and obscurations, the signs of dispelling sickness, and the signs of dispelling spirits. Each of those is also divided into three: actual, experiential, and dream signs, a total of nine subdivisions of the signs.

In the beginning, do not hope for those signs to happen; just keep practicing without expectations. When signs do occur, do not become attached, conceited, or inappropriately happy or sad. Think, "Such signs are just the avenues for the appearance of unimpeded interdependent connections. There is no real meaning, it is just illusion." Let go of hopes and fears and settle down. Then obstacles will not arise later and you will travel the path. The appearance of actual signs [of purification] stands on its own. If experiences that arise in the waking state appear clearly, then even a single occurrence may be considered as a sign. It is not so definite for dreams, but if the signs are extremely clear, occur repeatedly, and there is a noticeable change in your mental health when awake, then they can be considered genuine signs. An extensive presentation of signs can be found in the old books. Here, this visualization session does not actually contain a visualization, but the customary way to apply the arising of signs on the path does constitute a visualization. So this is the fifth round of visualization.

II. Main Practice Instructions

There are six parts: Fierce Inner Heat, Illusory Body, Dream, Lucid Clarity, Transference, and Intermediate State. If these are listed with their principal functions, they are (1) the Path of Methods, naturally blazing bliss-warmth; (2) Illusory Body, naturally liberated desire and anger; (3) Dream, naturally purified double delusion; (4) Lucid Clarity, naturally clarified stupidity; (5) Transference, buddhahood without meditation; and (6) Intermediate State, the victors' saṃbhogakāya. {15}

A. Naturally Blazing Bliss-Warmth, the Path of Methods

First, the natural blazing of bliss and warmth on the path of methods has three parts: (1) the preliminary, (2) the main practice, and (3) the concluding practices.

Session 6

1. Preliminary

In general, this is the guide for the main practice, but in terms of Fierce Inner Heat itself, it has its own preliminary called the Inner Space of Fire, the vital point of the body. It is also called the Fireball [or Wildfire] visualization of Inner Heat since it accelerates the generation of heat. In this practice, after you go for refuge and arouse the awakening mind, it is necessary to meditate on guru yoga as the initial preliminary. Therefore, meditate on yourself in the form of the deity, or sometimes it is appropriate to maintain pride as an ordinary person. Meditate as before on the complete fourfold seat above your head, but in this case of Fierce Inner Heat, the lotus in the seat is white rather than multicolored. If you meditate on the actual form of the guru who sits upon it, meditate that the guru is also white in color and radiates white light. If you meditate on the guru as Vajradhara, then definitely meditate on him being white like the autumn moon. On all occasions in the Six Dharmas, the meditation on the guru's actual form was said to be foremost and that has been the practice. But whether you imagine the actual form of the guru or the form of Vajradhara according to your preference, meditate on that very form with a blissful countenance, smiling amiably, and sending you continuous blessings. Then supplicate with intense feeling:

> Precious Guru, unified essence of all buddhas of the three times.
> For the sake of all sentient beings,
> bless me that the special absorption of bliss-warmth arises in my body.
> Bless me that the special absorption of bliss-emptiness arises in my mind.

Outer Visualization

Finally, the guru melts into the essence of elixir, which enters the crown of your head and dissolves. Your ordinary fully ripened karmic body, speech, and mind vanish into thin air like a rainbow, clean and pure. {16}

Transformed as the awakened body, speech, and mind of the awareness deity, you are the Conqueror Vajravārāhī with a red body, slightly menacing with a vajra pointing downward in the right hand and holding a blood-filled skull cup in the left. She is naked, wears the five bone ornaments, a crown of five dry human skulls, and a garland of fifty freshly severed heads. She stands with right leg extended on a supine human corpse with its head bent to the right, upon a lotus and sun seat, abiding in the midst of towering flames. She has three eyes, loosened hair, and so forth—the usual general attributes. In any case, imagine yourself as Vajravārāhī in form and attributes as well as you can, and hold that for a short time.

Inner Visualization

Then, with yourself clearly appearing in that divine form, turn your attention to the inside of the body. The inside of the body has no flesh, blood, bones, or any matter whatsoever; it is utterly empty. The outline of skin is also extremely fine, while the hollow interior is pervaded by red light that is the nature of heat. It is said to be like a red silk tent or a blown-up balloon. One is instructed to meditate on everything, including the roots of the hairs and the pores, as hollow cavities. In any case, your body appears clearly in the form of Vajravārāhī and is utterly empty inside. Imagine sequentially the utter emptiness from the top of the head to the soles of the feet and from the soles of the feet to the top of the head and down to the tips of the fingers and toes of the hands and feet, and focus on that. This is the inner visualization. When applying this as a guide of one's own experience, then it is most excellent to maintain both outer and inner visualizations for several days each.

Wildfire Visualization

For the actual Wildfire visualization,[5] from now on assume the physical vital point called sixfold binding stove.[6] That is, sitting with legs drawn up and crossed like a trellis. Place your right calf inside and the left outside. Cross your arms and with your hands grasp the opposite arms' biceps. {17} Rest your two elbows on your knees and hold your back straight. Maintain the rest of the standard physical vital points, such as the yogic gazes. Then, at the beginning of the session, expel the dead air three times, slowly and at length. Following this, the actual joining of the winds breathing exercise (*rlung sbyor*) is to inhale moderately and then press the upper wind down below the navel. The lower wind is held in its own place, so drawing it upward is unnecessary. The visualization is to imagine a foursquare formation of four fireballs in four places—directly in front of your navel, directly behind it, and at the right and left kidneys. The fireballs are round in shape, red in color, and hot to the touch. Here they are not exactly blazing with flickering tongues of flame, but imagine instead that they are about to ignite like coal before it is fanned or like red-hot burning iron balls. While holding the winds in a gentle breath (*'jam rlung*), rotate the belly once to the right and once to the left. That causes the four fireballs to collide violently and give off reddish sparks like the striking of flints. Imagine the whole inside of the body pervaded by glittering red light, making a rumbling sound in all parts of the body. When that becomes uncomfortable and you think you cannot hold it any longer, expel the breath slowly at first, strongly in the middle, and then finally exhale totally. This is one breath. Hold it as before and meditate on the visualization again. Dedicate the virtue at the end of the session.

Over the course of a few days, train only in applying the visualization for one breath and one right and left rotation of the belly. Gradually, after a few days, add one more right and left rotation each. Though there is no exact minimum number, it is taught that if you can perform twelve right rotations and twelve left rotations, you will gain the capability of fire. {18} In between the sessions, after you do the five-branch training[7] each time, train as much as possible in the yogic exercises of Drilling Stick and Drilling Base.[8] This is the sixth round of visualization.

2. The Main Practice of Fierce Inner Heat

This has four parts: (1) Eating the Food of Inner Heat, (2) Wearing the Clothes of Inner Heat, (3) Spreading the Seat, and (4) Riding the Windhorse.

Session 7

a. Eating the Food of Inner Heat

In this dharma tradition, this is the main visualization for Inner Heat. There are three levels of visualization depending on the differences [in practitioners'] wisdom and interest: (1) extensive, (2) intermediate, and (3) brief.

i. Extensive Visualization

First go for refuge, arouse the awakening mind, and practice guru yoga as before. Again, as before, imagine yourself as the deity with the empty space inside the body. After that, assume the vital points of the body with your legs placed in bodhisattva position, relaxed and wide. Place your palms on your knees with arms straight. The rest of the vital points conform to the standard practices. At the outset of this session, do the ninefold shake-up of dead air: the first three slow and long, the next three strong and short, and the final three twisting the torso while exhaling. These will be clear from looking at the actual practice.

Then clearly imagine your body with three channels, four chakras, and two syllables. Visualize the central channel, avadhūtī, as straight in the dead center of your body, neither to the right nor the left. In terms of front or back, it is slightly closer to the back. It has four characteristics: it is as straight as the trunk of a plantain tree, without kinks, curves, or turns; it is as clear as a sesame oil lamp, shining with its own light; it is as red as lac dye, like the color made from vermillion powder; and it is as thin as a lotus petal, which is extremely fine. The total thickness of its external shape is about that of a medium-sized arrow. It is said that the upper end of that central channel touches the cranial aperture. {19} However, you do not meditate on the actual bone of the cranial aperture but rather that the central channel reaches to a point two finger-widths below the crown of the head, directly below the aperture. Meditate on the lower end four finger-widths below the navel. That central channel is empty inside with both the upper and lower ends cut off. To its right is the red rasanā (Tib. *ro ma*) channel, and to the left the white lalanā (*rkyang ma*) channel. It is taught that these two channels measure about a fourth of the width of the central channel, or about the width of a wheat stalk; however you prefer to meditate on them is the same. Those two extend from the top of the head to four finger-widths below the navel, together with the central channel like three parallel lines. The upper and lower ends of the rasanā and lalanā are slightly longer, with the lower ends extending for four finger-widths and turning up into the lower end of the central channel. The upper ends of those two reach to one thumb-width behind the upper end of the central channel. From that juncture, they join up over the upper end of the central channel and cover it. Then they curve to the front, the rasanā ending in the right nostril and the lalanā in the left nostril.

In this manner, the central channel, rasanā, and lalanā are parallel except at the level of the navel, the level of the heart, the level of the Adam's apple at the throat, and two finger-widths below the upper end of the central channel. In those four places there are channel chakras (wheels) that are round at the hub like an empty ring. The rasanā, lalanā, and central channel are like a central axis, with [the channel chakras] wrapped around them like a belt. The hollow tubes of the channel "petals" fan out from that hub like the spokes of a parasol. The emanation chakra at the navel has sixty-four petals that appear like the spokes of an upside-down parasol. {20} The dharma chakra at the heart has eight petals exactly like the spokes of a parasol. The enjoyment chakra at the throat has sixteen petals like a raised parasol. The great-bliss chakra at the head has thirty-two petals like the spokes of a parasol. In all four chakras there is no separation of the outer rim and inner rim, and whatever the number [of spokes], they all touch the perimeter [of the central channel]. Meditate on them as red in color and glowing with red light like molten metal. Inside the central channel at the upper end is an upside-down white syllable *haṃ*. It has the nature of a vital drop, feels blissful and cool, and is about to melt. Inside the lower end of the central channel at the place where the three channels converge, there is a red upright syllable *raṃ*. It has the nature of fire and is extremely hot. Four finger-widths directly below the lower end of the central channel, near the anus, there lies a blue semicircular wind mandala. It is the nature of movement and functions as a seat, with its straight side facing forward. Meditate on all that.

Once you have clarified that basic visualization, slowly exhale the dead air one time. Then when the upper wind arises, inhale and press it down in a manner that leaves it below the navel. At the same time, draw up the lower wind, holding the joined winds at the navel. If you think it is rather uncomfortable and you are about to expel it, inhale as many small gulps of air as you can without letting out any of the air held previously. Push and press [your belly] to the right, left, and center in the area of the navel and hold the air as long as you can. When it makes you feel uncomfortable again, first let it out gently, then strongly, and finally empty it out. Train with those [breathing exercises] immediately afterward by inhaling and meditating as before. Until you become accustomed to this, {21} you can rest after four, eight, twelve, sixteen, twenty, twenty-four, twenty-eight, or thirty such breaths. It is inappropriate to stop whenever you want.

In the visualization, the air enters through the nose, travels down the rasanā and lalanā, and arrives at the junction of the three channels below the navel. By contracting the lower wind, a very fine blue wind from the wind mandala at the anus rises like a piercing spear and enters the lower end of the central channel. The three winds of the rasanā, lalanā, and the downward-clearing wind gather together and fan the *raṃ* syllable. This ignites the timeless awareness of inner heat, which blazes up from the *raṃ*. It burns like a candle, with a very sharp, fine point, like a red needle—fine, clear, and bright. It grows longer and longer. After taking a few breaths, imagine that it stays touching the *haṃ* in the head. Then gradually the *haṃ* melts and from it the stream of bodhicitta falls like a white silken thread stretching out. Imagine that it gets longer and longer until it dissolves into the *raṃ* at the navel.

In general, there are three kinds of visualizations for Fierce Inner Heat: visualizing only fire, visualizing vital drops, and visualizing blazing and dripping. Of those, this is the latter. There are also various styles such as "escape-and-chase," "brushing tangled hair," "half-pervading," and so forth. This constitutes the middle one. Both the blazing and the dripping in the middle of the central channel are said to be uninterrupted flows. However, given the basic context of the interior middle of the central channel, it is taught that you should meditate on the fire blazing in the anterior side and the bodhicitta falling in the posterior side within it. Wherever the firelight of blazing inner heat reaches, it creates the rumbling sound of heat inside the body. When the strand of whitish light of descending bodhicitta appears, think that the whole body is filled with bliss. {22} Alternate those two visualizations in your mind. Dedicate the virtue to awakening after each session. This extensive visualization is the seventh round.

For those of duller capabilities to get a taste of these meditations, it is effective to practice each one of these separately: the three channels, the four chakras, the syllables, joining the winds, and blazing and dripping.

ii. Intermediate Visualization for Eating the Food of Inner Heat

Dispense with the part about the four channel chakras along with their belt-like wraps around the center and just meditate on the rest as described above.

iii. Brief Visualization

As well as [what was eliminated in the middling visualization], also disregard the rasanā and lalanā channels. The difference here is that the two winds inhaled through the nose descend like spears cast to the right and left of the central channel and land six or eight finger-widths below the navel. When the lower wind is drawn up and meets these winds, it is as if they are struck and turned back up, thereby causing all the winds to enter the lower end of the central channel. You need to imagine that they activate the *raṃ*. The rest is the same.

Thus both the intermediate and brief visualizations are really contained within the extensive visualization and there is no need to treat them separately, so [all three] are included in the seventh round of visualization. The reason for that is that once the disciple has received all three from the guru, they only need to meditate on whichever one suits their own interests. But even though it is one round of visualization, it is fine to treat them as separate teaching sessions when explaining them.

Here, the classic guidebooks, such as the one created by the learned Venerable Gyaltsen Bum,[9] explain that during the preliminary practice of the Empty Space of Fire, one sits in the cross-legged vajra position, while during the main practice of Eating the Food of Inner Heat, one uses the position of the sixfold binding stove. {23} But with regard to the guru's teachings, these esoteric instructions have been explained out of order. We must only rely on the practice as it was described above. Eating the Food of Inner Heat is the main practice of Fierce Inner Heat. The source text states:

> One's own body is the means, with three channels and four chakras.
> The *A* blazes and *haṃ* drips, adorning the instances with four ecstasies.[10]

This is really the intended meaning. Meditation on the syllable *raṃ* is basically the meaning of meditation on the navel's short *A*. Although there is no actual meditation on the four chakras in the intermediate and brief visualizations, since there is the meditation on the completely perfect central channel, and since that very central channel is the core of the four chakras, they are in fact included [in the shorter visualizations].

Session 8

b. Wearing the Clothes of Inner Heat

This is to be done by someone familiar with the main visualization of Eating the Food of Inner Heat. For the outer visualization, do not engage in the idea of cold. Instead, meditate on your dwelling place as the nature of vajras or as if the ground and walls are molten iron, rumbling with the sounds of burning. Think of yourself in the deity's form, adorned with the five symbolic ornaments and wearing clothes of tiger and human skin. Imagine everything ablaze with lapping tongues of fire. For the inner visualization, imagine that a fire blazing from the *raṃ* four finger-widths below the navel fills the entire inside of the body. The vital physical posture is to sit with the knees drawn up. Although it is explained that the two hands encircle the knees, causing the breath to enter the interstices of the flesh, it is an arcane esoteric instruction. Rather, cross the hands inside, with the right palm covering the hollow of the left kidney and the left palm covering the hollow of the right kidney.[11] The knees encircle and press [the arms] from the outside. The vital point of the winds is to take two or three small breaths each time, in keeping with your physical strength. Between sessions, apply yourself to the yogic exercises of Drilling Stick and Drilling Base. This will produce warmth immediately. If you perspire, wear light clothing and wipe down your whole body. {24} If you have not meditated on the main practice of Eating the Food of Inner Heat, but you have practiced the Inner Space of Fire for a long time, it is suitable to do this meditation. This is the eighth round of visualization.

Session 9

c. Spreading the Seat

The outer visualization is the same as in Wearing the Clothes of Inner Heat except that in addition you meditate on a burning iron seat with the lotus and sun mandalas blazing and rumbling with tongues of flame while you sit there. For the inner visualization, turn your attention to an intense light from the red *raṃ* at the navel level. The vital point of the breath is to continually hold the gentle breath. If that is done during the day and in the evening, then when it is time to sleep, the best position is the cross-legged vajra posture, the middling is sitting with the legs drawn up, and the least is to raise [your head] with a pillow and lie on your right side, drawing the legs up to the chest, thus creating three "folds." Fall asleep while focusing on the *raṃ* at the navel. The purpose of this is that meditation on inner heat leads to the recognition of the lucid clarity of sleep. This way the continuity of warmth from daytime meditation will not be dissipated at night. This is certain to show results if the meditation is done after some training with either the Inner Space of Fire or Eating the Food of Inner Heat. This is the ninth round of visualization.

Session 10

d. Riding the Wind Horse

Someone who has meditated for a long time in the main visualization and the breathing exercises will have experienced the appropriate signs and qualities, having, as is said, "a gait equal to the supreme steed." Now, if you are a beginner in wind-training who has just taken up definite practice for one or two months were to meditate [on these practices], you would avoid disturbances of the channels and winds and compromised health when traveling or staying on the road. You would gain the benefits of physical training just by going or staying in itself. Furthermore, before setting out on the path, you should practice twenty-one rounds of breathing while doing the main visualization. Meditation in mere nonthought will also work. {25} Mainly, when it's time to go, cross your arms over your chest and hold gentle breathing. Visualize that two light-green winged wind goddesses pick you up by the armpits and carry you wherever you wish. In this case, the so-called round of breathing was explained before as taking four-times-four breaths. In a set of twenty-one, there are eighty-four breath [retentions]. This concerns beginners who have not gained proficiency in vase breathing. Those who can hold the breath for a long time do not need to do so many. Although it is not clear in the guidebooks, on these occasions it is not enough to merely cross the arms over the chest, holding the biceps. You must put your fists in your armpits when you cross your arms and then meditate that the wind goddesses lift you up. That is how it was taught by my root guru, the embodiment of all buddhas. This is the tenth round of visualization.

3. Concluding Practice Guide

This has two parts: taking the Empowerment of Existence and Naturally Liberating Obstructions.

Session 11

a. Taking the Empowerment of Existence

From the time you have received these esoteric instructions, at the conclusion of a meditation on Fierce Inner Heat, you must definitely do this meditation once to start a session break.

Upon a lion throne, white lotus, sun, and moon seat above your head, visualize the actual root guru or Vajradhara. Of course, either way is appropriate, but it is believed that meditating on the root guru him- or herself is more profound. In any case, you know that this white form radiating light is the union of all refuges. Offer the traditional sense offerings such as offering water and flowers, magnificent mansions and thrones, clothes, a treasure of jewels, wish-fulfilling trees, bountiful cows, the seven royal possessions, the eight goddesses of auspiciousness, and so on—in short, all the finest offerings from all times and directions. {26} This is the outer offering. Then offer the pledge substances, such as the five meats and five elixirs, consecrated as the elixir of timeless awareness. This is the inner offering. The presentation of a bliss-inducing consort of [an appropriate] family is the secret offering. Knowing that all of that is like illusion and dream is the offering of suchness. After you present these four offerings completely, say these words:

> Precious guru, unified essence of all buddhas of the three times:
> Outwardly I offer flowers and incense;
> inwardly, five meats and five elixirs;
> secretly, the timeless awareness of bliss-emptiness;
> and most secretly, the sublime offering of suchness.
> Please accept and confer the complete four empowerments.

Through your fervent supplication, a bright white bliss-inducing stream of awareness elixir rushes down from the guru's body. It enters through the top of your head and fills your body above the eyebrows. You receive the vase empowerment, and it bestows the spiritual powers of awakened body. Again the stream of elixir fills your body above the throat. You receive the secret empowerment, and it bestows the spiritual powers of awakened speech. Again the stream of elixir fills your body above the heart. You receive the wisdom-awareness empowerment, and it bestows the spiritual powers of awakened mind. Again the stream of elixir flows past the navel and so forth, filling the whole body to the soles of the feet. You receive the fourth empowerment, and it bestows all the spiritual powers of the awakened body, speech, and mind. The guru also fills up with light and melts, dissolving into you. The guru's awakened body, speech, and mind blend inseparably as one with your own body, speech, and mind. Settle in equipoise. After that, dedicate the virtue and begin the session break.

Before you receive this visualization from the guru, there is no issue. {27} But once you receive it, then it is required in this system of instructions for all kinds of Fierce Inner Heat visualizations to definitely meditate once in this way at the end of each session, since it has become like the concluding rite of the visualization and is included in the guides for concluding practices. In general, there is also a custom of meditating on this separately, not conjoined with any other visualization. Everything of significance is included in the vital point of taking the four empowerments from the guru's form, and since it is not polluted by being mixed with any elaborations, the potency of its blessings is tremendous. If you occasionally concentrate just on this practice for three, five, seven, or more days, it will become an unsurpassable enhancement for whatever other meditation you do. The reason that it is absolutely necessary to meditate on this at the end of practicing Inner Heat is that it stabilizes the meditative experiences of bliss and warmth from meditation on the main practice of Fierce Inner Heat; it brings down the winds stuck in the upper body; it heals the physical constituents that were harmed in various ways from exerting too much effort and allows you to extract the nutritious essence of meditative absorption; it guards against obstacles such as contamination in the session breaks; and, most of all, it generates timeless awareness by stabilizing the blessings. This is the eleventh round of visualization.

Session 12

b. Naturally Liberating Obstructions

In general, you should learn the details of removing obstructions from other sources. Just two topics will be covered in the course of this guide: the usual problems that occur while meditating on inner heat are the winds being stuck in the upper body, and the obstructions of *kunda* (generative fluid) below. There are some people who have both of these problems, but most will have one or the other. It is rare that other kinds of obstructions occur outside of a few individual cases.

Dispelling the Obstructions of the Upper Body

During meditation on Fierce Inner Heat in the path of methods, if there is pain in the upper torso, shooting pains in the head, or feeling mentally upset, [apply the following visualization]. {28} After practicing the preliminaries, imagine your own body as utterly empty. First do one or two sets of breathing, then imagine that there is a group of three round openings in the affected area, like a three-eyed gemstone. Make two fists and extend the arms in front, then with the back of the fists, strike above the breasts, and strike the ribs with the upper arms. At the same time, forcefully shout a short "*ha*." Think that the pain leaves through the holes like smoke or like a windstorm, billowing out and moving far away. Your body inside becomes utterly empty. If the entire body hurts, the special meditation is to imagine it as a sieve. If you cannot determine exactly which part of the body is in pain, and the mind is upset, then it is probably the function of wind at the heart. For that it is said to be good to meditate on a hole at the heart's white-black juncture (i.e., center of the chest). This is the twelfth round of visualization.

Dispelling the Obstructions of Kunda in the Lower Body

The best method is to dispel obstructions with an attitude that is free of denying or affirming. The middle method is to dispel them through empowerment conferrals and communal feasts. The least is to dispel them through visualizations and yogic exercises. So it is taught. It is further said that if excessive attachment and habitual clinging has caused the problems, they are dispelled by being free of denying or affirming. If caused by contamination and broken pledges, they can be dispelled by empowerment conferrals and communal feasts. If caused by emissions, they can be dispelled through visualizations and yogic exercises. Here, there is the option of applying the visualization of the sealed command to guard against emissions. However, since it is a sealed command, don't explain it in a large assembly; it is sufficient to mention it on the side.

This can be considered a separate session or not, as you like. But if that visualization is given to a few important disciples as an enhancement, then it would be considered the thirteenth round of visualization. {29}

In the usual sequence, there are seven visualizations related to Fierce Inner Heat that are described in the source texts.[12] Although not actually attested in the root verses, [there is a further] teaching to arouse or enhance bliss-warmth with the special Fierce Inner Heat of the Guru's Blessing. With that preamble, the Fierce Inner Heat of the Guru's Blessing should be taught on this occasion. However, the visualization for that must be learned elsewhere.

All of the preceding descriptions have presented thoroughly the Fierce Inner Heat that employs one's own body as the method. As a supplement to those, it is very important to implement the yogic exercises from the esoteric instructions of the source guides. Concerning the practices of Fierce Inner Heat based on another's body, a wisdom consort, there are pointed, profound esoteric instructions. But for the time being, we set them aside without comment. The learned and accomplished Zhönu Drup said:

> This glorious Shangpa Kagyu must emulate the life stories of the Indian Vajrāsana[13] and the Tibetan Sangye Langripa.[14] We are holders of the lineage of meditation in purity. We are not holders of the lineage of wanton behavior.[15]

B. Illusory Body, Naturally Liberated Desire and Anger

This instruction has three parts: (1) Relying on the Friendship of a Holy Guru for those of the highest capabilities, (2) Guidance without Interruption by Other Words for the average, and (3) Developing Meditative Absorption in a Single Sitting for the lowest.

1. Relying on the Friendship of a Holy Guru

This has two parts: (1) Integrating Devotion to the Guru and (2) Integrating the Unreal Nature of Whatever Appears.

Session 13

a. Integrating Devotion to the Guru

This section for those of the highest capabilities contains one major visualization for Illusory Body. In general, this is the foundation of all visualizations in the Five Golden Dharmas, not just for Illusory Body. So in this case as well, you must first complete going for refuge and arousing the awakening mind. Whether or not you meditate on Purifying Inner Space depends on your experience. {30} Then begin an investigation of everything pertaining to self and other.

"How is it? Generally there is no chance that anything composite is permanent. Specifically, all sentient beings of the six types of migrators do not transcend death. Furthermore, we will die soon, our time is uncertain, and nothing but the Holy Dharma will be of service at that time. From now on, we will have absolutely no need of food, clothes, possessions, influence, power, good or bad reputation, defeating enemies, protecting friends, and so on. Nothing at all will help. From now on, just happily let go, whatever happens." In this way, contemplate the unpredictability of death and the absence of necessities; train with intense yearning and then rest for a while in that.

Then visualize yourself instantly as the yidam deity. Regarding that, since Niguma's Six Dharmas are the intent of all tantra classes, it is appropriate to meditate on your special deity, whatever it is. Among those, it is certainly fine to meditate on whichever one of the principal deities in the Five Tantras' mandalas that you find agreeable, since it contains the quintessence of the meaning of all five tantras. The practice of the lineage since the time of the incomparable Rinchen Tsöndru[16] has been to meditate on Coemergent Cakrasaṃvara. Thus it is the succession endowed with the continuity of blessings. Therefore, meditate that you instantly become Coemergent Cakrasaṃvara, blue, with one face, embracing Vajravārāhī with two hands holding vajra and bell. He stands with left leg bent, pressing on black Bhairava, and right leg straight, pressing on red Kālarātri. Wrapped in a tiger-skin skirt, he is adorned with a crown of dry skulls, a garland of wet heads, the six bone ornaments, the crescent moon and crossed vajra in his hair topknot, and so forth. He is in union with red Vajravārāhī, who holds a flaying knife and skull cup. {31} They stand in the midst of a blazing bonfire.

At first, concentrate and visualize clearly. Then focus lightly on the deities' forms and just empty appearance, like an illusion. Let awareness relax inwardly. Then immediately meditate on the guru. The received method is to meditate on [the guru] above the head in the manner of one's family's chief deity. However, if that image is not easy, meditate on the guru in the space directly above your head. If you don't like that image, it is also acceptable to meditate on the guru facing you from the space in front. In any case, imagine a lion throne upon which is a stacked seat of a multicolored lotus, sun, and moon. Meditate on your own root guru siting there, glowing with a radiant complexion, magnificent and brilliant. In the case of Illusory Body and that of the other Five Dharmas, if you meditate on the guru as Vajradhara, you make his body color blue. However, in practice the main directive has been to meditate on the actual guru's form.

For an elaborate visualization, light rays radiate from the root guru's heart, invoking all the lineage gurus to melt into the root guru. The guru becomes the union of all of them. Similarly, the whole infinite expanse of peaceful and wrathful yidams are invoked and melt into the guru, who becomes the union of all yidams. All buddhas of the ten directions and three times are invoked and melt into the guru, who becomes the union of all buddhas. The Holy Dharma of scripture and realization are invoked in the form of letters and dissolve into the guru, who becomes the union of all dharma. All the noble sanghas of the greater and lesser vehicles are invoked and melt into the guru, who becomes the union of all sangha. All ḍākinīs, dharma protectors, and guards are invoked and melt into the body of the root guru, who becomes the union of all dharma protectors. That very root guru is the union of all gurus, yidams, buddhas, dharmas, sanghas, and dharma protectors. {32} If just hearing the guru's name can liberate one from all the bad existences of samsara, there is no need to even mention the results of supplicating. Think about that and many other approaches in order to bring intense devotion to your meditation.

Then you need to supplicate. Gather around you all sentient beings of the six kinds of migrators, primarily this life's actual parents, those enemies and obstructing spirits that would harm you, and the ground masters of the area where you are. Show physical respect toward the kind root guru by prostrating and circumambulating, verbal respect by supplicating, and mental respect by contemplating with undivided respectful devotion. Then when you chant the supplication, imagine that all sentient beings of the six kinds of migrators accompany you like a choir with the resounding of the supplication:

> Precious guru, unified essence of all buddhas of the three times,
> for the sake of all sentient beings,
> I pray to you to relinquish my self-fixation,
> to experience no needs,
> to master Illusory Body,
> to master Dream,
> and to attain the supreme spiritual power of Lucid Clarity
> Mahāmudrā,
> right now, quickly, on this very seat.

Pray that your devotion is strong enough to reach over and dissolve [into the guru] and then return and dissolve into you. For an expanded visualization, it is said that you imagine the murmuring sound of supplication coming from the four elements—stones, mountains, cliffs, plants, trees, forests—all of the animate and inanimate world. In this way, spend the main part of the session solely on devotional supplication. At the close of the session, the guru fills with light and dissolves, melting and becoming one with you. {33} In that state, relinquish all thoughts of past, present, and future; relax and settle in. In the session breaks, it is said one should cultivate the three intentionalities.[17] Alternatively, during this occasion for those of highest capabilities, the other two aspirations are less emphasized—it is the guru devotion that you need. That's how it was directly taught [to me]. Sometimes leave off other elaborations and meditate only on devotion. This is the thirteenth round of visualization.

Session 14

b. Integrating the Unreal Nature of Whatever Appears

After some time of meditating on the previous visualization, all appearances will become an unreal, insubstantial haze. All your current ideas about high and low, good and bad, near and far, that seem so true will vanish without a trace. This is not merely due to the effect of meditating on the lack of reality externally but arises naturally from within through the power of devotion.

When that occurs, that situation is called the arising of illusion-like experience. So then turn your mind to all appearances in that manner—self, other, environment, and inhabitants. "What? This all appears? It does. Is it real? It is not. It is like an illusion. It is like a dream." Thinking that, develop powerful intentionality. Afterward, look directly at that mind that is thinking "This is like an illusion; it is like a dream." There is nothing at all to hold on to. Relax into that and rest in equipoise. Whatever arises, do not fiddle with it. The essence of this practice is the previous integration of devotion to the guru. Within that state, you add the one further intentionality of illusion. Sometimes meditate that the guru melts into light and dissolves into you, and then meditate with intent on illusion. Sometimes the guru is before you or sits above your head, and in that state intentionally, meditate on illusion—whatever you prefer. {34} That is the fourteenth round of visualization.

2. Guidance without Interruption by Other Words for the Average

If you have taken this into practice as described but the applied virtue does not immediately arise, the problem is that your devotion does not measure up to the highest capability and you do not fit into that category. So now, for the Guidance without Interruption by Other Words for the average capability, there are two parts: (1) Meditating on One's Body as the Empty Appearance of the Deity's Form and (2) Integrating Whatever Appears as Illusory Body.

Session 15

a. Meditating on One's Body as the Empty Appearance of the Deity's Form

Practice from the refuge up through the supplication to the guru as in the instructions for those of highest capabilities. Do the supplications for half or two-thirds of the session. Then the guru melts into light and dissolves into you. Rest awhile in equipoise with your mind inseparable from the guru. There, when a thought spontaneously arises and increases, look directly at your body-mind while visualizing yourself clearly as the deity, and conduct an inspection: "How is it? This appearance of the deity's form is nothing other than my mind's perception. Apart from that, nothing in the least exists externally. This deity's form is only my mind, and mind is only the deity's form appearing here." This vigorous training with intentionality is the first vital point.

Again, look at the essence of mind: no actual valid thing is established. Other than a mere appearance, it has no outside, inside, or in between whatsoever. There is no way to say "it is truly like this." For sure it appears, but in reality it is not real. It is like an illusion. This vigorous training with intentionality is the second vital point.

Then by looking at the essence of the one who thinks "it is like an illusion," that intentionality itself subsides in its own ground. This wide-open stare that does not identify whatever arises is the third vital point. You need to meditate with the intentionality of those three vital points again and again. This is the fifteenth round of visualization.

Session 16

b. Integrating Whatever Appears as Illusory Body

The training is to progressively transfer those three vital points to all other appearances. {35} Begin by meditating on that visualization of your own body as the empty appearance of the deity's form. Then without allowing that to fade, first focus on your dwelling place and all your belongings. Train in thinking that they are nothing other than the mind's perceptions, that mind is also like an illusion, and that even fixation on illusion evaporates into basic space. Maintain the natural movement of naturally arisen pure awareness. Once you become familiar with that, train well with whatever you control—food, wealth, companions, servants, land, fields, and so forth—as well as the friends and enemies that are the objects of your desire or anger. Once you get used to that, gradually apply those three vital points to all appearances. In all the session breaks, meditate with intentionality on death and impermanence, devotion to the guru, and the unreal, illusory-like nature of whatever arises. Never be without one of those three. They are known as the three intentionalities. This is the sixteenth round of visualization.

3. Developing Meditative Absorption in a Single Sitting for Those of the Lowest Capabilities

For this, you must be free of the four frosts: too much movement is like frost for applied virtue, changing residence too many times is like frost for applied virtue, many plans is like frost for applied virtue, and much perverse discussion is like frost for applied virtue. The categories are (1) Making the Six Kinds of Migrators Arise as Illusion, (2) Integrating Sickness and Spirits as Illusion, (3) the sixfold set of qualities that develop, and (4) the natural arising of unattached illusion.

Session 17

a. Making the Six Kinds of Migrators Arise as Illusion

Begin with the refuge up through the supplication to the guru, the same as before, except that it is taught that you can spend one-third of the session on that. According to the actual presentation in the *Inventory*,[18] there are five supplications for both those of best and average capabilities, while only four supplications for those of least capabilities. {36} The reason for that is that the best and average practitioners supplicate with two separate lines: "Please let me accomplish Illusory Body. Please let me develop Dream," whereas for those of lesser capabilities, they are combined into the single line: "Please let me accomplish Illusory Body and Dream," effectively making four supplications. However, the actual practice and personal advice that have come down to us is that this division into three categories of best, average, and least capabilities is unnecessary. It does not matter whether all three types do five supplications or four supplications.

After the guru dissolves into you, focus your attention on the lower part of your utterly empty deity's form. There you imagine a tetrahedral source of phenomena, white and clear. Its narrow apex faces down and reaches directly above the anus. The wide-open side faces up with the front vertex at the navel and the other two vertices face the direction of the right and left kidneys. Imagine that it is radiant and clear with the nature of light. Turning your attention to this, the sentient beings of the six kinds of migrators appear within it in their various forms and their general distinct modes of body, possessions, color, shape, clothing, and attributes, along with their individual and varied ways of experiencing happiness and sadness. Imagine that they are packed into the source of phenomena.

Think, "All the habitual patterns of karma and afflictions that are the causes of taking birth as the variety of migrators are present in my mind stream and have arisen in the bodies of each of the six kinds." Also, reflect awhile on the following thought: "Below my navel there are root syllables that give rise to the appearances of the six kinds, and so those images arise there." Following that, more than imagining those very images to be the actual six kinds of beings, focus with the pinpoint of mind on the six kinds of beings below the navel and make all sentient beings throughout space the general object of visualization. {37} Then think, "How is it? They appear, but they are not real." Train vigorously with the intentionality that they are unreal. Also meditate with higher love and compassion, thinking, "It is so sad that they all cling to the unreal as if it were real and so wander in cyclic existence." Further, make a supplication while connecting with powerful feelings of guru devotion: "Guru, please offer them refuge from their sufferings in cyclic existence. Beloved guru, please consider them." Then, as you gaze with open attention at those six kinds of sentient beings, one of them disappears. Then a second disappears. Then one after another vanishes. In the end, the source of phenomena becomes empty inside. Focus on that. Further elaborations of the visualization after that, such as the disappearance of your body and the source of phenomena, are not necessary. Rest relaxed without fixation, free of all focus. When you can no longer stay in that state, envision the whole of the environment and its inhabitants and know: "It is like an illusion. Nonexistent yet appearing. Appearing while not real." That completes a single visualization. Meditate on it again and again. There are eight vital points on which to focus in this visualization: visualizing the source of phenomena, visualizing the six kinds of beings, training in the unreal nature of the six kinds of migrators, arousing compassion, supplicating the guru, resolving the six kinds of beings into emptiness, maintaining a natural repose, and intentionally cultivating apparent existence as illusion. It is said there is no other visualization more profound than this.

The practice during session breaks is solely the threefold intentionality regarding these subjects. However, merely thinking to train from the start in whichever of those three is preferable is not appropriate at just any time. {38} At the beginning, exert yourself in the methods of session-break training in whichever one is suitable. That will ensure training in each of the three separately. Finally, if you establish your intention by thinking, "I will stick with whichever of the three is appropriate," you will in fact never be without the appropriate one. For example, right at the start of the break, don the armor of thinking, "May the intentionality of death and impermanence always come to me," and then recall impermanence as much as you can during the session break. In that way, when you post the sentinel of mindfulness in the session breaks, the intentionality of impermanence will develop in most of the session breaks after just one or two months. When that happens, set it aside for a while and pursue guru devotion in the same way. Then, once that works, again set aside both of those and train in the same way with the intentionality of illusion. Once that occurs in most of the session breaks, afterward merely formulating the intention to stay with whichever of the three is suitable will be enough to ensure that happening. This is the seventeenth round of visualization.

Session 18

b. Integrating Sickness and Spirits as Illusion

Whereas the three guidebooks and supplements of old contain similar content with different enumerations and varying degrees of completeness, this is the definitive commentary. To integrate sickness, think, "This appearance of sickness will purify negative actions and obscurations and is encouragement for virtuous action. Therefore, it represents the compassion of the qualified guru. How kind!" Regard the sickness as the nature of the guru and supplicate intensely. Finally, rest in wide-open equipoise of these three inseparable: the guru, the sickness, and your mind. That is one way. Alternatively, think, "This appearance of sickness is a delusion. In the actual mode of being, there is no existent sickness or sick person. The nonexistent appearance of sickness is like the sickness in a dream." {39} Thus intensely apply the intentionality of recalling illusion and dream directly to that sickness. At the end, understand that the appearance of sickness is your own mind and rest in equipoise of illusory-like nature without particular focus. That is a second way. Or think, "This appearance of sickness is like an illusion in that it does not exist and yet it appears. What is my mind doing with this appearance?" Press the upper wind down forcefully. All sickness has gone down into the interior of the source of phenomena at the navel. The bottom of the source of phenomena grows longer and longer until it reaches far below the ground, and the sickness also descends with it. Imagine them both vanishing underground like a rainbow. That is a third way, from previous oral advice. So there are three integrations of sickness.

The integration of spirits also has three options. Once you understand that the harm done by spirits is a call to virtuous practice, it becomes the guru's compassion. Supplicate the guru and maintain a state where the guru, the harm, and your mind are all of equal value in their nature of clarity and emptiness. Alternatively, remember that the harmful demon spirit appears while not existing, and while appearing it is not truly established. It is like an illusion. It is like a dream. To fixate on it as real is totally deluded. Train vigorously with that intentionality. In the end, look at the essence of that spontaneously appearing harm-doer and rest in a wide-open state. Otherwise, meditate on the source of phenomena and six kinds of beings and so forth as before. Then visualize the apparent harm-doer in front of you. While keeping the recollection of illusion-like appearance, imagine that as you inhale, the spirit enters through your nose at the same time. {40} It arrives inside the source of phenomena at your navel. The source of phenomena has become huge. Hold your breath and twist around. The opening of the source of phenomena is drawn together so that there is no escape. That harm-doer now wanders through all the places of the six kinds of beings, seeing and experiencing their individual sufferings. It comes to believe in karmic cause and effect, its malicious mind is pacified, and it attains the awakening mind. Then when you breathe out again, that harm-doer is expelled through your nose. Imagine that it goes farther and farther away until it vanishes altogether. Or you can give it a torma to repay your karmic debts and request it to leave. Within all this there are six visualizations, but they are also counted as one major visualization or as two. Here they are combined into one. This is the eighteenth round of visualization.

c. The Sixfold Set of Qualities That Develop

This is an explanation of the benefits of Illusory Body to be given at the beginning of the meditation on the visualization for those of lesser capabilities. There is no new visualization here. The benefits are (1) the arising of warmth, (2) the stabilizing of the vital drops, (3) the refining and increasing of dreams, (4) the appearance of the regions of the six migrators, (5) the ripening and liberating of sentient beings, and (6) the natural arising of illusion.

(1) Since [Illusory Body practice] emphasizes the navel and the lower end of the central channel, which is the vital point of the area of the root syllable of Fierce Inner Heat, warmth rises up automatically. (2) Since you focus your mind on the lower end of the central channel, the winds are blocked there and that closes the channels, holding the vital drops and stabilizing them. (3) Since the root syllables of the six kinds of beings are inside the triangular channel knot at the lower end of the central channel, and because this targets the vital point, {41} in dreams you will be able to refine, increase,

emanate, and change the images of those six kinds and their various habitats simultaneously. (4) Since you apply wind-mind to the channels and constituents of the six kinds of beings, you will be able to ascertain the appearances of their hidden places. (5) Since this is meditation on the equality of self and other by means of guru devotion, emptiness, and compassion regarding all sentient beings throughout space, you will have the ability to ripen and liberate sentient beings. (6) The emanation chakra at the navel is the basis for the arising of delusion during waking time. When that vital point is targeted, it purifies the waking delusions and makes it possible for the realization of illusory body to arise of itself. And since that is the application of the vital point, this so-called realization of illusory body brings the nonconceptual deity's body of empty form, the natural arising of the whole apparent universe as an illusion.

d. The Natural Arising of Illusion Free of Attachment

This is not a special teaching just for those of lowest capabilities but rather an explanation of the signs of successful realization of Illusory Body in general. Meditation on Illusory Body reduces your current obstinate reification of attraction and aversion, high and low. In the end, the realm of all joy and pain, love and hate, will be emptied. You would not be pleased when a person to your right heaps on praise or displeased when someone on the left criticizes you. You won't be overjoyed at good news or profits concerning you and yours or displeased at hearing bad news or suffering loss. At that point, you have stabilized the experiential realization of Illusory Body. This is like the saying:

> Equality of sandalwood tree and ax
> is what we call free of attachment.[19] {42}

These last two subjects are not counted as rounds of visualization. They comprise one or two teaching sessions as appropriate.

C. Dream, Naturally Purified Double Delusion

In this guidance there are six parts: (1) recognizing dreams, (2) refining, (3) increasing, (4) emanating, (5) changing, and (6) ascertaining objective appearances.

1. Recognizing Dreams

This has two parts: (1) Instruction on the Vital Points of the Four Empowerments of Drops if self-recognized and (2) Relying on the Nine Infallible Vital Points if not recognized.

Session 19

a. Instruction on the Vital Points of the Four Empowerments of Drops if Self-Recognized

This basic visualization of recognizing dreams is the most important. For the guru yoga, all the general contents of the visualization are the same as in Illusory Body, except for the one change in the end of the supplication:

> Precious guru, unified essence of all buddhas of the three times,
> for the sake of all sentient beings,
> I pray to relinquish self-fixation,
> to be without needs,
> and to recognize dreams.

Everything else [in the later practices] also follows this pattern: the first two lines of the supplication is everywhere the same, and only the third line at the end is changed. Meditate on this guru yoga for one-third of the session, after which the guru melts into light and dissolves into you. In the center of your body, which has arisen as the clear empty form of the deity, is the central channel. It is white and radiantly clear like a crystal tube. The upper end reaches the inside of the cranium and the lower end the perineum. Visualize that inside the upper end of the central channel there is an upside-down white *haṃ* and in the lower end an upright red *hūṃ*. It is important in all cases to meditate while taking into account the wisdom that whatever arises is false in general and a dream in particular. {43} A pea-sized white drop breaks away from the *haṃ* in the head and arrives at the heart. Think that this purifies the affliction of stupidity and that the torso above the heart becomes light or blissful. Then a pea-sized red vital drop breaks off from the *hūṃ* at the perineum and arrives at the heart. This purifies the affliction of desire and the lower body below the waist becomes light or blissful. The two white and red drops meet at the heart and anger is naturally purified. The area of the heart becomes blissful or light.

Then focus your attention on those two drops chasing each other around inside the empty space of the central channel at the level of the heart. Their manner of circling around can be clockwise or counterclockwise, as you like. Recall the intentional notion of "this is indeed a dream" three or four times. The two drops circling around trying to capture each other barely touch. Focus on that while intensely training in the intentionality that it is a dream. The next [visualization] is the same except that you imagine bliss flowing into your body and mind as a result of the [two drops] touching. For this, also train with the intentionality of illusion. Then the white drop dissolves into the red one and disappears, or the other way around—either way, one dissolves into the other. As you focus on that, imagine that they vanish. Then rest for a while directly in that experience without thinking of anything at all. Again turn your attention to all the appearances of self and others and think, "All these appearances appear; in reality they are not real." In particular, think, "I have fallen asleep. All this appearance is actually a dream." Train vigorously with that intentionality. {44} This constitutes one visualization. Again, imagine the central channel and so forth over and over again, meditating repeatedly just on this.[20]

During the session breaks, replace the intentionality of Illusion with that of Dream so that the threefold intentionality becomes impermanence, devotion, and dream. Since the intentionality of dreaming is the main point, during all daily activities—whether walking, moving, resting, eating, or talking—constantly think, "I have fallen asleep. I am dreaming a dream. Surely it is a dream." If you maintain that, you will have no trouble recognizing dreams, so it is very important. You will quickly recognize dreams through meditating in this way.

However, the recognition of dreams is delayed in some people with weak karmic connections even if they meditate continuously like this during the daytime. They should not hope for recognition in a month or a month and a half, and not worry about the lack of recognition, but just let whatever happens happen. It is important to intensify intentionality. In general, it was said by previous practitioners of Nāropa's Six Dharmas that those of the highest capabilities might recognize dreams after a year. If you meditate for just a year, you will obtain stability in recognizing dreams. They hold that view. But in [Niguma's] dharma tradition, if you meditate in an isolated place with renunciation and disillusionment and without being affected by polluting stains or involved with conversation, then you will begin to have occasional recognition in seven or ten days' time. Then if you sustain the meditation without becoming dissipated or sloppy, you will recognize dreams in a period of three to four months and gain stability. Even if you don't continue to meditate, you will recognize the occasional dream. But those are chance occurrences and not reliable. Also, you might randomly recognize a dream one time right after you first meditate [on lucid dreaming], and with this new circumstance say, "I recognize dreams!" But then it doesn't happen again. This kind of recognition is not useful because it is not sustainable. {45} You must recognize dreams on the strength of the visualization and on the strength of intentionality. If you recognize dreams in that way and do not postpone your practice after a single recognition, lucid dreaming will increase and recognition will occur on a regular basis without difficulty. This is the nineteenth round of visualization.

b. Relying on the Nine Unerring Vital Points if Not Recognized

These are to boost the previous visualizations. In general, since the crucial four empowerments of the vital drop in self-recognizing dreams is extremely profound, using that to recognize dreams is an absolute must and will certainly produce those lucid dreams. So there is no great need for these enhancements. Nevertheless, if the former visualization does not produce recognition in a few months despite energetically meditating, then do these enhancements in sequence. The Nine Unerring Vital Points are three unerring points of time: dawn, daybreak, and sunrise; three vital points of body posture: full lotus, seated with legs drawn up, and reclining in lion pose; and three vital points of visualization: two that are nonconceptual and one that integrates concepts. Of those nine, here we will consider the three vital points of visualization.

Session 20

i. Extensive Vital Visualization for Recognizing without Concepts

Imagine the central channel with the two syllables as before. After that, clear away the dead air. As you inhale the upper winds, a white drop breaks off from the *haṃ* and arrives at the heart. As you draw up the lower wind, a red drop breaks off from the *hūṃ* and arrives at the heart. When you hold the joining winds, the two drops circulate in the heart. {46} Focusing on them with the intentionality of dreaming is the vase empowerment. When you again exhale, the white drop emerges from the right nostril and the red drop from the left. They swirl around at the point between your eyebrows. Focusing on that with the intense intentionality of dreaming is the secret empowerment. Those two drops fall in front of you. The white one becomes glorious Cakrasaṃvara and the red one becomes Vajravārāhī. They join as the form of coemergent union. Focusing on that with the intense intentionality of dreaming is the wisdom-awareness empowerment. Imagine that the mother dissolves into the father, imagine that Cakrasaṃvara dissolves into Vajravārāhī, and that also vanishes into the expanse of space. Resting in the equipoise of nonthought is the fourth empowerment.

Upon arising from that, train vigorously with the intentionality of dreaming. Meditate on that process again and again. In between sessions, maintain conduct as before. When you lie down to sleep at night, the coemergent couple in front of you vanishes into space; fall asleep within that very state without interference from any other thought. If you wake up during the night, it is best if you can meditate once on the complete visualization, but if you cannot, then cultivate the intentionality of dreaming. In the second half of the night, when there is a little time left for sleep, wake up and assume the physical posture and meditate with intense intentionality on that exact previous visualization. Afterward, when whichever of the three crucial times is upon you, and with whichever of the three crucial postures is appropriate, meditate on the sequence of the previous visualizations. In the end, when everything vanishes, go to sleep in that state without any other thoughts interfering. If you have strong familiarity with the meditation on the above visualizations of self-recognizing [dreams with the] drops from before, then you will recognize dreams on the first time. {47} Even without really strong familiarity, you will have lucid dreams after a few days and a few tries. This is the twentieth round of visualization.

Session 21

ii. Short Basic Visualization

Alternatively, learn this short basic visualization. Meditate on the guru yoga as before. Meditate on the guru in your heart, either in the form of your actual guru or white Vajradhara, with a white syllable *hūṃ* the nature of light in the heart. Meditating with both devotion in the guru and the intentionality of dreaming, mentally supplicate. Light radiates from the *hūṃ* and pervades all appearance. Think that it is a dream. All appearance melts into light and dissolves into you. That is the vase empowerment. Imagine yourself as the yidam and recall the intentionality of dreaming. That melts into light and dissolves into the guru at your heart. That is the secret empowerment. For that, also recall the intentionality of dreaming. The guru melts into light and dissolves into the *hūṃ*. That is the wisdom empowerment. Then think that the *hūṃ* also vanishes like a rainbow, and maintain that very experience. That is the fourth empowerment. Train vigorously in the intentionality of dreaming and meditate repeatedly on this visualization without regard for the number or duration of the sessions. That is how you must practice.

In the guidebooks of Jak[chen Gyaltsen Bum] and Sam[ding Zhönu Drup],[21] the dissolution of the environment and its inhabitants into oneself is not clear. Nor is the dissolution into lucid clarity in the daytime visualization. Apparently the practical application is somewhat hidden, but the learned adept Zhönu Drup also maintains that the [light] gradually radiates, as in the visualization for recognizing lucid clarity.

These two visualizations are designated as nonconceptual recognition because during their actual application, from the time of the dissolution of the visualization until you fall asleep, no other discursive thoughts should intervene. That means that you must remain without contemplation. {48} This is the twenty-first round of visualization.

Session 22

iii. Integration of Concepts

First do the preliminary as before, except that the four-spoke chakra at the throat becomes a four-petaled red lotus. Meditate that the red *oṃ* at the center of the lotus generates red light that permeates all areas of the throat. Hold the vase breathing or the gentle breathing. Before midday, set a powerful intention: "No matter what, I will grasp my dreams tonight. I will recognize dreams as dream." After midday, intensify intentionality by thinking, "I have fallen asleep. These appearances are dreams." In the evening session, set the intention by thinking, "Now dreams will soon come. I must know them to be dreams." Also, [the experience] between the current waking state of coarse appearances and before entering actual deep sleep is called conceptual thought between sleep and appearance. There are sensations such as sounds buzzing in the ears, or the body feeling numb and heavily pressed down, or tingling at the point between the eyebrows, and labored breathing. After that, vague impressions occur, such as the movement of humans and dogs, and the shapes of houses and roads, and such.

The movement of the undercurrent is clear, but the actions of a real dream are still somewhat unclear, yielding only vague and indistinct forms. This is said to be the thoughts between sleep and [waking] appearances. In this situation, vigorously train your intention by thinking, "I must recognize that as dream." On those three occasions, apart from changing the intentionality, the visualization is the same. While the way of grasping dreams during the three vital times with the three vital body postures is the same as above, here do not dissolve the visualization objects into emptiness and enter that state. {49} Instead, turn your attention to the *oṃ* syllable and think, "Now comes the thoughts between my falling asleep and appearances. I should identify this." By means of relying on moderate intentionality, not too intense, let yourself fall asleep. There, when thoughts occur between sleep and appearance, apply just a slight intentionality in thinking it is a dream. It is taught to squeeze the downward expelling wind [at that time]. However, if there is too much contrivance your sleep will disperse, so go to sleep within the state of slight intentionality. You identify the conceptual thoughts that occur between sleep and appearance, and also identify them by means of conceptual intentionality, so it is called integration of concepts. This is said to be an instruction through which it is impossible not to recognize dreams.

On this subject, the guidebooks of Jak, Sam, and Serlingpa[22] only mention the explanation of the *oṃ* at the throat as an aside and leave it at that. It is taught to meditate on the previous visualization as the daytime visualization, and to distribute the two nonconceptual visualizations. Alternatively, Jakchen says that in the enhancements of the two visualizations, one does not actually meditate on those two themselves but trains with the general intentionality of dreaming. These comments are made with reference to the understanding gained from oral esoteric instructions. This is the twenty-second round of visualization.

2. Refining Dreams

You need to refine the dreams once you have attained stability in recognizing them. This is the time to set aside the visualization for identifying dreams and concentrate solely on refining them. But if you continue to meditate regularly on identifying dreams, you may meditate on the visualization for refining dreams at the point when you recognize a few dreams each night. It is acceptable to practice both recognizing and refining at the same time. {50}

This has four parts: (1) Refining the Mind through the Body, (2) Refining the Body through the Mind, (3) Refining through Nairātmya, and (4) Refining through Intentionality.

Session 23

a. Refining the Mind through the Body

The practice is the same as in recognizing dreams up through guru yoga, except for a change in the intentionality [in the last line of the supplication] to ". . . and to refine dreams." Then for the main visualization, imagine that there is a huge chasm, like a cliff precipice, below the place where you are standing. Then imagine that you yourself are at the edge of that chasm, suspended about an arrow's length in the space above it. When you look down, you experience vertigo and become terrified. At that point, think, "I have fallen asleep. This appearance is a dream appearance. No reason to be afraid of that." Let go and allow yourself to fall. Just before you hit the ground, imagine that it all disappears into suchness, or that you can fly back up to the top where you stood on the edge. In this manner, refine the dream again and again. In this visualization you can appear as the yidam or in your ordinary form; it makes no difference in the meditation. There is also an explanation where you can leave one body at the edge of the precipice with another body tied to it by a cord of light that falls and climbs back out. This was not taught in the oral guidance. This is the twenty-third round of visualization.

Session 24

b. Refining the Body through the Mind

The preliminaries are the same as before. Imagine that there are large blue *hūṃ* syllables, the nature of light, in the nine orifices of your body as the yidam. In all of your pores there are infinite fine *hūṃ*s of vivid blue light covering the entire body without gaps. The tops of all the *hūṃ*s face inward. Train vigorously in the intentionality of lucid dreaming. Radiant clear blue light from all the *hūṃ*s radiates out like ropes of light shooting into your body. {51} The light gathers in and blends together, covering even from the outside of the body. The deity's shape is pervaded, and everything becomes a single globe of light. Again vigorously practice the intentionality of dreaming. That globe of light gradually vanishes from the edges, becoming smaller and smaller until it is the size of a fist, then a thumb, then a small pea, then a mustard seed, and finally is refined away altogether. Rest the mind in equipoise without thought. As conceptual thought arises, practice vigorously the intentionality of dreaming. This is the twenty-fourth round of visualization.

Session 25

c. Refining through Nairātmya

This is the same as before, except that in the main practice you visualize yourself as Cakrasaṃvara. Vajra Nairātmya is before you, blue, holding a flaying knife, blood-filled skull cup, and khaṭvāṅga. Meditate that she is blooming with youth and bliss. Visualize her size as no larger than one arrow's length, or one cubit, and no smaller than four finger-widths, or thumb size—whatever is comfortable within that range. Meditate that the syllables of the mantra *oṃ a svāhā* appear clearly at her genitals. Within a state of intense recollection of the intention of dreaming, repeat that mantra twenty-one times or however many is suitable. This instantly causes blue light rays to arise from it and strike your clear form as Heruka, intensifying its bluish radiance and vividness. Imagine that your whole body is filled with bliss. {52} Again, with the intentionality of lucid dreaming, turn your attention to the form of Nairātmya. This makes Nairātmya herself overflow and melt with the blue light rays and the experience of bliss. The light enters through the opening of the secret place of your Heruka form and pervades the whole body inside. It becomes more clearly blue and radiant than before. Imagine your whole body-mind filled with bliss. Think that this becomes brighter and brighter until it mixes with space and dissolves. Rest there awhile. Again practice with intense intentionality of dreaming and so on as before. Regarding this visualization, Khedrup Gyaltsen Bum said to meditate on a *hūṃ* at the tip of the organ, but this was not stated in the oral guidance. It was thought perhaps to be a mix-up from Sukhasiddhi's [instructions]. This is the twenty-fifth round of visualization.

Session 26

d. Refining through Intentionality

The preliminaries up through guru yoga are the same as before. In this case, there is no definite basic visualization; it is called refining through intentionality because you practice with the dynamic energy of intentionality alone, without a specific visualization. "My body that creates sickness and suffering is actually in bed. These appearances are dream appearances. This body also is the mental body of dream. These dream appearances and the mental body can be refined in whatever way I choose." Cultivate this intention continuously. Then if a pillar, wall, ceiling, or so forth appears before you, refine [the appearance] by passing through it without obstruction—up and down, back and forth. Additionally, practice such things as slipping through small windows; subjugating cliffs, water, fire, wild animals; and flying in the sky, entering the ground, walking on water, and so forth. In short, it is fine to practice with whatever comes to mind. But train especially with conceptual thoughts that are difficult to overcome, the type of things that you are attached to or the type that cause fear, anxiety, shame, and disgust. Sometimes shatter [those thoughts] upon contact, sometimes disregard them through the intentionality of dream and illusion, sometimes use fearless counteractive meditation, and sometimes readily vanquish them moment by moment. {53} This is the twenty-sixth round of visualization.

Refining the Mind through the Body is refining dream's dynamic energy. Refining the Body through the Mind is blending with lucid clarity, so [Dream and Lucid Clarity] are included in one practice. Refining through Nairātmya is blending with lucid clarity. Refining through Intentionality refines the dynamic energy, so the vital point of refinement of dreams is included in that practice. A single individual should meditate on whichever of those two [pairs] is appropriate.

3. Increasing Dreams

This has two parts: (1) Increasing Whatever Is Encountered and (2) Increasing for Whatever Is to Be Tamed.

a. Increasing Whatever Is Encountered

There are two parts to the first part: (1) Increasing Subtle and Coarse Four Elements and (2) Increasing Subtle and Coarse Sentient Beings.

Session 27

i. Increasing Subtle and Coarse Four Elements

The preliminaries are the same as before, except that the last line of the supplication is changed to "Bless me with the ability to increase dreams." Then, for example, if you see a clump of earth in front of you, think, "I have fallen asleep and this is a dream. Whatever way I increase will work." If you think of increasing it to two, it will become two. Likewise, in the beginning, alternate increasing from three to ten and so forth, then gradually gather them back into the original one. Ultimately, by training gradually and refining, you will gain the ability to increase [the dream object] to whatever you desire and gather it back into the original one.

By your meditating on this visualization again and again during the daytime, you will recognize dreams at night. Then recall this visualization for increasing and meditate on it [during the dream]. Despite this, there are some who cannot increase and gather back right away. In that case, meditate again with intense intentionality and after a few days, some capacity for increasing will develop and gradually will get better. {54} Some practitioners can increase dreams right from the start. Not only that, they are able to achieve emanating and changing dreams. Once you get used to practicing with something like a clump of earth and are able to expand and contract it, train successively in other objects. Train in coarse forms of the earth element, such as a mountain, down to a subtle one, such as a pebble or dust mote. Train in coarse forms of the water element, such as a river or lake, down to subtle forms, such as a drop of water. Train in coarse forms of the fire element, such as a huge conflagration, down to subtle forms, such as a spark. Train in coarse forms of the wind element, such as a big tornado, down to subtle forms, such as the breathing of a tiny creature. Here, "four elements" refers to all material phenomena that are without sentience. It means to train with everything included in the external environment. This is the twenty-seventh round of visualization.

Session 28

ii. Increasing Subtle and Coarse Sentient Beings

Preliminaries are the same as before. If you encounter a human or other being in front of you, think, "I have fallen asleep and this is a person appearing in my dream. I can increase them in any way." Increase that appearance from two or three up to ten, then gather it back and so forth as before. As this exemplifies, train with all sentient beings, such as horses and cows, that you actually see. Train with the large beings, such as horses and cows, down to very subtle ones, such as tiny insects. This is the twenty-eighth round of visualization.

b. Increasing for Whatever Is to Be Tamed

This has two parts: (1) Taming with Mundane Beings and (2) Taming with Transcendent Beings.

Session 29

i. Taming with Mundane Beings

The first, increasing whatever mundane beings are to be tamed, mainly concerns training with the forms of living beings. Training with nonsentient fire, water, and so forth is also a training, such as when one practices the increase of water as an antidote to fire. {55} Suppose you see something like a mouse before you. Think, "This is a dream mouse. I must increase something to tame it." Then a cat shows up, and you think that it can tame the mouse. Then, thinking that whatever you try to increase will increase, multiply the cat many times and do the visualization of taming. Similarly apply this by increasing hawks for small birds, wolves for dogs, tigers for other animals, lions for tigers, fire for lions, water for fire, cannibal demons for humans, and so forth. This is the twenty-ninth round of visualization.

Session 30

ii. Taming with Transcendent Beings

For increasing transcendent beings, when there is a spirit harmful to you or to others, imagine that the king of wrathful deities appears before you and binds that harmful spirit with lassos, tramples it underfoot, slashes it with weapons, burns it with fire, and terrifies it into an unconscious faint with the roar of wrathful mantra. Imagine that these and various other vanquishing methods render it unable to rise back up. Again, increase the number of such wrathful deities and imagine taming the spirit. Although any wrathful wisdom deity is certainly capable of taming all kinds of bad spirits, it is said that the following are most effective in terms of those to be tamed: Hayagrīva for taming gyalpo and tsen spirits, Vajrapāṇi for upper spirits, Garuḍa for ground masters and general malignant nāgas, Mañjuśrī Nāgarakṣā for cannibal nāgas, Acala for obstacles of devils, Uṣṇīṣa Cakravartin for curses, and Mañjuśrī-Vajrabhairava Mantra for bad spirits in general. This is the thirtieth round of visualization.

4. Emanating in Dreams

There are two parts in this instruction: (1) Emanating Whatever Is Encountered and (2) Emanating for Whatever Is to Be Tamed. {56}

a. Emanating Whatever Is Encountered

This has two categories: (1) Emanating as the Subtle and Coarse Four Elements and (2) Emanating as Subtle and Coarse Sentient Beings.

Session 31

i. Emanating as the Subtle and Coarse Four Elements

During the preliminaries, change the last line of the supplication to "Please bless me with the ability to emanate in dreams." All else is the same. Then, for example, if you see a clump of earth in front of you, think, "I have fallen asleep and this appearance of earth is dreamed earth. I also should emanate as a clump of earth like this." With this intention, you instantly become a clump of earth just like that. Then meditate for a while thinking, "This is certainly a dream." When that thought is interrupted and you become distracted by something else, cultivate intense intentionality for lucid dreaming. Meditate in this way, repeating it again and again. Apply the process exemplified here to all the other subtle and coarse elements. This is the thirty-first round of visualization.

Session 32

ii. Emanating as Subtle and Coarse Sentient Beings

This follows the process of the previous [visualizations on increasing]. If you see a person in front of you, think, "Oh! This is a dream person. I also should emanate as someone like this." Imagine that you instantly become like that. With the intention of dreaming, hold the mind there for a bit. Again, when that thought is interrupted, think, "This is a dream," and in that way go back and forth. The way to apply this to other living beings is the same as above. This is the thirty-second round of visualization.

b. Emanating for Whatever Is to Be Tamed

This has two parts: (1) mundane and (2) transcendent.

Session 33

i. Emanating as Mundane Beings

This is the same as before except that when you see something like a mouse, you think, "This is a dream mouse. I must tame it by emanating as a cat." {57} Immediately you become a cat. Imagine that you tame that mouse, leaving nothing behind. In that way, follow the process for the other examples. This is the thirty-third round of visualization.

Session 34

ii. Emanating as Transcendent Beings

For the sake of yourself or others, imagine that a demonic spirit that you have discovered is before you and think, "This is a dream demon. I must tame it." Immediately you become a big wrathful deity and—using the same previous methods of binding and beating into submission—destroy it without remainder. Think, "Ah, this is actually a dream. There is not a bit of a truly existent thing." Repeat this process again and again. The rest is the same as described above in the section on increasing dreams. "Increasing" means to increase whatever you find before you. "Emanating" means you yourself emanate. For the most part, increasing is a bit easier, while emanating is more difficult, so increasing is presented before emanating. Not only that, in the practice of emanating transcendent beings to tame whatever needs taming, before the visualization is mastered, you might be able to emanate yourself in a dream but unable to subdue the adversary. But if a wrathful deity arrives before you and tames it, subjugation can occur. It is said that the reason for that is the habitual pattern of clinging dearly to yourself as an ordinary human, which causes self-defeating despair. But when a deity stands before you, that is not the case. This is the thirty-fourth round of visualization.

5. Changing Dreams

This instruction has four parts: (1) Changing Subtle and Coarse Four Elements, (2) Changing Subtle and Coarse Sentient Beings, (3) Changing Various Deities' Forms, and (4) Changing into Empty Appearance Free of Attachment.

Session 35

a. Changing Subtle and Coarse Four Elements

In the supplication, change the last line to "Bless me with the ability to change dreams." {58} Other than that, there is no difference in the preliminaries. This is the same for the next three sessions. If there is something like a vase in front of you, think, "I have fallen asleep. This appearance of a vase is actually a dream. I can do whatever I want with a dream vase; if I try to change it, it will change." With the force of this intentionality, when you think that you must change this vase into a stove, it will become a stove. When you think of changing it to a pillar, it becomes a pillar, and so forth. Whatever you recall, the change happens accordingly, whether of the object's essence, size, shape, number, or color. In this way, when you are able to change something like a vase in various ways, train in the unending possibilities of changing inanimate objects—earth, water, fire, wind, rocks, mountains, cliffs, trees, forests, and so on—back and forth into various forms. This is the thirty-fifth round of visualization.

Session 36

b. Changing Subtle and Coarse Sentient Beings

This follows the same process. If you find a person before you, think, "This is my dream person. However I change it, it will change. It will change however I wish." If you think of changing it to a horse, it becomes a horse. Then change it to an elephant. Then again change it to an ox, a camel, and so on. Change living beings, such as humans and animals, back and forth into various forms. On these occasions of changing the four elements and sentient beings, you should change them into various indefinite colors, shapes, sizes, and numbers. This is the thirty-sixth round of visualization.

Session 37

c. Changing Various Deities' Forms

This is the same as previously, except that while you are within the state of intense intentionality of dream and the lack of reality, you meditate on yourself as the clear form of Coemergent Cakrasaṃvara. {59} Think, "What? I have fallen asleep. This appearance as a deity's form is a dream. I can change it to anything." Thinking that you as Cakrasaṃvara should be changed to Hevajra, you become Hevajra. Then again change to Guhyasamāja, then to Mahāmāya, then to Vajrabhairava, and so forth—changing into the essence of various yidam deities. In a similar way, change a single deity's color into various colors, such as white to blue, and that to red, and so forth. Also change the faces and arms to various indefinite forms, such as changing many faces and arms to few, few to many, or changing facial images and so forth to different ones, however you wish. This is the thirty-seventh round of visualization.

Session 38

d. Changing into Empty Appearance Free of Attachment

Previously you changed into various deity forms. Then you increased the size of the primary deity, changed all those that you increased, and trained vigorously in the intentionality that they are all like illusions and dreams. Now, by your looking openly at the appearance of the deity's form and the mind of the one to whom they appear, the illusion will be free of fixation on that deceit. Within that state, the lucid clarity of mahāmudrā without any frame of reference will arise on its own. Generate the principal deity's form from within that state and train repeatedly as before. By your training like that, during nighttime dreaming the meditation on any appropriate number of deities will occur. Then they will multiply even more. Finally, the deities' forms in your dream will fill all space yet without obscuring each other. All that will arise with three characteristics: bliss without attachment, clarity without concept, and appearance without intrinsic nature. {60} At that point, you have arrived at the natural state of the applied virtue of Dream, naturally purified double delusion.

The term "illusion" means the arising of near equanimity without reification regarding high or low objects that is the result of training with intentionality in the lack of reality during waking and dreaming. "Free from fixating on illusion" indicates an attitude of "What do I care; all this is merely the arising of deluded appearance." Then even that thought vanishes into the expanse, leaving you totally free of the fixations of denial or affirmation. That occasion, when you taste the experience of nonthought and bliss, is lucid clarity. It is also called mahāmudrā, as it is the abiding nature of the mind. When the clear, empty form of the deity arises spontaneously from within that state, it is also called mahāmudrā. "Bliss without attachment" concerns the time of the self-arising deity's form: although a vivid experience of bliss arises in both body and mind, you have no pride or conceit. And since you do not crave that bliss, there is no pleasure or displeasure whether it arises or not. "Clarity without concept" means that even though the form of a deity's body appears extremely clearly, it arises by itself without conceptual effort. As for "appearance without intrinsic nature," they say, "Although [something] appears, it is empty of true reality." This is very general, and naturally it does apply here. However, in this case the simultaneous arising of body, speech, and mind, as well as form, sound, smell, taste, and texture, arise in near equanimity to the perception of the single natural clarity of pure awareness. Apart from that, your felt experience is without any distinctions of entities whatsoever in those individual appearances. This is the thirty-eighth round of visualization. {61}

During these practices of lucid dreaming, the esoteric instructions on severing diffusion are very important, but since they are extensively elucidated elsewhere, they are not explained in the course of this guidance. The instruction known as *Direct Advice on the Required Severing of Diffusion* is also found elsewhere.[23]

6. Ascertaining Objective Appearances

This has four parts: (1) Clearly Knowing without Visualizing for those of highest capability, (2) Clearly Seeing Whatever You Think for average capability, (3) the Garuḍa of the Mental Body for those of lesser capability, and (4) Ascertaining Objective Appearances for those of least capability.

Session 39

a. Clearly Knowing without Visualizing

Even without effort in application, you see the hidden meaning of everything during all situations of waking life in the daytime and dreaming at night.

b. Clearly Seeing Whatever You Think

Whatever you focus on with intentionality in the daytime is seen arising at nighttime without any effort.

c. The Garuḍa of the Mental Body

The preliminaries are the same as before, except for changing the last line of the supplication to "May I ascertain objective appearances." For the actual visualization, cultivate an intense intentionality, thinking, "Tonight I will see such-and-such pure land of the Buddha" or "I will see such-and-such hidden thing." Then, thinking that it is actually a dream, imagine yourself as the yidam deity or some other appropriate physical form that you emanate. Imagine that you fly up into the sky and arrive there to see that place that you intended. In this way, the same will occur during the nighttime dreams. Here "garuḍa of the mental body" refers only to the ability to fly. However, some people also explain it to mean that you emanate as something like a garuḍa that can fly and go to those places. This is the thirty-ninth round of visualization. {62}

d. Ascertaining Objective Appearances

There are three esoteric instructions in this final section: (1) Illuminating Objective Appearances with Nairātmya, (2) Illuminating Objective Appearances with Vital Drops, and (3) Illuminating Objective Appearances with *A*.[24]

Session 40

i. Illuminating Objective Appearances with Nairātmya

The preliminaries are the same as before. Imagine a skull cup made of light below your navel, white on the outside and red on the inside. The blue syllables *oṃ a svāhā* inside it radiate with multicolored light rays. The light rays fill the source of phenomena and your body, and radiate out through the pores. Imagine that the external environment of the world is a divine palace and that the inner inhabitants, the sentient beings, are yidams. Imagine infinite offerings emanating from the tips of the light rays presented to all the hosts of yidam deities that were there all along and those that are new. Remember that the extent of all physical form is divine form, all sound is mantra, and all memory and awareness are illusion and dream. Again the light rays reabsorb and dissolve into the mantra syllables at your navel. That turns into the form of Exalted Vajra Nairātmya vibrating with the sound of the mantra. Present offerings and supplicate with, "May I ascertain objective appearances."

This is the definitive oral guide for the daytime visualization. Elsewhere, in the Jak system, when the light rays emanate from the mantra the first time, various yidams appear with Nairātmya in the lead. Then a second emanation [of light rays] presents the offerings. The former radiates from the right nostril and the latter from the left nostril. In the Samdingpa system, you meditate on the mantra inside a skull cup at Nairātmya's navel inside the source of phenomena at your navel. The light emanates just once, radiating from the right nostril. In both of these systems, there is no reabsorption of the light rays. This description of light rays reabsorbing into the mantra and the generation of the deity appears in Serlingpa's guidebook. {63}

The visualization for going to sleep at night is first to do the previous visualization one time, and after that, present the complete four offerings. Then supplicate with "Yidam Nairātmya, during the night tonight, please allow me to see infinite buddha realms and make vast offerings." If you have some particular minor desire in mind, then request that with "Please allow me to see such-and-such place." Then Nairātmya turns to face you. Imagine that the area of her heart becomes extremely bright and there you see the desired place appearing vividly like an image in a mirror. That will ascertain the objective appearances at the time of dreaming. It is taught that you may meditate on a source of phenomena in place of the skull cup. This is the fortieth round of visualization.

Session 41

ii. Illuminating Objective Appearances with Vital Drops

Do the preliminaries as before. Visualize yourself as the deity with the central channel in the center of the body. It is white and radiant, the nature of light, with the thickness of a bamboo cane. At the upper end, white *haṃ* faces head-down, and at the lower end, purple *hūṃ* stands right side up. At the navel, red short *A* (*a-chung*) also faces up. Exhale the dead air and then inhale, causing a white drop the size of a round pea to separate out from the *haṃ* and ascend to the heart. Contract the lower vital wind, causing a pea-sized purple drop to break off from the top of *hūṃ*. Draw in the belly, causing an extremely red drop the size of half a pea to break off the top of *A*. Both of those also arrive at the heart. The three essence drops merge into a single white drop, slightly red with a tinge of blue. {64} Focus your attention briefly on its radiance. Think that you will see the appearance of the place. At the same time as that intentionality, clear out the breath. Through that, pinkish light emerges from the drop at the heart and stretches out like a rope or a snake, leaving through the left nostril. It goes to whatever place you wanted to see. That light illuminates like a torch placed in a dungeon and you see the place vividly. Alternatively, it is also taught that you can make the light rays into a hollow tube and when you look through it you see the place. In this visualization, the vital point of winds and the red-blue vital drop come from the oral instructions. This is the forty-first round of visualization.

Session 42

iii. Illuminating Objective Appearances with *A*

Meditate on the preliminaries and the central channel as before. Within the central channel, meditate on a white *A* at the navel, radiant and clear—the nature of light. With the intentionality of lucid dreaming, meditate a bit on the vase breathing or gentle breathing. Transition to visualizing a string of white light rays stretching out from the *A* and emanating out through the central channel without obstruction, emerging from the nostrils and going to the area that you want to see. Then, like placing a torch in a dark dungeon, you can see clearly now. Or you can look through a tube of light, whichever you prefer. This is the forty-second round of visualization.

Regarding these three visualizations for those of least capability, a single individual does not necessarily need to meditate on all three; it is fine to do whichever one is appropriate. The point is that there is no specific order of former or latter. When explaining it to a group, the sequence of explanation according to the three old guidebooks is first Nairātmya, then Illuminating Objective Appearances with *A*, and lastly Illuminating Objective Appearances with Vital Drops. However, here the last two have been reversed because they are presented according to the extent of the visualizations: extensive, intermediate, and brief. {65}

In the instructions on *The Five Stages of the Secret Assembly*[25] and other sources, refining, emanating, and changing are classified as subcategories of refining dreams. In this teaching they are placed separately from refining, but this is not a contradiction because refining can be identified in a number of specific ways. In those other [sources], all [methods] of refining the dynamic energy of dreams are simply called refinement. Here, after recognizing that you are dreaming, the particular method to develop the dynamic energy of changing the dream in various ways that has not yet developed is refining. To increase that more and more, the three [methods of] increasing, emanating, and changing are done following refinement. Viewing the appearance of places is known as total freedom in dreaming, but it is merely a sign that qualities have developed. Also, one finds other esoteric instructions combining dream recognition and refinement into one. The latter is called a blend, such as [blending] Dream with Lucid Clarity, and so on. Here, it refers to such practices as Refining the Body through the Mind, Refining through Nairātmya, and the last two changing [practices of Changing Various Deities' Forms and Changing into Empty Appearance Free of Attachment].

In the instructions for Dream, if you do not first recognize that you are dreaming, then the very basic applied virtue of this dharma teaching is missing. So right from the start you need a grasp of dreams as dreams. For that reason, the instructions on recognition are presented [first]. Then you need to refine the dynamic energy in every way. In order to gain control over the appearances of dreams, there are the former and latter refining practices, increasing, emanating, the first two changing practices, and the appearance of places. To develop the main practice of supreme applied virtue in Dream itself, there are two practices: involving dreams in lucid clarity and involving dreams in the self-arising of the deity's form. For the first, there are the two middle visualizations of refining. For the latter, the last two changing practices: changing into various deities' forms and changing into empty appearance free of attachment. {66}

Understood in this way, the mindless words of certain arrogant scholars who say, "There are many instructions in Niguma's Six Dharma Dream practice but they are of little import" should be known as totally irrelevant nonsense. Everything in these Six Dharmas, from top to bottom, is of supreme benefit to beginners and triggers the immediate arising of signs of success. It is never like those "high" instructions explained by braggarts that have no benefit for beginners whatsoever. The self-made dharma of those fools is certainly not the excellent explanations based on scriptural dharma. Nor does this bloated deceit remotely resemble the practical teachings based on esoteric instructions. Of this I am sure.

D. Lucid Clarity, Naturally Clarified Stupidity

There are three parts to this guidance: (1) preliminaries, (2) main practice, and (3) concluding practices.

1. Preliminaries

This has four parts: (1) the roots are impermanence and disillusionment, (2) the branches are conduct and pledge substances, (3) the leaves are the innate radiance of the path of methods, and (4) the flowers that grow from supplications.

a. The Roots: Impermanence and Disillusionment

Meditate intensely with the attitude of needing nothing, which comes from the knowledge that you will definitely die, that the time of death is uncertain, and that everything in the cycle of the three realms and six migrations is suffering. To say nothing of those who have not upheld the guidance on impermanence before, even those who have maintained it need to meditate on it again on this occasion. In general, the inspiration for dharma practice is mainly meditation on death, impermanence, and disillusionment because this makes for a lucid and intelligent consciousness. This momentum strengthens, such that lucid awareness occurs even during dreams, facilitating the recognition of lucid clarity. Also, for those who are disillusioned, it acts as a whip to inspire their awareness so that even during deep sleep it is easy to recall. {67} For instance, if someone is hypervigilant during the daytime, they won't sleep much at night. Similarly, the Ḍākinī of Timeless Awareness said:

> As mortality arises in the mind stream, lucid clarity dawns.

b. The Branches: Conduct and Pledge Substances

As for conduct, it is said:

> Be leisurely in conduct and eat greasy food.
> Give up activity that makes you sweat.

Move very slowly like an invalid. Eat greasy food (i.e., heavy and nutritious) that is neither too much nor too little according to your physical constitution. It is advised to avoid activities that disturb the channels and winds and make you sweat, such as jumping, running, competitive sports, wrestling, and archery. Regarding pledge substances, in general you should arrange communal feasts and tormas for offering. Offer torma to the five classes of ḍākinīs. Also offer torma to the Swift-Acting Awareness Protector [Mahākāla] and make supplications. When offering torma, it is recommended to also offer incense of frankincense and mahāmāṃsa.

c. The Leaves: Innate Radiance of the Path of Methods

If you are already familiar with Fierce Inner Heat yoga, that meditation on a regular basis is sufficient and there is no need for anything else. If not, then first train with gentle breathing and vase breathing for one month each as a preliminary. During the visualizations of the main practice of Lucid Clarity, meditate on sessions of vital-wind practice either in the morning or in the evening to avoid becoming fatigued. The yoga of vital winds separates the elements of pure essence from the residue. Since lucid clarity arises from the radiance of pure essence, meditation on channels and winds is extremely important. {68} In general, of the Six Dharmas, Lucid Clarity is mainly explained in relation to the lucid clarity of sleep, and so Inner Heat and Lucid Clarity are counted separately. On the other hand, the most excellent method to generate daytime lucid clarity is Inner Heat. This is more powerful than any [visualizations of] dissolution, final dissolution, gradual dissolution, or some subtle vital-essence drops.

d. The Flowers That Grow from Supplications

As is said, "Devotion to the guru causes lucid clarity to arise." For lucid clarity to arise, guru devotion is very important. You may think, "But guru devotion is important in all meditation, why say that it is important only for Lucid Clarity?" In general, it's true that guru devotion sets up the auspicious connections for all practice. However, virtuous applications in the daytime can be achieved by your own efforts in meditation. While dreaming, there are various appearances of the dream itself and the coarse mind of thoughts and memories. When those occur, your daytime habitual patterns can guide you in the dream. Therefore, your own efforts and intentions effect your dreams; you need not rely on blessings alone. At the time of deep sleep, however, since there is no effortful recollection, the lucid clarity of dream must arise by itself; there is no reason for another meditation. The hope is in the auspicious connections from applying the vital points of the body and the conjunction of blessings of the guru and special deities.

Since these four preliminaries do not provide a basis for any new visualizations that were not presented before, they are not counted as separate cycles of visualization. They can be completed in one, two, three, or however many teaching sessions. {69}

2. Main Practice

There are four divisions in this Lucid Clarity: (1) recognizing, (2) integrating, (3) blending, and (4) ultimate lucid clarity.

a. Recognizing Lucid Clarity

This has three parts: (1) Recognizing Lucid Clarity Based on Nairātmya, (2) Recognizing Lucid Clarity Based on the Letter *A*, and (3) Recognizing Lucid Clarity Based on the Guru.

Session 43

i. Recognizing Lucid Clarity Based on Nairātmya

The preliminaries for this session are mostly the same as in Illusory Body practice. The difference is that when you meditate on the guru's actual form, it possesses the attributes and attire of the charnel ground, such as the hair being pulled up in a topknot, the six bone ornaments, the tiger-skin skirt, and so on. But if you meditate on the guru as Vajradhara, meditate on him as semi-wrathful Vajradhara Heruka with three eyes and all eight charnel-ground accessories. Change the last line of the supplication to ". . . and to recognize lucid clarity."

After that, imagine for a moment your ordinary form. On the cranial membrane below the skull, right at the crown, there is a lotus-sun seat the size of a split pea. On top of that and proportional with it, imagine Vajra Nairātmya. She is blue, holding a flaying knife and khaṭvāṅga. Her left leg is help up in dancing pose. Visualize her tiny form with prominent limbs. Meditate on a fine, razor-thin white *A* in her heart, clear and shining. Light rays emanate from it. First the brain, the nature of stupidity, is purified. Then the whole body is filled inside and the flesh, blood, and bones are purified. Imagine that your body becomes a body of light. It is said to be even better to meditate on yourself in the yidam's form, in which case, meditate on Coemergent Cakrasaṃvara. Focus your attention there on the letter *A* in Nairātmya's heart and meditate for a bit. {70} Then light rays emanate from that *A* and fill Nairātmya's form. Light rays radiate from her form and fill your whole body inside with brilliant light, like placing a lamp in a dark dungeon. Think that it shines forth from all your pores, turning all appearances into shining light. In this method alone, first focus on the *A* in Nairātmya's heart and then meditate on the light rays radiating and spreading, but focus on the *A* in the heart for longer. After practicing in that way a few times, let consciousness fall in its own place and relax into relaxation, resting for as long as you abide. Always meditate with this repeating process. Initially, you must exert effort for many days, but after meditating that way occasionally, an experience of abiding in nonconceptual lucid bliss will occur on its own. Don't entertain hopes and fears about this experience reoccurring. If it happens, it is enough to rest in that for as long as it lasts. When it passes, meditate as before with intense intentionality. When you go to bed at night, focus on the *A* in Nairātmya's heart and go to sleep. This is the forty-third round of visualization.

Session 44

ii. Recognizing Lucid Clarity Based on the Letter *A*

The preliminary is the same as before. Visualize the central channel, white and about the size of a bamboo cane, in the center of your body as the yidam. Inside that at the level of the navel or four finger-widths below the navel, as you like, imagine a white letter *A*, radiantly clear with the nature of light. Mentally hold that *A* letter for a moment. Light rays radiate from the *A*, filling up the inside of the central channel. Light rays emanate out of that and make the inside of your body extremely clear. Light rays shine out of your pores and infuse all appearance with vivid clarity. {71} When going to bed, focus on the *A* below the navel. The other ways to bring it into experience are the same as before. This is the forty-fourth round of visualization.

Session 45

iii. Recognizing Lucid Clarity Based on the Guru

Do the preliminary practice as before. Visualize yourself as the special deity with your root guru on a lotus-moon seat at your heart. If you meditate on the guru as Vajradhara, he is white with the usual attributes. If you meditate on the actual form of your guru, imagine that he or she has a glowing white complexion and radiates white light rays, smiling joyfully and with peaceful eyes. The body size is four finger-widths at the most or one thumb size at the least. Meditate that there is a vital drop at the heart, either radiant white tinged with red or else utterly white. The size should be relative to the guru's form: if you meditate on a four-finger-width body, then the drop is the size of a fava bean; if the body is thumb-sized, then the drop is the size of a small bean. This goes for anything in between as well. In any case, light radiates from that vital drop in the guru's heart and pervades the body with brilliant clarity, filling the mind stream with bliss. Light rays shine from every part of the guru's form, pervading your own body with brilliant clarity inside and out. Imagine that light rays stream from all your pores, suffusing all appearance with brilliant clarity. Focus your attention on the vital drop in the guru's heart for a prolonged period. Then again do the visualization of radiating light rays, alternating between them again and again to familiarize yourself. At bedtime, focus your attention on the syllable *hūṃ* in the guru's heart and lie down. {72} Other meditation styles are the same as before. This is the forty-fifth round of visualization.

This is the primary visualization for the main practice of grasping lucid clarity. That is because the dharma chakra at the heart is the main site where delusion occurs in deep sleep. If you meditate on the path by targeting that vital point, then it is also the main site where lucid clarity arises, the antidote for that delusion. But you may wonder if the other two methods are of any help in applying that vital point. Visualizations of that kind are not definite. In general, the best place for lucid clarity of deep sleep to arise is the heart. However, in the beginning, when it is difficult to insert the vital winds there, you can have the immediate experience of lucid clarity from the gathering of the winds if you target other places of the central channel. Then if you familiarize with that repeatedly, it will lead to the effortless confluence of winds and mind at the heart with just a minor shift in your intentionality. Lucid clarity itself will then arise easily. This method should also be applied to Dream and the others. Therefore, you do need to meditate with effort until you gain ability on whichever of these three visualizations for recognizing lucid clarity suits your mentality. It is not absolutely necessary for a single individual to meditate on all three.

Session 46

b. Integrating Lucid Clarity

Although there are two headings in the outline [of *The Inventory* by Khyungpo Naljor] for this—Integrating the Three Kāyas in the Daytime and Self-Arising of the Three Kāyas at Nighttime—in practice there is only one: Integrating the Three Kāyas in the Daytime. With regard to this, in the beginning the practice in the session breaks is very important. {73} It replaces the threefold intentionality explained in the context of Illusory Body—that is, the explanations of the root as a sense of impermanence and disillusionment and the supplication that grows the flowers. Accordingly, in the session breaks of Lucid Clarity practice, you need to meditate on impermanence and guru devotion as explained before in Illusory Body. Then, as a substitute for the necessary intentionality for recognizing illusion and dream in the practices of Illusory Body and Dream yoga, here you must apply the Integration of the Three Kāyas. In Samdingpa's guidebook, there is no clear distinction between sessions and session breaks. Jakchen states, "While focusing attention on the syllable *A*, maintain a balance between concentration and relaxation." We can understand this to mean that while visualizing the letter *A*, though awareness wanders, don't try too hard to prevent that distraction. It means to meditate [this way] at all times in equipoise and subsequent attainment, indicating meditation in both sessions and session breaks. In general, this instruction is certainly in keeping with the manner of placement during meditation sessions. However, the session practice has already been explained elsewhere, so here it applies only to the session breaks.

When you eat, walk, move, lie down, sit, and so on—during all daily activities—think that you must remember this Integration of the Three Kāyas. So set your intentions again and again while walking and sitting and so on. During whatever activities you engage, focus your attention directly on whatever happens, relax consciousness inward, and glance at your own nature just enough to recognize it. During those times, hold your gaze with wide-open unblinking eyes. Also, at first, even though it is a session break when you are supposedly resting in a leisurely way, just recalling this will cause sudden experiences. Then eventually you can even apply this to all busy activity. {74}

Furthermore, the clear aspect connected with whatever myriad appearances arise is the clarity of nirmāṇakāya. Looking openly at your own nature and not seeing anything at all is the emptiness of dharmakāya. Just the mere awareness and clarity of mind arises at once as a single taste, essentially inseparable, without any fabrication regarding the various appearances, and without any recognition [of them]. That is the innate awareness and innate clarity of saṃbhogakāya. That is the integration.

In this way, first train well in this applied virtue in the session breaks. After that, when you can mostly integrate that, recall any of the three intentions that are suitable for the occasion.

The three kāyas arise by themselves at night through the force of intense application of the visualizations during the sessions and the meditation of integrating the three kāyas during session breaks. When you grasp lucid clarity at nighttime in deep sleep, it is the natural arising of the three kāyas, the unity of clarity and emptiness. Regarding clarity during sleep, at this time myriad coarse appearances do not arise. Rather, it is the clear aspect of awareness itself and the various appearing signs of experience that arise. This is the forty-sixth round of visualization.

c. Blending Lucid Clarity

This has four parts: (1) Blending Clarity and Emptiness, (2) Blending Equipoise and Postmeditation Attainment, (3) Blending Day and Night, and (4) Blending Bliss and Emptiness.

Session 47

i. Blending Clarity and Emptiness

During meditative equipoise there is an experience of your mind not existing at all. That meditation is the condition for an experience of utter emptiness, as if there were nothing whatsoever. Even during the intervals between sessions, the thought occurs to you that all the things you face do not exist. That is the arising of the experience of unaccompanied emptiness. In those situations, whether in sessions or breaks, turn your eyes to the sky, rouse your awareness, and regard the basis of that utter emptiness. {75} Through that, you will gradually discover clarity in that emptiness and it will become emptiness-clarity. Also, during the sessions, when there are no conceptual thoughts, vivid clarity accompanied by joy and bliss will occur. There may be strong craving for that experience during session breaks. If a sense of self-complacency is present, that is the arising of the experience of unaccompanied clarity. Therefore, during all sessions and breaks, look at the essence of mind's pristine radiance and bare clarity and scrutinize it intensely. Through that it will vanish and leave nothing to recognize, as when tangible things disintegrate. Rest within that state without fabrication or contrivance. When you look at the mind, recall again and again that "it is like an illusion." Clarity and emptiness will arise. In this way, blend clarity and emptiness. This is the forty-seventh round of visualization.

Session 48

ii. Blending Equipoise and Postmeditation Attainment

In general, if you have genuine postmeditation attainment, it is not necessary to intentionally blend it with resting in equipoise. But here we are applying the terms *equipoise* (*mnyam gzhag*) to meditation sessions and *postmeditation attainment* (*rjes thob*) only to the intervals between sessions. Now during the sessions, resting momentarily in the empty clarity of mind without contrived effort may occur again and again, but in the breaks there is nothing other than that initial ordinary state. The experience of empty clarity just never happens. If that's the case, then when that slight experience arises, set the intention to blend it with whatever you are doing. For instance, repeatedly develop intentionality by thinking, "Now while I am doing circumambulations, I will nurture this experience." When you arise from a session of meditation, also hold the continuity of that thought with mindfulness. Even set up a sign to remind yourself, like something carried on your hand. {76} Then when the time comes to circumambulate, maintain the Integration of the Three Kāyas just as it was described, so that the experience of empty clarity in the meditation session will happen just as it was described. In this way, after a few days have passed, you will not need to exert great effort. Once you are familiar with it, other activities will all gradually be affected. This is the blending of the experiences of equipoise with postmeditation attainment. There is no need to blend the postmeditation attainment back into the equipoise. Some practitioners have excellent experiences in postmeditation, which will also be an enhancement of their experience in equipoise. But that happens automatically; it won't help to contrive it. This is the forty-eighth round of visualization.

Session 49

iii. Blending Day and Night

Even if experiences of empty clarity arise during the daytime sessions, they may not show up in the deep sleep of the nighttime. If so, rely on a suitable one of the three session visualizations. Then meditate with the vase breathing and intensely squeeze your awareness. When an experience of empty clarity arises, think with a modicum of intentionality, "Tonight when I sleep, this is exclusively what I will meditate on." Then, in the morning break, also develop your intention somewhat. In the afternoon and evening session breaks, it is important to train with intense intentionality. Then, at bedtime, hold a few gentle breaths and meditate on the visualization. Finally, turn your attention to your body and mind and go to sleep within a state of settled openness. That will definitely allow you to grasp the applied virtue of sleep. For some practitioners, the excellent applied virtue of the nighttime arises right from the start, and by merely recalling those experiences during the day, the applied virtue of the daytime is enhanced. {77}

This also happens automatically. In regard to Lucid Clarity, this [blending] occurs appropriately as needed. In the energy training of Dream, there are very many methods, since the nighttime experiences enhance the intentional focus in the daytime. This is the forty-ninth round of visualization.

Session 50

iv. Blending Bliss and Emptiness Inseparably

Tremendous bliss will arise in the joy brought on by experiences of mental clarity, emptiness, and nonthought. But it is not necessary to seek it out and blend it with emptiness. This will happen on of its own accord by knowing that the clarity itself is like an illusion. It *is* necessary to blend with emptiness in the experiences of melting bliss: the bliss from [practices with] another's body, the knowledge consort; the Inner Heat of one's own body as the method; the Illusory Body like that for those of lesser capability; the Vital Points of the Four Empowerments of Drops; or the likes of the three visualizations for grasping lucid clarity. Meditation on those practices causes the bliss-warmth of the winds dissolving in the central channel to arise. In such cases, it is necessary to blend [with emptiness]. This is not to say that you should blend immediately after each experience of bliss. That would dispel the experience, so don't do that. You only need to blend after the experience comes again and again and becomes stable. If you do not manifest pride and attachment, just looking at your own nature causes the unhindered appearance of bliss. Relax into that and let go without identifying it and maintain just that. That is sufficient. If attachment and conceit do arise, train with the intentionality of the illusion-like nature of that very bliss. Ultimately, when you rest in mahāmudrā, free of fixation on illusion, it becomes bliss and emptiness inseparable.

During all four of those occasions of blending, no matter what activity you are up to during the breaks, {78} all you need is to look repeatedly at whatever arises with the elephant's gaze and enter in open astonished awareness. At the time of resting in equipoise, with whatever experiences of conceptual clarity and emptiness arise and whenever you are applying the vital points of conceptual visualizations—at all those times it is crucial to enter that same state. Then again, in session or in break, know that happiness and suffering, high and low, and the eight worldly concerns are all like an illusion. This will destroy the reifications of good and bad, high and low, near and far—the celebrated categories of the modern world. This itself is important. This is the fiftieth round of visualization.

d. Ultimate Lucid Clarity

In the beginning, whether Lucid Clarity of the daytime or the nighttime, the first realization to arise will be the lucid clarity of inseparable clarity and emptiness. This corresponds to the path of accumulation. Then the lucid clarity of inseparable bliss and emptiness arises. This concerns the path of application. Then the lucid clarity of profound peace free of embellishment arises. This corresponds to arriving at each of the seven impure stages. Then the lucid clarity of consummate inseparability arises. This is the occasion of the three pure stages. After that is the lucid clarity endowed with dual purity; the dharmakāya of timeless awareness through perfect awakening. Of course, if one were to explain this subject extensively, there would be much more, but I will not elaborate here. In general, the term *lucid clarity* (*'od gsal*) here has been defined as the manner of realizing true nature, not as a category of the Lucid Clarity of sleep per se. There is no particular visualization here, so it does not count as a round of visualization. It could be taught in sessions as appropriate.

3. Concluding Practices

This has five parts: (1) general and specific sacred pledges; (2) removing obstructions, the self-purification of faults and mistakes; (3) enhancement practices that resolve doubt; (4) identifying special perceptions; and (5) divisions of daytime and nighttime, experiences and realizations. {79}

a. General and Specific Sacred Pledges

In general, it is important not to impair the training of whichever of the three levels of vows you have taken. Even previous experiences could degenerate if a fault or mistake occurs. Above all, the flawless sacred pledges of Secret Mantra must not be tainted by the root and branch downfalls. If those sacred pledges are damaged, forget about hopes for meditation; there won't be even a modicum of higher-realm happiness in this or the next life because you will go directly to the three miserable realms. This applies to sacred pledge in general. Furthermore, if you are able to practice all the sacred pledges of equipoise and postmeditation, those are also included in that. However, many kinds of activities to ensure that your oaths have not shifted may disturb the mind even more, so do not do that. Without ever parting from your practice or from devotion to the guru, do not compromise the kunda bodhicitta, which is the support of practice, and meditate on all ordinary objects of attraction and aversion as illusion-like without falling under their power. These are the sacred pledges particular to Lucid Clarity. Although here we say "lucid clarity," it does not refer only to the nighttime Lucid Clarity in the Six Dharmas but to all Lucid Clarity of daytime and nighttime. Therefore, it should be understood to apply generally to the blending with illusory body, as well as to the practices of Transference and Intermediate State because those are branches of Blending. Thus this sacred pledge covers all the sacred pledges.

b. Removing Obstructions, the Self-Purification of Faults and Mistakes

In general, the texts about dispelling obstructions connected with the path of methods is presented elsewhere. Here, empty clarity without fixation, empty appearance that arises by itself, and empty bliss without attachment are all the timeless awareness of experience. {80} The devil that is the antithesis of those is to get lost in fixating on regular conceptual thought. Therefore, look at the very nature of those thoughts and meditate on recognizing their self-liberated, self-purified, self-empty state. Furthermore, conceptual thought is mind, and mind is unborn and unlimited. With that vital point, look at whatever arises without contrivance or fabrication and autonomous perceptions will vanish. Remain in the natural movement [of thoughts] that do not incline toward either appearance or emptiness. Again, sometimes push it to extremes with the intense intentionality of knowing that all awareness and appearances of the various perceptions are like an illusion. Just these two methods will liberate you from all the sufferings of obstructions and erroneous directions.

c. Enhancement Practices That Resolve Doubt

Some teach that having conviction in one's own experience without any doubts enhances practice. Some teach that the two immeasurables are an enhancement. Apart from those, here is what you can do: refine the energy of intentionality of illusion and dream, and train vigorously in nonthought directly with the particular myriad appearances and objects of happiness and sadness, attraction and aversion. Generate the force of whatever intentionality is suitable in indefinite places, indefinite positions, and indefinite activities of going and staying. Meditating again and again this way is the outer enhancement. Occasionally meditating with intense focus unconcerned with life or death in the methods of conjoining vital winds and mind in the intense application of channels and winds is the inner enhancement. After each of those two enhancement practices, there will come a strong dynamic energy of awareness, generating the certitude of resolution. {81} Know it to be the guru's kindness and pray. It is good to meditate with compassion for sentient beings who do not have such realization. Do this if you need to enhance practice.

d. Identifying Special Perceptions

Since this is extensively presented elsewhere, there is no need for a detailed explanation at this point. However, having said that, there are indeed these four topics: (1) the perception of clarity, (2) the perception of nonthought, (3) the perception of bliss, and (4) the perception of unity.

First, for the clarity aspect of the experience of lucid clarity, there arise various appearances of signs during sleep, physical experiences, and mental experiences. Second, ringing in the ears, deep darkness, and oppressive heaviness will come. This is the wind-mind entering the central channel. Again, there will be experiences of shaking, quivering, fainting, and flailing limbs. This is the release of the channel knots. Further, there will be an experience like consciousness disappearing into the sky and a kind of trembling when experiencing the great clarity-appearance of nonthought. If you feel exultation and conceit about these, it will negatively impact your applied virtue. If you grasp them as the manifestations of sickness and spirits, they will become obstructions. Maintain a flexible attitude without liking or disliking what occurs. Third is the arising of bliss-clarity in body and mind. Fourth is the dawning of lucid clarity without effort or exertion in all times of day and night. So it is said.

e. Divisions of Daytime and Nighttime, Experiences and Realizations

On the occasions of meditating on new, mentally created [subjects], such as a deity's form or vital-essence drops, no matter the degree of clarity, it is neither lucid clarity nor the self-arising deity's form. {82} When awareness is tightened up and you rest in that with diligent thoughts of intentionality, you will think that mind abides just a little and that you are having experiences of bliss and clarity. When just that occurs during any circumstances of waking life, it is still not real lucid clarity. It is just the cause that can lead to lucid clarity. Therefore, whether in sessions or breaks, without exerting any purposeful effort in that particular situation, naturally arising mental clarity, bliss, and nonthought will dawn. That is called lucid clarity, whether it occurs in the day or the night. Also, around those times, if the deity's form suddenly arises as oneself or externally without particularly wanting it to, then that is called the self-arising deity's form of illusory body. It makes no difference if you are awake or dreaming.

Surely this must seem like the tall tales of a great meditator or the boastful complaints of sufferings endured in mountain retreats, at which tantric scholars and learned persons level criticism. But one can trust oneself when in one's own territory. I have direct personal experience and no reason to fear criticism. If we are able to meditate, all of us beginners, learned and ignorant alike, we do not need to suffer actual great hardships or wait for a very long time. When conditions are right, a little something will happen. Since that will benefit the mind, it will also provide immediate joy and comfort. Beginners such as ourselves cannot carry the practice of the unity of Illusory Body and Lucid Clarity that is commensurate with the stages and paths [of a bodhisattva]. But ultimately these practical steps for our current situation will become the effective cause of those states. It is like when we carefully cultivate small sprouts that will become an abundant autumn harvest in the end. {83}

There are two types of lucid clarity: the lucid clarity of experience and the lucid clarity of realization. Those two can be subdivided into the lucid clarity of the daytime waking experience and the lucid clarity of nighttime sleep. Dividing each of those four into lucid clarity with appearances and without appearances makes eight. The four categories with appearances can be further divided into four related to outer appearances and four not related to outer appearances, making eight. The four categories without appearances can each be subdivided into shallow lucid clarity and deep lucid clarity, again making eight. Adding all that up makes sixteen [categories of lucid clarity]. For the disciples in whom experiences have dawned, identify these categories and explain them in detail. This will introduce the practitioners to the type of lucid clarity they have experienced. For the disciples who have not had experiences arise, or in a group of people with various levels of experience, it is sufficient just to name these sixteen divisions.

Although Blending, Ultimate Lucid Clarity, and the five concluding practices are included in the outline of Lucid Clarity, one of the Six Dharmas, in fact they should be understood as guides for sustaining the experiences after one has already applied the instructions of Fierce Inner Heat, Illusory Body, Dream, and Lucid Clarity. These concluding practices contain many important vital visualizations to take into practice. However, since they come last in the sequence as instructions in the meditation subjects, they are not included in the divisions of the visualization rounds for immediate use. Add them in however many teachings sessions are appropriate.

These are called the four root dharmas, or Blending with Illusory Body. As for so-called Blending [and] Transference, there are many different categories of blending in the individual instructions of Lord Marpa the Translator that are not explained here.[26] {84}

In the tradition of this instruction, there are four types of blending, such as Blending Clarity and Emptiness. Further, there are what is known as the four or three wisdoms of Blending [and] Transference (*bsre 'pho*). The three wisdoms are the wisdom of mistaken wisdom, the wisdom of conventional wisdom, and the wisdom of ultimate wisdom. In the context of the great bliss that is accomplished through special techniques, when at first there is a mere arising of bliss, an attitude of attachment to this dissipating experience distorts it. This is misguided knowledge. Then the bliss arises of one's own mind like an illusion, which is the knowledge of conventional reality. That is the blending of the mistaken with the wisdom of knowledge of the conventional. The knowledge of the ultimate is the arising of the unfabricated experience of basic space. That is the blending of conventional knowledge with the wisdom of the ultimate knowledge. To recognize the arising of basic space directly in everything that arises is the blending of wisdom with any appearance. As that indicates, when just hazy appearances arise during waking hours, it is mistaken knowledge. When that arises as illusion, it is conventional knowledge. When there is natural freedom from fixating on that illusion, it is ultimate knowledge. When that is carried over to whatever arises, it is the blending of wisdom with any appearance. Similarly, when a lucid dream merely arises, it is mistaken; when you know that dream as illusion, it is conventional; and not fixating on that illusion is ultimate knowledge. When that is carried over into sleep, waking, and all states, it is the blending of timeless awareness with whatever appears. When you fall into unconsciousness in deep sleep, it is mistaken; when there is recollection of bliss and clarity within that, it is conventional; and when that remains naturally unfabricated, it is ultimate knowledge. When that seals the times of waking and dream, it is the inseparability of timeless awareness and whatever appears. {85}

According to this classification of the four wisdoms, the inseparability of timeless awareness and whatever appears is termed the "wisdom of the knowledge of unity." It is said that the self-arising deity's form during Illusory Body and Dream has aspects of all three: conventional, ultimate, and unity. More blendings have also been taught: the blending of the bliss of the Path of Methods [Fierce Inner Heat] with Illusory Body, the blending of the bliss-emptiness of Lucid Clarity with Dream, and the blending back and forth of Illusory Body and Dream. Thus the meaning of *blending* is to integrate inseparably [two or more practices] on the path.

Furthermore, if we are to explain the ground, abiding, and methods of blending, at this point the following must be understood. All delusion of samsaric beings can be subsumed into four states: waking, deep sleep, dreaming, and the passion of intercourse. Those four states obscure awakened body, speech, mind, and great bliss of the realm of phenomena [at the time of] the ground. Four timeless awarenesses on the path will dispel those obscurations: appearance-emptiness, awareness-emptiness, clarity-emptiness, and bliss-emptiness, respectively. In this context, awareness-emptiness is called nonthought. The primary practices [to remove those obscurations and develop those awarenesses] are, in order, Illusory Body, Lucid Clarity, Dream, and Fierce Inner Heat. The ultimate result of meditating on those is the actualization of nirmāṇakāya, dharmakāya, saṃbhogakāya, and sukhakāya. If those are correlated with the five types of timeless awareness, Illusory Body is the path to accomplish mirror-like awareness, Lucid Clarity is for equanimity awareness, Dream is for discriminating awareness, and Fierce Inner Heat is the timeless awareness of accomplishment of activities. Everyone agrees on those. As for the accomplishment of activities, it is taught that it corresponds in general to all four results, and it is also taught that both discriminating awareness and accomplishment of activities apply to Dream. {86} But in the teaching continuity of esoteric instructions, karmamudrā is explained as the path of accomplishment of activities. But there is no contradiction.

E. Transference, Buddhahood without Meditation

Transference of consciousness, which enables buddhahood without meditation, has two parts: (1) Transference according to the source texts and (2) a supplementary esoteric instruction.

1. Transference in the Source Texts

First, from the sources, there are four parts: (1) Transference in the Suchness of Dharmakāya, (2) Transference in the Union with the Yidam, (3) Transference in the Blessings of the Guru, and (4) Transference to the Unerring Celestial Realm.

a. Transference in the Suchness of Dharmakāya

At death, when mother and child lucid clarity meet, there is no more cause for any further deaths and existences. Since the bliss and emptiness of lucid clarity arises naturally to the yogin, they do not depend on the instructions of Transference above. They will be naturally liberated right then and there. There is no separate visualization here, so it is not counted as a round of visualization.

Session 51

b. Transference in the Union with the Yidam

The preliminaries are the same as in the section on Illusory Body, except that the last line of the supplication is changed to "Please bless me with buddhahood in the intermediate state." With yourself as the deity, meditate on whatever yidam you like in the space above your head. Though that is what is generally said, if it is not fixed, a foolish person's yidam will not be well calculated. Therefore, on this occasion, meditate on either Cakrasaṃvara or Hevajra at a distance of one arrow's length above your head. In the center of your body is the white central channel as it was described previously. The lower end reaches the perineum and is closed; the upper end touches the cranial aperture with its open end the same width as that of the aperture. Meditate on it as light and transparent, like an open skylight. Inside the central channel, clearly imagine your own mind as a white *A* at the navel, and the yidam's seed syllable at the lower end, a blue *hūṃ* that is the nature of vital winds. {87} At that point, clear away the dead air and hold the gentle breathing for a while. Concentrate intently on the *A* at the navel and the *hūṃ* at the perineum. Again as you exhale, make the sound of a long *hrīk* if you expel from the mouth or a long *hūṃ* if you expel from the nose, or don't make any sound as you forcefully clear out the vital winds. At that point, the *hūṃ* at the lower end is forceful and carries the navel *A* upward. The two stacked letters travel up through the central channel and shoot far out of the cranial aperture, reaching the yidam's heart. At that point, rest awhile in the way of no recollection without thinking of anything at all. In that situation, the vital winds will also fall naturally. In this way, meditate repeatedly some seven times. Afterward, the two stacked letters fall downward from the yidam's heart and enter your crown, traveling down the central channel. The *A* letter stays at the navel, and the *hūṃ* goes to the perineum. Imagine that they both become heavy. That is one short session of visualization. Meditate that way again and again. At the end of the session, after the two syllable letters have descended as before, the yidam melts into light and dissolves into you. Think that light radiating from the blue *hūṃ* becomes like a cover that firmly blocks the cranial aperture. Meditate in this way until the signs of successful transference begin to emerge. Then just meditate once on the visualization each day. This is the fifty-first round of visualization.

Session 52

c. Transference in the Blessings of the Guru

The preliminaries are the same as before. In the main practice, also meditate as before on the central channel. It is taught that within the central channel there is a white vital drop at the navel. It is also said that it is yellow or whatever. {88} But in practice, it is white with a yellow radiance and radiates light, like a karketana gem (chrysoberyl). Visualize it as round and rolled up, the size of a pea. Apply the breathing technique as before. That white-yellow drop projects far out of the crown of your head and dissolves into the guru's heart. After repeating this whole visualization seven times, do the visualization of the drop descending. Meditate on that drop resting in the navel, heavy, with an experience of bliss. That constitutes one short session. Meditate repeatedly on just that. At the end of the session, after the wind-mind falls to the navel, your loving devotion to the guru causes the guru to melt into light. It enters your cranial aperture and dissolves, filling your body and mind with bliss. Think that a white drop also blocks the cranial aperture on the crown of your head. Meditate in that way until showing signs of success. When applying those two methods of transference [at death], meditate only on the ascending transference [of the drop]. You won't need the return descent, and you also won't need to block the opening when the session ends. This is the fifty-second round of visualization.

d. Transference to the Unerring Celestial Realm

In general, this is included in the lineup of esoteric instructions. However, it is said to be a severely restricted precept and so has been sealed, not to be taught in a group. Therefore, you must learn it from another source. The Ḍākinī of Timeless Awareness herself taught five other methods subsumed in the subject of Transference, but they are not part of the regular outline.

2. Supplementary Esoteric Instructions

Now, there are many explanations of Transference in the source texts, but in practice it is taught that one should practice the Skylight of Timeless Awareness (*ye shes skar khung ma*). Of course, this is not because those original Transference methods were never practiced {89} but rather in consideration of the many practitioners who made this their main practice. There are two parts here: (1) the training and (2) the applications.

Session 53

a. Training

The preliminaries are the same as before. After the guru melts into light and dissolves into you, imagine your body becomes the empty hollow form of the deity. Meditate on the central channel as described in the yidam Transference. Inside the central channel, meditate on a white tetrahedral source of phenomena at the level of the navel. The fine tip faces downward, while the wide-open part faces upward with one vertex facing the front and the back surface [between the other two vertices] aligned with the back. Within that is the white letter *A*, situated without touching any support. Imagine it clearly the size of a small pea or a mustard seed. Other than the size, the rest of the visualization of the source of phenomena and the white *A* letter is the same as in the purifying inner space preliminary practice.

Exhale the dead air and then hold the vase breath forcefully for a short time. Focus intently on the white *A*. While holding the breath, slightly squeeze your belly toward your spine. The white *A* lifts up a bit and then returns to its former place. When you squeeze a little harder, it rises higher than before, and again comes to rest in its place. Then suddenly squeeze as hard as you can for an instant, forcing the vital winds to concentrate in the upper body. Visualize that the sides of the source of phenomena strike each other, which causes your mind as the white *A* to shoot up like an arrow through the central channel as if chased by the winds. It comes out of the cranial aperture and continues high into the sky. As it reaches higher and higher into space, imagine that it vanishes into the sky. Space, sky, and awareness—these three blend inseparably. {90} Rest openly just there. Do that visualization again and again, some seven times. Then, for the descent, a white *A* suddenly appears in the middle of the sky. It falls down through your cranial aperture and descends slowly down the path of the central channel. It lands in the center of the source of phenomena in the navel and remains there in its proper place, firm and heavy. This constitutes a single short session.

Meditate in this way again and again. In each long session there should be twenty-one or eleven or seven such short sessions. Practicing that way in four or six or so sessions a day will quickly bring the signs of success. There is no doubt that the relative best, middling, or least signs will occur in a week, or two weeks, or a month, depending on your degree of effort. The best sign is a lump swelling up on the top of your head, oozing pus from there, and so forth. Also, each time you do the visualization, if the two tendons in the back of the head stiffen, the eyes feel numb, or you become unconscious, these are also signs. The middling sign is just the lump on the head and, in front, something like the [neck] arteries stiffening. The least sign will be itching and pulsating on the top of the head. If these signs do not appear, it is said that you should do one of the two visualizations above. If you faint into unconsciousness for a long time by just meditating on the visualization that is the most clear, it is taught that covering your head with a bowl made of precious materials will prevent the problem of passing away. However, for this kind of problem it is best to strike your joints and do the forceful drop yogic exercises (*'bebs*). Once the signs have arisen, you should meditate on each visualization once a day. In general, if you refine the channel path through practicing Transference now, even if the transference visualization is not clear at the time of death, one can usually project out through the channel path since it was opened and cleared previously. However, it is not sure whether that will work every time, so better if there is a clear visualization to effect an infallible [transition]. If you set aside your interest in this meditation and a long time passes, it's possible that clarity will not arrive in the hour of your need. Therefore, in order to keep the continuity of training undiminished, this is a meditation for [a once daily] session. The remaining sessions should involve important meditations such as those of Illusory Body.

b. Application

This is the same as described before. When sure signs of imminent death arrive, do not be attached to your property. Offer it to whomever inspires you and donate to charity. Acknowledge and repair any grudges or exclusions that you [have created], in person or indirectly. Relinquish the attitude of attachment to those close to you. You must cut the ties of connection and meditate. At this point, there is also an explanation of transference using substances, which is good to practice but not indispensable. This is the fifty-third round of visualization.

Regarding everything up to this point, in Fierce Inner Heat practice you meditate on the central channel as red. For all the other practices, it is described in different ways in the many other guidebooks, such as white on the outside and red on the inside, and so forth. But in actual practice it is exclusively white. In the Skylight of Timeless Awareness practice, you need to meditate on the central channel as slightly wider when the source of phenomena is within it. It is the same in the Vital Points of the Four Empowerments of Drops. Of course, there is the explanation of the source of phenomena as white outside and red inside and so forth as appropriate. But other than the occasion of the Intermediate Stage, in the visualizations of the source texts for the other Six Dharmas, it is the oral tradition to always make the source of phenomena white. During the Path of Methods and Lucid Clarity, there is the custom of meditating on the whole body pervaded by the central channel, as described in all the old books. However, for beginners, this won't actually bring much benefit, so it is said to be unnecessary, and was not mentioned in the course of instruction. {92}

F. Intermediate State, the Victors' Saṃbhogakāya

This has four parts: (1) the Natural Arising of Dharmakāya in the Lucid Clarity of the First Intermediate State for the best, (2) the Natural Arising of the Victors' Saṃbhogakāya for the average, (3) the Natural Arising of Unrestricted Nirmāṇakāya for the lesser, and (4) instructions of general unerring vital points.

1. The Natural Arising of Dharmakāya in the Lucid Clarity of the First Intermediate State for the Best

This carries the same meaning as previous descriptions of the absence of something transferred or a transferring agent. The first intermediate state refers to the timeless awareness arising in the merging of mother and child lucid clarity when the mind at death transforms into the lucid clarity of empty bliss, since that arises during the first intermediate state. That is called the dharmakāya of death. When one arises from that state, instead of continuing through the intermediate states of ordinary individuals, the deity's form arises by itself like an illusion. That is called the natural arising of lucid clarity, but it should be understood as the natural arising *from* lucid clarity.

Those who have experienced the empty bliss and deity's form without interruption during waking hours and entered lucid clarity at all times in deep sleep, even if they have not finished the energy training of Dream, may have this natural arising of the pure vision of the deity's form. This is an individual to whom the dharmakāya arises naturally in the lucid clarity of the first intermediate state.

There is no separate visualization connected with this section. If you wish to explain these subjects in detail, do so in one or two or however many teachings sessions is suitable.

Session 54

2. The Natural Arising of the Victors' Saṃbhogakāya for the Average

The preliminaries stay the same as in Illusory Body, except that the last line of the supplication is changed to "May I attain saṃbhogakāya in the intermediate state." After the guru dissolves into you, regard yourself and all appearances. Train intensively with the thought "This is really the intermediate state of becoming." Cultivate strong disillusionment as well by recollecting the sufferings of the six kinds of migrators in cyclic existence and the shortcomings of afflictive desire and anger. {93} Contemplate this, thinking, "In this situation of the intermediate state, if there is delusion, it is really strong delusion; each thought of desire or anger can instantly turn into hell. Although meditation [during the time of] the path also brings powerful liberation, now a single moment of meditation here is more effective and enriching than months and years of meditation during waking life. Now I must not be deluded and fall under the power of afflictive emotions. I will meditate on the saṃbhogakāya of the victors as given me by my guru."

From within emptiness, a blue source of phenomena appears before you. Its tip is pointed down and its wide opening faces upward. Think, "To those without natural realization, this is the mother's womb. To those with realization, surely this is the actual palace of the Unsurpassed Pure Land (Akaniṣṭha)." Then you yourself arrive in its center. Your mind becomes the blue letter *hūṃ*, large and blazing with light. The light rays radiating from it strike the source of phenomena. Imagine that all the habitual patterns and karmic debts of your previous womb birth are purified. Similarly, all karma for womb birth is purified, and the doors to future births are blocked. The habitual patterns of the three other places of birth are consequently self-purified. With the thought "This is surely the intermediate state," meditate that the *hūṃ* is completely transformed and you instantly become Coemergent Cakrasaṃvara. Thinking, "This is surely the intermediate state," meditate on the guru upon a four-tiered seat on your head. Supplicate with single-pointed focus: "Please let me obtain the saṃbhogakāya now in this intermediate state." It is important to constantly develop the intentionality of thinking, "This is actually the intermediate state" at all times while meditating with this visualization. This is the fifty-fourth round of visualization.

Session 55

3. The Natural Arising of Unrestricted Nirmāṇakāya for the Lesser

Add this one after completing meditation on the previous visualization. {94} Think, "This is all the intermediate state; I can change all this appearance." As soon as you think all appearing form is the body of Cakrasaṃvara, everything stands up as the Heruka couple. As soon as you think of changing the entire range of sound into something like the seven-syllable mantra, that mantra itself resounds. During the day, meditate intently on all mental thoughts and memories—happiness and sadness, desire and anger, and so forth—as like illusion and dream. When dreams come up, merely recalling those three transformations will release you from all afflictions and sufferings. [This is the fifty-fifth round of visualization.]

Session 56

4. General Unerring Vital Points

On this subject most gurus say, "This is for the least of the lesser. These general infallible vital points, in terms of being a practice for those of the lowest capability, are explained immediately after fully completing the visualizations of unimpeded nirmāṇakāya, and exclusively as an addition to that meditation. Moreover, the last three Intermediate State visualizations do not stand on their own, but they are each added to the previous one." From one point of view, this is certainly true. However, if it is only taken in that way, then the name "general unerring vital points" loses its meaning. It is possible that this visualization should be added to the practices for the average practitioner. But to say it should also be added to the practice for those of lesser capability also makes sense. Since the teachings on the Intermediate State are subsumed into practices for highest, average, and lesser capabilities, there is actually no need to posit a fourth level. {95} The notes and clarification in *The Inventory* and the *Clarification* only mention general infallible vital points but do not connect it with the levels of capability. Therefore, it is appropriate as a visualization for either average or lesser. Meditating on this added visualization seems to give meaning to the term *unerring* (*chugs med*). As it is said:

> Guru, yidam, and illusory body;
> integrate these three constantly.
> For the great fears of intermediate state,
> unerring esoteric instructions are crucial.[27]

With intense intentionality for the intermediate state, meditate that among the six types of beings, all males, and particularly those who arouse your ire, are gathered on the right side of the source of phenomena where you are. Present the complete four offerings and say, "Please let me obtain the saṃbhogakāya in the intermediate state." All the females of the five types and especially those that arouse your desire are all gathered on the left side of the source of phenomena. After presenting the complete four offerings, supplicate with, "Please let me obtain the saṃbhogakāya in the intermediate state." Again, with devotion to the guru and the clarity of yourself and others as the deities' forms, generate powerful intentionality regarding the lack of reality [of those appearances], to be a support practice. Meditate again and again in this way. From the point of view of female meditators, the objects that arouse desire and anger are reversed. Although you should meditate that the blue source of phenomena where you are is extremely spacious and that they are all within it to the right and left sides, if that is difficult to visualize, it is said to be suitable to meditate that they are all in the space directly above or even outside [the source of phenomena]. {96} Also, my guru said that at first you as the yidam face the front side of the source of phenomena, but at this point turn to face the back of it because the six kinds of beings have changed into the forms of deities who come before you, and you need to make offerings and supplications to them. This is the fifty-sixth round of visualization.

On top of these fifty-six rounds of visualization, there is also the Inner Space Dispelling Sickness and Spirits, the last two subcategories of Illusory Body for those of lowest capabilities, Ultimate Lucid Clarity, the five parts of the concluding practices [of Lucid Clarity], and the [two] Transference practices in the first intermediate state. That makes sixty-seven teaching sessions in all.[28] Here, "teaching session" (*chos thun*) designates only the word guidances; the actual number of sessions are indefinite. If each visualization were assigned to each session independently of whether or not there is an actual session of visualization, we could call it sixty-seven visualizations [rather than teaching sessions].

III. [Conclusion]

namo guru

In this profound path of Niguma's Six Dharmas, there are four [styles of transmission empowerments]: (1) the extensive style wherein all the branches are presented in detail, (2) the intermediate style that condenses them in general, (3) the concise style that leaves no topic incomplete, and (4) the extremely concise style that condenses the vital points.

A. The Extensive Style wherein All the Branches Are Presented in Detail

Here, the empowerments for the Six Dharmas known as the Ten Permissions (*bka' bcu*) are conferred in full. At the juncture of completing the guidance in Dream, there were the explanations taken from the Illusory Body in a Single Sitting, the Natural Liberation of Fixation, the two refinement practices, the cycle of five visualizations, and so forth, as well as the extensive [instruction] on preventing excess (*'byams gcod*). At the juncture of completing Lucid Clarity, the recognition of the doors of perception in lucid clarity and the choices found in the supplementary writings were presented. However, the more recent practice is not to do those additional visualizations but to confer the empowerments in their entirety. {97} With regard to that, if you want to confer the empowerment during the specific time for each of the Ten Permissions, first confer the complete four empowerments of the Five-Deity Cakrasaṃvara. At the juncture following the general preliminaries, taking refuge, and arousing the mind of awakening, confer the empowerment of Five-Deity Cakrasaṃvara absorption empowerment, because it is the way of enhancing the yidam. Even though this isn't included in the actual Ten Permissions of the Six Dharmas, there is the empowerment of the Five Tantras' Deities absorption empowerment that is normally given at a suitable time during the guidance for Purifying Inner Space. When the guidance for the preliminaries is finished but Fierce Inner Heat has not yet begun, confer the particular permission (*sgos bka'*) for Fierce Inner Heat. Between Fierce Inner Heat and Illusory Body, do the particular permission for Illusory Body. Between that and the guidance in Dream, do the particular permission for Dream. Between that and the guidance in Lucid Clarity, do the particular permission for Lucid Clarity. These do not vary.

On this occasion of the extensive transmission, regarding the Great Empowerment of Illusory Body, some say that it is given directly in the midst of blending with illusory body, and they do it whenever suitable during the refining and increasing of dreams. Yet others say that since it is the conclusion of Blending, it should be done at the juncture after the main practice of Lucid Clarity. There's no great difference in those two, but I think the latter makes more sense. {98} Similarly, to do each of the particular permissions for Transference and Intermediate State during the instructions for each makes no difference. To give a general permission for both Transference and Intermediate States together, it would be best to do it at the end of the guidance on Intermediate State. In my opinion, it will work best to confer the Five-Deity Cakrasaṃvara absorption empowerment or the Five Tantras' Deities absorption empowerment, whichever of those two is appropriate, at the end of everything.

The Ten Permissions of the Six Dharmas are as follows: two permissions that open the door to blessings, two permissions that establish the blessings, and six permissions that are the main support of blessings.[29] The middle two are called the two general permissions, while the latter six are identified as the particular six permissions. There's no argument there. In the identification of the first two, however, some hold that they refer to the concise empowerments of Five-Deity Cakrasaṃvara and Five Tantras' Deities. Among those who hold that belief, there must be some who are unaware of the existence of an extensive empowerment for Five-Deity Cakrasaṃvara, while others seem not to know how to perform the empowerment because they don't understand the source text for the mandala ritual. Certain others say that while the major empowerment of the Five Deities is the ripening [empowerment] in Niguma's tradition, it is not specific to the Six Dharmas and so is not counted in the Ten Permissions. In short, in these later times, there were few who follow the tradition.

The reason for that is as follows. After Drogön [Sangye Tönpa] Rinpoche, during the time of the three learned adepts [Zhönu Drup, Shangtön Tsultrim Gön, and Gyaltsen Bum] and their direct disciples, while the practice custom spread, some supplements were created, such as *Garland of Offerings*.[30] It seems the actual rituals were lightened up, [details] were borrowed from other sources, the manner of implementing the practice was simplified, and the manuals that were composed were not very clear. Also, in general, the learned adept Zhönu Drup would never have given [the higher teachings] such as mahāmudrā or the Six Dharmas to anyone who had not received the extensive empowerments into an outer mandala. He was very strict about those restricted practices. The other two learned adepts did not keep such harsh restrictions, but they practiced along those lines. It was like that, and those who came later simply followed suit since this was the general custom of those great meditators. {99} They would only occasionally give the great empowerment of the Five Tantras' Deities in secret after many years and months of preparations. Unable to give the likes of the complete four empowerments all at once, they [preferred it if disciples] had previously received this or other appropriate extensive empowerments. When that did not happen, there arose a custom of giving the guidances even [to disciples who] never obtained the extensive ripening empowerments elsewhere, and without even the ripening Five-Deity Cakrasaṃvara. Subsequently, due to this being the gurus' practice, they had no great desire to bestow the extensive empowerment of Five-Deity Cakrasaṃvara, and this was the problem. They did not know how to do it. But when they needed to confer the Ten Permissions, they just replaced the extensive empowerment of Five-Deity Cakrasaṃvara by another [shorter absorption empowerment]. Furthermore, in this tradition of the Ḍākinī of Timeless Awareness, since the Six Dharmas are the bases and roots of the path, [their empowerments] do constitute the general ripening, so do not entertain the wrong idea of thinking something is contrary to the bases of the Six Dharmas. Thus, the two permissions that open the door to blessings are the two great and small empowerments of Five-Deity Cakrasaṃvara. The empowerment of the Principal [Deities] of the Five Tantras,[31] as it is concerned with yidam practice, is certainly connected pervasively to the Golden Dharmas in general. However, it is not counted in the actual twenty-five source permissions.[32]

This has shown the way to confer the extensive Six Dharmas with all branches complete.

B. The Intermediate Style That Condenses Them in General

The empowerments of opening the door to blessings are contained exclusively in the Great Empowerment of Illusory Body. These days, most masters follow this style. But [rather than] not doing the other permissions, it would be good to do them at the beginning of each [Dharma's] guidance. The two kinds of refinement and other subsidiary practices are unnecessary. {100}

C. The Concise Style That Leaves No Topic Incomplete

The Great Empowerment of Illusory Body must be conferred. In this manner of concise guidance, there are the two parts called the preliminaries and the main practice. The first, which is the Purifying *A* of Inner Space, is the first round of visualization. Although refuge and the mind of awakening must go before that, they are not counted separately.

In the main practice of the Six Dharmas, Fierce Inner Heat has three rounds of visualization: the preliminary is the Inner Space of Fire, the vital point of the body; the main practice is Eating the Food of Inner Heat; and the concluding practice is taking the Empowerment of Existence.

The three parts of Illusory Body are One's Body as the Empty Appearance of the Deity's Form, Integrating Whatever Appears as Illusory Body, and Making the Six Kinds of Migrators Arise as Illusion.

In Dream, recognizing has two: the Vital Points of the Four Empowerments of Drops in self-recognition and Integration of Concepts. For refining dreams, although it is said that one may choose a suitable pair of visualizations, basically there are the two: Refining the Body through the Mind and Refining through Intentionality. From the visualizations in Ascertaining Objective Appearances, Illuminating Objective Appearances with Vital Drops [is counted here]. Thus, in the basic outline of the Dream guidance, there are five rounds of visualizations in three categories: recognizing, refining, and [ascertaining] objective appearances.

During Lucid Clarity, [contemplating] impermanence and disillusionment, and guru devotion are done as preliminaries in the sessions. Make innate radiance the path of methods and make the pledge substances and integration the path of conduct during the breaks between sessions. Although it is said that one may meditate on whichever of the three visualizations for recognizing lucid clarity is appropriate, make just the recognition based on the guru the main practice. In that way, the guides on Lucid Clarity summarize the structure as: "recognizing and blending; in blending, there is blending clarity and emptiness and blending day and night." In total, there are three visualizations in Lucid Clarity: Recognizing Lucid Clarity Based on the Guru, Blending Clarity and Emptiness, and Blending Day and Night.

Transference has only the one visualization, that is the Skylight of Timeless Awareness. {101} Intermediate State has one major visualization by adding the integration of the Victors' Saṃbhogakāya with the Unerring Vital Points. So that makes seventeen major visualizations contained in the Six Dharmas.

D. The Extremely Concise Style That Condenses the Vital Points

This is the single-sitting practice that is explained elsewhere.[33]

[Concluding Verses and Colophon]

This distillation of the ḍākinī's speech,
a vase for the guru's profound expressions,

has been made without relying on
the multitude of writings there are.

Filling the mind to overflowing
with the continual stream of oral teachings,
one is skilled if one can put one's finger
on valuable secrets hidden in old books.

But without continual felt experiences,
how will mere compositions help?
It is crucial to plant in your mind
the guru's blessing stream of experience.

This sequence of extensive and concise visualizations for the profound path of Niguma's Six Dharmas was arranged without concealment or disorder by Tāranātha.

2. A Supplement to the Source Guide on the Profound Path of Niguma's Six Dharmas[1]

Tāranātha

namo guru
These are the oral instructions of Niguma, Ḍākinī of Timeless Awareness.

The Six Dharmas in a Single Sitting
and extensive oral instruction on the source guide,
with a selection of four profound guides:
Jeweled Light Garland,
Stainless Light Garland,
Ocean of Experiential Qualities,
and *Illusory Body in a Single Sitting*.
These six sets are definitely required
for experts on the Six Dharmas.

I. Six Dharmas in a Single Sitting

This is the profound path of the Six Dharmas rolled into a single sitting, which has preliminaries and main practice.

A. Preliminaries

There are two parts to the preliminaries: common and uncommon. The common preliminaries contain two practices: going for refuge and arousing the awakening mind. The uncommon preliminaries consist of the Purifying *A* of Inner Space and guru yoga. Three of these—refuge, awakening mind, and inner space purifier—are generally the same as in the extensive guidebook, except that the dissolution of the guru in the refuge object is left until after the arousing of awakening mind. Then the guru dissolves into oneself after doing the supplication of the inner space. After that comes the meditation on inner space. {105}

In guru yoga, meditate only on the actual form of the guru sitting on the complete four-tiered seat in the space in front of you. Meditate on the guru present since forever as the union of all refuge objects. You don't need elaborate visualizations such as gathering and dissolving [of each refuge object into the guru]. Then supplicate with intense yearning devotion:

> Precious guru, unified essence of all buddhas of the three times,
> for the sake of all sentient beings,
> I pray to you to relinquish my self-fixation,
> to experience no needs,
> to master Illusory Body and Dream,
> and to attain the supreme spiritual power of Lucid Clarity
> Mahāmudrā right now, quickly, on this very seat.

Supplicate intensely with only this prayer. It is sufficient to keep all sentient beings in your heart; you don't need the visualization of the six kinds of migrators actually supplicating along with you. Finally, the guru melts into light and dissolves into you. Rest in that equipoise for a little while.

B. Main Practice

1. Fierce Inner Heat

If you wish to practice Fierce Inner Heat, {106} assume the vital physical sevenfold posture of Vairocana as usual, except focus your eyes directly in front and place the palms of your hands on your knees. Meditate on yourself as Vajravārāhī with your body and mode of presence in accord. The inside of your body is empty and clear. In its center is the central channel with its four characteristics. Its length and so forth are the same as in the main text. Within that, four finger-widths below the navel, is a dark-red letter *raṃ* the size of a barley grain. At the navel is the sun-disk mandala, the size of a pea. Upon that, meditate on a fine, orange *A*-stroke, one finger-width high. Cultivate yearning devotion by thinking of it as essentially your root guru. Then imagine an upside-down white *haṃ* in your head and your root guru in the space above you, radiantly white and smiling, blazing with charisma. At the outset of this session, do the ninefold shake-up to expel dead air. Then meditate with the forceful fourfold breathing exercise.

Visualize that the wind enters into the lower end of the central channel and fans the *raṃ*. Tongues of dark-red fire blaze up four finger-widths high. This stimulates the *A*-stroke at the navel, the essence of fire. Crackling orange fire blazes up from the *A*-stroke, causing the *haṃ* in the crown of the head to slightly melt. The tongues of fire emerge from the cranial aperture and blaze expansively. Various offerings emanate from the tips of the flames. Imagine that they make the four complete offerings that delight the guru. The light of the flames presents offerings of bliss and warmth. That guru, the unified essence of all buddhas, melts into the elixir of bodhicitta, returning together with the flames and entering into the cranial aperture. The elixir mixes with the *haṃ* letter inside your head, and right away a stream of vital-essence drops falls down. As it reaches your throat, you experience ecstasy [and receive] the vase empowerment. As it reaches the heart, it causes sublime ecstasy; the secret empowerment. It dissolves into the *A*-stroke at the navel and bestows special ecstasy and the wisdom empowerment. From that, the elixir falls into the *raṃ* and you experience coemergent ecstasy and the fourth empowerment. Recollect this [from the previous description]. {107}

This meditation is similar to the regular blazing and dripping practice called Brushing Tangled Hair (*skra shad 'dzings pa*). The difference is that here you meditate that the fires of the *raṃ* and the *A*-stroke merge together and blaze, and that the dripping of the drops passes through the *A*-stroke and dissolves into *raṃ*. This combines three visualizations into one—Eating the Food of Inner Heat, the Inner Heat of the Guru's Blessing, and taking the Empowerment of Existence—so it is of great importance.

Also in this practice, when you focus your attention on the blazing of inner heat, forcefully expel the breath, hold it outside, and draw up forcefully inside. When you focus your attention on the falling vital-essence drops, violently inhale gulps [of air] and squeeze the two orifices of the downward-clearing winds. At all those times, keep the mind high in the sky. Push your belly out and twist your body while forcefully stirring up the energy [by shaking] and utter "*hal*."

This is an esoteric instruction of a second path of methods that completes the path in a single breathing exercise. It is a new teaching from a direct lineage. This is not explained as part of the teaching session on Fierce Inner Heat in a Single Sitting. It is very secret.

The general teaching here is called Six Dharmas in a Single Sitting. Furthermore, this yoga of Fierce Inner Heat is given the particular name of Fierce Inner Heat in a Single Sitting. The other [five dharmas] such as Illusory Body and so forth have not been separately designated each with the moniker "in a single sitting."

2. Illusory Body

You may meditate on your root guru in front, above your head, or in your heart. It is also suitable to supplicate the guru in whichever of those places or as dwelling throughout space.

> Father guru! Mother guru!
> Guru, consider me.
> Kind root guru, I pray to you.

Meditate with intense heart-piercing devotion and then relax into that state. Suddenly visualize yourself in the deity's form. Consider the appearance of yourself and all others: {108} "All of this is the deluded appearance of things that are nonexistent yet appear. Good and bad, happiness and sadness, desire and anger, high and low status, friends and strangers, prosperity and decline, likes and dislikes, praise and blame, and so on are all concerned with accepting or rejecting delusional reifications due to clinging to their solidity. How foolish of me! Why be concerned? In fact, it is an illusion, a dream."

Train vigorously with those thoughts and when you are beyond judgment, maintain that state without fabricating anything. All the practices for those of highest, average, and lesser faculties are included here.

Then immediately visualize yourself as the deity, or as your ordinary self, as you wish. Meditate according to the main course of the practice on the six kinds of beings and the source of phenomena below your navel in the clear, empty interior of your body, and so on, making those six kinds of migrators arise as illusion. The vital points of the practices for those of highest, average, or lesser faculties are each included here, but as they are combined into one meditation, it is considered a single round of visualization.

3. Dream

In Dream practice, there is recognizing, refining, and viewing objective appearances. The first is solely the Vital Points of the Four Empowerments of Drops for self-recognition. Meditate on the visualization for that just three times in close succession. After that, train with intense intentionality in the unreal nature of yourself and others, the habitats and inhabitants, enemies and friends, all enjoyments, and so forth. Within that state, settle without fabrication in whatever arises. Familiarize yourself with that again and again.

The second, refining dreams, is solely to Refine through Intentionality as described in the main text. However, the most important parts are the intentionality of illusion-like nature and to sustain a state of natural basic space.

Third, for Ascertaining Objective Appearances, meditate on a radiant clear white *hūṃ* in your heart, the nature of light. Rigorously cultivate the intentionality that all is dream and illusion and your desire to see the appearance of a place. Light radiates from the *hūṃ*, extending out like a rope. {109} It snares whatever place or thing you wish to see and pulls it in, dissolving into the *hūṃ* at your heart. The light from the *hūṃ* illuminates all appearance with shimmering radiance. Focus your attention there. During this practice, it is important to meditate with vase breathing. As is said:

> Cultivation of merit cuts through these three:
> nonrecognition, excess, and deviation.

This is held to be very important in the contexts of Dream and Illusory Body practices.

4. Lucid Clarity

Since it is the principal visualization for recognizing lucid clarity, you must definitely meditate on this based upon the guru. It is best if you have grasped it through that method. But if you have not grasped it, based on this especially potent [meditation on] the letter *A* you will come to it. Imagine a white *A* at the lower end of the central channel inside your body. Press down continually on the upper winds and continually draw the lower winds, until the *A* falls steadily down to the base of the perineum. It winds its way, constantly twisting, through the genital channel, and when it reaches the center of the vajra's glans it becomes shining blue in color. The head [of the syllable] turns back and faces inward. It tries to force its way out with great strength, but it cannot fit through the hole and remains there steadily. Focus intently on that for a moment. Again, rest there in startled wonderment, merely not blocking that appearance. Meditate on that again and again.

This way to grasp lucid clarity is the standard way and is highly praised for its ability to do that. You will come to recognize the lucid clarity of sleep by this alone. The visualization of Lucid Clarity in a Single Sitting in particular is only this latter one. The visualization based on the guru is a general supportive framework and is not the actual visualization for the occasion of the single-sitting practice.

Women who do the meditation based on the *A* visualize the lower end of the central channel extending eight finger-widths below the navel and meditate on that lower end. The vital points of the winds and so on are the same. {110}

If you intend to meditate on the entire practice of all these four main dharmas, begin by training with each one for two or three months to gain a bit of experience in them. After that, if you meditate on all four within a single day, practice Fierce Inner Heat at dawn or the early session, Illusory Body in the middle session, Dream in the afternoon session, and Lucid Clarity in the evening session. That is one way to arrange it, but not necessarily the only method. If you cannot meditate on all four dharmas in that way, you will still accomplish special meaning by meditating on three or two or even one.

The name "single sitting" is applied only to these four root dharmas. Transference and Intermediate State practices are considered supplementary, so it is said that they may be taught however extensively or briefly. Despite this loose status, in practice you should perform them as follows.

5. Transference

Meditate that the cranial aperture on your head is wide open like a skylight. It is similar to grasping lucid clarity based on the letter *A*, except that there is an *A* four finger-widths below the navel and as you exhale that *A* travels up the central channel to the cranial aperture. It shoots out into the midst of the sky like an arrow and vanishes high into the expanse. Imagine that the *A* reappears in the sky and falls down through your cranial aperture and down to the lower end of the central channel. It is taught that it is enough to meditate on just the alternating of [consciousness] going up and coming down; you needn't meditate on blocking the door [of the cranial aperture].

6. Intermediate State

This is the same as the meditation for those of average faculties in the source guidebook, starting from the meditation on the source of phenomena in front of you up to the guru above your head. In place of the unerring vital points, train in regarding the realms of the six kinds of migrators and all form, sound, smell, taste, and texture as illusion, and engage the intentionality of the intermediate state. {111} Clearly imagine [your future] parents' intercourse [that results in] womb or egg birth and, knowing that it is the intermediate state, transform them into the yidam couple. Remember that they are like an illusion and harbor no attachment to their reality.

These two subsidiary dharmas are minor portions of direct lineages. Similarly, this abridged style for a single sitting is an oral transmission, rarely written down in former times. There have been small changes to the second breathing exercise of Fierce Inner Heat, the [practices of] Ascertaining Objective Appearances, the Lucid Clarity of *A*, and these two subsidiary dharmas. These are also said to be from the direct lineages, though one finds Ascertaining Objective Appearances and Lucid Clarity in the old books as well. Everything else is exclusively the ancient esoteric instruction.

II. Sealed Visualizations

Now to explain the sealed [instructions] of necessary visualizations for the extensive and intermediate guidances (session 7 in *Tangdalma*).

This is a teaching session of Fierce Inner Heat in the regular course of Inner Heat of the Guru's Blessing. First complete the guru yoga from Fierce Inner Heat itself. [Then visualize] yourself as Exalted [Vajravārāhī] in a posture consistent with your own body. Remaining in your ordinary form is also acceptable. Either way, inside is the inner space of emptiness and clarity. The vital physical posture may be squatting with legs drawn up or cross-legged, whichever is suitable. In the center of your body, the central channel is said to be red and the width of an incense stick. The lower end begins four finger-widths below the navel and the upper end touches inside the crown of the head. The cranial aperture is very wide, said to be the size of a spindle. Meditate that the opening of the central channel and the cranial aperture are equal and open, commensurate with the width of the central channel. Within the central channel, at the level of the navel, is a sun seat upon which is your own root guru. The guru sits in cross-legged posture with hair drawn up in a bun, bone ornaments, and a tiger skin. Meditate on that guru as being the nature of fire that burns up whatever touches it. {112} In some of the old texts there is an explanation of meditating on *haṃ* in the head, but in practice that is not done. Then clear out the dead air and meditate intensely with the four-part breathing exercise.

Visualize that holding the joined winds (*rlung kha sbyor*) causes tongues of rumbling fire to blaze from the guru's body [at your navel]. The flames don't fit inside the central channel, so they blaze upward and out the cranial aperture, filling space with tongues of flame. They emanate various offerings that are presented to the guru, yidams, buddhas, and bodhisattvas who fill the space. The firelight itself becomes the offering of bliss. All of that melts into the elixir of bodhicitta and returns together with the flames. That elixir enters through your cranial aperture, travels down the central channel, and flows into the guru's form. Like oil poured on burning metal, it makes sounds of whistling, sizzling, and distant rumbling. Imagine that your whole body is filled with the rumbling and crackling of fierce tongues of fire.

Meditate on this for seven breaths or whatever is suitable. This practice enhances [the experience of] warmth. It is praised for relieving the pain of channels and winds. In general, since it evokes the guru's blessing, it is commended for dispelling all obstructors and developing all qualities.

The Empty Space of the Inner Channels

At first, meditate on the central channel as the size of a wheat stalk. Then it grows thicker and thicker until it is the size of a medium arrow shaft, then a horse whip. Then it shrinks narrower and narrower down to a wheat stalk. As you meditate on that, hold the gentle breath. Meditate on that for a few days.

Again meditate that the width of the central channel expands to the size of a wrist, then contracts to the size of a bamboo whip. Do that for a few days. Then meditate for a few days on it expanding to the size of an arrow quiver, then shrinking back to wrist size. {113} Then meditate for a few days on it expanding to the size of a body, then contracting back to the size of a quiver. During all those, meditate with the gentle breathing. Then train in expanding the central channel to the furthest extent that the mind can encompass and contracting it back down to the size of the body. In this, intensely hold the vase breathing. Then focus the attention on expanding the central channel outward until it vanishes in space, then when contracting it inward it becomes no bigger than a horse's tail hair. In this, the breathing exercise is either gentle or intense, it is not definite.

If you meditate on this at the outset, obstructions to the channels and winds won't occur. If you meditate on it in the middle, even though you focus on the visualization, it is a method for the wind-mind to enter into the central channel. If you meditate on it in the end, lucid clarity without center or circumference will dawn like the sky. It is taught that meditation on the energy channels brings about the realization of emptiness. However, sometimes only the experience of emptiness arises.

Dispelling Obstructions of Kunda in the Lower Body

In the section on Naturally Liberating Obstructions (session 12) there is the section on dispelling obstructions of kunda (generative fluid) in the lower body. There, it says, "The least is to dispel them through visualizations and yogic exercises." With regard to that, first hold some rounds of breathing [exercises]. Then meditate that in your secret place, at the bliss-sustaining chakra, is a red *hūṃ* with the top pointing inward and the lower hook (the vowel sign, *zhabs kyu*) facing outward. Also there is a red eight-petaled lotus with its stem inside the vajra channel (urethra), and its flower petals outside the gem (glans). Meditate that the lotus stem ends in a hook that attaches to the lower hook of the *hūṃ*. Meditate also that the central channel in the center of the body is wide open. Constrict the four muscles [of the arms and legs] and squeeze the belly up against the spine. Turn the tongue back and turn your eyes up to the crown. Make the uṣṇīṣa mudra facing backward with your hands above your head. Intensely utter a long drawn-out *hūṃ*.

The visualization is as follows: When it happens that the *hūṃ* in the secret place moves up with great force, its lower hook (*zhabs kyu*) pulls the lotus stem but the flower does not fit through the vajra's opening. {114} The vajra is inverted upward into the intestine and the *hūṃ* pulls it up through the central channel.[2] Imagine that the *hūṃ* and the inverted gem (*nor bu*) stretches above the crown of your head. Hold the breath outside for the duration.

Repeated meditation on this is highly praised for [stopping] emissions due to fullness, emissions due to desire, emissions due to underlying sickness, and emissions in dreams. It also stops the six kinds of emissions. However, for emissions due to lapses in sacred pledge, confession and renewal is recommended, and washing rituals for emissions due to contamination (*grib*). For both situations in common, communal feasts and torma offerings are said to be important.

Nairātmya

For the practices of Refining Dreams Based on Nairātmya (session 25) in the section on refining dreams, Illuminating Objective Appearances with Nairātmya (session 40), and Recognizing Lucid Clarity Based on Nairātmya (session 43), it is sufficient if you have made Nairātmya herself the yidam. If not, instantly create yourself as Nairātmya and diligently repeat *oṃ a svāhā* for one or two or three weeks. Make a small torma ball of dough decorated with meat and alcohol and consecrate it with the three seed syllables. Repeat *oṃ a ā i ī ṛi ṛī ḷi ḷī e ai o au aṃ svāhā* seven times and offer it. There is no definite time to send out that small torma. Once that has been done, during meditation on the main visualization, you should continue to meditate on the deity and offer torma. Recite one thousand mantras for the vase water. Use it to wash in the morning and before bed. In particular, it is important to recite the hundred syllables while washing your face and hands. If you do all this, since it is the power of the ḍākinīs' blessings, it is said that the visualizations will be sharp and come quickly. {115}

In the section on Lucid Clarity, Jakchen described Nairātmya as white, then again as light blue, either way. In the regular practice she is blue, so there are two styles.

The Essence of Severing Excess[3]

In the section on excessive insomnia, meditate that there is a four-petaled lotus at the throat and at the heart in the standard colors. A red *hūṃ* is at the heart and a red *oṃ* at the throat. A thread of red light emerges from the *oṃ* and encircles the *hūṃ* at the heart three times, wrapping tightly around. The rest of the thread turns back up and the tip attaches to the *āḥ* (*oṃ*?) at the throat. Focus your attention on the *hūṃ*. This will dispel insomnia.

For excessive delusion, visualize the throat the same as before and a white upside-down *haṃ* in the center of a four-spoked [chakra] in the crown of the head. Again a thread of light emerges from *oṃ* and wraps around the *haṃ* in the head. Imagine that the thread turns up again and its tip attaches to the *oṃ* at the throat. Then focus your attention on the *haṃ* at the crown. This is said to dispel excessive delusion. It is praised [as a remedy for] delusion that occurs immediately after recognition [of a dream].

For the excessive delusion of never self-recognizing dreams, in the context of Integration of Concepts (session 22), there is a red *oṃ* in the center of the four channel-petals at the throat. On the four petals are *a–nu–ta–ra*. Hold the vase breath and cultivate powerful intentionality for recognizing dreams. At bedtime, in a state of intense intentionality of dreaming, the *a* letter dissolves into the *nu*, that into *ta*, that into *ra*, and that dissolves into *oṃ*. While focusing the awareness on *oṃ*, go to sleep. That will clear up excess delusion.

Dispelling Excessive Delusion in Lucid Clarity

In general, this is the same as the regular way to recognize lucid clarity. First, depending on any of the visualizations, the best is to grasp lucid clarity on its own strength. {116} But since grasping lucid clarity is more difficult to get a handle on than in dreaming, if you are recognizing it on the strength of the visualization, it may take one month, or two months, or as long as three months, depending on the level of capability. Occasionally you might recognize it by accident a few times, but this is not assured. If, somehow, you regularly exert effort to that extent but still do not recognize lucid clarity, you need to use the forceful methods of the enhancement ritual (*spogs chog*). After focusing on that visualization a few times, if your sleep is pleasant and light, then you will quickly recognize lucid clarity. If your sleep is heavy and unpleasant, you continually fall back asleep, and you feel oppressed as if demons are weighing on you, that also is a sign that recognition will quickly ensue.

Make a great effort to meditate on this visualization for one month up to three months. Do not be rushed by hopes and fears, thinking, "Will I get it tonight or tomorrow night or not at all?" Let go of anticipation. Mostly it comes when you don't expect it.

Forceful Methods

This is the application of forceful methods if you never grasp lucid clarity. For this circumstance, think, "Now I will quickly recognize it in seven or so days." Present the communal feast offerings to the fellow disciples of your guru, confess and renew promises, and pray to recognize lucid clarity. Offer torma to the five classes of ḍākinī and Swift-Acting Protector every evening and request their activity to help in recognizing lucid clarity. For a week before [practicing], it is important to be diligent in washing and cleanliness and cautious with conduct and sacred substances. After that for three days, never sleep in the daytime and reduce nighttime sleep by a third or a fourth. Intensify the visualization and intentionality. {117}

The esoteric instructions of other traditions recommend not holding breathing exercises during the practice of Lucid Clarity because it will encourage dreaming. However, in this tradition the esoteric instructions teach that it is not a problem if dreams come. Dreams easily become lucid clarity; if dreams arise in the wake of lucid clarity, they are allies. It is taught that the natural arising of the deity's form comes from that. The meditation on the winds during this occasion of the enhancement ritual is considered crucial.

In the actual visualization, the heart channel [chakra] is in the form of a blue four-petaled lotus with a blue *hūṃ* in its center. Clearly visualize the four letters *a–nu–ta–ra* on the four petals, all of them blue. Focus on *hūṃ*. Recognize consciousness as empty awareness. Then light radiates from *hūṃ* and strikes the four letters. They fill up with light. The light radiates from that and fills your body. Light radiates from that, filling all that appears with light. Focus your attention again on *hūṃ* and maintain [the experience of] empty awareness and so forth. When you have repeated the process several times, all appearance melts into light and dissolves into you. Again focus your attention on *hūṃ*. Your body melts into light and dissolves into the five letters. Again focus your attention on *hūṃ*. The lotus and the four letters also dissolve into *hūṃ*. Focus on that. The *hūṃ* also vanishes like a rainbow; rest in wakeful equipoise within that state. At bedtime, focus your attention on the *hūṃ* and fall asleep in that state.

Recognition will come to most people following those methods. In case it does not, do the general torma offerings every evening for seven days as described before. It is taught that you should hide a single-piece authentic skull[4] under your pillow, although this is a concealed esoteric instruction.

In general, there is certainly nothing wrong with this. But the import is that if you can find two perfect skulls it is best, or if not, then one, {118} but if you cannot find even that, use two unbroken containers made of precious material. In each of them, make tormas of many excellent ingredients. Adorn them with a little human flesh, if available. Once you consecrate them, invite the guests. State that one of them will be offered as gratitude for recognizing lucid clarity, cover it with silk, and leave it thus concealed. The other one is to be dedicated, but just leave it as is and do not throw it outside of the retreat place. You should keep it as collateral, placing it at the head of your pillow. When you dedicate the torma, send it out with the smoke of frankincense and human fat.

In general, it is understood that when you sleep you should arrange for a companion who upholds their sacred pledges and who has experience to watch whether or not you are grasping lucid clarity. However, in practice this is not done because it is difficult to achieve for many reasons. From this point on, no one should see the tormas and sacred substances. It is said to be extremely important to do the practice alone. When recognition of lucid clarity occurs, in the morning give thanks by dedicating the torma that was held as collateral. However, don't throw it outside right away—keep it for three to seven days and refresh it every evening and rededicate it. Finally, one morning at the break of day, take it to the roof of the house or to a graveyard or mountaintop.

From the time that you have once recognized lucid clarity, leave the previous elaborations and enter strict retreat, paring it down to the visualization and intense intentionality. If you meditate in that way, continual recognition will come. Maintain that reduced practice and after one or two months you will attain a measure of stability. Other than the conditions caused by disturbance of the body's elements or contamination and such, you will certainly recognize [lucid clarity] once each night. By being attentive to minor experiences of bliss-clarity and merely recognizing them, they will happen again and again and the ability to maintain them for a longer time will come. {119} As for always recognizing lucid clarity at all times during deep sleep, this requires a very long time of familiarization and single-pointed meditation.

Besides, the mere lucid clarity of clarity-emptiness is held in common with applied virtue. The lucid clarity that is inseparable from bliss-emptiness is the main practice.

Problems during Both Dream and Lucid Clarity

If you cannot go to sleep while focusing on these visualizations of either Dream or Lucid Clarity, then meditate again and again on a dark-brown *muṃ* at the heart radiating light rays like a fog that pervades everything inside and outside of your body. Rely on heavy, nutritious food and move in a measured way to clear this up.

Sometimes you wake up as soon as you recognize dreams or lucid clarity, like a vehicle suddenly appearing out of water. This will be cleared up by focusing your attention in the center of the lower part of your body.

You might think that meditating repeatedly on the visualization in the daytime means that you should meditate repeatedly that way during sleep. Don't trouble yourself—relax. If you are overly worried about waking up when you recognize dreams or lucid clarity at night, then it *will* happen. So it is important to calm yourself.

Excessive insomnia (*sad 'byams*) is the name given to the condition of always waking up as soon as you recognize dreams or as soon as you recognize lucid clarity. If that happens, these methods will clear it up.

If at no time is there recognition of dreams and lucid clarity even though you continuously practice the visualization and intentionality, such that it makes no difference whether you meditate or not, that is called *excessive delusion* (*'khrul 'byams*). According to other esoteric instructions, such as in *Five Stages Complete in One Sitting*,[5] this is known as *excessive discipline response*.[6] If you become deluded immediately after recognizing dreams, this is called *less powerful excessive delusion* in the esoteric instructions of this tradition. In the well-known instructions of Nāropa, it is called *excess stubbornness* (*dred 'byams*). {120} This excess stubbornness does not often affect the lucid clarity of sleep, but it is common in this Dream practice, so methods to clear it up are important. Set your intention each time you fall asleep.

If dreams do not come once you have entered deep sleep when practicing recognition of dreams, or if sleep does not come when practicing Lucid Clarity, that is what's called *excessive emptiness* (*stong 'byams*). It will help to do a lot of breathing exercise during the day for this scarcity of dreams.

The problem of emission during deep sleep and Dream practice is called *excessive bliss* (*bde 'byams*). This has various causes, such as desire within the dream, habitual tendencies, and the influence of spirits. Whether for real or in dreams, when this happens the dynamic energy of dreams is usually compromised. It may seem that it makes no difference if it happens occasionally once or twice, but gradually it leads to deterioration. In particular, it will destroy the very roots of the virtuous application of Dream—the clarity-emptiness and the brilliant form of the deity. If this occurs even once during the practice of Lucid Clarity, it will lead to the deterioration of lucid clarity. If [emissions] are due to lapsed sacred pledge, or the influence of spirits, or fullness, even if you meditate again it will be distant and difficult to restore. In any case, the methods for clearing up all of those issues is in the section on Naturally Liberating Obstructions (session 12).

"Excessive" does not apply to one or two occurrences. It is a term for something that arises again and again, that has become entrenched as a really bad habit. Nevertheless, it is said to be very important to cut it off right from the start, before it becomes excessive. This concerns those who are very impatient and expectant. For those who continually practice without calculating results, at some point all excesses will end automatically.

Transference

In the section on Transference to the Unerring Celestial Realm (session 52), the preliminary is the same as in other source texts on Transference. {121} Meditate that in the space above your head there is a double-stacked tetrahedral source of phenomena, white outside and red inside. Its cause is bliss, and it arouses bliss. In its center is Exalted Vajrayoginī. She is red and brandishes a vajra with her right hand and a blood-filled skull cup at her heart with her left hand, a khaṭvāṅga in the bend of her elbow. She stands in a left-leaning pose with her legs in a wide stance. All her ornaments and accessories are totally complete. She stands on a seat of lotus, sun, and a man's corpse with its head facing to the left. She has an immeasurable entourage around her.

Visualize your own body in its ordinary form. Imagine the letter *raṃ*, the nature of fire, in the two soles of your feet and at the anus. Tongues of fire blaze up with a rumble from those letters, melting and boiling your whole body. It becomes the nature of the elixir of timeless awareness, as does the contents of the skull cup in Exalted Vajrayoginī's hand. She and all the entourage along with yourself drink of it, satisfying their mind streams with bliss. Meditate in this way three times. Then you become Heruka as sole father. Within your body is the central channel as usual. Visualize a white *A*, the essence of consciousness, at the navel and a blue *hūṃ*, the essence of vital winds, in the perineum, radiating light. Slightly hold the gentle breath.

When you exhale the breath, utter a long drawn-out "*hik*." At that time, the force of the winds of *hūṃ* in the perineum carries the *A* at the navel up through the length of the central channel and out the cranial aperture. Imagine that it enters through Bhagavatī Vajrayoginī's vagina and arrives at her heart.

The esoteric instructions in the old texts explain that you should repeat this visualization three times, after which you meditate that Vajrayoginī ascends to the realm of space, then descends, and so on. {122} However, this is not done in practice. Do the previous visualization seven times, each time these three—your own mind, Vajrayoginī, and emptiness—blend inseparably. Rest in the equipoise of that. In the end, your mind inseparable from Vajrayoginī's blessings in the form of white elixir with a red radiance emerges from her vagina. The stream of elixir enters the cranial aperture of you as the yidam. As it fills the crown chakra, you obtain the vase empowerment. Filling the throat, the secret empowerment; filling the heart the wisdom awareness; and filling the navel, the fourth empowerment. All the channels are filled with bodhicitta. The experience of bliss pervades all; rest awhile in equipoise. This is the meditation to be done again and again.

To conclude the session, Vajrayoginī and the source of phenomena melt into light, enter through the crown of your head, and dissolve into you. Imagine that there is a red upside-down letter *vaṃ* in the opening of the cranial aperture that radiates light rays that block the opening.

There is a short text on this called *Transference to the Unerring Celestial Realm.*[7] It is the one that says [in the colophon], "This is my, Khyungpo Naljor's, tradition, which I received from Ḍākinī Niguma." It is well known that the visualizations in the other general precepts of Transference and Intermediate State are called "transference to the unerring celestial realm." As well, a transference of Vajrayoginī's hand implement[8] has been identified as this, which is somewhat similar. The term "unerring transference" (*'chug med 'pho ba*) has also been applied to the *Red Khecarī Transference*. So it seems that unless it has been definitely established, [the correct] identification will become rare. {123} Please keep any new "unerring celestial realms" far away.

If there are practitioners who meditate on another's body based on this teaching, meditate in all guru yoga practices that the guru has the wisdom [partner] or that Great Vajradhara is with the mother. This is the traditional teaching.

Concluding Words

Niguma, crown jewel of a million glorious yoginīs with their heroes,
who purifies all flaws of this existence with the stream of elixir from the vase of her mouth,
and nurtures completely the hearts of the fortunate, who are sublimely fortunate to receive such as this,
since I have attained the appearance of some familiarity independently of others.

III. Summary of *Jeweled Light Garland*

namo guru

This is the essence of the practices in the source esoteric instruction *Jeweled Light Garland* by the incomparable [Mokchokpa] Rinchen Tsöndru.[9] It is a summary that targets the vital points of the three bodies of all esoteric instructions.

First is the fully ripened body (*rnam smin gyi lus*). Its basis is the three poisons from which it arises. Its cause is the impetus of karmic action. Its contributing conditions are the five elements that transform it. For those reasons, the afflictive emotions that fixate on the reality of things always rise up. The result of these causes is that there is no independence. The harm by the five elements occurs based on the external environment. Internally, sickness, enemies, and malicious spirits rise up. Actions and afflictions are first generated by mentation (*yid*). In the interim they accumulate as habitual tendencies, and in the end they fully ripen as happiness and suffering.

The body of habitual tendency (*bag chags kyi lus*) in dreams is more deluded than the delusion of this waking time. Afflictions, karma, and happiness and suffering rise up.

The mental body (*yid lus*) [of the intermediate state] is even more deluded than those two. The appearances of afflictions, karma, and suffering arise. {124} There, during the time of the mental body, the previous afflictions and so forth act as a cause and at that time all three—[afflictions, karma, and suffering]—as the contributing conditions. Then again the fully ripened body is created and so forth; one wanders [from body to body] like a cycling wheel.

You need techniques to purify the delusion of the fully ripened body. That would be the understanding of illusoriness as an antidote to the actual delusion of the mind and a method that targets the vital points of the body, since it was that delusion that acted as the cause for the body.

A. Illusoriness

This has two parts: (1) continual intentionality and (2) esoteric instructions on forceful methods.

1. Continual Intentionality

When all the sources of refuge, such as the lineage gurus, dissolve into the root guru, you make continual supplications. You train intensely in the intentionality that your own body and all appearances are not real, like an illusion. In all session breaks, also train with the intentionality of illusion by admonishing yourself with harsh [statements about illusoriness]. If you meditate like that but it still does not enhance your [realization of] illusoriness and impermanence in the daytime, and you don't recognize dreams at night, then you need the second part.

2. Esoteric Instructions on Forceful Methods to Recognize [Dreams]

In the daytime, engage in many fearless behaviors, such as running and jumping naked through an empty valley. Pray to the guru, yidam, and ḍākinīs to get to the point. At night, during the second half, assume one of three positions: cross-legged and leaning back, sitting with legs drawn up, or the lion's reclining position. Go to sleep while in a state of intense intentionality to transform dreams. There, you will come to realize various dreams.[10] [Blend them] when you wake from sleep. Understanding arising and appearance and ability to function will be liberating. Both in dreams and in the current perceptions—from the circumstances of their initial arising, the various changing perceptions after you remain in that state, and your ability to function from that very moment [of their arising]—in terms of those three, there is no difference [in dreaming and waking]. {125} And since their abiding nature is not even slightly existent, there is absolutely no difference. Think, "It is like an illusion" and cultivate fierce intentionality. By persistently meditating in that way, you will come to recognize dreams.

If you become apprehensive while refining dreams, it is because the hidden demon of clinging to the reality of here and now follows after you. In that case, think, "The body that produces sickness and suffering is in bed; this now is a mental body, so what is the reason for fear and such." Thinking that, refine whatever you recognize. Once it is somewhat refined, train in emanating and changing the four elements. Elevate your awareness and vital winds and soar above the sun and moon. Dive down to the depths and move through the ocean. Wander in the places of the gods and elsewhere. View the pure realms of Sukhāvatī, Potala, Wu-t'ai-shan, and Aḍakavatī. See the lords of the three families and request their teachings. Make offerings to the mandalas of Hevajra, Cakrasaṃvara, and others and request empowerment and instruction. Meditate on yourself and others—all the environment and its inhabitants of six kinds of beings—as the yidam deities in the mandala. Understand that these empty appearances are like an illusion.

Also, at first when you arise in the deity's form, if you then revert to your ordinary body, it is because the force of deluded habit adheres. Therefore, as soon as you wake up, meditate on the visualization and the intense intentionality of illusion. The illusion example is like your reflection in a mirror, to which you can address praise or blame without feeling pleasure [or displeasure]; meditate on that. Ultimate illusion is not real from the moment it arises; rest in that. Nondual illusion is the arising of the deity as appearance-emptiness. Blend appearance-emptiness bliss with example. Blend that with the ultimate. Blend that in unity.

Furthermore, the referents of the three examples of illusion, the freedom from desire, {126} the three wisdoms, the three [doors of] liberation, the outer and inner six perfections, the four seals, the four ecstasies, the three absorptions, and so forth are all included in that.[11] Apparitions of spirits in dreams and otherwise will all be naturally purified. The six kinds of migrators will arise as deities and the intermediate state will be purified, without doubt.

B. Methods That Target the Vital Points of the Body

Even though you practice along those lines, if at first [dreams] arising is difficult, in the middle refining is difficult, and in the end attaining stability is difficult, then in addition to devotion and the previous vital points of intentionality, you need esoteric instructions to target the vital points of the body.

Assume the vital physical posture of the reclining lion. Meditate on the lotus in the throat with red *oṃ* in its center and *a–nu–ta–ra* on the four petals. Cultivate the intentionality of recognizing or refining dreams. Have no doubts that this will enhance the Dream practice. The throat is the vital point where wind-mind gathers during four times: when about to enter dreams from the appearances of waking time; when sleep approaches; when sleep is upon you; and when about to have a dream. That is Nāgārjuna's instruction.

Also, in the center of the channel chakra in the heart, meditate on white light like a candle with a red tip four finger-widths high. Hold your awareness in that and constrict the breathing somewhat. If you meditate in this way day and night, then lucid clarity will arise both day and night. This kind of felicitous meditation instruction on Lucid Clarity—with clear, concise, and profound visualization—is not found elsewhere. It is taught as the instructions of the adept Lavapa.

Also, at the opening of the vital point between the eyebrows, imagine there is a vital drop—luminous white, oily, no bigger than a thumb, no smaller than a bean, and blissful. {127} Intensely insert wind-mind there. If this is accompanied by the intentionality of lucid clarity, then you will recognize lucid clarity. If it is accompanied by the intentionality of dreams, dreams will be recognized. This is mainly an instruction for realizing illusory body during waking life. It is similar to the [practice] during waking appearances of joining the winds at the throat chakra. It is taught as the approach of Yoginī Kalpa Zangmo.

In the life story of Venerable Mokchokpa, it is explained that these three instructions came from the lineage of Burgom.[12] Although that is certainly the case, this [instruction to] focus the attention on the letters in the throat is also contained in the section on enhancement practices for Lucid Clarity and Dream [in Niguma's Six Dharmas]. The vital drop between the eyebrows in found in the section on empowerment of Dream practice. Therefore, these instructions are related to the teachings of Ḍākinī Niguma. The practice of the candle at the heart is the same vital point as grasping lucid clarity in the vital drop, which is explained as the same basis of instruction blessings from both Lavapa and Niguma. Therefore they are not unrelated to the Six Dharmas of Niguma. Furthermore, other than Fierce Inner Heat, this [teaching] fully contains the basic esoteric instructions of all the complete vital points for blending [dream] with illusory body.

This concludes the esoteric instructions from *Jeweled Light Garland*.

IV. The Heart of the Six Dharmas from *Stainless Light Garland of the Path*[13]

In the section on the three preliminaries, going for refuge is not mentioned separately but should be added. Arousing the awakening mind is the same as usual. Guru yoga is done separately [for each dharma], basically the same as in the Illusory Body practice (session 13), except for the supplication: "I pray that realization of the mind of awakening and the realization of emptiness arise in my being." {128}

To begin [the main practices], go for refuge in the guru each time by saying:

> All sentient beings, my mothers, equal to the reaches of space,
> [go for refuge in the precious guru, the unified essence of all refuges.]

In the main practice of the Path of Methods, meditate on the Inner Heat of the Guru's Blessing. This is also said to be the [Inner Heat practice of] Riding the Wind Horse. Then meditate on receiving the Empowerment of Existence. There are these two visualizations.

In Illusory Body, meditate on the two techniques together: One's Body as the Empty Appearance of the Deity's Form and Making the Six Kinds of Migrators Arise as Illusion. In general, rely on seclusion with guru devotion as the support.[14] Do not befriend those who take refuge in this life. In all activities, keep to the realization that [all phenomena] lack any true nature.

In the context of the extensive Six Dharmas, these days one needs the revealed secret known as the particular permission of Illusory Body.[15] Take that in the style of a meditative absorption [empowerment]. In terms of this instruction [of *Stainless Light Garland of the Path*], it is said that blending becomes three times better than in the general practice of Illusory Body. Also it is the empowerment of Fierce Inner Heat: it is explained that to bestow this guidance, the actual empowerment of Fierce Inner Heat is conferred to open the door.

There are three visualizations for recognizing dreams. The first visualization is of a white *haṃ* in the top of the head and a pink *phaṭ* in the perineum. A drop of vital essence breaks off from the *haṃ* and becomes white Cakrasaṃvara. A vital drop breaks off from *phaṭ* and becomes Exalted [Vajravārāhī]. Their union [at your heart] pervades your body and mind with bliss. Meditate on the same thing in front of you. Cultivate the intentionality of recognizing dreams. At night, when going to sleep, the deities in front dissolve into the couple in your heart. That also [melts into] dazzling light that vanishes from the outside inward; then rest without visualization. The second visualization is self-recognition [based on] the Vital Points of the Four Empowerments of Drops. The third visualization, from the two [techniques for] Recognizing Dreams without Concepts, is the one based on the guru (session 21). Dreams are refined through intentionality. {129} Increasing, emanating, and changing dreams are also done in that [way]. For the visualization of ascertaining objective appearances, meditate as was explained [previously] in the section on [the Six Dharmas] in a single sitting.

In the esoteric instructions for grasping the lucid clarity of sleep, practice only Recognizing Lucid Clarity Based on the Guru.

This completes the heart of the meaning of the four root dharmas. Separate visualizations for Transference and Intermediate State are unnecessary. If you wish, follow the [instructions in] the extensive guidance. Great meditators who follow this style of practice have need of many significant points, which can be learned from the [actual text] taught by the protector of migrators, Sangye Tönpa himself.

V. Esoteric Instructions from *Ocean of Experiential Qualities*[16]

Some individuals who are attached to physical and verbal effort either cannot meditate on the Path of Methods or else are not interested in meditating on it due to their particular mindset (*blo rigs*). However, that does not disqualify them from practicing the completion phase of Secret Mantra. It is said that all paths are complete and correct within the three [practices] of Illusory Body, Dream, and Lucid Clarity.

The understanding of the free and endowed, difficult-to-find [human life], death and impermanence, and the shortcomings of cyclic existence will produce the intention to practice. Know that all the ground, path, and fruition are the unity of profundity and vastness. Arouse the awakening mind and the related four immeasurable attitudes toward sentient beings who do not realize this.

In the main part, first is Illusory Body for those of best, average, and lesser capabilities. The best is the [same as the practice of] the actual integration of devotion to the guru, except that here you visualize the guru's seat as only a lotus and moon and the guru's body as their actual one but adorned with the signs and marks [of perfection]. On the occasion of supplication, say, "[Precious guru], I pray to recognize illusion as illusion" and "I pray to recognize dreams as dreams." {130} That is what [the text] says, but that is not the only way. Since the meaning is the same in the source guidance, it is acceptable to follow that.

For those of average capability, the practice is One's Body as the Empty Appearance of the Deity's Form. The difference is that you train along the way in intentionality directly with all appearance: the appearing aspect is creation phase, the empty aspect is completion phase, and their inseparability points to great bliss.

For those of least capability, [the practice is] Making the Six Kinds of Migrators Arise as Illusion. The source of phenomena is white outside and red inside, and, in this context, just cultivate the intention of [recognizing] illusion; don't embellish with the other intentions.

In Dream practice, cultivate the intentionality of recognizing illusion and dreams during the daytime, and meditate on both self-recognition in the Vital Points of the Four Empowerments of Drops and the Integration of Concepts together in the nighttime. When you gain some degree of stability in those, add Refining Dreams through Intentionality. Then whatever dream you do recognize can be increased infinitely and so forth: recognizing, refining, emanating, and changing will all occur automatically in equal measure. For Ascertaining Objective Appearances, rely on the meditation of the vital drops (session 41), with the difference that the light of the drop draws in whatever place you wish to view and it dissolves into your heart. Also, when going to sleep at night, the viewed object and the drop at the heart are connected by a rope of light. Meditate that fear and so on are all like an illusion. On this occasion, give a short introduction to blending and transference by means of the four wisdoms.[17]

Then to grasp lucid clarity of sleep, you rely on the letter *A* (session 44). In the course of the guidance manual it states, "Measure four finger-widths below one's navel." However, a note, which is [the author's] own note, says "or at the tip of the organ."[18] This is a sublime vital point that accords with the tantras. It appears that this was the intent in *The Single Sitting* [texts]. {131} In the actual teaching, you meditate on a white *A* in the gem. Regarding the various appearances that arise from the bliss-emptiness of lucid clarity, it is said that the vital point is the deity's form arising naturally from lucid clarity. For more detail, see Drogön Sangye [Tönpa's] own exposition.

[General Comments]

Of those texts, *Jeweled Light Garland* was written in the style of a source text, so there is no editorial account whatsoever. This and the *Stainless Light Garland of the Path* do not constitute separate guidances, for it is said "there is nothing other than the Six Dharmas." There is talk that this arrangement of the Six Dharmas was set down before the command seal on written compositions was lifted and that they were composed as various concise manuals, like memoranda. Such things are said. But if it was a time before the command seal of the aural transmission was lifted on the Six Dharmas in general, writing such literary fragments would harm the command seal, and writing various things as memoranda would be highly inappropriate. These false statements that [they were written] so as not to forget things is not the case. Therefore, since both are the teachings of Drogön Sangye Tönpa, the seal was released.[19] One must understand that the minor variations in the visualizations are meant as options. Therefore, these two [texts] are for the worthy recipients of the instructions in the aural transmission of Niguma, Ḍākinī of Timeless Awareness, and they were given for the benefit of a few disciples who did not need the entire instruction cycle. Furthermore, special experiential realization arose in them and they reached the culmination [of spiritual practice]. It is not a contradiction that these texts summarize the points in the major guidance and yet are done separately, just as in Illusory Body in a Single Sitting. In that case, the learned great adept Khyungpo [Naljor] extracted Illusory Body in a Single Sitting and composed it separately, just as Drogön Sangye Tönpa wrote these two texts. {132} You should understand that in this case there is no difference in the quality of the authors.

Jeweled Light Garland and these two texts differ only in style—in being verse or prose and in the inclusion or not of analysis. Otherwise, their goals are the same. Therefore, whatever was suitable of the principal visualizations has been extracted from the extensive styles of guidance texts and put [into these short texts]. Nevertheless, each of the numerous guides had been blessed in their creation by those sublime beings [who wrote them]. Therefore, even now it is most excellent and fitting to lead devotees using those kind of guides in accordance with the disciples' individual mindsets.

In general, in the transmission of these extensive teachings in these word guidances, the words must remain uncorrupted and without errors of addition or duplication: you must definitely recall exactly what you heard from the guru. As for the meaning, in the experiential guides, it is not necessary to follow the exact order of the extensive guidebooks. The full measure of experience may be reached based on one individual visualization—or two or three—because they are all recognized as having a single foundation.

Those with no enthusiasm for meditating on the extensive or concise source guides on the Six Dharmas, but who are interested in claiming the name of Niguma's Six Dharmas, could just add however they want the Transference and Intermediate State practices to the former of these two [texts] and add Fierce Inner Heat to *Jeweled Light Garland* and the latter [text]. But if these additions are inserted into the main course [of the instruction], it runs the risk of polluting the speech of the adepts. So it is best to add them as separate texts.

Contrary to that, there are those who claim to have "a guidance of Niguma's Six Dharmas," such as the one composed by Lord Gendun Gyatso.[20] But Niguma did not speak those instructions, Khyungpo did not hear them, and none of the lineage gurus ever realized them. {133} Just calling such a fabrication "Niguma's Dharma" and running with it only deceives the fools with no clue about dharma. But, you may ask, what if it contains the genuine visualization sequence explained in another dharma system? Well, then why call it "Niguma's Dharma"? It is totally inappropriate to assign the term *Shangpa Dharma* to something without even a single visualization from the Shangpa Kagyu tradition.

VI. Illusory Body in a Single Sitting[21]

The [practice] called Illusory Body in a Single Sitting is indicated by the great learned adept Khyungpo in his *Inventory*:

> In the Illusory Body of the Single Sitting,
> there are four (eight) supplications and eight intentions.[22]

The four supplications apply [only to] the section on those of lesser [faculties]. The eight intentions are said to concern death and impermanence, guru devotion, knowing that you've gone to sleep, knowing illusion as dream, refining, emanating, and changing. The sequence of practice is going for refuge, arousing awakening mind, and the Purifying of Inner Space, which are to be done first. Then cultivate an intense feeling of disillusionment regarding death and impermanence and apply yourself diligently to the source text. The guru yoga is the same as in the main text for Illusory Body. After the guru dissolves into you, visualize yourself as the deity's form. Turn your attention to all external appearance and try to visualize that also as the deity's form. Visualize everything all at once and think, "All this is the perception of my mind. That mind is not real, it is like an illusion. Even more specifically, I have fallen asleep. All these appearances are actually dreams." Thus enhance both the intentionality regarding the lack of reality and the intentionality about dreams. {134}

In the session breaks, meditate without distraction on the three intentionalities together. Particularly add the intention for dreaming. At bedtime, train earnestly again in the intentionality of unreality and dreams, and then go to sleep in that state. Do not seek other instructions for lucid dreams; this is considered sufficient by itself. Afterward, continue with increasing, emanating, and changing dreams as taught in the extensive Six Dharmas. For more detail, there is a separate guidance manual by the learned and accomplished Gyaltsen Bum that you could look at.[23] Once you are sure of the source guides, you will see the meaning even in a few words.

This concludes the explanations of this genre of required sealed visualizations in the context of the Six Dharmas source guidance and the various important extensive and concise instructions.

Concluding Words

"This is the unerring profound meaning,"
but such a guarantee is extremely rare.
A teaching received just to draw folks in,
a mere approximation, fills the land.
Mostly fools with some interest
mainly enter into this dharma.
Mostly men and women
who rarely understand the profound meaning,
but few harbor evil or faulty attitudes.
Great ambition, eight concerns, and prejudice:
these three compete for prominence.
Faith, understanding, and compassion:
these three compete for obscurity.
Endowed with these six special features,

some slackers called "geshe"
lecture vainly of their own learning.
Since it doesn't sell to ordinary folks,
they hope to gather a motley retinue
and to this assembly with no knowledge of dharma
explain this teaching of false scripture,
where those knowledgeable in this dharma system
would not hear them teaching. {135}
Like the alphabet primer riddled by worms,
take that example to heart.
hey hey
We are certainly the fortunate ones
to have landed the guaranteed profound dharma.
The gurus have no need to hide
the dharma to engage—*emaho!*

A Supplement to the Source Guide on the Profound Path of Niguma's Six Dharmas was spoken by the vagabond Tāranātha.

maṅgalaṃ

3. Niguma's Yogic Exercises, Root and Commentary[1]

Tāranātha

oṃ svasti / namo guru

Releasing the channel knots, straightening the channels,
gathering into the central channel, and spreading through the channels
are four.
Standing and spreading, transforming, and pressing the torso are three.
One leg, two legs, twisting,
small-child style, and leaping are five.
The two openings are crossing and wide open.
Inserting in the central channel, drawing up in the central channel,
and gathering within the central channel are posited as three.
Vairocana, bent neck, Amoghasiddhi,
suppressing, equipoise, waving legs,
sudden stand, and threefold shake are eight.

Four are for channels, three are for vital drops,
five are for pain relief, two are for opening,
three are for the vajra dance, and
eight are for dispelling afflictions,
but if counted as one, that makes eighteen.

1. Cross-legged, twist the upper torso seven times.
2. Standing, [hands] on waist, heel-hop seven times.
3. Extend two hands from armpits to the sides of the thighs.
4. Sit down and massage the whole body.

5. Palms together above the head, strike the heels.
6. Extend the right and left fists, alternating.
7. Grasp the armpits and twist the upper torso.
   (8 & 9 are described as stick-jumping,[2] a practice not done now.) {139}
8. Stand with sole placed above knee, extend arms, hop.
9. Legs and arms in striking pose, three heel-hops.
10. Cover chest with intertwined fingers and twist three times.
11. Standing and sitting, rotate and shake the head.
12. After three heel-hops, fall to the ground.
13. Press the chest with one fist and fling out [the other].
14. Open mouth and eyes, extend, contract, and shake extremities.
15. Strike the chest, vulture[-like], shake, and circle.
16. Cross [arms], draw up, press down, open, and close.
17. Cover the biceps, and rotate the waist three times.
18. This is the dispelling of afflictive emotions:

[a.] With the mudra of awakening, twist right, left, above, and below.
[b.] Hook ring fingers, press the neck, twist the upper torso right and left.
[c.] Assume Amoghasiddhi mudra and strike the flesh.
[d.] To suppress, circle the blazing mudra, gaze with roving eyes.
[e.] Grasp the armpits, twist, and look again.
[f.] With equipoise [mudra] and vajra position, hold the belly tight.
[g.] Lying prone, wave legs, and knead dough.
[h.] Rise suddenly, point, and rotate in ten directions.
[i.] Triple shake-up, bind, extend, rub, and shake. {40}

In the Six Dharmas of Niguma, Ḍākinī of Timeless Awareness, these are the eighteen yogic exercises of the source guide on Fierce Inner Heat. If the last is divided by eight, there are twenty-five.

After one month of training the vital winds, do one week in the style of Fierce Inner Heat,[3] one week on the colliding Fireballs, one week on the main practice, one week on the Fierce Inner Heat of the Guru, and one week on Wearing the Clothes [of Fierce Inner Heat]. Then learn these yogic exercises and train with them again and again. When they don't tire you out and you don't need to concentrate, train in the particular visualizations for each session. Finally, all the visualizations in each session of yogic exercises will pertain to the relevant yogic exercise. If you exert yourself in practicing Fierce Inner Heat without break during each of the four or six meditation sessions [a day], immeasurable qualities will quickly arise for sure. Now to explain the meaning of the above summary.

1. Releasing the Channel Knots

Assume the vital points of the body while sitting in cross-legged vajra position. Draw the two hands up from the knees and plant them at the base of the thighs (groin). Twist the upper torso to the right and to the left seven times.

2. Straightening the Channels

Assume the basic vital body position as before. [When] the hands reach the groin, stand up suddenly and do a wind-jump [that raises the vital winds] (*rlung 'phar*). Holding the hands on the waist, rotate the belly to the right and to the left. Squeeze the anus each time while twisting the upper torso slightly to the right and left. After that, do a single heel-hop each and repeat [the sequence] seven times. Since this clears up disturbances of the channels, it is similar to doing [the practice called] Brushing Tangled Hair.

3. Gathering into the Central Channel

If this is done as an extension of the previous [exercise], it is sufficient to do just one wind-jump. If it is done separately, assume the basic posture of the second [exercise]. Make tight fists with your hands and extend them forcefully down the exterior of the thighs toward the posterior. Do two heel-hops and then a single leap-and-fall (*'phar rdeb*) Do this sequence seven times.

4. Spreading through the Channels

After expelling the breath, {141} first massage the head, then the upper torso, then the arms, then the lower body, then the extended legs. In particular, rub and strike the muscles of the four limbs against each other. This purifies the channels of those four [limbs].

5. Standing and Spreading

The basic posture is like that of the second one, except that the hands are gradually raised along the sides of the rib cage and extended up, and the palms come together above the head. Constrict the waist and push down on the downward-clearing wind. Draw up the life-force wind. Press down the chin strongly on the Adam's apple. Rather than the leap-and-fall, do very strong heel-hops. Repeat seven times.

6. Transforming

Assume the basic [standing] posture as before. Extend the clenched fists along the sides of the thighs. Leaving the left [arm at the] side of the body, forcefully extend and contract the right leg and arm. Extend and contract the fingers along with the limbs. Repeat this with the left side.

7. Pressing the Upper Torso

Assume the basic posture as before, except bind the chest by intertwining the fingers of the two hands to cover the chest and hooking the two thumbs under the armpits. Twist the upper torso to the right and left seven times. These [last] three will purify the vital-essence drops.

8. One-Legged Hop

The basic position is the same as in the second exercise. Place the sole of the right foot above the knee of the left leg. Open out the right knee. Extend both arms. Do three leap-and-falls. Do the same for the opposite side three times.

9. Two-Legged Hop

The basic position is the same as in the second exercise, except put the right arm and leg in front and rotate to the left, then raise them slightly higher. Stretch the hand and fingers straight out behind the right thigh. Stamp the heel on the ground in that direction. Do the same for the left. {142}

The eighth and ninth exercises are described in the sources as first grabbing hold of a staff with one hand and later with two hands and then lifting off, pole-vaulting a long distance. However, this practice is not done nowadays.[4]

10. Twisting

With fingers intertwined, squeeze the chest and armpits, apropos to the seventh exercise but standing up. While extending the head and neck, turn to the right and left three times. After that, expel the breath and sit down on the ground. Turn the head and upper torso three times. Then rise up halfway with the knees on the ground. The right hand remains as before, but reach around the back with the left hand toward the right hip and grasp it, thereby twisting the upper torso to the left. Do the same for the opposite side.

11. Small-Child Style

While sitting, rotate the head and shake the head three times. Then standing, rotate the head and shake the head three times.

12. Leaping

After three heel-hops, extend the clenched hands and land with the buttocks on the ground. Do that three times.

Those last five exercises purify both the vital winds and the vital-essence drops.

13. First Exercise to Open the Central Channel

Sit in cross-legged vajra position and straighten the body. Extend the two clenched hands directly in front. Strike and press near the breast with the left fist. Extend the right directly to the right of the buttocks for one cubit. Do that three times. Then do the opposite three times. This is called the crossing of right and left.

14. Second Exercise to Open the Central Channel

Do a wind-jump and then stand. Extend the hands and lie down on the belly. Open the mouth and eyes wide. Extend and contract the four limbs and forcefully shake them. This is called the *furthest opening.*

15. Inserting [the Winds] within the Central Channel

Stand up from the basic position. {143} Press down the winds, extend the hands, and beat the chest three times. Again extend the clenched fists to the side of the thighs and forcefully draw up the downward-clearing winds three times. Now extend the arms like the wings of a vulture and do three heel-hops. Then shake the body violently. Again clear out the winds, exhaling while shaking forcefully.

16. Drawing Up in the Central Channel

Stand and cross the right and left hands and put them under the armpits, squeezing the breasts with the forearms. Fill up the right-side ribs [and hold the breath]. Bend the head to the left and simultaneously draw up the vital winds on the right. Reverse it, bending over to the right and following suit on the left [by drawing up the winds]. Similarly bend the neck and pull and press forward. Also pull and press to the back.

17. Gathering within the Central Channel

Stand as before and cross the arms with the palms holding the right and left biceps. Rotate the belly three times to the right and three times to the left. Twist the upper torso to the right and left. Bend the waist back and forth to the right, left, and center, then regain control.

The two openings [of the channel] and three dances are counted separately but come together as one. So the two openings and inserting, drawing up, and gathering—these five—are called the yogic exercise of the vajra dance.[5]

18. Yogic Exercises to Dispel Afflictive Emotions

There are eight [or nine] subcategories:

a. Dispelling Stupidity [with] Vairocana's Mudra[6]

Make the mudra of supreme awakening at the heart and extend it in front. Twist to the right and left, up and down, striking the breast and belly.

b. Dispelling Agitation

Sitting in the cross-legged vajra position, hook the two ring fingers and with the other fingers press and bend the large ligament in the nape of the neck. Rotate to the right and left three times, twisting forcefully. Extend the hands above and slap the crown of the head with the palms three times. {144}

c. Dispelling Reproach[7]

Lift the two hands from the knees and slap the flesh of the buttocks and extend [the hands] in front and with the mudra of Amoghasiddhi. Hit the heart area and below the navel. Straighten the left arm and turn it out.

d. Suppressing Harm-Doers

Sitting in cross-legged vajra position, make the burning mudra to the right, left, center, and above, then slightly toward the back. Circle it three times to the right and three times to the left and, at the same time, open the eyes wide and rotate them as well with a powerful gaze.

e. Dispelling Anger with Akṣobhya's Mudra

Sitting in cross-legged vajra position, clap down the sides. Bind the center of the chest with the ten fingers intertwined and bend the elbows out, twisting to the right and left three times. Touch the ground with both hands, and look to the right, left, and center with a fearsome gaze.

f. Dispelling Pride with Amitābha's Mudra

Sitting in cross-legged vajra position, straighten the arms and place them firmly in the position of meditative equipoise. Raise the arms in that equipoise position and slam them into the belly, holding them there. Again straighten the arms and so forth, repeating three times. After that, expel the air and at the same time intensely utter "*ha*" three times.

g. Dispelling Desire

From the basic position, circle the right and left legs by turns three times and hit [the ground] with them. Then lay back and extend the right leg while contracting the left, and extend the left while contracting the right. Stretch the hands up in space and make the gesture of kneading dough.

h. Dispelling Greed, the Greater Descent of Great Bliss

From the cross-legged vajra position, stand up suddenly and spread the arms like a balance scale. Do a wind-hop (*rlung 'khrab*). Make the threatening pointing gesture, turning around to the right and left, up and down, front and back. Do one exhalation of the breath and extend the [mudra of] supreme generosity, raising the body. This is called sudden standing. {145}

i. Lesser Descent of Bliss

The so-called threefold shake is to shake the right and left arms from top to bottom and forcefully shake the upper torso [while exhaling]. Sit in the bodhisattva posture and do the threefold shake. Then cross the hands with the right hand above the left, palms facing up. With the left hand touching underneath the right, the left ring finger hooks the right ring finger. Extend that forward and turn them [inward]. Then reverse the position of the hands and turn them inward. Do this three times each with some force. Then extend the left fist straight out from the shoulder and rub the arm three times with the right fist. Then do the same for the right [arm]. Again do the threefold shake and finally a forceful fall (*'bebs*). This last exercise is called the threefold shake. It helps dispel regret, depression, and discursive thought.

[Colophon]

Most of these yogic exercises each have vital points of visualization that should be learned from the source text. These are the personal instructions of Niguma, Ḍākinī of Timeless Awareness. They are esoteric instructions for dissolving wind-mind in the central channel and releasing the channel knots, using one's own body as the primary means. They are the esoteric instructions for the supreme accomplishment of the path of liberation that are known as the eighteen physical trainings (*lus sbyong bco brgyad pa*). Regarding the sources of this, the oral directions are somewhat arcane, and they have been scattered among a great many words. There are many who do not know how to arrange them. Although it is possible for uneducated persons to make some collections of them, a practical application does not actually emerge clearly. Since I saw that the practice was close to disappearing, in order to save it and spread it, I, Tāranātha, having attained some degree of devotion in the glorious Shangpa Kagyu, have laid it out clearly without restriction.

Tangtong Gyalpo and the Direct Lineage

Introduction

The following five chapters were composed by the great adept Tangtong Gyalpo (1361?–1485), "King of the Empty Plain," one of the five names bestowed on him by the ḍākinīs, which he lists right at the beginning of the first text. These texts present his versions of the practices on the Six Dharmas, Amulet Mahāmudrā, Three Integrations, Immortal Body and Mind, and the dharma protector Six-Armed Mahākāla. In the introduction to his book *King of the Empty Plain*, translator Cyrus Stearns sums up some of his achievements:

> This heroic figure became legendary because of his contributions to the mystical traditions, his exceptionally long life, and his innovative achievements in the fields of art, architecture, and metallurgy. Tangtong's life and teachings are intertwined with divine madness, visionary revelation, demon exorcism, the quest for immortality, the relationship of human beings with their environment, and the process of ultimate enlightenment. He is famous in Tibet and the Himalayan regions for building many iron suspension bridges and is thus known by the epithet "Iron-Bridge Man" (Lcags zam pa). The great master also constructed many stūpas—architectural symbols of enlightened mind—that were strategically located according to geomantic principles in order to control the wild energy of the landscape.[1]

Tangtong Gyalpo figures prominently in all areas and schools of Tibetan Buddhism, and the Shangpa tradition is no exception. He received the long transmission (*ring brgyud*) of Niguma's teachings that had been passed down through the one-to-one lineage until Sangye Tönpa from the master Jangsem Jinpa Zangpo (b. 14th century). At that time, he entered a wilderness retreat to practice them, and there had his first vision of Niguma herself, who granted special transmissions in what is known as a direct or short lineage (*nye brgyud*).[2] In the twofold category of all Shangpa lineages, these long and direct lineages that originated with Tangtong Gyalpo are known as the Iron Bridge tradition (*lcags zam lugs*) or Tang tradition (*thang lugs*), while all other Shangpa divergent lines, twenty-four in total, are counted together as one. In that sense, and in many others, Tangtong Gyalpo's teachings stand apart. Even some of his other compositions that are not specifically Shangpa have been incorporated into the Shangpa curriculum, such as the widely practiced Avalokiteśvara sādhana *Filling Space with Benefit for Beings.*[3]

Collection of Essentials is the general name for the Shangpa teachings that Tangtong Gyalpo received in three visionary encounters with the Ḍākinī Niguma, and contained in a supplemental volume of his *Collected Works.* They were written down much later (probably 1458) after his third vision in which Niguma granted her permission to do so. They are among the few texts actually signed by him as the Madman of the Empty Valley. They have been passed down in the Shangpa Kagyu line that is distinct from those of his other traditions, as well as from other Shangpa lineages. Finally, they were received by Jamyang Khyentse Wangpo both from his teachers and in a visionary meeting with Tangtong Gyalpo himself in 1834, when he was fifteen years old.[4]

Vital Words of Instruction on the Six Dharmas of Niguma is a thorough explanation of each of those doctrines, and covers the same basic topics as *Tangdalma* in chapter 1, explicitly following Niguma's root text, the *Vajra Lines of the Six Dharmas.*[5] Most of the subjects are explained in a pleasantly succinct and practical way. The one exception, however, is the teaching on the practices for the intermediate state, or bardo. Here we find a very clear and detailed presentation of the stages of death, what signs and experiences to expect at each stage, and how to apply the practices.

Guidance in Amulet Mahāmudrā and *Guidance in the Three Integrations* are likewise brief and lucid but do not leave out any of the vital points for the application of those practices. *Guidance in Immortal Body and Mind*, generally known as Immortal and Infallible (*'Chi med 'chugs med*) or Naturally Liberated Immortality (*'Chi med rang grol*) joins what were originally two separate practices. The first was based on Virūpa's *Attaining Immortality of the Body* (*Amārasiddhimūla*), a confusing and seemingly corrupted version of yogic postures and breathing techniques to attain actual physical immortality through thirty-two exercises. The second was Niguma's *Immortal Mind Root Text* (*Amāramahājñāna*), which employs a more creation-phase approach and mahāmudrā-style pointing out of the mind's deathless nature. Both of those were introduced and translated in the first volume of Shangpa practices, *The Treasury of Precious Instructions, Volume 11: Shangpa Kagyu*. Fortunately, Tangtong Gyalpo here uses the second approach for both subjects, which is the form that they came to be practiced in the Shangpa lineage. In other contexts, Tangtong Gyalpo is renowned for not only his own longevity but for a number of teachings and rituals for achieving it.

Guidance in the Six-Armed Awareness Protector is the one text here not found in the *Collection of Essentials* or elsewhere. Swift-Acting Awareness Protector Six-Armed Mahākāla ("Chakdrukpa"), is considered a wrathful emanation of compassionate Avalokiteśvara. This is the dharma protector of the Shangpa Kagyu and held dearly as a profound and esoteric practice. It was given to the great Indian adept Maitrīpa by Śavarīpa, and then passed to Khyungpo Naljor, who brought the protector to Tibet. It is said that Tangtong Gyalpo received the thirteen empowerments of Protector, which are found later in this volume, from the meditation master Zangpo Pal,[6] and he conferred the empowerment on multiple occasions.

4. Collection of Essentials

Vital Words of Instruction on the Six Dharmas of Niguma, Ḍākinī of Timeless Awareness[1]

Tangtong Gyalpo

namo lokeśvaraya

"The one who is ineffable, spontaneously present, and unconditioned,
the union as blissful saṃbhogakāya, arising to tame anyone,
Vajradhara with three kāyas and seven aspects,"[2] and so on.

Lords, see me with understanding, most kind gurus.
Think of me with affection, host of yidam deities.
Protect me at all times, Three Precious Jewels.
Remove adverse conditions and achieve conducive ones, ḍākinīs and
protectors.

I—King of the Empty Plain, Madman of the Empty Valley, Extractor of the Essence of Any Food, Equalizer of Any Occurring Conditions—have gathered into one place the essential extract of all the teachings of the Great Vehicle. The explanation of this special instruction of the aural lineage of Niguma, Ḍākinī of Timeless Awareness, has two parts: (1) the person who is the support for practice and (2) the actual practice.

I. The Person

This should be someone who has received the empowerment into the mandala either of the Five Tantras' Deities or of Cakrasaṃvara; who possesses sacred pledge, faith, and diligence; and who has fully assimilated the preliminary teachings such as death and impermanence, karmic cause and effect, the shortcomings of cyclic existence, and so forth. {149} As it states in Niguma's *Vajra Lines*:

> Matured by four empowerments, faithful, and diligent,
> having first [experienced] impermanence, weariness, [and samsara's] deficiencies,
> whoever strives at this sublime path
> will awaken in six months, a year, or in this lifetime.[3]

II. The Actual Practice

This has two parts: (1) the preliminaries and (2) the main practice.

A. Preliminaries

In the space before you appears a jeweled throne supported by eight lions. On that, the stem of a lotus with a thousand petals arises from *paṃ*. Upon that, the mandala of the sun with a hundred thousand light rays arises from *raṃ*. And upon that, the moon mandala arises from *āḥ*, reaching the extent of the billionfold universe. There are various cushions of silk and so on, upon which sits my root guru in the form of Great Buddha Vajradhara. He is blue, with one face and two hands, holding a vajra in the right and a bell in the left, crossed over his heart. He sits with two legs crossed in vajra position, his naked body adorned by bones and jewels. {150} He smiles amiably. His loose locks fall down to his waist. Just seeing his form purifies negative actions and obscurations. Just hearing his voice is certain to place one in the state of a nonreturner. Imagine this appearing with no intrinsic nature. Before him you and all sentient beings go for refuge from the very bottom of your hearts:

> All sentient beings, my mothers, equal to the reaches of space,
> from today until the heart of awakening, go for refuge in the guru.
> We go for refuge in the Buddha. We go for refuge in the dharma.
> We go for refuge in the sangha. We go for refuge in the yidams.[4]

Repeat one hundred or so times. Then the four immeasurable meditations:

May all sentient beings, my mothers, equal to the reaches of space, have happiness and the causes of happiness.
May they be free from suffering and the causes of suffering.
May they never be separated from happiness that is free of suffering.
May they dwell in equanimity, free of happiness or suffering, close or distant, attachment or aversion.

Arousing the mind of awakening:

I will attain the state of a buddha for the sake of all sentient beings. Therefore, I will engage in the stages of applied virtue with body, speech, and mind.

Supplicating the gurus:

I supplicate Great Buddha Vajradhara.
I supplicate Ḍākinī Niguma.
I supplicate adept Khyungpo Naljor.
I supplicate Mokchok Rinchen Tsöndru.
I supplicate Great Nyame Kyergangpa.
I supplicate Lama Sangye Nyentön.
I supplicate Dharma King Sangye Tönpa.
I supplicate wise adept Shangtön Chöje.
I supplicate Great Gyalwa Mupa.
I supplicate Lama Dorje Zhönu.
I supplicate Tsenden Namkhai Naljor. {151}
I supplicate Jangsem Jinpa Zangpo.
I supplicate adept Tsöndru Zangpo.

Bless me to naturally produce bliss-heat on the Path of Methods.
Bless me to naturally liberate desire and anger in Illusory Body.
Bless me to naturally purify double delusion in Dream.
Bless me to naturally dispel stupidity in Lucid Clarity.
Bless me to awaken without meditation in Transference.
Bless me with the victors' saṃbhogakāya in the Intermediate State.

Supplicate intensely with this or whatever verses are suitable.

B. Main Practice

This has six parts: (1) the Path of Methods, naturally blazing bliss-warmth; (2) Illusory Body, naturally liberated desire and anger; (3) Dream, naturally purified double delusion; (4) Lucid Clarity, naturally awakened stupidity; (5) Transference, buddhahood without meditation; and (6) Intermediate State, the victors' saṃbhogakāya.

1. Path of Methods

This has three parts: (1) preliminaries, (2) main practice, and (3) concluding practice.

a. Preliminaries

This has three parts: (1) The Purifying *A* of Inner Space, (2) the Inner Space That Dispels Sickness and Spirits, and (3) the three special signs of inner space.

i. The Purifying *A* of Inner Space

Meditate as before on the guru as white adorned Vajradhara upon a lotus from *paṃ* and moon-disk mandala from *āḥ* above your head. Dissolve all the gurus and yidams into that. Then supplicate:

> Precious guru!
> Bless me to dispel sicknesses and bad spirits.
> Bless me to purify negative actions and obscurations.
> Bless me that special meditative absorption arises in my mind stream.

Take the Empowerment of Existence as described below, then say "*A*." Imagine a source of phenomena (tetrahedron) with each of its three vertices level with your midbrow and right and left ears. It is white inside and out, utterly empty, the size of your body. Meditating on that again and again without distraction purifies all negativity, obscuration, [corruption from] misappropriated and ransom offerings, and damaged sacred pledge. {152}

ii. The Inner Space That Dispels Sickness and Spirits

The source of phenomena's three vertices each point toward the larynx and two bases of the ears. It is white both outside and inside, with the lower tip reaching the perineum. Within it, imagine your own unborn mind as white *A*. Repeat "*A* - *A*" as many times as appropriate. Thereby the *A* melts into light and becomes elixir in essence and white as camphor in form, cooling to the touch. Imagine it able to soothe all sickness from heat.

Again, the source of phenomena's three vertices each point toward the two breasts and the spine directly behind them. It is red both outside and in. Within it, imagine your own unborn mind as a red *A*. Then, repeating as before, the *A* melts and becomes elixir in essence and red like molten copper in form, hot to the touch. Meditate that it is able to pacify all sickness from cold.

Again, the source of phenomena's three vertices each point toward your navel and two kidneys. It is maroon both outside and inside. Within it, imagine your own unborn mind as a maroon *A*. Then repeating as before, the *A* melts and becomes elixir in essence and maroon like the refined essence of melted butter in form, soft to the touch. Imagine that it is able to pacify all sickness of the vital winds.

Again, a black source of phenomena's three vertices each point toward a spot four fingers below the navel and the two hips. Within it, imagine your own mind as a black *A*. Then repeating as before, the *A* melts into light and becomes elixir in essence and boils like molten bronze in form, extremely hot to the touch. Imagine that it is able to burn up all sickness, spirits, negativities, and obscurations. Then repeat *A* and meditate that it causes all sickness as purple shapes; all spirits as scorpions, snakes, and so forth; and all negativities and obscurations as pus, blood, and liquid coal that exude from all the pores and lower orifices while inside the body crackles and sparks with burning. {153} By continuously meditating without distraction on these visualizations, you will accomplish them when you experience that whatever sickness and spirits you targeted are all pacified. Alternatively, it is also appropriate to meditate on each later source of phenomena situated within the immediately previous source of phenomena.

iii. The Special Inner Space of Three Signs

The signs of purification of negative actions are the rising sun, flying through the sky, arriving on the rooftop or a mountain peak such as a snow mountain, landing on the water without sinking, showing up naked without shame, washing, wearing spotless white clothing, and so forth. The signs of purging sickness are diarrhea and vomiting, exuding pus and blood, and perspiring profusely. Signs of expelling bad spirits are scorpions, snakes, spiders, frogs, tadpoles, and bugs leaving the body. All of those signs can occur for real or as a visionary experience or in dreams, and so on—however they occur.

b. Main Practice

This has five parts: (1) The vital point of the body: Inner Space of Fire or four attributes of the central channel, (2) Wearing the Clothes of Fierce Inner Heat, (3) Eating the Food, (4) Spreading the Seat, and (5) receiving the Empowerment of Existence.

i. The Vital Point of the Body: Inner Space of Fire

Imagine yourself as Vajrayoginī and assume a sitting posture with your two legs drawn up and crossed [at the calves] and the soles of your feet on the mat. Cross your arms and grasp the right and left biceps [with the opposite hands]. Place your elbows on your knees and bend the neck slightly. This is called the sixfold-binding-stove posture. Meditate on the guru above your head as before, and pray:

> Precious Guru!
> Bless me with the arising of bliss-warmth meditative absorption.
> Bless me with the arising of bliss-emptiness meditative absorption.

After you request the Empowerment of Existence, clearly visualize the central channel that extends from inside the crown of the head down to the perineum. It has four attributes: it is straight as an arrow, hollow inside like copper coins [with holes in the centers], red as a lac flower, and glossy as sesame oil. {154} To its right is the red rasanā channel and to the left the white lalanā channel, both entering the central channel at the lower end. Both the rasanā and lalanā have coiled channel knots at each of the four places—navel, heart, throat, and head. At the head, the [upper ends] of the rasanā on the right and lalanā on the left branch into four lesser channels: two go to the right and left of the mouth, two go to the two nostrils, two go to the eyes, and two go to the ears, open like cobra hoods. At the opening of the anus is the arrow of vital winds, its tip hung with blue banners. The tip of the arrowhead, between the rasanā and lalanā, enters the central channel. On the tip of the arrow is a fire from *raṃ*, the size of a deer pellet. Visualize this flame with five attributes: fine at the base, sharp at the point, bulging in the middle, hot to the touch, and red in color. Imagine the white syllable *haṃ* hanging upside down inside the central channel in the top of the head.

Then, after slowly clearing out the dead air, slowly inhale equally [into two nostrils] while drawing the vital winds in and down. Then slowly draw up the lower wind, joining the upper and lower winds at the navel. By that, the lower winds move, causing that fire to blaze up below the navel in a shape like a porcupine [quill]. Taking another breath makes it blaze up to the navel. At the third retention of the breath, it arrives at the heart and its heat causes drops from the *haṃ* letter in the head to fall like a string of pearls. Imagine the drops striking the fire at the heart with a sizzling sound. The fire does not go out, nor does it flicker—these are profound vital points that are very important.

By that process, first warmth will arise, then bliss, then the meditative absorption of bliss-emptiness. Thus it is like the root of the Six Dharmas. As Niguma herself said [in the *Vajra Lines*]:

> One's own body is the means, with three channels and four chakras.
> The *A* blazes and *haṃ* drips, adorning the four instances with four ecstasies.
> Uniting with the wisdom's khagamukhā,
> the dissipating and nondissipating four ecstasies arise in sequence.[5]

ii. Wearing the Clothes of Fierce Inner Heat {155}

The physical posture and visualization are the same as the previous practice, except that the palms of the crossed hands cover the right and left kidneys. Think that at the navel and directly behind it and at the right and left kidneys there are four balls of fire the size of [bird] eggs. By joining the winds as before, you will experience the warmth arising quickly, which is the accomplishment. If an elderly person does this, the fireballs should be imagined as the size of pigeon or duck eggs.

iii. Eating the Food of Fierce Inner Heat

The physical posture is the same as before, but add this to the visualization: Breathe out a white water-wind, and [breathe in] and hold a red fire-wind. The joining of the winds causes a fearsome fire to fall from the palate.[6] Meditate on this filling the entire belly inside with red fire. In this, since the occurrence of obstructions is imminent, apply the following in response to your own experience. First expel the air-wind, then expel the fire-wind, then expel all winds with the colors described below. Then visualize inhaling and holding the yellow earth-wind by the roots of the teeth. By your joining that with the wind drawn up from below the navel, the belly fills with yellow radiance. Then it fills with a white radiance by holding the white water-wind from the palate. Then it fills with a red radiance through holding the red fire-wind from between the teeth. Then the belly fills with blue radiance through holding the blue air-wind and joining the upper and lower winds. With those methods, heat will come swiftly and obstructions will be minor.

iv. Spreading the Seat of Fierce Inner Heat

In addition to the physical posture and visualization described above, at bedtime curl up in the sleeping-dog posture with your right side underneath. As you exhale, imagine that red fire emerges continually from your nostrils and fills inside all your bedding with red radiance. Hold the breath slightly and meditate.

v. Receiving the Empowerment of Existence

Meditate on the guru above your head as before. Light radiates from the guru's heart and invokes all the gurus, yidams, buddhas, and bodhisattvas in the form of Vajradhara, who dissolve [into the guru's heart]. {156} Present your body and all possessions to the precious guru, the embodiment of all. Say:

> Precious guru, please confer upon me the Empowerment of Existence.

With that supplication, a stream of white elixir emerges from the guru's big toe. [It enters through your head and] fills down to the eyebrows. Think that physical stains are purified and you receive the vase empowerment. On the path, you are empowered to meditate on creation phase and manifest the resultant nirmāṇakāya. Red elixir emerges and fills down to the throat. Think that verbal stains are purified and you receive the secret empowerment. On the path, you are empowered to meditate on the completion phase and manifest the resultant saṃbhogakāya. Blue elixir emerges and fills down to the heart. Think that mental stains are purified and you receive the wisdom-awareness empowerment. On the path, you are empowered to meditate on combined creation and completion phases and manifest the resultant dharmakāya. Finally, the guru melts into light and dissolves into you. Think that the guru's awakened body, speech, and mind become inseparable from your body, speech, and mind. Physical, verbal, and mental negativities and obscurations along with habitual patterns are all purified. You receive the fourth empowerment. On the path, you are empowered to meditate without embellishment and manifest the resultant fourth kāya. That purifies all negative acts, obscurations, and damages and violations of sacred pledge; prevents obstructions; engenders the absorptions that have not yet arisen; and increases those that have more and more.

c. Concluding Practices

This has two parts: (1) Naturally Liberating Obstructing Forces and (2) Riding the Horse of Vital Winds.

i. Naturally Liberating Obstructing Forces

Imagine that there are terrifying, fierce eyes in the three places of your two breasts and midway between them, and the three corresponding places on your back. Meditate that all the pores from your crown to your soles are like the *eyes* (i.e., holes) in a sieve or colander. From those eyes, all sickness as the color purple; all spirits as scorpions, snakes, frogs, tadpoles, and so forth; and all negativities and obscurations in the form of liquid coal are expelled out like water pouring through a sieve. {157} Hold the joining of winds while contemplating that. If obstruction of the kunda (sexual fluid) in the lower body occurs, yogic exercises and visualizations of descending, holding, reversing, and spreading will clear it up.

ii. Riding the Horse of the Vital Winds

This is the esoteric instruction for the second concluding practice. Think that there are blue wind goddesses at both your armpits and both soles. Put your two vajra fists under your arms. Mainly expel the earth-wind and inhale and hold the air-wind. Join upper and lower winds, and think that you circle the four continents and Mount Meru. Once the winds are trained, think that the four goddesses are carrying you in the air when you move. When you hold the breath and arrive back, you will move like the excellent horse. Concerning these practices, Niguma taught [in the *Vajra Lines*]:

> The inner space purifier gathers the quintessence in three vital points,
> and to quicken the heat, the Six Dharmas, Inner Heat in sequence:
> rabbit descending, holding, reversing, spreading, and blending with vital winds.
> Adorn with undissipating, great, nondual, timeless awareness.[7]

2. Illusory Body, Naturally Liberated Desire and Anger

This has three parts: (1) Relying on the Friendship of a Holy Guru for those of the highest capabilities, (2) Guidance without Interruption by Other Words for the average, and (3) Developing Meditative Absorption in a Single Sitting for the lowest.

a. Relying on the Friendship of a Holy Guru

After doing the preliminaries as before, visualize your root guru as Buddha Great Vajradhara seated on the lotus-moon seat above your head. He is blue and holds a vajra in the right hand and a bell in the left, crossed over his heart. He sits with two legs crossed in vajra position, his naked body adorned by bones and jewels. He smiles amiably and has three eyes. His loose hair falls over half of his body, and he is adorned by the marks and signs of an awakened being, shining with the brilliance of one hundred thousand suns. Imagine the radiating light rays blessing your mind stream. {158} Imagine all the sentient beings that you are leading into his presence supplicating with a low murmuring sound:

> Precious guru, bless me to realize nonself.
> Bless me to abandon fixation on a self.
> Bless me to refine Illusory Body.
> Bless me to actualize Lucid Clarity Mahāmudrā.

Thus pray with intensity and make this request:

> Precious guru, please confer the manifest empowerment on me.

With that supplication, the empowerment is conferred as before in the path of methods. At the end, rest for a long time in the state of equipoise, your body, speech, and mind inseparable from the guru's awakened body, speech, and mind. After arising from that state, in all daily activities and all mental activities, think, "Ah! Appearances do appear but their reality is not real. It is illusion. Alas, it is a dream."

The supplications of Integrating Devotion to the Guru on the path and Integrating the Unreal Nature of Whatever Appears are both taught separately, but here they are uniquely combined. Since just this is the main practice in all Vajrayāna approaches, if you energetically cultivate this experience one-pointedly, it is the fastest way to traverse all paths. As it states in *Actualization of Timeless Awareness*:

> The stages of the levels and paths will be traversed
> in months and years through devotion to the guru.
> If you never part from the guru's appearance,
> you dwell constantly with the buddhas.[8]

And from Niguma:

> The stages of the levels and paths
> are traversed on the strength of devotion.
> The sublime vital point of the tantras' intent
> is never to part from the guru's manifestation.[9]

b. Guidance without Interruption by Other Words

For those of average capabilities, do the guru yoga as before. Then think:

> Alas! All sentient beings born in the past are dead. Those born now will also die. Of all the sentient beings existing now, not even one will get out alive and remain. {159} I too will most certainly die. Not only that, our time on earth is uncertain and there are many causes of death but few that sustain life. I'm afraid I will die soon.

Meditate until such time as you disengage from any idea of accomplishing something for this life, lofty or lowly. If you think, "Oh what if I die?" [know that] after death you will not cease to exist. If you die without realizing the single meaning of the abiding nature, there will be no place to go other than whichever of the six realms of beings is fitting. And in whichever place you are reborn, there is nothing other than the experience of suffering; never a chance for happiness. So it is not nice. Contemplate that and meditate until such time as an uncontrived desire to attain buddhahood arises. Meditate again and again with recollection and intention, thinking, "Ah, this is all a dream, all an illusion."

Then a lotus from *paṃ* and a moon from *A* appear. Upon that seat, *hūṃ* radiates light that makes offerings to the noble ones and performs the welfare of sentient beings. The light returns and completely transforms into oneself as white Cakrasaṃvara holding vajra and bell crossed over the heart and adorned by bones and jewels. To one's perception, a form does exist, but a tangible form does not exist. Meditate on appearance with no intrinsic nature, like a reflection in a mirror. Contemplate how such forms as the deity's color, implements, jewels, accessories, and posture are nothing other than an invention of your mind and do not exist out there. So think, "Such appearances do appear, but their reality is not real. It is illusion. Alas, it is a dream."

Furthermore, whatever appearance occurs as an object of mind—whether of the environment or its inhabitants, close or distant or neutral, happy or sad—continuously say, "It is illusion, it is a dream" without interruption by other words, such as idle conversation. {160} In your mind, also never let your intentionality of recollecting illusion and dream diminish. The teachings of [visualizing] one's own body as the deity's form of appearance-emptiness, and the integration of whatever appears as illusion are uniquely combined here. It states in the *Sutra of the Questions of *Kumāraprabha*:

> It is said "all phenomena are illusions and dreams."
> Whoever says and recalls these words

will be released from the bonds of existence
and definitely awaken in this very life.[10]

c. Developing Meditative Absorption in a Single Sitting

If not a single experience has arisen based on those methods, then it means you are of the least capability. So the third option for those of lesser capabilities is to develop absorption in a single sitting. Do the preliminaries as before. Visualize yourself clearly as Cakrasaṃvara. Below the navel is a source of phenomena with the following colors in order from the bottom up: black, yellow, light brown, maroon, red, and white. Meditate on the beings within them as, respectively, hell beings, hungry ghosts, animals, humans, demigods, and gods. Once you have focused with single-pointed attention on that, think and say, "All of this is illusion. It is a dream." Until such time as all the appearances become unreal illusion, meditate on a single seat without letting it cool off. Moreover, whatever appearances occur—whether harmful ones such as sickness, spirits, and so forth or good and pleasant and so forth—repeat "It is illusion, it is dream" and contemplate that. [The four instructions called] Making the Six Kinds of Migrators Arise as Illusion, Integrating Sickness and Spirits as Illusion, the Sixfold Set of Qualities That Develop, and the Natural Arising of Illusion Free of Attachment are all included in this single practice. You will understand by meditating. For a concise version, meditate on the six kinds of beings within the source of phenomena that is white outside and red inside. Then contemplate as before and all the qualities of naturally arising illusion will develop.

Regarding all these, Niguma gave her personal instructions on cultivating experience with this verse:

Illusory Body, unreal, is for those of highest, average, and lesser
capability:
with constant devotion, with one's body, and whatever appears,
integrate them as the deity's form of empty appearance, free of
attachment. {161}
Desire and anger naturally liberated, the fourteenth stage will be
attained.[11]

3. Dream, Naturally Purified Double Delusion

Also in Niguma's [*Vajra Lines*] it states:

> Whoever has completely abandoned all ideas,
> should constantly maintain the vital point of intention for dreaming.
> Double delusion will be naturally purified and the qualities
> of the stages of the path of illusion will naturally arise at all times of day and night.[12]

Instruction for the Natural Liberation of Dream's Double Delusion from the aural lineage includes six topics: (1) recognizing, (2) refining, (3) increasing, (4) emanating, (5) changing, and (6) viewing objective appearance.

a. Recognizing Dreams

This has two parts: (1) the preliminaries and (2) the main practice.

i. Preliminaries

This is similar to the previous preliminaries, but in the guru yoga visualize your root guru on the lotus-moon seat above your head as red Buddha Great Vajradhara, crossing the vajra and bell over his heart, with ornaments and attributes the same as before. Supplicate with:

> Precious guru, bless me to recognize my dreams.
> Bless me to refine my dreams.
> Bless me to increase my dreams.
> Bless me to change my dreams.
> Bless me to look into objective appearance.
>
> Please confer upon me the full four empowerments.

With that supplication, a white *oṃ* emerges from the *oṃ* in the guru's forehead and dissolves into your forehead. You receive the vase empowerment, which purifies physical stains and empowers you to meditate on creation phase as the path. Red *āḥ* emerges from the *āḥ* in the guru's throat and dissolves into your throat, purifying verbal obscurations. You receive the secret empowerment, empowering you to meditate on completion phase as the path. Blue *hūṃ* emerges from the *hūṃ* in the guru's heart and dissolves into your heart, purifying mental obscurations. You receive the wisdom-awareness empowerment, empowering you to meditate on combined creation and completion as the path. Finally, the guru melts into light and dissolves into you. {162} Your body, speech, and mind and the guru's awakened body, speech, and mind become inseparable. Rest in that state for a long time. Your physical, verbal, and mental obscurations along with habitual patterns are all purified. You receive the fourth empowerment. Think that you will actualize the four kāyas. This precedes the Six Dharmas, such as Dream practice.

ii. The Main Practice of Recognizing Dream

This has two parts: (1) self-recognition and (2) infallible [vital points].

A) Self-Recognition

A pea-sized white drop emerges from the *haṃ* letter in the crown of your head and arrives at your heart. A pea-sized red drop from the perineum ascends to your heart. Then that red drop chases that white drop round and round, making a swirl of vivid colors at the heart. Focus your attention on that and recall the intentionality for dreams and illusion. In this way, the circling of the drops is the vase empowerment, when they nearly touch it is the secret empowerment, when they touch it is the wisdom-awareness empowerment, and when they dissolve into one another and vanish into light and you are left with no idea of a reference point—then you have received the fourth empowerment. Meditate like that again and again. When you are about to sleep and the drops dissolve into each other and disappear, you may recognize dreams within that state of nonthought. The way to recognize them is to take many naps. Then, whether you have a gentle dream or a nightmare, think, "Ah, this is a dream" and recognize it.

B) Infallible Vital Points

This was created with nine topics, but it can be subsumed into three: vital points of body, vital points of time, and vital points of visualization. First, the vital point of the body posture is sitting with legs drawn up. Second, the vital point of time is first light, before the sun rises. Third, the vital point of visualization is threefold: two that are without conceptual thought and one with conceptual thought.

1) The First Vital Point of Recognizing Dreams without Concepts

A white drop descends from the *haṃ* in the crown of your head and a red drop ascends from the perineum; they meet at the heart. They chase each other around as before. Focus your attention on their circling and think, {163} "Ah! I have fallen asleep. This is in my dream." Recall this with intense intentionality. When about to fall asleep, the white drop exits through the right nostril and the red one through the left nostril, circling around in a colorful swirl at the point between your eyebrows. Focus attention on that and recall the intention of illusion and dream. Then the white drop becomes white Cakrasaṃvara holding vajra and bell crossed over the heart. The red one becomes red Vajravārāhī holding flaying knife and blood-filled skull cup. Focus your attention on their circling around and think, "This is illusion. This is a dream." Finally, Vajravārāhī dissolves into Cakrasaṃvara, who dissipates into light. Then sleep in a nonconceptual state and recognize that you are dreaming.

2) The Second Vital Point for Grasping Dreams without Concepts

Say, "This naturally pure basic space is purified of the adventitious stains that are to be cleared away." Imagine yourself as Cakrasaṃvara with a thumb-sized Cakrasaṃvara on a lotus and sun in your heart that is emanating light, and think, "I have gone to sleep. This is in a dream." On the verge of sleep, you dissolve into the Cakrasaṃvara in your heart. That also vanishes into light. Within that nonreferential state, recognize that you are dreaming.

3) Recognizing Dreams through Conceptual Thought

The body posture for Dream practice is sitting with legs drawn up. The time is from first light until sunrise. The basis of recognizing dreams is the letter *haṃ*. The place of dreams is the throat. Therefore, imagine the emanating light of the white *haṃ* letter in your throat. The essence of dream is the discursive thoughts just before falling asleep. Therefore, once you have gone to sleep but before the arising of obvious dreams, this is where dim thoughts of people and so forth arise and you can recognize them with attentiveness. Without opening your eyes, think, "This is happening in a dream" and recognize it. That way it is impossible not to recognize it as a dream. {164} However, if you still do not recognize it, then meditate on white Vajra Nairātmya holding flaying knife and skull cup within your cranium on the cranial membrane, as if she is hovering in space. Then it is impossible not to recognize. If you do this continuously, it can be a big hindrance, so then leave it.

b. Refining Dreams

This has four parts: (1) Refining the Mind through the Body, (2) Refining the Body through the Mind, (3) Refining through Nairātmya, and (4) Refining through Intentionality.

i. Refining the Mind through the Body

Meditate on yourself as white Cakrasaṃvara holding vajra and bell. Think, "This is a dream. In dreams, I can refine things however I want." Then, throw yourself into an abyss or something and think that you vanish into light.

ii. Refining the Body through the Mind

Meditate that you appear clearly as Cakrasaṃvara with blue *hūṃ* at the point between the eyebrows and in each of the joints. Their light refines your body into the deity's form of mahāmudrā, and it is refined within that state of clarity-emptiness without fixation.

iii. Refining through Nairātmya

Imagine yourself clearly as Cakrasaṃvara with a white downward-facing *hūṃ* inside the gem [of the sexual organ]. Focus attention on that visualization and think, "This is a dream," while uttering *hūṃ* aloud. The *hūṃ* turns to face upward and becomes white Vajra Nairātmya holding flaying knife and skull cup, entering your body inside with trembling bliss and then melting into light. Your whole interior body is filled with white light and finally disappears altogether. Rest within the state of mahāmudrā.

iv. Refining through Intentionality

Whatever you see, whether subtle or coarse, in the environment or its inhabitants, think, "It is a dream," then refine by passing back and forth through it.

c. Increasing Dreams

This has two parts: (1) Increasing Whatever Is Encountered and (2) Increasing for Whatever Is to Be Tamed.

i. Increasing Whatever Is Encountered

Visualize the mandala of earth and think, "This is a dream. I can increase whatever appears in a dream." Then increase one to ten, then ten to a hundred, then a hundred to a thousand, a thousand to ten thousand, {165} that to a hundred thousand, and so on—as far as your mind can encompass—then gradually reverse and meditate that they fill all of space. After that, increase the mandala of water as before, then the fire mandala, and after that increase the wind mandala as above. With this as an example, increase whatever you see—subtle or coarse forms of the elements or of sentient beings—thinking that it is a dream as before.

ii. Increasing for Whatever Is to Be Tamed

There has two parts: (1) taming with mundane beings and (2) with transcendent beings.

A) Taming with Mundane Beings

After you have increased an external adversary, such as insects, then tame them by increasing yourself as many birds to eat them, and so forth. For something like birds, you emanate something like hawks and tame them. Similarly wolves for dogs, tigers for wolves, lions for tigers, cannibal demons for humans, and so forth—emanate the appropriate opponents for each of them to tame them by killing, binding, beating, and so on.

B) Taming with Transcendent Beings

Emanate as the king of garuḍas for something like nāga adversaries, Hayagrīva for something like Pekar, Mañjuśrī Jñānasattva for something like nāga devils and nāga cannibals, wrathful Vajrapāṇi for something like yakṣas and cannibals, and so forth. For each bad spirit, emanate whatever wrathful being is known to be its opponent power and tame it by vanquishing, swallowing, beating with implements, burning in bonfires, and so forth.

d. Emanating Dreams

This was illustrated by [the instructions for increasing dreams].

e. Changing Dreams

Think that you can change this mandala of the earth into that of water, change the water mandala into that of fire, the fire mandala into that of wind, and the wind mandala into space, where it vanishes. Then look at the essence. This is the transformation of the world environment. To change the sentient beings that inhabit it, change hell beings into hungry ghosts, hungry ghosts into animals, animals into humans, humans into demigods, demigods into gods, and gods into mahāmudrā. {166} Similarly, change this impure world into a pure realm and so forth, thus gaining stability in dreams. During all of this, it is important to remember that this is just a dream and dream appearances can be changed into anything.

f. Viewing Objective Appearance

The physical posture and preliminaries are the same as before, except imagine that you appear clearly as the yidam with a source of phenomena or a skull cup below the navel. It is white outside and red inside and filled with elixir. Then white Vajra Nairātmya, holding flaying knife and skull cup and dancing, leads infinite yidam deities inside through your right nostril. Think, "Yidam deities, please let me ascertain objective appearance." Again Nairātmya leads them out through the left nostril and they remain in space. With a symbolic hand gesture, they show you first the places of hell, then of hungry ghosts, animals, humans, demigods, gods' realms, and finally Sukhāvatī and the other pure realms. Contemplate this both day and night and meditate until such time as objective appearance is ascertained. Occasionally investigate the arising, abiding, and ceasing of the appearances of the environment and its inhabitants. Become absolutely certain that they are apparitions of your own mind. Then after investigating the arising, abiding, and ceasing of mind, rest in equipoise within a state of mahāmudrā, the unity of appearance and emptiness.

In this, the best is to apprehend clarity with no frame of reference. Average is to see clearly whatever you think. Lesser is to soar in space with the mental body. And the least is to see the object of visualization. In this latter, there are some [practices] called Raising Objective Appearance with Nairātmya, Natural Clarity of Objective Appearance with [the Syllable] *A*, {167} and Illuminating Objective Appearance with Vital Drops. You will gain accomplishment by practicing just these elaborations, they are so profound. *ithi*

On those occasions, if obstructions arise such as excessive delusion, excessive insomnia, or excessive bliss, supplicate the guru with devotion, do communal feasts and torma offerings for the yidams and dharma protectors, and see the visualizations for clearing away obstructing forces in Mokchokpa's *Severing Excess*.[13]

4. Lucid Clarity, Naturally Awakened Stupidity

This has three parts: (1) preliminaries, (2) main practice, and (3) conclusion.

a. Preliminaries

Contemplate impermanence and the shortcomings of cyclic existence. Eat nutritious food and remain peaceful in your daily activates. Meditate persistently to generate the path of methods. Offer communal feast and torma to the guru, yidams, ḍākinīs, dharma protectors and guards. Devotion is the vital point of Lucid Clarity, so earnestly supplicate the guru.

b. Main Practice

This has four parts: (1) recognizing, (2) integrating, (3) blending, and (4) ultimate lucid clarity.

i. Recognizing Lucid Clarity

First, Recognizing Lucid Clarity Based on the Letter *A*: Imagine yourself clearly as Cakrasaṃvara with a radiant, stainless white *A* at the heart. Its light fills the body inside. Then meditate on your body as totally brilliant white inside and out, and recognize that. If you don't recognize it, then imagine yourself as white Cakrasaṃvara with an identical thumb-sized version of Cakrasaṃvara on a lotus and moon in your heart. In that heart, imagine a white *A* the size of a mustard seed radiating light. {168} The light emanating from that makes the whole body brilliantly white inside and out. Meditate on the light radiating from all the pores in the body and turning the entire environment and its inhabitants into clear light—then it will arise. If you don't recognize it by that, then there is Recognizing Lucid Clarity Based on a Vital Drop.[14] With yourself as thumb-sized Cakrasaṃvara, imagine a white drop the size of a sesame seed emanating light at the point between your eyebrows and focus with single-pointed attention on that. If you meditate without any distraction, [lucid clarity] will surely arise. Otherwise, there is Recognizing Lucid Clarity Based on Nairātmya. As explained before in the section on Dream, meditate that Nairātmya seems to hover in the space at the cranial membrane while the skull itself is like a conch dome. By this, lucid clarity will be recognized.

ii–iv. Integrating, Blending, and Ultimate Lucid Clarity

The last three parts are elaborations for after lucid clarity has arisen. These and the enhancement practices have been clearly elucidated in the guidebooks of previous masters according to the *Vajra Lines* and Khyungpo Naljor's summary.[15] Those and the introduction by the guru are sufficient.

c. Concluding Practices

Make sure you are not touched by downfalls of the root and branch sacred pledges. In particular, do not lose even a trickle of the white element, since the vital drops are the refined essence of timeless awareness in Lucid Clarity [practice]. Further dispelling of obstructions, enhancements, identification of the doors of perception of lucid clarity, experiential realization, the differences of daytime and nighttime practice, and other subjects will be clarified in the commentaries of previous gurus.

Concerning these practices, Niguma states [in the *Vajra Lines*]:

> Lucid clarity arises through devotion to the guru and
> the great bliss with and without dissipation, the yogic gazes
> cause bliss, clarity, and nonthought inseparable to arise naturally.
> Adorn the preliminaries, main part, and conclusion with the vital points of time.[16]

5. Transference, Buddhahood without Meditation

In the *Vajra Lines*, Niguma said:

> Nothing transferred, no transference; this is for the very best.
> The average and lesser abandon desire and anger
> and with joy and devotion, project upward with single-pointed focus.
> Adorn this with aspiration prayers.[17]

This practice has three parts: (1) transference directly based on the view for the best, (2) transference based on illusory body for the average, and (3) transference through aspirations for the lesser.

a. Transference Based Directly on the View for the Best

With your own mind free of all extremes of elaboration, such as an object or agent of transference, you rest single-pointedly in the state of bliss, clarity, and nonthought like the radiant essence of space. {169} This is also called transference to dharmakāya suchness.

b. Transference Based on Illusory Body for the Average

This has two parts: (1) transference to the yidam and (2) transference to the guru.

i. Transference to the Yidam

This has two parts: (1) training and (2) application.

A) Training

Meditate with heightened clarity on the yidams standing on the lotus and sun above your head: blue Cakrasaṃvara with four faces and twelve arms embracing the mother. Mother Vajravārāhī, red, holding flaying knife and skull cup, embracing the father. Make offerings to them. Supplicate fervently:

> Yidam, Glorious Heruka, please lead me to the celestial realms.

Heruka says:

> Child of good family, come on up.

With this permission, your own mind becomes a [sphere of] white light. It enters and rises up the central channel, then projects far out from the cranial aperture and dissolves into the hearts of the yidam couple. Then imagine that the yidam couple also dissolves into the heart of saṃbhogakāya as four-faced, twelve-armed Cakrasaṃvara in Akaniṣṭha. Focus single-pointed attention on a white *A* in their hearts. Then again that *A* becomes a white light that comes down and enters through your cranial aperture, becoming a white *A* as it arrives at the heart. Focus your mind on that. Train in that way again and again. The signs of successful training are, in the best case, swelling on top of the head that oozes blood or lymph. The middling is throbbing and so on, and the least is itching in that area. In all cases, it is possible that the consciousness leaves the body. This can be prevented by pressing a container made of precious substances on your head.

B) Application

At some point, when you are stricken by the signs of death, offer feasts and tormas to the guru and yidam. Abandon all attachment, aversion, and stupid [indifference] based on three types of objects—pleasant, unpleasant, [and neutral]—such as your body, possessions, friends, and family. {170} According to the visualization described above, transfer your mind with single-pointed attention and so not return to the body.

ii. Transference to the Guru

A) Training

The preliminaries are the same as above. With yourself as the yidam, meditate on your root guru in the form of Vajradhara on a lotus-moon seat above your head. He has the attributes and ornaments as described in Illusory Body instructions. Offer the seven-branch service and repeat again and again:

> Precious Buddha Guru, I supplicate you.
> Please lead me to the place of the celestial realm.
> Please bless me to attain right now the supreme spiritual power of mahāmudrā.

With that supplication, you receive permission as before. Your mind becomes a white light that enters the central channel and moves upward. It projects through the cranial aperture and beyond, dissolving into the guru's heart. The guru then vanishes into light. Rest within the state of nonthought. Alternatively, it dissolves into the guru's heart as Cakrasaṃvara in Akaniṣṭha, as before.

B) Application

This should be understood from the previous directions.

c. Transference through Aspirations for the Lesser

Ordinary people who cannot manage these visualizations should abandon attachment and aversion at the time of death and then make pure aspiration prayers to be reborn in the pure land, and so on. They should perform positive acts of great blessing such as chanting the names of the buddhas.

There is a separate oral instruction for Transference to the Unerring Celestial Realm. It is an esoteric instruction for the radical method of transference to the awakened state for the very sinful. *ithi*

6. Intermediate State, the Victors' Saṃbhogakāya

In general, one could explain all phenomena of samsara and nirvana in terms of six intermediate states (*bar do*): (1) the spontaneously present intermediate state of intrinsic nature, (2) the intermediate state of meditative stability in absorption, (3) the intermediate state of birth and death of the karmically ripened body, (4) the intermediate state of habitual dreaming, (5) the intermediate state of the reverse order dying process, and (6) the intermediate state of the arising order in becoming. {171}

Here, we are concerned with the three main intermediate states to be refined: the intermediate state of life, between birth and death; the intermediate state of dream, between sleep and waking; and the intermediate state of becoming, between death and rebirth. Of these, meditation on Illusory Body is the method that refines the first. Refining and increasing dreams is the method that refines the second. The present subject concerns the methods to refine the intermediate state of becoming. Niguma's *Vajra Lines* states:

> In the intermediate state, [recognize] appearance and so on as lucid clarity, as the deity's form,
> and take rebirth as nirmāṇakāya to tame whomever.
> The vital point is aversion.
> Desire, anger, and jealousy are refined by the deity's form of lucid clarity.
> The two obscurations are naturally purified and three kāyas actualized.
> Form, sound, water, earth, dissolve appearance, increase, and so on.
> One should know the progression of dissolution of the eighty natures.[18]

There are two parts in this practice: (1) how to train in the intermediate state of becoming in one's current circumstances and (2) how to attain awakening by practicing in the intermediate state after the arising of the lucid clarity of death.

a. How to Train in the Intermediate State of Becoming in One's Current Circumstances

Think, "Alas! I've died and arrived in the intermediate state. Without a material body, I leave no footprints behind. Without the white and red elements of my body, the external sun and moon don't shine. Even my shadow does not appear. These are signs of being in the intermediate state. My precious guru told me to recognize the intermediate state and to practice the victors' saṃbhogakāya. Now that time has come. I have nowhere else to place my hopes. Guru and Jewels, think of me!" Thus supplicate. The best practitioners settle directly on the view, the average meditate on Illusory Body, and the lesser make pure aspirations.

Then sometimes think, "I'm in the intermediate state. The signs are sometimes a huge abyss that is deep gray, sometimes deep red, and sometimes a deep black. These must be what my guru taught as the three places of terror. I have nowhere else to place my hope," and so on, meditating as before. {172}

Again, on some occasions think, "I'm in the intermediate state. As the earth-winds withdraw, there are sounds of mountains crumbling and I seem to fall below them. As the water-winds withdraw, there are sounds of a huge river and I seem to be carried away by it. As the fire-winds withdraw, there are crackling sounds of forest fires and so on and I seem to be burning. The force of the air-winds withdrawing makes the sound of a great karmic gale, and I seem to be blown away. My guru told me about four terrifying sounds that arise in the intermediate state—these are them. I have nowhere else to place my hope . . . (etc.)." Meditate as before.

Then sometimes think, "I have died, and now I'm in the intermediate state. The place is unpredictable: sometimes a shrine room or something like a home appears, sometimes a cave or a hut. The companions are unpredictable: sometimes a pleasant divine boy or girl appears as my friend; sometimes unpleasant demons and cannibals and so forth appear as my companions. The food is unpredictable: sometimes elixir, but sometimes rotten food and so forth appear that I imbibe through their odors. The clothing is unpredictable: sometimes I appear to be wearing rags and such, sometimes silks and such. The appearances are also unpredictable: now I appear in my own country and then suddenly I appear to have arrived in another country. Refuge is unpredictable: sometimes it appears that I go for refuge under a bridge, or a bench, or a tree. My guru told me about the six unpredictable signs of the intermediate state. I have nowhere else to place my hopes . . . (etc.)." Meditate as before.

Furthermore, think, "I have died and arrived in the intermediate state. Yesterday, when speaking with my relatives, they answered, but now I cannot elicit a reply. As food I eat odors. {173} I pass unobstructed through mountains and so forth, instantly arriving wherever I please." When eating food, making conversation, getting dressed, and so forth—in short, during all four kinds of activities—think, "Alas, I have arrived in the intermediate state . . . (etc.)" and supplicate with "I have nowhere else to place my hopes. Guru and Jewels, think of me!" Within that state, the best settle directly in the view, the average meditate on Illusory Body, and the lesser make pure aspirations.

b. How to Attain Awakening by Practicing in the Intermediate State after the Arising of the Lucid Clarity of Death

(1) The Natural Arising of Lucid Clarity in the First Intermediate State for the best, (2) the Natural Arising of the Victors' Saṃbhogakāya for the average, (3) the Natural Arising of Unrestricted Nirmāṇakāya for the lesser, and (4) general vital points for unerring integration.

i. The Natural Arising of Lucid Clarity in the First Intermediate State

In cases of gradual death, first there is the manner of dissolution of the five objective appearances. Form dissolves into sound and the eyes see forms a little less clearly. When sound dissolves into smell, the ears don't hear sounds. When smell dissolves into taste, the nose cannot perceive smells. When taste dissolves into textures, the tongue cannot perceive essential tastes. When the phenomena of textures dissolve into the vital winds, the body cannot feel touch accurately and the body's complexion deteriorates.

Then the way the elements dissolve: First earth dissolves into water and the body's strength declines. Saliva and mucus begin to drip. When water dissolves into fire, the moist parts such as the tongue, mouth, and nose all dry up. When fire dissolves into wind, the body's warmth contracts inward from the extremities. When wind dissolves into consciousness, outer and inner breathing stops. When consciousness dissolves into lucid clarity, during the first instant the white constituent of refined essence that is the nature of water and abides in the form of the letter *haṃ* within the head, descends. The external sign of that is a white radiance like the rising moon. The internal sign is a smokelike haze or a mirage-like shimmer radiating five-colored light rays. {174} At that time of so-called appearance, the first instant of nonconceptual timeless awareness arises. The force of that [appearance] blocks the thirty-three thoughts that come from anger. At that time anger won't arise even for a deadly enemy.

After that, the red constituent of refined essence that is the nature of fire and abides at the navel in the form of the short *A* of inner heat, blazes upward. The external sign is like the sunrise. The inner sign is the arising of red sparkles like fireflies. At that time of so-called increase (*mched pa*), nonconceptual timeless awareness grows clearer than before and you remain relaxed without fixation. That is the occurrence of the second instant. Its force blocks the forty thoughts that derive from desire, and at that point desire will not arise even for a divine boy or girl.

When the two white and red constituents first meet at the heart, vital winds and mind enter between them. The outer sign is dense blackness like night. The inner sign is a refreshing nonconceptual state of clarity, like a steady flame unmoved by wind. At that time of so-called attainment (*thob pa*), there is nonconceptual timeless awareness free of all fixation to clarity. Resting relaxed in that state is the occurrence of the third instant. Its force stops thoughts that derive from stupidity.

The wind-mind that had entered between the white and red constituents now enters into the central channel. The outer sign is a pale radiance like the break of day. The inner sign is like the striking radiance of the sun in the autumn sky. An experience of bliss-emptiness arises. At that time of so-called full attainment (*nye bar thob pa*) of intrinsic lucid clarity, there is freedom from all stains of clinging thoughts. The timeless awareness of bliss, clarity, and nonthought occur in this fourth instant. {175} That timeless awareness causes all eighty natural concepts in all their aspects of subtle and coarse to dissolve into lucid clarity. This is also called intrinsic lucid clarity, the palace of dharmakāya lucid clarity, or the naturally arising lucid clarity of the first intermediate state.

Practitioners of the highest capability who have previous experience with lucid clarity will recognize this as lucid clarity itself because they identify this intrinsic lucid clarity with the lucid clarity of previous meditation, like a meeting of mother and child. Since they remain single-pointed within that state, there is no need to enter the intermediate state of becoming. They are awakened as dharmakāya. And while not wavering from that unborn dharmakāya, the two form kāyas arise naturally as spontaneous presence that remains until all of cyclic existence is empty, taming whomever in whatever ways to mature them and establish all sentient beings in liberation. The *Display of Timeless Awareness Tantra* states:

> Individuals who recognize lucid clarity
> will not see the city of the intermediate state.
> Form kāyas will arise to benefit others,
> as, for example, wish-fulfilling gems.[19]

This is just from the point of view of gradualist practitioners. For instantaneously [realized practitioners], that particular sequence is not definite. For an ordinary person, the dissolution of elements and so forth at death is like the way experiences arise in meditation for a yogin. So it is uncertain whether the first occurrence is of smoke or mirage and so forth. In short, the Victor's sutras and the teachings of a guru with authentic meditation and one's own meditative experiences—these three must be in accord. When knowledge and experience part ways, it is the cause for regret, and desperate boasting is a big problem. Those who would claim to be practitioners, take care!

ii. The Natural Arising of the Victors' Saṃbhogakāya for the Average

A person of average capabilities who cannot settle into the lucid clarity of the first intermediate state must enter the intermediate state of becoming. They must strive in order to attain the saṃbhogakāya in the first week. Up to the first three and a half days of that week the appearances of the last life's body, region, home, wealth, possessions, friends, and relatives arise. In that time, it is difficult to understand that it is the intermediate state. When three and a half days have passed, glimpses of the future body will arise fleetingly, and it becomes difficult to maintain the appearance of the last life's body. When pained by hunger and thirst and other afflictions, you go to your previous friends and family to take food and drink. But they won't even reply to your request, let alone give you food and drink. Once you see them calling your name, weeping and wailing, you'll think, "Ah, I am dead," and recognition will dawn. At that point, you'll think, "My holy guru told me to recognize the intermediate state and practice the victors' saṃbhogakāya. That time has come." That understanding happens on the strength of previous familiarization, and you may now awaken as the victors' saṃbhogakāya in the intermediate state.

Sometimes supplicate the guru with thoughtful intention and remember that all appearances are your own mind's appearances, and all the appearances of your mind are illusion and dream. Then meditate on yourself as the yidam deity and the world environment as the palace with the inhabiting sentient beings transformed into gods and goddesses. The force of your previous meditation causes you to appear as the victors' saṃbhogakāya adorned with the major and minor marks—appearance without intrinsic nature, clarity without concept, and bliss without attachment. The deity's form is dharmakāya in essence, saṃbhogakāya in form, and nirmāṇakāya's enlightened activity. Those three combined as mahāsukhakāya arises of itself. That will remain until all of cyclic existence is empty, taming whomever in whatever ways to mature them and establish all sentient beings in liberation. {177} If you have meditated previously, your intermediate state consciousness will be thirty times clearer than your current consciousness. So there is no way not to attain awakening. Meditate without entertaining doubts.

iii. The Natural Arising of Unrestricted Nirmāṇakāya for the Lesser

If you have not attained awakening in the first week because your previous meditation was not powerful enough, you have turned out to have lesser capabilities. It is therefore possible that you will remain in the intermediate state for forty-nine days. You will think, "I have died and now am in the intermediate state" and feel great suffering. After that, desire will arise in regard to father or mother, male or female, and so on. Jealousy and envy will also arise based on that desire. That establishes the connection for taking rebirth in cyclic existence. Therefore, at the time that you think "I have died," also think, "Alas! By the power of attraction and aversion arising, I will take a rebirth of in cyclic existence. Rather than that suffering, I will now attain the supreme spiritual power in the pure realm of great bliss." Also think, "All these appearances of the intermediate state are illusions and do not truly exist," and supplicate the guru. Then imagine before you a dark-blue source of phenomena. Your own mind as a blue *hūṃ* is inside it. Five-colored light rays radiate from that and purify the habitual patterns and stains of the five kinds of migrators. Think that it blocks the door to a womb. Then meditate on the *hūṃ* completely transforming into your mind as the yidam couple. Also meditate on all the male and female appearances in the intermediate state that evoked attachment and aversion as the male or female yidam, and make offerings and supplications. All sound is mantra and all thought and memory is the mahāmudrā of the deity's form. Rest in equipoise within that state for a moment. The entire external environment and internal inhabitants and your own body of empty appearance free of attachment will naturally arise as nothing but the appearance of nirmāṇakāya, and it will be impossible not to attain awakening at that point.

iv. General Vital Points for Unerring Integration

A sense of disillusionment with cycle existence is the vital point for the Intermediate State in all three cases of practitioners with best, average, and lesser capabilities. {178} Therefore, remember intentionality and develop intense disillusionment while supplicating the guru. Meditate on appearances of male and female—in short, on oneself and others, the entire environment and all its inhabitants—as the divine palace with its yidam couples. Never allow your mindful intention of emanating and changing [appearances] to diminish. More extensive explanation can be learned from the teachings of previous masters. This explanation is a mere summary of the oral instructions on the Six Dharmas of Niguma.

In conclusion, in these degenerating times of conflict, the force of beings full of perverse views makes people who arrogantly claim to be Buddhists mostly resemble merchants at the market selling watered-down milk. They pollute the teachings of past masters and the Victor's words with their own contrived ideas and deceive themselves and others. But once you join your own experiences to the teachings and directories of the past, you will possess the totally pure view. Then when you forbear any hardships in practicing these special esoteric instructions and single-pointedly take them into your experience, in this life or during the intermediate state you will definitely attain awakening and then travel to the sacred celestial realm. Here, Niguma states [in the *Vajra Lines*]:

> In the degenerating time of conflict when wrong views disturb our mind streams,
> genuine dharma is as daytime stars and turtle fur.

In a time when perverse dharma is bartered as the milk of ethical behavior,
cherish meditative experience adorned by scriptures and inventories.

Those who practice this sublime path
will naturally arise as the three kāyas, inseparable bliss-emptiness
immediately, in this life, or in the intermediate state,
and will go to the totally pure celestial realm.[20]

Thus she spoke and sealed the instruction.

Colophon

This *Collection of Essentials* from the personal instructions on the Six Dharmas of Niguma was collected from the personal instructions of all the gurus and included in one place by the Madman of the Empty Valley at the Shelkar Lhadong retreat center of Tarpaling, where I realized them through practice. With that exemplar, I fully completed it at the sublime sacred site of Riwoche on the day the ḍākinīs gather, the tenth of the seventh month in the year of the Tiger. The scribe was Lodrö Gyaltsen, holder of the ten precepts. May meditative experience and realization increase like the waxing moon.

maṅgalaṃ bhavantu

5. Niguma's Auxiliary Practice, Guidance in Amulet Mahāmudrā[1]

Tangtong Gyalpo

namo guru

Spontaneously present unconditioned great bliss,
saṃbhogakāya Great Vajradhara and others;
I bow to all the gurus,
and now explain mahāmudrā.

The instruction on Amulet Mahāmudrā by Niguma, Ḍākinī of Timeless Awareness, has three parts: (1) preliminaries, (2) main practice, and (3) conclusion.

I. Preliminaries

This has two parts: (1) common and (2) uncommon preliminaries.

A. Common Preliminaries

Imagine in the space before you a jeweled throne with a lotus and moon seat. Upon that is the essence of your root guru in the form of white Cakrasaṃvara with one face and two hands holding vajra and bell crossed over his heart, adorned by bones and jewels—an appearance with no intrinsic nature. Before him you go for refuge, meditate on the four immeasurables, and arouse the mind of awakening. Then offer a mandala, recite the hundred syllables, and supplicate the lineage of gurus. Meditate exhaustively on death and impermanence, karmic cause and effect, and the shortcomings of cyclic existence. Meditate on love and compassion until you feel it even for your enemy through recognizing all beings as your own mother, recalling their kindness, and so forth. {183} These are the standard practices.

B. Uncommon Preliminaries

This concerns resting directly in the three naturally settled states. With your body as the yidam deity, sit with your legs crossed in vajra position. Place your two hands in the mudra of equipoise, straighten up your spine, slightly bend your neck, look straight ahead with relaxed eyes, touch the tip of your tongue to your palate, leave the lips before your teeth, and lock your arms with the elbows turned inward as a substitute for a meditation support stick. Properly assume these vital points of the body. Then relax the four channels and four tendons. This is the naturally settled state of the body. Do not try to close or open your lips, and remain free of verbal utterances. This is the naturally settled state of the speech. Rest without any contrivance, including the desire to meditate with the idea that holding a yogic gaze is meditation. This is the naturally settled state of the mind.

To abide in that state with a hiatus of openness is the measure of the preliminaries. {184} Something like that is called ordinary mind (*tha mal gyi shes pa*). All beings experience it occasionally in certain circumstances, such as resting after exhaustion. Not recognizing that is the cause of their wandering in cyclic existence. Therefore, grasp it with mindfulness no matter which of the six sense objects appear to the six sense organs during all four daily activities. Look directly at the essence [of that appearance] and you will fully experience empty clarity without fixation. Recognize that "now my preliminary practice has dawned" and settle in that with startled openness.

If, on that occasion, consciousness continues to proliferate outward due to a lack of previous meditation experience, then apply the enhancement practices. Observe with logical analysis what there is that can be identified in external objective appearance. What can be identified internally in the body? What can be identified in the secret level of the mind? After such observation, if you cannot find anything to identify, then settle within that state. If your mind continues to project out to appearances, then [consider] that objective appearance itself. Whence did it arise in the first place? Now where does it dwell? Where will it go in the end? Don't rest with a vague understanding but make a thorough search. If this becomes a hazy state without identification, then recognize it with mindfulness and settle into that state. Investigate it in that way.

Also, watch the mind that investigates—whence does it arise, where does it go, and where does it stay? When you observe the investigation itself, if you notice that mind has become scattered, look directly at the essence of that and intensify awareness with no distraction at all. When you remain serenely single-pointed without any thoughts whatsoever, rest in equipoise in that very state. If you follow those directions but conceptual thought still proliferates, then get a hold with mindfulness. As soon as a thought arises, cut off its trajectory completely and settle. On all those occasions, maintain a nonjudgmental attitude toward whatever experience arises. If that never works and thoughts still proliferate, to get a hold of it with mindfulness follow the aftermath of a thought to see where it goes. You will gain complete resolution by recognizing the hidden flaw of thoughts, [which is that they do not truly exist]. {185} When you meditate in that way without distraction, there is no doubt that the experience of empty clarity without fixation will arise. After fulfilling the instructions for the preliminaries through those methods, do the burglar's pointing-out introduction.[2] The signs of success are that physical and verbal acts cannot rob [the experience]. The enhancement practices are to blend the vital winds in deity practice and so forth. You should learn the process of visualization for blending the winds in mahāmudrā.

Now for a short presentation of the required practice of holding the breath. Assume the correct vital points of posture and let the winds (or breath) move evenly. Then first exhale blue wind-wind. Then exhale red fire-wind. Then exhale white water-wind. Then exhale yellow earth-wind. Then exhale colorless space-wind. As you exhale, think that all [those winds] have departed through all your pores. Then, first slowly inhale earth-wind through the nostrils while drawing up the lower wind. Focus your attention on the yellowness at the navel and hold it. When you can no longer hold it, slowly exhale. After that, draw in the water-wind to the heart and hold as before. Then draw in the fire-wind to the throat and hold as before. Then draw in the wind-wind to the head and hold as before. Then draw in the space-wind through all the pores and hold as it pervades the entire body. Alternatively, it is appropriate to do it in pairs: earth-wind with fire-wind and water-wind with wind-wind.

II. Main Practice

A. Naturally Free of Four Faults

The abiding nature of your mind is emptiness and unity beyond unity or separation, yet it is too close to see. This fault causes us to wander in cyclic existence. This is like your own face, [which you cannot see until] you come across the right condition of a clear mirror wherein you see your reflection. {186} Likewise, when you meet the mirror of the holy guru's instructions and put them into practice, you can see the mind's abiding nature. Mahāmudrā arises in oneself, but it cannot be indicated by examples or metaphors, so it is too profound to recognize. You can rest in the naturally settled states any time, but it is too easy to believe and so you are distracted. The three kāyas arise in oneself but they are too fine to comprehend and thus certitude does not arise. These faults that prevent decisiveness are the cause of wandering in cyclic existence. So now abandon those four faults. Once you rely on the guru's esoteric instructions, you will recognize what is self-evident, develop certainty, and with absolute decisiveness maintain nondistraction.

B. Ultimate Natural Arising of the Four Kāyas

At the time of resting in the naturally arising mahāmudrā, which is free from all equipoise, postmeditation, and mental fabrication, a variety of things arise. That is the natural arising of nirmāṇakāya. Nonconceptual freedom from fixation on that clarity is the natural arising of dharmakāya. The arising of bliss in that nonconceptual clarity is the natural arising of saṃbhogakāya. The indivisible nature of those three is the natural arising of the ultimate mahāsukhakāya. The nonconceptual aspect of that suchness is the timeless awareness of things as they are. The variety of appearances to be known without fixation is the timeless awareness of things in their multiplicity. The inseparability of those two aspects is the inseparability of basic space and timeless awareness.

To enhance those [experiences], contemplate the wretchedness of all those who wander in cyclic existence due to attributing notions of *me* and *mine* to the fact that all phenomena are empty and hence nonself. Supplicate with yearning devotion. Rest in the openness of all of that at all times. The measure of stability in the main practice is that there is not even an iota of something to meditate on, yet there is not even an instant of distraction. You remain continually within that state of nonconceptuality day and night, during all activities. {187}

III. Conclusion

In short, the conclusion is to recite perfectly pure dedications and aspirations such as the following. This is the sublime esoteric instruction.

> From within a state of inseparable emptiness and compassion,
> I vanquish the poison of referencing a dedication object or act.
> In the knowledge that there is no dedication in the realm of
>   phenomena,
> may all virtue be dedicated to omniscient buddhahood.

[Colophon]

From the quintessential auxiliary practices, this guide to the view, a summary of the practice of Amulet Mahāmudrā, was written by the Madman of the Empty Valley, having applied my own madness. It was composed in the sublime sacred site of glorious Riwoche. The scribe was Lodrö Gyaltsen, holder of the ten precepts.

sarva maṅgalaṃ

6. Niguma's Auxiliary Practice, Guidance in the Three Integrations[1]

Tangtong Gyalpo

namo guru

The practice of the Infallible Three Integrations on the Path from the auxiliary cycle of the aural lineage of Niguma, Ḍākinī of Timeless Awareness, has three parts that are based on appearances: (1) integration of the guru, (2) integration of the yidam, and (3) integration of illusion.

I. Integration of the Guru Based on Appearances

A four-petaled lotus arises from *paṃ* in the space before you. In its center and on each of the four petals moon mandalas arise from *A*. In the center, the root guru appears as white Cakrasaṃvara with one face and two hands holding a vajra and bell crossed over his heart. White Hevajra holding vajra and bell crossed at his heart is on the petal in the east, yellow Guhyasamāja holding vajra and bell crossed at his heart is in the south, red Mahāmāya the same as above is in the west, and green Yamāntaka holding a flaying knife and blood-filled skull cup above and below his heart is in the north. Visualize them all adorned by ornaments of bones and jewels. White *oṃ* is in their foreheads, red *āḥ* in their throats, blue *hūṃ* in their hearts, and multicolored *hūṃ* in their navels. {188} Light radiates from those and invokes the gurus, deities, and buddhas in the forms of awareness beings identical to those [visualized], into which they dissolve. Invoke the five families, who confer empowerment. With that, all the deities become crowned by the buddhas of the five families. Then supplicate:

> Precious guru, please confer the actual empowerment on me.

A white *oṃ* emerges from the guru's forehead and dissolves into your forehead. You obtain the vase empowerment and so forth, as in the previous section on Fierce Inner Heat. A red *āḥ* emerges from the throat and dissolves into your throat. A blue *hūṃ* emerges from the heart and dissolves into your heart. Then the four deities in the four directions dissolve into the principal figure. The principal and his seat melt into a colored array of light and dissolve into you. Rest in equipoise in that state.

Then meditate on the preliminaries, including going for refuge, arousing the awakening mind, contemplating death and impermanence, and so on. With yourself visualized clearly as the yidam, meditate on your root guru with a brilliant smile and radiant form, sitting on a lotus-moon seat above your head. Imagine, with yourself in the lead, all sentient beings earnestly supplicate:

> Precious guru, I pray to you!
> Bless me to relinquish fixation on the self.
> Bless me with the feeling of contentment in my being.
> Bless me to refine Illusory Body and Dream.
> Bless me to actualize Lucid Clarity Mahāmudrā.

Whatever forms appear, think, "These are all my holy guru." In particular, whether they are beautiful forms that inspire attachment or unattractive forms that inspire aversion, and so on—never forget your conviction that they are the guru. {189} Then think, "This is how the guru will liberate me from cyclic existence and establish me in the state of awakening. How kind!" Do prostrations, offerings, and all the seven branches of service. Then be absolutely certain that whatever appears is the guru. Be certain that the guru is your own mind. Be certain that your mind is free of embellishment. Take into practice the unity of appearance and emptiness, and within that state, make pure prayers of dedication and aspiration.

II. Integration of the Yidam Based on Appearances

Moon mandalas appear on the center and petals of the four-petaled lotus before you. Cakrasaṃvara is in the middle, white with a blue radiance, with one face and two hands holding vajra and bell while embracing his partner, and adorned by bones and jewels. On his lap, red Vajravārāhī holds a flaying knife and skull cup while embracing her partner. White Ḍākinī is on the eastern petal, green Lāmā in the north, red Khaṇḍarohā in the west, and yellow Rūpiṇī in the south. They all brandish flaying knives with their right hands and hold blood-filled skull cups to their hearts with their left hands, with khaṭvāṅgas in the crooks of their elbows. They stand with their right legs extended, pressing down on the corpse that is their seat, and their left legs partially bent in dancing posture. All of them are adorned by bones and precious jewels, and stand amid blazing fire. Then, as before, the awareness beings enter them. Imagine that after they receive empowerment they become crowned by the five families.

> All tathāgatas, please confer the actual empowerment on me. {190}

With that supplication, the three seed syllables arise as before from the three places of the principal figures. They dissolve into your three places. You receive the three empowerments. The respective obscurations of body, speech, and mind are purified. On the path, you are now empowered to meditate on creation phase, completion phase, and the unity of creation and completion. The result will be the actualization of the three kāyas. Then the four goddesses dissolve into the principal couple. They in turn become a colored mass of light that dissolves into you, bestowing the fourth empowerment. Think that all your obscurations are purified. Meditate with heightened clarity on yourself and all apparent forms as the Cakrasaṃvara couple—appearance without intrinsic nature. Present offerings to them. Then recite the yidam's seven-syllable essence mantra. With all apparent form visualized as the yidam, meditate on the audible sound of the mantra and know that all sound is mantra. In this way, decide for sure that all appearance of deity and mantra is your own mind and that your own mind is free of embellishment. Meditate on that. Afterward, do the dedication.

If this is to be practiced in a single session, meditate on the guru above your head and supplicate. Cultivate decisive certainty that your body and all appearance is the yidam, that all sound is the empty resonance of mantra, and that all thought is illusion and dream. In short, never be apart from the guru on your head, your body as the yidam, and your speech as supplication or mantra recitation. Never separate from [the knowledge that] all food and drink is elixir, that all thought and memory is illusion and dream, and that the command guards and dharma protectors go before you. Practice in that way. This is the heart of the sutras and tantras. {191} Since it is like the ḍākinīs' vital heart, practice it without hesitation. It is the esoteric instruction that definitely produces awakening in a matter of months or years.

III. Integration of Illusion Based on Appearances

Decide for certain that all appearance is the mind and that mind is illusion and dream. Then put into practice the refining, increasing, emanating, and changing of nighttime dreams as presented in the Six Dharmas. In short, the Integration of Appearances on the Path [applies to] visual objects whether beautiful or not, auditory objects whether pleasant or not, olfactory objects whether fragrant or not, gustatory objects whether delicious or not, tactile objects whether soft or not, and mental objects whether pleasant phenomena or not. Look directly at the essence [of those perceptions] and don't block their appearance, but don't become fixated. Rest without distraction in the state of empty clarity without fixation.

The practice of those three teachings will produce the following results. Uncommon devotion in the guru will be born. All appearances will fade away through the natural arising of illusion. The self-recognition of dreams will lead to refining, increasing, emanating, and changing them, and the ascertaining of appearances. In the daytime, the nonconceptual clarity of mahāmudrā will dawn. In the nighttime, the deity's form will appear by itself and unlimited lucid clarity will arise. These experiences will occur just as they were described, so have no doubts and put them into practice.

[Colophon]

These esoteric instructions on the infallible Integration of the Guru, Integration of the Yidam, and Integration of Appearances from the quintessential auxiliary practices was composed at the sublime sacred site of Riwoche by the Madman of the Empty Valley in conjunction with his own experiences. The scribe was Lodrö Gyaltsen, holder of the ten precepts. {192} These [compositions] describe mainly just the visualization sequences of the meditations and so are very concise. However, just this will accomplish your purpose; meditate and you will understand. If you wish to offer an explanation, you must realize the teachings through the textbooks by past masters who commented upon the *Vajra Verses*.

7. Niguma's Auxiliary Practice, Guidance in Immortal Body and Mind[1]

Tangtong Gyalpo

namo guru

Here is appended the esoteric instructions of the quintessential auxiliary practice, Immortal Body and Mind. To practice this, refine the vital channels, drops, and winds with the thirty-two physical yogic exercises.[2] Then take a comfortable seat and assume the vital points of the body posture—either sitting with the legs drawn up or cross-legged. First go for refuge, arouse the awakening mind, and practice the guru yoga.

Then contemplate in this manner: Regarding so-called death—is it the body that dies or the mind that dies? If you think it's the body, then is it the fully ripened body that dies or the body of habitual patterns? It is not the first because this body is merely inert matter consisting of a bunch of flesh, blood, bones, skin, and so forth. How can that die? If it can, then why don't earth and stones and so on die? The body of habitual patterns also does not die. If it could die, then dreaming of death would effectively cause death. Thus people who dream of dying in a dream would never wake up because once dead, they would not revive. Think about that. In short, *death* is a designation for nothing other than the mere fact that the mind no longer dwells in the fully ripened body once the propensity of one's previous karma runs out. Therefore, so-called death has no true existence. Keep meditating until you ascertain for sure that the body is deathless.

If you think it is the mind that dies, then counter that with the practice of this special instruction called *Natural Liberation of One's Mind as Immortal.*[3] {193} First go for refuge and arouse the mind of awakening. Then instantly imagine yourself as blue Cakrasaṃvara standing on a lotus, sun, Bhairava, and Kālarātri, with right leg extended stomping on Kālarātri's belly and left leg bent, pressing and bending black Bhairava's head. With one face, two arms, and three eyes, Cakrasaṃvara grimaces and bares his teeth. A jewel is on the tip of the bound topknot of hair on top of his head, with a new-moon crescent on the left and a crossed vajra on the front. His two hands hold vajra and bell while embracing Vajravārāhī. He wears a crown of five dry human heads, a necklace of fifty fresh wet heads, and six bone ornaments. With his tiger-skin skirt loose, he displays the nine dance poses. In his lap, the red mother Vajravārāhī threatens wicked beings with the flaying knife in her right hand and embraces her partner with the left while holding a blood-filled skull cup. She is naked with three eyes and loosed hair. She is voluptuous with full breasts. She is adorned by the crown of five dry skulls, necklace, and five bone ornaments, her left leg outstretched and right leg wrapped around Cakrasaṃvara. Both of them stand in the midst of a blazing fire of timeless awareness. Meditate clearly on that and supplicate the guru above your head.

I. Preliminaries

There are three parts to engage the practice. First, for the preliminaries, imagine a blue *hūṃ* at Cakrasaṃvara's hairline emanating blue light so bright that it obscures even the extremely clear form of the deity. {194} The light that emerges from the *hūṃ* illuminates from the point between the eyebrows up. Then it extends down to the nose, including the eyeballs, illuminating the three staring eyes. Then the light gradually continues down to the throat, heart, navel, and perineum, illuminating everything from there up. Finally it moves to the knees, calves, and toenails—meditate until all of it arises in limpid lucidity. That constitutes the outer refinement of the father deity. Then again blue light emerges from the *hūṃ*. It descends through the cranial aperture to the nose and then the throat, turning everything above them clear blue. Then it continues down to the heart, navel, perineum, knees, calves, and toes—meditate on everything above that as being the nature of a limpid blue radiance. That is the inner refinement of the father. Similarly, imagine a red *vaṃ* at the hairline of the mother deity's head radiating red light rays. Red light refines the mother both outwardly and inwardly as before. Meditate particularly on the red radiance of her bhaga and breasts—this is the visualization of color.

Then visualize sequentially [starting with] the father's third eye: the topknot of hair, the way of holding the vajra and bell, the face with four canine teeth bared, the manner of standing, the grace, the bonfire, and so on, visualizing each one clearly. This is the meditation on shape. Meditate in the same way on each shape of the mother.

Then [meditate on] Cakrasaṃvara's crown jewel, crescent moon, crossed vajra, and the six bone ornaments—wheel, earrings, necklace, bracelets and anklets, belt, and smeared human ashes—and the crown of dry human heads and the long garland. Also, meditate on Vajravārāhī's five bone ornaments (minus the ashes), and the crown of dry heads, long garland, and so forth, meditating on each of them by turn. This is the visualization of ornaments.

Meditate in this way on the two, father and mother, as the union of empty clarity and great bliss—natural lucid clarity. {195} From the perspective of clarity, their [features] are unmixed and totally complete. From the perspective of emptiness, there is no established intrinsic nature whatsoever, only the nature of light. Contemplate that and think, in the same way, this very mind of mine appears in the form of a deity, but apart from that there is no valid existence in the external sense. Meditate until you are sure. The metaphors are dreams and water moons. Although you dream of various objects in a dream, the objects have not actually come into the dream, nor has your mind gone over there to [those objects]. Sleep distorts the mind such that the mind itself appears in myriad forms. Other than that, there is nothing truly existing. You should understand this by the metaphor of the moon reflected in water. Similarly, examine your own mind that appears vividly as the deity's body. Where does it come from? Where does it go? Where does it stay? Resolve that it does not come from anywhere, nor does it go anywhere, nor does it stay anywhere; it is the unity of clarity and emptiness free of the extremes of embellishment. Such a mind inseparable from the deity's form has not been seen by all the past buddhas, nor will it be seen by all those to come, nor is it seen by them now. Contemplate that and meditate.

II. Main Practice

In the meditation on immortality of the mind, which is clarity-emptiness with no real intrinsic nature, there are four visualizations of deathlessness.

A. Sickness does not exist in that mind of clarity-emptiness that even the buddhas of the three times have not seen. The appearance of sickness is the appearance of contamination of your mind by karma and incidental afflictions. {196} Ultimately there is no cause for sickness. Without a cause, there can be no resulting sickness. Contemplate that and meditate until you realize that mind has no sickness.

B. In such a mind, death does not exist. So-called death is just a designation for the apparent separation of this inert body and incidental discursive thought. If you really investigate it, there is no passing on and no thing that passes on. Meditate until such time as you are certain of the emptiness of no valid existence whatsoever.

C. In such a mind as that, observe whether or not there is the cause of buddhahood. There is no cause of buddhahood. The nature of mind at the time of being a buddha and at the time of being a sentient being are both lucid clarity and emptiness inseparable. The term *buddha* is merely a designation for that totally pure nature of mind that is free of all incidental blemishes. Contemplate that and meditate.

D. When you think that way about the empty clear nature of your mind as the deity's form, then cyclic existence does not exist. Since samsara has no valid existence, those who cycle in cyclic existence also do not exist. Contemplate that and meditate until you are absolutely certain that cyclic existence is the deluded appearance of your own mind.

III. Conclusion

Meditate without distraction to produce certitude, becoming absolutely resolved that your mind is deathless as described. If this is enhanced with supplicating the guru, meditating on compassion for sentient beings, and dedicating the merit for all beings to attain perfect awakening, then even those who have committed the five acts of immediate retribution will be enlightened at death or in the intermediate state, let alone fortunate ones with few obscurations who meditate constantly. If the form [of the deity] arises completely or even partially at death, then like the mechanism of a cannon or a stone thrown into a still pond or the fifteenth day when the full moon arises as the sun sets, you will attain awakening as the victors' saṃbhogakāya. {197} Without ever leaving dharmakāya, the two form kāyas continuously and spontaneously enact the welfare of beings by doing whatever it takes to tame them.

Without such instructions as these, exerting great effort in practice will just result in meaningless exhaustion, like churning water to produce butter. But to have such instructions and put them into practice is to extract the vitality of all the sutras and tantras and drink it, curing the chronic disease of delusional karma and affliction. Then you will certainly go to the celestial realm. You need to practice with such instructions. There are no esoteric instructions more profound than these in all of India and Tibet. Indeed, it is a teaching by which intelligent men and women with diligence will awaken in a single lifetime. With the logic of these [instructions], observe whether both this corporeal body and this clear empty mind fall from cyclic existence to buddhahood or not, and whether or not they fall from buddhahood to bad migrations in cyclic existence and to happy existences, and so forth. Meditate until you become absolutely certain that body and mind are infallible.

[Colophon]

This concludes the clarification of the visualization sequence of Immortal and Infallible from the cycle of quintessential auxiliary practices through which ardent practitioners will be enlightened in a single lifetime. I, the Madman of the Empty Valley, brought them into my experience according to the ḍākinīs' teachings. The whole composition of the main and auxiliary quintessential instructions was written between the eighth day of the sixth month and the fifteenth day of the seventh month in the year of the Tiger at the sacred site of Riwoche. The scribe was Lodrö Gyaltsen, holder of the ten precepts.

To properly practice this Holy Dharma, cut the ties to this life. {198} Then will it become your ultimate strategy for accomplishing life's great meaning. Everyone, exert yourselves vigorously with diligence!

8. Niguma's Auxiliary Quintessential Practice, Guidance in the Six-Armed Awareness Protector[1]

Tangtong Gyalpo

Homage to Guru-Protector inseparable.
Homage to Swift-Acting Avalokiteśvara.

Here, as an auxiliary quintessential practice, is added the practice of Guru-Protector Inseparable by Lama Khyungpo Lotsāwa-Paṇḍita. The yogin who is to obtain the blessings of this protector should, in a secluded place, first go for refuge and arouse the awakening mind. Then [visualize] an eight-petaled multicolored lotus that arises from *paṃ* above your head. In its center, a moon-disk mandala arises from *A*, and upon that a multicolored vajra cross from *hūṃ* marked with a multicolored *hūṃ* at its center. From that, radiating light rays make offerings to the noble ones and purify the negativities and obscurations of all sentient beings. They gather back and completely transform into multicolored Vajrasattva with one face and two arms. His right hand holds a multicolored vajra and his left hand holds a vajra-handled bell while embracing his partner, multicolored Mother Vajragarvā, who sits in his lap. She has one face and two arms and holds a flaying knife in her right hand and feeds the father with a blood-filled skull cup in her left hand. They are both adorned by bones and jewels. White *oṃ* is in their foreheads, red *āḥ* at their throats, blue *hūṃ* at their hearts, and multicolored *hūṃ* at their navels. Those letters radiate light that invokes all the gurus, yidams, and buddhas in the form of Vajrasattva.

> *jaḥ hūṃ vaṃ hoḥ*—they become indivisible [with the visualized form]. {199} Bhagavat, I pray to you to cleanse and purify

> all negative acts, obscurations, faults, downfalls, and stains that I have accumulated in lifetimes since beginningless cyclic existence.

Through supplicating with that, five-colored elixir arises from the *hūṃ* in their hearts. It fills both the couple's forms and flows from the places of their union. That enters through the cranial aperture at the top of your head. All negativities and obscurations in the form of liquid coal comes out from your lower orifices and two soles. Imagine that while repeating the one hundred syllables. At the end say:

> I, through the darkness of ignorance . . . (*bdag ni mi shes rmongs pa yis* . . . etc.).

Vajrasattva dissolves into oneself. Imagine yourself as multicolored Vajrasattva, holding in the right hand a multicolored vajra at the heart and a vajra-handled bell at the hip with the left, with right leg slightly bent and left straight, adorned by silks and jewels. Then, in the space in front of you, a lotus arises from *paṃ* and a sun seat from *raṃ*. Upon that, from *gaṃ*, imagine white Gaṇapati fallen on his back, with a white *hūṃ* on top of him. Light radiates from that and annihilates all evil ones. Imagine that the light gathers back in and from it arises Glorious Awareness Protector, white with one face and six arms, his two legs in the standing position. In his first right hand he holds a wish-fulfilling jeweled flaying knife, in the middle a skull rosary, and the last fiercely rattles a ḍamaru. In his first left hand he holds a blood-filled skull cup, in the middle a trident, and in the last a vajra lasso. He has three round, red eyes, a gaping mouth, and bared fangs. {200} His eyebrows and beard tufts are brilliant. His orange hair streams upward. He has a crown of five dry skulls, a garland of fifty blood-dripping wet heads, and is adorned by the six bone ornaments and snakes. He wears a tiger-skin skirt tied with a green silk belt. His belly protrudes and his limbs are thick and solid. His forehead is smeared with vermilion. Large and small bells decorate his arms and legs. He wears a wet elephant skin. Buddha Akṣobhya crowns his head. He stands amid the blazing fire of timeless awareness.[2]

Perform the consecration of his three places and the invocation and indwelling of the awareness being. Then imagine that a finger span above his head is a lotus and sun seat, upon which is your root guru, white, with one face and two arms. The right hand holds either a skull ḍamaru or a precious gem, the left holds a golden bangle bell, and the two legs are in the standing posture. The guru is adorned by various decorations of silks and jewels, with a peaceful and smiling countenance. Meditate that just seeing the body of the guru purifies obscurations and just hearing the voice definitely establishes you in the stage of no-return. Light rays radiate from the heart and invoke all the root and lineage gurus and yidams, who dissolve into the guru.

If you wish to do the recitation, [imagine that] a white mantra string arises from the *hūṃ* in Protector's heart, enters your mouth, and dissolves into your navel, purifying and incinerating all sickness, spirits, negativities, and obscurations, while reciting the mantras: {201}

> *oṃ vajra mahākāla kṣiṃ kṣetra vighnān vināyaka hūṃ hūṃ phaṭ phaṭ svāhā*
> *oṃ vajra nara kriṃ kriṃ hūṃ hūṃ phaṭ phaṭ svāhā*

Repeat however much is suitable. However, if you do not recite the mantra, there is no fault of omission.

In short, by your intense devotion and faith in the inseparable guru and protector, unimaginably immeasurable light rays arise from the guru and strike the protector, causing him to blaze with the nature of light. He rattles the ḍamaru. Think of the guru inseparable from the protector. Then from the protector dark-reddish light rays, the nature of bliss, radiate and cause the guru to blaze with the nature of bliss. Guru rattles the ḍamaru and bell. Think of the Protector inseparable from the guru, and recite the supplication.

> *namo buddhāya / namo gurubhyaḥ / hevajra vīra vīreṇīyī ḍāka ḍākinī joka jokiṇī sarva buddha bodhisatvaya śvaraṇaṃ gacchāmi*

> *kye kye!* Glorious holy gurus, root and lineage gurus who dwell in the ten directions and three times, please grant your blessings. Host of yidam deities, please grant your blessings. All assemblies of buddhas and bodhisattvas, please grant your blessings. All hosts of heroes and heroines, ḍākas and ḍākinīs, yogis and yoginīs, please grant your blessings. Deity hosts of glorious Six-Armed Awareness Protector, do not obscure your timeless awareness. Do not restrict your power and ability. Do not delay

your compassion. Do not calculate the distance of your blessings. All of you: grant your blessings through your bodies, grant your blessings through your speech, grant your blessings through your minds, and grant your blessings through inexhaustible awakened body, speech, mind, qualities, and activities. Bless me right now. Bless me quickly. Bless me on this very seat. {202}

I supplicate Great Buddha Vajradhara.
I supplicate glorious Śavarī the Mighty.
I supplicate Lord Maitrīpa the Great.
I supplicate adept Rāhula the Great.
I supplicate adept Khyungpo Naljor.
I supplicate incomparable Rinchen Tsöndru.
I supplicate glorious Kyergangpa the Great.
I supplicate Lama Sangye Nyentön.
I supplicate Chöje Sangye Tönpa.
I supplicate Khedrup Shangtön Chöje.
I supplicate Muchen Gyaltsen Palzang.
I supplicate Khedrup Dorje Zhönu.
I supplicate unequaled Namkhai Naljor.
I supplicate Bodhisattva Jinpa Zangpo.
I supplicate wild father Tangtong Gyalpo.
I supplicate Six-Armed Awareness Protector.
I supplicate Guru-Protector Inseparable.
I supplicate Protector-Guru Inseparable.

Continue with this and

Guru-Protector inseparable, please confer on me the complete four empowerments.

Through supplicating many times, a white *oṃ* emerges from Protector's forehead and dissolves into my forehead, purifying physical obscurations . . . (etc., as usual). A red *āḥ* emerges from his throat and dissolves into my throat . . . (etc.). A blue *hūṃ* emerges from his heart and dissolves into my heart . . . (etc.). Then the guru dissolves into the Protector. Protector melts into light and

> dissolves into me; as though facing a reflected image in a mirror, mind rests in equanimity.

Think that physical, verbal, and mental obscurations are purified and that you have obtained the four empowerments. Then dedicate by saying:

> To the Guru-Protector inseparable
> I go for refuge with devotion.
> May I dispel every affliction
> of all sentient beings.

If you see or hear or even write this verse in gold lettering to wear around your neck, even if you have committed the five acts of immediate retribution, {203} you will actually see [Guru-Protector] in the intermediate state and come to dwell on the three pure levels. If you possibly must enter the intermediate state, [Guru-Protector] will definitely look after you there.

Additionally, it is also suitable to meditate on the Protector as black with a white radiance. That is the same as before, except for the following: Upon the lotus-sun-Gaṇapati seat in the space before you, golden-black Protector adorned with accessories is in standing posture. As previously, the root guru is on a lotus-moon seat above his head, this time with a body like molten gold, one face and two arms, and holding a wish-fulfilling gem in the right hand and a golden small bell in the left. Meditate on that with the decorations and accessories as before. Through supplicating as before, the guru dissolves into the protector, and the protector into oneself. Remain within that state. Do the dedication as before.

Again, dark-red Protector stands before you on a similar seat, with red root Guru on a lotus and sun above his head. Guru holds a ḍamaru in the right hand and a precious gem in the left, adorned as before with decorations and accessories. Supplicate as before, receive the empowerments, and dedicate.

Again, meditate on dark-green Protector standing before you on a similar seat, the hand implements and so forth the same as before. Green root Guru upon a lotus and sun above his head holds a ḍamaru in the right hand and an elixir-filled vase in the left, adorned as before with decorations and accessories. Supplicate as before, receive the empowerments, and dedicate.

Again, meditate on a black source of phenomena with a black upside-down *hūṃ* inside. By your uttering "*hūṃ*," that source of phenomena becomes the seat of lotus, sun, and Gaṇapati. {204} Meditate that the *hūṃ* turns right side up [and becomes] blue-black Awareness Protector with the decorations and accessories as before. Visualize his retinue of harm-doers (yakṣas) and the goddess according to the source texts. Invoke the awareness beings and so forth as before. Above his head, your root guru is deep blue with one face, two arms, and wrathful accessories, sitting in the midst of a blazing bonfire. The right hand holds a ḍamaru and the left hand holds the mighty sovereign wish-fulfilling gem. Meditate that the decorations, accessories, and manner of sitting are the same as before. Supplicate, receive the empowerments, and dedicate as before. It is also suitable to make the guru white in color.

Again, in the space in front of you, meditate on the lotus-sun-Gaṇapati seat, upon which is Awareness Protector of various colors, with the ornaments, accessories, and hand implements the same as before. Above his head, on a lotus and moon, your root guru is variously colored, holding a ḍamaru in the right hand and the mighty sovereign gem in the left, with a countenance both peaceful and wrathful. Meditate on the same ornaments and accessories and supplicate as before. Receive the empowerments, then rest your mind in the intrinsic nonexistence of appearances. Afterward, make the totally pure dedications.

If you meditate in that way without distractions for seven months, that in itself will produce enlightenment. If you meditate for one session every daybreak, you will obtain the dharmakāya and rūpakāya at death. If even once you make a connection with the empowerment, even if you have committed the five acts of immediate retribution, it is impossible that you would not reach enlightenment in the intermediate state. In this vein, Śavarīpa stated:

> If you meditate on the mighty sovereign
> on the crown of Awareness Protector,
> imagine the brilliance of light rays,
> and supplicate without distraction,
> you will attain awakening in years or months.
> For seven generations do not disseminate
> this Guru-Protector inseparable. {205}
> Awareness Protector came
> to such as me, Śavarīpa,

spoke on three occasions and
sealed this command, then went into the sky.
Ema!—this amazing, wonderful dharma—
do not spread beyond a one-to-one transmission.[3]

Practice this teaching. This esoteric instruction on accomplishing Guru-Protector Inseparable in an auxiliary quintessential dharma cycle was done by the Madman of the Empty Valley by applying my own experience, at the great holy site of Riwoche. The scribe was Lodrö Gyaltsen, holder of the ten precepts. Do not teach it to those who have not obtained the subsequent permission and esoteric instructions. It is extremely profound. *ithi*. Virtue!

Method and Wisdom

The Six Dharmas and Mahāmudrā

Introduction

The two texts that follow represent a clear and concise instruction on the two main approaches of Vajrayāna: the path of methods (*thabs lam*) and the path of wisdom (*shes rab lam*), or liberation (*grol lam*). Here, the first is the Six Dharmas of Niguma, a completion-phase practice, which are yogic techniques involving physical and mental constructs. The second is mahāmudrā, the Great Seal, which is ultimately without constructs.

The Single Sitting: Words of the Ḍākinī of Timeless Awareness is Jamgön Kongtrul's beautiful practical guide to Ḍākinī Niguma's Six Dharmas that could, with practice, be implemented in one session. Coming after Tāranātha's incredibly thorough exposition in *Tangdalma*, this might seem redundant. But by the same token, it is more approachable and pared down to the bare necessities while offering some crucial new details. For example, in the preliminary practices there is a precise description of the fundamental practice known as the ninefold shake-up of dead air, which has not been found elsewhere in these two volumes. On the other hand, the main practices are reduced to fundamentals: Fierce Inner Heat involves only Eating the Food of Inner Heat, Dream practice involves only recognizing and refining dreams, and so on. The whole text is divided into three main sections (though only two are in the outline). The general instructions explain the minimal components to thoroughly practice these Six Dharmas that is consistent with the traditional approach. This would be hard to do in one session, although how to divide them into the four sessions of one day is suggested. The special esoteric instructions are extremely pithy and short versions that more readily lend themselves to a single session, perhaps as a way to maintain the Six Dharmas as a daily practice after completing an extended retreat. Finally, a section called "General Valuable Vital Points on Everything" concludes the text with crucial aspects of all meditations, such as devotion and compassion.

Amulet Mahāmudrā or Three Naturally Settled States Guidance Manual is the only mahāmudrā instruction by Kongtrul's predecessor, the great master Jonang Tāranātha, that is included in his *Treasury*. It is also beautiful and practical, and incredibly profound. I would venture that Kongtrul found this instruction so perfect he had nothing to improve upon and did not include his own mahāmudrā instruction. The text follows the traditional format based on Niguma's teachings: the preliminary of three naturally settled states (including precise instructions on calm abiding and higher insight), the main practice of freedom from the four faults that prevent realization of the nature of mind, and the resulting natural arising of the three kāyas, as well as enhancement practices. Tāranātha divided the text into visualization or contemplation sessions like many of his other practice instructions. These aide the practitioner in the smooth progress toward hopefully inevitable realization.

Although a person might prioritize either the path of methods or skillful means requiring physical effort or the so-called "lazy" path of wisdom or liberation, each according to their own propensities, the smart way is to incorporate both approaches presented in these two texts.

9. The Single Sitting, Words of the Ḍākinī of Timeless Awareness

A Concise Guide to Niguma's Six Dharmas, the Root of the Golden Dharmas of the Glorious Shangpa[1]

Jamgön Kongtrul

Great bliss, pervading the static and moving
in myriad forms from a single nature,
born from the stages of the profound:
I bow to the unsurpassable.

I present the Six Dharmas in a Single Sitting
that is taught explicitly in all tantras,
the legacy of a million supreme adepts
that grants timeless awareness through practice.

These are the indisputable words of the Ḍākinī of Timeless Awareness that combine the essence of the completion phase of all the highest tantras, such as the culminating five teachers.[2] It is the heart essence of Khedrup Khyungpo Naljor and the others, all of them in their final lives as bodhisattvas. It is the highest degree of spoken dharma that immediately produces confidence. It can be found extensively in the books of old, especially in the collected works of Venerable Drolwai Gönpo (Tāranātha).[3] There are certainly numerous manuals on single-sitting practices by him and other noble ones. Here I will condense the profound quintessence of those texts and adorn them with new instructions from the transmission of the ancient lineages. {209}

In general, this is the daily practice for someone who has obtained the permissions that open the door and grant blessings and in whom some appropriate experiences of the four root dharmas has arisen. Even if they have not arisen, it is for one who has fully received the great guidances. This has both (1) general and (2) special esoteric instructions: the general instructions comprise (1) the preliminaries and (2) the main practice. There are (1) common and (2) uncommon preliminaries.

I. General Instructions

A. Preliminaries

1. Common Preliminaries

These are the general, well-known four contemplations that refine the mind stream. But since they must precede all practice, here I will present a cursory clarification. Assume the usual posture on a comfortable seat in an isolated place. Contemplate as follows and intensify your resolve:

> This human body adorned with eight freedoms and ten endowments is more difficult to find than a wish-fulfilling gem. But due to many life-threatening conditions, it is impermanent and cannot be assured to last even for today. Once I die, only the results of my good or bad actions will hold sway. All sentient beings throughout space are also tormented in this way by the proliferation of samsaric sufferings. {210} Since the precious guru is the only sovereign who can give us refuge from this suffering, I have no other hope than you.

The actual common preliminary in this doctrine's own system has two parts: (1) going for refuge and (2) arousing the mind of awakening.

a. Going for Refuge

Imagine the area as a pure realm. In the space before you appears a four-tiered seat consisting of a lion throne, multicolored lotus, sun, and moon. Upon that is your kind root guru in his or her actual form, with a brilliant countenance, charismatic and radiant with light, smiling at you with pleasure. Develop the certainty that the guru is the embodiment of the union of all the Three Jewels and Three Roots in the ten directions and three times. Completely entrust yourself while thinking, "Guru, consider me." Imagine that all mother and father sentient beings throughout space also go for refuge along with you. Recite as much as you can:

> All sentient beings throughout space, my mothers, take refuge in the precious guru, the gathered essence of all refuges.

You do not dissolve the refuge objects at this point.

b. Arousing the Mind of Awakening

Think, "There is not a single sentient being that has not been my parent. They are very dear to me, but they are destitute, involved as they are in cyclic existence with its endless suffering. I must repay their kindness to me by helping them, and not just partially. In order to establish them in the totally unified state of Great Vajradhara, I will meditate on the path of methods of the aural lineage." Say:

> For the sake of all sentient beings throughout space, I will attain the state of perfect omniscient awakening. {211} To that end, I will take up the practice of the profound path of Niguma's Six Dharmas.

Recite that again and again.

When you come under the refuge of the Jewels
and develop the attitude of a great being,
without regressing on the path of freedom,
all activity becomes the cause of awakening.

2. Uncommon Preliminaries: The Purifying *A* of Inner Space

Again visualize your root guru as before and with intense feelings of devotion say:

> Precious guru, unified essence of all buddhas of the three times:
> for the sake of all sentient beings,
> I pray to you to pacify all my sickness and spirits,

to purify all my negative acts and obscurations,
and for special meditative absorption to arise in my being.

Do that supplication as much as you can. Then the guru melts into light and enters through your cranial aperture, refining away the brain, which is the nature of stupidity. Your head above the neck becomes like a water bubble, white and soft to the touch. [Within the head] is a white tetrahedral source of phenomena, empty inside, radiant, and clear like a crystal vase. [It is suspended upside down] with its sharp apex facing downward at the throat. The broad side with its three vertices faces upward with one vertex level with the eyebrows and the other two vertices at the temples by the right and left ears, just touching [the inside of the skin outline]. Right in the center of that source of phenomena is a radiant clear white letter *A*—the embodiment of your unborn mind inseparable from the guru. Half of the letter is within the source of phenomena and half protrudes above the rim, suspended in space without support. First concentrate on that and focus your mind. {212} Afterward, hold the mind there by balancing your consciousness between concentration and relaxation. When unable to maintain that, quietly recite short *A* twenty-one times. This causes a stream of white elixir to cascade down from the *A*. It fills the source of phenomena to the brim and splashes over the opening, filling and washing your whole body inside and out. All beginninglessly accumulated negativities, obscurations, habitual tendencies, [corruption from] misappropriated funds, profit from the sale of images, contraventions and errors in sacred pledge, and such exude out through your pores and orifices in the form of liquid smoke or liquid coal and slither away darkly. The filthy substances of your body also dissolve and are expelled, while the elixir washes the outside of the body. The black soot goes far under the ground and disappears. Imagine that your body becomes a polished crystal vase filled with elixir like an unobstructed white rainbow. Then relax consciousness. When this is intended as a separate practice, the visualization and recitation are repeated. However, the initial guru yoga is sufficient.

This visualization has two branches: pacifying sickness and pacifying spirits. For sicknesses of heat, imagine that cool white elixir soothes red sickness. For cold sicknesses, red-hot elixir pacifies sickness that appears white and thick. For sicknesses of the vital winds or a combination [of winds, bile, and phlegm], yellow, oily elixir pacifies bluish thick sickness, and so forth. Wherever that sickness is located, a hole forms in front of it and it passes outside. Think that it is totally cured.

For spirits, the elixir that falls from the letter *A* becomes the specific antidote to each spirit: wrathful deities descending like hail, fireballs, molten bronze rivers, and the roar of mantras. Meditate that the spirit is totally annihilated without remainder, and rest in equipoise.

What is to be refined has never existed.
What refines is the letter of the unborn itself.
All elaborations are pacified; meaning the middle way.
This way of refining is unequaled by all others. {213}

B. Main Practice

1. The Six Dharmas

a. Naturally Blazing Bliss-Warmth, the Path of Methods

This has three parts: (1) the preliminary, (2) the main practice, and (3) the concluding practices.

i. Preliminary

The preliminary of Fierce Inner Heat is the vital point of the body called the Inner Space of Fire or Inner Heat Wildfire.[4] Visualize yourself as Coemergent Cakrasaṃvara or in your ordinary form. Above your head is a vast and wide bejeweled throne supported by eight lions. There, on a seat of white lotus, sun, and moon sits your root guru, white as the autumn moon and smiling. Meditate on the guru's waves of blessing. If you tend toward wrong ideas or when you need to increase devotion, it is all right to meditate on the guru as Vajradhara. However, the special feature of these Six Dharmas is the meditation on the guru in his or her actual form. With the intense longing of devotion through multiple means, such as the notion described above, that the guru is the embodiment of all refuges, say:

> Precious guru, united essence of all buddhas of the three times.
> For the sake of all sentient beings,
> bless me that the special absorption of bliss-warmth arises in my body.
> Bless me that the special absorption of bliss-emptiness arises in my mind.

Through your supplicating with intense feeling, the guru melts into the essence of elixir, which enters the crown of your head and dissolves, refining away your fully ripened karmic body. You become Exalted Vajrayoginī, dark red, with one face and two arms. The right hand is slightly menacing with a vajra pointing downward and the left holds a blood-filled skull cup to the heart. She wears a crown of the five dry human skulls and is bedecked with a garland of fifty freshly severed heads. Three eyes, loosened hair, and five bone ornaments adorn her. She stands in the posture of right leg extended on a white human corpse with its head bent to the right, upon a lotus and sun seat, amid towering flames. {214} Imagine that the inside of your bodily form is utterly empty down to the pores and is like a red silk tent. The vital point of the body is the sixfold-binding-stove position, sitting with the legs drawn up and the calves crossed, the right inside and the left outside, forming a cross. The two hands are also crossed, grasping the opposite biceps, with the elbows resting on the knees. Keep the backbone straight and rest the gaze straight ahead. Visualize a foursquare formation of four fireballs—directly in front and in back of your navel and at the right and left kidneys. They are round, red, and very hot, about to erupt into flames, like red-hot burning iron balls.

Without stopping that visualization sequence, expel the dead air three times with long, slow exhalations. Inhale slowly and press the upper winds down below the navel. Hold the lower winds in place without drawing them up. Rotate the belly once to the right and once to the left, causing the fireballs to collide. Imagine that the whole inside of your body fills with the glittering red and crackling heat of the pink sparks of fire. Hold the gentle breath, ignoring the discomfort. When unable to hold it longer, expel the breath slowly at first, strongly in the middle, and then finally exhale totally. Do this four or eight times, holding down the breath as you are able. When you have practiced for a time, gradually add the rotations [of the belly], once to the right and once to the left. When you can perform twelve right rotations and twelve left rotations, you will gain the capability of fire. After doing the five-branch training, train as much as possible in the yogic exercises of Drilling Stick and Drilling Base, which will swiftly arouse the heat.

ii. Main Practice: Eating the Food of Fierce Inner Heat

The vital points of the body are to sit with your legs in bodhisattva position, relaxed and wide, your palms on your knees with arms straight, teeth and lips resting naturally, and the gaze as described above. The spine is straight and the two big toes are turned inward. {215} Visualize yourself as Exalted Vajrayoginī with the central avadhūtī channel in the center of the empty internal space. The channel has the four characteristics of being straight like a medium-sized arrow, fine, radiant, and red. Its upper end reaches the cranial aperture, and its lower end is four fingers-widths below the navel. The openings of both ends are cut and inside they are clear and empty, like a bamboo stalk that has been cut straight through. To its right is the red rasanā channel and to the left the white lalanā channel, both about the thickness of a wheat straw. The three channels run closely parallel, except that the lower ends of the two are four finger-widths longer and turn back to just enter into the lower end of the central channel. The two upper ends are one finger-width behind the central channel and bend straight from there. From that juncture their ends come together, covering the top of the central channel, then curve to the front and terminate at the two nostrils. Within the upper end of the central channel there is a white upside-down syllable *haṃ*, blissful and cool. Inside the lower end of the central channel, at the place where the three channels converge, there is a red upright syllable *raṃ*, extremely hot. Four finger-widths directly below the lower end of the central channel, near the anus, there is a light-blue semicircular wind mandala with its straight side facing forward, extremely volatile. Clearly visualize all that.

For the ninefold shake-up of dead air, the first three are slow and long, the next three strong and short, and for the final three twist the torso while exhaling. Press the thumb of the right hand against the base of the ring finger, with the little finger also bent. Place the middle finger behind the index finger and press the left nostril. With the left hand, make a fist with the thumb inside and put it under the right armpit and press down with the right arm. The elbow squeezes the right breast as you completely exhale once from the right nostril. {216} Then reverse it and exhale once from the left. Then once again exhale from the right. Relax a little and refresh the visualization of the empty space. Again, slowly clear out the dead air once. Then inhale and with the upper winds press down below the navel. Also draw up the lower winds slightly and hold the joined winds.

In the visualization, the winds all enter through the nostrils and travel down the rasanā and lalanā, arriving at the juncture of the three channels. Blue wind from the wind mandala rises like a piercing spear and enters the central channel. The three winds [of the rasanā, lalanā, and the downward-clearing wind] fan the *raṃ* syllable, which produces a fine, pointed line of fire, clear and radiant, blazing steadily higher. After a few breaths, it strikes the *haṃ* in the head, causing a stream of white bodhicitta to fall. As this lengthens, meditate that it dissolves into the *raṃ* at the navel. It is said that the intention is mainly to focus on the blazing and dripping of the fire in front and the vital drops in back. Alternate your intention between the sound of heat inside your body wherever the light of fire occurs and vibrating bliss in whatever course the light of the bodhicitta takes. Hold your breath as long as you can. When it becomes somewhat uncomfortable, inhale as many small gulps of air as you can without letting out any of the air held previously. Push and press your belly to the right, left, and center in the area of the navel. When you can't [hold the breath any longer], let it out as before and then immediately inhale and meditate. If you need to rest, take a break after four, eight, sixteen (etc.) times; not just whenever you want to. Do not do this practice either at dawn or dusk, or at noon. At first, begin the breath-holding practice at the times when [the breath] moves from the left or equally [from both nostrils]. This and the acts of adopting or abandoning the evil winds and so on should be learned elsewhere.

iii. Concluding Practices: Taking the Empowerment of Existence

Visualize the guru and seat as before. Imagine that you present the four complete and perfect offerings: the outer offerings of manifold excellent substances and offerings from all times and directions; the inner offerings of sacred pledge and elixir of awareness; {217} the secret offering of a bliss-inducing wisdom consort; and the suchness offering of knowing that the three spheres are like an illusion and a dream.

> Precious guru, unified essence of all buddhas of the three times:
> Outwardly I offer flowers and incense;
> inwardly, five meats and five elixirs;
> secretly, the timeless awareness of bliss-emptiness;
> and most secretly, the sublime offering of suchness.
> Please accept and confer the complete four empowerments.

Through your fervent supplication, a bright-white bliss-inducing stream of awareness elixir falls from the guru's body. It enters through the top of your head and fills your body above the eyebrows. Physical stains are purified, and you receive the vase empowerment. It fills your body above the throat. Verbal stains are purified, and you receive the secret empowerment. It fills your body above the heart. Mental stains are purified, and you receive the wisdom-awareness empowerment. It fills the whole body. All stains of the three doors are purified, and you receive the fourth empowerment. The guru melts into light and dissolves into you. The guru's awakened body, speech, and mind blend inseparably as one with your own body, speech, and mind. Settle in equipoise.

This practice has very great purpose and blessings, so on this occasion of Fierce Inner Heat it must be done each time without fail. If you meditate with ardent intentionality, it will become the most excellent of all enhancement practices. For the natural liberation of upper and lower obstructions, consult the source texts.[5]

Actual bliss-emptiness of mahāmudrā
rises quickly through this gift,
the heart of all victors: caṇḍālī,
the ultimate accumulation and purification.

b. Illusory Body, Naturally Liberated Desire and Anger

Imagine that you are dark-blue Cakrasaṃvara with two hands holding vajra and bell, crossed [around Vajravārāhī]. He is adorned with the six symbolic ornaments and marked by the crescent moon and crossed vajra in the hair topknot, wearing a garland of wet heads and a tiger-skin skirt. {218} He stands with left leg bent and right leg straight, pressing on Bhairava and Kālarātri. He is embraced by red Vārāhī holding a flaying knife and skull cup. They stand on a lotus-sun seat in the midst of a blazing bonfire. Visualize the guru upon a four-tiered seat on your head as in the practice of Purifying Empty Space. If you meditate on the guru as Vajradhara, make him blue. Light rays emanate from [the guru's] heart and invoke from the ten directions all gurus, yidams, buddhas, bodhisattvas, heroes, ḍākinīs, sangha members, and dharma protectors. They dissolve into the guru, who becomes the embodiment of the union of all the Jewels, and appears as just that. Develop intense devotion with thoughts such as "Just hearing the guru's name liberates from the bad propensities of cyclic existence, let alone actually supplicating." Imagine the murmuring sounds [of supplication] from all six kinds of sentient beings and so forth—the whole environment and its inhabitants—and say:

> Precious guru, unified essence of all buddhas of the three times,
> for the sake of all sentient beings,
> I pray to you that I relinquish my self-fixation,
> have no needs,
> accomplish Illusory Body,
> and cultivate Dream.
> Please bless me to attain the supreme spiritual power of Lucid Clarity Mahāmudrā right now, quickly, on this very seat.

When you supplicate intensely, the guru dissolves into you. This visualization alone, praised for its profundity, has eight vital points: (1) One's own body as the deity's empty clear form contains in its lower part a white source of phenomena, the nature of light. This has three vertices: one at the navel and two facing the two kidneys. Its narrow point is at the perineum and its wide opening faces upward. Focus on that briefly. (2) {219} Within that, you meditate on immeasurable sentient beings of the six kinds, each with their individual bodies and functions, densely packed into the source of phenomena. You think, "These are manifestations of my own karma and habitual tendencies for taking birth as each of those kinds of migrators." Also recall, "Below my navel are the root letters that cause the arising of the appearances of the six kinds of migrators, and so their forms have arisen." (3) You make the sentient beings throughout space the object of your visualization and then turn your mental reckoning on the six kinds of beings at the navel. Think, "Do they appear? They appear. Are they real? They are not. They are like an illusion, like a dream." Rigorously meditate on that. (4) You think how sad it is that they all cling to what is not real as being real and wander in cyclic existence. Thus develop distinct compassion. (5) You supplicate the guru to afford them lasting refuge from the sufferings of cyclic existence: "Beloved guru, please consider them." (6) One of them disappears, then a second disappears. The source of phenomena gradually becomes empty inside. You focus on that. (7) You rest relaxed without fixation, free of all focus. (8) When you can no longer remain in that state, you envision the whole of the environment and its inhabitants and resolve that it is nonexistent yet appearing, like an illusion.

During session breaks, increase the power of your meditative absorption by constantly cultivating the intentionality of impermanence, devotion, and illusion. Learn about how to integrate all good and bad conditions, such as sickness and spirits, from the source texts.

Meditate on this essence of all Sutra and Tantra:
the deluded machinations of samsara vanish
and the six qualities will arise automatically.
Infinite appearance and emptiness—amazing!

c. Dream, Naturally Purified Double Delusion {220}

i. Recognizing Dreams

Visualize your body as that of the yidam and meditate on the guru on your head as before during Illusory Body. The supplication is the same as before, except that the last line changes to "... and to recognize dreams." After fervently supplicating, the guru melts into light and dissolves into you. In the center of the empty space of your body, which has arisen as the clear, empty form of the deity, the white central channel stands like a crystal column. The upper end reaches the head and the lower end the perineum. Meditate that inside the upper end of the central channel there is an upside-down white *haṃ* and in the lower end an upright red *hūṃ*. It has also been taught to meditate on the upper and lower ends of the central channel as very thin and the middle as being thick, like the shape of a fish. In any case, when you meditate on it in a way suitable to your own disposition, it's best to imagine it no wider than your forearm and no narrower than a bamboo cane. If the central channel is wide, it is easy for the [visualized] vital drops to circulate in it, but if it is narrow, it is a little difficult. In all cases, the only important thing is to meditate while taking into account the knowledge that whatever arises is false in general and a dream in particular. Then a pea-sized white drop breaks away from the *haṃ* in the head and arrives at the heart. This purifies stupidity. Your torso above the heart becomes light and blissful. A pea-sized red vital drop breaks off from the *hūṃ* at the perineum and arrives at the heart. This purifies desire. Your lower body below the waist becomes light and blissful. The two white and red drops meet at the heart and anger is naturally purified. Imagine the area of the heart filled with bliss and lightness. Within the state of intense intentionality regarding their lack of true existence and dreamlike nature, focus your attention on those two drops chasing each other around inside the empty space of the central channel at the level of the heart. Their manner of circling around can be clockwise or counterclockwise, as you like. {221} This is the vital point of the vase empowerment. Then imagine that the two drops circling around trying to capture each other barely touch. This is the secret empowerment. Then imagine that their touching each other causes your body and mind to experience a thrill of bliss. This is the wisdom empowerment. Finally, one drop dissolves into the other and then vanishes, and you rest without a reference point. That is connected with the vital point of the fourth empowerment. In between [these visualizations], intensely recall a few times the notions that these are not real but a dream. In the session breaks, always maintain the intentional contemplation of impermanence, devotion, and dreams.

ii. Refining Dreams

Once you have stabilized the recognition of dreams, there is the second phase of refining them. In this context it is to refine the dreams through intentionality. The practice is the same as in recognizing dreams up through guru yoga, except for a change in the supplication to ". . . and to refine dreams." There is no definite [visualization] because you practice with the dynamic energy of intentionality alone. Think, "This mental body of dream can be refined in whatever way I choose." Cultivate this intention continuously. Pass through pillars, walls, and so forth without obstruction. Practice slipping through small windows and so on. Practice direct subjugation of particular frightening situations, such as those involving fire, water, wild beasts, earthquakes, and so forth. Fly in the sky and penetrate under the ground. Train especially with conceptual thoughts that are difficult to overcome, the type that cause shame and disgust. Sometimes [remember that] they are unreal. Sometimes use counteractive meditation. In these ways, refine through intentionality in the daytime and actually refine dream appearances at night. Learn about increasing and other Dream practices from the source texts. You should also know the esoteric instructions concerning the profit ritual if you don't recognize [dreams], stabilizing them when you do, severing diffusion, and other important instructions.

When all dreamlike phenomena
are always known to be like dreams,

the womb of sixfold beings' existence stays empty.
The clear empty deity's form arises by itself. {222}

d. Lucid Clarity, Naturally Clarified Stupidity

In the standard preliminary, meditation on the pain of impermanence produces disillusionment. The main practice is the recognition of lucid clarity. You appear clearly as Cakrasaṃvara. Your root guru is on a complete four-tiered seat on your head, adorned by the eight charnel-ground attributes, such as the hair topknot, bone ornaments, and tiger-skin skirt. If you meditate on the guru as Vajradhara, meditate on semi-wrathful Heruka with three eyes. Change the last line of the supplication to ". . . and to recognize lucid clarity" and supplicate fervently with powerful devotion. Within the white central channel at the level of your heart, a thumb-sized figure of your root guru sits on a white four-petaled lotus and moon seat, white and emanating light rays. In that guru's heart is a white pea-sized vital drop emanating light. Focus there and rest in equipoise. The light that emanates from that suffuses the guru's form and fills the mind with bliss. Light rays come from that form and pervade your own body, which then radiates light rays out of all its pores. Meditate that all appearances are pervaded by its brilliance. Focus on the drops at the guru's heart and the emanation of light rays again and again. In between visualizations, let consciousness fall in its own place. Sometimes bliss, clarity, or nonthought will arise automatically, but just continue without hopes and fears. At bedtime, focus your attention on the vital drop or on a mercury-colored *hūṃ* in the guru's heart. In the session breaks, recall impermanence and devotion to the guru. In particular, apply the Integration of the Three Kāyas: remain with your eyes in the unblinking elephant's gaze, relax consciousness, and sustain the intrinsic essence of whatever arises. The aspect of clarity in the various appearances is nirmāṇakāya. {223} The emptiness aspect that recognizes its own essence is dharmakāya. Those two inseparable in the natural clarity of reflexive awareness is saṃbhogakāya. That knowledge is the integration [of the three kāyas]. The stubborn reification of the eight worldly concerns is destroyed. Without getting lost in the regular course of discursive thought, they are self-liberated and self-purified. This one thing is important to everything. Blending and the concluding practices, such as dispelling obstructions and enhancing, can be found in the source texts.

Shifting concepts are purified in basic space.
The false cave of samsara's ignorance collapses.
Lucid clarity, with or without appearance,
is handed over by this heart blood of instruction.

e. Transference, Buddhahood without Meditation

Here we will use the supplementary esoteric instruction, the Skylight of Timeless Awareness. Visualize your own body as the yidam and meditate on the guru on your head, and so on, the same as in the section on Illusory Body. Change the last line of the supplication to "Please bless me with buddhahood in the intermediate state." The guru dissolves into you. In the center of your body's inner space is the white central channel. It is the width of [anywhere between] a forearm and a bamboo cane. The lower end reaches the perineum and is closed; the upper end touches the cranial aperture and is wide open. Inside the central channel is a white source of phenomena at the level of the navel. The fine tip faces downward while the open part faces upward with one vertex facing the front and the other two vertices facing right and left. Within that is the white letter *A*, suspended without touching anything. Imagine that it is very fine and clear and about to levitate. Clear out the dead air three times, then hold the vase breath forcefully for a short time. Focus on the white *A*. Draw up the lower wind. Slightly squeeze your belly toward your spine. The white *A* lifts up a bit and then returns to its former place. When you squeeze a little harder, it rises higher than before and again comes to rest in its place. Again, squeeze as hard as you can. At the same time, the sides of the source of phenomena strike each other. {224} The wind force causes the white *A* to shoot up like an arrow through the central channel. It comes out of the cranial aperture and continues high into the sky, then vanishes. Space, sky, and awareness—these three blend inseparably. Rest openly just there. Do that visualization some seven times. For the descent, a white *A* suddenly appears in the sky. It falls down through your cranial aperture and descends slowly down the central channel. It lands in the center of the source of phenomena in the navel and remains there, firm and heavy. Imagine vibrating bliss arising in your body.

This constitutes a single short session. At first, while you are training, meditate again and again until you show the signs. In daily practice, you don't need to do the visualization more than once. In the session breaks, meditate that the upper end of the central channel is closed.

Regardless of good or bad karma,
one is transported to pure celestial realms.
In just seven days the final goal is attained.
Even lesser folks who try this much—amazing!

f. Intermediate State, the Victors' Saṃbhogakāya

The preliminaries stay the same, except that the last line of the supplication is changed to "May I attain saṃbhogakāya in the intermediate state." After the guru dissolves into you, train intensively with the thought "This really is the intermediate state of becoming." Cultivate strong disillusionment with the sufferings of cyclic existence and the shortcomings of desire and anger. Think, "In this intermediate-state situation, a moment's thought creates lasting happiness or severe suffering. No matter what, I must not be deluded." Meditate on a blue source of phenomena in front of you. Its tip is pointed down and its wide opening faces upward. Think, "To those without realization, this is the mother's womb. To those with realization, this is the palace of the Unsurpassed Pure Land." Then you arrive in its center and become the blue letter *hūṃ*, large and blazing with light. {225} The light rays radiating from it strike the source of phenomena, purifying all the previous and current habitual patterns and karmic debts of womb birth in the six realms. The doors to future births are blocked. The habitual patterns of the three other places of birth are consequently self-purified. Meditate that the *hūṃ* completely transforms and you instantly become Coemergent Cakrasaṃvara with the guru upon a four-tiered seat on your head. Supplicate with single-pointed focus: "Please let me obtain the saṃbhogakāya in this intermediate state." All physical appearance is that of the Cakrasaṃvara couple. The extent of sound is the seven-syllable mantra. All thoughts and memories in the mind are dreams and illusions. Within that state, become utterly convinced that nothing truly exists.

Imagine that in the right side of the source of phenomena, all those who arouse your anger and all males become Cakrasaṃvara. All those that arouse your desire and all females on the left side of the source of phenomena become Vajravārāhī. Present the complete four offerings. Female practitioners should reverse the objects that produce desire and anger. It is most important to constantly cultivate devotion, the deity's form, and the conviction that everything is the intermediate state, while knowing them to be unreal.

Like irrigation water from a cut-off pipe,
concepts change course in the intermediate state
and you won't enter another life in existence;
it is crucial to familiarize from now on.

[Concluding Remarks]

At first, meditate on the four root dharmas until you have some kind of experience of each of them. Then, if you meditate on all of them in their entirety, do Fierce Inner Heat in the morning, Illusory Body at midday, Dream in the evening, and Lucid Clarity at night. Meditate on the auxiliary dharma cycles whenever it is convenient. If you cannot practice all six dharmas, separate out whichever one[s] you prefer and meditate on that. {226} Refuge, awakening mind, and Purifying Inner Space must all go first. If you wish to meditate only on Fierce Inner Heat, apply the vital points of the body, the empty space of fire, three or four breathing [cycles], and meditate on Eating the Food of Inner Heat as much as you are able. After that, take the Empowerment of Existence one time. Just this can be done in four or six or however many sessions. This applies to the others as well. This concludes the concise explanation of the essential Six Dharmas as it is explicitly presented in the source and subsequent guidebooks.

II. Special Esoteric Instructions

To meditate on the four root dharmas individually in single sittings, first go for refuge, arouse awakening mind, and purify inner space as before. Do the general guru yoga, meditating in the manner of the Purifying Inner Space. Do the supplication with intense feeling:

> Precious guru, unified essence of all buddhas of the three times,
> for the sake of all sentient beings,
> I pray to you that I relinquish my self-fixation,
> have no needs,
> accomplish Illusory Body,
> and cultivate Dream.
> Please bless me to attain the supreme spiritual power of Lucid
> Clarity Mahāmudrā right now, quickly, on this very seat.

Supplicate intensely. On this occasion, you only need to know that the guru is the union of all Jewels and to keep all sentient beings in your thoughts; you do not need to do the visualizations of dissolving back [into the guru] or the supplications by the six kinds of migrators. At the end, the guru dissolves into you and you rest in equipoise.

A. Inner Heat in a Single Sitting

The vital points of the body are the same as the general seven-point posture of Vairocana, except that the gaze is to look straight ahead and the two palms rest on the two knees. {227} Meditate on yourself as Vajravārāhī—the manner of sitting and so forth in harmony with your own body. Ornaments, seat, and so on are the same as usual. In the middle of the clear, empty interior of the body is the central channel endowed with the four characteristics but without the rasanā and lalanā channels. Its length and other attributes were described before. Within it, four finger-widths below the navel, is a dark-red letter *raṃ*, the size of a barley grain. At the level of the navel, on a sun seat the size of a pea, is an orange *A*-stroke, one finger-width high and very fine. Meditate on that and cultivate a sense of devotion, thinking that it is the essence of your root guru. At the upper end of the central channel is a white upside-down *haṃ*. Think of your guru in the sky above, white and smiling and blazing with charisma. Do the ninefold shake-up of dead air, then forcefully hold the breath with the four-stage application practice. The actual winds enter [through the nose] on the left [and right][6] of the central channel and, like a piercing spear, enter the lower end and fan the *raṃ*, causing a dark-red flame to rise up four finger-widths. This provokes the *A*-stroke, the guru's essence, to blaze up with crackling orange flames. The *haṃ* at the head heats up and its flames come out the cranial aperture, spreading widely. The complete four offerings emanate from the tips [of the flames] and the offering of bliss-warmth comes from the light of the flames, all presented to the delight of the guru. That embodied essence of all buddhas melts into the elixir of bodhicitta and, together with the flames, enters through the cranial aperture and mixes with the *haṃ* in the head. A flow of vital drops stretches down to the throat. This [bestows] ecstasy and the vase empowerment. It arrives at the heart: sublime ecstasy and the secret empowerment. It dissolves into the *A*-stroke and the navel: special ecstasy and the wisdom empowerment. Elixir then falls from that and dissolves into the *raṃ*: coemergence and the fourth empowerment. Remember that this is the meaning [of the visualization]. {228} Again, meditate on the blazing and dripping like the Brushing Tangled Hair practice of regular Inner Heat practice, except that here you meditate that the fires of the *raṃ* and the *A*-stroke merge together and blaze, and that the dripping of the drops passes through the *A*-stroke and dissolves into *raṃ*. This combines three visualizations into one: Eating the Food of Inner Heat, the Inner Heat of the Guru's Blessing, and taking the Empowerment of Existence. Thus it is said to carry great blessings and importance.

For this occasion, focus your attention on the blazing that occurs when you forcefully expel the breath, hold it out, and draw up from inside. Focus your attention on the melting when you inhale forcefully and squeeze the two doors of the downward-clearing winds. At all times, keep the mind high in the sky. Push out your belly and then twist your body while forcefully stirring up the energy and say "*hal.*" The entire path of methods is completely contained in this single practice of vital winds. It is an extremely secret esoteric instruction from the direct lineage. This single-sitting practice is not a meditation to start with. Do this meditation as a daily practice and enhancement practice after achieving a degree of warmth in the path of methods from the source.

B. Illusory Body

It is acceptable to meditate on your root guru on your head, in your heart, or elsewhere. Supplicate the guru in a particular place or even dwelling throughout space:

> Father guru! Mother guru!
> Guru, consider me.
> Kind root guru, I pray to you.

Meditate on intense heart-piercing devotion and then relax into that state. Suddenly visualize yourself in the deity's form. Think about the appearance of yourself and all others: "All this is the deluded appearance of nonexistent things. Good and bad, desire and anger, the eight worldly concerns, and so on are all concerned with accepting or rejecting delusional reifications. {229} What's there to be concerned about? In fact, it is an illusion, a dream." Train vigorously with those thoughts, and when you are beyond judgment, maintain that state without fabricating anything. Then immediately visualize yourself as the deity or as your ordinary self if you wish. Meditate on the source of phenomena below your navel as in the regular practice. The vital points of the practices for those of highest, average, or lesser faculties are here condensed into one meditation.

C. Dream

Recognizing dreams is the same as in the main course of instruction. Meditate three times in succession on the Vital Points of the Four Empowerments of Drops for self-recognition. After that, train with intense intentionality in the unreal nature of yourself and others, the environment and its inhabitants, enemies and friends, all enjoyments, and so forth. Within that state, settle without fabrication in whatever arises. Familiarize yourself with that again and again. Refining dreams is also the same as explained before, with the most important vital points to continue the mode of intentionality in illusion-like nature and natural repose. If you wish to ascertain objective appearances, meditate on a bright clear white *hūṃ* in your heart that radiates light. Rigorously cultivate the intentionality that all is dream and illusion and your desire to see the appearance of a place. Light radiates from the *hūṃ*, extending out like a rope. It snares whatever place or thing you wish to see and pulls it in and dissolves it into the *hūṃ* at your heart. The light from the *hūṃ* illuminates all appearance with shimmering radiance. Focus your attention there. During this practice, it is important to meditate with vase breathing. To develop the applied virtue from Illusory Body and Dream, you need the accumulation of merit as a support. As was said:

> Cultivation of merit cuts through these three:
> nonrecognition, proliferation, and deviation.[7]

D. Lucid Clarity

Although what was explained before is the fundamental visualization, if you cannot grasp lucid clarity no matter what you do, the following is especially potent. Imagine a white *A* at the lower end of the central channel inside your body. Press down continually on the upper winds and continually draw the lower winds, until the *A* falls steadily down to the base of the perineum. {230} It winds its way, constantly twisting, through the genital channel, and when it reaches the inside of the gem (glans), it becomes a brilliant blue color. The head [of the syllable] turns back and faces inward. It tries to force its way out with great strength, but it cannot fit through the hole (urethra) and remains there steadily. Focus intently on that for a moment. Again, rest there in startled wonderment, merely not blocking that appearance. Meditate on that again and again. For women, meditate on the lower end of the central channel that reaches eight finger-widths below the navel. The rest is the same. This method of grasping lucid clarity is especially profound.

E. Transference

Meditate on a white *A* in the lower end of the white central channel within your body and visualize that the cranial aperture is wide open. At the same time as you exhale the breath, the *A* that is four finger-widths below the navel travels up the central channel to the cranial aperture. It shoots out into the sky like an arrow and vanishes in the expanse. Rest for a bit in equipoise. Imagine that the *A* reappears in the sky and falls down through your cranial aperture and down to the lower end of the central channel. It is taught that you needn't meditate on blocking the door [of the cranial aperture] and so on but just the alternating of [consciousness] going up and coming down. You should know, however, that the practices of Transference to the Unerring Celestial Realm or the Skylight of Timeless Awareness should precede this practice.

F. Intermediate State

The section on the Intermediate State was clarified earlier according to the source guidebook. However, here you do not do the cycle of visualizing the objects of desire and anger within the source of phenomena as deities. Train with the intentionality that the abodes of the six kinds of migrators and all good and bad form, sound, smell, taste, and texture is an illusion and the intermediate state. Visualize the intercourse that results in womb birth, egg birth, and so on, and transform that into the yidam couple's union by the intentionality of the intermediate state. {231} By knowing that to be illusion, maintain the state of nonattachment.

[Conclusion]

This extremely profound way of practicing the Six Dharmas in a Single Sitting comes from the uninterrupted oral teachings and some instructions of the blessing transmission that were actually taught by Ḍākinī of Timeless Awareness in a direct lineage to Venerable Kunga Drolchok.[8] If you practice this until actual signs of success appear, take as your main source the extensive big guide with sixty-seven basic visualizations or the medium guide that has only seventeen visualizations.[9] Practice the visualizations from the class of sealed precepts as circumstances permit. Once you get a taste of meditative experience, it is really good to be content with just what has been presented here. Since all the vital points are contained here, both mother and child [versions], if you are able to put them into practice, you will accomplish your purpose with just this much. Also, if you are interested in extracting something like just the Illusory Body or Dream practices, you should learn them separately from the single-sitting practices.

General Valuable Vital Points on Everything

Your root guru is the union of the Three Jewels and Three Roots. Know that all other adjunct gurus are manifestations of that root guru. In general, the unshakable devotion that sees your guru as superior to even the Buddha is the indispensable life support of the path of Secret Mantra. In particular, as glorious Mokchokpa said:

> Illusory Body ascertains Lucid Clarity. Dream ascertains Illusory Body. Faith and intention ascertain Dream. The teacher of faith and intention is the guru. Therefore, everything depends on the root guru.[10]

We can understand how important this is for maintaining the path of methods. That and to integrate it on the path by apprizing the unwavering recollection that your own mind's emptiness is dharmakāya, appearance is nirmāṇakāya, and their inseparable innate awareness and innate clarity is saṃbhogakāya. {232} Within that state, exert yourself in whatever breathing practices you can—vase breathing, gentle breathing, or intermediate breathing. Know that what arises from that—the clarity-emptiness or bliss-emptiness—is all like an illusion. Rest without fixation in the state of mahāmudrā. By blending these experiences of resting in equipoise with all activities in postmeditation attainment, they will quickly become stabilized. Always avoid loss of kunda bodhicitta, and do not get lost in ordinary thinking—these are the yogin's sacred pledges.

By meditating in that way, whatever experiences arise in body, speech, or mind—gentle or rough, high or low, happy or sad—you understand to be illusion and dream without pleasure or displeasure, rejecting or accepting, hopes and fears. Then maintain that flexibility. This is the supreme dispelling of obstructions. Know that whatever good or bad thing happens, such as progress in your practice of virtue, is exclusively the guru's compassion. Make supplication and devotion the sole foundation of your path. Pass the time with an altruistic mind that generates nothing but loving-kindness and compassion without bias toward all sentient beings who lack realization. This is the root of enhancement practices and the welfare of migrators.

Through meditating in such a way, at some point, without making any effort on purpose, the lucid clarity of mental bliss, clarity, and nonthought will arise by itself without center or boundaries. That and the appearance of the clear radiant deity's form will arise suddenly without any actual idea of wanting to create it. This is called the natural arising of the deity's form of illusory body. This inseparability of profundity and clarity has equivalent qualities to the clear realization of the noble ones.

Furthermore, Khedrup Khyungpo Naljor said:

> Once you practice just these dharmas, such as Illusory Body, Dream, and so forth, you don't need to be afraid of oppressive dreams, or the omens from various ḍākinī transformations, {233} or the various displays of apparitions that will come. You will have my blessings at all times and situations.[11]

The yidam deity [Tārā] gave these concise instructions to Öntön Kyergangpa:

> The vital point of Illusory Body is its lack of reality; destroy reification.
> The vital point of Dream is intentionality; integrate it on the path.
> The vital point of Lucid Clarity is devotion; attain it through prayer.
> The vital point of altruism is compassion; renounce prejudice.[12]

These four vital points cover all the bases of instructions. Put them into practice without carrying the four frosts [that damage] applied virtue: movement, changing residences, many plans, and perverse views.[13] Now in this time of degenerations, it is mostly difficult for the signs of success to manifest as described in the source texts due to the influence of the doctrine having become a mere reflection [of its former state]. Nevertheless, if you practice in this case, there is a prophecy given by the two ḍākinīs of timeless awareness to Khyungpo Naljor that they will nurture with compassion his disciples and later lineage disciples and lead them to the celestial realm of pure empty bliss. And Khyungpo himself said:

> There will never be someone better than I, or even someone equal. Also, all those who hold my lineage will be preeminent among all others, so it will consist only of those with excellent cultivation.[14]

He spoke the truth. The gurus of this lineage, such as the five precious ones, were mostly in their last lives as bodhisattvas. They had received prophecies concerning their ability to provide refuge from the lower realms through all contact such as seeing, hearing, recalling, or touching them. Each of those adepts promised their blessings for experiential realization for as long as the lineage remained unbroken. {234} My teacher, the master of adepts Karma Zhenpen Özer,[15] and those before him developed the experiences of the Six Dharmas exactly as described in the source texts. They saw the yidam deities and actualized the realization of the two inseparable truths. This is not just a pseudo-pure manner of explanation by mere words. These are instructions that one can believe in; the warmth of their blessings has not dissipated.

In general, there is no doubt that supreme and common spiritual powers will be attained just by hearing once or seeing with faith these teachings, not to mention actually putting them into practice. Free of faults, full of qualities, and certain to bring awakening in a matter of months or years, the Golden Dharmas of the single lineage is praised as transmission from lineage [master] to lineage [master]. The great adept Khyungpo stated:

> These instructions of mine are superior to others. Given at the beginning, they are helpful from the start. Given in the middle, they are helpful along the way. Given in the end, they are helpful to conclude. Therefore practice them with great diligence

> without doubt or a conflicted mind. They were received from the guru, the actual Buddha. They attract the actual ḍākinīs. Real qualities arise. They possess the transmission of the lineage. They have the ḍākinīs' blessings. They are replete with the power of instructions. Practice them! Those with the best faculties will awaken in the fully ripened body, the average in the body of habitual patterns, and the least in the intermediate state—it's impossible not to get enlightened. I am sure that there is nothing like my transmission legacy and vital instructions in all of India or Tibet.[16]

He praised them again and again in this way, and impartial adherents of other schools also strew the flowers of praise, raising the banner of fame to the pinnacle of existence. However, it was predicted that when the lineage passed down, these Golden Dharmas would either be interrupted or become watered down like milk sold in the market. {235} This is what has happened. Many imitations and corrupted versions have turned it into a mere reflection. The legacy of the direct lineage fell to Kunga Drolchok and hence to Omniscient Drolwai Gönpo [Tāranātha], who saw with timeless awareness the vital points of the uninterrupted esoteric instructions and so illuminated without deviation the intentions of the Seven Jewels. This is only the essence of that.

[Concluding Verses and Colophon]

Though it is a very degenerate time,
adepts who preserve this Golden Dharma
have taken me in. What good fortune!
Thinking of their qualities, I am full of faith.

Whatever mistakes I've made in writing this,
I confess before the guru, the Buddha.
To engage with mere words and no practice
will incur the ḍākinīs' punishment.

May seeing, hearing, or recalling this
beget miraculous birth in the realm of great bliss.

Held by the great adept Khyungpo and his spiritual heirs,
may we attain the great celestial realm.

I, Yönten Gyatso, born into the Khyung clan and engaged with interest in the Shangpa teachings, composed this text according to the earlier and later teachings that were given by the fearless, wise, and loving one with light rays, [Jamyang Khyentsé Wangpo], who attained primordially the state of a great vajra master. It was completed at Palpung Monastery, at the isolated retreat Dechen Ösal Ling, on the morning of the day of the ḍākinīs' gathering, a time of auspicious astrological conjunctions. May it be the cause for the glorious Shangpa Kagyu to spread all over the earth.

10. Amulet Mahāmudrā or Three Naturally Settled States Guidance Manual[1]

Tāranātha

namo gurave

Amulet Mahāmudrā or Three Naturally Settled States, is an instruction of Niguma, Ḍākinī of Timeless Awareness. The preliminaries of this guidance, such as contemplations on the difficulty in attaining a free and endowed human birth, impermanence, suffering, and so on, are the same as the standard versions. Going for refuge, arousing the awakening mind, and the Purifying *A* of Inner Space are the same as in the Six Dharmas. The preliminary to individual sessions is guru yoga. This is otherwise the same as in Illusory Body practice, except that many mandalas are offered and the supplication to recite is:

> [Precious guru, unified essence of all buddhas of the three times,
> for the sake of all sentient beings, I supplicate you]
> that I may relinquish self-fixation,
> that I may have no needs,
> that I may realize Lucid Clarity Mahāmudrā.

I. Actual Guidance

The actual guidance has three parts: (1) the preliminary, Three Naturally Settled States; (2) the main practice, Naturally Free of Four Faults; and (3) the conclusion, the Naturally Arising Three Kāyas.

A. The Preliminary, Three Naturally Settled States

This has two parts: (1) the guidance on calm abiding and (2) the guidance on higher insight.

1. Calm Abiding

This has two parts: (1) the basic visualization and (2) the enhancement.

a. Basic Visualization

Visualization Round 1

You have already abandoned all meaningless activities of body, speech, and mind. {239} From now on, until you have attained a modicum of stability in your meditation, relax your efforts toward intentional virtue, not to mention unvirtuous and neutral acts. Physically, assume the seven-point posture of Vairocana. Verbally, after clearing out the dead air three times, give up even doing breathing exercises, let alone talking, and remain in a settled state. Relax your mind without contrivance. That is the first round of contemplation.

Visualization Round 2

When various discursive thoughts proliferate, recognize them right away, abruptly cut them off, and then settle.

Visualization Round 3

If the undercurrent of thought becomes excessive, as soon as you become aware of it, promise yourself that from now on, nothing like this will ever happen again. Your resolution to be mindful in recognizing thoughts as they arise will clear this up.

Visualization Round 4

At that time, if your consciousness becomes unclear and forgetfulness increases, this is the fault of dullness (*bying ba*). Tighten your awareness, turn your eyes upward, and meditate in open places or on rooftops. Standing up and so forth will eliminate dullness. {240} If you become irritable or restless, it is [the fault of] agitation (*rgod pa*). You should relax and gaze downward. If your mind is distracted by the pleasures of the senses, develop detachment by recollecting impermanence and suffering.

b. Enhancement

This has three parts: (1) training with indefinite gazes, (2) training with various dharma activities, and (3) training with various activities.

i. Training with Indefinite Gazes

Visualization Round 5

Gaze with your eyes high and nearby, such as at the center of the ceiling, or far away, such as at the top of a mountain or the expanse of the sky, and rest in equipoise.

Visualization Round 6

Gaze down and nearby, such as at the bottom of a wall, or far away, such as at the base of a mountain, and rest in equipoise.

Visualization Round 7

Gaze straight ahead at something close, like a wall, or distant, like a mountain scape, and rest in equipoise.

ii. Training with Various Dharma Activities

Visualization Round 8

It is said, "Blend with reciting sutras, repeating mantras, and various conversations." That is, at first blend with the recitation of sutras and so forth with which you are familiar. Then gradually blend with all kinds of recitation as you are able.

Visualization Round 9

At first blend with short mantras, then blend with all recitation.

Visualization Round 10

At first, blend with the sounds of the elements, such as water. Then blend with many people chattering and doors shutting and so forth. Then blend with other people's conversations. Rest with mindless openness on those vivid sounds.

iii. Training with Various Activities

Visualization Round 11

When eating, eat in a naturally settled state. When walking, also practice that way. Even when speaking, do not abandon that naturally settled state. At first, practice with less weighty subjects that don't need much concentration. Eventually you can practice with everything. {241} Thus, whether pleasure, pain, joy, sorrow, fear, anxiety, disgust, and so forth—you will practice blending the naturally settled state with all objects that provoke high or low conceptual thoughts. Everything will be included within your previous practice of virtue.

2. Higher Insight
[a. Preliminary]

The higher insight practice of seeking the mind [will be explained] from the point of view of the guru's oral transmission, where it occurs in detail. First, after resting in the vital points of the aforementioned three naturally settled states, search from within a state of relaxation. This is the preliminary of every [higher insight practice].

[b. Main Practice]

The main practice consists of seven visualization sessions: (1) searching for mind's essence, (2) searching for its beginning and ending, (3) searching for objective appearances, (4) searching for conceptual thought, (5) searching for the difference between the existence or nonexistence of objective appearance, (6) searching for the difference between the existence or nonexistence of conceptual thought, and (7) gaining certitude in natural basic space.

i. Searching for Mind's Essence

Visualization Round 1

Look fixedly at mind's essence and begin a thorough investigation. Once your efforts have ceased of their own accord and you experience that there is no way to say, "This is it," let go in the naturally settled state. That is the first round of contemplation.

ii. Searching for Its Beginning and Ending

Visualization Round 2

Look at mind only without concept. Is it something stable and permanent that never arises nor ceases? There is nothing at all that causes it to arise or cease. If nothing creates or stops it, how did it arise? When it abides, how does it abide? What is its color and shape? Where is the outside and inside? When it ceases, how does it cease? When you make these kind of analyses, there is no way to identify it. Peace!

iii. Searching for Objective Appearances

Visualization Round 3

When you see form with your eyes, look for the essence of that vivid sight of forms. Investigate carefully whether that is the same or different from mind's keen sparkling awareness. {242} Apply the same process to sounds heard by the ears and so on.

iv. Searching for Conceptual Thought

Visualization Round 4

Again, is there a difference between this sudden arising of conceptual thought and the abiding nature of mind? Examine whether those two are the same or not. When thoughts arise, how do the arise? During the time from their arising until their ceasing, what is the manner of their existence? Once they cease, what is the manner of their cessation? Examine this closely.

v. Searching for the Difference between the Existence or Nonexistence of Objective Appearance

Visualization Round 5

What is the difference between the mind at the time of seeing form with the eyes and the mind at the time of not seeing form? If that difference exists, examine how it exists, and if it does not exist, examine how it does not exist.

vi. Searching for the Difference between the Existence or Nonexistence of Conceptual Thought

Visualization Round 6

Thoroughly investigate whether there is a difference in the quality, clarity, and emptiness of the mind when thoughts are present and the mind when they are absent. The end of those four methods of searching is the dissipation of the focus, so maintain solely that state.

vii. Gaining Certitude in Natural Basic Space

Visualization Round 7

All these appearances are definitely in your mind. When you examine the mind thoroughly, there is nothing to identify, and you settle within that very state. At this point, the lack of identification when you search a great deal is not that there is nothing at all; while empty, a variety arises. Empty awareness feels naked, vivid, bright, and sharp. Settle fully in that inexpressibility. These are the seven [methods] of higher insight.

Thus there are eighteen rounds of contemplation in the preliminary practice of the Three Naturally Settled States. Khyungpo said that of his gurus, Niguma primarily created the preliminary, Maitrīpa primarily the main practice, and Sukhasiddhi primarily the concluding practices. {243} In this context of the preliminary practice, you should develop realization.

B. The Main Practice: Naturally Free of Four Faults

[1. Preliminary]

First is the burglar's pointing-out method by means of the blessing [empowerment]. Construct a blue source of phenomena as the mandala. There, upon the mañji (tripod), place a large torma, stick in an arrow with silk attached, and adorn it with fine ornaments. In front, arrange offering tormas, general offerings, and feast substances. Consecrate them as usual. The ritual master meditates that he or she is Coemergent Cakrasaṃvara according to the visualization descriptions (*mngon rtogs*). Cleanse the mandala and tormas in front with *sumbha* . . . and purify with *svabhāva* . . . (etc.). Recite the torma ritual from the creation of the Protector through the [mantra] recitation. Then have the disciples wash. Distribute and collect the flowers and so forth. The disciples offer a mandala three times. Have them focus attention for a little while on themselves as Coemergent Cakrasaṃvara according to the visualization description. Then have them meditate instantly on the Protector in the front visualization.

Above the Protector, imagine the lineage gurus all around and in their midst is Awareness Ḍākinī Niguma. She is dark brown, holds a ḍamaru, skull cup, and khaṭvāṅga, and stands in the posture of dance, adorned by bone ornaments. She is in the prime of life. Imagine the presence of buddhas, bodhisattvas, hosts of mandala deities, and hosts of millions of ḍākinīs of the five families.

Imagine that this actual mandala that has been prepared is the realms of the billionfold universe filled with gold, and think that it is offered to all the deities. Master and disciples together consecrate the feast and tormas. For the consecration ritual, use the consecration according to the inner offering of any yidam practice. {244} Say *oṃ hrīḥ ha ha hūṃ hūṃ phaṭ* with *oṃ akāro* . . . (etc.) added to the end. First offer to the guru and yidam. Then offer to the Protector and retinue as in the torma ritual. Offer to the ḍākinīs with *oṃ sarva ḍākinī saparivāra akāro* . . . (etc.). While they hold flowers in their joined palms, have the disciples repeat this supplication three times:

> "I go for refuge to the buddhas present in the ten directions.
> I go for refuge to the dharma present in the ten directions.
> I go for refuge to the sangha present in the ten directions.
> I pay homage and go for refuge to the guru, yidam deities, and Six-Armed Awareness Protector with his retinue of deities.
> Root and lineage gurus, hosts of yidam deities, please grant me your blessings to directly recognize the realization of mahāmudrā.
> Ḍākinīs, dharma protector guards: please prevent any outer or inner obstacles to my reception and practice of mahāmudrā."

Encourage [the disciples] to have yearning devotion to the root guru. Have them settle into the natural resting state of the winds with the vital points of physical posture. Then imagine that all the gurus, yidams, and ḍākinīs with their hosts melt into light and dissolve into the disciples themselves. Relax a moment in that. Then say:

> Look steadily at your own essence.

Let them rest in equipoise for a while.

> The present mind is free of all identification. This naked vividness is itself unborn mind dharmakāya, also called ordinary mind or the naturally settled state. From now on, maintain just that without contrivance at all times during equipoise or subsequently. {245}

Do the mandala offerings, aspiration prayers, and so on as usual.

2. The Main Visualization

The preliminary for the session is as above. Again and again set the intention with "I will recognize with attention all mental stillness and movement."

For the main focus, when mind abides, turn inward and just recognize that. Rest in an uncontrived way. Whatever perceptions of objective appearance or discursive thought occur, don't particularly pay attention; neither deny nor affirm, accept nor reject. Whatever arises, rest evenly in the mere recognition of it. While not blocking the thought itself, maintain that state of wakefulness. But do not get lost in nonrecognition at all. With constant recognition, from then on when there is mental movement, let it move. If it gets away, let it go. Particularly strive at mindfulness. This is "not an iota of meditation, not a moment of distraction." This itself is the introduction to natural freedom from the four faults:

> Too close to recognize.
> Too profound to grasp.
> Too easy to believe.
> Too excellent to comprehend.[2]

The first fault is the lack of self-recognition. The second is that, although our ordinary mind reveals itself on multiple occasions—such as during our previous death or the experience of physical exhaustion—it was not introduced by our guru's instructions and it cannot be known by any other means. The third is that given the lack of anything to be done by anyone, smart or stupid, we cannot trust it intellectually. The fourth is that we simply cannot comprehend the fact that our mind's intrinsic nature is that of a buddha.

When you merely recognize all [thought] that moves or abides, there is natural empty clarity. Therefore, it is meaningless to alter or fabricate whatever arises. {246} When you understand that there is nothing whatsoever in all cyclic existence and its transcendence apart from this intrinsic nature of clarity and emptiness, those faults are naturally liberated.

C. The Conclusion: The Naturally Arising Three Kāyas

This has two parts: (1) the actual introduction to the three kāyas and (2) its enhancement.

1. Introduction to the Three Kāyas

Once you self-recognize that the uncontrived freshness of your previous ordinary mind was always the naturally arisen unity of clarity and emptiness from the beginning, you can be certain that its emptiness is dharmakāya, its clarity is nirmāṇakāya, and their unity is saṃbhogakāya. Having engendered certitude, maintain that naturally settled state itself. When you have that felt experience, you recognize each moment of mind as the three kāyas, and each moment of thought as their intrinsic nature. Once you have that kind of experience, you must always maintain it.

2. Enhancement

This has two parts: (1) enhancement and (2) dispelling obstructions.

a. Enhancement

This has three parts: (1) enhancement based on immeasurable devotion, (2) enhancement based on immeasurable compassion, and (3) enhancement based on special methods.

i. Enhancement Based on Immeasurable Devotion

Generally, devotion arises automatically when realization is born and compassion arises naturally for sentient beings who do not have that realization. Nonetheless, to meditate again on devotion and compassion is like adding dry wood to the fire—it increases greatly and becomes an incomparable enhancement of the path. Meditating intensely on devotion and compassion while repeatedly meditating on path mahāmudrā becomes the means to realize the ultimate.

In general, *devotion* (*mos gus*) means decisively regarding your root guru as the real buddha, their mind as dharmakāya, all their conduct and awakened activities as the two form kāyas at work for the benefit of others, and their essence as the embodiment of all buddhas, bodhisattvas, yidams, ḍākinīs, and dharma protectors in one. {247} The guru led you to your own nature, so you will never ever be able to repay that incredible kindness. Supplicate one-pointedly with intense devotion. The devotion to the guru will transform your mind so that when natural uncontrived timeless awareness arises vividly, you rest in that state of equipoise.

ii. Enhancement Based on Immeasurable Compassion

All sentient beings have been your kind parents. Yet since they do not recognize their own minds, with afflictive emotions they accumulate karmic actions and wander around in cyclic existence. Think and also say, "This is certainly lamentable." Finally, settle serenely in a state free of distinction between the objects of compassion and the one engendering compassion.

iii. Enhancement Based on Special Methods

This has three points:

> Blending ordinary mind with vital winds
> will stop conceptual thought and ignorance.

This means to settle into the equipoise of mahāmudrā with an uncontrived mind, and then forcefully hold the vase breathing. Since this causes the vital winds and the mind to converge as one, it increases realization more and more.

> Blending lucid clarity of the deity's form with vital winds,
> felt experience will become like the waxing moon.

Meditate on yourself as Coemergent Cakrasaṃvara, appearing yet without intrinsic nature, like the moon's reflection in water. That unobstructed appearance of the deity's form is itself uncontrived and fresh. To grasp [its] lucid clarity with mahāmudrā, forcefully squeeze the vital winds. The deity's form thus enhances mahāmudrā and increases experience.

> Blending unity consciousness with vital winds
> actualizes the resultant three kāyas.

Meditate on yourself as the clear empty deity's form and the other's body as the wisdom partner. Or, according to "one's own body is the means,"[3] the experiences of Fierce Inner Heat and Lucid Clarity seal the deity's form. {248} Hold that deity's form with mahāmudrā and distinguish it, then meditate. In speech, forcefully hold the vase breath. The clear form of the deity is nirmāṇakāya, the nonconceptual mahāmudrā is dharmakāya, and bliss is saṃbhogakāya. The vital winds act as a support for those three. The practice of the three kāyas at the time of the path causes the mind's abiding nature from the time of the ground to become actualized in the manner of the result. As long as the rootless state is not yet manifest, it is important to persevere in giving up busyness and meditating in isolation.

b. Dispelling Obstructions

Instructions to dispel obstructions, such as those of inverted channels and winds, are a branch of the Path of Methods, such as the Six Dharmas and so forth, and so they are common knowledge and will not be explained here. Here, the uncommon removal of obstructions concerns efforts to not be bound by the glue of [mere] meditative experience and not to stray into prioritizing appearance or emptiness.

Attachment to any one of the three [meditative experiences] of bliss, clarity, and nonthought is a deviation. Therefore, whatever joy and bliss arises in body and mind, whatever aspect of radiance or clarity occurs in your awareness, and whatever experience of nonthought dawns in the bright emptiness, leave it behind without the attachment of being pleased with it. If your meditative experience becomes too thick, as if you cannot break it, don't meditate; just let yourself go in whatever appearances you enjoy. When bliss, clarity, and emptiness disintegrate, the abiding nature arises starkly.

Attachment to the reality of mind's appearing aspect, clarity aspect, and mental perceptions arises. If this degenerates into gross fixated attachment to desire and anger, imagine that it is like an illusion and, after searching and not finding, let it go. Through that it will arise as empty.

Since there are no distinctions in the essence of one's mind, you might think that there is no need to be concerned with the results of actions. If such a wrong view develops, think about this: Although the results of action are not true, in a conventional way, the results of causes are inevitable. Fire is not true, but it burns wood. Water is not true, but that does not stop it from being wet. You must develop belief in karmic results and practice accordingly.

Abiding without fixation on the clarity and emptiness of mind is calm abiding. You need to dispel dullness and agitation. All appearance is mind.

If you are able to directly experience it without identifying all the abiding and moving, that is the birth of higher insight. If you can maintain an uncontrived state by recognizing the nature of whatever arises, the realization of the main mahāmudrā practice is born. When whatever you think in your mind and any appearances arise, without needing to rely on mindfulness and effort, the clarity and emptiness of recognizing your own nature in everything is continuous. That is called rootlessness and is the final culmination of meditative experience.

This is the direct instruction by Tāranātha for the benefit of Khyenrab, the spiritual friend from the eastern region of Kongpo.

Two Celestial Goddesses

Introduction

The two celestial goddesses, White Khecarī and Red Khecarī, are forms of Vajrayoginī and are often addressed as such. Khecarī, or Khachöma (*mkha' spyod ma*) in Tibetan, means "she who engages in space" and is essentially synonymous with *ḍākinī* (*mkha' 'gro ma*), "she who moves in space" (like one's awareness). Their pure land or celestial realm is called Khecara (*mkha' spyod*), and it is the destination for their practitioners, particularly for the transference of consciousness practices based on these two goddesses, but also part of the Transference practice of the Six Dharmas.

Khyungpo Naljor received these practices from Niguma, but the source texts, or vajra lines, for White Khecarī are credited to Atiśa, from whom Khyungpo Naljor received them again on his return to Tibet. Similarly, he received the Red Khecarī again from Rāhulaguptavajra in Tibet. Both of those sources are found in volume 11 of *The Treasury of Precious Instructions*. Another source seems to be a brief collection of texts found in two places in the *Shangpa Texts* called *Red Khecarī's Sādhana, Empowerment Ritual, and Hand Offering or Defilement Removal*. The first of these is based on Rāhula's instructions, while the others are not attributed. The collection is presumably by Sangye Tönpa Tsöndru Senge. According to Kongtrul, the reading transmission for any but the Transference practices have been broken, so it is those that are mainly performed or practiced for the benefit of the dying. As he says in the following text, "Therefore the continuity of the practice of this profound dharma itself has declined and left us destitute." This is a shame since they contain very enticing and profound practices such as the ones presented here. Kongtrul summarizes the essence of the practices as follows:

> Bhagavatī, the Vajra Queen, manifesting the radiance of the [red] sun and [white] moon, is aroused through the especially exalted supplication and the vital points of visualization. The

> caṇḍālī (fierce inner heat) of bliss-emptiness blazes up based on the release of passion at each of the chakras in the four places. Through those very supports, one comes to engage in the space (*mkha' spyod*) of great integral unity.[1]

In *Releasing the Knots of the Central Channel*, Kongtrul gathers what he can find from the extant sources and creates the means of accomplishing them in the form of complete sādhanas, divided into three main parts: White Khecarī, Red Khecarī, and the combined practice of White and Red Khecarīs. Each of those has subdivisions for use in particular ritual situations and includes all the necessary elements of liturgical practice. It is interesting that in his general liturgy for all Five Golden Dharmas, he had declined to provide one for the Khecarīs, referring the reader to the Especially Exalted Supplication,[2] and offers only a brief description in *The Sealed-Knot Vajra*.[3] His willingness to impart detailed notes for these secret practices may depend on the circumstances and disciples for whom they were written.

In Praise of Vajrayoginī (Skt. *Vajrayoginīstotra*) by Atiśa Dīpaṃkara (982–1055?) is the often mentioned Especially Exalted Supplication. It is also known as *In Praise of White Khecarī* in the Shangpa literature. This praise, along with the very brief source text by Atiśa mentioned above, are held in great esteem. Just reciting this beautiful praise as a supplication is in itself sufficient for receiving the blessing.

White Khecarī Transference is by Lochen Gyurme Dechen (1540–1615) of Riwoche. This great translator, who signs here as "the bilingual one" (*skad gnyis smra ba*), figures prominently in the Shangpa lineage, and especially in the lineage of the great adept Tangtong Gyalpo. Recognized as an emanation of the Indian master Maitrīpa, Gyurme Dechen received the Shangpa teachings primarily from Jonang Kunga Drolchok (1507–1566). His notations can even be found as an integral part of Niguma's *Vajra Lines of the Six Dharmas*. His main heir for the Shangpa tradition was the Sakya master Ngawang Chödrak (1572–1641), the author of many related texts. Here, Gyurme Dechen recounts the circumstances of Tangtong Gyalpo's visionary encounter with Ḍākinī Niguma when she granted him the instructions of the Khecarī practices. It is the identical narrative he gives in his biography of Tangtong Gyalpo, *A Jewel Mirror in Which All Is Clear*, written in 1609.[4] He writes that while Tangtong Gyalpo recorded all the other teachings from Niguma, he did not commit these instructions to writing beyond two illustrations, presumably because of their arcane nature. He then claims that this text is in fact those instructions, including an explanation of the two examples, given to him by Kunga Drolchok. The actual Transference of Consciousness instruction is very brief and somewhat unclear, but it can be clarified with reference to Kongtrul's instruction above.

Red Khecarī Transference by Lama Rāhula is essentially the same as the *Red Khecarī Sādhana* by the same author in volume 11. Indeed, that text is named as *Vital Drop Transference* in its colophon, as it is here. Rāhulagupta, a disciple of Maitrīpa and one of Khyungpo Naljor's primary masters, granted him the transmission for Red Khecarī, and most of the other instructions that he had already received from Niguma, on the occasion of miraculously visiting him in Tibet. As with *White Khecarī Transference*, this ancient instruction is fleshed out in the first text by Jamgön Kongtrul.

11. Releasing the Knots of the Central Channel

A Practice of White and Red Khecarīs[1]

Jamgön Kongtrul

namo guru vajravārāhī yai

In the realm of phenomena, source of every victorious one,
the light of great bliss blazes, wearing local clothing,
radiant as the moon and the sun: I bow to you.
I explain the profound yoga according to the adept transmission.

The learned adept Khedrup Khyungpo Naljor received the entire cycle of maturing and liberating instructions of both of the celestial goddesses (Khecarīs) from the Awareness Ḍākinī Niguma, Red Khecarī from the black adept Rāhula, and White Khecarī from glorious Atiśa. He merged the blessings from all of those traditions into a single stream to form the basic practices.

White Khecarī

If you wish to practice the yogas of creation and recitation of White Khecarī, the preliminary is to go for refuge and arouse awakening mind using the special version in the Six Dharmas, but changing the last line.[2] Alternatively, repeat three times the general prayer that begins "Buddha, dharma, and supreme assembly . . ." (*sangs rgyas chos dang tshogs mchog* . . . etc.) and meditate on the four immeasurables.

oṃ svabhāva śuddhaḥ sarva dharmāḥ svabhāva śuddho 'haṃ

From within emptiness, I appear instantly as Cakrasaṃvara. In the space before me is a white tetrahedral source of phenomena, radiating light rays. Made of bliss, it arises as bliss. In its center is a white letter *hrīḥ* radiating white light rays that purify the negativities and obscurations of all sentient beings. {253} The light reabsorbs and completely transforms into Vajrayoginī. She is white as the autumn moon, beautified by a hint of red radiance. She is charming and in the prime of youth. She smiles fiercely with a passionate attitude, her eyeteeth slightly bared. Her black hair falls loosely over her back. She glares with her three bloodshot eyes roving through space. She wears a tiara of five dry skulls and a garland of fifty fresh heads. In her right hand she brandishes a flaying knife and holds a blood-filled skull cup to the side with her left hand. Her two legs bend around the side of her back and rest on her shoulders, showing the anthers of her open lotus. With a slender waist and full thighs and vulva, her body is swollen with bliss. She is adorned by the five symbolic ornaments and sits amid a bonfire with three-pointed white flames. White *oṃ* marks her forehead, red *āḥ* her throat, and blue *hūṃ* her heart. Offering goddesses emanated from my heart present the offerings.

oṃ vajra puṣpe . . . (etc. to) . . . *śabda āḥ hūṃ* {254}

Praise:

Glorious Vajra Ḍākinī,
wheel wielder of the ḍākinīs,
five awarenesses and three kāyas—
homage and praise to the protector of migrators.

Supplicate with devotion:

Exalted Vajrayoginī, please grant me your blessings.

Through the force of that supplication:

> White, red, and blue light rays radiate from the *oṃ āḥ hūṃ* in Vajrayoginī's three places. They invoke white, red, and blue light rays that are the nature of the awakened body, speech, and mind of all the ten-direction buddhas and bodhisattvas. Those dissolve into the three seed syllables, from which white, red, and blue light rays emerge, coiling around one another. They travel down the length of the central channel, emerge from her bhaga, and dissolve into my three places. All obstacles of negativities, obscurations, sickness, and spirits are purified. My body, speech, and mind are in essence Vajrayoginī's awakened body, speech, and mind. Cakrasaṃvara and Vajrayoginī appear individually and yet are essentially one in the inseparability of method and wisdom.

In this meditative absorption, focus with single-pointed attention and in a state of knowing everything as illusory, recite:

> *oṃ oṃ oṃ sarva buddha ḍākinīyai vajra varṇanīyai vajra vairocanīyai hūṃ hūṃ hūṃ phaṭ phaṭ phaṭ svāhā*

Repeat this three million, two hundred thousand times or however much is possible. At the end of the session, repeat the offerings and praises as above. Supplicate three times with

> Exalted Vajrayoginī, please lead me to the pure realm of Khecara.

Then meditate on the visualizations of Transference as found below, or just continue here with

> Vajrayoginī melts into light and dissolves into the top of my head, filling my body full with the elixir of bliss and bestowing the blessings of vajra body, speech, and mind.

Rest in the equipoise of Lucid Clarity Mahāmudrā. When you arise from that, dedicate the virtue to awakening. In between all sessions, integrate on the path by regarding all appearances as the deity's body, like illusion. {255} Enjoy food and drink with the understanding that it is the elixir of timeless awareness. All sensory pleasures are the deity's natural appearance of great bliss. At this point, if you would like to offer torma, then follow the description below.

Body Blessing

Now, what's called the body blessing is a profound final dissolution connected with the completion phase. While meditating on Vajrayoginī on the crown of your head, imagine red bodhicitta flows from her lotus at the secret place, enters through your cranial aperture, and fills your body to the brim with redness the nature of light. Special bliss arises joyfully (*sing sing ba*) in your being. Like the condensation of breath on a mirror, your body dissipates from the outer edges inward and gathers into your heart. Finally, relax within emptiness. Settle awareness in limpid radiance. Arise again in the forms of Cakrasaṃvara or Vajrayoginī.

Secret Blessing

In what's called the secret blessing, imagine White Khecarī at the tip of your gem. She melts into reddish light and enters the passageway, completely filling up your body. The afflictive emotion of desire is cleansed and purified. Meditate as above that your body becomes the nature of light, red, full, and so forth. This is lauded as especially good for desire.

Repairing Sacred-Pledge Violations

The method to repair violations of sacred pledge based on that is to first arrange whatever offerings you have, go for refuge, and arouse awakening mind.

> Before me is a lotus and moon seat, upon which is my root guru, with a radiant body and smiling countenance, sitting within clear light.

Increase the offerings, whether actually laid out or mentally emanated, and offer them through just the force of your meditative absorption or by reciting suitable verses. Meditate with fervent faith and devotion, and make fervent supplications. For a short, general version:

Precious guru, unified essence of all buddhas of the three times:
Outwardly I offer flowers and incense;
inwardly, five meats and five elixirs;
secretly, the timeless awareness of bliss-emptiness;
and most secretly, the sublime offering of suchness.
Accept them and purify all violations of my sacred pledge.
Please grant me the supreme spiritual power of mahāmudrā on
this very seat. {256}

Perform the confession with standard verses such as "Guru vajra holder . . ." (*bla ma rdo rje 'dzin pa* . . . etc.), or else using the particular version of recalling and naming [each of] the sacred-pledge violations, such as a lack of respect for your root guru. Then:

White Khecarī is at the point between the guru's eyebrows. White light rays radiate from her secret place, touching all the buddhas and bodhisattvas and pleasing their bodies with offerings. From between their eyebrows, white awareness elixir emerges and enters the guru's head, arousing undissipating bliss. Again, a stream of white light rays emerges from Khecarī's secret place and enters my midbrow point. All negative acts and obscurations, including violations related to the guru's body, are cleansed and purified.

Recite the three-*oṃ* mantra one hundred and eight times. Finally, imagine the following:

Khecarī arrives from afar and dissolves into the point between my eyebrows.

Repeat that formula:

Red Khecarī is at the guru's throat. Red light rays radiate from her secret place, touching all the buddhas and bodhisattvas and pleasing their speech with offerings. From their throats, red awareness elixir emerges and enters the guru's throat, arousing undissipating bliss. Again, a stream of red light rays emerges from

> Khecarī's secret place and enters my throat. All negative acts and obscurations, including violations related to the guru's speech, are cleansed and purified.

Recite the three-*oṃ* mantra one hundred and eight times.

> Khecarī arrives from afar and dissolves into my throat.
>
> Blue Khecarī is at the guru's heart. Blue light rays radiate from her secret place, touching all the buddhas and bodhisattvas and pleasing their minds with offerings. From their hearts, blue awareness elixir emerges and enters the guru's heart, arousing undissipating bliss. Again, a stream of blue light rays emerges from Khecarī's secret place and enters my heart. All negative acts and obscurations, including violations related to the guru's mind, are cleansed and purified.

Recite the three-*oṃ* mantra one hundred and eight times.

> Khecarī arrives from afar and dissolves into my heart.

Rest lucidly in the mahāmudrā of the deity's form and sustain it for a long time. Finally, dedicate the virtue to awakening. Yogins who have completed the required recitations should learn how to accomplish the Khecara [long-life] pills and other practices from the source texts.

Transference

Instructions for the auxiliary yoga of the fast path of the Transference of Consciousness that is held in common with the long lineage are taught in the ancient texts. Here I will present the uncommon version according to the direct lineage.[3] This can follow immediately after the above meditation, recitation, and supplication. Otherwise, if it is to be done separately, first go for refuge and arouse the awakening mind.

Within your ordinary body, the central channel is as straight as an arrow. {257} Its color is white and vividly clear, the nature of light. The lower end reaches the perineum and the upper end the cranial aperture. At the crown of your head is White Khecarī, youthful, attractive, and swollen with great bliss. Her attributes are the same as usual. Her lotus and the upper end of your central channel are in contact. Focus very precisely on that.

Then your skull from the eyebrows up melts into light, which blends with the [contents of] the bhañja (skull cup) in [Khecarī's] hand. Your body from the navel up, including all corporeal matter, flesh, and blood, melts into that skull cup, becoming awareness elixir. She drinks it and is pleased. Within your central channel at the level of the navel, the essence of your vital winds integrated with your mind is the white letter *A*, blazing with light and ready to lift off. Visualize a blue *hūṃ* facing upward at the tip of your sexual organ. Fervently supplicate. Slightly hold a gentle breath. Mentally recite the three-*oṃ* mantra. Pull up from the bottom of the belly and clear out the breath while uttering a long sound of *hik*. Visualize the force of the vital winds of the *hūṃ* offered up to the *A* at the navel, which then shoots right out from inside the central channel like a shooting star. It enters Vajrayoginī's secret place and arrives at her heart. Your mind and Vajrayoginī's mind and emptiness—these three blend inseparably. Rest in that equipoise.

Again, visualize the *A* and the *hūṃ* and so forth as before, repeating that visualization seven times. Then your mind and Vajrayoginī's blessings inseparable become white elixir with a reddish tinge. It emerges from her secret opening, enters through the crown of your head, and fills the four chakras. You receive the four empowerments. In the end, your entire body is filled with bodhicitta and you experience pervasive bliss. Rest in equipoise.

All of that is one short session. Repeat it again from the visualization of the central channel, and keep training as many times as works in each session. When your interest wanes, Vajrayoginī melts into light and dissolves into your head. Think that your cranial aperture is blocked by a golden vajra cross marked with the letter *haṃ*.

For a shorter visualization, say *hik* after the supplication, making the *A* letter lift off from the navel in the central channel. It enters Vajrayoginī's secret place and arrives at her heart. She flies to Khecara, then returns. {258} By uttering *ka*, the *A* letter again falls to the navel in the central channel. Repeat this a number of times. Finally, the *A* melts into the form of elixir and, with your body visualized as before, enters your cranial aperture and becomes the essence of heavy *A* at your navel. Block the cranial aperture. [The practice that includes] the departure of Khecarī constitutes one style. Train in this way until you produce signs [of success].

If you utilize them yourself when dying or apply them for another dying being, the consciousness does not come back down. Raise it up repeatedly until the signs appear. In the end, imagine that Vajrayoginī departs higher and higher into the sky's realm and then maintain unembellished recognition of your nature. It is said that if you practice this Exalted [White Khecarī] as a yidam without interruption, diligently doing the offerings and supplications on the tenth days of the waxing and waning moon, you need have no doubt that you will go to the celestial realm of Khecara.

Red Khecarī

If you wish to practice the yoga of Red Khecarī, the sequence of creation and recitation is preceded by going for refuge and arousing the awakening mind. Then:

> *oṃ svabhāva* . . . (etc.)
> From within emptiness, I appear as Coemergent Cakrasaṃvara radiating five-colored lights. Before me is a double-stacked source of phenomena, white on the outside and red on the inside. It arises as bliss-emptiness. In its center is a seat of a lotus, sun, and human corpse. In its center, the red letter *vaṃ* completely transforms into Vajrayoginī, with a complexion of vermilion. Her three bloodshot eyes glance around. She bares her fangs and slightly grimaces wrathfully with a fierce expression. She is in the prime of youth, with a slender waist and full thighs, vulva, and breasts. She is naked with her hair loose and flowing over her back, beautiful and attractive. In her right hand she holds a vajra pointing down and with her left a blood-filled skull cup held high as she turns to drink from its stream of bliss. In the crook of her left arm is a white khaṭvāṅga, the nature of methods. She is adorned by a tiara of five dry skulls, a garland of fifty fresh skulls, and the five symbolic bone ornaments. Her right leg is extended, pressing on the heart of the human corpse. Her left leg rests behind her shoulder. {259} She stands in the midst of a blazing fire of timeless awareness.

If you wish, make offerings with *oṃ vajra puṣpe* . . . (etc.) and offer praises with "Glorious Vajra Ḍākinī . . . (etc.)." It is also acceptable to skip the offerings and praises. Then supplicate:

> Exalted Vajrayoginī, please grant your blessings.
>
> Light rays from the short *A* in my navel strike the source of phenomena. All habitual tendencies are purified. Light rays radiate from Exalted Vajrayoginī's secret lotus. They strike me, purifying all negativities and obscurations.

Visualize that and recite the three-*oṃ* mantra. At the end of the session, recite the offerings, praises, and supplication. The yoginī visualized in front melts into light and dissolves into you. Dedicate the virtue. For the yoga of session breaks, follow the procedure in the White Khecarī.

The Uncommon Completion Phase

Very clearly visualize yourself as Vajrayoginī with the empty internal space. At your navel is a red eight-petaled lotus radiating light rays of five colors. Imagine that the stamens are candle lights, four finger-widths high. The vital point of the body is to hold the vase breath with its four applications as usual and to let your gaze fall to the tip of your nose. When you are about to lose [holding the breath], apply [methods to prolong it such as] swallowing, causing the bliss-warmth of inner heat to blaze. Blend this with the experience of illusion to naturally raise the illusory body. Placing [the attention] in the throat induces lucid dreams; at the heart, lucid clarity; and at the secret place, gains control of the downward-clearing [vital winds]. When you control them, meditate on the inner heat in karmamudrā and jñānamudrā. Then it is said that meditation on lucid clarity of the final dissolution, as described in the context of White Khecarī, will bring the accomplishment of the ultimate lucid clarity of unified bliss and emptiness. This is the enlightened view of Rāhula and Atiśa.

Transference

When you meditate on Transference in this, [imagine] a blue source of phenomena that is the nature of a womb, and within it your own mind as a deep-blue *hūṃ* radiating light rays. The obscurations of the womb and the habitual tendencies toward that birthplace are purified. The *hūṃ* completely transforms into yourself as the sole hero Cakrasaṃvara. Meditate on the appearance without intrinsic nature, radiating five-colored light rays.

If this is done in connection with the above creation phase and recitation, do the offerings, praises, and supplication, and imagine that Vajrayoginī comes to the top of your head. {260} If it is done separately, precede it with going for refuge and arousing the awakening mind, and then visualize that Vajrayoginī appears instantly above your, Cakrasaṃvara's, head. As before, her two legs rest on your shoulders. Her vulva, like an open red lotus, touches your cranial aperture. At your navel, the essence of your wind-mind is a white *A* ready to ascend, trembling as if buffeted by wind. It looks up and sees, through the clear opening of the cranial aperture, Vajrayoginī's secret place. With the intense yearning to go there, supplicate three times.

A white light ray, like a spider's silk, wends its way from her heart and reaches the *A* at your navel. Like a magnet meeting iron, the string pulls it up through the cranial aperture and into her bhaga. It reaches her heart with a snapping sound. Yoginī quickly ascends into the sky, going higher and higher, and arrives at Khecara, where she disappears like a rainbow. Rest in awareness without thought. Like clouds forming in the sky, Yoginī reappears and arrives back, again placing her two feet on your, Cakrasaṃvara's, shoulders. As she sits there, your mind as the letter *A* breaks off from her heart and descends to your navel, where it again looks upward, and so forth. Repeat the process. During this time, it is crucial to hold the gentle breathing. You can say *hik* [and *ka*] audibly or mentally.

At the end of the session, the *A* falls to your navel. After that, Vajrayoginī melts into light and dissolves into the crown of your head. Alternatively, [visualize that] pink bodhicitta flows from her lotus and fills the four chakras of your body. You obtain the four empowerments and are pervaded by undissipating bliss. Vajrayoginī comes through your cranial aperture and arrives at your navel. Imagine that the timeless awareness of nondual bliss and emptiness is born. Rest in equipoise. Finally, imagine that your cranial aperture becomes solid, the nature of vajra. The working application [at the time of death] is the same as in White Khecarī.

White and Red Khecarīs

Torma Offering

If you wish to offer tormas in the session breaks to both White Khecarī and Red Khecarī, first place a torma of various food and drink in the palm of your left hand. Join the right thumb and ring finger, and cleanse and purify.

> From within emptiness, a white letter *A* becomes a vast and wide skull cup, white on the outside and red on the inside. {261} It is completely filled inside with the five meats marked by *hūṃ - bhrūṃ - oṃ - jriṃ - khaṃ* and the five elixirs.
>
> *oṃ āḥ hūṃ* (repeat three times)—it becomes the elixir of sacred pledge.
> *oṃ āḥ hūṃ* (repeat three times)—it becomes a vast ocean of elixir of timeless awareness.
>
> Exalted Khecarīs appear before me surrounded by an immeasurable entourage of awareness ḍākinīs. *pheṃ!* Deities and retinues extend their tongues of light-ray straws to drink it and are delighted by undissipating bliss.

Repeat three times the three-*oṃ* mantra with the added three seed syllables to offer the torma. Then offer with *arghaṃ* . . . (etc.), praise with "Glorious Vajra Ḍākinī . . . (etc.)," and request awakened activity with "Accept this torma I offer to you . . . (*mchod sbyin gtor ma 'di bzhes la*) . . . (etc.). Repeat the hundred syllables and supplicate for forbearance. Then:

> Exalted ones with their entourages melt into light and dissolve into me.

After the request for awakened activity, if you wish, you can also offer general tormas to the dharma protectors. Take the tormas to a clean place.

Hand Offering

If you wish to do the hand offering before other rituals, such as the tenth-day offerings, consecrate the inner offering as in the torma ritual [above].

> A five-petaled lotus appears on the palm of my left hand.

Place a drop of the inner offering in its center and on the four petals in a counterclockwise order.

> *oṃ vaṃ / haṃ yaṃ / hriṃ maṃ / hriṃ hriṃ / hūṃ hūṃ / phaṭ phaṭ*
> Those seed syllables completely transform into the forms of the six armor heroines.

Offer with *oṃ vajra puṣpe* . . . (etc.) and the inner offering with the three syllables.

> The five elements of my hand are consecrated as the nature of the five families. All the deities dissolve into my hand.

Do the consecration of offerings as usual, or just say *oṃ vajra spharaṇa khaṃ* to mentally consecrate them. Create the deity visualization with "On the wrist of my left hand is a source of phenomena . . . (etc.)."[4] Present the outer offerings with *oṃ vajra yoginī arghaṃ pratīccha svāhā* . . . *pādyaṃ* . . . *oṃ vajra puṣpe āḥ hūṃ* . . . (etc.). Present the inner offering with the three syllables. Recite the eight-line praises that appear below. Supplicate to accomplish your wishes:

> Exalted Vajrayoginī, please grant me all supreme and common spiritual powers without exception. {262} Especially, please guide me to the celestial realm of Khecara.

Do the hundred syllables and the request for forbearance. Make the mudra of embrace at the forehead and say:

> *oṃ yoga śuddhaḥ sarva dharmāḥ yoga śuddho 'haṃ*
> The deity melts into light and dissolves into me.

Alcohol Offering

For this tradition's uncommon alcohol offering or hand offering or removal of all defilement, fill a qualified kapāla with alcohol.

> Instantly I become Exalted Vajrayoginī.

Say the three-*oṃ* mantra while tracing a source of phenomena with your left ring finger [on your right palm in the case of] White Goddess and a two-tiered one on your left palm for Red Goddess.

> The skull cup becomes a source of phenomena as a celestial palace. Inside it, all the alcohol becomes the mantra's bright white seed syllables[5] with the white letter *hrīḥ* above them [radiating white light rays] . . . (etc.).

For Red Khecarī, substitute "red" for "white" and "red letter *vaṃ*," etc. Continue with the creation-phase ritual [of either deity] up through the offerings and praises. Imagine that the three-*oṃ* mantra syllables are touching [each other] like in a necklace and visualize them as if they could be touched.

> The goddess's body and the mantra's syllables emit light rays the nature of elixir. In particular, naturally occurring bodhicitta falls blissfully from her bhaga and fills the skull cup.

Visualize that and do the recitation as much as you can. Afterward:

> The deity and the mantra melt into the nature of elixir, filling the skull cup.

As you repeat each mantra, sprinkle drops in conjunction with the meditation chant. Then:

> All the gurus, yidams, ḍākinīs, and dharma protectors are pleased and delighted by this undissipating bliss in their body, speech, and mind. Innumerable small thick-limbed bodies of Vajrayoginī dissolve into my own three places. Sickness, spirits, negativities, obscurations, defilements, and all things unclean are cleansed and purified. The dwelling place is utterly filled with [forms of the] Exalted One and reverberates with the natural humming sound of the mantras.

Partake of [the elixir] with an especially vivid visualization of yourself in the deity's form, like an illusion. {263}

> All violations of sacred pledge of body, speech, and mind, and all bad karma, negative acts, and obscuration are cleansed and purified. The timeless awareness of coemergent bliss and emptiness arises.

It is taught that by such practice you will quickly see the yidam and realize coemergent bliss-emptiness. You may sprinkle this alcohol offering on feasts, tormas, and even use it to wash yourself. It is important to keep it secret, out of sight of those who lack sacred pledge. You can learn other methods of removing defilements from the teachings of Drogön [Sangye] Tönpa.[6]

Brief Offering for the Tenth Days of the Waxing and Waning Moon[7]

Smear a clean platform with the five cow products.[8] For White Khecarī, arrange upon that the mandala of a white source of phenomena surrounded by a white circle of fire, with a white sphere or heap in the center. On top of that, place a mirror suitable for inscribing and as you say *sumbha ni*... (etc.), smear it with alcohol and vermilion power. Take a gold-nibbed pen in your left hand and as you recite the essence mantra, write the three-*oṃ* mantra string within the center of the vajra source of phenomena.

The process is the same for Red Khecarī except for the following: the mandala is a red double-stacked source of phenomena,[9] outlined by a double white border (*re kha*) around the edges and a vajra in the middle. Arrange five heaps of flowers on that. In the center of the mirror and double-stacked source of phenomena, *vaṃ*[10] is encircled by the three-*oṃ* mantra. Draw seven *āḥ* letters around the edges of that, the armor mantras in the six corners, and [six] joy swirls by the six [outer concave] sides. Upon that, place seven piles of flowers.

In both cases, the best method is to draw the mandalas on cloth and always keep them. If you don't happen to have a gold-nibbed pen and other implements, you can gather them just in imagination. On occasions where you have neither a drawn nor a powder mandala, it is sufficient to draw, with alcohol, a mandala on your hand and place piles of grain. In any case, put a torma of many excellent ingredients before the mandala and arrange the two water offerings, sense offerings, and any other offerings in a counterclockwise order in the shape of a source of phenomena. Put the feast articles to the right and the dharma-protector torma and general tormas to the left. Arrange the inner offerings, preliminary torma and whatever other requisite articles in front of you. {264} Cleanse the preliminary torma with *sumbha ni* . . . (etc.) and purify with *svabhāva* . . . (etc.). Consecrate it with *oṃ āḥ hūṃ ha hoḥ hrīḥ*.

Invoke the guests:

> *pheṃ vajra āralli hoḥ / jaḥ hūṃ vaṃ hoḥ / vajra ḍākinī samayastvaṃ dṛśya hoḥ*

Offer with *oṃ kha kha khāhi* . . . (etc. three times) and *arghaṃ* . . . (etc. through) . . . *śabda*.

Request activity:

> Whoever lives in this place—
> gods, nāgas, yakṣas, rākṣasas, or others—
> I offer this torma for the secret activity.
> Genuinely accept it and
> may we yogins and our retinues . . . (etc.).

With *sumbha ni* . . . (etc.), expel obstructors and cleanse and purify the place and articles.

> From within emptiness, *hūṃ* produces a protection circle. Within it, a celestial palace with completely perfect characteristics arises from *bhrūṃ*. Inside that, *oṃ āḥ hūṃ* produces cloudbanks of vajra offerings that generate undissipating bliss, filling the bounds of space, continually in time and place.
>
> *oṃ vajra arghaṃ svāhā* / . . . *pādyaṃ* . . . *oṃ vajra puṣpe āḥ hūṃ* / (etc. to) . . . *śabda*

Consecrate by saying:

> *oṃ sarva vida pūra pūra / sura sura / āvartaya āvartaya hoḥ / oṃ vajra spharaṇa khaṃ*

Then, if you wish to do an extended ritual, follow the Principal Deities of the Five Tantras or the Five-Deity Cakrasaṃvara from the self-creation through the recitation, dissolution, and rearising of the deity. Or, in brief:

> Instantly I become the form of Glorious Coemergent Cakrasaṃvara.

Repeat the seven syllables one hundred times. Do the hand offering and alcohol offering described above. Cleanse and purify the mandala in front.

> From within emptiness, in the space before me is a white, tetrahedral source of phenomena . . . (etc.).

Continue with the self-visualization of White Khecarī through to the blessing of her three places.

> Light rays radiate from her heart and invoke Vajrayoginī and her entourage from the lands of Oḍḍiyāna and the great city of Khecara—*vajra samājaḥ*.

Circle with the blazing mudra at your forehead.

> *pheṃ*
> From the pure, unembellished dharmakāya,
> saṃbhogakāya displays in the way of illusion.
> Vajrayoginī, with your host of ḍākinīs,
> arise from the basic space of mahāmudrā. {265}
> With your intention for beings' benefit,
> please come here this instant.
> *oṃ vajra āralli hoḥ* . . . (etc.).
>
> Exalted Khecarī is surrounded by a host of the four ḍākinīs and others, such as the five classes of awareness ḍākinīs, as numerous as atoms. Above her are the root and lineage gurus, around her the host of yidam deities, and below her the Swift-Acting Awareness Protector and other dharma protectors and guards, as vast as an ocean. They are invoked and become indivisible with the deities visualized before me—*jaḥ hūṃ vaṃ hoḥ*.

Make offerings, praises, and supplications as above. With the vital points of the visualization, do a bit of the mantra recitation. Again refresh the offerings and consecrate them:

> These supreme waters of mantra,
> pure and flawless and pleasing,
> I offer to you with good faith
> please accept whatever you like.
> *oṃ śrī vajrayoginī sapārivāra arghaṃ pratīccha hūṃ svāhā*

Repeat this, replacing "water" and "*arghaṃ*" with "washing water" and "*pādyaṃ*."

> Flowers, incense, light,
> perfume, food, and music,
> I offer to you with good faith:
> please accept it and be pleased with me.

To the above mantra, [substitute] *vajra puṣpe* through *śabda āḥ hūṃ*. Then if you like, you may recite the full offerings, beginning with "The flower of genuine joy . . . (etc.)" and the offering of fabric with ". . . soft and light . . ."[11]

> From my heart radiates *a ā / i ī / u ū / ṛi ṛī / ḷi ḷī / e ai / o au / aṃ aḥ*. The syllables completely transform into the sixteen offering goddesses that emanate out, filling the sky. *oṃ vīṇe vajrī huṃ hūṃ phaṭ*

Likewise replace with *vaṃśe . . . mṛdaṃge . . . muraje . . . hāsye . . . lāsye . . . gīti . . . nṛtī . . . puṣpe . . . dhūpe . . . āloke . . . gandhe . . . rūpa . . . rasa . . . sparśe . . . dharmadhātu vajrī ṇī*
These are the offerings made by the sixteen awareness goddesses.

> Whatever is excellent throughout time and space—
> form, sound, smell, taste, and texture—
> when I offer with devotion to you, Exalted One,
> please accept it and grant the highest supreme powers. {266}
> *oṃ śrī vajrayoginī saparivara rūpa śabda gandhe rasa sparśe pratīccha svāhā*

The skilled completely fill this realm
with the seven precious possessions;
the wise offer them daily
for the sake of their desired spiritual powers.
oṃ śrī vajrayoginī saparivara śabda mahāratna āḥ hūṃ

Consecrate the inner offering and offer it by flicking drops. Add the three syllables to the three-*oṃ* mantra and recite:

Venerable Khecarī, mother of all victors,
and five-family ḍākinīs—into your mouths *oṃ āḥ hūṃ*.
Vajradhara and others filling space,
root and lineage gurus—into your mouths *oṃ āḥ hūṃ*.
Cakrasaṃvara and others, the yidam deities,
pervading the interspaces—into your mouths *oṃ āḥ hūṃ*.
Protector sister and brother, oath-bound dharma protectors,
covering the ground—into your mouths *oṃ āḥ hūṃ*.
All beings from four modes of birth in five states,
imagined as Yoginī—into your mouths *oṃ āḥ hūṃ*.

Taste the elixir [while saying] the three syllables.

oṃ sarva tathāgata anurāgaṇa vajra svabhāva ātmako 'haṃ
Here there is no beginning, middle, or end.
No existence and no transcendence of it.
No self and also no other.
This is supreme great bliss itself.

Rest in equipoise with that thought to complete the offerings. If you are interested in a longer series of offerings, take them from other similar sources. Then do the eight-line praise, adding the sounds of cymbals and drums.

oṃ
Bhagavatī Vajravārāhī, Exalted One,
invincible mother of the three worlds, awareness goddess,
sovereign who dispels fears of spirits, great vajra,
undefeated power on the Vajra Seat, undefeated by others,

magic eyes that desiccate poison, fierce one, wrathful one, barer of fangs,
terrifying, killing, destroying, totally victorious over others,
Vajravārāhī, you stun, stupefy, and paralyze,
I bow to great Yoginī, sovereign of desire, ḍākinī.
hūṃ hūṃ phaṭ

Also do the one verse praise:

Glorious Vajra Ḍākinī,
[wheel wielder of the ḍākinīs
with fivefold awareness and three kāyas;
homage to the protector of migrators.] {267}

Vajra Ḍākinīs, however many there are,
who cut the bonds of concepts,
and fully enter worldly activity:
I bow and praise all of you.

Four elements radiate from the navel center
with dharmakāya and saṃbhogakāya.
She who gathers the ḍākinīs,
Exalted One, I bow and praise you.

Do just this much, or if you are able and willing, recite any appropriate praises, such as the two kinds of praises to White Khecarī by Jowo Je [Atiśa] or praises to the Red Khecarī from other sources. Then continue with this praise:

Bhagavatī, mother of all victorious ones,
the real perfection of wisdom of the realm of phenomena,
with the body of undissipating coemergent bliss-emptiness,
Vajra Queen, I bow at your feet.

I present vast clouds of outer, inner, and secret offerings;
sincerely confess every individual fault;
rejoice; request the turning of the dharma wheel;
supplicate you to remain always; and dedicate this to awakening.

I go for refuge until I attain awakening
and arouse the awakening mind in the highest vehicle.

I will take the four empowerments, stay on the path of sacred
pledge,
refine my being in blessings, meditate on the two phases,
enjoy the three wonderful conducts, and so forth:
I will rely on all approaches.

With stable meditative absorption, I will accomplish unrestricted
activity,
gather the three messengers, attain the eight powers,[12] and so on,
imbued with the ability to perform the benefit of migrators,
may I attain the state of glorious Heruka in this life.

At this juncture, offer the torma. Consecrate it as explained before, then continue with "Exalted ones and retinues extend their tongues . . . (etc.)," including the offering, praises, and request of awakened activity.

Then for the feast offering, follow the feast offering of Five-Deity Cakrasaṃvara called *Increasing Awakened Activity*.[13] {268} At the beginning of the descent of blessings, add:

oṃ
The immutable joyous realm of Akaniṣṭha
in the pure bliss-emptiness of Khecara,
Lady Perfection of Wisdom
renowned as Vajrayoginī,
surrounded by ḍākinīs of three regions,
I practice following in your footsteps:
please come here to grant your blessings.

Since this is a condensed [version of the feast], there is no need to do the words of symbolic offering and accepting, such as "Regard the phenomena here . . . (etc.)."[14] Consecrate the leftovers. It is sufficient to offer with just the moderate *oṃ kha kha* . . . (etc.). Afterward, refresh the offerings and consecrate them. Present the outer offerings with just the mantra. Present the inner offerings by adding the three syllables to the essence mantra. Recite the eight-line praise. Supplicate for your desires with this and other prayers:

> Exalted Vajrayoginī, please grant me all supreme and common spiritual powers without exception and guide me to the celestial realm of Khecara.

Repeat the one hundred syllables three times, and

> Inferior mantras, inferior rituals,
> inferior actions—whatever I've done:
> main epitome of the profound and sublime,
> Goddesses, it is reasonable to forbear.
>
> Authentic goddess and authentic pledge,
> the authenticity of their words are supreme.
> May that truth become the cause
> for those goddesses to accept me.

Say that and other aspiration prayers. If you have a representation [of the deity], let the awareness beings from the front visualization remain in that. The pledge beings melt through the crown of your head, dissolve, and so forth as in the self-visualization, and then dedicate the virtue. If you do not have a representation, both the pledge and awareness beings dissolve into you. Send the guest deities back to their own places with *sarva gaccha*. Recite the *Sealed Word of Auspiciousness*[15] or any appropriate verses spoken directly [by the masters] in order to create happiness and well-being.

[Conclusion and Colophon]

The White and Red Khecarī practices are well known as the flowers of the Five Golden Dharmas that form the core of the Shangpa teachings. However, apart from the continuity of textual transmission (*lung*) of the three permissions for blessing,[16] some ancient texts, and the guidance tradition of Transference, the records (*yig cha*) have mostly not survived. {269} In the case here, though there are certainly suitable records of the works created by excellent adepts of the past, [no one has] witnessed even the texts, let alone their transmissions and permissions. Therefore, the continuity of the practice of this profound dharma itself has declined and left us destitute. So, taking the excellent teachings of the all-knowing Venerable One as a basis, I gathered the quintessential intent of the ancient writings and whatever extra adornments that were appropriately consistent and justifiable and made this clear arrangement.

With faith in this dharma and a mind to benefit others,
I audaciously compiled what I thought was proper.
Though my childish mind has strayed from the profound meaning,
I confess the contradictions and errors to the guru and gods.

May the Vajra Queen nurture all migrators.
In the joyous palace of liberation, Khecara,
may I become lord of the assembly with compassion's power
to guide all migrators to that celestial realm.

Karma Ngawang Yönten Gyatso, with undivided trust in this profound dharma, completed this composition at Devīkoṭi Tsadra Rinchen Drak, the remote retreat of glorious Palpung, on the gathering of the ḍākinīs celebration during the waning moon.

12. In Praise of Vajrayoginī, the Especially Exalted Praise[1]

Atiśa Dīpaṃkara

Sanskrit: *Vajrayoginīstotra*
Tibetan: *rDo rje rnal 'byor ma la bstod pa*

Homage to Vajra Khecarī.
Khecarī appears from *hrīḥ*.

You rest in space on a pure lotus and moon,
since you ease the torment of afflictions.

[Your body] is youthful and very beautiful,
in the manner of a sixteen-year-old.

You are the color of the autumn moon, radiating light,
since you are untouched by the flaws of cyclic existence.

You call *hūṃ* and *phaṭ*, the echoes of empty sound,
since you wake us from the sleep of ignorance.

Your mind is the unity of nonduality,
coemergent bliss and emptiness.

Your two legs rest behind your two shoulders
so that we may enjoy the space.

Your bhaga swells wide open
since you lead migrators to the celestial realm.

Your lower body sports bone ornaments
to show methods and wisdom are not dual.

Your body is full with rising breasts
since you are passionate and full of bliss.

You brandish a flaying knife in the right hand
since you sever ignorance at the root.

You raise a skull cup to space with the left
since you drip with nondual elixir.

Your face is smiling and wrathful
since the welfare of beings delights you.

Your three eyes look intensely into space
since you see the buddhas of ten directions.

Your head is crowned by five dry skulls
since you completely perfect the five kāyas.

Your dark-blue hair is jet black
since true reality is immutable.

Your braids with bones press on your back
since you suppress habitual afflictions.

You proudly wear a lovely silk-ribboned tiara
since you possess a charming air.

You are fully decorated in precious gems:
tiara, earrings, armbands, {272}
choker, garland, necklace,
bracelets, and anklets,
since all good qualities adorn you.

A string of fifty human heads forms your garland[2]
since you abandon all conceptual thought.

You dwell within a mountain of white fire
since the firewood of afflictions burns up.

Masses of rainbow lights surround you
since you possess the meaning of illusion.

I pay homage and praise Khecarī,
I bow and praise you who guide
to the pure celestial realm of Khecara
if those with faith, diligence, and sacred pledge
supplicate you with offerings and praises.

Goddess, remain before me in space
bless my body, speech, and mind,
and as soon as my body and awareness part,
please take me straight to the heart of Khecara.[3]

Composed by Paṇḍita Dīpaṃkara and translated by the paṇḍita himself and Lotsāwa Rinchen Zangpo.

13. White Khecarī Transference[1]

Lochen Gyurme Dechen

oṃ svasti

Exalted Yoginī amid the swirling light waves
of the rainbow, mighty one of celestial space,
anointed with the autumn moon's radiance, is youthful.
With agility she changes and displays anything at all:
she clearly shows the fortunate ones
the supreme mandalas,
and in the same instant bestows
the timeless awareness of great bliss.

The name Naiguptā (or *guhya*)[2] means "definitely concealed" or "she who is definitely secret." Abbreviated, it becomes Niguma, who is renowned as a mighty lady who moves through space with an immortal rainbow body. She actually revealed her face in visionary experience to the great universal emperor of adepts known as Tangtong Gylapo, whose fame resounds like thunderclouds completely filling the sky's expanse. She conferred the four empowerments in their entirety in the supreme great mandala and he was completely filled with the youthful vitality of the four ecstasies. At that time, they fully engaged in every form of the great secret conduct, such as questions and responses, symbols and countersymbols, and the delightful enjoyment of the amazing pleasures of a communal feast.

On that occasion, she opened the magical esoteric instructions for the individual vajra lines by means of their three [levels of interpretation]: direct, implied, and concealed. In particular, she bestowed the extremely profound instructions on Transference of the Infallible White and Red Khecarīs, together with the teachings by means of two examples sealed by her command. From his practice of these instructions, Tangtong Gyalpo mastered an unimaginable repertoire of attainments, such as the instantaneous display of countless physical forms in a single moment, the clairvoyant knowledge of others' minds, and the ability to actually transfer his and others' [consciousness]. {274}

Later, on the peak known as glorious Riwoche in Latö Jang, in the adept's own residence, he was granted permission by the ḍākinī and subsequently committed this profound path to writing as the *Collection of Essentials* and affiliated texts.[3] However, the oral instructions for the Transference practices of White and Red Khecarīs were transmitted only by drawings illustrating two examples. Apart from those, he had not written a record of the oral advice, and so it was not widely known.[4] He stated in the *Collection of Essentials*, "There is a separate oral instruction for Transference to the Unerring Celestial Realm." This is that [instruction].

Within your body, the central channel is straight as an arrow, radiantly clear, and the nature of light. The lower end reaches the perineum and the upper end faces the cranial aperture. Above your head, Exalted White Khecarī embodies the experience of great bliss. Meditate that her lower body is right above your cranial aperture. Then the inside of your head above the eyebrows melts into light, which dissolves into the vessel that sustains bliss in Khecarī's hand and becomes indivisible with it. Then your body from the navel up—including all corporeal matter, flesh, and blood—is consecrated as elixir in that skull cup, which is presented as offering to Khecarī. At that time, the Khecarī who sits on your central channel is like a bird landing on a treetop. That is the first example.

With the outside of your body not visualized, only the central channel appears. It is like a derelict stupa that has collapsed, leaving only the central axis (*srog shing*). That is the second example.

Exalted Khecarī visualized above your head appears youthful and attractive, with small, round nipples. Her two legs rest on the back of her shoulders, clearly displaying her bhaga, the source of great bliss. Focus your attention there. {275} This image is an unsurpassable skillful method to draw your consciousness upward.

These [teachings represent] the drawn examples of the great adept [Tangtong Gyalpo's] own uncommon esoteric instructions. They were given to me joyfully by Venerable [Kunga] Drolchok Rinpoche, so they are not muddled by the mud of my own inventions.

The awareness ḍākinī's moist breath has not faded
from the profound instructions of Khecarī Transference
that comes from the lineage of the heroic adepts
and now rests in the drop in my heart's center.

Thus, delighting in the elixir of this profound path,
exhorted by command of Venerable Ngakgi Wangpo,[5]
I, the bilingual one (Lochen Gyurme Dechen) in this great nation,
compiled this during the tenth day, when the ḍākinīs gather.

sarva maṅgalaṃ Virtue!

14. Red Khecarī Transference[1]

Rāhulagupta

namo guru
Red Khecarī's Transference of Consciousness practice has three parts: (1) the preliminary, (2) main part, and (3) conclusion.

I. Preliminary

Set up the mandala as in the short text. Arrange six tormas. Do the five offerings and the kapāli and so forth for the prelude. Then relate the story of how Lama Rāhula and Lama Shangpa met.[2] Have [the disciples] imagine Exalted Lady surrounded by the lineage gurus on a mandala of vermilion and do a brief refuge and awakening mind prayer.

II. Main Practice

Now meditate like this: Imagine before you there is a blue tetrahedral source of phenomena. Imagine within it a blue *hūṃ*. Light rays radiate from that and purify the obscurations of the womb. They return and fully melt [the *hūṃ*], which transforms into oneself as Sole Hero Cakrasaṃvara holding a vajra in the right hand and a bell in the left. Visualize this as appearance without intrinsic nature, radiating light rays of five colors. Then meditate on the vermilion mandala as a double-stacked tetrahedral source of phenomena, white on the outside and red on the inside, made of bliss and arising as bliss with the nature of light. Within it is Vajrayoginī. With yourself as Cakrasaṃvara, imagine a white drop within the navel, the essence of the syllable *A*. Imagine five-colored light rays radiating from that, purifying the obscurations of the womb for oneself and others. Then the essence of your mind in the form of that *A* rises up in a flash of white and arrives at your heart. From there it leaves through the left nostril and moves out to melt into Vajrayoginī's heart, leaving your body empty. With that impetus and the sound of impact [when *A* strikes the heart],[3] Vajrayoginī rises far up and shoots like an arrow as far as the celestial realm of Khecara. {278} Do this meditation seven times with such visualization.

Afterward, think that Khecarī descends in a flash from Khecara and comes to sit on the crown of your head with her two legs apart. From her lotus a stream of white bodhicitta with a tinge of red trickles down and enters your cranial aperture, filling your whole body with bodhicitta. Focus on the visualization of the expanding wave of undissipating bliss while saying the three-*oṃ* mantra a number of times and playing music.

The bodhicitta reaching the crown center is the vase empowerment; the throat is the secret empowerment; the heart is the wisdom-awareness empowerment; and the navel is the fourth empowerment. Rest your mind for a moment in that.

Then Vajrayoginī dissolves through your cranial aperture and arrives at the navel. Think that emptiness pervades bliss and the experience of nondual bliss-emptiness is born. Rest within that state without contrivance. Now meditate without a break in sessions.

III. Conclusion

At the time of dying, meditate as before. Then think of that drop at your navel as Vajrayoginī, the essence of your consciousness. She rises up from the navel and goes far out from your cranial aperture, all the way to Khecara. Rest within unborn mahāmudrā. Until your breath stops, meditate again and again with focused attention on that visualization. That will take you to Khecara.

[Colophon]

This completes the instructions of Lama Rāhula called *Vital Drop Transference* that blocks the five birthplaces all at once. It is said that just by receiving the empowerment, one will not be born in the five birthplaces, so have confidence.

Sukhasiddhi, Ḍākinī of Timeless Awareness

Introduction

Sukhasiddhi was one of the main Indian teachers of Khyungpo Naljor. She along with the ḍākinī Niguma represent the deep source of the Shangpa lineage in two powerful and mysterious women. The story of Sukhasiddhi, whose name translates into Tibetan as Dewai Ngödrup, "Spiritual Power of Bliss," is recounted in the first text of this section. As with Niguma, she also was born in Kashmir, which during their time (10th–11th centuries) was still a locus of tantric practice. And again like Niguma, she was said to receive teachings directly from the Buddha Vajradhara. The details of her story are both compelling and somehow familiar, with multiple layers of meaning. It begins with her in the situation of a sixty-year-old housewife who makes the unforgivable "mistake" of feeding a starving beggar (perhaps a siddha) rather than hoarding food for her family, after which she is banished from her home. She fends for herself with a home-brew start-up, which leads to her encounter with the beer-drinking forest yogi called Virūpa. This Virūpa is not the same as his counterpart of the same name famous for the vajra lines in the Sakya tradition. She receives esoteric instructions and initiations from this "Shangpa Virūpa," the result of which finds her transformed into a beautiful young woman of sixteen. Though the material that Khyungpo Naljor received from Niguma and brought back with him from India forms the foundation of Shangpa practice, his relationship with Sukhasiddhi, with its hints of intimacy beyond that of teacher-disciple, is reflected in the special esoteric character of the practices presented below.

Sukhasiddhi also figures prominently in the Pacification (*zhi byed*) and Severance (*gcod*) traditions. In the Severance tradition, she appears in the lineage directly after the Buddha Tārā, presumably a position indicating her ability to channel Tārā's direct teachings, as with those of Vajradhara. Āryadeva the Brahmin comes after her in the lineage. This Āryadeva, not to be confused with Nāgārjuna's Āryadeva, was the maternal uncle of the great South Indian adept Dampa Sangye (also known as Pa Dampa), who spent years in Tibet propounding teachings that became known as the Pacification of Suffering. This Āryadeva the Brahmin also authored the only Indian text that is regarded as a source for the Severance tradition that was developed by the great Tibetan yoginī Machik Lapdrön.[1] Dampa Sangye is positioned after Āryadeva the Brahmin, but Sukhasiddhi is also counted as one of Dampa Sangye's fifty-four human male and female teachers, specifically one of the "ten ḍākinī gurus that introduced intrinsic awareness."[2] Dampa gathered pithy verses, or dohas, from his numerous Indian masters, presented in four somewhat overlapping anthologies found in the Tibetan canon. Those attributed to Sukhasiddhi certainly reveal her as a ḍākinī who points out the nature of awareness:

> Releasing the power in awareness
> naturally dissolves conceptual thinking,
> and one abides in naked awareness.
> This is the instruction of Sukhasiddhi.[3]

and

> Make it real;
> you'll not turn back.
> That's Sukhasiddhi's perspective.[4]

This ability is emphasized in the iconography of Sukhasiddhi in Tibetan tangkhas as a youthful white beauty pointing with her finger up to "unborn space." The important connection with Dampa Sangye would explain his surprising appearance in artistic depictions and some of the visualizations in the following Shangpa texts. There have been a number of close encounters and crossovers between these traditions, such as with Sangye Nyentön Chökyi Sherap and other Shangpa lineage holders.

The following texts are mostly from ancient and rare sources. Some versions are contained in other collections, most notably in Kunga Drolchok's *One Hundred and Eight Teaching Manuals of Jonang*, and in various Shangpa anthologies. Many of the old texts present similar content in slightly different ways, leading one to suspect the existence of multiple editions that went separate ways over time. They tend to contain interlinear notes by an unknown editor (here in small font). The first set of older texts have Sanskrit titles and occasionally identify the author and translator. For instance, the first title is actually a set of four distinct texts, as the title indicates: *Sukhasiddhi's Story, Indian Source Text, Secret Sādhana of the Navel Emanation Chakra, and Empowerment Ritual.* The first of these is the well-known tale, related above, of Sukhasiddhi. The lineage as it appears in the colophon identifies the recipient as a certain Jampa Rinchen Zangpo. He is positioned right where one would expect to find Jonang Kunga Drolchok. (Could it be one of his names?). *Sukhasiddhi's Indian Source Text* is identified in its colophon to be the *Secret Sādhana Practice of the Navel Emanation Chakra.* This might have been brought to Tibet by Khyungpo Naljor, and was translated as usual by Lendarma Lodrö. However, Tāranātha states otherwise.[5] With the same name, the *Secret Sādhana of the Navel Emanation Chakra* is by Sangye Nyentön Chökyi Sherap, and begins with an homage to his teacher Kyergangpa. Another edition in *Khyungpo's Collected Works* states that both of those texts were based on the *Ocean of Vows Latter Tantra*, a very common but not extant source for ancient Shangpa literature. Finally, the *Empowerment Ritual* has the same information as the above, with Khyungpo Naljor and Lendarma Lodrö as the preservers of what must be taken to be Sukhasiddhi's actual teachings.

The two texts in chapters 16 and 17, which are really considered as one, were authored by Jamgön Kongtrul himself. *Bringing Down the Rain of Great Bliss: A Lineage Supplication for the Profound Path of Sukha's Six Dharmas* and *Fast Path of Integral Unity: Awareness Ḍākinī Sukhasiddhi's Profound Path of Creation and Guidance on the Six Dharmas* present the lineage and Kongtrul's systematic practical instructions for the two phases: the creation phase of deity visualization and the completion phase of the Six Dharmas of Sukhasiddhi. These are the same six as those of Niguma and of Nāropa. Here there is a sense of more karmamudrā-style visualizations or in-person practices that somehow fit with Sukhasiddhi's character. There is also reference to particular elaborations based on Bodong Chokle Namgyal's direct transmission on longevity from the two ḍākinīs in the conclusion. This, and Sukhasiddhi's Six Dharmas and mahāmudrā instructions are the ones still in practice today. Kongtrul's colophon makes that clear:

> In general, in the dharma cycle of Awareness Ḍākinī [Sukhasiddhi], Nairātmya's inner guidance and the cycle of Vārāhī's secret sādhana came from Khedrup Khyungpo himself and later were directly received by the great Nyentön. From among the few

> highly valuable teachings of incredibly profound instructions, such as the *Three Nails of Creation Phase* [and] the *Navel Emanation Chakra*, these days most of the ancient writings are no longer extant, other than in the reading transmissions and what's included in the *One Hundred Teaching Manuals [of Jonang]*. However, the basis is these two: this Six Dharmas and the mahāmudrā timeless awareness. Khedrup Khyungpo retrieved these Golden Dharmas through his difficult labors and precious treasure. Because of that, those with noble minds in the future will maintain its continuity and, having obtained its blessings, will readily attain the two spiritual powers through effort in just these main practices. This is the assured promise of the Ḍākinī of Timeless Awareness.

The next set in chapter 18 contains six ancient texts from the cycle of oral instructions (*zhal gdams kyi skor*). In some sources they appear under the title *Blazing Light of Bliss-Clarity*. These include oral instructions on the four empowerments (although four empowerments are not apparent); on introducing the nature of mind; on the sādhana practice; on the Navel Emanation Chakra; on close attainment; and on the esoteric instructions of the Three Nails. This set includes mainly practices involving the visualization of the sexual union of Sukhasiddhi (in essence the buddha Nairātmya) and Virūpa (in essence Hevajra), facilitated by Dampa Sangye (in essence one's guru). How does Dampa do that? By providing his bamboo cane or flute as a conduit for the flow of elixir between the visualized couple and one's cranial aperture so that it fills the body with bliss. Bliss is the main focus of all of Sukhasiddhi's oral instructions. In Kongtrul's list of practices in *The Beryl Key*, one original text on Sukhasiddhi's Six Dharmas is missing here, perhaps because he included his own commentary on that subject. Most of these short texts were bestowed by Sukhasiddhi directly in a visionary encounter on Sangye Nyentön Chökyi Sherap (1175–1255), the sixth of the initial Seven Jewels of the one-to-one lineage.

Chapter 19, *Sukhasiddhi's Introduction to Mahāmudrā*, is likewise teachings that were transmitted directly to Sangye Nyentön, as he is also known. This contains two texts: the actual practice advice for mahāmudrā, and instructions from the aural lineage, sometimes called the whispered lineage. This latter includes five techniques for resting, ten methods for integrating, and five convictions for vajra-like meditative absorption. Due to the complexity of the ancient materials with multiple texts lumped together under a single title, a brief outline is provided here:

Chapter 15: *Sukhasiddhi's Story, Indian Source Text, Secret Sādhana of the Navel Emanation Chakra, and Empowerment Ritual*
- I. Sukhasiddhi's Story
- II. Indian Source Text
- III. Navel Emanation Chakra Secret Sādhana
- IV. Empowerment Ritual
- V. Additional Instructions

Chapter 16: *Bringing Down the Rain of Great Bliss: A Lineage Supplication for the Profound Path of Sukha's Six Dharmas*

Chapter 17: *Fast Path of Integral Unity: Awareness Ḍākinī Sukhasiddhi's Profound Path of Creation and Guidance on the Six Dharmas*

Chapter 18: *Sukhasiddhi's Cycle of Oral Instructions and Instructions on Three Nails*
- I. Four Empowerments Oral Instructions
- II. Introduction [to Mind] Oral Instructions
- III. Sādhana Oral Instructions
- IV. Navel Emanation Chakra Oral Instructions
- V. Close Attainment Oral Instructions
- VI. Esoteric Instructions on the Three Nails

Chapter 19: *Sukhasiddhi's Introduction to Mahāmudrā*
- I. Introduction to Mahāmudrā
- II. Aural Lineage Instructions

15. Sukhasiddhi's Story, Indian Source Text, Secret Sādhana of the Navel Emanation Chakra, and Empowerment Ritual[1]

Khyungpo Naljor and
Sangye Nyentön Chökyi Sherap

I. Sukhasiddhi's Story[2]

Sanskrit: *Sukhasiddhi*
Tibetan: *bDe ba'i dngos grub kyi lo rgyus*
The Story of Dewai Ngödrup, "Spiritual Power of Bliss"

Homage to the glorious Exalted Ḍākinī!

Of the thirty-eight hundred thousand great cities of Kashmir, this takes place in a northwest city. In that city there lived a couple with three sons and three daughters. Those eight family members were extremely poor and becoming destitute, with nothing but a single jar full of grain for provisions. They wouldn't eat that, so they covered it and hid it. Then the three sons went south in search of food, the three daughters went north, the father went west, [and the mother stayed home]. When a poor starving beggar came asking for something to eat, the mother opened the jar of grain, cooked it up, and gave it to him.[3] Meanwhile, the father, not finding anything to eat, had become famished and thin. He thought, "At home there was that full jar of grain to eat, I need to get that," and he turned back. The three sons also hadn't found anything, so they went back. The three daughters hadn't found anything and likewise returned. {281} As if they had consulted one another, they all returned at the same time. They said, "Mother, please give us the jar full of grain. We have grown thin with hunger and will be depleted." The mother replied, "I thought you all would return with food, so when a destitute beggar came here begging for food, I gave him the grain; there is nothing left." The husband and three sons said, as if with one voice, "You did something like this before and it did not make us happy. This time you did not come [with us] to look for food, and you exhausted our stores. Now get out of here." So they banished her from home.

Then the old woman left Kashmir and traveled west, arriving in the country of Oḍḍiyāna. There in Oḍḍiyāna, all who are born as males are exclusively heroes and all who are born as females are exclusively heroines. It is said that innate awareness is naturally brightened by merely reaching that holy place. Sukhasiddhi gathered some grain seeds and by cultivating them she produced a load of grain. {282} She carried that into the village and became a beer merchant.

At that time, there was a black master named Virūpa or Avadhūtipa living in the forest with his mudra (female partner) Avadhūtima, with whom he practiced secret conduct. That yoginī frequently came to purchase beer. When she bought beer from that old woman beer seller, the woman always sold her beer that was more delicious than any other. The old woman asked, "Yoginī, to whom do you convey this beer that you buy?" She replied, "I take it to an excellent yogi who lives in the forest up there." "In that case, there is no need to pay for it," said the old woman, who then chose the best of the beer for her to take.

Virūpa questioned her, saying, "Yoginī, how is it that you come with only the finest beer without even needing to pay for it?" She replied, "There is a faithful one unlike our previous beer merchants. I [told her] that I take the beer to my excellent guru who lives in the forest. Faith arose in her and she sent the beer." Virūpa said, "Yoginī, I must definitely deliver that old woman from the three realms. Bring her here." The yoginī went to the old woman's place and said, "My guru Virūpa told me to bring the beer seller because he must deliver her from cyclic existence. Will you come?" The old woman was very intrigued and came to meet the yogi carrying a jug full of beer. Venerable Virūpa conferred the complete fourfold empowerment of the Secret Sādhana of the Navel Emanation Chakra right on the spot. {283} He also taught her the creation and completion phases, the Six Dharmas, and magnetizing activity, including the three kinds of gathering.[4] Sukhasiddhi became a ḍākinī of timeless awareness at that time.

When her husband and children exiled her from Kashmir, she was fifty-eight years old.[5] After reaching Oḍḍiyāna and becoming a beer merchant, she was sixty. By the time she met Virūpa and received the empowerments, she was sixty-one years old.

One evening, on the strength of attaining spiritual powers, her fully ripened body of a sixty-one-year-old was naturally purified and transformed into a rainbow body. She appeared youthful and in the prime of youth, her body utterly white, her silken hair falling loose down her back, like someone at the stage of a sixteen-year-old on whom one could never tire of gazing. She dwells in the sky at the height of seven tāla trees (palmyra) and is known as the Awareness Ḍākinī Sukhasiddhi. That ḍākinī became the actual Bhagavatī Nairātmya. She was also the secret consort of Virūpa, who was identical with Hevajra. Even now, never passing away, she is constantly present in the six times,[6] watching all beings of the three realms with her timeless awareness. Beyond that, she makes a special appearance to those with pure outlook to teach them dharma. For all those who practice the secret sādhana and supplicate her, she actually manifests her blessings and enables them to attain all the supreme and common spiritual powers. Therefore, those who hear the life story of that awareness ḍākinī, or even just hear her name, will develop great devotion.[7]

[Khyungpo Naljor's account:]

> Deeply moved by the seeds of faith, I, Khyungpo Naljor, traveled all over India. {284} Then, above the forest of sandalwood trees, in the midst of swirling light seven palmyra trees high in the sky, I saw her from afar, surrounded by innumerable ḍākinīs. Then I came before her and, after prostrating and circumambulating, I offered her five measures of gold and requested authentic instructions. She conferred the complete uncommon empowerment as well as oral instructions on the creation and completion phases of the secret sādhana, the Six Dharmas, and the three gatherings. In particular, she granted the especially elevated vital points to attain buddhahood in just years or months and every vital point of Secret Mantra. Of my four root gurus, the one who was especially kind to me was Sukhasiddhi. Her first kindness was to teach me many transmissions. Her middle kindness was to

> become my secret consort and bestow every empowerment. The final great kindness was to give me all the empowerment practices with oral instructions. Furthermore, she was never apart from me while anywhere in India and Tibet and always grants blessings and confers the complete four empowerments. The really great kindness was to continuously teach the vital points of Secret Mantra. Future generations of disciples will also accomplish this revealed secret sādhana.

Lama Mokchokpa said:

> One time while I was practicing at Dingma, I saw Sukhasiddhi face to face for the first time. At that time she conferred the complete four empowerments and gave many teachings. Then one time when I was staying in practice on the cliffside of Mokchok, Sukhasiddhi came and made many prophecies. From that time on she has never left me.

Lama Kyergangpa said:

> When I went to the Magical Appearance (Jokhang temple) in Lhasa, this Sukhasiddhi taught me many completion-phase practices. {285} She always confers the complete four empowerments. She is never apart from me for even a moment.

Sangye Nyentön said:

> I had gone to Kyergang and was staying in some caves when I saw Sukhasiddhi face to face. Three times she said, "Yogi, rest awareness without support." We have not been apart since then. She gave me the specially elevated instructions of the four empowerments and made many prophecies. She proclaimed, "If you and your disciples wish to attain enlightenment in just years or months, stay in remote places and secretly practice this secret sādhana."

The lineage of succession is Chöje Tönpa, Khedrup Shangtön, Khetsunpa [Zhönu Drup], Khyungpo Tsulgön, Ritrö Rechen, Shangpa Karpo, Sangye

Palzang, the one named Namkha, and incarnate Rinpoche Sangye Chökyi Kunga Tashi Ngawang Gyaltsen Palzangpo.[8] That holy one gave it to me, Jampa Rinchen Zangpo, with love.

II. Sukhasiddhi's Indian Source Text

Sanskrit: *Vajravārāhīguhyasādhanāma*
Tibetan: *rDo rje phag mo'i gsang ba'i sgrub pa*

Homage to glorious Vajrayoginī.

Regarding the subject of the ḍākinī (in Oḍḍiyāna), the mandala is vermilion. You appear as Vārāhī with a (red) source of phenomena at the navel. In its center is a four-petaled lotus with *oṃ-mo* in its center, *ha-'o* in front, *ri-'o* on the right, *ni-'o* in the back, and *sa-'o* on the left [petals]. They are all red in color (with green outlines). They have the nature of intoxicants. Red light rays with the shape of hooks radiate from those sets of letters. {286} They draw in the ruby-colored magical abilities of magnetizing from all buddhas, bodhisattvas, heroes, and ḍākinīs, which dissolve [into those letters]. Their magical ability has the form of red light. It is planted at the point between the eyebrows (the heart also occurs) and the secret place of the visualized one. Like kiṃśu leaves moved by the wind, the practice consort[9] along with sense pleasures cannot help but gather on the lotus. Then the source of phenomena's opening draws closed. Light rays of the unmoving letters are planted in the two places as before. The lotus ([moves] very quickly), as if motionless. The rapid, uncontrollable circling causes the practice consort along with the sense pleasures to become (thoroughly red) like vermilion. Look with threefold nakedness (of the partner's body, speech, and mind). Exert effort in single-pointed focus on threefold nonabiding (of body, speech, and mind). Then the three gatherings (of humans, ḍākinīs, food and wealth) and the three arisings (of physical well-being, verbal ability, and mental realization) will occur. Seven hundred thousand (mantras) will make you the lord of the world. In six months you will attain the fourteenth level. Control comes through a passionate mind. Supreme [powers] come through nonconceptual mind. Keeping secret and silent and free of doubt is the sacred pledge.

The *Secret Sādhana Practice of the Navel Emanation Chakra*, [from the *Ocean of Vows Latter Tantra*],[10] revealed by Ḍākinī Sukhamasiddhi[11] is complete.

Translated by Lotsāwa Lendarma Lodrö. I, Khyungpo Naljor, brought it into my experience.
maṅgalaṃ

III. Sukhasiddhi's Secret Sādhana of the Navel Emanation Chakra[12]

The awakened heart abides within lucid clarity. {287}
Knowing appearance and sound as illusion, unattached,
the deity's body enacts the welfare of migrators.
I bow to the glorious Kyergangpa.[13]

This instruction of vital points of the ḍākinī has two subjects: [the ritual service of] (1) approach and of (2) near accomplishment.

A. Approach

This has two parts: (1) meditation on creation phase with recitation and (2) completion phase.

1. Creation Phase with Recitation

This has three parts: (1) preliminaries, (2) main practice, and (3) conclusion [which appears after completion phase].

a. Preliminaries

Stay in a pleasant, isolated place, such as a mountain retreat, and sit on a soft, comfortable seat. Sit tight with the positions of meditative stability. [Develop] love, compassion, and the awakening mind first, then supplicate three times with *hūṃ*.

b. Main Practice

The practice of the main part is conveyed in the tantra:

> Once burned by the light of the letter *A*,
> there is nothing at all that will not be achieved.

Meditate on yourself as Vajravārāhī the instant you think of it. Then meditate that within the central channel in the center of the navel is a single four-petaled lotus with anthers. Its front petal is light blue, the right is red, in back is white, and the left petal is yellow. Meditate clearly on the shape and colors. Imagine a white *A* radiating light in its center. On the front petal is a light-blue *ha*, on the right is a red *ri*, in back is a white *ni*, and below that [on the left] is a yellow *sa*. Meditate clearly on those letters.

Now imagine in the space before you Bhagavat Hevajra indistinguishable from Black Ācārya Virūpa. Below him is Venerable Indian Dampa holding a cane flute (*sba'i gling bu*) in his hand with which to bless you. {288} Meditate that those two dwell amid immeasurable buddhas and bodhisattvas dispersed around them like massing clouds. Your strong devotional faith in them causes the three letters *oṃ āḥ hūṃ*, like a string of pearls, to emerge from the hearts of primarily Hevajra, and all of the buddhas and bodhisattvas. The [letters] come through Dampa's flute and enter through the cranial aperture at the crown of your head and descend down the central channel, finally melting into the *A* at the navel. Contemplate the expanding undissipating bliss. Do the full measure of going for refuge.

Through that you do not come under the ḍākinī's control; it is the vital point to bring ḍākima under *your* control.

Now recite the four letters above (*ha ri ni sa*) at a barely discernible whisper. White light rays radiate from the *A* at the navel. They dissolve into the four letters and burn them until they become like burning iron. Meditate on scintillating bliss. The lotus below uncontrollably spins counterclockwise intensely; meditate on that going round and round. Constantly maintain that visualization of the lotus spinning as the letters do not spin while doing however much of the recitation.

When you grow tired of that, light radiates from the *A* at the navel. It travels up the central channel and emerges from the cranial aperture and hooks the bliss of all the goddesses that fill space, pulling it through your cranial aperture. That dissolves into the *A* at the navel. Meditate on the increasing, undissipating bliss. In a similar way, meditate that the light rays from *A* draw all the bliss from a ghandarva girl, a brahmin girl, a caṇḍāla girl, a nāga girl, and a human girl. That is the creation phase with recitation.

2. Completion Phase

This regular ordinary mind—
don't pollute it with concepts of meditating. {289}
Rest relaxed within the uncontrived state.
Just being without any frame of reference
is called mahāmudrā.

c. The Main Parts, Concluding Practices

By your meditating in that way,
all phenomena, the appearance and sound of things,
are understood to be like illusions,
so without attachment, daily activities
will serve as virtue of body, speech, and mind,
compassionately striving for the welfare of beings.

The completion of the [recitation] approach marks the second [stage]—engaging in the close attainment.[14] As explained: "Once the approach of three hundred thousand recitations is done, there is nothing at all that will not be accomplished." That is to say, once three hundred thousand recitations are finished, then you begin the near attainment, which should be learned directly from the guru.

The guru's precious instructions
that solicit the ḍākinī by vital points
were written down just as they were spoken.
Ḍāki, please don't scold me for this.
The virtue I dedicate to beings' welfare.

The secret sādhana of the ḍāki's vital points is finished.

IV. Sukhasiddhi's Empowerment Ritual[15]

namo guru
If you wish to confer the blessing on others, find a pleasant, isolated place, sweep it, and sprinkle it with water. Arrange images of the gurus and Jewels. Put up excellent *putsa*.[16] Apply a mixture of the five elixirs and alcohol to

the cleansed ground in the four corners and draw there a four-petaled lotus within a circle. Make the front petal light blue, the right petal red, the back petal white, and the left one green, as above. The center is outlined with a black circle. In the center is black *hūṃ*. Draw the letters *ha ri ni sa* from the front clockwise, the same colors as the lotus petals. On top of that place the mañji. {290} Smear a mirror with the alcohol-elixir mixture and cover it evenly with vermilion powder. Draw on it the four-petaled lotus with its five seed syllables as before, and place the mirror on the opening of the mañji. (Then go for refuge, arouse the awakening mind, visualize yourself as Hevajra, and do the recitation.) Meditate on the black *hūṃ*s above [on the mirror] and below [in the mandala] as Black Master Virūpa inseparable from Hevajra. (Meditate that Sukhasiddhi is to Hevajra's left.) Regard the letters as the essence of the four ḍākinīs and imagine the letters' forms as their bodies. Imagine the pledge beings below.

If you have them, surround [the mandala] with the five kinds of putsa.[17] If not, then arrange whatever you do have. Place the three tormas behind. Put elixir pills in a skull cup full of alcohol and place it in front of you. Consecrate the inner offerings (as usual). Do the vajra and bell prelude. (Present the consecrated offering and the inner offering. Do the praises, present the tormas, and do the self-induction.) Gather the disciples and place them in rows. Settle comfortably on your own seat. With the pride of being the yidam deity, sprinkle the disciples with the consecrated alcohol to protect from obstructors (with *sumba ni* . . . etc.). Then lead the disciples through contemplations (of the free and endowed difficult-to-find human birth, etc.), the confession of negative acts, the common going for refuge, arousing the awakening mind, (and the five-branch path, etc.) according to the tradition of the transcendent perfections. Then the disciples do prostrations and offer flowers with sincere devotion. (Then give the permission of the mantra and the other branches.) The guru cleanses the offerings and presents them to the deity. Supplicate for blessings, (saying, "Virūpa *hūṃ* Sukhamasiddhi *haṃ*"). [Then instruct the disciples:]

> Meditate on yourself as Cakrasaṃvara with a four-petaled lotus at the level of the navel inside the central channel. {291} Visualize the front petal of that lotus blue, the right one red, the back white, the left yellow, and the middle is black with a white *A*. The front petal has a light-blue *ha*, the right a red *ri*, the back a white *ni*, and the left a yellow *sa*. Then imagine all the buddhas and bodhisattvas in the space in front of you. Above them,

> from *hūṃ*, meditate on Hevajra inseparable from Virūpa. To the left of that, from *hūṃ*, meditate on Nairātmya inseparable from Sukhamasiddhi. Above your head is Dampa holding a cane flute that touches your central channel [at the cranial aperture]. Imagine the guru in front of Dampa and supplicate with "Venerable Virūpa *hūṃ* Sukhasiddhi *haṃ*" three times. That causes the three letters *oṃ āḥ hūṃ*, like strings of pearls, to emerge from the hearts of all of the buddhas and bodhisattvas, primarily the three: Virūpa, Sukhasiddhi, and Dampa. The letters come through Dampa's flute and descend, entering your central channel, finally slowly dissolving into the four letters. Meditate that this reduces the power of your transgressions. Then say, "I go for refuge in the triad of guru, yidam, and ḍākinī." Do the full extent of going for refuge in that supplication.

Then with the physical sitting posture, have [the disciples] meditate on the visualization above while the guru also meditates on the visualization. Supplicate and play the music, blowing and rattling [the instruments]. The manner of descent to body, speech, and mind accords with general custom.

The Actual Empowerment Conferral

This has two parts: (1) the four empowerments of the vase and (2) the empowerment conferral of the six goddesses.

First, supplicate for the vase empowerment three times: {292}

> "In the manifest mandala of refuge,
> full as a bag of sesame seeds:
> please confer the empowerment on me."

Then:

> Just as the gods bathed him
> as soon as he was born,
> just so I bathe your body
> with pure divine water.

oṃ sarva tathāgata vajra abhiṣiñca tu māṃ

Saying that, confer the vase empowerment (on the crown, etc.). Supplicate for the secret empowerment three times:

"Just as Awakened Vajra granted
the great offering to the Buddha,
grant me this today, Vajra Space,
in order to protect me."

The hosts of mandala deities
from the three secrets of ten directions,
honored by all in the three realms,
the great empowerment of the vajra is conferred.

Say that with the mantra and give the bodhicitta on their tongues. Supplicate for the wisdom-awareness empowerment three times:

"All the buddhas of the ten directions
gather the awareness elixir of three realms
fully into the pathway of the vajra;
grant the empowerment conferral of great bliss."

On top of them the hosts of deities bestow
the awareness consorts to generate bliss;
the wisdom empowerment of the Victor's heir.

Say that with the mantra to give the empowerment. Supplicate for the fourth empowerment three times:

"Epitome of omniscience, awareness, and compassion:
principal one, please confer empowerment on me."

Assume the positions of the yogic exercises: slightly cross the legs, hold your left hand at your heart in the threatening gesture, and with your right hand bring the thumb to the little finger [with the other] three fingers raised, and stare with alert eyes. {293}

In empty space, which lacks awareness,
tame the root of mind with awareness.
Tame the root and rest relaxed.

That is the fourth empowerment.

Empowerment by the Six Goddesses

Meditate on yourself as Cakrasaṃvara. Light radiates from the *A* at the navel. The goddess appears before you, white with a yellow radiance and a lustrous complexion. She possesses the experience of bliss and is youthful and charming, adorned by rainbow light (*pa nya tsa li ka*) and various jewels. Imagine light rays radiating from her secret place. Meditate clearly on that secret place. Then five-colored light rays radiate from a blue-black *hūṃ* in the tip of your organ. They go into [her] source of phenomena and fill all the radial channels, increasing bliss. Exalted Lady is brought toward you intensely by the light rays of bliss. Then from inside your organ [the light] goes up to Exalted Goddess, filling all the channels. Her bliss increases. Press down strongly on the lower winds and compress the belly. Meditate on nondual bliss-emptiness. Again one time light radiates from the *hūṃ*, invoking the bliss as above. Undissipating bliss expands in your body.

Meditate on nondual bliss-clarity.
Then Exalted Goddess
embraces you in nondual unity.
Method and wisdom churning,
warmth evokes the vitality of bliss.
The mother's self-arising sun flow,
that abundance of bliss
from the vajra, from within the interior
moves upward and
fills all major and minor channels.
Bliss fills your being and expands,
undissipating bliss increases in your body.
Your body changes to the color of ruby;
the mother is overpowered.
Your *kunda* radiates there, {294}

increases in the mother,
red complexion grows on the white;
the mother overpowers the father.
Thus the couple's light is stirred up.
When bliss fills your being,
intensely compress the lower winds.
Bliss reveals the truth of emptiness,
emptiness prevents attachment to bliss;
nondual bliss-emptiness is supreme awareness.
The red lasts long, the white is brief.
Understand supreme vital points.
In great bliss of the deity's empty form,
rest without thought in the clarity.
In this state of the nondual couple,
do the recitation of the mantra:
oṃ ha ri ni sa and so forth.
Through that, all stains of attachment
to deity's form mahāmudrā are purified;
free, self-arising purity arises.
Taming anyone is spontaneously present,
that is the ultimate fruition.
Gandharvī, brāhminī, caṇḍālī,
human, and nāgī likewise.
White is the four empowerments.
Blue is the four ecstasies.
Brown is the four instances.
Dark brown again is four [empowerments].
Ruby is the four kāyas.

Then enjoy the communal feast. Offer torma. Send out the leftovers. The deities of the mandala are gathered into the master's navel. Do whatever confessions of omissions and additions that you like, then rest in equipoise.

[Concluding Verse and Colophon]

This esoteric instruction of blessings
is written down just as the guru spoke it.

I request the ḍākis to have patience.
I dedicate the virtue to the welfare of beings.

The record of the empowerment, vital instructions of the Ḍākima, is finished.

V. [Additional Instructions][18]

namo guru

Meditate on a source of phenomena below the navel. Within the source of phenomena imagine a four-petaled lotus. On its center is *oṃ*, in front *ha*, to the left *ri*, to the back *ni*, and to the left *sa* or *svāhā*. Meditate on those letters as red. Light rays radiate from those seed syllables, striking all the buddhas and bodhisattvas. {295} The light rays draw in all their strength and ability, which dissolve into the seed syllables. The opening of the source of phenomena closes. Press down slightly on the upper winds and repeat the mantra.

The vital point of magnetizing humans, wealth, and food depends on the navel chakra of emanation. Visualize yourself as Vajravārāhī and the khaṭvāṅga as the male consort, each with bodhicitta. The bodhicitta dissolves into the male object.[19] Meditate on scintillating bliss. That male's red bodhicitta enters your body. Meditate that your body clearly becomes red. Verbally repeat the mantra *oṃ ha ri ni sa svāhā*. Bliss is drawn from below the navel of the divine girl. This is profound meaning. It is secret. *ithi*

[Visualize yourself] either as the essential form of Cakrasaṃvara or the mother's essence as Vajravārāhī. Your white bodhicitta touches the mother's lotus and the white develops a red radiance. Think that you experience bliss. It gathers back and you magnetize it. Imagine that the white with the red radiance imbues you with undissipating bliss. Recite "*oṃ ha ri ni sa*, bliss is drawn in from beneath the goddess's navel." Gather the object of engagement and meditate on mahāmudrā. *ithi*

namo guru

Visualize yourself instantly as Cakrasaṃvara. Light rays radiate from the *A* at the navel. Before you is the divine girl, white with a yellow radiance, wearing fine clothing and adorned by all the precious ornaments. Light rays of five colors radiate from the deep-blue *hūṃ* at the tip of your organ and enter the lotus of the goddess in front. Imagine that the goddess experiences bliss. [The light] gathers back in and enters up your organ. Meditate that undissipating bliss increases. {296} At that time, while the visualization is continuously drawing up, it is important to pull up the lower winds. Then the goddess in front joins in union with you and you gather the bliss into yourself. Meditate on the undissipating bliss-emptiness inseparable of the mahāmudrā of the deity's form.

maṅgalaṃ

16. Bringing Down the Rain of Great Bliss

A Lineage Supplication for the Profound Path of Sukha's Six Dharmas[1]

Jamgön Kongtrul

Hero Heruka's great bliss delights
the heroine Yoginī of invincible space,
their united divine forms: the adept Virūpa
and Sukhasiddhi, mighty one of the tenth level.

Lord Khyungpo, chief of all adepts in the Land of Snows,
Mokchokpa, heir of the single-lineage vajra legacy,
Chökyi Senge, the real Avalokiteśvara,
Nyentön Rigongpa, the hidden buddha,
Tönpa Drogön, releasing vajra knots.

Tsangma Shangtön, Rikpa Dorje,
Khutön Tsul[trim]gön, supreme guide Chöpal Zang,
Tsultrim Gyaltsen, Khyenrab Chökyi Je,
Zhönu Chödrup,[2] Semkyi Dudrol (Kunga Drolchok),
Lhawang Drakpa, Jetsun Drolwai Gön (Tāranātha),
Trinle Wangmo, Yeshe Gyatso,
Nyingpo Lodrö, Drupnye Kunzang Wang,
Tsewang Norbu, Trulzhik Chöying,
Kunzang Chöjor, Lozang Tutop,
Nyima Chöpel, Losal Tenkyong,
Khyentse Wangpo, the real Mañjuśrī. {299}

Root and lineage gurus who show the ripening and liberating path,
yidams, ḍākinīs, with hosts of dharma protectors,
I supplicate you! Please grant your blessings.

Unborn elixir cleanses karma, afflictions, sins, and obscurations.
The path of divine mantra refines attachment to ordinary appearance.
Changeless bliss of melting arises from blazing and dripping exercise.
Self-liberated illusion destroys fixation on the reality of delusion.
Double-deluded appearance naturally arises as divine form.
Lucid clarity's sun dispels the darkness of ignorance.
Death's secret passage hastens one to the great celestial realm.
Intermediate state's delusion arises as the victors' saṃbhogakāya.
Having three indestructible essences brings longevity.
Bless me to attain in this very lifetime
the supreme state of Vajradhara unity.

Written by Yönten Gyatso in order to fulfill the aspirations of the lord nephew [Jangchub Sempa Lodrö Zangpo, attendant of Jamyang Khyentse Wangpo]. Virtue!

17. Fast Path of Integral Unity

Awareness Ḍākinī Sukhasiddhi's Profound Path of Creation and Guidance on the Six Dharmas[1]

Jamgön Kongtrul

Chief Ḍākinī of Timeless Awareness
known as Spiritual Power of Bliss, {300}
great mighty one of the tenth level,
I bow to you, inseparable from my guru.
The secret words of the vajra holders
are the great adept Khyungpo's heart essence.
An aural lineage not polluted by sophistry,
the guru's oral transmission is clearly presented.

From among the Five Precious Jewels of the [Shangpa] Kagyu lineage that are the secret vajra words of the aural lineage not polluted by the words of ordinary people or the intellectual flaws of sophists, that effortlessly grant in a single lifetime the citadel of integral unity, the one that, like the heart's radiance, was passed as a concealed teaching in the lineage from one fortunate individual to the next, the profound secret that was not proclaimed all over the place, the ḍākinīs' heart blood—this is it. However, due to the [scant] fortune of the times, the branches of the source [texts] are mostly kept in the ḍākinīs' own abode, but the root instruction is well preserved. The explanation of how to conveniently put that into practice has three parts: (1) the preliminaries, (2) the main practice, and (3) the conclusion.

I. Preliminaries

This has two parts: (1) common refuge and awakening mind and (2) uncommon purifying inner space.

A. Going for Refuge and Arousing the Awakening Mind

Since this is the special [method for] maturation, the person who would ripen their being and train with the four contemplations that turn the mind should sit on a comfortable seat in an isolated place with the [physical] positions of meditative stability. In the space before you is a jeweled throne supported by eight great lions, upon which is a seat of a multicolored lotus, sun, and moon. On that is your root guru, the epitome of the awakened body, speech, mind, and the vajra awareness of all buddhas. The guru's form is incomparably charismatic, smiling slightly, resting in the equipoise of numerous approaches to meditative absorption. If just hearing the guru's name liberates from cyclic existence and the lower realms, what is there to say about supplicating for whatever your exigencies? Imagine that you and all sentient beings headed by your parents go for refuge all together. Say:

> All sentient beings, my mothers, equal to the reaches of space, go for refuge in the precious guru, the unified essence of all refuges. {301}

Repeat that seven or more times.

> For the sake of all sentient beings throughout space, I will attain the unified state of Vajradhara. To that end, I will practice the profound path.

Repeat that three times to arouse the awakening mind.

B. The Purifying *A* of Inner Space

This has two parts: (1) the preparation and (2) the main practice.

1. Preparation

For the supplication, imagine that you and all sentient beings are supplicating:

> Precious guru, unified essence of all buddhas of the three times,
> for the sake of all sentient beings, I supplicate you to bless me
> that I may relinquish self-fixation,
> that I may have no needs,
> that I may cultivate Illusory Body and Dream,
> and that Lucid Clarity Mahāmudrā arises to me.

Supplicate many times. On the strength of your intense devotion, the guru above your head melts into light and dissolves into you.

2. Main Practice

Remain in your ordinary form. Visualize that inside your head is a white tetrahedral source of phenomena made of light. Of three vertices, one faces the midbrow and the other two face in the direction of the right and left ears. Its narrow apex faces down and the wide opening faces upward. In the center of the empty interior there is an unsupported white letter *A* that protrudes slightly above the opening of the source of phenomena. Meditate on that and fix it in your mind. The repetition of "*A*" twenty-one times causes a stream of white elixir to fall from the *A*. It completely fills up the inside of the source of phenomena. All sickness, spirits, negativities, and obscurations accumulated since beginningless lifetimes are purified. Think that your body becomes empty clarity, the nature of light.

II. Main Practice

This has two parts: (1) the phase of creation of the support [of the visualized deity] and (2) the phase of completion of the supported [interior subtle body]. {302}

A. Creation Phase

When doing just the meditation-recitation separately, first do the refuge, awakening mind, and the four immeasurables. Then continue to here with the purifying of empty space. Afterward, add *svabhāva* . . . (etc.) to purify in emptiness.

From within emptiness—inside a protection circle of the vajra ground, enclosure, latticework, tent, canopy, and blazing fire—is a celestial palace complete in all respects. In its center, upon a lotus and sun, you instantly become Ḍākinī Sukhasiddhi, white as a conch shell. Her hair falls down loose and she is adorned by bone ornaments. She holds a skull cup full of elixir with her right hand and lifts her left hand in the mudra of pointing to the unborn. Her two feet are in a dancing posture. She stares with wide-open three eyes. She has the form of timeless awareness, with *oṃ* at the head, *āḥ* at the throat, and *hūṃ* at the heart. Light radiates from the [letters] and invokes the awareness being—*jaḥ hūṃ vaṃ hoḥ*—that becomes indivisible from the pledge being. Focus your attention on that and recite *oṃ sukhasiddhi hūṃ* a bit to evoke her presence.

In your navel center is a four-petaled lotus with *A* at its center and *ha ra ni sa* arrayed clockwise on the petals. Visualize all the letters as white with a red radiance. The mantra recitation makes light radiate from the letters in the navel. The light draws all knowledge, love, and ability of all the buddhas and bodhisattvas, the capacity to magnetize the five classes of ḍākinīs, four great kings, ten direction protectors, and so on, and the vital essence of the world's five sense pleasures. Imagine them returning in the form of white and red light rays that dissolve into the letters at the navel. Recite the five letters as much as you can: *a ha ri ni sa.*

More particularly, if you will accomplish the empowerment ritual, the transformations of the vital profound visualizations by means of threefold nonabiding[2] is clarified in the ancient texts.

At the end say:

> In empty space, which lacks awareness,
> with awareness tame the root of mind.
> Tame the root and rest relaxed.[3] {303}

Recall the meaning and rest in equipoise.

Here, "mudra pointing to the unborn" just means that [Sukhasiddhi's] finger of her left hand is lifted up toward the sky. The guidebook of Khyenrap Chöje[4] offers different ways of visualizing as follows: Her right hand is in the trident mudra at the heart, indicating the three kāyas. Her left hand in the threatening gesture reveals the unborn. It states that her two legs are in a squatting position, but this would seem to relate to the context of completion phase.

B. Completion Phase

1. Fierce Inner Heat

From the Six Dharmas:

> First Fierce Inner Heat, the path of methods,
> the body's vital point is to assume the sixfold stove [posture].

Exhale as in the practice of the ninefold shake-up of dead air. Visualize yourself as Sukhasiddhi, empty inside like a silk tent. In the center, level with the navel, is a red four-petaled lotus of fire, with a red letter *A* in its center. Of the four petals, *ha* is in the east, *ri* in the south, *tu* in the west, and *sa* in the north, all of them red. Those seed syllables are slightly higher than the lotus. At the anus, imagine a green wind mandala arisen from *yaṃ*. First, slightly contracting the lower winds causes the wind in the anus to stir. That strikes the lotus at the navel, making the red color even brighter and hot to the touch. It begins to spin counterclockwise, round and round. Focus intently on that visualization. Gently press down the upper winds and hold the joining [with the lower wind]. Visualize a thumb-sized flame of fire arising from the *A* in the navel. It possesses three qualities: red in color, hot to the touch, and essentially the nature of bliss. After a few rounds of breathing (*rlung khug*), the *A*'s red light rays invoke the four seed syllables from the [four] directions. They also blaze with fire endowed with the three qualities. First they pervade the entire inside of the body at the navel; imagine bliss-warmth arising. After becoming familiar with that, imagine [the fire] pervading in stages to the heart and to the throat. Finally, think that your whole body is filled with sparkling red firelight. {304} During all those [stages], mentally recite *a ha ri ni sa*.

[Perform] a vase breath with the standard four applications.[5] Though it is not actually taught in the ancient writings, since it is a general branch of the Six Dharmas, doing the yogic exercises if you are able will be very good and enhance the practice. Through that, first there will arise a bodily sensation of warmth. Then the mental sensation of melting bliss is invoked on top of that. Then nonthought will arise effortlessly and you will vividly see the true face of higher insight. If warmth starts to arise, do not relax your efforts; and when bliss arises, without following the mental sensation of conceptual thinking, just focus on the yogic gaze with awareness of the space between your eyebrows. Through blending the outer and inner spaces, you will understand the unchanging true face of the integral unity of bliss-emptiness. That is the actual goal of the path of methods.

2. Illusory Body

Meditate on the guru on a four-tiered seat above your head and fervently supplicate as before. Visualize your body as the ḍākinī, empty inside, and the lotus at the navel with the five seed syllables. Beneath that is a tetrahedral source of phenomena, white outside and red inside. The lower point touches the perineum and rises up from there. Within it are the sentient beings of the six kinds of migrators, each experiencing their own kind of suffering: heat and cold for the hell beings, hunger and thirst for the hungry ghosts, and so forth. Imagine it like an illusion, without a core, rising and fading like mist. Think with compassion on how all these beings grasp as real what is unreal and wander in cyclic existence under the power of that delusion. How pitiful! Think, "Though all this does arise; in reality, it is not real. It is illusion. It is dream." Intensely cultivate that intentionality.

Hold the joined winds while doing the mental recitation. This causes light to radiate from the *A* in the navel. It strikes the four letters and light radiates from them as well. That strikes the six kinds of beings within the source of phenomena, cleansing and purifying all the sufferings from negativities, obscurations, and violations. Imagine them all staying there in shimmering light. Contract the lower winds. Think that the lotus spins intensely counterclockwise. {305} Focus your mind on the six kinds of beings inside the source of phenomena. Produce the intense intentionality of remembering illusion and dream. When the session ends, let the source of phenomena, outside and inside, vanish by itself.

Light rays radiate from the *A* at the navel and emerge from your cranial aperture. The god's girl is radiant white. Her lips are edged. (This refers to the lotus.) Her eyes are lined. (This refers to the drawing on the upper eyelids.) Below the waist she is naked and the lotus at the secret door is open. [The light] penetrates the bhaga and summons the bliss, exciting the [lotus] stamens and drawing out all the streams of blissful bodhicitta. That enters the top of your head and fills your whole body inside. Especially imagine that [the bodhicitta] melts into the seed syllables at the navel, generating immeasurable bliss. Hold the joined winds.

Apply the same process to the gandharva girl, who is blue; the yellow brāhminī, the pink human, the light-yellow nāgī, and the brown caṇḍālī. Their bliss is drawn in as before. By your nurturing a natural state of illusion, your whole body fills with great bliss and, on the strength of that, all appearance will arise as great bliss. Through that practice, illusion arises naturally, dreams are recognized, the winds are controlled, and warmth arises—all this occurs at the same time. It is said there is no greater enhancement of applied virtue than this.

3. Dream

Meditate on the guru in the heart and supplicate as before. In particular, fervently supplicate with, "Bless me to grasp dreams." Clearly imagine the navel lotus, (the natural experience of bliss-warmth), with the five letters. Light rays radiate from the *A* and strike the four letters. They spin forcefully and emit red light rays the nature of bliss-warmth. Think that your whole body inside becomes clear. In the intervals of those [visualizations], think, "It is a dream," and fervently develop that intentionality continuously while holding the joined winds and mentally reciting. In particular, meditate with single-pointed focus in the evening and when going to sleep. {306} Finally, imagine that the four seed syllables dissolve into the *A*, and the *A* disappears into light. Fall asleep within that state and recognize dreams. If you do not recognize them, then in the gap between appearance and sleep, when thoughts are dim (*hrib pa*), which is itself the seed of dreams, think, "This itself is a dream," and find the balance between concentration and relaxation. In this way it is impossible not to recognize them.

Once you attain stability in grasping [the fact that you are dreaming], you refine the dreams. Think, "These appearances throughout the daytime are dream appearances. This body is a mental body. Both of these are not truly existent, so I can do anything." Switch various things back and forth between big and small, good and bad, or change the deities' forms, seed syllables, hand implements, and so forth that are not definite. Refine all of that without fixation, resting in the equipoise of mahāmudrā. Then that will also occur in your dreams.

When you become familiar with that, you can advance to increasing, emanating, and so forth, in accordance with other [explanations] of the Six Dharmas.

For [the practice of viewing] objective appearances, light rays from *A* cause the other four seed syllables to turn into the nature of light. Think that by those means the whole body quivers, like a blown-up balloon, and rest your mind without fixation in empty clarity. When you go to sleep, think of whatever hidden place you wish to visit, such as a pure realm. The light rays emitted from the *A* illuminate that place and you arrive via the path of light. Once you have looked or become accustomed to it, focusing your mind there will ascertain it accordingly. Devotion is important for this occasion, so understand how to properly change the final sentences of the supplications [to specifically supplicate for this practice] and so forth.

4. Lucid Clarity

Practice guru yoga as before, fervently supplicating to recognize lucid clarity. Clearly visualize the lotus with five seed syllables at the navel, all white. Do the wind [exercises] and mental recitation. White light rays radiate from *A*, and the four seed syllables blaze with light. Crystal-white light rays come from the lotus and seed syllables, like the striking of sun rays, and fill your insides. {307} Imagine everything outside and inside becomes a mass of shimmering white light. Rest your mind for a long time in uncontrived empty clarity—brilliant wakefulness.

Particularly in the daytime, focus with unwavering attention on the unborn white *A*, the nature of your consciousness. In the evening, and especially when going to sleep, meditate intently and maintain the splendor of nonconceptual clarity. If sleep ends, the four seed syllables dissolve into *A*. Focus your attention on the *A* as the nature of light without any interruption by conceptual thought and go back to sleep. It is said to be impossible for lucid clarity not to arise and impossible to lose it once it has arisen.

There are many subtle divisions and important points concerning lucid clarity, such as thin or thick, subtle or coarse, different experiences and realizations, and so forth.[6] Nevertheless, when you have fallen asleep, if vivid appearances are accompanied by mindful awareness, that is designated as recognition. When you get used to that, even in the daytime the naked empty clarity will arise, brought on by the strength of the nighttime's virtuous practice. If you persistently sustain it, you will quickly gain mastery over the lucid clarity of joined day and night.

5. Transference

This has two parts: (1) training and (2) application in action [at death].

a. Training

In the guru yoga practice, after the first four lines of the supplication, add "Please let my consciousness transfer to the pure celestial realm." Visualize the white lotus in your navel with the four letters, and practice the breathing exercises and recitation to collect your mind. The hole in the top of your head is the size of a spindle, vividly clear. Imagine the four letters as the four elements. The letter *ri* dissolves into *ha*, that into *ni*, that into *sa*, and that dissolves into *A*. This corresponds to the dissolution stages of the elements [at death]. That *A* is there ready to blaze up; contracting the lower wind causes the winds to stir from the anus and strike the *A* at the navel. {308} It ascends up like a shooting star through the cranial aperture and flies far away. Think that it vanishes in unborn space. Repeat this twenty-one times in each session and train for the signs to show. At the end of a session, the white *A* appears clearly from space, falls through the cranial aperture, and lands heavily at the navel. This forcefully produces the body's heat. Think that your cranial aperture is blocked by a crossed vajra.

b. Application

When the signs of impending death are clear and the methods such as cheating death have not deterred it, confess your faults and vow [to desist from them]. Offer your body and possessions to the guru and Jewels, energetically cutting your entanglements. Verbally shout "*hik*"—your mind as the letter *A* blends with space and then does not come back. At death, lie down in the position of a reclining lion. It is said that having done the transference of consciousness in that way, it is impossible not to go to the celestial realm. It is the vital point of forcefully attaining buddhahood for great sinners.

According to the guidance manual of Khyenrab Chöje,[7] during the training, the ḍākinī holds a flaying knife and skull cup, and one thinks of the lotus petals as the essence of the four elements. The *A* letter flies and falls. During the application at death, the four lotus petals dissolve into the ḍākinī. Those four [seed syllables], having dissolved into the *A*, then ascend.

6. Intermediate State

Change the end of the supplication in the guru yoga to "Please let me attain the victors' saṃbhogakāya in the intermediate state." Clarify the lotus with the seed syllables at the navel. Through your breathing exercises and mental recitation, the *A* radiates light. The essence of the forms of the four seed syllables are the goddesses with one face and two arms, holding flaying knives in their right hands and blood-filled skull cups in the left. The light strikes their form; imagine shimmering light. Sometimes rest openly without distraction in the essence of self-arising nonconceptual clarity. Sometimes do the mental recitation. {309} Again white light rays radiate from *A*. They penetrate the secret places of the four ḍākinīs. Imagine their vivid great bliss. In all those contexts, think, "Alas! I am dead. All the appearances are intermediate state appearances. This body is also the mental body of the intermediate state. All appearances of the six consciousness groups are the aggregates included in the four names.[8] Nothing at all here is real." Whatever appears, whatever resounds, integrate all of it into the path of the intermediate state.

Again, sometimes think, "I must be sure to avoid wandering through the entrance to the womb; I must become buddha in this very intermediate state." Imagine your own body as the rainbow-like empty appearance of the deity's form, the environment as a celestial palace, the appearance of its inhabiting sentient beings as deities, sound as mantra, and thoughts as the unembellished nature of phenomena in lucid clarity. In particular, think of all males and objects that inspire anger as Hevajra, and all females and objects that produce desire as Nairātmya. If you get used to resting in such equipoise for a long time, it is impossible that the self-arising deity's form will not arise in your dreams. When that occurs, it is said to be impossible not to get enlightened as the saṃbhogakāya in that intermediate state. If you have good recollection and awareness in the present, and powerful intentionality, then when the deluded appearances of the intermediate state arise, first you recognize them; then, because of your meditation on the path, you are instantly liberated at that moment. Thus, the root of all approaches depends on mindful recollection and awareness.

III. Conclusion

This has two parts: (1) the main part and (2) the particular elaboration.

A. Main Part

At the end of all sessions of creation and completion phases, do the *Sealed Word Dedication*[9] if you know it. If you don't know it, then do general Mahayana aspiration prayers and in particular the aspiration of integral unity. Seal that with actual and associated dedications [while maintaining] the complete purity of the three spheres. {310} Whatever yoga you have been pursuing during equipoise, maintain that same one with mindful awareness at all times in subsequent attainment. Keep the continuity of mindful intentionality from the practices of Illusory Body, Dream, Intermediate State, and so forth. Avoid like poison the causes of deviations in applied virtue such as doubt, laziness, pride, and wrong views. Rest in equanimity without engaging in the conditions that hinder virtue: faults and qualities, good and bad, hopes and fears, affirming and denying, and rejecting and accepting. Take as your support for everything the supreme enhancements of applied virtue: devotion, pure view, and compassion. Through persistence in the crucial practice, proliferating thoughts will be severed from the inside, delusions will vanish like mist, qualities will arise automatically, and you will manifest the state of integral unity.

B. Particular Elaboration

Here is a description of a method of further elaboration. If you wish to take up the practice of longevity that Bodong Kunkhyen Jikdral the Great received in a direct lineage,[10] you do not need to do the refuge, awakening mind, and the four immeasurables if you have done them previously. Purify all phenomena by saying *svabhāva* . . . (etc.).

From within emptiness, you instantly become glorious Coemergent Hevajra. Before you in space is a circular vajra enclosure. Within it is a multicolored lotus with a hundred thousand petals; its center is a swirling ocean of milk filled with various gems. The trunk of a wish-fulfilling tree rises in its midst, with branches, leaves, flowers, and ripened fruit. In its center, on a lion throne with a seat of lotus, moon, sun, and antelope skin, your root guru is indivisible from the Ḍākinī of Timeless Awareness, Spiritual Power of Bliss (Sukhasiddhi). She is white with a red glow, with one face and two arms. Her right hand rests on the seat near her right hip. {311} Her left hand makes the trident mudra facing her heart. She is beautifully adorned by silks, jewels, and bone garlands. She sits in a squatting posture with legs drawn up and crossed [at the ankles] in a pavilion of swirling rainbow light. The letter *oṃ* is at her forehead, *āḥ* at her throat, and *hūṃ* at her heart. Light from those letters radiates out and invokes the awareness beings—*vajra samājaḥ / jaḥ hūṃ vaṃ hoḥ*—they become indivisible. Again light rays from the heart invoke the empowerment deities. They confer empowerment, fill her body, and purify stains. The excess water rises up and becomes the crown ornament of Coemergent Hevajra couple.

Offer:

> *oṃ jñānaḍākinī sukhasiddhi vajra arghaṃ pratīccha svāhā* (similarly with) . . . *pādyaṃ* . . . (etc. then) *oṃ vajra puṣpe āḥ hūṃ* (through) . . . *śabda* . . . (and) *oṃ pañca kāmaguṇa mahāsukha āḥ hūṃ*

Praise:

> Lovely and charming, youthful as a sixteen-year-old,
> with the radiant form of empty bliss in basic space,
> you dwell within the ineffable unborn state;
> I praise the Spiritual Power of Bliss.

In her heart, on a moon-disk mandala, is the letter *hūṃ*, white with a red radiance. The multicolored mantra string circles clockwise around it.

> *oṃ āḥ guru ḍākinīye sukhasiddhi āyurjñāna siddhi mem prayaccha*

Repeat that as much as you can. Immeasurable multicolored light rays radiate from the mantra string and strike the entire environment with its inhabitants and all the sugatas of the ten directions. It invokes their compassionate blessings and all their flavor, potency, and refined essence, which dissolves into the awareness ḍākinī. Immeasurable light rays as the elixir of immortality flow down from her into your cranial aperture and fill your whole body. The mass of all negative acts, obscurations, faults, downfalls, and stains accumulated during beginningless lives in cyclic existence is cleansed and purified. {312} Think that the immortality [elixir] with its threefold essence blesses you with the accomplishment of the supreme nirmāṇakāya guru.

At the end, present the outer offerings as above and the inner offering with *oṃ āḥ hūṃ*. Supplicate:

> You attained rainbow body of indestructible essence,
> the illusory form of coemergent lucid clarity
> and great bliss—saṃbhogakāya;
> Sukhasiddhi, consider me!

The front-visualized guru Awareness Ḍākinī, along with the seat and throne, melts completely into light. Her awakened body, speech, and mind become indivisible from your body, speech, and mind as the yidam. Thus the four empowerments are obtained in one sitting. Think that the obscurations of the four circumstances are purified and the ultimate four kāyas are attained. Rest intrinsic awareness in the effortless state of phenomena's nature for as long as it abides. Finally, arise in the form of integral unity and do the dedication and aspiration.

In general, in the dharma cycle of Awareness Ḍākinī [Sukhasiddhi], Nairātmya's inner guidance, and the cycle of Vārāhī's secret sādhana came from Khedrup Khyungpo himself and later were directly received by the great Nyentön. From among the few highly valuable teachings of incredibly profound instructions, such as the Three Nails of Creation Phase [and] the Navel Emanation Chakra, these days most of the ancient writings are no longer extant, other than in the reading transmissions and what's included in the *Hundred Guidances* [*of Jonang*]. However, the basis is these two: this Six Dharmas and the Mahāmudrā timeless awareness. Khedrup Khyungpo retrieved these Golden Dharmas through his difficult labors and precious treasure. Because of that, those with noble minds in the future will maintain its continuity and, having obtained its blessings, will readily attain the two spiritual powers through effort in just these main practices. This is the assured promise of the Ḍākinī of Timeless Awareness.

[Colophon]

For those with faith, diligence, and sacred pledge,
this brings attainment of the real Vajradhara
in a year or six months.
This dharma system, not merely rumored as
the heart of the path of methods and wish-fulfilling gem,
I've explained as best I can for its increase and duration.
Through this virtue may I and all others
gain the supreme spiritual power of great bliss.

At the time of receiving this dharma system of the heart's drop directly from the great all-knowing all-seeing Mañjughoṣa, the aspirations of the master of highest knowledge, my lord nephew Lodrö Zangpo contributed the conditions; I, Yönten Gyatso, wrote this in the monastic seat of Palpung, in the style of a memorandum of the guru's oral transmission. The intended meanings of the ancient writings were also gathered in their entirety for further clarification. May this benefit the doctrine and sentient beings. Let virtue prevail!

18. Sukhasiddhi's Cycle of Oral Instructions and Instructions on Three Nails[1]

Sangye Nyentön Chökyi Sherap

[I. Oral Instructions of Four Empowerments]

namo guru

I write the oral instruction of the four empowerments
of the Emanated Navel Chakra Secret Sādhana.[2]

Precede this with arousing the mind of awakening. Instantly you become Cakrasaṃvara as a solitary hero holding vajra and bell. Meditate that as form, you exist as body; as touch, you do not exist as substance; and you possess the experience of bliss. Light rays from *A* at the navel move up through the cranial aperture. On the tips of the rays are goddesses, white with red radiance. Youthful and voluptuous with full breasts, their young bodies are charming, beatified by jewels and various divine Pāñcālikā garments.[3] Their front sides and lotuses are very vivid with a glow of passion. Just seeing or hearing or touching them causes immeasurable arousing bliss. Imagine that one such venerable goddess arrives before you.

With yourself visualized as Cakrasaṃvara, imagine a dark-blue *hūṃ* at the tip of your gem (glans). {317} Five-colored light rays from that radiate up into the secret place of the goddess in front. She faints in bliss. The light rays capture the bliss and bring it inside the gem; bliss flows up—*tri li li*, warmth spreads—*chi li li*. Think that as you contract the lower winds intensely, the timeless awareness of nondual bliss-emptiness arises in your being.

Again light radiates from *hūṃ* and goes up the lotus and brings back all the bliss, which goes up the gem. That bliss itself is utterly lucid; the timeless awareness of nondual clarity-emptiness arises in your being.

Again light radiates from *hūṃ* and goes up; intoxicated by bliss, [she] comes to embrace you and have intercourse. From the place of union, the dewdrops of passion come drop by drop; [you] quiver with bliss—*tril tril ba*—and your whole body is pervaded by bliss. Contract the lower wind intensely. Then at the hole in the gem, the channel of the goddess's bliss and the red bodhicitta penetrate and by vigorously drawing up the lower winds, {318} the red bodhicitta that is all inside the gem flows up—*tri li li*; warmth spreads—*chil li li*. Red [bodhicitta] continuously arises in the secret place and fills up below the navel, arousing intense bliss. As the redness completely fills up to the heart, to the throat, and to the crown of your head, your whole body is filled with bliss. Then as your bliss turns you as red as the color of coral, your splendor overpowers the mother. One white [bodhicitta drop] emanates to the goddess's vagina and she faints in bliss. Meditate on the white with a radiance of red. In this way, both female and male faint in bliss; remain within the nondual bliss-emptiness. This is also counted as the four upward-supporting ecstasies.[4]

This is also applied to the white gandharvī with a green radiance, the green brāhminī with a white radiance, the red caṇḍālī with a white radiance, and the yellow nāgī with a white radiance. The human [girl] is whatever [color] pleases you. Meditate thus on all six sequentially.

[Concluding Verse]

The four empowerments were directly received
from Ḍākinī Spiritual Power of Bliss
by this guru with three [qualities][5]—
Sangye Tönpa Rinpoche, who gave it to me.[6]
This vital heart of the hero [and] ḍākinī
enlightens you in just a year or months.
ithi

II. The Oral Instructions of Introduction[7]

Homage to all holy gurus.

The introduction of one's own mind's mahāmudrā in the nonduality of the ḍākinī and one's own mind:

> With the physical yogic exercise (legs slightly crossed, left hand in the threatening gesture at the heart, the right thumb and little finger grasped and the other three raised),
> in empty space, which lacks awareness,
> with awareness (visualize) taming the root of mind (looking with sharp eyes).
> Tame the root and rest relaxed.

Overcome inabilities. Cut entanglement. Reverse attachment. Transform perception. {319} Banish activity. Leave the crowded country. Understand [difficult] conditions as spiritual powers. Understand suffering as the nature of phenomena.[8] (Control what is desired, give up what is not desired, let the six consciousness groups go dumb. By that, all cyclic existence and transcendence is naturally free. So it is said.) Release and draw out intrinsic awareness. Do not spread the aural lineage among people.

By your practicing like that, auspicious interconnections will actually arise just as they are. You will attain the state of a vajra holder in this very life, and your abilities and qualities and continuous spontaneous awakened activities will ripen and liberate sentient beings until the ocean of cyclic existence is emptied.

This is the legacy of instruction bestowed by the Ḍākinī: Release and draw out the faculties, clarify intrinsic awareness,[9] reinforce strength, and hold with mindfulness the root [of mind] (as unborn). The introduction to one's own mind [as] ḍākinī (called mahāmudrā of unborn mind) brings appearances (and all ḍākinīs) under control. This concludes the oral instruction of the secret sādhana.

III. Oral Instructions on the Sādhana[10]

Bowing at the feet of the holy gurus
I write the oral instructions of the Secret Sādhana.

Precede this with the self-visualization. Instantly you create yourself as Exalted Lady with the central channel appearing clearly. Imagine at the navel a four-petaled lotus, the front petal light blue, the right red, the back white, and the left yellow. Imagine a white *A* in the white center of the central stamen. Then imagine all the buddhas and bodhisattvas in the space before you. Meditate on *hūṃ* becoming Hevajra indivisible from Virūpa in front of them, and to their left, from *haṃ*, Nairātmya indivisible from Sukhasiddhi. {320} Above your head is Dampa holding a cane flute in his hand that touches your central channel. Think of your guru sitting in front of Dampa and supplicate three times with "Venerable Virūpa *hūṃ* Sukhasiddhi *haṃ*."

That causes the three letters *oṃ āḥ hūṃ*, like strings of pearls, to emerge from the hearts of all of the buddhas and bodhisattvas, primarily from those three: Virūpa, Sukhamasiddhi,[11] and Dampa. The [letters] come through Dampa's bamboo flute and descend, entering the central channel, finally dissolving into the four letters. Meditate that this reduces the potential of transgressions. Then say, "I go for refuge in the triad of guru, yidam, and ḍākinī." By doing the full measure of practice, you will not come under the ḍākinī's control; it is the vital point to bring the ḍākinī under your control.

Then for the recitation, imagine light emanates from the white *A*. It dissolves into the secret place of the letter, which is the goddess in essence. The potential of transgressions is reduced; bliss vibrates and light suffuses. Think that and then recite the four letters fully but just barely audible.

Now, if you wish to recognize and refine dreams, [imagine] light rays radiate from *A*. Think and say aloud, "All the lotus array is illusion. This is a dream." During all daily activities, remember the intentionality of illusion and dream.

To bring under control, all the objects of accomplishment are drawn in by the *A*'s light rays and dissolve into the letters and lotus. Then intensely arouse intentionality and passion.

If you want bliss, contract the lower winds, causing the lotus, which is the nature of bliss, to circle. {321} As it touches your flesh, think that special bliss is aroused. If you wish for warmth, light rays the nature of heat radiate from *A*. Red light the nature of heat radiates from the four letters and the lotus, filling all your insides. Think that, burned by the heat, you almost faint. The lotus spins rapidly; focus your consciousness on that without distraction while your body becomes a fireball.

If you want the natural arising of the deity's form, the ascertaining of objective appearance, the clear appearance of lucid clarity and such,[12] and for the perceived appearance to arrive quickly, imagine that the *A* at the navel and the four letters are the nature of light and maintain undistracted attention day and night. In particular, with the light of *A* inside your body in general and especially the entire inside of the navel filled with light, focus without distraction on the clarity of *A* within that light. With that as the main visualization, it is said to be important to maintain stable visualization when you sleep or move about and so forth.

When you grow tired of the recitation and that visualization, dissolve it in bliss. Light radiates from *A*, filling all of space. It draws in the form of red bodhicitta from the divine girl's secret place. Imagine that it dissolves into the four letters and you feel vibrating bliss. Do the same for the other five.

Whatever you control, emanate immeasurably many and offer them to Exalted Lady. It is said this is the profound way that accomplishes meditative experience.

There is absolutely nothing that has been left out of the oral instructions of this Secret Sādhana. The esoteric instructions of vital points that produces supreme and common spiritual powers in a matter of years or months is the lineage of Sukhasiddhi. {322}

IV. [Navel Emanation Chakra][13]

Bowing at the feet of the holy gurus
I write the oral instructions of the Navel Emanation Chakra.

Instantly you are generated as Exalted Lady. Imagine at the navel, from *E* (*A*?), a tetrahedral source of phenomena, white outside and red inside. Within that is a four-petaled red lotus. From its center, to the front is *ha*, to the right *ri*, to the back *ni*, and to the left *sa svā hā*. Light radiates from those seven seed syllables. It draws in all the magnetizing ability and awakened activity of all the buddhas and bodhisattvas, which dissolve into the letters, lotus, and source of phenomena. Imagine the reddening of the seed letters and the abundance of magnetizing ability. Those letters, endowed with dazzling brilliance of all that ability and activity, radiate light. Think of the three existences filled with the five sense pleasures all becoming red light. Imagine all the sense pleasures of all sentient beings drawn back in and imagine experiencing the brilliance of the three existences. In that way, all the sense pleasures are gathered into the source of phenomena, and the letters and lotus become the nature of brilliance. Again, red light rays radiate from the seed syllables like hooks and whatever practice consort is to be achieved powerlessly appears and dissolves upon the lotus. Then imagine the red guru upon the letters. The opening of the source of phenomena closes and red light comes from the guru. It strikes the practice consort, and their body is filled with red. Imagine their body, speech, and mind as naked. That is, their naked body prostrates without clothes; naked speech speaks of devotion, naked mind is great forceful faith and devotion, yearning and yearning, unable to bear separation [from you]. {323} Imagine that and think of the lotus spinning rapidly while the stationary letters emit light. The nonabiding of the body is movement; the nonabiding of the speech is recitation; and the nonabiding of the mind is the male's love, the female's passion, and the gem's intense longing.[14] Think the practice consort also dissolves, and bow repeatedly with devotion to the guru.

Based on the *Secret Sādhana of the Navel Emanation Chakra* by Lama Shangpa (Khyungpo Naljor), it is impossible that all supreme and common spiritual powers will not arise—such is this oral instruction.

V. Close Attainment

In the context of close attainment, meditate on yourself as Exalted Lady. If you have fulfilled it, do the recitation as in the main text. If not, then with yourself generated as Exalted Lady, the best is if you have the practice consort before you. If not, then visualize them clearly or, alternatively, imagine the light from *A* summoning them and the four-petaled lotus with letters within the source of phenomena [and so forth], as you have [previously] meditated. Then rest in the nonabiding body of movement, the nonabiding speech of recitation, and the nonabiding mind of phenomena's nature. Then audibly say, "*ha ri ni sa*—joy!" The lotus in the source of phenomena uncontrollably spins rapidly. Its light rends all the major and minor channels and that practice consort faints in bliss. A red stream of bodhicitta flows from her secret place, as if the stopper had been pulled. It beads up below your right big toe. You become completely red. Through that radiance, imagine that the consort becomes red and mentally intoxicated and becomes faithfully devoted. This is called "summoning bliss from below the goddess's navel [with] *oṃ ha ri ni sa*." That bliss is gathered into you. *ithi*

VI. Esoteric Instructions of the Three Nails[15]

These are instructions on the Three Nails that Ḍākinī Sukhasiddhi bestowed on Dharmaprajña.[16] {324}

guru ratna / cakrasaṃbhara / śrīyoginī / namo
Homage to Ḍākinī Spiritual Power of Bliss.

Specially exalted Three Nails instruction
of the Secret Sādhana Navel Emanation Chakra:
the nail of the guru on the head,
(the nail of) yidam Cakrasaṃvara at the heart,
(the nail of) the four ḍākinīs at the navel.

First, with devotion to the guru,
if you wish to traverse (ten) levels and (five) paths in years (and) months,
sit with crossed legs on a comfortable seat,
and accomplish the awakening mind and four immeasurables.
Visualize oneself as Vajrayoginī
with [red] color and hand implements.
On your head, upon a lotus (and) sun
imagine a black letter *hūṃ*.
Light radiates from it and accomplishes the two purposes, (ripening and liberating sentient beings and offering to the buddhas).
Light returns and transforms the *hūṃ*
into Virūpa and Hevajra;
imagine them to be indivisible.
Inside of your vajra's vase, (the gem),[17]
is a red source of phenomena
and within that the white letter *A*.
Light radiates, achieves two purposes, and returns.
Meditate that *A* is Nairātmya
inseparable from Sukhasiddhi.
Then join the two winds,
clearly visualized above and below (as Virūpa and Sukhasiddhi).
Twisting your body to the right
makes Nairātmya come to the navel.

Twisting to the left, she comes to the heart.
By that joining of right and left
she goes from the throat to the crown.
From the cranial aperture she (fully) embraces the father.
They enter into nondual union.
Imagine the spreading of nondissipating bliss.
Meditate on your root guru
in front of them.
Meditate clearly on the guru
and the Hevajra couple. {325}
Imagine the buddhas, bodhisattvas,
and hosts of ḍākinīs all around.
With (single-pointed focus) on that without being distracted (elsewhere),
fervently supplicate with long *hūṃ*. (Say, "Virūpa *hūṃ* Sukhasiddhi *haṃ*.")
If you supplicate with single-pointed attention
three times each day and night,
outer and inner obstacles will subside and
the three gatherings (of ḍākinīs, food, and wealth) will actually occur.
Especially, (Ḍākinī) Spiritual Power of Bliss
will grant you blessings in person and spiritual powers (both supreme and common).
You will traverse ten levels and five paths in years and months.
This is the uncommon supplication (unlike others).

Yidam Cakrasaṃvara is in the heart
of yourself as Exalted Vajrayoginī.
If you meditate without distraction on
that clarity without concept and recite the mantra,
it will also arise naturally in your dreams.
That is the actual saṃbhogakāya.

The (third), nail of four classes of ḍākinī in the navel:
The light of *A* burns;
if you practice threefold nonabiding (of body, speech, and mind),
you accomplish the supreme and common in years and months.
This secret practice of near attainment
of Exalted Vajrayoginī
gathers and summons, and gathers bliss.

First do the recitation of going for refuge.
Then for the vital point of the practice consort,
meditate clearly (as in the sādhana) in the source of phenomena,
on the four-petaled lotus with seed syllables
as being the nature of light.
Then light rays from *A*
evoke the vital points of the four syllables.
Audibly saying "*ha ra ni sa*—joy"
creates the condition for
light rays from the lotus and four syllables
to fill up all the greater and lesser channels.
The practice consort's bliss increases,
and the cause of bliss is movement (from all the channels). {326}
The sun of the radiance of the four elements
comes out as if the plug were pulled.
You appear clearly as Exalted Lady.
Imagine beneath the right big toe,
the flower rolled up in a bead.
You and whoever the practice consort is
become the color of lac dye.
Imagine (the consort's) devotion (to you and) bliss increasing.
Clarifying three nonabidings (body as deity, speech as mantra, mind as the nature of phenomena) is crucial.

Then the application of summoning.
Imagine as before the lotus and seed syllables
in the celestial palace of excellent features, the source of phenomena.
In particular, the *A* is red
and emits red light rays
that go to the secret place of the four letters.
Warmth evokes the place of (the letters') bliss
and the lotus uncontrollably spins (turning to the right).
A lotus breaks off [from] the lotus
and comes from the self-occurring flower.
Imagine underneath the right big toe it gathers
uncontrollably into beads, [then] press.
The lotus breaking off and the pressing
and the red light rays radiating

fill the channels and increase the bliss.
With red body, devoted and relaxed,
she cannot bear to look; the flow of the sun
uncontrollably gathers under foot.
Meditate by turn on the breaking off and the self-occurring [flower].
Recite the mantra as before.
Afterward dissolve into the secret place.

The previous fulfillment of the recitation requisite,
the clarity of yourself, and of the front visualization:
these three converge and moment by moment
you meditate without distraction in nonabiding.
The three gatherings and the three arisings (physical bliss, verbal ability, mental realization),
will be achieved in just years and months.

The stages of gathering the bliss
by the water stream of especially exalted four empowerments
should be conferred on other worthy recipients (having done the mandala, etc.).
When doing the practice yourself {327},
do from the recitation of refuge (through) the full measure of practice.
Then you are Cakrasaṃvara
with light radiating from *A* in the navel.
The goddess is white with a brilliant (golden) radiance,
she is youthful and charming with a blissful glow,
adorned by various jewels and Pāñcālikā's (divine garments).
That light strikes her secret place
and she arrives before you.
Meditate clearly on her secret place.
Then on the tip of your organ
the blue-black *hūṃ* radiates light rays
of five [colors] to the source of phenomena,
filling the channel spokes and increasing bliss.
Light rays of bliss from that
gather forcefully on their return.
They move up inside your organ
and all your channel spokes are filled (by Exalted Lady).
Bliss is born and

forcefully raising the lower wind joins (the goddess's) belly.
Meditate on bliss and emptiness inseparable.
Once again light radiates from *hūṃ*
and draws in the bliss as above.
Undissipating bliss increases in your body.
Meditate on clarity and emptiness inseparable.
Then the goddess, Exalted Lady,
embraces you in nondual [union].
The churning of method and wisdom makes warmth
that evokes the vital points of bliss;
the mother's self-arising sun flow.
That excellent abundance of bliss
goes up inside the vajra
and fills all the greater and lesser channels.
Bliss fills your being and expands.
Undissipating bliss increases in your body.
Your body turns the color of *rakta*,
controlling the mother.
Your own kunda radiates over
and the mother's bliss expands.
The (mother's color is) white with a red radiance;
the mother is controlled by the father.
Thus the couple is shaken by light. {328}
When your being is filled with bliss,
the forceful contracting of the lower wind
and the meaning of emptiness is revealed by bliss.
[But] do not let emptiness attach to bliss;
supreme timeless awareness is nondual bliss-emptiness.
The red lasts long, the white is short.
Understand the supreme vital points.
Rest without thought in the clarity of great bliss
in the deity's form of empty appearance.
Do the recitation within that state
of the nonduality of mother-father:
reciting *oṃ ha ri ni sa* and so on.
Through that, the mahāmudrā of deity's form
free of all stains of clinging,
becomes self-arising purity,

spontaneously present for all disciples.
That is the ultimate fruition.
Practice in the same way with [partners of]
gandharva, brahmin, caṇḍāla, human, and nāga.
This uncommon fourfold empowerment
if practiced by worthy recipients,
will produce the three gatherings and three arisings.
In particular, (Sukhasiddhi said), "I will grant you spiritual powers.
The Exalted Lady, as those six [partners]
will be seen in months or years, and become the mother consort.
You will proceed to the thirteenth level."

These words were spoken by Sukhasiddhi
in the autumnal time of precious sources,
at Rigong, the ḍākinīs' gathering place,
where she remained for seven days.
(Sukhasiddhi) conferred four empowerments (to Sangye), taught the vital points (of Secret Mantra),
and prophesied authentic pure great bliss.
So the tamer of beings, Sukhasiddhi,
taught Nyentön Dharmaprajña (Chökyi Sherap).
The (ḍāki's) exact words are written down (by Nyentön).[18]
This carries (Sukhasiddhi's) command seal of [no] more than one (disciple).
ithi / maṅgalaṃ

19. Sukhasiddhi's Introduction to Mahāmudrā[1]

Sangye Nyentön Chökyi Sherap

I. Introduction to Mahāmudrā

namo
Ḍākinī's pointing out of intrinsic awareness:
in empty space without distinction,
tame mind's root with awareness.
Tame the root, then rest naturally.

Creation phase and recitation completed,
place the left fist at the heart,
and raise up the right fist.
Stare nakedly at the center of the sky
unobstructed by wind or sun.
Heighten awareness and reverse the faculties [inward].
Wake up consciousness, tighten the body,
and slightly holding the winds,
meditate on an *A* in your navel.
It courses up the central channel, out the cranial aperture,
flies into space, and disappears.
The nature of phenomena free of elaboration,
the nature of mind free of elaboration,
free of elaboration within space itself;
rest in freshness without contrivance.
Without corruption caused by concepts,
press awareness by *phaṭ*, then evoke it.

Rest freshness in freshness itself.
Without distraction caused by concepts,
without loosening equanimity through laziness,
relax within the uncontrived state
of this natural condition of ordinary mind.
There is nothing at all to meditate on here,
discard any idea of wanting to meditate.
Rest awareness in its own innate disposition.

Afterward realize all phenomena—
consciousness, appearance, and sound—as dream and illusion.
Without attachment to anything, for the sake of beings,
rest within the state of unequaled awareness.
This is the Ḍākinī's heart advice.

Alternatively, after gathering the bliss,
rest in innately pure ordinary mind,
unpolluted by thoughts of wanting to meditate,
and relax into that uncontrived state.
Only the absence of any reference whatsoever
can be called mahāmudrā.
ithi

II. Aural Lineage Instructions

guru ḍāki namo
This instruction from the aural lineage has three parts. (1) Through the five techniques for resting, just as you can see the limpid mandala by looking into a silver-white mirror, {330} the introduction to mahāmudrā of both the ḍākinī and your own mind is this:

With the physical exercise,
in empty space without distinction,
tame mind's root with awareness.
Intensify the root, then rest relaxed.
Rest without support.
Rest without fixation.
Rest without a rester.

(2) Integrate the practice on the path through ten methods:

Overcome inability. Cut entanglement. Reverse attachment. Transform perception. Disrupt behavior. Leave the crowded place. Understand conditions as spiritual powers. Understand suffering as the nature of phenomena. Draw out awareness. Do not spread the aural lineage among people.

(3) Develop vajra-like meditative absorption through five convictions:

Be convinced that mind is empty. Be convinced that emptiness is dharmakāya. Be convinced that dharmakāya is continuous. Be convinced to be without hopes and fears. Be convinced there is no samsara and nirvana.

This concludes Sukhasiddhi's aural lineage, which is none other than the single lineage.

Sangye Nyentön proclaimed that the instructions of the aural lineage should not leave one's mouth. Do not discriminate. Do not sell for wealth. Do not leave it deliberately. Give it to the worthy without concealing it.

I humbly offer *Sukhamasiddhi's Introduction to Mahāmudrā*, a profound Golden Dharma. It is complete.

Lineage Supplications for the Six Dharmas of Niguma

Introduction

The first two supplications for Niguma's lineage are called supplications with "attached location" (*gnas sbyar ma*). That is a style of prayer that begins each quatrain with the location of the supplicated master—sometimes actual places, sometimes pure realms, and sometimes totally abstract mind states. In his catalog to the collection, Jamgön Kongtrul describes them as "attached-location supplications to both the long lineage and the direct lineage."[1] The first, *Supplication to Niguma's Lineage*, is for the lineage that comes through the great adept Tangtong Gyalpo, then through some Sakya masters down to Jamyang Khyentse Wangpo. This is the Tang tradition (*thang lugs*), usually indicating the direct transmission that he received in visionary encounter from Niguma. However, Tangtong Gyalpo also received the long lineage of Niguma's teachings from Jangsem Jinpa Zangpo and Jakchung Tsangma Shangtön, named here among many other masters in what appears to be the long lineage.[2] An added section carries the lineage through Kongtrul to Norbu Döndrup, who was the retreat master at Tsadra Rinchen Drak after Kongtrul, and Kalu Rinpoche's teacher.

The second supplication, *Clouds of Blessing*, appears to be the long Jonang lineage, coming as it does through Kunga Drolchok. There is an addition of the last verse ("Bless me . . . etc.") added by Kongtrul, signing as Guṇa, and taken from the "Tangtong tradition"; in other words, from the first text here. In *Among Tibetan Texts*, Gene Smith asserts this supplication was written by the seventh Drukchen, Kagyu Trinle Shingta and supplemented by Kongtrul.[3]

Trinle Shingta appears in the lineage of the third supplication, *Shower of Great Bliss*. In the table of contents of the earlier Kundeling edition of *The Treasury*, these three supplications are noted as being misplaced in the publication. They certainly seem randomly placed here, maybe as a consequence of that, as it seems to have followed suit in dividing them up. In another text of Shangpa liturgies, these three are found together.[4] I have taken the liberty of reuniting them here, albeit diverging from the order in this Shechen edition.

20. Supplication to Niguma's Lineage[1]

Jamgön Kongtrul

namo guru bhyaḥ

I supplicate the kind root guru
on a sun-moon seat above my head.
I pray to you, precious guru,
I supplicate; bless my mind stream.

I supplicate Buddha Great Vajradhara
in the palace of Dharmadhātu Akaniṣṭha.
I pray to you, precious guru,
I supplicate; bless my mind stream.

I supplicate Niguma, Ḍākinī of Timeless Awareness,
in the dark forest of sandalwood groves.
I pray to you, precious guru,
I supplicate; bless my mind stream.

I supplicate Khedrup Khyungpo Naljor
in the glorious monastery of Zhangzhong.
. . . (etc.; add the last two lines)

I supplicate incomparable Rinchen Tsöndru
in Shang Lhapu Mokchok Monastery.
. . .
I supplicate Öntön Great Compassion
in the central upper valley of Kyergang Monastery.
. . .

I supplicate Nyentön Bepai Naljor
in the cliffside monastery of Upper Yol.

. . .

I supplicate Khedrup Tsangma Shangtön
at the glorious monastery of Jakchung Palgön.

. . .

I supplicate Muchen Gyaltsen Palzang
at the monastery of the upper outskirts of Mu.

. . .

I supplicate Lama Dorje Zhönu
at the secluded place of a hundred haunted grounds.

. . .

I supplicate Tsenden Namkhai Naljor
at the glorious monastery of Mudzilung.

. . .

I supplicate Jangsem Jinpa Zangpo
at the northern monastery of Dorjeden.

. . .

I supplicate Drupchen Tangtong Gyalpo
on the peak of glorious Riwoche.

. . .

I supplicate lineage-holder Lodrö Gyaltsen
at the hermitage of the new Mangkhar Monastery.

. . .

I supplicate Khedrup Palden Darpo
at the forest retreat of secluded Purong.

. . .

I supplicate Jetsun Sönam Tsemo
at the graveyard of glorious Zhegön.

. . .

I supplicate Kalzang Gyurme Dechen
at the joy swirl *evaṃ* on Practice Mountain.

. . .

I supplicate Khenchen Ngawang Chödrak
at the dwelling place of Labrang Fortress.

. . .

I supplicate Jamyang Sönam Gyaltsen
at the dharma palace of Increasing Virtue.
. . .
I supplicate Ngawang Tenpa Rabgye
at the secluded place of Secret Mantra Great Bliss. {332}
. . .
I supplicate Mangtö Sönam Chöpel
at the secluded place of Tromolung.
. . .
I supplicate Kunga Lekpai Jungne
in the great school of Tashi Chö.
. . .
I supplicate Jamyang Sönam Palzang
at the excellent vajra place of Dokshe Monastery.
. . .
I supplicate Pakchok Chönyi Yeshe
at the palace of Samdzong Chöde.
. . .
I supplicate Tsungme Yeshe Gyalchok
at the herb valley of Mudrupachok.
. . .
I supplicate Yongdzin Mati Tsenchen
at the great dharma school of glorious Sakya.
. . .
I supplicate Jamgön Vajraratna
at the cliff fortress of Jagyur Dorje.
. . .
I supplicate Jamyang Khyentse Wangpo
at the center of the learned nonsectarian assembly.
. . .
[I supplicate Jamgön Yönten Gyatso
in the palace of pure, unbiased outlook.
. . .
I supplicate Norbu Dönkun Drubpa
in the palace of bliss-emptiness equanimity.
. . .][2]

I supplicate my kind root guru
in the dharma palace in my heart.
. . .
I supplicate the yidam, deities of [Five] Tantras
in the victors' mandala of my body.
. . .
I supplicate dharma lords, heroes, and ḍākinīs
in the country's twenty-four sacred sites.
. . .
I supplicate Swift-Acting Awareness Protector
in the Cool Grove Charnel Ground.
. . .
I supplicate sisters and brothers, vajra siblings,
in indefinite meeting places of pure minds.
I pray to you, precious guru,
I supplicate; bless my mind stream.

Bless me that bliss-warmth self-blazes on the Path of Methods.
Bless me that desire and anger self-liberate in Illusory Body.
Bless me that double delusion self-purifies in Dream.
Bless me that stupidity self-clarifies in Lucid Clarity.
Bless me to attain buddha without meditating in Transference.
Bless me as the victors' saṃbhogakāya in the Intermediate State.
Bless me to realize Lucid Clarity Mahāmudrā.

21. Clouds of Blessing

Supplication to the Guru Lineage of the Profound Path of Niguma's Six Dharmas[1]

Jamgön Kongtrul and Kagyu Trinle Shingta

namo guru

I supplicate the kind root guru
on a sun-moon seat above my head.
I pray to you, precious guru,
I supplicate; bless my mind stream.

I supplicate Buddha Great Vajradhara
in the palace of Dharmadhātu Akaniṣṭha.
I pray to you, precious guru,
I supplicate; bless my mind stream.

I supplicate Niguma, Ḍākinī of Timeless Awareness,
in the dark forest of sandalwood groves.
. . . (etc.; add the last two lines)

I supplicate Khedrup Khyungpo Naljor
in the pure realm Blissful in the north.
. . .
I supplicate Mokchokpa Rinchen Tsöndru
in the pure realm Abhirati in the east.
. . .

I supplicate great Öntön Kyergangpa
in the pure realm Arcimat in the east.
. . .
I supplicate Nyentön Bepai Sangye
in the pure realm Avakīrṇakusuma in the east.
. . .
I supplicate Drogön Sangye Tönpa
in the pure realm of the eastern stainless abode.
. . .
I supplicate Khedrup Tsangma Shangtön
in the presence of Dharma Lord Tönpa.
. . .
I supplicate Khyungpo Tsultrim Gönpo
in the pure realm of Padmovyūha.
. . .
I supplicate Jadral Ritrö Rechen
in the divine palace of Tuṣita above.
. . .
I supplicate Shangkarwa Rinchen Gyaltsen
in the palace of Shambhala in the north.
. . .
I supplicate incomparable Sangye Palzang
in the pure realm of divine Akṣobhya Monastery.
. . .
I supplicate Drupchen Namkha Gyaltsen
in the pure land of past lord gurus.
. . .
I supplicate Gyagom Lekpa Gyaltsen
in the realm of lotus flower stamens.
. . .
I supplicate [Kunga] Drolchok Semkyi Dudrol
in the royal realm of impartial openness.
. . .
I supplicate Chöku Lhawang Drakpa
in the dharma palace of the upper-cliffs site.
. . .

I supplicate Venerable Tāranātha
in the pure realm of the physician king's palace.
. . .
I supplicate Venerable Yeshe Gyatso
in the sacred site of Lotus Light Palace.
. . .
I supplicate Jampa Yönten Gönpo
in the pure realm of nirmāṇakāya, pure abode.
. . .
I supplicate Jalu Gönpo Paljor
in the pure realm of Khecara, site of lucid clarity. {334}
. . .
I supplicate Drupchok Gönpo Drakpa
in the site of the pure realm of Abhirati.
. . .
I supplicate Khyapdak Gönpo Namgyal
in Yangdzong, the site of elixir stream.
. . .
I supplicate Rikdzin Tsewang Norbu
among the rocks of outer Oyuk.
. . .
I supplicate Kagyu Trinle Shingta
in the assembly hall of sudden ḍākinīs.
. . .
I supplicate Kunga Gelek Palbar
in Mokchok's pleasure grove of practice.
. . .
I supplicate Kunga Lhundrup Gyatso
at the seat of former special exalted ones.
. . .
I supplicate Drupchen Kagyu Tenzin
in the pure realm of Trulzhik's Abhirati.
. . .
I supplicate Chokzik Karma Lhaktong
in the palace of self-arising saṃbhogakāya.
. . .

I supplicate Karma Zhenpen Özer
in the monastery of samsara-nirvana equality.

. . .

I supplicate prince Lodrö Taye
in the midst of unbiased learned adepts.

. . .

I supplicate Karma Tashi Özer
in the palace of love and compassion.

. . .

[I supplicate Drupwang Norbu Döndrup
in the palace of unattached bliss-emptiness.]

. . .

I supplicate the kind root guru
in the all-pervading wheel of great bliss.

. . .

(From Kagyu Trinle Shingta to here was newly added by Guṇa)

I supplicate brothers and sisters, vajra siblings,
in indefinite meeting places of pure minds.

. . .

I supplicate the yidam, deities of [Five] Tantras
in the victors' mandala of my body.

. . .

I supplicate Swift-Acting Awareness Protector
in the Cool Grove Charnel Ground.

. . .

I supplicate dharma lords, heroes, and ḍākinīs
in the country's twenty-four sacred sites.

. . .

Bless me that bliss-warmth self-blazes on the Path of Methods.
Bless me that desire and anger self-liberate in Illusory Body.
Bless me that double delusion self-purifies in Dream.
Bless me that stupidity self-clarifies in Lucid Clarity.
Bless me to attain buddha without meditating in Transference.
Bless me as the victors' saṃbhogakāya in the Intermediate State.
Bless me to realize Lucid Clarity Mahāmudrā.

The seven lines of the supplication beginning with the Path of Methods were not included in previous [versions]. However, they were filled in by Guṇa (Jamgön Kongtrul) from the attached-location supplication in the Tangtong tradition.

22. Shower of Great Bliss

A Concise Supplication to the Lineage of Profound Teaching of Niguma's Six Dharmas[1]

Jamgön Kongtrul

Vajradhara, pervading lord of everything;
Niguma, secret sublime delight;
Khyungpo Yogi, with five culminations;
Mokchokpa, king of supreme spiritual power;
Öntön Kyergangpa, bodhisattva at the stream's end;
Nyentönpa, dancer in illusion's integral unity;
Lord Tönpa, gone to buddhahood in one lifetime;
Tsangma Shangtön Tsultrim Bumpa, the honorable;
Zhönu Drup, sealed by the awareness mudra;
Gyaltsen Bum, the desired learned righteous adept;
Tsultrim Gön, desired emanation in existence;
Rechenpa, blazing with the brilliance of sublime caṇḍālī;
Rin Gyalwa [Shangpa Karpo], drenched in illusion's elixir;
Sangye Pal, accomplisher of wind-mind as deity's form;
Namkha Gyal, illuminated by the light of bliss-emptiness;
Lekpa Gyal[tsen], appearance dissolved into native mind;
[Kunga] Drolchok, lord of the Vajra Queen;
Chöku Lhawang Drak, full of undissipating bliss;
Drolwai Gönpo, glorious secret heruka;
[Yeshe] Gyatso, regent of embodied awareness;
[Jampa] Yönten Gön, taking up deliberate conduct on the path;
Gönpo Paljor, gone in a rainbow body;
Gönpo Drakpa, equalizer of samsara and nirvana;
[Gönpo] Namgyal, intoxicated by coemergent joy;

Rikdzin [Tsewang Norbu], leader of a million learned adepts;
[Kagyu] Trinle Shingta, real holder of the white lotus;
[Kunga Gelek] Palbar, a hundred lights of virtue and realization;
Kunga Lhundrup [Gyatso], treasure revealer of abiding nature;
[Ngawang] Lodröpa, always guided by beautiful Khecarī;
Lord Karma Lhaktong, hidden buddha;
Zhenpen Özer, receiver of wind-mind empowerment;
my root guru, holder of the treasury of instructions:
I supplicate with intense undivided longing.

Your body is Guhyasamāja, your speech Mahāmāya, {458}
your mind Hevajra, your qualities Cakrasaṃvara,
and your activity is Bhairava, all inseparable.
Holders of the golden rosary of profound instructions
from the king of learned adepts, Khyungpo Naljor,
I supplicate you with intense yearning from my heart.
With deep compassion, grant your blessings for spiritual powers.

Bless me that bliss-warmth of fierce inner heat blazes.
Bless me that illusion arises by itself without attachment.
Bless me that the deities' forms arise in dreams.
Bless me that lucid clarity arises without interruption.
Bless me to achieve the unerring celestial realm.
Bless me to attain the three kāyas in the intermediate state.
Just hearing your name tears existence asunder.
Bless me to quickly attain the state of the great adept Khyungpo
and then lead all migrators throughout space.

[Colophon]

By the command of Jampai Pal, the delightful adept of the profound inner path of yoga, and also drawn from my own respectful desire for something short, Dewai Dorje (Jamgön Kongtrul) made this supplication in the abode of strong yearning. Let virtue prevail.

Four Deities Combined

Introduction

This classic Shangpa practice involves visualizing oneself as Cakrasaṃvara with one's guru as the Buddha Vajradhara couple above one's head. In front of Vajradhara is the special Shangpa lineage dharma protector Six-Armed Mahākāla, with the deities Vajrayoginī, two-armed Avalokiteśvara, and Green Tārā in the other directions. As an elaborate form of guru yoga practice, one visualizes receiving their blessings within oneself. Meditation on the Vajradhara couple grants highest spiritual powers, meditation on the Protector dispels outer hindrances, while Tārā dispels inner hindrances, meditation on Avalokiteśvara increases compassion, and on Vajrayoginī enhances bliss. Thus all the bases for spiritual progress are covered.

The practice originates with the great Indian adept Śavarīpa, who passed it on to his accomplished disciples Maitrīpa and Rāhula. Sukhasiddhi also held this practice, as indicated in the opening homage of Jamgön Kongtrul's first text here, *Naturally Luminous Timeless Awareness*. This is the main sādhana with the visualization description included as the liturgy. It follows the general format of creation-phase practice, culminating with the taking of empowerment to receive the full blessings.

The most important origin story is recounted in the second text, Kongtrul's guidebook on the practice called *Radiant Light of Timeless Awareness*. This involves the transmission to Khyungpo Naljor by Hidden Yogi, Rāhulaguptavajra, during his miraculous visit to Tibet. Kongtrul's account is ultimately based on an Indian source text called *Two Histories of the Four Deities*.[1] With its interlinear notes attempting to clarify the arcane verse style, one can embellish somewhat on the main points below. The story focuses on Rāhula, and appears to be written by him in first person. It recounts his birth and the appearance of the four deities at that time. Then after some training in the dharma, he falls ill with smallpox (*'brum nag*) at the age of twenty-one. In this near-death condition, the four deities appear again as they did at his birth and predict that the disease will purify his previous bad karma, and that he will go on to do great things and finally end up in the celestial realm of Khecara. With their blessings he, of course, recovers. It seems this is the origin of the label "four blessing deities" (*byin rlabs lha bzhi*). Rāhula continues his studies with their blessings and more visionary encounters. The deities and his human mentors encourage him several times to go to Tibet, where the forlorn inhabitants are in dire need of spiritual guidance. Rāhula does just that and spends seven or eleven months transmitting these and many other teachings to Khyungpo Naljor. In this ancient account, before Rāhula departs, he praises Khyungpo's noble intentions and apparently his patience, echoing the words that his teachers had previously used:

> Those in the vajra land of the North
> don't understand karmic consequences, equate sin with virtue,
> wish to sever the blessings of Caṇḍi [ḍākinī],
> don't rely on gurus, are without sacred pledge,
> and while dharma just enters their ear holes,
> if one explains it after close examination,
> they mostly go right to hell.[2]

He then flies away to India, stopping briefly in Nepal to attend a feast.

23. Naturally Luminous Timeless Awareness

Four Deities Combined Practice, a Profound Dharma of the Glorious Shangpa Kagyu[1]

Jamgön Kongtrul

namo gurave
Blessings of Sukhasiddhi and Rāhula
on lineage holders to lineage holders.
I bow before the four deities
and explain their simple daily practice.

Fortunate people who have obtained its permission and procedural guide may do this condensed essential practice. There are three parts: (1) preliminaries, (2) main practice, and (3) conclusion.

I. Preliminaries

To go for refuge, repeat this three times:

> All sentient beings, my mothers, equal to the reaches of space,
> go for refuge in the precious guru, the unified essence of all refuges.

To arouse the mind of awakening, repeat this three times:

> For the sake of all sentient beings, I must attain the unified state of Great Vajradhara. To that end, I will engage the profound dharma, Four Deities Combined Practice.

II. Main Practice

This has two parts: (1) creation-phase recitation and (2) taking the uncommon empowerment.

A. Creation Phase Recitation

oṃ vajra rakṣa rakṣa hūṃ phaṭ
In the center of the vajra protection circle and blazing fires,
I appear clearly in the form of glorious Cakrasaṃvara.
Above my head is a source of phenomena, great bliss,
white outside and red inside, the nature of light.
Within is a four-petaled lotus, sun and moon in its center.
Upon that, from *hūṃ* a *hūṃ*-marked vajra completely transforms
into the guru, Great Vajradhara, the radiance of space, {337}
with one face and two hands holding vajra and bell, embracing his own light:
Vajradhātviśvarī, who holds a flaying knife and skull cup.
They are adorned by silks, bones, and precious jewels,
sitting in vajra posture in a boundless expanse of light
of blessings and timeless awareness.

In front of them, on a seat of sun and suppressed Gaṇapati,
from *hūṃ* a *hūṃ*-marked flaying knife becomes
the Awareness Protector with one face and six arms.
He is the color of rain clouds, with three eyes and four snarling fangs,
orange beard, eyebrows, and hair blazing upward.
He holds flaying knife, skull rosary, and ḍamaru in his three right hands
and blood-filled skull cup, trident, and lasso with the three left hands.
He is adorned by dry and wet skulls, bones, [five] snake types,
a smear of vermilion, bells, and little bells.
His head is beautifully crowned by royal Akṣobhya.
He has an elephant-skin cloak and tiger-skin skirt.
He sports a standing posture in the midst of blazing bonfire.

To the right, on a sun, red *hṛīḥ* becomes a *hṛīḥ*-marked flaying knife
that completely transforms into red Vajrayoginī. {338}
She is youthful and smiling, with an expression of laughter.

Her three eyes glance left, her locks fall loosely.
Her right hand holds a flaying knife downward, threatening,
and her left holds up a skull cup full of elixir for her to drink.
She bears a khaṭvāṅga and wears the five symbolic ornaments.
She stands with right leg extended, trampling Bhairava and Kālarātri.

In back, on a moon seat, *hrīḥ* becomes a *hrīḥ*-marked white lotus
that completely transforms into pure white Avalokita,
his right hand with a vase grants refuge,[2]
his left holds a white lotus stem to his heart.
The locks of his hair are crowned by Amitābha.
He is seated in the posture of right leg extended and left drawn in.

To the left, on a moon, *tāṃ* becomes a *tāṃ*-marked utpala,
and completely transforms into green Exalted Tārā.
She is charming as a sixteen-year-old, crowned by Amoghasiddhi.
Her right hand gives refuge, her left holds a blooming utpala.
With ornaments, she deports majestically with right extended and left drawn in.

All of the deities are marked with *oṃ āḥ hūṃ* in their three places.
Light radiates from the *hūṃ*s, invoking the Three Roots and Three Jewels
in the forms of the guru and four deities, who then dissolve [into the visualized forms].
jaḥ hūṃ vaṃ hoḥ—they become the united essence of all refuge sources.

> Precious guru and group of four deities: outwardly I offer flowers and incense; inwardly five meats and five elixirs; secretly the awareness of bliss-emptiness; and more secretly the offering of suchness. These and other special unimaginable offerings I present for your pleasure. Partake of them and please grant your blessings.
>
> Door for the entry of every blessing,
> place of attainment of every spiritual power,
> deities for dispelling every obstacle:
> I bow to the guru and four deities.

Some holy masters have suggested substituting a seven-branch service and mandala offering for these offerings and praise. {339}

Focus on the guru in the center with devotion and repeat the mantra:

namo buddhāya / namo guruhe / vajra vīra vīriṇī / śrī ḍāka ḍākinī / joka jokinī / sarva buddha bodhisatvāya śaraṇaṃ gacchāmi kyai

A stream of elixir falls from Guru's form,
enters the crown of my head, fills my body, and purifies
negatives, obscurations, faults, downfalls, sickness, spirits, and obstacles.
I have attained the blessings of Guru's three secrets.

Focus on the protector in front and repeat the mantra:

oṃ vajra mahākāla kṣiṃ kṣetra vighanāṃ vināyāka hūṃ hūṃ phaṭ phaṭ svāhā

A stream of elixir falls from Protector's form,
enters the crown of my head, fills my body, and purifies
negatives, obscurations, faults, downfalls, sickness, spirits, and obstacles.
I have attained the blessings of Protector's three secrets.

Focus on Vajrayoginī on the right and repeat the mantra:

oṃ vajra nara kraṃ kraṃ hūṃ hūṃ phaṭ phaṭ svāhā

This recitation is the actual mantra presented in the ancient texts. In some later practices, it is taught to recite the three-*oṃ* mantra here.[3]

A stream of elixir falls from Yoginī's form,
enters the crown of my head, fills my body, and purifies
negatives, obscurations, faults, downfalls, sickness, spirits, and obstacles.
I have attained the blessings of Vārāhī's three secrets.

Focus on Avalokita in the back and repeat the mantra:

oṃ maṇi padme hūṃ / oṃ vajra rakṣa namaḥ samanta hūṃ phaṭ

A stream of elixir falls from Exalted One's form,
enters the crown of my head, fills my body, and purifies
negatives, obscurations, faults, downfalls, sickness, spirits, and obstacles.
I have attained the blessings of Exalted One's three secrets.

Focus on Tārā on the left and repeat the mantra:

oṃ tāre tuttāre ture svāhā

A stream of elixir falls from Tārā's form,
enters the crown of my head, fills my body, and purifies
negatives, obscurations, faults, downfalls, sickness, spirits, and obstacles.
I have attained the blessings of Tārā's three secrets.

When you do this for the sake of accumulating the recitation, repeat the *namo buddha* mantra a bit more, and the other four in equal measure. {340} If you do this at the beginning of Protector's recitation practice, it is said to bolster Protector's recitation itself. In the course of [other] guidances, it is taught to principally recite Yoginī's three-*oṃ* mantra. These [authors] apparently had in mind Yoginī as the main practice. Here, as a daily recitation, just repeat all the mantras in equal numbers, such as one hundred or seven times each. On occasions when you are unable to do the elaborate version, skip the verses of the individual visualizations and after just the praises repeat each mantra three times. Then say:

A stream of elixir falls from the guru and deities,
enters the crown of my head, fills my body, and purifies
negatives, obscurations, faults, downfalls, sickness, spirits, and obstacles.
I have attained the blessings of the guru's and deities' three secrets.

B. Taking the Uncommon Empowerment

At the conclusion of either the long or short session of recitation-meditation, augment it with repeating the five mantras or by repeating *namo buddha* . . . (etc.) three times, as supplication.

> Light rays radiate from the *hūṃ* in the guru's heart
> and gather in the four deities: Avalokita to the head,
> Tārā to the throat, Great Black to the heart,
> and Yoginī to the navel; light radiates again,
> invoking the victors and their heirs.
> They completely fill up the guru's body.

Draw up the lower wind and hold the vase breathing or the intermediate breathing.

> Wind stirs in the secret place, igniting fierce inner heat at the navel.
> That emerges from the cranial aperture, heats the source of phenomena,
> strikes the guru's form, and the deities melt in bliss.
> A stream of elixir emerges, enters the crown of my head,
> fills above the throat, and purifies physical negativities and obscurations.
> I obtain the vase empowerment; the blessings of awakened body enter.
> It fills above the heart and purifies verbal negativities and obscurations.
> I obtain the secret empowerment; the blessings of awakened speech enter.
> It fills above the navel and purifies mental negativities and obscurations.
> I obtain the wisdom empowerment; the blessings of awakened mind enter.
> It fills my whole body and purifies negativities and obscurations of all three doors.
> I obtain the fourth empowerment; all blessings are perfectly complete.

The source of phenomena dissipates in light; the guru dissolves
into me;
my three doors become inseparable from the three vajras. {341}

III. Conclusion

This has two parts: (1) resting in equipoise and (2) the activities in the session breaks.

A. Resting in Equipoise

Maintain that very state of the inseparable merging of the guru with one's own mind for as long as it lasts, without any fabrication, restriction, or affirmation—just mere recognition.

B. Activities in the Session Breaks

When you arise from that, without letting mindful awareness dissipate, seal with dedication and aspiration prayers:

All buddhas at all times
possess the state of Great Vajradhara.
Through my virtue may I attain that
and may all migrators also attain it.

Conduct for the sake of perfect awakening
and any conduct after perfect buddhahood
was praised by the Awakened Vajra;
may I practice those two conducts.[4]

Then go about your activities.

[Concluding Verse and Colophon]

Good for dispelling obstacles and enhancing practice
in a matter of years or months,
after meditating on this yoga of profound dharma
may as many beings be freed as atoms in the realm.

Karma Ngawang Yönten Gyatso wrote this according to the guru's teaching transmission to make the connection with the required practices for those dedicated to accomplishment in the secluded retreat of Kunzang Dechen Ösal Ling. Let virtue prevail!

24. Radiant Light of Timeless Awareness

A Guidebook on the Four Deities Combined Practice, a Profound Dharma of the Glorious Shangpa Kagyu[1]

Jamgön Kongtrul

namo guru caturdevāyā

I bow to the glorious guru who bestows supreme spiritual powers,
and to the four blessing deities who dispel outer and inner hindrances
and enhance good qualities.
I will briefly clarify the guidance sequence.

The great learned adept Khyungpo Naljor received the complete heart essence of one hundred and five Indian adepts, principal among whom were the two ḍākinīs of timeless awareness. The great individuals who held this long lineage tradition of Shangpa Kagyu always mastered the perfectly complete precepts of authoritative texts and instructions from the vast ocean of the profound dharma of Sutra and Mantra and were exclusively those who were grounded in the experience of supreme accomplishment. Of the four or five well-known instruction cycles that have continued to the present time, here I will explain the stages of guidance of the Four Deities Combined Practice, the instructions of the great adept Rāhulagupta, with whom this practice is primarily associated. He was a South Indian who had attained the state of an immortal awareness holder and reached the heights of supreme accomplishment. This presentation has two parts: (1) the brief story of the origins of the lineage and (2) the extensive explanation of the actual stages of guidance that came from [that lineage]. {345}

I. Story of the Origins of the Lineage

The four deities were revealed in visionary experience to the great adept mighty Śavarīpa, and he taught their method of accomplishment (*sādhana*). Master Maitrīpa listened to those teachings and arranged the sādhana. Clearly the learned adept Khyungpo received it from this [master], as he said he had "the constant blessings of the four deities." Besides, it was primarily from [Maitrīpa that Khyungpo also] received the Awareness Protector.

But the main source of this lineage of instructions is the great adept Rāhulaguptavajra. He was born in the south of India, in a land blessed by Vajraḍākinī called Elabhiśa. As soon as he was born into the royal caste, he saw the four deities face to face and was blessed by them. When he was young, the residual karma from previous lives ripened as severe illness, causing a sense of sadness. He entered the dharma and trained until he was very learned in all sutras and tantras. He relied on the instructions of Guṇasāgara, Ratnasāgara, and others, easily attaining the common spiritual powers. Ultimately he attained the longevity of an awareness holder and the supreme accomplishment of mahāmudrā. {346}

Rāhula was requested by his accomplished gurus to [visit] Khyungpo Naljor while Khyungpo was doing a solitary retreat at Penyul Jokpo (*'phen yul 'jog po*). He was sent off in the manner of a dharma path, leaving India at daybreak and miraculously arriving before the sun rose in Tibet. He stayed a while, giving Khyungpo Naljor many profound instructions, such as White and Deep-Blue Protectors (*mgon po dkar mthing*), and the Chariot of Vital Winds.[2] In particular, he bestowed the cycle of Four Deities Combined Practice with its supplemental material. Khyungpo took it to heart in practice and became a great adept, such that his disciples with pure karma could actually perceive him in the forms of the four deities. He in turn passed the practice to Mokchokpa and others, and from there the system of transmission of the blessings and instructions has continued without interruption to the present. I supplicated Jamyang Khyentse Wangpo for them. That great person who is inseparable from Great Vajradhara and holds the secret treasury of the entire corpus of common and uncommon mysteries of our Vajrayāna, who dwells on the great level of the exalted ones beyond human [experience], kindly granted it to me.

Here I have gathered the special direct lineage of the sādhana actually imparted to Mokchokpa Rinchen Tsöndru by the four deities and explanations and permissions that Spiritual Power of Bliss (Sukhasiddhi) gave to some lineage holders. In general there are two explanations: the practice of the four deities separately and the combined practice. Of those, the subject to be explained on this occasion will be the Four Deities Combined Practice.

II. The Actual Instructions of Those with That Lineage

This has three parts: (1) the stages of the preliminaries, (2) main practice, and (3) conclusion.

A. Preliminaries

1. Session Preliminary

The session preliminary is to take a comfortable seat and assume the physical vital points of posture as usual. Expel the dead winds and settle into mindfulness.

2. Guidance Preliminary

The guidance preliminary has two parts: (1) going for refuge and (2) arousing the awakening mind. {347}

a. Refuge

In the space before you, on a lotus-sun-moon seat on a lion throne, your actual root guru, who is the unified essence of the Three Jewels and all refuge sources, appears in the form of Great Vajradhara. You and all others, the whole range of migrators throughout the reaches of space, with your three doors combined in unison, go for refuge with single-pointed mind from now until attaining awakening. Repeat as much as you can:

> All sentient beings, my mothers, equal to the reaches of space,
> go for refuge in the precious guru, the unified essence of all refuges.

b. Awakening Mind

Think, "Sentient beings throughout space, however many there are, have all been exclusively kind parents to me. They wander in the ocean of suffering in cyclic existence with no chance to escape—how pitiful! In order to liberate them from cyclic existence, I must definitely attain Great Vajradhara's state of integral unity quickly." This is the awakening mind of aspiration.

Then think, "In order to attain that, I must cultivate the experience of the profound yoga of Four Deities Combined Practice that comes from an aural lineage consisting exclusively of adepts, a short path that gathers into one profound vital point the stages of the path of Vajrayāna. Through that, I will quickly attain the state of the guru and four deities and place all sentient beings in that state as well." This is the awakening mind of engagement. Verbally recite:

> For the sake of all sentient beings, I must attain the unified state of Great Vajradhara. To that end, I will engage the profound dharma, Four Deities Combined Practice.

Repeat that a number of times. Then rest without reference to the refuge objects.

B. Main Practice

This has two parts: (1) the yoga of creation-phase recitation and (2) taking the profound empowerment. {348}

1. The Yoga of Creation Phase Recitation

By your saying "*oṃ vajra rakṣa rakṣa hūṃ phaṭ*" there appears a protection circle with vajra ground, enclosure, lattice, tent, and canopy, with a blazing fire of awareness outside. In its center, on a seat of the sun disk with Bhairava and Kālarātri, you appear clearly as Bhagavat Coemergent Cakrasaṃvara within an expansive mass of light. Above your head is a source of phenomena, brilliantly clear and unsullied, the nature of light, white outside and red inside. The lower vertex touches your cranial aperture while the wide opening faces upward. It arises as bliss and expands bliss. In its center is a fully blossomed four-petaled multicolored lotus with stamens that rise a cubit in height. Upon them, on a stacked seat of the sun and moon, blue *hūṃ* becomes a blue vajra marked by *hūṃ*. That completely transforms into the essence of your root guru in the form of Great Vajradhara, the color of radiant vaiḍūrya. His two crossed hands hold vajra and bell, embracing Vajradhātviśvarī, who holds a flaying knife and skull cup. They are both adorned by bones and precious jewels, and clothed in silks. They sit in vajra posture and lotus posture [respectively], radiating the boundless light of blessings and timeless awareness.

On the lotus petal in front, on the sun-disk mandala, white Gaṇapati lies face up.[3] On that seat, black *hūṃ* becomes a flaying knife marked by *hūṃ*. That completely transforms into Swift-Acting Awareness Protector, Six-Armed Mahākāla. He is as dark as the clouds at the end of time, with three round red eyes, and fangs bared in his open mouth. His orange eyebrows, whiskers, and hair stream upward like flames of fire. His forehead is smeared with a drop of vermilion, and Akṣobhya crowns his head. He holds a meteorite flaying knife in his top right hand, a skull rosary in the middle hand, {349} and fiercely rattles a sandalwood ḍamaru in the lower right hand. He holds a skull cup filled with human blood in his upper left hand, a trident in the middle hand, and a vajra lasso in the lower left hand. He wears a crown of five dry skulls and a garland of fifty wet skulls dripping with blood. He is adorned by the six bone ornaments and bunches of five types of snake, with bells and small bells on his arms and legs. He is short and stocky, with thick limbs and protruding belly. His upper body is cloaked in a wet elephant skin, and he wears a wet tiger-skin skirt cinched by a green silk belt. His legs are in standing posture, [with right foot raised] as if mobilized to move. He stands in an expanse of blazing flames of timeless awareness.

The lotus petal to the right of the guru has a sun seat upon which a red *hrīḥ* becomes a flaying knife marked by *hrīḥ*. That completely transforms into Exalted Vajrayoginī, who is red with a maroon radiance, youthful as a sixteen-year-old. As she smiles, her eyeteeth protrude slightly. Her three eyes glance to the left. Her right hand holds a flaying knife downward, and her left holds up a skull cup full of elixir for her to drink. She has a khaṭvāṅga in the bend of her left elbow and is adorned by the five symbolic ornaments. She stands with right leg extended, trampling on Bhairava, and the left bent, pressing on Kālarātri. The rays of her timeless awareness blaze everywhere.

On the lotus petal in back of the guru is a white *hrīḥ* on a moon mandala, which becomes a white lotus marked by *hrīḥ*. That completely transforms into Exalted Avalokita, the color of the moon. He is peaceful and smiling, adorned by all the silks and precious ornaments. His hair is piled on top with locks falling loosely, crowned by Amitābha. {350} His right hand holds a vase with the mudra of supreme generosity, and his left hand grasps the stem of a white lotus flower with thumb and ring finger at his heart; the full blossom is near his left ear. He sits in the position of right leg extended and left contracted, within an expanse of rainbow light.

On the lotus petal to the guru's left, upon the moon, green *tāṃ* becomes a green utpala flower marked by *tāṃ*. It completely transforms into Exalted Tārā. She is green and in the prime of youth, in form like a sixteen-year-old, adorned by silks and jewels. Her right hand is extended upon her knee in the mudra of supreme generosity. Her left hand in the mudra indicating the Three Jewels holds at her heart the stem of a green utpala flower that blossoms near her ear. She is crowned by Amoghasiddhi. She sits in the position of right leg slightly extended and the left drawn in, within the light of her own radiance.

Meditate clearly on those five—the principals and entourage—as appearance with no intrinsic nature. All five are marked with white *oṃ* at their foreheads, red *āḥ* at their throats, and blue *hūṃ* at their hearts. Light rays radiate from the *hūṃ*s, invoking the gurus, yidams, buddhas, bodhisattvas, heroes, ḍākinīs, and hosts of dharma protectors and guards, all in the forms of Vajradhara and the four deities. Imagine that they dissolve into the respective deities visualized above your head. Say *jaḥ hūṃ vaṃ hoḥ* and imagine those deities above your head become the unified essence of every source of refuge.

Imagine that goddesses emanate from your heart and present the outer sense offerings, the inner five elixirs and five desirables, and the secret offering of the bliss-emptiness arising from intercourse. Rest the mind in the uncontrived meditative absorption of the natural purity [of those offerings, and say:]

> Precious guru and group of four deities: Outwardly I offer flowers and incense; {351} inwardly five meats and five elixirs; secretly the awareness of bliss-emptiness; and more secretly the offering of suchness. These and other special unimaginable offerings I present for your pleasure. Please partake of them and grant your blessings.

After just saying that, it is acceptable to go directly to the recitation [of mantras as] supplication. According to the guru's teaching transmission, however, it is advised to do [more] offerings and praises at this point. If you are interested, then directly after the offerings described above, do the extensive praises that consist of one verse for each deity:

One whose [kindness makes great bliss itself
arise in that very instant,
guru whose body is like a jewel;
I bow at the feet of the vajra holder.][4]

Wicked one with a cannibal's body,
[terminator bodhisattva,
destroyer of the three-tiered cities;
I pay homage to you, fierce one.][5]

Glorious Vajra Ḍākinī,
[wheel wielder of the ḍākinīs,
with fivefold awareness and three kāyas;
homage to the protector of migrators.][6]

White body unblemished by flaws,
[with the perfect buddha as crown,
compassionate eyes look upon migrators;
I pay homage to Avalokita.][7]

Gods and demigods bow their crowns
[down to your two lotus feet.
You are the liberator from all poverty;
homage to Mother Tārā.][8]

Or a short praise:

Door for the entry of every blessing,
place of attainment of every spiritual power,
deities for dispelling every obstacle:
I bow to the guru and four deities.

Regarding this, some holy masters have said that as a substitute for the offerings and praises, one could do the seven-branch service and mandala offering. If you wish to do so, there is nothing contradictory, so recite any appropriate verses for the seven-branch service and the *Mandala of the Sealed Word*[9] after the offerings and praises. Then, without letting your attention wander to anything else, recite with intense powerful yearning the individual mantras in the manner of a supplication and meditate on the visualization of the elixir falling and purifying. First elixir falls from Guru Vajradhara's body. It enters the crown of your head and fills your body, cleansing and purifying negativities, obscurations, faults, downfalls, sickness, and bad spirits. Think that you obtain the blessings of the guru's awakened body, speech, and mind all at once while saying the mantra:

> *namo buddhāya / namo guruhe / vajra vīra viriṇī / śrī ḍāka ḍākinī / joka jokinī / sarva buddha bodhisatvāya śaraṇaṃ gacchāmi kyai*

Apply the same formula to the rest. {352} By your devotion to the Protector, a stream of elixir falls from Protector's body. It enters your crown, fills your body, and purifies all negativities, obscurations, faults, downfalls, sickness, and bad spirits. In particular, boundless tiny replicas of the Protector arrive, falling like rain, and enter inside your body. They noisily devour raw all your sickness, spirits, negativities, and obscurations. Think that the blessings of Protector's awakened body, speech, and mind enter your being, and repeat:

> *oṃ vajra mahākāla kṣiṃ kṣetra vighanāṃ vināyaka hūṃ hūṃ phaṭ phaṭ svāhā*

Then, by your supplicating Yoginī, a stream of red elixir falls from Vajrayoginī's secret place. It enters your crown, fills your body, and purifies all negativities, obscurations, faults, downfalls, sickness, and bad spirits. Think that you obtain the blessings of Yoginī's awakened body, speech, and mind in your being, and repeat:

> *oṃ vajra nara kraṃ kraṃ hūṃ hūṃ phaṭ phaṭ svāhā*

Then, by your supplicating Avalokita, a stream of white elixir falls from Exalted Great Compassionate One's body and from the vase in his hand. It enters your crown, fills your body, and purifies all negativities, obscurations, faults, downfalls, sickness, and bad spirits. Think that you obtain the blessings of Avalokita's awakened body, speech, and mind in your being, and repeat:

> *oṃ maṇi padme hūṃ / oṃ vajra rakṣa namaḥ samanta hūṃ phaṭ*

Then, by your devotion to Exalted Tārā, a stream of elixir falls from Tārā's right big toe. It enters your crown, fills your body, and purifies all negativities, obscurations, faults, downfalls, sickness, and bad spirits. Think that the blessings of Exalted Lady's awakened body, speech, and mind enter your being, and repeat:

oṃ tāre tuttāre ture svāhā

Complete the main part of the session with those recitations and visualizations. In the later transmitted teachings, it says to recite primarily the three-*oṃ* mantra for Yoginī's recitation practice while reciting the others somewhat less. {353} Some say that this will enhance the Protector's recitation accumulation, and so forth. These statements were apparently made in relation to those whose practices focus mainly on those particular yogas. Here, in general, do the recitation of the guru's supplication slightly more and the other recitations in equal amounts.

2. Taking the Uncommon [Profound] Empowerment

Recite the series of five mantras three times in the manner of a supplication and arouse intense devotion. Light rays radiate from the letter *hūṃ* in Guru Vajradhara's heart and invoke the surrounding four deities. Imagine Avalokita dwelling at Guru's crown, Venerable Tārā at the throat, Awareness Protector at the heart, and Vajrayoginī at the navel. Light rays radiate again from Guru's heart and invoke from the ten directions all the gurus, yidams, buddhas, bodhisattvas, heroes, ḍākinīs, awareness dharma protectors and guards in the forms of the four deities. Think that they fill up the whole inside of the guru's body, like grain fills a barrel, with their individual aspects.

Then instantly visualize the three channels and five chakras in the center of your empty body. At the lower end of the central channel is an *A*-stroke like a barberry thorn (*skyer tsher*). Clearly visualize a wind mandala near the secret and anal openings. Hold the joined breath or, if unable, slightly contract the lower winds to join [them] with the awareness winds. That causes the wind to stir at your secret place, striking the *A*-stroke at the navel; the red fire of timeless awareness of the inner heat blazes fiercely. It emerges from your cranial aperture and strikes the source of phenomena, greatly heating it. {354} That in turn heats up the deities, causing the blazing of unbearably great bliss. All the body deities melt fully into elixir. A stream of elixir emerges from the place of union of the deity couple and enters you through the crown of your head. As it fills above the throat, it purifies physical negativities and obscurations. You obtain the vase empowerment; the blessings of awakened body enter. As it fills above the heart, it purifies verbal negativities and obscurations. You obtain the secret empowerment; the blessings of awakened speech enter. As it fills above the navel, it purifies mental negativities and obscurations. You obtain the wisdom-awareness empowerment; the blessings of awakened mind enter. As it fills the whole body, it purifies negativities and obscurations of all three doors. You obtain the fourth empowerment; every blessing of the three vajras enter you.

Finally, the source of phenomena vanishes by itself into space. In great delight, Guru melts into light and dissolves into you. You also dissolve into emptiness. Imagine that the guru's and your own mind blend inseparably.

C. Conclusion

This has two parts: (1) maintaining the abiding nature and (2) entering the session breaks.

1. Maintaining the Abiding Nature

After the guru dissolves into you, assume the sevenfold position with your body. The vital point of speech is to dispel the dead air with the ninefold shake-up. Let the two movements fall naturally. The vital point of mind is not to follow after any thoughts of the three times nor entertain any ideas of good and bad, affirmation and denial, or hopes and fears. Just maintain wide-open consciousness and self-recognizing mindfulness without any contrivance of acceptance or rejection. Train at first with tight focus, in the middle relax loosely, and finally rest in the awareness of your native state without losing the vitality of mindfulness. Rest in that equipoise as long as it lasts.

2. Entering the Session Breaks

Upon arising from that, begin the activities of session breaks. Always remain in the state of knowledge that whatever appears is the guru, the yidam, illusion, and the nature of phenomena. Make the following aspiration: {335}

May all sentient beings be happy.
May all sentient beings be free of sickness,
May they achieve the very path
that leads to buddhahood.

I shall free those not freed
I shall liberate those not liberated.
May they come to dwell right now
in the treatise of yoga's temple.

Say verses of auspiciousness:

May there be auspiciousness of the guru and yidam,
the total perfection of good qualities.
May there be auspiciousness of ḍākinīs and dharma protectors.
who accomplish all awakened activity.

Dedicate the virtue:

All my accumulation of virtue
I do not at all claim as my own,
but dedicate to the supreme realm of reality
for the sake of all beings without exception.

After dedicating the virtue to unsurpassed awakening with this and other prayers, undertake your devotional activities.

The yoga of Guru Vajradhara bestows supreme spiritual powers in this life. Since, in doing this practice, the stages of the path depend on both dispelling obstructions and enhancing [meditation], Protector dispels outer hindrances, Tārā dispels inner hindrances, Avalokita enhances outer love and compassion, and Vajrayoginī enhances inner bliss-warmth. These are well known as the culminations [of these practices]. Through practicing them, [one can] in a single session completely perfect the stages of the path of Vajrayāna; thus it is an especially exalted profound vital point. Not only that, as is said:

> Accomplished in three months without distraction,
> meditating without fail in each session at dawn
> accomplishes supreme and common spiritual powers.

Since this is what grants the two powers in a matter of years and months, those with sufficient merit and intelligence in regard to the Holy Dharma should undertake this as the heart of their practice. {356}

[Concluding Verse and Colophon]

Four Deities, the supreme gift of the golden garland of adepts,
written as a guidebook according to the oral teachings,
concise, clear, and shared here for fortunate ones to engage;
may their display of its fulfillment pervade the world.

The incomparably kind and all-seeing Jamyang Khyentse Wangpo, lord of a hundred families, kindly granted this profound guidance with its blessing [empowerment] and at the same time he granted permission for the writing. It was composed at the upper retreat of Kunzang Dechen Ösal Ling as a requisite practice for those endeavoring in practice there. I, Karma Ngawang Yönten Gyatso, who is steeped in much study, composed this from the teaching transmission of my guru without pollution by the sediments my own fabrications, at the secluded retreat of Devīkoṭi. Let virtue prevail!

Liturgical Practices and Supplications

Introduction

A Wish-Fulfilling Gem is an elaborate offering ritual, commonly known as a "guru puja," compiled by Jamgön Kongtrul using well-known prayers, sections borrowed from works of Venerable Tāranātha and others, and held together with his own writings and structural outline. Although it is complete and quite beautiful in itself, generally it forms the basis for a day[s]-long offering ritual that includes parts or wholes of many other texts, some of which are included in these two Shangpa volumes. For example, prayers and practices such as the two lineage prayers with attached locations (chs. 20 and 21 above), the supplication to the masters' lives (ch. 26), their songs of experience (ch. 30), the torma-offering rituals of the Ḍākinīs of the Five Classes (ch. 32) and of the Protector (ch. 35), the feast ritual of the Five-Deity Cakrasaṃvara (ch. 18 in volume 11), and the Shangpa aspiration prayers such as that of Niguma (ch. 29). All of this is strung together by a procedural outline (*las rim*) but subject to the chanting master's discretions according to time—whether limited or stretching to many hours or days in order to fulfill the expectations of special occasions.

Garland of Uḍumbara Flowers is Jamgön Kongtrul's very long supplication of longing for all the former masters of all Shangpa lineages. Uḍumbara flowers are described in the permission for the Great Empowerment of Illusory Body: "Omniscient ones in this world / are like uḍumbara flowers, / appearing every few hundred years, / and possibly not appearing at all."[1] Botanists say the plant does not bear flowers at all. In any case, the point of extreme rarity is well taken, though the implication is that all thirty of these lineage masters (and Kongtrul includes himself) are just that rare. A very exceptional lineage! The prayer is written in the style of "supplication to the life stories" or "biographical supplication" because it references certain events in the life or previous lives of each master, some more than others. These remarkable events are merely suggested here, but they should remind the reader of the full stories as found in their biographies and histories (and even in the songs of experience in chapter 30), inspiring faith and confidence. Generally, however, the examples here are somewhat thin on actual events and thick on dithyramb, which one might also find inspiring. As mentioned above, this prayer would be added as a liturgy in the long devotional rituals done in monastic or retreat settings.

Verdant Tree of Faith: The Life Story of the Glorious Holy Guru is Tāranātha's supplication to Jonang Kunga Drolchok, of whom Tāranātha was the recognized incarnation. He is never actually mentioned by name, but the prayer includes previous lives and deeds, his visionary experiences of deities and masters, and his actual teachers and studies. Kunga Drolchok's own "autobiographical record" of many of his teachers can be found in *The Treasury of Precious Instructions, Volume 18: Jonang.*

Jamgön Kongtrul then supplements this with his own similarly styled prayer to Tāranātha, called *Flowers of Faith*. Kongtrul considered himself an incarnation of Tāranātha, and thus also of Kunga Drolchok, establishing the spiritual continuity of this Shangpa Jonang lineage.

Finally, Niguma's *Aspiration of the Sealed Word* is one of the most profound and beloved of the Shangpa prayers, always added at the end of long practice sessions alongside those of Khyungpo Naljor and the more recently composed aspiration prayers for the Shangpa lineage by Dilgo Khyentse Rinpoche (1910–1991) and Kyapje Kalu Rinpoche (1905–1989). The ancient writings of the Shangpa lineage such as this one by Niguma and several by Khyungpo Naljor often have the appellation of "sealed word" (*bka' rgya ma*), meaning not only that they are approved or official but also recalls the command seal that Niguma gave originally to Khyungpo Naljor that the teachings be given to only one disciple at a time for seven generations, after which the seal would be lifted. Although Niguma's aspiration is undoubtedly ancient (if not original), it somehow seems very contemporary.

25. A Wish-Fulfilling Gem

Offering Ritual for the Lineage Gurus of Shangpa Kagyu, Protectors of Beings[1]

Jamgön Kongtrul

namo guru jñānaḍākinī yai

Those who obtained this from Vajradhara,
female adepts of integral unity beyond training,
the two awareness ḍākinīs inseparable from my guru:
I bow at your feet.

All supreme and common spiritual powers
depend solely upon the guru.
So those fortunate to please such a one
will have all their desires amply fulfilled.

Even better, abandon all other acts
and undertake the genuine guru offering.
It is the heart of flawless instructions
and all sutras, tantras, and treatises.

For practitioners with devotion and the good fortune to believe that the guru is the united essence of all rare and sublime Jewels, this is "the heart of practice." If you have the resources, decorate a clean place with an arrangement of ornaments and articles. In the middle, place the drawn images and other representations for the feast and request [the holy beings'] presence. Offer a mandala and mainly the two waters and sense objects, along with however much clean and pure offering substance you have on hand, without being stingy. On special occasions, such as the fourteenth day of the first winter month [that commemorates] when the learned adept Khyungpo Naljor attained manifest awakening in great all-pervasive dharmakāya, put up extensive feast substances. {359} If you are bereft of supplies, or you are like a simple yogin, it is sufficient just to offer the mandala and whatever sense offerings you have collected. The main thing is an attitude of definite renunciation of cyclic existence and faith in the goal of supreme spiritual power. With sincere devotion coming from your inspiration from the life stories of the lineage gurus, first go for refuge:

> All sentient beings, my mothers, equal to the reaches of space, go for refuge in the precious guru, the unified essence of all refuges.

Say that a number of times, then arouse the mind of awakening:

> All sentient beings, equal to the reaches of space, must attain the unified state of Great Vajradhara. To that end, I will practice the profound path of guru offering.

Repeat that three times, then dispel obstructors.

> Instantly I become glorious Cakrasaṃvara and Vajrayoginī.
>
> Gods, demigods, secretists (*guhyaka*),
> body putrefiers (*kaṭapūtana*), and any others,
> who abide in body, speech, or mind;
> hosts of obstructors, listen to me!
> I have the strength of glorious Vajra,
> engaging fully the circle of protection,
> my form of blazing vajras
> will scatter those born of three bodies.[2]
> If some of you transgress me anyway,
> you will be totally crushed; nothing else.

Fiercely set the boundaries, saying:

oṃ sumbha nisumbha [hūṃ hūṃ phaṭ / oṃ gṛhṇa gṛhṇa hūṃ hūṃ phaṭ / oṃ gṛhṇapāya gṛhṇapāya hūṃ hūṃ phaṭ / oṃ ānayaho bhagavān vidya rāja hūṃ hūṃ phaṭ]

Multicolored light radiates and gathers,
creating a blazing vajra tent in all directions.
Outside it the bonfire of awareness blazes,
making a totally secure protection circle.
oṃ vajra cakra rakṣa bhrūṃ hūṃ

For the consecration of offerings, visualize the cleansing water:

oṃ vajra amṛta kuṇḍalī hana hana hūṃ phaṭ

Repeat twenty-one times to consecrate, then sprinkle [the offerings], using that same mantra to cleanse and *svabhāva* . . . (etc.) to purify.

From within emptiness, from *bhrūṃ*, the dwelling place becomes a jeweled celestial palace with all levels and characteristics complete. In its center, arising from *oṃ*, is a vast and wide precious vessel, within which *hūṃ* melts and becomes the offerings made of divine ingredients—drinking water, washing water, flowers, incense, light, perfume, food, music, and so forth—excellent offering substances that fill the whole sky realm with their virtues.

oṃ vajra arghaṃ svāhā / oṃ vajra padyaṃ svāhā / oṃ vajra puṣpe āḥ hūṃ / oṃ vajra dhūpe āḥ hūṃ / oṃ vajra āloke āḥ hūṃ / oṃ vajra ghandhe āḥ hūṃ / oṃ vajra naividya āḥ hūṃ / oṃ vajra śabda āḥ hūṃ

Play music for the descent of blessing. Then accomplish the supports for accumulation:

In the vast pure realm perfectly arrayed
is an unimaginable mansion marvelously decorated,
an incomparable house built of vajra gems.
In the middle of this wide celestial palace of freedom,

on a lion throne, white lotus, and full moon,
sits my root guru as the awareness ḍākinī,
Sukhasiddhi, white with a red radiance.
Her hair is loose, three eyes staring, {361}
right hand holding an elixir-filled skull cup,
left in the mudra of pointing to the unborn,
adorned by bones, two legs in dancing stance,
her awareness body rests in the midst of rainbows.

Above her head the sixth buddha Vajradhara
and Vajra Nairātmya are in union.
Around the principals, in four directions [clockwise],
Venerable Ḍākinī Mighty Niguma is in front,
dark brown with three eyes gazing at space,
holding a hand drum, skull cup, and vajra khaṭvāṅga,
adorned by bones, sitting with two legs in half-lotus.

The Victor's heir Maitrīpa outfitted for yogic conduct,
accompanied by Ratnadevī and Gaṅgādhari.[3]
Rāhulagupta in the style of an immortal adept,
and Puṇyākara as a great paṇḍita monk.
In between are the one hundred and fifty learned adepts
in the garb of paṇḍitas, yogins, and ḍākinīs.

In front of them, master of the practice lineage, Lord Khyungpo,
wears the three dharma robes and a red paṇḍita hat,
his right hand touches earth, his left rests in repose,
as he sits on a lotus-sun seat, relaxing in half-lotus.

Then the holders of the jewel garland of the precept lineage,
from the six great heart sons of the transmission
in succession down to my own root guru.
Most are pure meditators wearing saffron robes,
though some are indefinite, engaging yogic conduct, and so on,
interested in whatever tames whomever, they arise in glory.
But they all are confident in realizing the unborn.
The mystery of awakened body, speech, and mind is unimaginable.
They rest in constant equipoise of a hundred doors of absorption,

miraculous deliberate conduct always accomplished without bias. {362}
Their deeds of awakened activity pervade ten directions and three times.
The brilliance of their blessings of compassion blazes immeasurably.

Above the gurus are the yidam deities all around,
and buddhas, bodhisattvas, heroes, and yoginīs,
with an ocean of dharma protectors and oath-bound ones,
arising as the display of the glorious gurus' three secrets
to whomever believes in the guru as buddha;
they appear actually present before them.

Although at this point you don't really need the invocation and supplication to be present, the following is presented for the sake of the less experienced beginners, to make it simple to understand:

Sublime beings with the vision of nondual timeless awareness
have gone to the dharmakāya and won't arrive here.
Yet with great love, may your form kāya emanations
please come here as an offering field for the faithful.
ratna guru saparivāra vajra samājaḥ

Lords, it is good you have come for migrators' sakes.
Partake of these water offerings that I will present
and remain comfortably on this pleasing seat
until all the acts of offering are complete.

oṃ pravara satkara arghaṃ pratīccha svāhā

Similarly with . . . *padyaṃ* . . . to offer the two waters. Then:

oṃ padma āsani samayas tvaṃ

Imagine that [those awareness beings] become indivisible with those previously visualized. Then either do actual prostrations or join your palms together:

Totally pure form, faultless and unmistaken,
prolific melodious speech encompassing all knowledge,
mind of knowing suchness, vast and profound;
I bow to the glorious guru, the actual three vajras.

You forever forsook two obscurations and habitual patterns
and perfected all qualities, possessed of two purities,
you manifest two kāyas for the sake of self and others;
I bow to the sender of emanations throughout samsara and nirvana.

If someone follows you with an unwavering mind,
instantly blessings bestow the highest path of awakening,
or else one's excellent desires and emancipation; {363}
I bow to you who surely gives what is sacred.

Coemergent integral unity, the real great bliss of three existences,
liberates all migrators in three realms with nonreferential
compassion.
Inexhaustible qualities of knowledge, love, and power;
I bow to you, unwavering purity of the realm of phenomena.

The natural appearance of your single timeless awareness
emanates clouds of every buddha and their heirs.
Your liberation story of two truths knows no bounds;
I bow to the united essence of all buddhas.

Pervasive master, lord of the wheel, Vajradhara,
Nairātmya and Venerable Virūpa,
birth mother of all victors, Spiritual Power of Bliss,
and mighty one of ten levels, Niguma; I bow.

I bow to Maitrīpa and Puṇyakāra,
Rāhula, and all hundred and fifty learned adepts,
Khyungpo Naljor, Rinchen Tsöndru,
Öntön [Kyergangpa], Nyentön, and Chöje Tönpa.

I bow to Khedrup [Shangtön], Khyungpo Tsultrim Gön,
[Ritrö] Rechen, Shangkar, Sangye Palzangpo,

Namgyal, Lekgyal, Drolchok, Lhawang Drak,
and to the great Venerable Tāranātha.

I bow to Gyaltsen Palzang, great Dorje Zhönu,
Namkhai Naljor, Jangsem Jinpa Zang,
mighty adept Tangtong Gylapo, and others;
to all the gurus of long and direct lineages.

Present the outer offerings.

I offer all actual and imagined flowers
with nice colors, good shapes, and satisfying fragrance,
such as coral tree, utpala, and water lily,
to the assembly of glorious gurus, the supreme refuge. {364}

oṃ ratna guru saparivāra vajra puṣpe pūja megha samudra spharaṇa samaye hūṃ

I offer all actual and imagined incense
with delicious aromas when their fine ingredients are sensed,
such as aloe, sandalwood, and snake heart[4]
to the assembly of glorious gurus, the supreme refuge.

oṃ ratna guru saparivāra vajra dhūpe pūja megha samudra spharaṇa samaye hūṃ

I offer all actual and imagined light
with brilliant illumination of all things to dispel darkness,
such as lamps, fire, moon, sun, and body radiance,
to the assembly of glorious gurus, the supreme refuge.

oṃ ratna guru saparivāra vajra āloke pūja megha samudra spharaṇa samaye hūṃ

I offer all actual and imagined perfume
with the supreme touch of bliss when their sweet scent is spread,
such as camphor, musk, compounded scents,[5] and others
to the assembly of glorious gurus, the supreme refuge.

oṃ ratna guru saparivāra vajra gandhe pūja megha samudra spharaṇa samaye hūṃ

I offer all actual and imagined food
with fine color and nutritious flavor of bliss when tasted,
such as jackfruit, sugarcane, and blood soup,
to the assembly of glorious gurus, the supreme refuge.

oṃ ratna guru saparivāra vajra naividya pūja megha samudra spharaṇa samaye hūṃ

I offer all actual and imagined music
with sweet melodies and profound meaning when heard,
such as big drums, horns, cymbals, and lutes,
to the assembly of glorious gurus, the supreme refuge. {365}

oṃ ratna guru saparivāra vajra śabda pūja megha samudra spharaṇa samaye hūṃ

I offer the soft, light fabric of the gods
to clothe the form of your immutable vajra.
When I offer with undivided faith,
may I also obtain the vajra body.

oṃ ratna guru saparivāra vajra vastraya āḥ hūṃ svāhā

Lord, though you have no hunger or thirst,
[I offer] drinks of milk soup, syrup, and elixir,
together with vast amounts of food
imbued with color, smell, and taste,
all added into this excellent food.
Please accept in ever-excellent great bliss.

Spiritual Power of Bliss, principal of the mandala,
inseparable from my supreme guru,
all the precept lineage is your emanation,
therefore I pay homage from my heart.

As for me, I have more faith
in a single pore of your body
than for all other sources of refuge.
Not through folly; there is a reason:

In all the tantras the victors praised you
as higher than all buddhas,
and said the same in all sutras and such.
I bow to you who are ever praised by the victors.

The victors' heirs and guides in ten directions,
regarding you as the Awakening Vajra,
paid homage and offerings in the four times
of every day and proclaimed this:

"The parent of all the tathāgatas
is you, our teacher."
Teacher, vajra holder, to you
we pay homage and go for refuge.

There is more good merit in offering
a drop of sesame oil to your body
than offering the supreme jewel realm
to the victors for incalculable eons.

If you ask for what reason:
all buddhas' timeless awareness comes from you.
I will abandon all other offerings
and offer and bow to you, Venerable One.

All spiritual powers of the three vajras
abide in your awakened body, speech, and mind.
But you do not abide anywhere; {366}
your great wonder is lucid clarity equaling space.

In this time of strife, beings have no fortune
to see the real Vajrasattva.
I bow to those who practice in a master's body
and accept offerings out of love.

To tame migrators, their five aggregates
are the fivefold awareness in five-family mandalas.

The four immeasurable goddesses in the mandala
indicate the four elements—so marvelous.

Their eyes and so forth are the eight bodhisattvas,
their joints and so forth are the pure ten wrathful ones,
their bodies and so forth are vajra females:
I pay homage to the forms of timeless awareness.

"Your body is subject to birth and death."
I'm ashamed and regret all such mistakes,
and moreover sincerely acknowledge them.
May I manifestly become like you.

The thirty-seven factors of enlightenment
are surely part of the Bhagavat's body.
The crown is the five families, all the pores
are surely the arhats; I bow to you.

The worldly gods are your seat,
the three existences are surly you, Guru.
You are surely the Three Jewels,
creator of the three precious ones.

Not with mere hypocritical words,
from now until the heart of awakening,
I sincerely go for refuge,
and pay homage with utmost faith.[6]

At this juncture, do the standard thirty-seven-heap extensive mandala and this *Mandala of the Sealed Word*:

The sublime mandala exquisitely arrayed,
majestic mountain in the center, four continents and lesser lands,
the illuminating sun and moon circling, beautifying.
Outside the iron mountains, between them rolling oceans adorn.

Jewels, wish-fulfilling trees, bountiful cows,
seven royal emblems plus the treasure vase, the eighth,

harvest that needs no toil, water with eight qualities,
unimaginable clouds of outer, inner, and secret offerings. {367}

This delightful and pleasing mandala
offered by a yogin who seeks to achieve both purposes,
I offer on the strength of my diligence
to guru, yidam, and the ocean of victorious ones.

This yogin, descendant of all the buddhas,
offers this excellent, pleasing mandala.
Please remove the mass of defects, faults, and stains,
and grant the supreme and common spiritual powers.[7]

Sacred wheel, gem, queen, minister,
elephant, supreme steed, and army commander,
the seven precious emblems of royalty,
I emanate and offer to the supreme guru.

Precious swords, skins, gardens, mansions,
seats, garments, and boots,
I offer to the guru and mandala deities;
please accept them and grant me blessings.

The victors' fulfilled wishes in goddess style:
goddesses give bliss of form, sound, smell, taste, and texture
[with] mirror, lute, incense burner, food vessel,
fine soft cloth, and *padma bhañja*.

Goddesses who play clay drums, resting on khaṭvāṅgas,
with bodies white, blue, yellow, red, and green.
Goddesses with beautiful form, sweet sound, fragrance, and
  nutrition.
Goddesses who mature the haughty through blissful youth.
Filling all space: I offer to the guru and deities.

Goddesses in perfect rapture of luminous illusory supreme bliss,
with lutes, flutes, kettle drums, and clay drums;

goddesses of laughter, charm, song, and dance;
goddesses of fine flowers, incense, light, and perfume;
goddesses of form, taste, touch, and source of phenomena:
sixteen goddesses with aspects of joy perfectly complete.
May this display by the vajra consort's joy {368}
please your vajra mind, Heruka.

Sacred ponds for bathing,
divine clothing blissful to touch,
garuḍas, bulls, peacocks,
oxen, horses, and other supreme mounts.
Wish-granting cows, source of desires;
crops that grow without cultivation;
wish-fulfilling trees; supreme fruits;
and excellent vases: filling all space, I offer.

I offer my body and possessions,
and all my virtue from the three times.

I offer realms filled with precious jewels:
gold, silver, pearl, chrysoberyl,
sapphire, diamond, ruby,
emerald, coral, Jambu gold,
moon crystal, and mountains of seven gems,
as numerous as atoms in the realm, I offer.

Utpala lotus in five colors,
three colors of nutmeg flowers,
karnikar-tree flowers,
chinaberry flowers, ornamental jasmine,
and oleander flowers,[8]
I offer you by the powers of meditation.

Fearless lions, jeweled throne,
excellent seat of lotus, sun, and moon.
Earrings, bracelets, anklets,
necklaces, and perfect rings,
golden sashes carried for offerings,[9]

crowns with silk scarves, long garlands,
red, gold, white, black,
and pale-yellow victory banners.
Also clothing of various kinds,
many flower garlands,
canopies hung with silken
arrows and curtains, so beautiful.
Also I offer food and drink
through deep quiescence.

Gold in the hundreds of thousands,
a variety of precious jewels,
cloth of a hundred fabrics interwoven,
elephants, horses, and estates,
good spouses and children,
male and female servants and siblings,
with intelligence and inspiration
I offer myself as well. {369}

Food of the five elixirs,
the very stuff of spiritual powers;
supreme food of the five lamps,
the principal pledge of all buddhas;
supreme drink of flawless peace,
the five ingredients for [making] intoxicants:
honey, molasses, grain, composite, and tree sap;
I offer these as the nature of wisdom.

oṃ āḥ hūṃ
From the union of method and wisdom together,
melting bliss, the nature of perfectly pure appearance,
completely pervades the three realms.
May this secret offering please you.

Your form is without hollow spaces,
neither flesh, bones, nor blood,
like rainbows in the sky;
I bow to the teaching of your body.

Your form is without disease or filth,
without feelings of hunger or thirst,
since the whole world follows you;
I bow to teaching of worldly deeds.

Nothing to cling to, like the moon in water,
all phenomena do not abide anywhere.
Without pride and nowhere abiding:
homage and praise to you, the inconceivable.

Going and sitting and also sleeping,
in all regular activities
you always remain in equipoise:
homage and praise to you, the inconceivable.

Illusion-like meditative absorption
while projecting great magical manifestations
is equilibrium in the lack of various distinctions:
homage and praise to you, the inconceivable.

Free of the three realms,
equal to space,
unsullied by desires:
homage and praise to you, the inconceivable.

Not dependent on the aggregates,
constituents, and sense fields;
completely free of misapprehensions:
homage and praise to you, the inconceivable. {370}

Without concepts and without conceptuality,
your mind is totally nonabiding,
unimaginable awakened mind:
homage and praise to you, the inconceivable.

Just as space does not abide anywhere,
free of embellishment and untainted,

your mind is equal to space:
homage and praise to you, the inconceivable.[10]

Migrators are seen like the moon in water,
what's heard is like echoes, genuinely engaged,
mind beyond misery seen as a mirage,
so with food and drink, which are like the sky,
smell is sensed like the scent of sky flowers,
mentation pervades like the sun and the moon,
genuine abiding is like the Supreme Mountain,
like dreaming of a young love in a dream.
Conventions are like expressions of illusory mirages,
their actual nature like the source of coemergent bliss,
while existence has no intrinsic nature, unimaginable mind,
always arising, is the sugatas' sublime path: homage and praise.[11]

Profound peace, free of embellishment, the native state,
appearance and emptiness, these two are not two.
Wonderful, this view free of thought:
I bow to you, the innate play of great bliss.

The nature without expression, thought, or utterance,
is experience of bliss without fixation on bliss or emptiness.
Wonderful, relaxing in meditation without effort:
I bow to you, the innate play of great bliss.

Natural lucid clarity, without rejecting or accepting,
is pure of incidental stains of dualistic fixation.
Wonderful, the natural coemergent fruition:
I bow to you, the innate play of great bliss.

This concludes outer, inner, secret, and suchness offerings and the praises. Then recite extensive or concise supplications as appropriate. {371} In particular, recite the two lineage prayers in the style of attached locations and others at this juncture.[12] Then, if you have time and want to do the elaborate version:

You whose kindness causes
great bliss to arise instantly:
vajra guru with jewel body,
I bow at your lotus feet.

Emptiness and compassion inseparable,
your body with seven aspects of union,[13]
Vajradhara's integral unity of bliss and emptiness:
pervasive lord of all families, I bow before you.

Birth mother of all buddhas of the three times,
granting spiritual powers to children of the lineage,
ḍākinī of undissipating timeless awareness,
Sukhasiddhi, I bow before you.

Coemergent perfection of wisdom,
unshakable treasury of all mysteries,
mighty Ḍākinī Niguma,
Vajra Queen, I bow before you.

Blessed by the lord of retreat [Śavarīpa],
holder of the secret treasure of essential meaning,
victors' heir, just hearing your name is meaningful:
Maitrīpa, I bow before you.

Yoginī, whose knowledge and realization equals
the great masters of supreme accomplishment:
supreme mistress of the secret celestial realm,
Ratnadevī, I bow before you.

The great energy of awakening mind perfected,
you maintained the doctrine at the Vajra Seat;
seeing, hearing, recalling, and touching you is bliss:
Puṇyākara, I bow before you.

Specially blessed by the four deities,
you attained the state of mahāmudrā;
your vajra body still lives:
Rāhula, I bow before you.

Supreme master of the mind of awakening,
lamp that illuminates the darkness of Tibet,
renowned throughout the three worlds:[14]
Atiśa, I bow before you.

Graciously accepted by Bhagavatī,
you protected Śākyamuni's domain:
acclaimed as like a second Buddha,
Abhayākara, I bow before you. {372}

Heart son of great paṇḍita Nāropa,
on the far shore of vast esoteric instructions:
lord protector of many living beings,
Great Dha Bodhisattva, I bow before you.

You know various countries and languages,
treatises, and so forth without studying,
by just concentrating on your subtle body:
Tathāgata[rakṣita], I bow before you.

Adept of impartial deliberate conduct,
your power and activity are unhindered:
lord of attainment with fearless confidence,
Amoghavajra, I bow before you.

With thorough knowledge of the scriptures,
you enacted unimaginable benefit for others
and enjoyed wondrous celebrity:
*Matibhadra, I bow before you.[15]

Perfectly skilled in knowledge, realization, and ability,
gaining supreme power in the intermediate state,

you became a mighty yogi:
Vairocanarakṣita, I bow before you.

Inseparable from Yamāntaka,
you slew the clans of barbarian extremists
and accomplished all actions by mere thought:
Kamalarakṣita, I bow before you.

Manifesting the real Vidāraṇa mandala,
you placed your vajra and bell in the space:
paṇḍita who sees the three times,
Advayavajra, I bow before you.

With blissful resplendent glow of great bliss
and charm that one never tires of seeing:
chief of the ḍākinī hosts of three sacred sites,
Samantabhadrī, I bow before you.

Reaching the culmination of levels and paths,
your timeless awareness of yogic realization blazed:
lady who holds the vajra secrets,
Sumati, I bow before you.

Freely moving through the space of awareness,
you look after the fortunate ones
with your variety of emanated forms:
Kanakaśrī, I bow before you. {373}

You journeyed below the earth,
and with the power of the sword
help the demigod beings even now:
Gaṅgādhari, I bow before you.

Lalitavajra, Sukhavajra,
Dharmapala, Āryadeva,
Bhandapa, and the other learned adepts:
one hundred and fifty, I bow before you.

Adorned by the three higher trainings,
emanated from Amitābha's heart,
Bodhisattva, any connection is meaningful:
Langri Tangpa, I bow before you.

Knower of all things, you attained the ten powers,[16]
holder of the secrets of awareness ḍākinīs,
you are the very essence of the Five Tantras:
Khyungpo Naljor, I bow before you.

Amazing bodhisattva in your final existence,
you soared freely in space like a bird:
with power over wind-mind, Mokchokpa,
Rinchen Tsöndru, I bow before you.

You mastered a hundred doors of absorption;
with immeasurable compassion you guide migrators:
Avalokiteśvara Kyergangpa,
Chökyi Senge, I bow before you.

In the form of Buddha Hevajra,
with Awareness Protector at your service:
mighty one of the tenth level, Rigongpa,
Great Nyentön, I bow before you.

Master of five kāyas in immutable bliss-emptiness,
you bound the net of heroes and ḍākinīs:
lord of migrators who lifted the vajra seal,
Sangye Tönpa, I bow before you.

You refined buddha realms, matured migrators,
and displayed unsurpassable miracles:
Khedrup Lord Tsangma Shangtön,
Tsultrim Bum, I bow before you.

In your unthinkable life of liberation
were recollections, absorptions, and clairvoyance:

great Khedrup Samdingpa,
supreme Zhönu Drup, I bow before you.

You hold the heroic conduct of a victors' heir,
liberating through seeing, hearing, recalling, or touching:
supreme Khetsun Jakchenpa, {374}
Gyaltsen Bum, I bow before you.

You emanated in existence with intention
to dredge the depths of cyclic existence:
great bodhisattva known as the second Khyungpo,
Tsultrim Gönpo, I bow before you.

You released the knots of dualism in basic space
and brought the four elements under control,
consummating deliberate conduct: Rechenpa,
Sangye Senge, I bow before you.

You perfected the great skill of twofold knowledge
and the five eyes of totally pure vision arose:
descendant of the Victor, Shangkarwa,
Rinchen Gyaltsen, I bow before you.

You blazed with brilliant light of bliss-emptiness
and realized samsara and nirvana as illusory body:
with supreme spiritual power, Kuklungpa,
Sangye Palzang, I bow before you.

Whatever arose you purified as an awareness wheel
and accomplished unimpeded action and powers:
amazing great adept of supreme spiritual powers,
Namkhai Gyaltsen, I bow before you.

Free of rejecting or accepting samsara or nirvana,
you saw all phenomena as manifest buddhahood:
hidden buddha, Gyagompa,
Lekpa Gyaltsen, I bow before you.

Accepted by the Awareness Ḍākinī,
your knowledge, ability, and activity equaled the sky:
great hero adept, Jamgön,
Kunga Drolchok, I bow before you.

Treasure holder of the aural lineage instructions,
crown jewel of millions of adepts:
mighty yogi, Draktöpa,
Lhawang Drakpa, I bow before you.

Vajradhara in the times of strife,
fearless knower of all things,
lord of secrets Heruka,
Tāranātha, I bow before you.

Essence of the single timeless awareness
dancing in the manifold manifestations, {375}
teacher and student inseparable, supreme regent,
Yeshe Gyatso, I bow before you.

With qualities of innate and acquired learning,
you matured others and could liberate them:
ablaze with glorious blessings, Dzongtengpa,
Yönten Gönpo, I bow before you.

You consummated ascetic deliberate conduct
and your rainbow body left for the celestial realm:
amazing magnificent renunciant,
Gönpo Paljor, I bow before you.

You stabilized the two phases
and mastered Mantra's ten principles:[17]
endowed with all qualifications, supreme master,
Gönpo Drakpa, I bow before you.

You perfected experience and realization's great energy,
and reached the full measure of meditative warmth signs;

you have inconceivable qualities of a mighty adept:
Gönpo Namgyal, I bow before you.

You dwelt fully in the pure levels
while your various emanations helped beings:
incomparable awareness holder,
Tsewang Norbu, I bow before you.

Though you are awakened since forever,
yet your continuous compassion guides migrators,
protector of the Himalaya, Lord Drukpa,
Trinle Shingta, I bow before you.

Great Maitreya in the guise of saffron robes,
ornament of the world in the time of degenerations,
master of the practice lineage, eyes of the world,
Tenpai Nyinje, I bow before you.

Holders of the ancestral lineage, exemplifying their lives,
epitome of realization, Mokchokpa,
Kunda Gelek Palbar, and
Lhundrup Gyatso, I bow before you.

Eight worldly concerns discarded like straw,
you planted the victory banner of remote practice:
great person who destroyed delusion (Trulshik),
Kagyu Tenzin, I bow before you. {376}

Delusions dissolved into the central channel's basic space,
and pure appearance arose continuously:
yogi with the ability to emanate and transform,
Karma Lhaktong, I bow before you.

Unaffected by harm from the four elements,
you saw the yidam deity countless times,
and gained control over appearance and mind:
Karma Zhenpen, I bow before you.

[Prophesied in all the sutras and tantras,
you mastered longevity and awakened activity,
your deeds were those of a second victor:
Lodrö Taye, I bow before you.

A thousand-petaled lotus of ethics blossomed,
love's fragrance permeated the ten directions,
and the fruit of creation and completion hung heavy:
Zhiwai Nyingpo, I bow before you.

Planting the victory banner of attainment in one life,
you departed to the domain of great nonmeditation
and achieved the wondrous rainbow body:
Norbu Döndrup, I bow before you.]

[The last three verses are supplications added by Karma Rangjung Kunkhyab.][18]

Vajradhara and Nairātmya,
Virūpa, Sukhasiddhi,
Niguma and Vajrāsana,
and Rāhula, I bow before you.

One hundred fifty great learned adepts,
Khyungpo Naljor, Mokchokpa,
Öntön, Nyentön, Drogön,
and Tsangma Shangtön, I bow before you.

Famous throughout the three worlds,
worldly protectors bowed at your feet:
world protector, great Nyaktön,
Gyaltsen Palzang, I bow before you.

You mastered the qualities of the path
such as magical display and clairvoyance,
yet engaged in hidden deliberate conduct:
Dorje Zhönu, I bow before you.

You broke the bonds of existence,
with qualities of renunciation and realization:
unimaginable sky yogi without compare,
Namkhai Gyaltsen, I bow before you.

You crossed the ocean of two accumulations,
and readily mastered emptiness and compassion:
guide of migrators, bodhisattva,
Jinpa Zangpo, I bow before you.

Lord of the assembly of heroes and ḍākinīs,
wheel monarch of an ocean of adepts,
with mastery over life, Iron-Bridge Builder,
Tangtong Gyalpo, I bow before you.

Just like wish-fulfilling gems,
you spontaneously achieve the two purposes:
holders of the teaching system of glorious Shangpa,
gurus of the lineage, I bow before you. {377}

Master of the whole doctrine of the Buddha,
crown of all those learned and accomplished,
dwelling fully on the level of the exalted ones,
Khyentse Wangpo, I bow before you.

The six heart sons of Shangpa,
the three learned adepts, and others
from the disciple lineage of the monastic seat,
all great beings, I bow before you.

Great Jikdral, father, sons, and others,
nurtured by Niguma and Sukhasiddhi,
those who spread the profound instructions,
sublime adepts, I bow before you.

Essence of Hevajra, Guhyasamāja,
Mahāmāya, Cakrasaṃvara,

and Vajrabhairava,
glorious guru, I bow before you.

Inseparable from buddha, vajra,
jewel, lotus, and action ḍākinīs,
and from Swift-Acting Awareness Protector,
glorious guru, I bow before you.

Three Jewels and Three Roots,
are contained in your one actual form:
the single sufficient sovereign, highest refuge,
glorious guru, I bow before you.

The glorious vajra holder
incarnated as a master in the age of strife,
you have done this incredible deed:
glorious guru, I bow before you.

You display your three secrets in various lives,
attuned to different characters, abilities, and interests,
with skillful means and great compassion:
glorious guru, I bow before you.

The problems of flaws fully expended,
and all good qualities perfected,
giver of gifts to victors and heirs,
glorious guru, I bow before you.

Bad destinies are averted by just hearing your name,
blessings are granted by supplicating you, {378}
necessities accrue by relying on you with devotion:
glorious guru, I bow before you.

[Seven-branch prayer]

I hold you as the supreme refuge
from now until the heart of awakening,

precious root and lineage gurus,
like wish-fulfilling gems.

I prostrate to you who are worthy of worship
together with all beings equaling space,
our bodies equaling atoms, voices of praise,
and minds in single-pointed devotion.

I forever offer to those worthy of offering
Samantabhadra's display of offering clouds,
and the roots of virtue from my three doors,
encompassed by my sky-like mind.

I confess with sincere regret and shame
the big obscuration since time immemorial,
along with the hidden misdeeds and such;
protector of migrators, grant purification.

I rejoice with respect and delight
in the lives of liberation led by great beings
that are amazing and unsurpassed,
and in any good deeds in existence or peace.

Please dredge up the depths of cyclic existence
through dharma doors in harmony with all types,
and in particular, turn the wheel of the single path
traversed by the victors and their heirs.

Please remain firm as the immutable vajra,
manifesting to our senses' sphere of experience
in form kāyas without arising and setting,
since the continuity of dharmakāya is eternal.

I dedicate this merit shared in common
with the roots of merit of all migrators,
to the accomplishment in just one lifetime
of the guru's deeds of the three secrets.

May I be held by the compassionate hands
of the dharma monarchs and their heirs,
and complete real realization on the path,
to spontaneously achieve the goals of self and others.

May I never displease the guru,
for there is no other victorious one,
but be able to achieve only their pleasure {379}
by rendering all manner of service with three doors.

May the blessings of always pleasing the guru
cause our minds to merge inseparably,
and may renunciation and realization, like a full vase,
be transferred to my stream of being.

May I be granted the realizations of the life
and secrets of the guru's speech,
and with the ability to retain it well,
be fortunate to spread and increase it.

May I be born into a Vajrayāna family,
be accepted by a guru, keep sacred pledge,
never be apart from vajra and bell,
and dance in the arena of timeless awareness.

May I grasp the vajra mysteries,
realize the import without accepting or rejecting,
and by accomplishing unbiased deliberate conduct,
become a lamp for the whole world.

May I also gain glory and influence,
good health and vajra longevity,
and plenty of resources in harmony with dharma,
so I can spread the doctrine in a hundred directions.

May I be born in Sukhāvatī as soon as I die
if I fail to achieve supreme spiritual power now,

and in the instant that I am born there,
come before Khyungpo and his heirs.

May I be able, through my many emanations,
to dispel the two obscurations of all those
with whom I had good, bad, or neutral connection,
and guide them there to Amitābha's pure realm.

May I quickly attain everything
in the lives of root and lineage gurus,
and become a guide like yourself,
who liberates beings from the ocean of existence.

The profound practice sequence of the gurus
brings the level of a buddha in one life;
by the truth well spoken by Vajradhara,
may all these aspirations by accomplished.

Also do the regular confession.[19] At this point recite whatever appropriate seven branches that you are able. If you are interested in doing a communal feast, follow the liturgy of the Five-Deity Cakrasaṃvara feast offering created by Venerable Kunga Drolchok,[20] except add the following at the beginning of the descent of blessings: {380}

oṃ
In the great pervasive realm of phenomena,
from the heart of all samsara and nirvana,
the lord over all the families
is known as the glorious guru,
and is surrounded by buddhas and heirs.
I will train following your footsteps;
please come here to grant your blessings.

In the place that bestows undissipating bliss,
the forest of medicinal sandalwood trees,
the queen mother Vajra Nairātmya
is known as Sukhasiddhi,
surrounded by the three seats complete.[21]

I will train following your footsteps;
please come here to grant your blessings.

Offer torma to the Swift-Acting Awareness Protector, such as the *Concise Torma Ritual*.[22] If you have practiced it, offer a feast torma with *Ḍākinīs of the Five Classes Torma Offering* as a supplement.[23] Once the feast and the leftovers are complete, continue:

It is said that two thousand commoners equal one brahmin,
and likewise two thousand flawless brahmin monks
and two thousand folks with the eyes of awareness
equal the offering field of a single vajra master.
Therefore, lord protector vajra master,
you are the most excellent field, none more eminent.
Victor, if one pleases you, it is repeatedly said,
one will attain omniscience and timeless awareness.

Offerings made to the master, Vajrasattva,
create all merit, serve as all hardship,
vanquish negativity, calm suffering,
and free one from the depths of existence. Homage!

It is said that if one thus offers respectfully to you,
compared to offering to all the ten-direction victors,
preventing plagues and other misfortunes,
one will surely attain the supreme spiritual power.

I offer my virtue, body, and possessions in three times,
without any clinging to the offering substances, {381}
and my practice of prayer, mantra, mudra, and meditation;
I present all outer, inner, and secret offerings.

It is said that all those who scorn you
will be killed by rulers, fire,
poison, plague, and rogues
and then cook in hell forever.
To scorn and malign you
is to scorn and malign all buddhas.

One who treads on or ridicules
your bedding, seat, shoes, or parasol
will fail in enterprises and fall ill.
To step over your body's shadow
is said to be like destroying a stupa.
I confess each such act that I have done.

To unequivocally criticize the master
prevents accomplishment even in dreams.
To appreciate the master's qualities
is not ever a fault.
Pondering the qualities is spiritual power;
speaking of faults spoils spiritual power.
I acknowledge and confess all such faults
that I have committed with careless three doors.

The merit of each hair on your body
cannot be matched even in part
by all the enlightened activity
of the victors of the three times.
I rejoice with highest inspired faith
in the inexhaustible merit created
by you, your chosen disciples,
and whoever worships and honors you.

Though one trains for a million eons in study,
contemplation, and meditation of sutras and tantras,
it is said that without the guru's esoteric instructions,
one will never receive their blessings.
To obtain the guru's transmission
is to get supreme spiritual power effortlessly.
I request you to turn the profound dharma wheel
so that you may liberate us from our bonds. {382}

Since it is the guru's kindness that illuminates
lucid clarity coemergent with great bliss
and the emptiness of everything,
if I do not receive the master's blessings,

I have toiled to no end.
Bereft of the guru, I will not succeed
in practices of mantra and mudra;
I supplicate you to not transcend misery.

Lord of the gods in the higher realms,
wheel-wielding monarch on the earth,
lord of the hooded nāgas underground,
the letter *oṃ* in the pure, supreme Vedas,
guru, father, mother, ancestor,
friend, and protector of migrators,
conqueror of flaws, site of all qualities,
holder of vajra yoga, I bow to you.

Ever-present timeless awareness pervades
the whole world without coming or going.
Leader of the people, lord of sages,
like a wish-fulfilling gem, you protect
all the poor and vulnerable people.
Terrified by unbearable cyclic existence,
I rely on you from now and ever after
with heartfelt faith of body, speech, and mind.

For vajra practitioners, accepting the master
is often said to be the root of all sacred pledge.
Just as offering inferior intoxicants and dry burnt offerings
are fruitless types of religious practice
that are transitory and meaningless when performed,
the dharma without a master will not be productive.
Therefore, as the most important of all sacred pledges,
I will endeavor to keep the sacred pledge with my master.

At all times and in all circumstances,
may I accomplish my glorious guru's activity.
May I accomplish whatever pleases you,
and abandon anything that does not please.
When you are delighted, it is much better
than all of us attaining supreme awakening.

If somehow you are not pleased, then in this life
even attaining awakening is not the supreme goal. {383}

By the power of collecting together
all my and others' virtue from the three times,
may I actualize sacred supreme spiritual power in this life
and always please and make offerings to my guru.

For those of us incarcerated in cyclic existence,
there is no other refuge than you, our guide.
I supplicate you continuously with devotion:
please watch over us with unfailing compassion.

May the vajra master's body and my body
be inseparable and blessed as the vajra body.
May I achieve whatever the glorious guru says
and our speech be inseparable as vajra speech.
May I hold the whole treasury of mind's secrets
and our minds merge, inseparable and blessed.

May I become like you, the real Vajradhara,
seeing and realizing actual unborn lucid clarity,
by uniting creation and completion, inseparable method and wisdom
within the emptiness-compassion of unified bliss-emptiness.

May I see the guru as the actual Buddha,
have vast absorptions of tranquility and insight inseparable,
and with flawless pure conduct in body, speech, and mind
become liberated from this cyclic place of dualism.

Through the boundless supreme means of massive blessings beyond thought or word,
bless me now with supreme spiritual powers and the four kāyas,
to place all migrators throughout the reaches of space in the supreme vehicle
and quickly fill all realms with benefit and happiness.

Again earnestly supplicate for your desires by means of the seven-branch service and then also recite:

> Precious one, source of the mind's desires,
> lord protector, this is my request to you:
> let the Buddha's Holy Dharma, source of benefit and happiness,
> flourish through study, contemplation, and practice. {384}
>
> Let the virtuous friends who hold the doctrine, freedom guides,
> be free of sickness, spread their awakened activity,
> and place ever-suffering migrators
> in the happiness of freedom.
>
> Let all those who diligently practice the Holy Dharma
> complete the profound path of devotion to the guru,
> perfect renunciation and realization, attain the guru's state,
> and accomplish immeasurable benefit for others.
>
> Let us, in the meantime, in all circumstances,
> always be accepted by the sublime guru,
> please the guru with body, possessions, and virtue,
> and with your love receive the blessings.

Taking the four empowerments:

> My prayer causes the entourage to melt into light
> and dissolve into the guru's body with its three-place letters.
>
> White light rays from the guru Awareness Ḍākinī's forehead
> dissolve into my forehead and I receive the vase empowerment.
> Physical negativities and obscurations are purified
> and the blessings of awakened body enter my being.
>
> Red light rays from the guru Awareness Ḍākinī's throat
> dissolve into my throat and I receive the secret empowerment.
> Verbal negativities and obscurations are purified
> and the blessings of awakened speech enter my being.

Blue light rays from the guru Awareness Ḍākinī's heart
dissolve into my heart and I receive the wisdom-awareness
empowerment.
Mental negativities and obscurations are purified
and the blessings of awakened mind enter my being.

Again white, red, and blue light rays from the three places
radiate all at once and dissolve into my three places.
I receive the fourth empowerment, purifying habitual patterns of
my three doors.
The blessings of vajra awareness enter my being.

Sukhasiddhi raises the mudra of the unborn,
considers me with delight, and bestows the introduction:

> In empty space, which lacks awareness,
> tame the root of mind with awareness.
> Tame the root and rest relaxed. {386}

My mind and space blend inseparably.
Like the sky, my mind relaxed in its own state
is free of identifiable birth or cessation, center or boundary;
I rest relaxed awhile without conceptual thought.
Uncontrived freshness is self-arising and serene,
effortlessly focused within spontaneous presence.

Bless me that the glorious guru's awakened form
and my body merge inseparably as vajra body.
May I achieve whatever the glorious guru says
and our speech be inseparable as vajra speech.
Bless me to hold the whole treasury of mind's secrets,
and for the guru's mind and mine to merge inseparably.
Bless me to achieve all acts that delight the guru
and to equal the guru's acts of awakened activity.

May I keep the guru as a crown on my head,
hold the vajra and bell in my hands,
recite the sovereign secret mantras with my voice,
and meditate on integral unity with my mind.

For the confession of faults [in performing the ritual], recite the hundred syllables.

> Whatever ignorant faults I have accumulated
> through carelessness and lack of understanding,
> I confess in your presence, loving master,
> the nature of compassion: please forbear.

Dissolution phase:

> Supreme refuge, you have enacted the welfare of migrators.
> Although the dharmakāya is not subject to change,
> please move your form kāyas toward my body
> and bless me with your great loving-kindness.

> In great delight, the guru Awareness Ḍākinī melts into a globe of light rays and dissolves into me. My three doors and the guru's awakened body, speech, and mind become inseparable, like water poured into water.

Rest in equipoise for a long while within an uncontrived state. {386} If you know it and are so inclined, do the *Aspiration of the Sealed Word* and any other appropriate aspiration prayers of the Mahayana. Then the *[Sealed Word of] Auspiciousness*:

> Qualities fully perfected like the snow mountains,
> from which blessing rivers quench fortunate disciples,
> you who reveal my mind as coemergence;
> may there be auspiciousness of the sublime gurus, dharma
> sovereigns.

> You watch over practitioners as your children,
> ever together like a body and its shadow,
> giver of spiritual powers to those with sacred pledge;
> may there be auspiciousness of the yidam deities.

> You take care of practitioners holding vows
> and properly accomplish various awakened activity,

such as pacifying, enriching, controlling, and subjugating;
may there be auspiciousness of the dharma protectors.

Apparent existence self-liberates like illusion and dream,
that is the experience of uninterrupted great bliss
in the space of empty clarity of mind mental engagement;
may there be auspiciousness of great-bliss mahāmudrā.

Whether they support and offer[24] to practitioners
or treat them with contempt,
everyone will be placed on the path of awakening;
may there be auspiciousness of incomparable awakening mind.

However many states of auspiciousness there are
in all of cyclic existence and its transcendence,
like the course of a great river of abundance;
may there be auspiciousness for all beings always.

May merit rise like the sovereign Supreme Mountain,
great acclaim spread everywhere like the sky,
and long life, health, and others' welfare be spontaneously present;
may there be auspiciousness of an ocean of supreme qualities.[25]

Afterward, do not discard whatever offering morsels are left in desecrated places or where there is careless behavior.

[Concluding Verses and Colophon]

May whatever merit has accrued from writing down
the means to make offerings to gurus of the Shangpa tradition,
primarily the ḍākinīs of timeless awareness, {387}
go toward all migrators obtaining the sublime guru.

May I quickly accomplish
those inconceivable life stories
of the glorious Shangpa Kagyu
and become the total glory of migrators.

May whoever comes into contact with this
be brought to the pure land of Sukhāvatī
by the great adept Khyungpo and his heirs
and receive the prediction of their enlightenment.

This was faithfully composed with the permission from the venerable dharma king who knows and sees everything, Jamyang Khyentse Wangpo, coupled with my own strong interest. I, Karma Ngawang Yönten Gyatso Lodrö Tayepai De, have an innate propensity of undivided faith in this particular lineage. I took Venerable [Tāranātha] Rinpoche's blessed teachings as the specific basis and added whatever new material was worthy.[26] At the practice place of Vajracittakoṭi, on the holy day of the Victor's descent from the god's realm, it was composed during a single session on the very virtuous positive conjunction of the astrological juncture of accomplishing awakening. May it become the cause for the widespread flourishing of the great precious teachings of the Shangpa Kagyu, the guide for migrators.

26. Garland of Uḍumbara Flowers

Supplications to the Lives of the Amazing Jewel Lineage of the Glorious Shangpa Kagyu[1]

Jamgön Kongtrul

Melody of the Vajra: Supplication to All-Pervasive Great Vajradhara

Epitome of all families, without beginning or end,
a single entity encompassing the stable and moving in unity,
the nature of lucid great bliss in an awareness body—
pervasive lord Vajradhara, I supplicate you.

Free of all embellishment, awakened in emptiness,
the secret space of Vajra Queen's bhaga,
city of great freedom, source of phenomena—
original manifest awakening, I supplicate you.

Nondual, immutable, unbiased,
great desire, neither desire nor excellence,
entity and not entity, extinguished,
timeless awareness, bodhisattva Samantabhadra,
no affliction and great affliction,
coemergent, glorious bodhicitta, holding vital drops,
glorious Kālacakra Vajra,
methods and wisdom, epitome, yoga—
with numerous names, I supplicate you.

Emptiness and compassion inseparable, changeless great bliss
beyond the four extremes of existence and nonexistence,

the very essence of all sugatas, those gone to bliss,
ultimate timeless awareness, I supplicate you. {391}

Knowledge and knowables unified, well beyond
the extremes of embellishment, every cause and effect
seen at once by the one timeless awareness—
dharmakāya without compare, I supplicate you.

Echoes of emptiness rise like the shining sun,
kāyas and pure lands with five certainties appear
with no intrinsic nature everywhere like the sky—
completely perfect saṃbhogakāya, I supplicate you.

As artist, person, supreme, and so on, pure and impure
reflected forms, with fully bloomed lotus eyes,
diverse emanations enacting the welfare of migrators,
manifesting in whatever way tames them, I supplicate you.

Various bodies and all forms of speech,
all aspects of changeless bliss in integral unity
with supreme emptiness of all forms, inconceivable mystery,
inexhaustible continuous wheel, I supplicate you.

Six families, twelve principles of truth, sixteen of suchness,
one hundred families, infinite families,
the many dancing in the experience of the one—
pervading lord of all families, I supplicate you.

Pervading all phenomena impartially,
caring incessantly for beings everywhere,
abiding eternally without increase or decrease—
effortless accomplishment of great purpose, I supplicate you.

Essence of natural lucid clarity during the ground,
yoga of undissipating bliss-emptiness on the path, {392}
reaching the result of separation as ultimate two purities—
great renunciation, I supplicate you.

Like the eight metaphors: illusion, dream, mirror divination,[2]
you unerringly see without concept the extent of all knowledge
and the manifest subject itself just as it is—
great realization, I supplicate you.

Engaging nonreferential compassion ceaselessly
in spontaneous effortless welfare for every being
for as long as space endures—
great being, I supplicate you.

Pure unobscured earth, water, fire, wind, space,
sun, moon, and consciousness
have limitless power, ever faultless, and so on—
endowed with eight qualities, I supplicate you.[3]

Permanent, very cool and painless,
single, changeless, blissful, flawless,
joyful, and always in clear equipoise—
endowed with eight flavors, I supplicate you.

With inconceivable awakened body, speech, and mind,
limitless miracles, pervading all situations,
transforming, achieving purpose, and arousing awakening mind—
endowed with eight masteries, I supplicate you.

Complete enjoyment, union, great bliss,
no intrinsic nature, completely filled with compassion,
kāyas and awareness uninterrupted and unceasing—
endowed with seven aspects,[4] I supplicate you.

Subtle body, light to touch, all pervasive,
genuine attainment, total illumination, reliable,
great might, producing all one's desires—
endowed with eight superiorities, I supplicate you.

No intrinsic nature, reflexive awareness spreads,
having no obscuration, without conceptual thought,

all entities are seen as appearing reflections—
endowed with awareness of the profound, I supplicate you.

The domain of merit and awareness appears,
and by observation the whole of reality is engaged;
utterly meaningful conduct is the awakened activity—
perfect timeless awareness of vastness, I supplicate you.

Without partiality of object or time,
inseparable essence, undifferentiated suchness,
seeing the equality of all phenomena without concept—
timeless awareness of pervasiveness, I supplicate you.

Uninterrupted, with no phenomena that hinders, {393}
utterly removed from the most subtle atoms and change,
beyond even the conceptual realm of the victors' heirs—
timeless awareness of permanence, I supplicate you.

Body in union, mind in unchanging bliss,
compassion's form, concepts dissolve in close union,
vital winds blocked, melting bliss actualized in bodhicitta—
perfect unchanging bliss, I supplicate you.

Born of emptiness, karmic appearance and suffering ended,
the body of immutable wind-mind arrives anywhere,
not opposing the known, the body of perfect marks and signs
emanates multitudes of replicas; I supplicate you.

Not two, abiding without concept in the innate nature
of all phenomena as infinite appearance,
achieving all welfare in an unwavering state—
integral unity of perfected aspects, I supplicate you.

One timeless awareness sees clearly all phenomena,
realizes every equality of knowables distinctly,
and knows without thinking what tames those to be tamed—
endowed with fivefold awareness, I supplicate you.

Ten powers, four fearlessnesses, eighteen unique attributes,
great compassion for beings, undissipating awareness
of the twenty-one categories, and so on—
perfect qualities of dharmakāya, I supplicate you.

Thirty-two excellent marks, eighty secondary signs,
sixty limbs of melodious speech, and so forth;
those two form kāyas for others' benefit—
source of all qualities, I supplicate you.

Effortless, spontaneously present continuum
permanently places all beings on the steps to enter the path
with awakened activity that ensures definite good and consummation
for beings to be tamed who equal space; I supplicate you.

May I also not remain in extremes of existence and peace,
but quickly accomplish the unified state of Vajradhara,
the mighty one of four kāyas, presiding lord of all entities,
and always engage the inexhaustible ornamental wheel.

Melody of Timeless Awareness: Supplication to Awareness Ḍākinī Niguma

Vajra Queen, mother of all the victors, {394}
dark brown, adorned by bones, engaging space,
granting supreme spiritual power to the fortunate—
Venerable Niguma, I supplicate you.

In the amazing land of the Kashmir valley
emanated from Madhyāntika's blessings,
in the city known as Incomparable in the world,
you took sublime birth, I supplicate you.[5]

In Śāntivarman's pure Brahmin family sphere,
Nārotapa and you, Ḍākinī of Timeless Awareness,
as brother and sister, matured as a pair
like the sun and moon, I supplicate you.

Manifest emptiness endowed with all supreme aspects,
you appear in the body of the progenitor of all victors,
though in the illusory form of worldly existence,
you abandon craving rebirth, I supplicate you.

Gone beyond levels and paths innumerable times before
so that in this life the naturally occurring achievements
found in your life of liberation are unimaginable—
ḍākinī of coemergence, I supplicate you.

Without depending on intentional ascetic training,
just the advice of mighty adepts gracing your ears
brought integrated mastery of all dharmas—
self-liberated great bliss, I supplicate you.

The subtle and profound meaning of tantras and instructions—
knowing one liberates all—develops potent twofold knowledge
that really sees without obscurity the true nature of phenomena—
glorious female adept, I supplicate you.

In the empty expanse, binding mind, eyes, and winds,
you see the forms produced by spring's [vital drops] in the dhūti,
reflected vajra forms such as smoke arise all at once—
the stage of approach perfected, I supplicate you.

The life-force [wind] Rāhu[6] is blocked and falls to the belly,
life-force and downward-clearing [winds] join in the six chakras,
stopping the movement of the six elements, sun, and moon—
the stage of near attainment perfected, I supplicate you.[7]

Beyond the three seals, the incomparable Great Seal
causes the innate light of unchanging coemergent bliss
to [manifest] tenfold illusory body with all its faculties—
the stage of attainment perfected, I supplicate you.

By blocking twenty-one thousand six hundred winds,
that many [kinds of] unchanging bliss were obtained,

bodhicitta stabilized in the crown and the levels instantly traversed—
the stage of great attainment perfected, I supplicate you. {395}

Through proximate-cause conduct, you reveled in pleasures,
Vajradhara nurtured you and though of equal fortune,
your kāya of integral unity of [the stage of] training
enacts the welfare of all beings; I supplicate you.

All phenomena became manifest without obscurity,
you attained inconceivably millions of doors of absorption
and gained control over the secret treasury of all victors—
mother of all victors, I supplicate you.

Body of bliss, emptiness and compassion inseparable,
epitome of common and supreme emanations of the sugatas,
mighty one of the tenth level, glorious guide of migrators—
adorned with bones, I supplicate you.

Please lead with your great nonreferential compassion
all grandmother sentient beings wandering in cyclic existence
from the ocean of fathomless and endless suffering
to the pure land of expanding, undissipating happiness.

Lovingly nurture those fortunate to have entered the path,
pacify all adverse conditions, obstructors, and obstacles,
increase our meditational experience and realization,
and bless us to complete the five paths and ten levels.

Melody of Great Bliss: Supplication to Awareness Ḍākinī Sukhasiddhi

Giver of undissipating coemergent great bliss,
full with the radiance of sixteen-year-old youth,
mistress of the entire ḍākinī assembly of three places—
Spiritual Power of Bliss, I supplicate you.

You manifested as a pauper in a Kashmiri household,
trained in realization on the path,

and perfected faith and great compassionate energy,
diligently giving without attachment; I supplicate you.

For past eons as numerous as sands of the Ganges,
you completed accumulations of merit and awareness.
That training manifested as awakened karmic propensity
and you renounced your home; I supplicate you.

In the land of Oḍḍiyāna in the west, source of mysteries,
the males are heroes and the females heroines.
Your enlightened potential was awakened
just by arriving in their midst; I supplicate you. {396}

You sold flavorful beer as a living, showed magical methods,
and sent twice-strained rice beer with the yoginī
for Avadhūtī,[8] the forest dweller, and with faith
made a close connection; I supplicate you.

Venerable Virūpa accepted you as a disciple
and conferred the complete four empowerments of secret practice.
Instantly your fully ripened body of sixty-one years changed
to that of a youthful sixteen-year-old; I supplicate you.

In one instant you truly traversed all levels
from the path of interiority to the great vajra level
and manifested the vajra form of pure rainbow body—
mighty one of the celestial realm, I supplicate you.

You became the actual coemergent Vajra Nairātmya,
remaining in cyclic existence as long as it takes,
keeping the six watches over migrators in the three realms—
Bhagavatī, I supplicate you.

You grant real blessings in response to supplications,
with compassion always hold close the lineage holders,
and grant supreme and common powers in just years or months—
great compassionate one, I supplicate you.

Your form body appears as Vajrayoginī for migrators' sakes,
a flower of such exquisite form that one never tires of looking,
blooming with anthers of the signs and marks of awakening—
perfection of wisdom, I supplicate you.

Your speech teaches according to migrators' dispositions
the nature of emptiness through infinite dharma doors
with invincible echoes for all circumstances—
Brahmā's voice of sixty tones, I supplicate you.

Your sublime mind of lucid-clarity mahāmudrā,
the true space vajra of bliss-emptiness inseparable,
undissipating, coemergent, pervading everything—
source of all dharma, I supplicate you.

Epitome of active qualities of freeing and maturing,
subject of an unimaginable life of liberation,
just hearing your name bestows undissipating bliss—
wish-fulfilling jewel, I supplicate you.

Uniting in bliss with all victors and bodhisattvas,
wherever four elements exist you emanate forms,
like an excellent vase, a gem, or a wish-fulfilling tree—
spontaneously present activity, I supplicate you. {397}

With impartial compassion shown to all equally,
you guide the fortunate to the celestial realm
with a loving expression and compassionate smile—
sole friend of the many beings, I supplicate you.

Show your loving face and joyfully grant prophecies
to lineage holders, your supplicating children.
Confer empowerment of great vajra awareness
and grant the blessings of inseparability with you.

Melody of Loving-Kindness: Supplication to Great Master Maitrīpa[9]

Your great qualities equaled the reaches of space,
your fame spread throughout India and Tibet,
master of mahāmudrā, Lord Maitrīpa,
Advayavajra, I supplicate you.

A tīrthika paṇḍita from a brahmin family,
you met Nārotapa and converted to Buddhism.
You received suitable empowerments and instructions
that awakened the karma of former training; I supplicate you.

At Nālandā you ordained in the doctrine.
When in dispute you attended all-knowing Ratnākaraśanti
and many learned adepts, becoming an indisputable scholar,
raising the victory banner of scholarship; I supplicate you.

You entered Vikramaśīla Monastery,
and while alternating teaching and practice,
you saw the face of Vajrayoginī, mother of the victors,
who graced you with prophecy; I supplicate you.

You knew the time had come to support absorption
with the inner conduct, practiced secretly.
You changed your beer and woman into milk and a bell
for those who caught you; I supplicate you.

When the sangha expelled you from that place,
you left and spread a leather seat on the River Ganges,
where you gained countless further abilities,
common and uncommon; I supplicate you.

Since you had not yet realized suchness,
you went to the Śrī Parvata slopes, as the yidam prophesied,
and, joined by Prince Sāgara, you sought
an accomplished guru; I supplicate you.

Although exhausted, emotional, and wretched,
your resolve to fulfill your hopes never shifted. {398}
After six months of single-pointed prayer,
you achieved your desire; I supplicate you.

You met Lord Śavarī with two women attending
and he taught you with profound symbols.
Empowerments and instructions nurtured the abiding nature
and you received permission to teach; I supplicate you.

Awareness arose of seeing the ultimate nature just as it is
and you became chief of boundless heroes and ḍākinīs.
In Bodhgaya you taught widely on mental nonengagement
and it flourished; I supplicate you.

At Śītavana charnel ground you played with revitalizing corpses
while Mahākāla accomplished all your wishes.
You practiced yogic gazes and emanated various forms,
keeping solitude in mountain retreat; I supplicate you.

You matured many fortunate Indians and Tibetans,
such as Gaṅgādharā, Ratnadevī,[10]
and the four great ācāryas,[11]
who went to the pure realm; I supplicate you.

In the intermediate state you achieved supreme mahāmudrā,
and your supreme awareness body dwells throughout space.
In the north, your activity of Tantra's essence continues
for as long as the Buddha's dharma; I supplicate you.

Master Maitrīgupta, son of the victors,
think of me, your devoted child, with loving compassion.
Bless me to realize the innate suchness,
inconceivable coemergent mahāmudrā.

Melody of Natural Occurrence: Supplication to Glorious Great Vajrāsana[12]

Like the sun, you illuminate the darkness of beings' minds,
like the moon, you wax full the mandala of knowledge and love—
master of the Sage's doctrine, Vajrāsana,
Puṇkyākara, I supplicate you.[13]

Born in excellent prosperous Malabar in the exalted land of India[14]
into a brahmin household that practiced the pure conduct
and was never associated with unvirtuous actions,
the positive indication of blessing arose; I supplicate you.

You took rebirth intending to glorify the doctrine.
With your innate intelligence and without attachment
to your good caste, form, or accumulated wealth,
you practiced for the two purposes; I supplicate you. {399}

Having seen happiness and wealth as a dream,
definite renunciation raged like the fire at time's end
and you took ordination in the doctrine at Nālandā—
accomplisher all good purposes, I supplicate you.

The force of previous training kept you free
of the stains of natural flaws, former violations,
or associating with them even in dreams—
genuine great arhat, I supplicate you.

You received the heart essence of hosts of adepts, yogins,
and paṇḍitas in the east, west, and center of India,
and filled that ocean of learning with gems of discernment—
source of all needs, I supplicate you.

You were peerless in the ten topics of knowledge,
especially in the ways of outer and inner Secret Mantra,
desireless and unhindered great renunciant, you gained omniscience—
mighty one of highest knowledge, I supplicate you.

Though you inherited from millions of the fortunate,
the fathomless and vast jewel treasury of instructions,
as if gathered from all the nāga king's learned adepts,[15]
saving it for others; I supplicate you.

In Magadha, source of all the victors of the fortunate eon,
you held the Sage's doctrine boldly with knowledge and liberation[16]
like the mandala of the moon amid stars and constellations—
guide of the assembly, I supplicate you.

On the lion throne at the heart of Mahābodhi,
you attained the state of fearless lord of dharma.
The Victor prophesied your name Vajrāsana—
your fame pervades the world, I supplicate you.

On the sole path traversed by victors and their heirs,
your sublime mind of awakening is as stable as Meru
and falls everywhere impartially like cool rays of the moon—
chief of Buddha's heirs, I supplicate you.

Through your mastery of the common secret treasury
and uncommon one, such as *Jewel Ocean Tantra*,
you gained command of two spiritual powers—
victorious vajra holder, I supplicate you.

Your incomparable bodhisattva activity
totally trained disciples without partiality. {400}
You made the region and is inhabitants most auspicious
and became an object of faith for those who saw or heard you—
meaningful to connect with, I supplicate you.

At Śākyamuni's royal seat, you maintained his activity
as the crown ornament of all Indian and Tibetan adepts.
The world with its gods pays homage to you—
lion of humans, I supplicate you.

May I also keep the discipline, complete study, reflection, and meditation,
refine awakening mind, achieve beings' welfare impartially,

be able to shine like the sun on the Sage's doctrine,
and quickly attain the liberated life of a sublime being.

Melody of Peace: Supplication to the Great Fearless Ācārya Abhayākaragupta

As famous as the sun and moon in Jambudvīpa,
you enacted buddha activity at Bodhgaya—
supreme omniscient one in the age of conflict,
Abhayākara, I supplicate you.

Born into the royal caste in Jārikhaṇḍa in the south,[17]
from a young age you studied grammar and logic
and the Vedas with their branches to the end,
going beyond tantras and classics; I supplicate you.[18]

In the pleasure grove, the beautiful form of Vajrayoginī
exhorted you and you went to Bhangala,
where you studied as a scholar of all Sutra and Mantra.
Upholder of the piṭakas, I supplicate you.

You ordained and acted as a Vinaya holder,
and sought out empowerments and instructions throughout India.
In all dharma traditions and especially in tantric Mantra,
your highest knowledge flourished; I supplicate you.

Glorious Sauripa accepted you as a disciple,[19]
Vajravārāhī urged you to teach and compose,
you meditated in charnel grounds and attained absorption—
endowed with bodhisattva abilities, I supplicate you.

You taught many activity practices from the tantras,
gained the power of truth and the awareness of signs,
revealed a treasure under a pauper's hearth, and so on—
endlessly amazing, I supplicate you.

You became abbot of Bodhgaya,
glorious Nālandā, and Vikramaśīla,

and continuously turned the wheel of dharma—
tamer of worthy disciples, I supplicate you. {401}

When you composed a commentary to the *Eight-Thousand*,[20]
buddhas in ten directions proclaimed it auspicious with one voice.
Flowers rained down when you composed the *Vajra Garland*[21]
and Vārāhī entered your body; I supplicate you.

When you composed *Ears of Grain*,[22] beginning, middle, and end,
Cakrasaṃvara, Hevajra, and Kālacakra granted good luck.
Likewise for the other erudite, meaningful treasures
and countless treatises; I supplicate you.

Like leaving a voice message for future generations of migrators
about the profound meaning of the victors' and their heirs' intent,
since it would be difficult for the doctrine to arise thereafter,
you were prophesied to have an effect; I supplicate you.

While building a temple in the western land,
you held a begging bowl to the sky and Jambhala filled it
with food and drink and supportive provisions—
all views and thoughts achieved, I supplicate you.

Crown jewel of all Mahayana followers,
praised by Śravakayānists as a Vinaya holder,
great reformer of the Victor's doctrine—
famous in the ten directions, I supplicate you.

Your powerful abilities of knowledge and compassion
were abundantly perfected and the Sage's doctrine
was upheld, protected, and spread in your life that equals
that of the world's ornaments; I supplicate you.

Many Indian and Tibetan learned adepts of that period
became your students; after your activities were complete
you went to a peaceful place and in the intermediate state
gained supreme power of mahāmudrā; I supplicate you.

By the virtue of supplicating, may I find masters like you
to nurture me in all my lives and enjoy the freedom
of the jewel treasury of renunciation and realization
while spreading and sustaining the precious doctrine.

Melody of Jewels: Supplication to the Great Adept Rāhulaguptavajra[23]

The stack of many precious atoms of your three accumulations[24]
built up your qualities as Mount Meru in the center of four continents,
adept to whom a million deities adhered—
Rāhulaguptavajra, I supplicate you.

In the south of India, the region of Elabhiśa (Elabhaśa) {402}
at the special sacred site of Vajraḍākinī,
in the city of Bhiraji (Bhiriji), into the royal caste
you were born like a sal tree; I supplicate you.[25]

At that time, with light, sweet sound, and good scent,
the four emanated deities revealed their forms of awareness;
the wonderful signs of virtue began then—
Devasatva, I supplicate you.[26]

You learned the Holy Dharma until you were twenty.
At twenty-one, when afflicted by sharp vajra[-like] pains,
a mighty yogin and four deities blessed you,
saying that previous bad karma would be exhausted through illness
and predicting your ascent to the celestial realm in this life; I supplicate you.

For five days in the presence of self-manifesting Tārā
you did fasting practice, your parents bound you in chains,
but Vajrayoginī freed you and blessed you
with prophecy; I supplicate you.

At the acclaimed temple of Vikramaśīla
you learned well the Sage's entire basic training

and from many paṇḍitas and adepts you heard
the complete sutras and tantras; I supplicate you.

While you meditated in the meaning of profound Mantra,
the guru urged you to abide in avadhūtī conduct,[27]
but with your scholar's pride you delayed.
Later, even concentration couldn't accomplish practice.

You cut your tongue and limbs with a knife
as Guṇasāgara had commanded you.
At that moment you perceived the four deities
and your body was restored; I supplicate you.

Avalokiteśvara, Vajrayoginī,
Exalted Tārā, and Swift-Acting Awareness Protector
taught you dharma in person whenever approached
and granted blessing and powers; I supplicate you.

You followed the command of Jñānasāgara
to submerge in water for seven days;
leeches sucked your blood and you nearly died—
karmic obscuration uprooted, I supplicate you.

The adept yogins encouraged you
to use your miraculous powers to visit Tibet.
Your wondrous apparitions appeared to learned adept Khyungpo
Naljor
and granted many profound instructions and practices.

Beginning with the four blessing deities and so forth, {403}
you inducted several fortunate ones in the emanated mandala.
Then you returned to the Exalted Country
and arrived instantly; I supplicate you.

At the most steadfast vajra land in the south,
you renounced distraction, establishing that place for practice.
You attained the supreme spiritual power of mahāmudrā
and the state of an immortal awareness holder; I supplicate you.

In the forested hills known as Black Mountain,
you dwell as the vajra rainbow body—
wondrous and amazing one who consummated the training,
supreme mighty adept, I supplicate you.

May I also exhaust all stains of twofold obscuration
so that the sun of timeless awareness arises within
to vanquish the incidental darkness of ignorance
and attain the vajra awareness holder in this life.

Melody of Devotion: Supplication to Khedrup Khyungpo Naljor[28]

Great learned adept, unrivaled in the three times
in the Sage's doctrine, source of all good virtue,
amazing incarnate of five culminations—
Khyungpo Naljor, I supplicate you.

You manifested great awakening since forever,
yet with ceaseless compassion for disciples
your emanations fill space and the realm of phenomena—
three kāyas perfected, I supplicate you.

Born at Nyemo, the holy spot in Tibet's central province,
the moment the signs and marks of an emanation appeared
the adept Amogha blessed you
and made a prophecy; I supplicate you.

"This child, an incarnation, will go to India
and collect the heart essence of all paṇḍitas and adepts
that will ripen and liberate all migrators.
His various emanations will train disciples.
He will proclaim essential Mahayana dharma, free of extremes,
and the lion's roar of ultimate Secret Mantra, inseparable
bliss-emptiness,
will be heard in the ten directions.
His body will become Cakrasaṃvara, {404}
his speech, the epitome of Mahāmāya,

his mind, glorious Hevajra,
his supreme emanation place, Guhyasamāja,
and his bliss-holding secret place, Yamāntaka.
Once these mandalas are arrayed in his body,
they will actually manifest to his disciples.
Further, he will transform into various yidams
to train innumerable people difficult to train.
His life span will be one hundred and fifty years.
At the end, when it's time for the vanquishing deed,
he will display various omens and miracles.
Then he will pass on to the pure realm Sukhāvatī
that is praised by all victors and become a buddha,
turning the wheel of the Mahayana dharma.
Future generations of all people with faith
will no doubt also go to that realm of the victors."

After saying these words, that guru adept departed
like a bird in the sky; I supplicate you.

Descended from the marvelous Great Khyung clan
blessed by ever-excellent awareness appearing as King of Light,
you mastered letters, astrology, and mind sections of Bön,
nurturing disciples in that discipline; I supplicate you.

You learned dzogchen's three classes from Jungne Senge,
mahāmudrā classics and instructions from Kor Nirupa,
and became a second Teacher in each of those doctrines—
natural and acquired great talents perfected; I supplicate you.

With the force of previous training you traveled to India
and in Bodhgaya you met the second Buddha, Vajrāsana,
receiving the three baskets, the four tantras, and so forth,
and assimilating them; I supplicate you.

"In a former lifetime, as the Victor foretold,
you were a śrāvaka with great magical powers;
no Indian scholar could be your teacher."
Thus he praised your inconceivability; I supplicate you.

As [Vajrāsana] foretold, you went back to the cold regions
where Langri Tangpa, a magical emanation of Amitābha,
was raising the freedom flag of pure conduct—
second mighty Sage, I supplicate you. {405}

You traveled seven times to Nepal and Tibet
carrying rare jewels and gold without sparing yourself,
enduring hardships without concern for your life—
great being, I supplicate you.

You attended one hundred and fifty Indian scholars,
among whom fifty were particularly learned adepts,
and four were your especially exalted root gurus.
Of those, the two awareness ḍākinīs heard teachings directly
from the sixth [family], Great Vajradhara, saṃbhogakāya.
You pleased them and received ultimate instructions,
resolved misunderstandings, and practiced with single focus—
holder of supreme and common spiritual powers, I supplicate you.

In the acacia forest of sublime Sosadvīpa,
the royal mother, Vajra Queen Niguma,
entrusted Vajradhara's secret treasury to your single lineage—
mighty one of the tenth level, I supplicate you.

In the joyous Medicine Grove, Nairātmya
as Sukhasiddhi conferred empowerment and prophecies.
The elixir of her instructions held special blessings—
regent of the sixth buddha, I supplicate you.

In the emanated mandala of Advayavajra,[29]
you received empowerment and transmission
and heard Lord Maitrīpa's mahāmudrā and protector teachings—
served by dharma protectors, I supplicate you.

At Bodhgaya you held a huge offering ritual,
amazing sights and signs continued for ten days;
praised in chorus by gods, humans, scholars, and adepts—
champion in the three regions, I supplicate you.

Swift-Acting Awareness Protector is the very unity
of all gurus, yidams, ḍākinīs, and dharma protectors.
He promised in person to be the destined deity
of you and your lineage; I supplicate you.

Great adept Rāhula, who was nurtured by the four deities,
visited you bearing instructions; you received tantras, sādhanas,
esoteric instructions, and rituals beyond count
and were shown amazing miracles; I supplicate you.

You conferred empowerments in many emanated mandalas,
averted an assault of enemies and obstructors with an emanated army,
and were taught a treasure chest of visualizations by Mañjuśrī—
actual expeller of sickness and spirits, I supplicate you. {406}

When you emanated as death's messengers and divine maidens,
those clinging to permanence developed remorse and enthusiasm.
You passed through cliffs, appeared in single and multiple forms, and so on—
conjurer of illusion's apparitions, I supplicate you.

As the guru ḍākinī foretold, you went to Shang in Zhangzhong,
and beginning there, founded one hundred monastic centers,
covering the land with study, teaching, meditation, and practice—
lamp of the doctrine, I supplicate you.

Your body as the nine emanated deities of Hevajra
really appeared with the Five Tantras' deities in your five places.
Upon one hundred and eight dharma thrones you emanated—
teacher of dharma, I supplicate you.

Through the supplication of the gods of the four great kings' abodes,
for seven months you subsisted on the food of absorption
and sat cross-legged in space at the height of a palmyra tree,
turning the dharma wheel of Mahayana; I supplicate you.

"You fulfilled the guru's intentions, satisfied the gods, liberated people,
and did the deeds for the Buddha's doctrine."

Flowers rained down and the sound of *a la la* resounded—
commended by gods, I supplicate you.

Your emanations suppressed the jealousy of a large college,
and the seeds you planted in the morning on a wide plain
during a time of famine ripened by the afternoon,
nourishing many; I supplicate you.

The Great Mother in Akaniṣṭha granted the threefold [teaching of] the unborn,
Amitābha in Sukhāvatī granted the longevity practice of the elixir vase,
and Avalokita in Potala granted meditative absorption
in all-pervasive compassion; I supplicate you.

You traveled to the sacred lands of Alakāvatī and Oḍḍiyāna,
where Vaiśravaṇa and Yoginī [Siṃhamukhā] conferred empowerment
and gave you secret tantric instructions on blazing and gathering—
master of any desired absorption, I supplicate you.

Tanglha, Shampo, Madrö, and the other strong gods
offered their life essence and you conferred empowerment,
bound them under oath, and assigned them as the doctrine's guards—
Heruka Great Glory, I supplicate you.

In the ground of your disciples from U-Tsang and Kham,
Meutön Drime formed the trunk of wisdom,
Yorpo Gyamo, the spreading branches of altruism,
Ngultön Rinwang, the expanding leaves of compassion, {407}
Latö Könkhar, the bright flowers of love,
Zhangom Chöseng, the core sap of Lucid Clarity,
and Mokchok, the ripe fruit of Illusory Body and Dream.
These were the principals, the ultimate six disciples
predicted by the guru ḍākinī to be your equals.
The ultimate assembly of eighteen thousand
was given teachings and matured over many years.
At the end of your final life of one hundred and fifty years,
four classes of great kings, the gandharva king, and so forth,

the nine great worldly gods supplicated you not to pass on.
You considered that with compassion and love,
and taught dharma and made predictions; I supplicate you.

Amitābha displayed the array of Sukhāvatī pure realm
and proclaimed, "You are in your final life as a bodhisattva
and will become genuinely awakened in Sukhāvatī.
Whoever trains by following you
and hears the name of Amitābha
will be born in Sukhāvatī by a great miracle.
The [next] three lineage holders will awaken in Abhirati."
Recipient of prophecies, I supplicate you.

"My transmission legacy of vital instructions are unique;
those of highest, middling, and least capability
will be awakened in the ripened, habitual, or intermediate body."[30]
Thus did you guarantee it; I supplicate you.

"Those with faith, pray to me in Sukhāvatī!
You will undoubtedly be born there."[31]
Saying that, you displayed a multitude of forms—
epitome of ten powers, I supplicate you.

You manifested Five Tantras' deities and the four blessing deities
and others in your body and taught the dharma.
The sky filled with rainbows and the sound of music
while a great rain of flowers fell; I supplicate you.

In the midst of amazing sights, you left for Sukhāvatī,
with body forms, relics, auspicious swirls, and so forth,
to draw in the faithful with countless relics—
endowed with fourfold liberation, I supplicate you.

Wonderful sights proliferated for three weeks.
The ḍākinīs saw your casket as divine form that liberates on sight {408}
and made real offerings and light rays that shone in four directions—
Buddha's equal, I supplicate you.

By the power of faithfully recording this prayerful drop
from the ocean of your inconceivable life of liberation,
please nurture and bless me and all those connected with me
so that we actualize your life story in our own lifetimes.

Venerable Khyungpo, our unfailing supreme refuge,
stay on the lotus-moon seat on the heads of all migrators
and with your kindness of unceasing compassion,
please grant supreme and common spiritual powers.

Melody of Wonder: Supplication to the Incomparable Mokchokpa[32]

Victor's heir who spontaneously accomplished the two purposes,
the indisputable lord of adepts
who was predicted by the awareness ḍākinī,
Venerable Mokchokpa Rinchen Tsöndru, I supplicate you.

Born in Lhapu at Shang, into the Sheu clan,
once you entered the dharma, you relied properly on the guru,
resolved misunderstandings, and through practice
gave birth to absolute certainty; I supplicate you.

You met a man carrying [books], but you disdained study,
so you committed yourself to seek instructions.
Khampa Aseng[33] gave you profound creation and completion
teachings of the sovereign tantras; I supplicate you.

You received Rechungpa's creation and completion teachings
from Burgom [Nakpo],[34] and when you endeavored in their practice,
you showed signs to enemies, saw the face of Exalted Yoginī,
and attained meditative absorption; I supplicate you.

With Kön[chok] Khar, Yorpo [Gyamo], Dorje Gyal[tsen], and others
you studied many classic instructions, mainly the perfection of wisdom.
Especially, the great adept Khyungpo accepted you as a disciple
and you pleased him in many ways; I supplicate you.

He granted you every instruction he had received
from his four root gurus to whom he offered gold,
and he even made you the holder of the one-to-one lineage.
You always saw the five deities in his body; I supplicate you.

You actualized illusion-like absorption, {409}
realized all by knowing the one, invigorated your knowledge,
and once you subdued all the noxious spirits,
you made many migrators happy; I supplicate you.

You received the vast and profound Holy Dharma
from Akṣobhya, the two awareness ḍākinīs,
Indrabodhi, Vajrayoginī, and especially Heruka
in visionary experiences; I supplicate you.

When you met the incomparable Gampopa, with delight and love
he said that you were his spiritual child in many lives
and directly introduced you to the nakedly seen dharmakāya,
causing simultaneous liberation of thought; I supplicate you.

He entrusted the mahāmudrā legacy lineage to you,
and you perfected the skill in meditative absorption.
You said from then on discursive thought never arose—
bodhisattva in your final existence, I supplicate you.

For twelve years in the cliffs of Mokchok
you renounced human food and practiced with single focus.
At that time Acala, the four deities, the Awareness Protector,
and the ḍākinīs actually visited; I supplicate you.

During the ritual observance of Shangpa's holy day,
the guru Amitābha came and bestowed the central channel's elixir.
You actually saw pure buddha realms as numerous as dust motes
on each atom; I supplicate you.

Others saw your emanations that overwhelmed and destroyed,
and when you sat cross-legged in space, the fortunate ones had faith;

you nurtured them and gathered countless disciples,
maturing and liberating all; I supplicate you.

To hear your name or voice, or to see your holy residence,
or just to have faith and devotion induces meditative absorption
and leads to immeasurable liberation—
any connection is meaningful, I supplicate you.

When you conferred empowerment of the Five Tantras' Deities,
they actually appeared in your five places and in the sand mandala,
and all the fortunate disciples saw them—
source of blessings, I supplicate you.

Buddha's attendants arrived from Sukhāvatī
to accompany you there, but you refused; {410}
you lived for three more years turning the dharma wheel—
protector of pupils, I supplicate you.

"I will go from here to the eastern realm of Abhirati
where I will attain awakening on the level of Radiant Light.[35]
Then I will be a teacher only of the Mahayana,"
you proclaimed with the lion's roar; I supplicate you.

"All my lineage holders who pray to me there
will be born in that sublime pure land," you said,
and you displayed countless amazing apparitions,
then left for Radiant Light realm; I supplicate you.

Miraculously, you returned on a path of light
and invested the protector of migrators with the [dharma] lineage
and entrusted Sherap Repa with the status of the family lineage
to ensure continuity; I supplicate you.[36]

Sovereign of the dharma, Venerable Mokchokpa,
consider my supplication with loving compassion,
bless me with your awakened body, speech, and mind
and please lead me to the realm of Radiant Light.

Melody of Faith: Supplication to Great Öntön Kyergangpa[37]

Great clouds of love amass in luminous space,
a rain of compassion falls on the fields of disciples
and ripens the fruit of two spiritual powers—
Kyergangpa Chökyi Senge, I supplicate you.

In India you were Prajñāvarman and others,
very famous masters and hidden yogins;
your many emanations trained countless disciples—
lord of compassion, I supplicate you.

In China you brought misbehavers to the dharma
and taught cause and effect, and emptiness and compassion
to cannibals and monkeys as appropriate to their species[38]—
spreader of emanations to whoever is tameable; I supplicate you.

Nurtured by Avalokiteśvara in all your lifetimes,
you spontaneously accomplished the two purposes.
Here in the Himalayan region, your various emanations
also accomplished the Exalted One's activity; I supplicate you.

Born in Uru, protector of migrators, you ordained at Kyergang
and learned Sutra from All-Seeing Bal.[39] {411}
At [Draklha] Lupuk you received Avalokita's empowerment and instructions
from the adept Chegom; I supplicate you.

After three and a half years of intense hardship
you became accomplished and were blessed
by the sight of Avalokiteśvara and Yamāntaka,
your constant companions; I supplicate you.

You received the complete instructions of the lineages
of Rechungpa from Tsari Gompa and of Atiśa from Penpukpa.
Conditions led to the direct realization of your mind
as unborn dharmakāya; I supplicate you.

When you met Venerable Mokchokpa,
Awareness Protector welcomed you and became your servant.
Authorized as the single lineage holder, clinging to appearances collapsed
and absorption's great energy perfected; I supplicate you.

Avalokita always graced you with the Holy Dharma,
the Five Tantras' deities gave profound esoteric instructions,
many adepts and ḍākinīs instructed you
and gave teachings; I supplicate you.

When you traveled to your dharma seat of Kyergang,
Awareness Protector with his retinue actually came along
carrying offerings to present to the guru's seat,
and worshipped you with respect; I supplicate you.

With prescience you impartially tamed migrators,
Varuṇa offered you the nāgas' gemstone,
and with totally pure three spheres, thrice [you gave all]
to please your guru; I supplicate you.

In Oḍḍiyāna you received the great empowerment
and sādhana of Hayagrīva from Padma Tötreng,
and, as Padma commanded, the complete instructions
from Nyemo Zhuye;[40] I supplicate you.

You enjoyed the profound, quintessential instructions from many adepts,
such as Zhangom [Chöseng],[41] around whom ḍākinīs clustered like clouds.
With only your meditative absorption, dhāraṇī, and water,
you protected countless destitute migrators; I supplicate you.

Light rays radiating and absorbing from the eleven faces [of Avalokita]
purified your and others' sickness, spirits, and obscurations; absorptions arose.
Dampa [Sangye] taught Pacification; Hevajra father and mother
taught confession [using the Sanskrit] alphabet; I supplicate you.

The Great Compassionate One encouraged you to train disciples:
"In degenerate times this practice tradition I have taught
will spread and future followers will see me directly." {412}
Beings' welfare equaled space; I supplicate you.

After this life you took miraculous birth in Sukhāvatī
and heard the Victor's teaching; again in Oḍḍiyāna
your conduct of Mantra brought many migrators
to the state of vajra holders; I supplicate you.

Then in the presence of Akṣobhya in Abhirati realm
you perfected the conduct of purity and became a buddha
in the world of Vaiḍūryaprabha pure realm.
You lead lineage holders there; I supplicate you.

"I will be the tathāgata Glory of Immaculate Space,
live for one thousand years, have nine hundred thousand followers,
and transform fifty-six thousand [sessions] of the Holy Dharma."
Fearlessly you made this promise; I supplicate you.

"It is meaningful to see, hear, recall, or touch me.
Those who pray to me will all become advanced bodhisattvas
in the pure realm of Abhirati in the east." You said this
and entered equanimity in the realm of phenomena; I supplicate you.

Compassionate Öntön, the real Avalokita,
quickly grasp the hook of compassion
and bless us disciples who have bad karma
to accomplish the welfare of self and others.

Melody of Blessing: Supplication to Great Sangye Nyentön[42]

Vajradhara in the guise of a spiritual mentor,
you perfected every excellent quality,
Hidden Buddha Nyentön of Rigong,
Chökyi Sherap, I supplicate you.

Born into the śāla-like [Nyen] clan in lower Yol,
you had an innate, uncontrived attitude of detachment;
without clinging to your body or any possessions,
you perfected transcendent generosity; I supplicate you.

With intense renunciation you became a monk,
learned dharma, discipline, madhyamaka, logic, and the perfections,
guarding your higher training as your very eyes—
you perfected transcendent ethics; I supplicate you.

Not intimidated by sickness, spirits, and adverse conditions,
you endured great hardships for the sake of the Holy Dharma
and responded to all harm with helpfulness—
you perfected transcendent patience; I supplicate you. {413}

You clarified misunderstandings with the lamp of study,
applied endless perseverance in the wisdom of reflection,
and actualized the result of undistracted meditation—
you perfected transcendent diligence; I supplicate you.

You were nurtured by Öntön, Great Compassionate One,
who bestowed the complete single lineage of Ḍākinī's secret words.
You saw all appearance, sound, and phenomena as unreal, like rainbows,
and self-arising illusion was born; I supplicate you.

Hevajra, Vārāhī, Avalokiteśvara, and Tārā
granted you the elixir of the dharma.
In particular, through Sukhasiddhi's pointing out,
your realization equaled space; I supplicate you.

Awareness Protector accomplished your orders for action,
Varuṇa acted as your servant and subject,
the great classes of worldly gods and demons requested empowerment,
and you brought them to dharma; I supplicate you

Day and night, in illusion and dream, deities arose naturally
and the timeless awareness of nondual bliss-emptiness

completely eclipsed the deluded concepts of ordinary appearance—
you perfected transcendent meditative stability; I supplicate you.

Following the command of Durtrö Nakpo,
Latöpa came from India by miraculous powers
and gave you the yogic exercises of immortality.[43]
Your secret handicap was liberated in basic space; I supplicate you.

Following the guru's orders, you stayed at Rigong retreat
in the way of a hidden yogin and nurtured the fortunate.
You wandered in pure realms of victors in the ten directions—
master of the tenth level, I supplicate you.

The eighty great adepts and others actually arrived
and stayed for three days, conferring empowerments and teachings.
They spoke prophecies, then left flying through the sky—
foremost heir of the victors, I supplicate you.

Your awareness of the unborn was constant during and after
meditation,
you saw all phenomena precisely like the moon's reflections in water,
and you were empowered and gained the six super cognitions—
you perfected transcendent wisdom; I supplicate you. {414}

When lightning bolts struck you thirteen times,
they became blazing meteorites adorned with flowers.
You sent back the ḍākinī envoys and with your vajra body
trained your disciples; I supplicate you.

You were entreated by goddesses and rākṣasas [to make a statue],
and when the materials were all collected, an emanation
of Awareness Protector sculpted and dissolved into it,
making a self-created Protector; I supplicate you.

"Those in whom boundless devotion arises for you,
the epitome of Great Vajradhara, will be enlightened.
I too will bless them in the future."
Thus spoke Sukhasiddhi; I supplicate you.

"Whoever sees, hears, or recollects you
will never fall back into error
but will be born as your disciple."
Gurus and deities repeated; I supplicate you.

When your work here with disciples was complete,
you left for the eastern realm of Avakīrṇakusuma,
where you awakened as the victor Padmaśrī—
turner of the dharma wheel, I supplicate you.

Knower of the world, Victor Nyentönpa,
look here with your unveiled buddha eyes at us wanderers
who have bad karma, bad bodies, and bad circumstances.
Please mature and liberate all sentient beings.

Melody of the Lion: Supplication to Drogön Chöje Sangye Tönpa[44]

Like a wish-fulfilling gem, you make our wishes come true;
just hearing your name protects us from fear of bad existences.
Protector of migrators, dharma lord teacher,
Tsöndru Senge, I supplicate you.

Born into the Yangal Karpo clan, a lineage of Shen Bön practice,
in Kharek Tsaisilma, your signs and marks were manifest.
In all your activities, the experience of dharma increased
and propensities of previous training awoke; I supplicate you.

At the age of nine, an emanation of Machik appeared. {415}
She gave the Severance dharma empowerment conferred on the mind,[45]
the single-lineage oral instructions, and made prophecies—
single son of the ḍākinī, I supplicate you.

You viewed cyclic existence as a prison or hellish firepit,
with an intense sense of futility and renunciation you ordained
and studied Sutra and Tantra with many tutors—
Lion of Speech (Mañjuśrī), I supplicate you.

In the presence of an adept of Zangyul you were recognized
as the prophesied emanation of Amitāyus,
seventh in the lineage of Siddharājñī, Queen of Adepts[46]—
recipient of the single lineage, I supplicate you.

When you came before Sangye Nyentön,
many heroes and ḍākinīs welcomed you.
Your first dharma connection was instructions on the three bodies.[47]
You saw your guru as Buddha; I supplicate you.

You accomplished all at once the Illusory Body and Dream practices
of refining, emanating, and increasing; perfected the great energy of
absorption;
and utterly destroyed all grasping to the reality of appearances—
great delusion destroyer, I supplicate you.

From Vajradhara through the [Seven] Jewel lineage
all in turn predicted that you would train all the disciples.
Fortunate one to completely receive the aural lineage
of Golden Dharma precepts, I supplicate you.

In the daytime, inconceivable, inexpressible mahāmudrā;
in the nighttime, spontaneous lucid clarity with three aspects;
self-arising nature of integral unity arose—
you perfected the victors' three kāyas; I supplicate you.

Your body cast no shadow and you clearly saw
sentient beings' thoughts from their lives in the three times.
Your attention to afflictions of leprosy, spirits, and chronic disease
instantly cured them; I supplicate you.

When you conferred empowerment, the heroes and ḍākinīs
built the mandala and displayed their individual forms.
People entered the dharma by hearing your name;
just seeing you produced supreme absorption; I supplicate you.

At Meditation Cliff, Ḍākinī Niguma gave you
a rosary of one hundred and eight pearls,

foretelling an equal number of hidden adepts
that you would mature and liberate; I supplicate you. {416}

You gave experiential guidance, as your guru commanded,
impartially to high and low, good and bad, old and young,
such that the fame of your name
reached far shores; I supplicate you.

The world with its six great continents
and lesser regions was filled with your student adepts;
you brought many hundreds of thousands to spiritual maturity
through your unthinkable life of liberation; I supplicate you.

As prophesied by the lord couple of the sixth family,
once the garland of Seven Jewels had ended,
you released the vajra knot, and as long as the doctrine remains,
you will be the guide to emancipation; I supplicate you.

In order to inspire those who cling to permanence,
you completed your altruistic work and departed to the eastern realm
amid rainbows, flower showers, earth tremors, and wafting incense;
gone to Avakīrṇakusuma, I supplicate you.

Your amazing remains emanated countless relics of deity forms
as a support for the offerings of gods and humans,
remaining a field of merit for the faithful until the end of existence,
not diminishing but increasing; I supplicate you.

Dharma lord unrivaled in the three regions,
look from your pure realm with eyes of awareness,
arouse the power of your compassion for your supplicants,
and bless us with awakening in one lifetime.

Melody of Glory: Supplication to Khedrup Tsangma Shangtön[48]

The flower of your marks and signs smells of the three trainings;
the stamens of knowledge and love are your flawless beautiful form;

seeing, hearing, or recalling you relieves longing—
Shangtönpa Khedrup Chöje, I supplicate you.

Leaves of morality grew from the stem of your free and endowed life,
the lotus of absorption bloomed from the firm ground of study and
reflection,
and the fruit of experiential realization was nectar ripe for the
picking—
Tsangma Shangtön, I supplicate you.

Born amid auspicious portents of virtue
to parents of the Rwa clan in the Shang region,
your renunciation, devotion, and boundless compassion
was beyond childish behavior; I supplicate you. {417}

You held the victory banner of unblemished ethics,
guarding as your life even minor points of training.
Unrivaled in explanation, debate, and composition,
you broadened study and reflection; I supplicate you.

You dedicated all your possessions to the dharma,
never disobeyed the guru's words even in jest,
and left the schemes of this life far behind,
intent on accomplishment in one life; I supplicate you.

Just the sight of Rigong Chöje Tönpa's face
inspired your uncontrived devotion;
meditative absorption was born and within seven days
you perfected the Six Dharmas; I supplicate you.

"You are the first to drink the elixir of the single lineage,
fortunate one who was prophesied as my foremost disciple."
Thus [Sangye Tönpa] made you the unrivaled holy spiritual son—
undisputed learned adept, I supplicate you.

"In this and future lives, you will benefit countless beings,
attain the fourteenth level in Sukhāvatī, and

go to the celestial realm with the lineage holders."
Recipient of that prophecy, I supplicate you.

Vajravārāhī granted you introduction to the four empowerments.
You received guidance in Ati, and as soon as you practiced the gazes,
you reached the culmination of awareness, infinite lucid clarity.
Deluded appearance subsided in basic space; I supplicate you.

All obstructions and flaws were released in great bliss,
you saw outer and inner apparent existence as infinite purity;
and with Tārā's blessing, equipoise and postmeditation blended
continuously—
surrounded by ḍākinīs, I supplicate you.

You displayed all the signs of a nonreturner,
your body, not affected by vermin, shown with pure radiance;
just seeing your face transformed people's perceptions—
Great Compassionate One incarnate, I supplicate you.

All disease and demons were dispelled just by your spit,
anyone with faith who saw, heard, or connected with you
experienced the absorptions of illusion, lucid clarity, and so on
arising effortlessly; I supplicate you.

Full of qualities, you lived in a hidden way,
renouncing possessiveness of all material things, {418}
with only your cushion and one day's provisions—
ultimate renunciant, I supplicate you.

After achieving tremendous welfare for migrators,
you departed for the pure realm amid amazing miracles,
such as ḍākinī envoys who filled the whole of space;
you left prolific relics, I supplicate you.

Glorious guru, with your hook of compassion,
quickly pull us from the swamp of cyclic existence;
in this life, fulfill our wishes that accord with the dharma,
and in next life, let us attain the state of the three kāyas.

Melody of Renown: Supplication to Khedrup Samdingpa Zhönu Drup[49]

The epitome of a flawless life, unchanging sublime realization,
unwavering compassion, unrestricted super cognitions,
and meaningful awakened activity—
Samdingpa Zhönu Drup, I supplicate you.

In Lower Nyang Valley, praised for its one hundred qualities,
in an eminent household you entered a ḍākinī's womb.
You were born, and when four years old, the sight of an adept's dwelling
generated your meditative absorption; I supplicate you.

At Nartang dharma college you took ordination from Chimpa
and studied all the sutras, tantras, treatises, and instructions.
You became a learned monastic, perfecting profound wisdom—
unrivaled in discernment, I supplicate you.

Retinue, possessions, and all the prosperity of this life
you shot far away from you like drops of spittle.
You engaged in boundless virtue through intense hardship—
king of ascetics, I supplicate you.

You attended eighty-three authentic learned adepts;
your mind merged with theirs and fully absorbed their heart essence.
You obtained encouraging predictions and permissions—
empowered regent, I supplicate you.

You supplicated Sangye Tönpa on the road to meet him
and experienced meditative absorption in illusion and dreams;
just by seeing his face your conceptual patterns
were liberated in dharmakāya; I supplicate you. {419}

You were at the head of the [opening of the] single lineage
and granted all the profound dharma like a full vase:
"You are the chosen heir of my dharma; now help others!"—
thrice you obtained such permission; I supplicate you.

With unbearable compassion you ignored your own happiness
and with unwavering diligence floated in the state of dharmakāya,
never again subject to deluded perceptions,
only lucid clarity day and night; I supplicate you.

You experienced the intent of the great completion
and the precious instruction [of the Path with Its Result];
you clearly saw the pure lands and the six realms of migrators—
endowed with eyes of timeless awareness, I supplicate you.

In numerous haunted places, without concern for life or limb,
your powerful deliberate conduct of emptiness and compassion
controlled your own perceptions and outshone those of others.
You reached the ultimate sphere of activity; I supplicate you.

When you were making aspirations in the presence of the guru,
Kagyu lamas came and bestowed their blessings.
You never wavered from the timeless awareness
of appearance and mind as kāyas and pure lands; I supplicate you.

After countless beings who saw, heard, or touched you
were established in freedom, you departed for Sukhāvatī
amid unimaginably amazing signs and emanations
equaling the reaches of space; I supplicate you.

Dharma king, Khedrup Rinpoche,
regard us with love from your pure realm,
liberate all migrators from miserable existences,
and increase the virtuous doctrine of the practice lineage.

Melody of Liberation: Supplication to Khetsun Jakchen Gyaltsen Bum[50]

Your vast flawless aspirations had no end or boundary,
you were filled by a precious treasure of marvelous qualities—
learned and righteous Sangye Palden Jakchenpa,
Gyaltsen Bumpa, I supplicate you.

You assumed an emanated form in a family of adepts,
literacy flowed automatically without study, your intellectual skill grew,
and all the teachings came into your mind at first sight— {420}
magical emanation for any trainees; I supplicate you.

You accepted all basic precepts and rejected what is to be rejected,
with renunciation you perfected chaste morality,
with unquenchable thirst you drank the elixir of study,
the fame of your erudition spread; I supplicate you.

When you practiced Severance regularly, the ḍākinī blessed you,
ordinary drink turned to flavorful elixir,
Great Black One showed himself and dispelled obstacles—
natural yogin, I supplicate you.

Great Tsangma Shangtön accepted you as a disciple
and granted all the teachings and oral transmissions.
The certitude of experiential realization sprang up like summer's
scenery—
Victor's successor, I supplicate you.

In numerous haunted places you mastered your sphere of activity
and applied yourself to undistracted practice in isolated places.
You attained visionary experiences of the guru and yidams,
and prophecy from the ḍākinī; I supplicate you.

You saw all realms of samsara and nirvana by the radiance of lucid
clarity,
received the empowerments of five precious gurus,
were granted all the texts, appointed proprietor of the aural lineage,
and entrusted with beings' welfare; I supplicate you.

Merely seeing your face transformed others' perceptions;
when you turned your attention their sickness and spirits vanished.
Just desiring the dharma, disciples could experience absorption—
you brought appearance and mind under control; I supplicate you.

Once you manifested the form of the yidam deity;
sometimes the heroes and ḍākinīs rendered service;
the nine great beings bowed and obeyed you—
public lord of adepts, I supplicate you.

You wrote down the instructions of the Three Roots
exactly as you received them, ensuring the essential continuity
of the practice lineage for as long as the Sage's doctrine exists—
benevolence beyond thought, I supplicate you.

After benefiting millions of fortunate beings,
you departed for the blissful realm amid great miracles,
such as teaching the dharma from multiple bodies
and emanating countless relics; I supplicate you. {421}

Learned and righteous great buddha,
bless us, the fools who have entered the degenerate age,
so that we realize our own mind as the real dharmakāya
and achieve all our wishes in accord with the dharma.

From then on, the seats, disciples, and lineages of Jak and Sam were boundless; one is incapable of covering them. However, as it is my own lineage tradition and extremely important, [the following is an attempt].

Melody of the Lotus: Supplication to Khyungpo Tsultrim Gönpo[51]

The mandala of compassion expanded in the space free of elaboration,
the light of blessings dispelled the darkness of many living beings,
your emanated form was produced as the appearance of awareness—
Tsultrim Gönpo, I supplicate you.

From the sky of dharmakāya's realm without birth, cessation, or
abiding,
the clouds of saṃbhogakāya appear endowed with five certainties,
and the variety of taming magical emanations
trains beings throughout space; I supplicate you.

The root of existence is severed in the heart of awakening
and the victors' activity fully pervades an ocean of realms,
but the special pure land where you dwell
is Sukhāvatī; I supplicate you.

You visibly assumed the mode of a brave bodhisattva
[with activities] such as upholding the Victor's dharma,
transforming [the world into] a pure realm, and maturing many
migrators—
inconceivable life of liberation, I supplicate you.

In the world afflicted by the five degenerations,
with the highest love imbued by the strength of compassion,
you willingly displayed existence in the cool north
of this world Endurance; I supplicate you.

You perfected renunciation and realization,
and without a speck of concern for your own benefit,
in order to guide disciples on the path of emancipation,
you entered the stages of the doctrine; I supplicate you.

Your three secrets immaculate, the golden mountain;
your dharma robes between sessions shrouding it in red light;
your higher trainings, the sun and moon mandalas,
dispelling the darkness of the three realms; I supplicate you.

Your sea of study teemed with gems of knowledge,
the wave sets of amazing contemplation rolled in, {422}
the mountain of your meditation was higher than Meru
adorned by four continents; I supplicate you.

At the feet of Tsangma Shangtön Tsultrim Bum
you practiced the approach phase; the nectar essence of the aural
lineage
pooled within your heart and you tasted meditation,
causing realization and liberation to arise instantly; I supplicate you.

The buddhas and bodhisattvas made predictions,
completely blessing you as a yogin adept,
making you lord of the ḍākinī assembly of the three sites—
teacher by apparitions of four [ways to] train; I supplicate you.[52]

You saw upon one atom pure lands equaling all atoms in the universe
and projected countless emanations to all of them,
teaching unimaginable dharma approaches in all languages—
performer of Buddha's activity, I supplicate you.

You discussed the teachings with victors and exalted ones,
conversed about experience with supreme adepts,
and engaged in deliberate conduct with ḍākinīs—
unimaginably awesome, I supplicate you.

Those who see, hear, recall, or touch any part of you
are assured of the lasting bliss of total liberation.
You pacify the noxious minds of spirits and savages,
planting the sprout of awakening mind; I supplicate you.

Like the unified essence of all the lives of freedom
of learned and righteous adepts of India and Tibet,
you are unrivaled in the three worlds—
known as the third Khyungpo, I supplicate you.[53]

You granted fortunate ones the full treasury of secrets,
then departed to the blissful realm amid great miracles.
Again, with unimaginable manifestations,
you trained your disciples; I supplicate you.

May the blessings of your three secrets
enter the body, speech, and mind of all living beings,
and the continuous wheel of your life story fill like clouds
the realm of reality so that we may live equal to you.

Melody of Mysteries: Supplication to Jadral Ritrö Rechen[54] {423}

In the snowy mountain fastness, like the mighty five-faced [lion][55]
in the site of your isolated retreat, with fourfold disregard,[56]
you fearlessly practiced deliberate conduct—
Jadral Ritrö Rechen, I supplicate at your feet.

From your state of complete awakening you manifested here
to your sublime essential family; once you saw the pleasures and wealth
as a hollow plantain tree in a kingdom of dreams,
you made your life meaningful; I supplicate you.

Once you saw all places in cyclic existence, high or low,
to be the very nature of suffering, like slaughterhouses,
and even supposed happiness as the cause of suffering,
renunciation welled up from within; I supplicate you.

Once you saw that even the wealth of powerful gods and humans
was ultimately impermanent like a dancing lightning bolt,
without even a sesame seed's worth of lasting effect,
you attained conclusive revulsion; I supplicate you.

Once you knew that the deceptive allure of the eight worldly
concerns—
such as honor, gain, and fame—was like an island of cannibals
where free life is murdered, you gave it up even in dreams
and bid farewell to cyclic existence; I supplicate you.

Without purposeful pretense or insistence from others,
the strength of faith in superiors and compassion for inferiors
blazed like the fire at time's end, neither increasing nor decreasing—
Victor's son, great bodhisattva, I supplicate you.

With a mind for correct dharma practice, such as relying on a mentor,
you were like a swan gliding into a lotus pond,
completely perfecting the liberated life of a holy being
with immaculate intent and conduct; I supplicate you.

In particular, with undivided faith you placed your crown ornament
at the lotus feet of the third Khyungpo, pleasing him in many ways
and receiving the quintessential profound secrets—
successor of the Victor, I supplicate you.

The brilliance of sublime caṇḍālī blazed,
you realized all phenomena of samsara and nirvana as illusory body,
entered the equilibrium of lucid-clarity mahāmudrā,
and perceived double delusion as the deity's form; I supplicate you.

You savored unchanging bliss and emptiness, {424}
overwhelmed apparent existence, and banished deluded appearance in
basic space
through a hundred modes of deliberate conduct,
which inspired the fortunate ones; I supplicate you.

In degenerate times, you saw that many migrators were deceived
by the counter-dharma behavior of devils and their ilk
and made sure they didn't fall under the influence of fake dharma
by perfecting the genuine dharma; I supplicate you.

Your radiant body cloaked in white cotton robes,
you sing the glorious songs from the doha melodies,
and the warmth of your intent turned toward destined ones
imbues their mind streams with vajra awareness; I supplicate you

Mighty yogin, on the strength of your compassion
rescue my mind from the precipice of anti-dharma,
bless me to renounce existence and be a dharma king
in the glorious mansion of enlightenment.

MELODY OF TOTAL PURITY: SUPPLICATION TO KHYENDEN SHANGPA KARPO[57]

Your flawless knowledge was as wide as the sky,
your nonreferential compassion bottomless and limitless,
and your awakened activity unimaginable—
Shangkarwa Rinchen Gyaltsen, I supplicate at your feet.

Liberated from extremes of permanence and nihilism,
without leaving the realm of reality, with great compassion energy
you emanated in various forms according to beings' inclinations
and trained disciples in the three times; I supplicate you.

Just as the masses of clouds are one in the sky's sphere,
so too there are many physical expressions of lineage holders,
but they are one value in the awareness ḍākinīs' realm,
so you willingly took existence; I supplicate you

In a young beautiful body, the fortune of higher realms,
like a lotus born in the desolation of a swamp,
you were born in the world but not sullied by its flaws—
you inspire wonder, as with the gods; I supplicate you.

In the ocean of naturally occurring confident accomplishment,
countless rivers of your acquired studies were gathered;
in the joyous city of foundational qualities of higher ethics
you ascended; I supplicate you.

You attended unbiased masters of valid cognition
and imbibed the essential nectar of their instructions. {425}
In particular, through Ritrö Rechen, lord of the ḍākinīs,
you realized the meaning lineage; I supplicate you.

The profound extract of Vajradhara's intention,
the uncorrupted secret words of the Awareness Ḍākinī,
the path of method's Six Dharmas, the path of liberation's
    mahāmudrā—
you diligently practiced them; I supplicate you.

You joined rasanā and lalanā, the sun and moon set in their course,
in the central channel by using forceful means, fully binding them;
you conquered impure karmic winds in the city of outflows
through yogic exercises; I supplicate you.

You attained stability in unchanging melting bliss,
perceived form, sound, and thought like water moons,

and became the peer of heroes and yoginīs—
achiever of great bliss-awareness, I supplicate you.

Like the sun lord in the cloudless sky,
the sun of awareness rose in your pristine mind,
knowledge of the nature and extent of things grew,
and you saw the truth of phenomena's nature; I supplicate you.

Like the continuous descent of a waterfall,
equipoise and postmeditation were equal in your stable mind;
you felt bliss, clarity, and nonthought without increase or decrease,
and perfected experience and realization; I supplicate you.

Like the unshakable Meru, king of mountains,
you were never moved by deluded thoughts or conditions;
you didn't seek elsewhere but found buddha within you—
actualizing the result, I supplicate you.

You went to the royal seat of accomplishing integral unity for yourself,
inconceivable awakened activity for others,
defeated the unfortunate and nurtured the fortunate—
propagator of the Kagyu succession, I supplicate you.

Bless us to meet a mentor who shows the path to freedom,
engage the sublime path of secret Vajrayāna,
effortlessly engender the actual realization of the path,
and reach the culmination of the secret path.

Melody of Elixir: Supplication to Nyame Sangye Palzang[58]

You arose as the full glory of the Buddha's doctrine,
in particular, the sublime master of the Kagyu doctrine, {426}
totally without rivals; peerless Kuklungpa,[59]
Sangye Palzang, I supplicate at your feet.

You dwelt on a pure level; during the great empowerment
your full-moon body appeared clearly in the vessel of disciples;

you magically displayed anything at all
to benefit the doctrine and migrators; I supplicate you.

Your powerful aspiration did not waver with the temptation
of worldly happiness—for dharma's excellent conduct
you spit out the droplets of glory and wealth and set out
in pursuit of permanent happiness; I supplicate you.

Once you saw that nondharmic people who pretended otherwise
were creating the causes leading sooner or later to bad existences,
you sought the infallible essence of the authentic
doctrine of the Teacher; I supplicate you.

Your wish-fulfilling morality was renunciation of the three realms,
not just refuge from fear or aspirations for higher realms;
you set the noble mind of awakening on the tip of the victory banner—
source of benefit and happiness, I supplicate you.

You realized the meaning of knowing and knew all knowable
phenomena,
saw the meaning of the unborn and unrestricted love dawned,
traveled the inner path and with outer abilities
trained a variety of disciples; I supplicate you.

You eagerly tasted the essence of Sutra, Mantra, and instructions
from learned adepts, but the supreme guru of previous connection
was wise Shangpa Karpo, who accepted you as a disciple,
awakening your karmic destiny; I supplicate you.

You enjoyed the great gem treasury of aural lineage as your own
and the springtime of your experience and realization
grew like the medicinal herb valley of summertime—
holder of the precious lineage, I supplicate you.

You released all the knots of the impure channels,
dissolved the movement of dualism within the central channel,
and achieved unchanging bliss of the moving vital drops—
overlord of adepts, I supplicate you.

Grasping with mind-made effort vanished in basic space;
deluded thoughts of ordinary attachment subsided in their own
ground;
within the great infinite purity of whatever appeared,
the wheel of timeless awareness arose; I supplicate you.

You saw relative appearances as instructive examples, {427}
actualized the perspective of the absolute as dharmakāya,
and danced in the timeless awareness of their united great bliss—
blessing the animate and inanimate; I supplicate you.

You converted whoever you contacted to the Holy Dharma,
conveyed fortunate ones to buddhahood in a single lifetime,
and even pacified the minds of nonhuman evil spirits,
bringing all appearance under control; I supplicate you.

Through your impartial practice of secret deliberate conduct,
you reached the culmination of victory in all directions,
and from the vajra path you actualized the state
of integral unity beyond training; I supplicate you.

Externally, may the cave of eight worldly deceptions collapse;
internally, may the light of the unchanging bliss of melting blaze;
secretly, may I directly see the dharmakāya beyond concepts;
and may I quickly achieve the liberated life of Nyame Sangye.

There is not much available information in the life stories of the four gurus beginning with Khyungpo Tsultrim Gönpo until here, so these supplications consist of just general praise.[60]

Melody of the Unsullied: Supplication to Tokden Namkha Gyaltsen[61]

Like the mandala of the sun in the expanse of the sky,
you held the victory banner of precious Kagyu doctrine
in the Snowy Ranges, without comparison—
Namkha Gyaltsen, I supplicate at your feet.

You were free of the fetters of embellishment
and had long since abandoned rebirth, but for those in training
you appeared through the power of compassionate aspiration
and displayed any emanations; I supplicate you.

In a country where many excellent learned adepts arose,
there are sublime sites blessed by Padma, the second buddha;
especially exalted was the new monastery of Shangpu,[62]
where you intentionally took birth; I supplicate you.

You saw the purity of the Jeu family and Zhang clan
and decided you should enter the womb
amid amazing signs of virtue and with blessings
of your parents' bodies and minds; I supplicate you.

The wish-fulfilling sapling of your beautiful form
took birth with a suffused fragrance of virtue, {428}
and perfectly formed limbs, the fortune of higher realms,
and smiling flower of three trainings; I supplicate you.

Always conscientious of mindful awareness,
you were untainted by the slightest stains
of acquired or innate unvirtuous flaws—
exemplary righteous one, I supplicate you.

You served many adepts, such as Vanaratna[63] [and] Chokle Namgyal,
placing the dust from under their feet on your head;
with devotion, intelligence, and persistent effort
you became their heart son; I supplicate you.

You internalized the words of Buddha and treatises,
including the three vehicles and four tantra classes,
and gained the fearless poise of explanation, debate, and composition,
surpassing all competitors; I supplicate you.

You wholly imbibed the heart essence of the adept named Sangye,
and with no concern for hardship, remained in isolation

practicing absorptions of creation and completion
and mastering them; I supplicate you.

Bliss-warmth blazed on its own, undissipating bodhicitta stabilized,
appearance [realized] as untrue, lucid clarity arose day and night,
and you perfected Dream practice, visiting all the pure realms—
master of the sights and super cognitions, I supplicate you.

During equipoise you actualized lucid clarity of dharmakāya;
in subsequent attainment, the power of your effortless compassion
tamed the mind streams of all humans and nonhumans—
master of appearances, I supplicate you.

In visionary encounters you saw and caused others to see special deities
such as Kālacakra, Vārāhī, Avalokita, peaceful and wrathful deities;
clouds of ḍākinīs and dharma protectors accomplished activities
of whatever you requested; I supplicate you.

Drops of your saliva healed sickness and spirits,
your mere focused attention dispelled obstacles,
and the wheel of your works and deeds spread
the Buddha's doctrine; I supplicate you.

In one day of study, your confidence arose from within;
in one month of yoga, you became adept; in one year, you had arrived;
in one lifetime, you taught and practiced as a buddha—
such praise pervaded the earth, I supplicate you.

With unhindered ability to explain the intent of Sutra and Tantra, {429}
your two stages perfected, and the sights and super cognitions,
you gathered countless disciples with qualities
of scripture and realization; I supplicate you.

On the fifteenth day of the waxing moon, with wonderful portents
such as permeating sweet fragrance, sounds, and light,
you entered the equipoise of lucid clarity's realm of reality—
diffusing great clouds of emanations, I supplicate you.

May we be born in the realm of Abhirati, where the glorious guru
attained full awakening, and taste the elixir of three vehicles.
May every migrator who sees, hears, recalls, or touches you—
all beings to be tamed—be completely matured in that realm.

Melody of Lucid Clarity: Supplication to Muchen Gyaltsen Palzang[64]

Your awakened activity was as vast as the sky,
your renown as bright as the sun and moon,
your qualities as limitless as the ocean—
Gyalwa Mupa Chenpo, I supplicate you.

Avalokiteśvara emanated for the sake of migrators
as the son of an adept lineage in the Nyak family;
a rain of flowers fell and the ground shook in six ways—
protector of the world, I supplicate you.

Blessed by the great bodhisattva of Tropu,
who foretold your future as a glorious protector of beings;
from the time you were small your life of an exalted one
brought joy to all migrators; I supplicate you.

You put on your head the dust from under the feet
of many holy ones, such as Jamyang Rinchen Gyaltsen,
and learned the sciences, collections, tantras, and instructions,
gaining indisputable eloquence; I supplicate you.

You pursued the higher tenet systems at the place of glory
and attained stability in the two stages and awakening mind;
the renown of your great qualities
spread around the globe; I supplicate you.

The Mongol emperor [Ayawara] invited you to Tāitu Palace
where you benefited beings in unimaginable ways;
your ascetic practice at the emanated site of Chubar[65]
culminated in renunciation and realization; I supplicate you.

When you came into the presence of Khedrup Shangtön,
he followed Protector's prophecy and with pleasure {430}
gave you the entire profound teaching instructions—
gone to the heights of accomplishment; I supplicate you.

At the invitation of the Mongol emperor Genpa Chenpo,
you liberated Mongols, Sogdians, Uighurs, and folks of Minyak—
countless people of multiple ethnicities and languages—
establishing them in freedom; I supplicate you.

The leaders of gods, nāgas, and humans, with their retinues,
and all the scholars and adepts unanimously declared
you to be the chief of bipeds and the crown jewel
of the three worlds; I supplicate you.

The buddhas and their heirs, Avalokita and others,
spread near-perfect happiness in the Land of Snows
when you arrived in the presence of Amitābha—
Great Compassionate One, I supplicate you.

Dharma lord, teacher of Nyak, Gyaltsen Palzangpo,
remember your devoted children with love—
place me and those like me, embodiments of suffering,
felicitously on the level of total liberation; I supplicate.

Melody of the Innate: Supplication to Khedrup Dorje Zhönu[66]

Your free and endowed life was adorned by the three trainings;
the gem of your study, reflections, and meditation was inexhaustible.
You brought fortunate disciples to buddhahood in one life—
Dorje Zhönu, I supplicate at your feet.

Your family of highest capabilities was fully awakened,
you attended many spiritual mentors and trained in many traditions;
in particular, the sovereign Mupa Chenpo appointed you
head of the aural lineage; I supplicate you.

You traversed over long distances as if flying,
undaunted by cold, like the mandala of the sun,
bliss-warmth blazed naturally and you levitated—
master of the ultimate path of methods, I supplicate you.

You reached the culmination of illusion and dream,
led your life with the sights and super cognitions,
with the power of gods and humans, even devils were no concern,
free of the bonds of eight worldly concerns; I supplicate you.

Your inner qualities were beyond the mind's scope,
but your deliberate conduct was outwardly hidden, {431}
you firmly planted the victory banner of practice—
sublime adept, dharma lord, I supplicate you.

As you counted many years, you showed no signs of aging,
your physical appearance was blissful and bright
with the supreme suppleness of the four quintessences—
lord adept of immortality, I supplicate you.

Amazing, magnificent, sublime being named Vajra,
may your compassion enter migrators such as myself
so that we fulfill life and accomplishment
and reach the state of a supreme adept.

Melody of Integral Unity: Supplication to Muchen Namkhai Naljor[67]

Great being who actualized buddhahood in the pure realm,
taught the Mahayana dharma to the Buddha's heirs,
and benefited others by emanations in the impure realms—
Namkha Gyaltsen,[68] I supplicate at your feet.

In exalted India [you were] Paṇchen Sūryagarbha;
you transferred to the womb of accomplished parents
who were blessed by Great Compassion and Vajrapāṇi
and were born amid virtuous signs; I supplicate you.

You appeared as a child but possessed unhindered clairvoyance,
and you became disgusted with all worldly activities;
as faith and the energy of wisdom and compassion grew,
your sublime liberation family was awakened; I supplicate you.

You attended many spiritual mentors, such as Gyalse Tokme,
and trained in erudition through the expressing media of the Tripiṭaka
while the content expressed in the three trainings
completely filled your mind stream; I supplicate you.

In particular, you received from Lord Muchen and Dorje Zhönu
the experiential guidance, and through your lifelong meditation
bliss-warmth blazed on its own, illusion arose on its own, and so on—
perfected qualities of the path of methods, I supplicate you.

You pursued practice night and day without wavering,
enjoyed the food of undissipating meditative stability,
settled into the evenness of a hundred absorptions and arose—
increasing the highest great accumulation; I supplicate you.

You were nurtured by sugatas, yidams, and ḍākinīs,
and held the sights and super cognitions of giving up attachment; {432}
you saw all the migrators in the intermediate state
and cared for them with total compassion, I supplicate you.

You gave refuge to the sick who were gripped by fear
just by your mere attention, like the physician king,
and with your limitless bodhisattva activity
you became protector of all beings; I supplicate you.

Whoever saw, heard, recalled, or touched you will not regress.
Though you had abandoned the signs of birth and death,
to disciples you appeared to go simultaneously to many pure realms,
displaying magical illusion; I supplicate you.

You emanated countless relics for the sake of the faithful
so that all the gods and humans can forever make offerings;

your amazing signs will be uninterrupted
and your blessings unthinkable; I supplicate you.

Incomparable Venerable Namkhai Naljor,
may this child's supplication activate your compassion:
pacify adverse conditions to the accomplishment of Holy Dharma
and bless us with attaining the wished-for conducive conditions.

Melody of Accomplishment: Supplication to the Great Adept Tangtong Gyalpo[69]

Great Compassionate One and mighty Hayagrīva
inseparably united as Padmākara Vajradhara
displaying the illusory emanation as refuge for beings—
Tangtong Gyalpo, I supplicate at your feet.

Omniscient Dolpopa, [knower of] the buddhas of three times,
returned in your adept's body to train those difficult to train.
Ḍākinīs of timeless awareness gave you a single overall name
enhanced with five excellent names; I supplicate you.[70]

In Latö Jang your vajra marks and signs appeared;
urged by the Exalted One you rejected home and took ordination,
and rainbows and flowers fell when your hair was shorn—
Honorable Tsöndru Zangpo, I supplicate you.[71]

While training in the classic traditions, you fell into a state of
absorption,
yet you mastered all the teachings without studying;
right from the start you displayed countless miracles—
self-arisen great adept, I supplicate you.

Infinite dharma doors were disclosed to you
by buddhas, bodhisattvas, yogis, and yoginīs
in virtuous, low caste, and mendicant styles
of five hundred genuine gurus; I supplicate you.

While doing your practice at Tarpa Ling, {433}
you actually met Great Vajradhara with the five-family buddhas,
the eight bodhisattvas, the ten wrathful ones, and the [five] goddesses;
you received the profound path and many other profound teachings—
free of the darkness of two obscurations, I supplicate you.

Your compassion was impartial, you knew all there is to know,
controlled your own experience, mastered the four actions,
liberated your mind stream with realization, perfected deliberate
conduct,
and outshone the eight worldly concerns; I supplicate you.

In all the great sacred sites you made many aspirations
and met past adepts and hosts of yidam deities;
in all the charnel grounds you partook of communal feast
with the heroes and ḍākinīs; I supplicate you.

"When humans and nonhumans in the snow lands,
and animals, the sick, deaf, blind, poor, and so on
see, hear, or recall your form, in the short term their fears will subside
and ultimately they will reach higher realms or definite goodness
and the Holy Dharma of the Mahayana will spread.
Especially, subdue the barbarians on the borderlands."
Again and again you were entreated in this way
by Avalokita and Exalted Tārā; I supplicate you.

The Bhagavat disclosed infinite dharma doors,
Aṅgaja taught you the perfection of wisdom,[72]
Heruka and Yoginī conferred empowerments
and entrusted the tantras; I supplicate you.

In the Charnel Ground of Blazing Skeletons,
great glorious Virūpa accepted you and bestowed
the complete Path with Its Result and pledge substances,
which stopped your excretions; I supplicate you.

Three times Awareness Ḍākinī Niguma came
and gave you complete empowerments and instructions,

engendering unimaginable miracles and super cognitions—
scribe of the instructions, I supplicate you.

On the island of Tāmradvīpa,[73] the great adept Śavarī
blessed you with the introduction to mind's nature;
at Blazing Rock the supreme adept [Vararuci] visibly entrusted
Mahākāla as your protector; I supplicate you.[74]

On the peak of Copper-Colored Mountain in the Land of Demonesses,
the guru's three kāyas as the Lord of Uḍḍiyāna [Padmasambhava]
gave countless empowerments and teachings of the Eight Great
Sādhanas and others,
and made prophecies; I supplicate you.

Vajrasattva granted you Atiyoga teachings,
at the ḍākinīs' behest you saw to the people of Tibet, {434}
and in the barbarian lands, with immeasurable miracles
you tamed and converted them; I supplicate you.

With your great miraculous abilities you traveled
to every major and minor place in the world—
India, Nepal, Kashmir, Khotan, Oḍḍiyāna, China, Mongolia,
Dawa, Neling, Kalinga, Priyangku, and others.[75]
You manifestly liberated the fortunate individuals
and used various skillful means to ensure that the others
would mature as your disciples in the future—
you covered the earth with dharma; I supplicate you.

You placed worthy recipients in celestial realms, regardless of age,
achieved the respectful service of even wild animals,
tamed and bound under oath the eight tribes of gods and spirits,
and controlled the four elements; I supplicate you.

You built numerous iron bridges to span the rivers,
the liberation-upon-seeing Auspicious Stupa of Many Doors,[76]
multiple images in the jeweled or Gar style,
and other countless threefold supports; I supplicate you.

You set up geomantic focal points to suppress Mongol armies,
arranged excellent supports as antidotes to elemental disturbances,
and through your aspirations you provided long-lasting refuge
from the fears of sickness and famine; I supplicate you.

Medicine Buddha gave you death-defying elixir,
Amitāyus gave you longevity pills,
you lifted the fear of sickness, spirits, and untimely death
from all migrators; I supplicate you.

When you showed your body in the border country Kāmata,
the king and ministers who were engaged in sinful acts
tried to burn and drown you, but they were converted
to being faithful Buddhists; I supplicate you.

You had six supreme children, eight supreme close sons,
five awareness ḍākinīs, sixteen hidden ḍākinīs,
eighteen pledge ḍākinīs, thirty-seven male and female awareness holders,
fifty-eight people with karma, five hundred nonreturners,
one million eight thousand capable of benefiting others, and more,
whom you matured and liberated, then gathered instructions in eight parts—
investiture of regents; I supplicate you.

Your actual body lived for one hundred and twenty-eight years;
on the fourth day of the miracle month, when your luminous orb rose
into space, in response to the yearning melody of your heart son,
you displayed a form body in the sky in front of him; I supplicate you.

When supplicated again, your cubit-high body appeared {435}
at your practice place and stayed for a week in clear light.
Your amazing physical relics remain firm without changing
as an offering object for gods and humans; I supplicate you.

Hereafter, you will appear to your fortunate disciples,
regardless of distance, to bestow uninterrupted blessings
with your activity for Tibet's well-being—
kindness beyond belief, I supplicate you.

Avalokiteśvara, great adept, dharma lord,
your compassion never tires or lapses—
please show your face and bless us,
the unlucky beings living in the end-times.

Sublime adept, may I quickly attain
a life span, realm of disciples, life example,
and powers of aspiration just like yours
and liberate all migrators throughout space.

Melody of Coemergence: Supplication to Gyagom Lekpa Gyaltsen[77]

You manifested the dance of the original state in the space of awareness,
the brilliance of indestructible lucid-clarity bliss blazed,
and you were worshipped as supreme among adepts—
Gyagompa Lekpa Gyaltsen, I supplicate at your feet.

You totally rejected the prison of samsara's bustle
and engaged in the pure conduct of the doctrine of definite goodness,
your previous training in virtuous dharma awakened—
great being, I supplicate at your feet.

With many learned and accomplished spiritual mentors
you studied the general teachings of Sutra and Tantra;
in particular you received the entire long tradition
of the glorious Shangpa Kagyu; I supplicate you.

Drupwang Namkha Gyaltsen accepted you as a disciple,
and you practiced diligently day and night without wavering;
the qualities of experience and realization grew like the waxing moon—
mighty yogin, I supplicate you.

The two supreme minds of awakening flowed constantly through your heart,
but you would not exploit some short-lived awakened activity,
so the [activities of] subjugation, protection, and so forth
were accomplished by Awareness Protector; I supplicate you.

Though your life story revealed unimaginable skills,
such as your physical transformations and so on,
you always acted responsibly with common deliberate behavior—
hidden buddha, I supplicate you. {436}

You invested the hero adept of Mañjunātha[78]
as regent overlord, [ensuring that] the river of Kagyu adepts
will flow for as long as the Sage's doctrine remains—
amazing awakened activity, I supplicate you.

For others' sake, you left a portion of your remains
and through the endless proliferation of emanated relics
you placed many fortunate ones in a place of freedom—
your deeds fulfilled, I supplicate you.

By the virtue of my supplication, may the stains of two obscurations
in the mind streams of myself and migrators be permanently purified
and may the three kāyas arise naturally by directly seeing
the face of innate dharmakāya, coemergent lucid clarity.

Melody of Maturing and Liberating: Supplication to Venerable Kunga Drolchok[79]

Foretold by the Victor, upholder of the conduct, mighty adept,
in order to spread the essential doctrine in the Himalaya,
you manifested as the hero adept Mañjunātha;
Kunga Drolchok, I supplicate at your feet.

When the full moon of your rebirth arose in Lowo Mentang[80]
it was as if the lotus plant from the heavens
that keeps the color and fragrance had bloomed,
like spring's glory; I supplicate you.

When the flower of your marks and signs was threatened by elemental
turmoil,
as soon as you befriended the morning sun of the Sage's doctrine,
you were victorious over the onslaught of obstructions,
finding dharma's meaning within; I supplicate you.

In the central region, with knowledge and liberation,
without hesitation you entered the lotus lake, joyful as a swan,
and meditated in courageous conduct at a tender age,
releasing mind's knots; I supplicate you.

The strength of former training awakened, you effortlessly knew the
 piṭakas,
Sarasvatī entered your throat, evoking the powers of discernment
in the three ways of erudition, such as eloquence—
your clear intellect was captivating; I supplicate you.

Your crown jewel [guru] made prophecies and encouragement,
four jewels gave you the vital points of instruction,
two great paṇḍitas[81] cleared up the net of doubts—
spontaneous accomplisher of intentions, I supplicate you. {437}

Two renunciants enhanced your realization:
Ngakgi Wangpo aroused your interest in terminology;
and in particular, Lord Gyagom, the real Vajradhara,
entrusted mind's treasury; I supplicate you.

In outward manner, you were bound by the training of pure prātimokṣa;
inwardly, you had perfect control of the mind of awakening;
secretly, you upheld the deliberate behavior of Mantra—
sublime sovereign, I supplicate you.

Lord of secrets Yamāntaka dispelled obstacles,
Hevajra father-mother, Cakrasaṃvara,
Vajrayoginī, and other special deities
blessed and nurtured you; I supplicate you.

Mistress of the celestial realm, Venerable Niguma,
granted the Six Dharmas, Awareness Protector, and others,
and you realized lucid clarity without center or boundary—
recipient of the amazing direct lineage, I supplicate you.

In Sosadvīpa you joined the great Ḍākinī and her gathering
for communal feast and she made a prophecy;

your realization increased in blending equipoise and postmeditation—
protected by Ḍākinī like a son, I supplicate you.

Mitrayogin gave you the *Threefold Meaning of the Essence*,[82]
Bhāviveka conferred the dharma empowerment of symbols,
dharma protectors such as Mighty Strength Thief and Vaiśravaṇa[83]
acted as your servants; I supplicate you.

You perceived whatever arose as the play of illusion;
with a natural attitude free of fixation and contrivance
you behaved without attachment like a small child,
but all your acts became dharma; I supplicate you.

"I am a person with whom any connection is meaningful;
seeing, hearing, recalling, or touching me prevents bad existences."
So you promised with undeceiving words—
protector of many beings, I supplicate you.

You collected all the streams of instruction in the snowy lands,
exemplified by [giving] Niguma's guidance more than one hundred times;
after spreading your altruism throughout the reaches of space,
you departed for the celestial realm; I supplicate you.

Again, all over India, Tibet, Oḍḍiyāna, Drāmiḍa,
and indefinite places where there were beings to be trained,
your many emanations purified the realm of disciples
and they gained unsurpassable awakening; I supplicate you.

Accomplished hero, nurture me in all my lives {438}
so that the inexhaustible ornamental wheel of my three secrets
manifests clouds of oceans of infinite liberated lifetimes
equal to yours, illustrious one.

Melody of the Profound: Supplication to Chöku Lhawang Drakpa[84]

Glorious pervading lord, changeless vajra body,
indestructible melody of inexpressible vajra speech,

great bliss of integral unity, the equality of vajra mind—
Lhawang Drakpa, I supplicate at your feet.[85]

Your vajra body was adorned by flawless youth,
all the qualities of the profound path arose in glory,
with a fearless attitude of deliberate conduct
your great energy was perfected at birth; I supplicate you.

Your sublime vajra family was awakened from the start;
though free of dualistic acceptance and rejection
you simulated renunciation of illusory cyclic existence
to draw various types to the dharma; I supplicate you.

You held close upon your head and pleased in the three ways
the vajra master, sublime one free of mind's knots,
and attained the totally perfect blessings of his three secrets—
cherished by that holy one; I supplicate you.

With great effort in the two phases, the quintessence of Vajrayāna
carried you to the culmination of accomplishment.
The force of your meditation brought highest wisdom, desireless and
  unhindered—
master of the sights and super cognitions, I supplicate you.

The force of your devotion made you see everything as the guru,
you perfected inner heat and bliss-emptiness blazed like fire,
you controlled illusion and could variously emanate and change,
your pure perception thoroughly pervaded; I supplicate you.

Dualistic wind-mind dissolved in the avadhūtī,
phenomena of samsara and nirvana nakedly arose as dharmakāya,
not a speck of hopes and fears, certainties and doubts, dos and don'ts—
king of renunciants, I supplicate you.

With the power of great vajra timeless awareness
you showered real blessings on all fortunate ones,
and with realization you subdued by splendor others' perceptions—
mighty yogin, I supplicate you. {439}

You saw daytime appearances as illusion and dream,
nighttime appearances spread in pure great lucid clarity,
everything dawned as the sphere of unified great bliss—
finalized experience and realization, I supplicate you.

With the blessings of the ḍākinīs of timeless awareness
you enjoyed the feast circle with the three emissaries,[86]
and sustained the royal guise of a great adept without pretense—
Venerable Draktö, I supplicate you.

Your distribution of the elixir of total liberation
[made disciples] vassals protecting the domain of adepts;
lord of liberators, Venerable Lhawang,
you made meaningful investiture, I supplicate you.

You held the golden rosary of the amazing Kagyu,
and by giving an inexhaustible river of blessings
your great waves of deeds benefited the Shangpa doctrine—
unrivaled sublime being, I supplicate you.

May I rely on the unmistaken holy one and receive your blessings,
arrive at the culmination of the secret path, and attain spiritual powers.
Grant your blessings that the profound long tradition increase without
  a break
and that I may accomplish a life of liberation such as yours.

(Here one should add the supplication spoken by Jonang Jetsun Rinpoche.)[87]

Melody of Virtue and Goodness: Supplication to Venerable Glorious Lama Karma Zhenpen Özer[88]

Holder of a life story of inconceivable secrets,
to ordinary viewers you practiced hidden deliberate conduct;
mighty adept with whom any connection is meaningful—
Zhenpen Özer, I supplicate at your feet.

Sincere renunciation arose freely from within,
you kept the pure brahmin conduct of Śākyamuni's doctrine,

you spontaneously learned reading and writing by the blessings
of Exalted Lion of Speech; I supplicate you.

Unbidden, Dark-Red [Guru Drakpo] with Fire Garland
revealed himself and dispelled all your outer and inner obstacles. {440}
You visited with numerous authentic masters
and drank dharma's elixir; I supplicate you.

Öntön appeared and said that [you were] the hidden yogin
who would imbibe the quintessence of the Shangpa dharma
and other instructions received from Karma Lhaktong
just as Venerable Mokchok's manifestation promised; I supplicate you.

When you practiced mind training, you became sick for three years,
but you overcame it in the space of emptiness and compassion.
With unimaginable diligence in ascetic practice,
you gained experience of the instructions; I supplicate you.

You perfected the meditative absorptions of Fierce Inner Heat,
Illusory Body, Dream, and Lucid Clarity,
and visibly displayed undeniable outer signs
such as expelling sickness and spirits; I supplicate you.

You abandoned the eight worldly concerns even in dreams,
never pretended agreement just to save face,
turned away from worldly schemes as if from rot—
king of renunciants, I supplicate you.

You abandoned self-fixation, and with reverse meditation of equalizing
the sickening fear of the tangible and intangible,
you enhanced your practice and perfected deliberate conduct—
mighty yogin, I supplicate you.

Unimaginable experience and realization was born,
the adepts, deities, and ḍākinīs showed themselves,
dharma protectors and oath-bound ones accomplished activities—
lineage holder of former masters, I supplicate you.

You mastered magical transformations such as invisibility,
explicitly understood hidden phenomena such as evolution of elements,
and displayed emanated forms to those with pure vision,
such as that of Marpa Lotsāwa; I supplicate you.

You resolved any circumstances directly on the path
by the indefinite variety of tögal conduct—
yogin who controlled appearances [as] mind,
Karma Maṇi, I supplicate at your feet. {441}

You spread the practice lineage for fortunate disciples,
whoever had good or bad connections with you did not regress,
completing your activity, you remain in the great lucid clarity—
sublime form of timeless awareness, I supplicate you.

Glorious precious guru, supreme recollection,
remain always with unwavering compassion
with your heart-stamen in the center of my head's mandala,
and grant the blessings of your awakened body, speech, and mind.

Melody of the Auspicious Coil: Supplication to All-Knowing Jamyang Khyentse Wangpo[89]

You know the nature and extent of all there is to know,
with nonreferential compassion you consider all migrators your children—
king of dharma, capable of emptying the pit of cyclic existence,
Khyentse Wangpo, I supplicate at your feet.

Sole father of the victors, Exalted Mañjuśrī,
fills the realm of reality with manifestations to train beings.
You took birth intentionally in these degenerate times
as a glorious protector of doctrine and migrators; I supplicate you.

In a medicinal valley of four kinds and ten virtues in Amdo,[90]
in the emanated place of activity to train migrators,
after five sublime observations such as of a pure family,[91]
you manifested an emanation body; I supplicate you.

All the supreme guides with timeless awareness
with one voice made prophecies of a holy being,
gods and humans praised you as lord of beings
for your extraordinary behavior; I supplicate you.

You set foot all over U-Tsang and greater Tibet
and attended over one hundred masters, pleasing them in three ways.
Without fatigue or regret, you thoroughly sought the Holy Dharma
with boundless resolve; I supplicate you.

When doing practice in Sachen's cave,
the mudra of your special deity dissolved into your heart,
fully releasing the eight great treasures, [such as] confidence,
perfecting the energy of twofold knowledge;[92] I supplicate you. {442}

You excelled at the five classical sciences and their branches,
such as grammar, logic, art, healing, calculation, and poetics,
and your fame spread everywhere in the region
of the Himalayas; I supplicate you.

By a mere glance at the texts you plumbed the depths
of vinaya, abhidharma, madhyamaka, prajñāpāramitā, and tantras.
You gained infallible retention and displayed it overtly
as the wheel of stability (Mañjuśrī); I supplicate you.

The jewel ornament of your pure discipline attracted fortunate ones,
the smiling face of your absorptions magnetized their mental powers,
the elegant grace of your knowledge shook the three levels—
mighty one of three trainings, I supplicate at your feet.

With spotless dharma vision you saw any topic's depth and breadth,
your explanation, reasoning, and composition were open and
    unrestricted,
and all your deeds and activities were free of the stains of delusion,
inspiring the confidence of gods and humans; I supplicate you.

You hid your inner qualities like the oceans' treasures
while praising and honoring the slightest qualities in others.

You gave up cherished possessions as if they were grass
for the sake of the doctrine and beings; I supplicate you.

You mastered vast retentions, absorptions, and super cognitions,
becoming worthy of offerings by people in the three worlds,
yet you never became haughty and would take on great hardships
for a single word of the Holy Dharma; I supplicate you.

You were indifferent to any worldly actions and plans,
such as preserving the explanations of pseudo-dharmas.
Like a fearless lion, you engaged in ever-excellent conduct—
unrivaled on this earth, I supplicate you.

Every stream from the source texts and esoteric instructions
in the long traditions of the Eight Great Chariots of practice lineages
collected in your mind's lake, establishing the continuum of maturation
and liberation,
and extending the doctrine's life; I supplicate you.

You provided disciples with training supports without bias
from the great chariot of the completely perfect doctrine of the Sage;
without falling into sectarianism, you became the crown jewel
of all the tenet systems; I supplicate you. {443}

All your activity was done exclusively to benefit others,
your company was meaningful, you showed many amazing sights,
and you produced an inconceivably great accumulation of merit—
mighty one on the tenth level, I supplicate you.

The Oḍḍiyāna couple, Vimalamitra, dharma kings
and successors, Chöwang, Omniscient [Longchen], and so on—
gurus and yidam deities of many lineages
blessed you and granted spiritual powers; I supplicate you.

Especially, Master Mañjuśrīmitra granted you
the secret treasury of Sutra and Tantra and blessed you
with the awareness body inseparable from himself,
fully waking your knowledge and realization; I supplicate you.

With great affection, the uncle-nephew lineage [of Sakya]
conferred empowerment and entrusted you with their tantras.
Many other Indian and Tibetan scholar-adepts nurtured you repeatedly
in real life, visionary experience, and dream; I supplicate you.

When you entered the [Guhya]samāja mandala [conferred by] the
supreme teacher of the So [system],
the power of the wisdom empowerment refined residues of aggregates
and elements
and transformed into Vajrasattva's three secrets—
sublime overlord of all families, I supplicate you.

The mother of the victors, Vajra Queen nurtured you,
and apparent existence dawned as the wheel of infinite purity;
you clearly saw the mandala of your vajra body—
supreme chief of adepts, I supplicate you.

You could gather the ḍākinīs of the outer and inner three places,
the timeless awareness of the three blazes increased,[93]
and the auspicious connection of the three conducts culminated—
great mighty yogin, I supplicate you.

The karmic propensities from many lifetimes awoke,
you found a million streams of sacred images, holy substances,
rare *pustaka* (books) of sutric and tantric scriptural teachings
that flowed into the ocean of your life; I supplicate you.

You possessed the six lineages and mind treasures, pure visions,
aural lineages, recollected [teachings], and reconcealed treasures;
you gained the domain of the seven precious transmissions—
turner of the dharma wheel, I supplicate you.

You controlled your own perceptions and subdued others with
splendor,
accomplished the four activities without even trying, {444}
and recruited ḍākinīs, dharma guards, and powerful haughty spirits
to accomplish your commands; I supplicate you.

You matured and liberated millions of fortunate ones
through countless profound and vast dharma wheels;
you lived an inconceivably exalted life of freedom—
epitome of compassion, I supplicate you.

By my single-minded supplication of undivided devotion,
from this time until I attain awakening,
may I never be apart from you, glorious sublime guru,
and once you accept me, may I manifest such a life as yours.

By my service of properly pleasing you in three ways,
may I attain your mind's essence and consummate practice,
completely perfect the qualities of the levels and paths,
and attain the state of mighty Vajradhara.

May there be no obstacles to practice that accords with dharma,
and by gaining mastery of the dharma of scripture and realization,
may I spread the Sage's doctrine across the world
and become a sovereign of the dharma like you.

Melody of the Ever Excellent: Supplication to the Glorious Guru

[In this supplication to himself, the underlined words spell out Jamgön Kongtrul's names. First is Karma Ngawang Yönten Gyatso Trinle Kunkhyap Pal Zangpo:]

> Sublime illuminator of the Karma Kagyu doctrine,
> powerful one in speech, vast ocean of qualities,
> wave sets of your virtuous activity pervade everywhere,
> glorious excellence, I supplicate at your feet.

[Lodrö Taye:]

> You studied, reflected, and meditated on the ten sciences,
> [and] subjugation, protection, all-knowingness and its branches,
> your intellect free of attachment or hindrance
> is endowed with boundless discernment; I supplicate you.

[Padma Gargyi Wangchuk Trinle Drodul Tsal:]

Great powerful Padma and others nurtured you,
you upheld the awareness mantras of compassionate lord of the dance,
with the energy of awakened activity to train migrators—
glorious sublime guru, I supplicate you.

You were born into the Khyung clan, to a family of adepts,
the karmic propensities of previous training woke the virtuous dharma,
and you collected the conducive conditions for the two cycles—
amazing marvelous one, I supplicate you.

With rejecting harm to others as a basis, you practiced restraint;
with helping others as a basis, you endeavored in the training precepts;
and with clarity in the two phases of every visualization description,
you were thus a threefold vajra holder, I supplicate you.

You relied on many learned adepts, guides, and tutors;{445}
with diligence and noble motivation you plunged into the ocean of Sutra and Tantra;
and with the fine gifts of the jewels of classic and esoteric instructions,
you relieved the poverty of fortunate ones; I supplicate you.

According to the vajra command of the Omniscient One of Oḍḍiyāna,
the accomplished leaders who reveal treasures
prophesied you as an emanation of [the translator] Vairocana,
investing you with power; I supplicate you.

Sublime visionaries—Victor [Karmapa] and his heirs,
Chokgyur Dechen Lingpa, and Jamyang Khyentse Wangpo—
proclaimed you an emanation of Tāranātha and Gyurme Dorje
and honored you as an excellent teacher; I supplicate you.

You had the pure view to preserve the Victor's doctrine impartially,
the noble motivation to accomplish beings' welfare impartially,
and the style of conduct that directly integrates whatever arises—
holder of a holy life, I supplicate you.

In the remote site of Tsadra Rinchen Drak
you planted the victory banner of lifelong practice
and performed acts of teaching, composing, and transmitting—
spontaneous achiever of two purposes; I supplicate you.

As clearly extolled in the vajra scriptures,
you created images of Heruka's body, speech, and mind
to benefit migrators for as long as
the doctrine remains; I supplicate you.

On the strength of devotion and inevitable interdependence,
may I never be apart from the glorious, supreme guru.
May we come together in the celestial great city
and attain the sublime place of Vajrasattva.

May your three secrets remain firm as a vajra,
forever beating the drum of the profound and vast dharma,
so that I and others will complete all paths of goodness.
May our wishes be spontaneously achieved and the glory of virtue
  and goodness blaze.

[Colophon]

Without even a tiny speck of laudable qualities, to write such self-praise is a fool's errand. Nevertheless, I could not refuse the urgent request of the diligent practitioner and holy Lama Pema Norbu.[94] {446} I, Yönten Gyatso, a person of three preoccupations,[95] wrote this by hand. Let virtue prevail.

Melody of Achieving All Goals: General Aspiration to Conclude

All glorious gurus, the real buddhas,
please come here with great, nonreferential compassion,

sit upon the lotus-sun seat in the space before me
and think of me, your faithful, devoted child.

I and all migrators, with bodies as numerous as atoms,
bow respectfully in body, speech, and mind, and pay homage.
With melodious sounds of an ocean of diverse harmonies
I praise you in every way and supplicate.
I offer my body and possessions, real and imagined,
as an ocean of Samantabhadra's offering clouds.
I regretfully confess and vow not to repeat the sins, obscurations, faults, and downfalls
accumulated since beginningless time or arising naturally.
I rejoice from the bottom of my heart in all the virtue,
flawed or not, in all cyclic existence and its transcendence.
I beseech you to turn the dharma wheel of the three vehicles
according to beings' capabilities, for as long as their realms exist.
I request that you remain steady and everlasting like a vajra
in the state of continuous, nonreferential compassion.
I dedicate all good actions starting with this, and in the three times,
to the swift achievement of the glorious guru's
awakened body, speech, mind, qualities, and activities,
for myself and all migrators throughout space, my parents.

May all the gurus nurture me with their compassion,
may disrespect or wrong views never arise for even a moment,
may I please you in three ways through many types of service,
and ultimately merge my mind as one with yours.

In all my lives may I never be separated from you,
the venerable masters, not even for an instant.
May I see what you do as good, hold what you say as true,
and be inseparable from the guru's three secrets. {447}

By the power of my prayer made with sincere faith,
may I live this one life commensurate in all ways
with the lives of liberation of all those holy ones
from Vajradhara down to my own root guru.

[Colophon]

The charred logs of this ordinary person's words
may not have the blazing brilliance of blessings,
yet through the virtue of composing with devotion alone,
may I be inseparable from all the gurus.

Though I have no inherent good qualities,
I have been embraced by genuine gurus
and obtained the blessings of lineages such as this.

With the noble intention to benefit the doctrine and migrators,
I, the lucky one with three preoccupations,
Ngawang Yönten Gyatso, wrote this supplication
on the hillside of Tsadra Rinchen Drak,
on the holy day of the Victor's descent from the gods' realm.

May these supplications, like the strings of the sitar
with melodies of an ocean of diverse harmonies,
fall on the ears of beings in the three places
so that they too take up the song.

Let virtue prevail.

27. Verdant Tree of Faith

The Life Story of the Glorious Holy Guru[1]

Tāranātha

namo guru bhyaḥ
Homage to the holy gurus.

Supreme special deity Mañjughoṣa, lord of adepts,
beloved Holy Dharma that teaches the essential meaning,
and the assembly who performs its amazing activity—
I pay homage with a mind of sincere faith.

Through your long cultivation of limitless two accumulations,
you [took birth in] the excellent central spot of Tibet,
which is comparable to the teaching hall of Indra—
to your miraculous manifestation I bow in homage.

According to the prophecy of Kunzang Drupai Wangpo,
an emanation of Mañjuvajra by the name of Dorje
would take birth in the translator's family [of Ra Lotsāwa]—
to your birth as a sublime guide I bow in homage.

When troubled by disturbances of the four elements,
the lord of adepts appeared as Fiery Protector (Jvālānātha)
to dispel outer and inner obstacles.
I bow in homage to you.

At that time, your wind-mind entered the avadhūtī,
you saw countless victors and their heirs in the sky,

and the former imprint of Vajrayāna was fully awakened,
increasing the strength of your faith; I bow in homage.

Your compassionate commitment to all beings increased
without being shown or encouraged by others;
you followed the Mahayana, deities, and awareness mantras
and complete understanding arose within; I bow in homage.

You understood letters and such by yourself
and effortlessly comprehended just by hearing
many subjects, such as the Jātaka tales,
pleasing those around you; I bow in homage.

At the young age of seven you taught many sādhanas
such as for Hevajra, Vajrayoginī,
Acala, Tārā, and Mañjuśrī—
foremost of the brilliant, I bow in homage. {450}

You relied closely on the teachings of wise Jampa [Lhundrup],
learned the Tripiṭaka and its commentaries,
and all five sciences such as grammar and logic—
to the unrivaled Lion of Speech, I bow in homage.

You stayed close to the lotus feet of the one named Kunga [Gyaltsen]
and received the three levels of vows;
countless tantric empowerments, transmissions, and instructions
completely filled your being; I bow in homage.

You completed the sādhana practices of an ocean of mandalas,
and did vital completion phase of an ocean of Secret Mantra,
devoting yourself day and night to accomplishment.
Teacher of the path enjoyed by the victors, I bow in homage.

You knew well the precise intent of Sutra and Tantra,
and the systems of explication, debate, and composition;
you were without compare in these three realms.
To you, an ocean of qualities, I bow in homage.

You mastered the collection of an ocean of tantras
and comprehended the interpretations of a million learned adepts
of exalted India and the Himalaya fastness
without mixing them up; I bow in homage.

You actualized illusion-like meditative absorption
and totally subjugated the obstacles and obstructors
that appeared as signs in your dreams by actualizing
the profound meaning of emptiness; I bow in homage.

Buddhagupta and other accomplished Indian gurus
gave you the essential elixir of oral instructions;
you listened well and became master of the extraordinary
ocean of profound meaning; I bow in homage.

The supreme vajra master, the primordial lord,
your connection during your succession of countless lives,
[again] became your root guru, the embodiment of all lineages,
and your minds merged inseparably; I bow in homage.

When you received the ultimate meaning from him,
the primordially abiding nature arose naturally as coemergence
and you actualized all phenomena as essential dharmakāya.
To the lord of existence and quiescence, I bow in homage. {251}

You taught the Holy Dharma, infinitely profound and vast,
attained the ultimate lineage where all [lineages] become one,
and actualized the profound awareness of completion phase.
To the original victor of great bliss, I bow in homage.

You attained the signs of special transmission blessings
of the sixteen great charioteers of exalted India
and wheel-wielding adepts beyond count.
To the guru, dharma king, I bow in homage.

You actualized the twelfth vajra stage
concordant with the exalted path of Vajrayāna

and became the regent of mighty Vajradhara
in this age of conflict; I bow in homage.

When exerting yourself in the sādhana of Cakrasaṃvara,
the yidam deity who had nurtured you throughout your lives,
you saw signs that you had become that Heruka.
To the master of boundless wonders, I bow in homage.

While you were receiving Tārā's four empowerments,
a host of ḍākinīs blessed and purified your body,
and everything took the form of tantric texts.
To the lord of Secret Mantra teachings, I bow in homage.

You saw the actual mandala in the sky,
Āryadeva cleared away the web of your doubts,
Śāntideva taught the meaning of the *Guhyasamāja Tantra*,
and you attained the absorption of dharma continuity; I bow in homage.

While resting in equipoise of the Six-Branch Yoga,
you perfected the signs of virtue from the start;
many actual signs appeared indicating your control of vitality,
and you saw uncontrived timeless awareness; I bow in homage.

While resting in equipoise of the glorious Guhyasamāja's meaning,
by Mañjuśrī's compassion you saw the suchness of all phenomena.
By the blessings of the king of wrathful ones, Yamāntaka,
you became a powerful master; I bow in homage.

When resting in the equipoise of the meaning of yoga's ultimate mystery,
your body's clear appearance as the deity's form stabilized
and you attained the gathering of messengers of the three places
and coemergent great bliss; I bow in homage. {452}

Because you were of such pure heart,
many supreme adepts such as Saraha, Śavarīpa, Lūhipa,

Ghaṇṭāpa, Jālandhara, Śāntigupta, and others
revealed themselves in your dreams; I bow in homage.

You severed all doubts concerning them;
when you were elucidating the intent of the tantras,
countless heroes and ḍākinīs used symbols
to introduce the profound meaning; I bow in homage.

The one called Śākya from Tuṣita visited you,
Maitreya actually blessed you
and you attained the signs—
continual spiritual enrichment, I bow in homage.

You obtained all the dharma directives of the holy ones,
sublime masters such as Padmasambhava, Gampopa,
and the one endowed with four reliances.
Nurtured by sublime spiritual masters, I bow in homage.

Perfect in study and reflection, joyful in single-minded practice,
you have covered the earth with your cycle of dharma—
incomparably wonderful, precious guru,
with an attitude of deep respect I bow in homage.

Tāranātha wrote this in response to the disciples' requests.

28. Flowers of Faith

A Supplement to Venerable Tāranātha Rinpoche's Biographical Supplication[1]

Jamgön Kongtrul

Son of the Victor, you became father of all victors;
renouncing existence and quiescence, you are lord of all existence and
quiescence;
glorious Cakrasaṃvara in the guise of a lama—
Drolwai Gönpo, I supplicate at your feet.

In the past, at the royal palace of Śrāvastī
you were the main athlete with incredible strength.
The mind of awakening arose in the presence of Vipaśyin[2]
and you attained its sure wonder; I bow in homage.

Thereafter, you always accompanied buddhas,
displayed the special conduct of a bodhisattva,
and fully matured disciples' buddha nature
with countless miraculous emanations; I bow in homage.

Among the five hundred bodhisattvas around Śākyamuni,
you developed an exceptionally pure intellect.
You donned the armor of an impartial doctrine holder
of the essential definitive meaning; I bow in homage.

In various bodies as siddha, vidyādhara, ṛṣi, paṇḍita,
minister, brahmin, householder, and plebeian,

you upheld the Buddha's doctrine and dredged the depths
of cyclic existence; I bow in homage.

In the east, in Vigataśoka with Tathāgata Cambhaka,
you were a universal monarch
with eight bodies appearing at once
on Meru's peak and elsewhere; I bow in homage.

Likewise in other worlds and here in Tibet,
you showed many emanations at the same time;
of those the chief guide Viṣnurājā, hero of Oḍḍiyāna,
was the emanation basis; I bow in homage.

Heruka entrusted you with a treasury of secrets;
the Sage authorized you as the master of all dharma;
the eight bodhisattvas blessed you as the source
of all Sutra and Tantra; I bow in homage.

Avalokita praised you as a bodhisattva guide of beings;
Ākāśagarbha gave you the higher trainings;
Exalted Tārā continuously appeared and prophesied, {454}
raising your awareness; I bow in homage.

Padmākara inducted you into the circle of blood drinkers;
Yeshe Tsogyal conferred empowerment by profound symbols;
Ḍombī Heruka empowered you as the lord of the ḍākinīs
of the three places; I bow in homage.

Candragomin introduced you to meditative absorption;
Ārya[deva] washed away your pain during illness;
Goddess Sarasvatī granted you the power of eloquence—
to your unimaginably vast awareness, I bow in homage.

The eighty great adepts, translators, and yogins,
when supplicated, each taught you dharma in person
and Abhaya inducted you into the great mandalas
of infinite tantras; I bow in homage.

[Ḍākinī] Guhyajñānā conferred four secret empowerments;
ḍākinīs actually granted you all-conquering excellent medicine;
at Devīkoṭi, the Ḍākinī's directives openly displayed[3]
the Six Dharmas; I bow in homage.

Luhipāda introduced you to great bliss;
you enjoyed the feast gatherings in the three circles;
you received prophecy that all who saw, heard, recalled, or touched you
on passion's great path would be liberated; I bow in homage.

To Oḍḍiyāna, Copper-Colored Mountain, and Shambhala
you traveled with miraculous feet and drank the elixir
of oral instruction from Indrabhūti, Padmākara,
and the great Śākī; I bow in homage.

Vajravārāhī, Kālacakra, and Guhyasamāja
conferred the empowerment of great light and gave assurance:
"Your commentaries on the meaning of the tantras are good"—
lord of secrets of vajra dharma, I bow in homage.

Mañjuśrī as Dark-Red Vajrabhairava conferred empowerment
and granted the prophecy of vanquishing the hordes of devils.
With the blessings of the eight great adept gurus,
you fathomed the depths of dharma; I bow in homage.

With the descent of awareness [beings], your pure outlook pervaded
regarding all appearance, sound, and thought.
Your vajra songs freed thoughts and awakened awareness
in your karmically connected entourage; I bow in homage.

Rainbows and flowers appeared when you performed great deeds,
such as conferring empowerments, offering rituals, and teaching;
ḍākinīs' symbolic songs and fragrances pervaded throughout {455}
as miraculous apparitions manifested; I bow in homage.

You restored the long tradition and cleared up confusions,
brought forth new, previously unknown conveyances,

and otherwise reinforced the foundation of the doctrine's supreme vehicle
of the essential definitive meaning; I bow in homage.

The omniscient dharma lord showed you Sukhāvatī realm of bliss,
granting the dharma domain of nonreturning.
Great Butön placed the dharma crown on your head,
making you master of the Sage's doctrine; I bow in homage.

The host of gurus and nonsectarian learned adepts
joyfully shouted, "Well done!" when you completed practice
and said, "In three lifetimes you will attain enlightenment,"
with a lion's roar; I bow in homage.

Powerful dharma protectors who had seen the Buddha
became your servants and offered their life-force essence.
Mahākāla Sister-Brother and their retinues accomplished
whatever you requested; I bow in homage.

In this life, you engaged in deeds by means of the view.
In the future, in Drāviḍa, you will spread Sutra, Illusion, and Mind[4]
and more, turning the wheel of the awakened activity
of Padma Tötrengtsal; I bow in homage.

Encouraged by Vārāhī, Tārā, Kṛṣṇācārya, and Padma De,
heroes and ḍākinīs presented you with full offerings
of song, dance, parasols, drums, bells, and bliss-inducing elixir.
You departed for infinite pure realms; I bow in homage.

The abodes of the demons shook, and in infinite worlds
amazing sights and so on heralded the state of absorption.
Positive indications of accomplishments pervaded everywhere—
awareness woman's great being, I bow in homage.

In Oḍḍiyāna, you appear as Vīryarāja,
in Drāviḍa in the manner of Bliss, Sukhanātha,
in Vaiḍūryanirbhāsa and Sukhāvatī
you manifest as a tenth-level lord; I bow in homage.

In essence, you are Coemergent Jālasaṃvara,
to ordinary folk, in the world called Lokābhaḥ (Luminous),
you will attain awakening as the sugata Sūryatilaka—
to your unimaginable manifestations I bow in homage.

In exalted India, the likes of Abhayākaragupta
will not come again—you are such a person. {456}
You surely attained the level of the sixth Buddha's regent,
incomparable Heruka, glorious guru:

I bow with respect and present clouds of offerings.
I confess all faults and rejoice in virtue.
I entreat you to turn the dharma wheel and always remain.
I dedicate all virtue to the attainment of your state.

May I replicate Kunga Nyingpo's life of liberation
in awakened body, speech, mind, qualities, and activity.
May I spread the good word, victorious in all directions,
and bind all migrators in the ḍākinīs' net.

May I never be separated from you, Tāranātha,
in this life or the next, in between, or in dreams.
May I attain the secret treasury and achieve impartial deliberate conduct,
and become enlightened in the play of great-bliss union.

May I always accomplish acts that please the Venerable One,
may blessings enter my being and my awakened activity
be ever inseparable from yours, lord,
may auspicious glory pervade the world.

[Colophon]

I wrote this supplement to [Tāranātha's] *Verdant Tree of Faith: The Life Story of the Glorious Holy Guru* because some previous holy masters' compositions were too long or too short or their transmission had not lasted. It is written in the manner of a faithful supplication for myself and others by Karma Ngawang Yönten Gyatso at the secluded retreat of Palpung. Let virtue prevail.

29. Niguma's Aspiration Prayer of the Sealed Word[1]

Niguma

Sanskrit: *Āryapranidhanarāja*
Tibetan: *'Phags pa smon lam gyi rgyal po*

Homage to all the buddhas and bodhisattvas.

May the prolific compassionate activity
of the many victors in ten directions and three times
accomplish all these prayers of mine
just as they are expressed.

May I please my guru with immeasurable devotion
from this time on and in all circumstances,
filling space with offerings of pure bodies and enjoyments[2]
so their activity flourishes and is never absent.

May I never, in all lives, meet false ācāryas,
bad gurus, bad companions, and bad benefactors
when hearing, explaining, meditating, and practicing,
but attend excellent gurus and thereby attain awakening.

May I have good family, health, eloquence,
good form, charisma, and strength in all my lives,
and with a natural long life, dedicated friends,
wealth, and dharma, be respected by all.

May I be free of discord and in harmony with all
wherever I am born, throughout my lives,
and be perceived as lovely, attractive, and fascinating
by those who see, hear, recall, or touch me.

May I be protector, refuge, hope, and champion
to all sentient beings throughout space;
all their hopes and desires
justly fulfilled by me.

May I train alongside friends who wish me well,
body, speech, and mind joined in a single aspiration,
never separate from this moment on
in the sublime happiness of our pure perception. {460}

May I be a wish-fulfilling gem wherever I am born,
raining down a boundless cornucopia
of desires as soon as they are thought,
placing all beings in a state of happiness.

May all migrators wherever I stay
be free of illness, bad spirits, strife, and poverty;
and with long life, health, dharma, and wealth,
may auspiciousness and well-being abound.

May I, in this life and in all lives,
gain access to the sky-treasure of wealth
and dispense the four gifts in the ten directions,
maturing and liberating beings through ten perfections.[3]

May my superb wisdom, without desire or limitation
for all phenomena of cyclic existence or transcendence,
bring every sphere of what's knowable in the three times
into sharp focus within a single instant.

May I be graced by the flawless three trainings
and honored by the world, with its conflict-free gods,[4]

establishing all migrators in supreme ethical discipline
to fully perfect all their excellent qualities.[5]

May I be content in remote retreat with food and clothes,
and without a moment of outer or inner obstacle,
gain ultimate experience, realization, and activity
that matures and liberates every migrator.

May all the powerful gods and arrogant demons,
without need of a moment of exhortation or worship,
offer me their life force and obey like servants
to guard the doctrine with mighty magical powers.

May I manifest love and compassion
to pacify the mutual hatred and harm
of all sentient beings in the three realms
so they dwell in a mother's love for her only child. {461}

May dharmakāya manifest at the time of my death
before the cessation of the vital elements,[6]
form kāyas arise to spontaneously help others,
and my remains and relics continue to draw beings.

May I make offerings throughout the ages
to the multitudes of buddhas of the eon
who dwell in all the pure lands of the victors,
and fill space with Samantabhadra's offering clouds.

May I perceive the ocean of totally pure realms,
and with totally pure conduct and limitless wisdom,
perfectly behold all the oceans of dharmas
and realize the whole ocean of timeless awareness.

May I actualize the victors' melodious speech,
and with my Brahmā voice resounding through space,
teach the dharma in the languages of all people
and place all beings without exception in Buddha's state.

May I actualize the absorption of boundless illusion
like Samantabhadra's liberation through illusion,
to instantly establish upon every atom
the buddha bodies and realms without exception.[7]

May my aims, absorptions, and activities
be as boundlessly deep and fathomless
as the realms of beings and depths of the oceans,
the reaches of space, and the infinite realm of reality.

May I emanate countless universal monarchs
to fulfill beings' hopes, rule the dharma domain,
gain dominion over all realms throughout space,
and place all beings without exception in happiness.

May I become a sovereign supreme healer
instantly to soothe the pains of living beings
when they are worn out by suffering
in the future age of disease and warfare. {462}

May I gather thick clouds of abundance to fill the sky
and rain down five sense pleasures in all directions,
replete with food, drink, fine cloth, silver, gold, and wealth,
for the times of hunger and thirst in the age of famine.

May the efficacy of my bodhisattva activity
teach every being throughout the reaches of space,
in whatever way will benefit each one,
until the ocean of cyclic existence is empty.

May I completely subdue all migrators not tamed
by the victors of the ten directions and three times,
those haughty beings who took the wrong path,
and place them instantly in the state of a buddha.

May my effortless self-arising awakened activity,
spontaneously beneficial and uninterrupted,

mature and liberate all sentient beings
so long as they remain in cyclic existence.

Victors of the ten directions and three times,
when they were ordinary folks and bodhisattvas,
aroused awakening mind, aspired through countless eons,
completed two accumulations, and gained enlightenment.

Then they matured and liberated countless beings
by mastering vast qualities of excellence.
May the full extent of my aspirational activity
join as one with their aspirational activity.

May the spontaneous vast benefit for others
arising from these aspirations of mine
be wholly fulfilled when entreated by anyone
filled with faith, devotion, and the awakening mind.

May all that is excellent, auspicious, and joyful
everywhere in cyclic existence and transcendence
flow constantly like the course of a great river
to suffuse all directions for myself and others.

This concludes Niguma's *Sovereign of Noble Aspirations.*

Songs of Experience

Introduction

An Ocean of Blessings Meaningful to Hear[1] is a collection of verses from various spiritual masters in the long Shangpa lineage, spanning over a thousand years. Such expressions of spiritual experience (*nyams mgur*), or "songs of realization," were in evidence from as early as the seventh century CE, usually written in the late Middle Indo-Aryan dialect of Apabhraṃśa.[2] Many such verses from the mahāsiddhas, the great adepts of India, were brought into Tibet with the spread of Buddhism and found their way into Tibetan canonical collections. Of particular note are the collections attributed to Saraha, the Great Brahmin, and to Dampa Sangye, the South Indian who spent considerable time teaching in Tibet.[3] The custom of expressing near-ineffable spiritual experience in poetry and song was taken up enthusiastically by indigenous Tibetans. Most famously, perhaps, by the great yogin and poet Milarepa, whose so-called Hundred Thousand Songs (*mgur 'bum*) are sung, recited, and studied to this day.[4] Such collections are also known as a multitude or "ocean" of song (*mgur mtsho*), such as the one here.

But the term *song* (*mgur* or *mgur dbyangs*) should be understood in a very broad sense as verse or poetry. Other terms used here are *vajra lines* (*rdo rje tshig rkang*), referring to ancient "original" lines spoken by figures such as Niguma, and *doha*, which technically means verse composed in couplets but has become a more general term almost synonymous with *mgur* while retaining some sense of Indian antecedents. It is not known whether most of these verses were actually voiced in tuneful song by their creators or written down as poetry. The sense is that any expression of verse is said to be "sung." Perhaps "poetry reading" would be more precise. In Tibet it became a popular practice for monastic or lay assemblies to recite the songs during religious ceremonies as a way of honoring the ancestral lineage, learning about the lives of the masters, and supplicating for their blessings.

Such is the case for the collection here. Kongtrul mentions it specifically for inclusion in his guru puja, *A Wish-Fulfilling Gem*, in chapter 25 above. This collection was not included in Kongtrul's *Treasury of Vast Precepts*. So his express purpose may have come to mind afterward, setting him to gathering verse from various sources, described in his colophon:

> The precious Kagyu tradition considers singing vajra songs extremely important and so the custom has spread widely. But the long tradition of the Shangpa Kagyu has not spread much in this context, so even texts containing the songs of that lineage of adepts have become like daytime stars. I have gathered these mainly from their biographies and similar sources, and supplemented them from the [songs of] the later lineage wherever appropriate. Whatever sublime quintessence of the elixir of the profound dharma from this lineage was to be found is now contained in this golden receptacle of former virtue.

The first five entries are of Indian origin. Beginning with Buddha Vajradhara's verse, as received by Niguma, these persons represent the most important Indian sources of Shangpa teachings. Some verses, such as the few examples of the prolific "singer" Maitrīpa, will be found in canonical sources. The Tibetan lineage begins, of course, with Khyungpo Naljor, forefather of the Shangpa lineage. His songs, and those of his direct successors, are amply supplemented with narratives of their lives, taken mostly from their biographies. Verses of the masters closer to Kongtrul's time may be taken from their respective collected works. The list of masters is not inclusive—perhaps they did not all compose such verse—but those that Kongtrul deemed the most significant are beautifully represented by their devotional and sometimes iconoclastic style of song. Here is the lineup:

Buddha Vajradhara (eternal)
Niguma (10th–11th centuries)
Sukhasiddhi (10th–11th centuries)
Maitrīpa (986–1063)
Rāhula (10th–11th centuries)

Khyungpo Naljor (978–1128 or 1050–1140)
Mokchokpa Rinchen Tsöndru (1110–1170)
Öntön Kyergangpa Chökyi Senge (1154/1143–1217)

Sangye Nyentön Chökyi Sherap (1175–1255)
Drogön Sangye Tönpa Tsöndru Senge (1207–1278)
Khedrup Tsangma Shangtön (1234–1309)
Tangtong Gyalpo (1361?–1485)
Kunga Drolchok (1507–1566)
Jamyang Khyentse Wangchuk (1524–1568)
Jonang Tāranātha (1575–1634)
Lochen Gyurme Dechen (1540–1615)
Losal Tenkyong (1804–1865?)
Jamyang Khyentse Wangpo (1820–1892)
Jamgön Kongtrul Lodrö Taye (1813–1900)

30. An Ocean of Blessings Meaningful to Hear

Collected Vajra Lines, Dohas, and Melodious Songs of the Glorious Shangpa Kagyu[1]

Compiled by Jamgön Kongtrul

Glorious Vajradhara's regents are the mighty bodhisattvas on the tenth level in the unbroken succession of indisputable adepts renowned throughout the three worlds as the protectors of migrators in the Shangpa Precept Lineage (Shangpa Kagyu), adorned by many amazing and exalted qualities. I pay homage and bow respectfully before their lotus feet.

Vajradhara, the sixth lord pervading over all [buddha] families, expressed verses of direct guidance (*dmar khrid*) of the profound Vajra Secret Tantra via the innate sound of the indestructible vajra nāda.[2] From that time forth, the successive garland of jewel [adepts] in the instruction lineage all captured the realm of the true nature, the dharmakāya, and the brilliance of their experiences and realizations blazed high. Those profound experiences burst forth as the laughter of vajra melodies of doha that resound throughout space. The purpose of those [spiritual songs] is to inspire yogins' devotion and faith; to encourage their renunciation and aversion; to enhance greater and greater meditative experiences; to arouse courage in the timeless awareness of realization; to please the heroes and ḍākinīs; to liberate from the perils of obstructions and obstacles; and to satisfy countless human and nonhuman migrators through the supreme gift of the Holy Dharma.

Therefore, to respectfully proclaim a small portion [of those songs], {465} I ask you to first commence with the stages of the preliminaries and the visualizations for meditate absorption. (With that encouragement, repeat the following three times.)

> All sentient beings, my mothers, equal to the reaches of space, go for refuge in the precious guru, the unified essence of all refuges. (Repeat three times.)
>
> For the sake of all sentient beings, I must attain the unified state of Great Vajradhara. To that end, I will engage in the sequence of recitation of the doha vajra melodies. (Repeat three times.)

With those triple recitations, go for refuge and arouse the mind of awakening. Those who take up these songs must give up their thoughts of being ordinary and dwell in the stages of the yoga. In order to bring that clearly to mind, [recite the following:]

> The environment and its inhabitants are the pure celestial realm. The dwelling place is the celestial palace of great liberation, completely decorated and arrayed inside and outside, containing immeasurable offering articles. The assembly gathered here becomes the glorious mandala of the five herukas. From our hearts, great light rays that illuminate all buddha realms radiate and invoke the gurus, victors, and their heirs as a circle of awareness that fills the space in front—*vajra samājaḥ*.
>
> Gurus, victors, and heirs,
> yidams, heroes, and yoginīs,
> you play in all-pervasive dharmakāya
> with no signs of coming or staying. {466}
>
> Yet your magical emanations of awareness to tame whomever
> appear real to our mind-space of devotion.
> Remain here until your purpose is accomplished
> and bless this mandala of the assembly.
> *padma kamalāya stvaṃ*

Offer the *Mandala of the Sealed Word*: "Sublime mandala exquisitely arrayed . . ." (*bkod pa shin tu mdzes pa'i maṇḍal mchog . . .* etc.)[3] and the regular confession: "I go for refuge to the Three Jewels . . ." (*dkon mchog gsum la bdag skyabs mchi . . .* etc.).[4]

Respectful devotional supplication is the lead-in to the songs. The confidence of experience and realization is the follow-through of the songs. Expressing auspicious joy and appreciation is the concluding finale of the songs. This indeed is the practice of the precious precept lineage. Therefore, begin with intense longing of undivided faith in the root and lineage gurus, victors, and heirs. This has the power to banish ordinary perceptions, forcefully transform our frame of mind, and raise awareness through realization. Please properly prepare that way for the section on the songs with this supplication:

namo guru

I supplicate the benevolent root guru,
Vajradhara, pervading lord of all families.

I supplicate glorious Heruka,
Cakrasaṃvara who binds the net.

I supplicate Niguma, Ḍākinī of Timeless Awareness,
in the realm of undissipating bliss-emptiness mandala.

I supplicate Mother Sukhasiddhi
in the celestial realm of saṃbhogakāya.

I supplicate the one hundred and eight adepts
in the emanated palace of taming whomever.

I supplicate Khedrup Khyungpo Naljor,
ḍākinīs' son with Five Tantras' culminations.

I supplicate Venerable Mokchokpa,
bodhisattva in his final life, holder of the single lineage.

I supplicate Venerable Kyergangpa,
Avalokiteśvara in the body of a pure meditator.

I supplicate Venerable Nyentön the Great,
pervasive lord of the six families in a hidden way.

I supplicate Venerable Sangye Tönpa,
exemplar of the lives of the Seven-Jewel lineage. {467}

I supplicate the three learned and accomplished lords,
the ground where the Kagyu rivers fall.

I supplicate the lineage of glorious Jak and Sam,
who had amazing lives of awakened activities.

I supplicate Venerable Tsultrim Gön, Ritröpa,
and Shangkarwa Rinchen Gyaltsen.

I supplicate Venerable Kuklungpa, Namgyalwa,
and Gyagom Lekpa Gyaltsen.

I supplicate Venerable Tangtong Gyalpo,
who achieved immortality nurtured by ḍākinīs.

I supplicate glorious Kunga Drolchok,
who subdued beings by deliberate conduct.

I supplicate Venerable [Chöku Lhawang] Draktöpa,
who manifested the real intent of dharmakāya.

I supplicate Venerable Tāranātha,
Heruka, glorious lord of secrets.

I supplicate the succession of sublime persons,
holders of the glorious Shangpa Kagyu.

I supplicate the yidams of Five Tantras
in the centers of the indestructible five chakras.

I supplicate the ḍākas and ḍākinīs of timeless awareness
in the five-colored drops of the body's subtle essence.

I supplicate Swift-Acting Awareness Protector
from the charnel ground of compassionate display.

Outwardly, may designations of deluded appearances collapse.
Inwardly, may I realize the inseparability of the relative and ultimate.
In between, may I actualize the very nature of dharmakāya
and empty the pit of cyclic existence in the three realms.

Buddha Vajradhara

Great Vajradhara, the sixth sovereign overlord of all the families, sang these vajra lines of the abiding nature to his own appearance as Ḍākinī of Timeless Awareness [Niguma] by way of the uncreated natural self-sound, revealing cyclic existence and its transcendence as the nature of mahāmudrā.

Emaho! Ordinary mind—amazing! {468}
The preliminary is three naturally settled states.
The main practice is the four faults free in their own ground.
The ultimate is the naturally arisen four kāyas.

The preliminary's sacred pledge is a vajra secret.
Enhancement is supplication and compassion.
Integration is seeing that suchness in whatever appears.
Actualization is being without meditation and without distraction.

Blending is integrating nonthought on the path.
The yogic gaze of lucid clarity is enhancement.
After waking, blend nonthought with clarity.
Lucid clarity in the day, night, and intermediate state:
see the natural arising of the three inseparable kāyas.

This is the single word that discloses the ultimate meaning
that no one knows is hidden in their mind stream.
Familiarize and stabilize nonmeditation and nondistraction.
Then you will traverse the grounds and paths right away.
With no mental engagement, the two obscurations are pure on their own.
The resultant naturally arising three kāyas are spontaneously present.

All sutras and tantras teach this, but it is naturally concealed.
You should learn it directly from the guru's blessing.

In the dharmakāya sky, lightning of five poisons flashes
from the clouds of conceptual thought—see great timeless
awareness.

Without mental engagement, free of all hopes and fears,
I bow to you, ordinary mind.

Khedrup Khyungpo Naljor entreated Ḍākinī of Timeless Awareness for these very vajra lines by offering five hundred gold pieces. He put it inside a heart-like amulet box and wore it constantly.[5]

Niguma

The Awareness Ḍākinī called Nigupta was the sister of glorious Nārotapa. She was a self-manifesting yoginī, a mighty bodhisattva on the tenth level, who was actually nurtured by Vajradhara. She taught these vajra lines of *Naturally Free Mahāmudrā*.[6]

I bow to you, mind itself,
the wish-fulfilling gem.

Wishing to attain perfect awakening,
visualize your own body as the deity
to purify ordinary thoughts.
Be devoted with a pure noble heart to the guru.

Don't dwell on the guru or yidam,
don't bring anything to mind,
such as whether things are real or not real. {469}
Rest within the uncontrived native state.

Your mind without distraction is dharmakāya.
Nondistraction from that is the vital point of meditation.
Realize the great freedom from limitations.

The variety of desirous and hateful thoughts
that strand you in the ocean of cyclic existence:
sever them as intrinsically nonexistent
with the sharp weapon of the unborn.
If the tree is cut at the root,
the branches will not grow.

Just as bubbles arise and dissolve
in the water of the limpid sea,
in that way conceptual thinking is nothing
other than the nature of phenomena.
Don't see it as a problem—relax.

Whatever arises, whatever is born, that itself
without fixation is free in and of itself.
Appearance, sound, and phenomena are your own mind.
Aside from mind, there are no phenomena.
Mind is free of the elaborations of arising and cessation.

By knowing that suchness of mind,
even when engaging in the five sense desirables,
you will not leave the nature of phenomena.

For instance, one who goes to the golden isle
cannot find dirt and stone even when sought.
In the equality of the great realm of phenomena,
there is no rejecting or accepting, no equipoise or subsequent
attainment.

At whatever time this is actualized,
at that time it becomes spontaneously present.
You become like a wish-fulfilling gem
who fulfills the hopes and desires of beings.

You should understand this as applicable to the levels
of highest, intermediate, and lesser personal capacity.

Sukhasiddhi

Awareness Ḍākinī Sukhasiddhi was fully initiated into the emanated mandala by the great glorious Virūpa. She actualized the realization of the eighth level in a single evening and encountered the real Vajradhara. She became inseparable from Bhagavatī Nairātmya. She granted this essential teaching to her fortunate disciples.

Disengaged from the objects of the six senses,
nonrecollection is the path to transcendence.
No conceptual thought is the realm of phenomena,
free of mentation—that is mahāmudrā. {470}

Don't meditate! Don't meditate! Don't mentally meditate!
Mental meditation is the machination of conceptual thought.
Concepts bind you to cyclic existence.

In empty space, which lacks awareness,
with awareness tame the root of mind.
Tame the root and rest relaxed.

Maitrīpa

The great mighty adept, glorious Śavarīpa accepted him as his disciple and predicted his attainment of supreme mahāmudrā in the intermediate state. Chief of infinite heroes and ḍākinīs, master of instructions in the essential meaning of the abiding nature through mental nonengagement, this is the sovereign Maitrīpa [also known as] Advayavajra. While he was living in a hidden manner at Vikramaśīla Monastery, the other monastics saw him indulging in alcohol and consorts, and they expelled him. So he went to the River Ganges where he spread out a mat of a kṛṣṇasāra pelt (black spotted antelope), used his staff as an oar, and paddled off while constructing this song.[7]

To attend a venerable guru is joy.
To drink the elixir of instruction is joy.

To taste that experience is joy.
To have no experience at all is joy.

The view without hopes and fears is joy.
If it is spontaneous, more's the joy.

Meditation without dualism is joy.
If it is without reference point, more's the joy.

Conduct without moral choice is joy.
If it is fearless, more's the joy.

To view the mind with the mind is joy.
To sever the deviance of hope and fear is joy.

To roam in remote mountain retreats is joy.
The view without hope and fear is joy.

To leave homeland and relations is joy.
To live on alms for food is joy.

To eat the food of great bliss is joy.
To wear clothes of lucid clarity is joy.

To carry the path of the messenger is joy.
To focus the gaze on the nose tip is joy.

Having said that, he sailed unhindered straight out over the water. Then everyone understood that he was an accomplished adept and with regret prostrated to him from the shore. {471} That great master guru, when he was at the mountains of Śrīparvata in the south, touched the dust from under Venerable Hermit [Śavarīpa's] feet and requested the empowerment conferral of mahāmudrā. At that time, he sang this vajra song to ascertain the abiding nature of things.

hūṃ hūṃ
Cyclic existence and transcendence are indivisible,
existing like the waves on the water.

Buddhas and sentient beings are not two,
like poison before and after its mantric antidote.

Mind itself is one but with many perceptions,
like crystals changing colors under different conditions.

Various things arise and yet are your own mind,
like all waters will taste of salt in the sea.

Letting go of real and unreal reveals original mind,
like the remains of a bird's tracks in space.

As a single small lamp banishes
the dense dark of a thousand years,

each instant of realizing one's mind resolves
the dense blur of cyclic existence's passions.

The yoga of uniting method and wisdom
stills the conceptual waves of pain in cyclic existence.

A water-purifying gem put in mud
disappears, can't spread, and can't move.

But as soon as mahāmudrā realization arises,
the sky-like mind pervades and expands.

Clarity without concept is like space,
appearing without self-nature like a water moon.

Clarity without fixation, like rainbows,
is indescribable, like the pleasure of youth.

Without direction, free of all boundaries,
untainted by bias, nothing obscures it.

Stainless, like a crystal ball in the mud,
mind is free of hopes and fears, like a lion.

Undivided like a river, the mind of great bliss
shines impartially like the light of the sun and moon.

Ema! How wonderful this self-manifestation.
Rest in its native state, yogin.

Here, do not contrive anything at all;
the uncontrived is dharmakāya itself. {472}

Contrivance blocks the view of the exalted path,
so let the elephant of mind go free.

If you know that, it is the heart of yoga;
the fruit of awakening is attained without practice.

All the hard work is done without acting.
You attain spiritual powers without practicing.

You gain the ultimate result without meditating.
The three existences were liberated since forever.

No need to deny or affirm anything here.
This is the vajra song ascertaining the view.

Emaho!
If you want to meditate on the innate abiding nature,
no need to calculate the seasons, stars, and constellations;
when you remember the king of time, the time is right!

Don't seek for a remote mountain retreat;
this mountain of your body is the best hermitage.

Don't purposefully reject distractions;
knowing the variety as mind will be an ally,
like the grasses in a forest fire.

Don't set retreat boundaries or create registers;
keeping silent is the best retreat.
Rest relaxed like a tuft of cotton wool.

Give up doing and creating mental supports;
don't restrain consciousness—let it go.

If sinking or agitation arise, look directly at them.
Gradually abandon whatever harms the mind.
If anger or desire arise, know that it's a devil.

Resting in uncontrived mind is buddha.
Rest relaxed during all walking, lying, or sitting.

If the root of all discursive thought is mind,
since there is no mind, no thought exists.

If only a support for spontaneous presence arises,
anger and desire cannot arise to the yogin.
Therefore, a realized yogin—what a happy mind!

If only a way without reference points is found,
prejudice cannot occur to the yogin.
Consciousness without bias—what a joyful feeling! {473}

If only an uncontrived continuum arises,
dos and don'ts cannot occur to the yogin.
Not to negate or affirm, reject or accept—what fun!

If only an awakening mind of equality arises,
self and other cannot occur to the yogin.
The equality of self and other—what a fair plan!

Rest in the state of three existences' primordial liberation.
This is the vajra song ascertaining the meditation.
ithi

Emaho!
A conscientious mind is the best conduct.
Don't be careless; exhibit mindful awareness.

Whatever you do, don't set limits.
Do anything at all, like an infant.
Behave without artifice, like a little boy.
Be fearless, like a lion.
Have no doubts, like an elephant plunging into water.
Enjoy clean and unclean, like a dog or pig.
Frequent all places in equal taste, like a fly.
Don't suppress what arises, like a crazy person.
Be aimless, like a born carnivore.
Go everywhere, like the wind element;
such movement without attachment is best.

Whatever you experience, apply the seal of the unborn.
This is the vajra song ascertaining the conduct.

In native mind itself without hopes and fears
you attain ineffable absorption through nonminding,
you attain the changeless view through the unborn,
you attain unbiased conduct through nonfixation,
you attain inconceivable results through the unconditioned,
and all hard work is completed without doing anything.

You'll meet constant companions without gathering
and inexhaustible treasures without accumulating.
Like an excellent vase or the wish-fulfilling gem,
these self-occurring results are incredible.
This is the vajra song ascertaining the result.

Rāhula

Born in southern India, Vajrayoginī and the other special four deities actually looked after him and granted blessings. {474} After he attained the undying vajra body, he miraculously traveled to Tibet and back again. He still lives in the forested hills of the Black Mountains, accomplishing the welfare of migrators. The mighty yogin adept Rāhulaguptavajra taught this oral instruction on practicing the inconceivable.

[Homage to the bodhisattvas!][8]
Homage to the gurus!

Their intentions in short are the practice
of the four immeasurables of yoga.
Though inconceivable, I will explain.

In the empty nature of cause and effect,
immaterial form, nondual sound,
and nonreferential result arise effortlessly,
as in the example of rain without thunder.

Therefore fortunate yogins enter
the deliberate conduct of selfless nature.
This variety of apparent existence
is unreal, empty, and without identity;
its very essence totally pure.
In the compassion of such a state,
buddhas and beings are no different.

Nonmeditation, nonthought, natural clarity
without center or circumference is the meaning of the middle
[way];
meditate on mind's nature like that.
Meditate with compassion on the sickness and spirits
of the sentient beings who don't realize that.

Rest in evenness and meditate with equanimity
on whatever is right before you.
With that, at all times and circumstances
you will accomplish the meaning of nonduality.

The meditation[9] instruction of the aural lineage:
The form of all buddhas united as one,
and the very minds of all are a white letter *hūṃ*.
Meditate on that in the hearts of self and others
as a vital drop upon a sun seat.
Imagine [as it emanates and returns back][10]

it is that which tames migrators
and purifies all afflictive emotions.

That is the meaning of the nondual;
the suchness of the deity has no intrinsic nature.

After you meditate on compassion in that way, {475}
the unimaginable thought
is to be of benefit; think in that way.

In my, the yogin's, own heart
is a pea-sized eight-petaled lotus.
From that [comes] white and red clear light,
between which is Agni's white *oṃ*.
It has nothing to do with physical yoga;
it is absolutely unimaginable.

Whoever does this yogic meditation
will realize nondual timeless awareness.

That clarity without awareness is dharmakāya.
In such subtle yoga as this,
clairvoyance dawns and nonduality is realized.
The intrinsic nature of joy will arise
and you will gain the result, equanimity.

Some people stay with the meditation of four deities.[11]
Some rely on verbal recitation.[12]
They do not understand how to meditate on the nondual.

This oral instruction for others' welfare
from the lineage passed from mouth to mouth
has been explained by Rāhula.[13]

In keeping with the predictions of his accomplished gurus, Rāhulagupta, the adept of immortality, left the exalted land of India one morning at dawn. With magical abilities he traveled to Tibet and arrived right at daybreak in Penyul Jokpo, the place where the learned and accomplished Khyungpo

Naljor was doing his spiritual practice, thus showing him a miraculous display. Rāhula stayed for eleven months, during which he gave many common and uncommon instructions. When it was time to return to India, Lama Shangpa [Khyungpo Naljor] accompanied him as far as Mangyul, where Rāhula granted these "Vajra Lines in Six [Syllables in Six Verses]."[14]

The root of suffering
is fixation on self.
Without hate or desire,
settle in evenness.

Life changes and ends but
is not done; born again.
Care for cause and effect,
uphold sacred pledge.

Since nature is union,
this rainbow-like body
appears without substance. {476}
Always remember that.

This life's desires will come,
next life's path will be shown
by Buddha-like gurus.
Always remember that.

Until you are stable,
you're busy and upset.
Like a wounded gazelle,
practice alone yourself.

Beings in this age of war
have great pride and envy.
Like a lamp in a vase,
hide your good qualities.

Rāhula sang that song and then took his leave by way of the sky. Instantly he arrived at the Vajra Seat and presided at a communal feast.

Khyungpo Naljor

namo guru

His name is renowned throughout all the buddha realms, completely pervading them. Beings of the three realms along with the gods bow their hair crowns to the mirror gems of his toes. In the Himalayan regions he was unrivaled and without any comparison. Great Khedrup Khyungpo Naljor Tsultrim Gönpo spoke these verses himself, summarizing the essence of his life of freedom:

I, Khyungpo Naljor, bow with respect
to the guru, yidams, ḍākinīs, and dharma protectors.
In order to benefit lineage holders of future generations,
I will narrate some of my life. Please listen respectfully.

I, a humble monk, was born at Nyemo Ramang
in Gangkarda, into the noble Khyung clan.
My father was called Khyung Gyaltak
and my mother was Gozang Tashi Kyi.
When I entered into her womb,
my parents and local people became happy.
I emerged from the womb in the Tiger year.
At that time, the Indian adept Amogha said:

"This child, an incarnation, will go to India
and collect the heart essence of all paṇḍitas and adepts
that will mature and liberate all migrators.
His various emanations will train disciples. {477}
He will proclaim essential Mahayana dharma free of extremes,
and the lion's roar of Secret Mantra, inseparable bliss-emptiness,
will be heard in the ten directions.
His body will become Cakrasaṃvara,
his speech the epitome of Mahāmāya,
his mind glorious Hevajra,
his emanation place supreme Guhyasamāja,
and his secret place bliss-holding Yamāntaka.
Once these mandalas are arrayed in his body,
they will actually manifest to his disciples.

Further, he will transform into various yidams
to train innumerable people difficult to train.
His life span will be one hundred and fifty years.
At the end, when it's time for vanquishing conduct,
various omens and miracles will be displayed.
Then he will pass on to the pure realm Sukhāvatī
that is praised by all victors and become a buddha,
turning the wheel of the Mahayana dharma.
Future generations of all people with faith
will no doubt also go to that realm of the victors."

After speaking those words, that great adept
returned to the exalted land of India like a bird in the sky.
My parents reported this prophecy when I was five years old.
By the time I was ten I had mastered writing and calculation.
At twelve, as was the custom of my paternal ancestors,
I studied the mind teachings of Bön, dzogchen, and mahāmudrā.
Then, carrying a decent amount of gems and gold dust,
without regard for my own life and with great difficulty,
I traveled to the lands of India and Nepal seven times.
I studied with one hundred and fifty sages in India,
particularly fifty learned and great adepts,
four especially exalted root gurus,
and two awareness ḍākinīs who truly heard teachings
from the saṃbhogakāya, the sixth buddha Vajradhara.
I pleased them and received their ultimate instructions. {478}
I resolved my misconceptions and did focused practice,
by which I attained both supreme and common spiritual powers.[15]

That was a short account of his life. Now listen respectfully. As described in his own words, Khedrup Shangpa Dugupa[16] first became learned in the Bön doctrine and attained spiritual powers. Then he heard teachings on the three classes of great completion (*rdzogs chen*) from Jungne Senge, and studied the Indian source tantras of mahāmudrā, the Great Seal, with Kor Nirupa, and so forth. He studied many such sources and instructions, and became highly proficient in all of them. But his former karma was awakened, and at the age of fifty he left for India. There he studied with one hundred and fifty learned adepts, four root gurus, two ḍākinīs of timeless awareness, and so on. He practiced and learned unimaginable approaches to the dharma from the greater and lesser vehicles, common and uncommon.

First, this song about meeting Vajrāsana Puṇyāgupta, one of his especially exalted four gurus:

> I, Khyungpo Naljor,
> developed a huge and deep fear
> of samsara's unbearable sufferings.
> This never-ending cyclic existence
> means boundless suffering of birth and death,
> and unimaginable sufferings of bad existences.
> Dying is easy; its living that scares me to death.
>
> Karma follows into the next life,
> and we cycle helplessly in samsara.
> Nothing will help me and all living beings
> other than getting to know death.
> In the face of death, whose time is uncertain,
> I ignored my health for the sake of dharma,
> and without concern for my life or limb,
> I did not depend only on the country of Nepal
> but went straight to the home of the thousand buddhas,
> where our Teacher manifested as Buddha:
> the Vajra Seat of Bodhgaya, India.
> There, I met the one whom the Great Sage
> had prophesied to be the second Buddha—
> glorious Vajrāsana. {479}
>
> When I actually met him face to face,
> I offered him five hundred gold pieces from Gulang.[17]
> I thought I had met the actual Buddha;
> my hairs stood on end and tears welled up.
> Great devotion arose from deep inside me,
> and I joined my palms and said this:
>
>> "Once I become a fully ordained khenpo,
>> I request the root of the doctrine, the Vinaya.
>> Once I have aroused the mind of great awakening,

I request the teachings of the Mahayana.
Once I have received ripening empowerment in Secret Mantra,
I request liberating creation and completion."

I entreated him with those words,
and the glorious Vajrāsana
smiled with pleasure and spoke:

"In the hinterlands of the red-faced demons,
people are disturbed by wrong views and doubts.
They seek various teachings but can't practice them.
Not matured themselves, they try to help others.
They are jealous and critical of each other;
laypeople who have heard tell of dharma.
You, who come from such a country,
are an intrepid person of faith
who fears birth and death.
To seek the unerring Holy Dharma
you traveled here to India
with great hardship at the risk of your life.
You—lucky Khyungpo Naljor.
In a former life, in the northern Himalaya,
you were a śrāvaka with boundless miraculous powers
who became known as Great Miracle Worker.
At that time, you tamed misinformed heathens,
gods, nāgas, yakṣas, bhūtas,
and all the groups of people.
You circled the assembly of śrāvakas
and flew to the sky like a bird.
Mountains and water didn't hinder you.
You showed various emanated forms,
appearing as one or many and so forth.
Since you became that great arhat,
I and other wise men of India
are unable to be your preceptor. {480}
In the north of the Land of Snows
lives Langri Öden,[18] of golden color,

an emanation of Buddha Amitābha.
Go there and ask him to be preceptor
for your full ordination.
Here at the Vajra Seat in Magadha
and other sacred sites,
I will grant your requests
for Vinaya, the Perfections, and Secret Mantra
and teach them however you like."[19]

He said that and acted as the preceptor for the novice monk ordination, giving him the name Tsultrim Gönpo. However, Guru Vajrāsana's nose began to bleed, [a sign that] he couldn't change his name from Khyungpo Naljor. At that point the guru exclaimed, "Khyungpo *dzoki mahā phala phala.*" First he gave him the reading transmission for the Vinaya and taught him the treatise *Vinayasūtra.*[20] Then gradually he taught him all the source texts and instructions of Sutra and Mantra.

The most excellent of all was the cycle of the Five Tantras' Deities practiced within a single mandala, which is based on the root and explanatory tantras of the *Jewel Ocean Tantra*. This is Khyungpo Naljor's verse about how he received that empowerment and instruction:

The special features of the sublime instructions,
empowerments, tantras, and sādhanas
of the Five Great Tantra Classes are these:

The liberation tantra of Cakrasaṃvara
teaches the cause, path, and result.
To accomplish great bliss,
the vajra of awakening mind
is the practice of bliss itself.

Glorious Guhyasamāja,
essential Mahāmāya,
quintessential Hevajra,
great Magical Illusion (Mahāmāya) able to eat great ecstasy,
glorious Binder of the Wheel (Cakrasaṃvara),
and wrathful Vajrabhairava:
these are the five culminating teachers.

They are the very integral unity
of tantras of both methods and wisdom.
First, in the ripening path of empowerment
there are outer, inner, and secret [aspects].

In the path there are two stages:
creation phase and completion phase. {481}
Creation is appearance, and completion emptiness,
integrated like the moon reflected in water.
Completion involves one's own body, another's body,
and their union as bliss and emptiness inseparable.

The results are supreme and common spiritual powers.
The common are the eight actions and eight great feats.
The supreme are the four kāyas with their activities
that arise spontaneously on their own to tame whomever.

If trained individuals with karmic connections
exert themselves with single-pointed focus
and keep sacred pledges, they will surely succeed.

One's own body is the path of means,
another's body is the action mudra.
This vital point of integrating desires
comes through a sublime lineage:

Exalted Master Nāgārjuna
who received prediction of Buddha.
The one called Kaṃpala
who attained mastery based on lucid clarity.
Kukuripa the Great
who emanated dogs as mudras.
The one called Lūhipa
who gained powers eating fish guts.
And glorious Harikela[21]
blessed by the presiding deity.

From all of them the succession came to
Ḍombipa, Kusulu, and Mahāvajra,
who brought them together.
Glorious Śrījñāna,
Vairocanarakṣita,
Sumati the yogin,
Tathāgatarakṣita,
Amoghavajra,
and glorious Vajrāsana
is the lineage that came down to me.

Then from Venerable Śrījñāna, Vairocanarakṣita, Ḍākima Kanakaśrī, and others, Khyungpo Naljor received innumerable teachings on Sutra, [the Mahayana path of] characteristics, and the Secret Mantra sādhanas and instructions on outer and inner tantras. When it was time for him to depart, he offered thirteen pieces of gold to Guru Vajrāsana on the summit of Mount Malaya. During the tenth-day offering rituals, he saw sights and received prophecy. He composed these verses about what happened:

Flowers fell like rain from the sky, {482}
heroes and ḍākinīs filled the space,
sounds and light and rainbows trembled.
When we made offerings to the gods,
Vajrāsana spoke these words:

"Son of good family, return to Tibet.
Liberate many sentient beings,
disciples in the Land of Snows.
In the future, these teachings
will be spread by a yogin
who holds your lineage.
He will receive all this dharma,
and with an altruistic mind, whatever happens
he will teach the unerring way of the bodhisattvas
and reach the level of complete nonabiding.
Eventually there will be many realized disciples.

"Of the four major classical tenet systems,
a difference is fully delineated between
the vehicle of characteristics and the vajra vehicle:
one takes the cause and the other takes the result as the path.

"The stages of direct perception and inference
[examined through] the four great axioms
are ascertained by the three natures.
That is the process for philosophical debate.

"The vehicle of the perfections and Secret Mantra
share the thirty-seven factors of enlightenment
and differ in regard to the five paths.[22]
To use the incidental concise meaning as the path
is called the process for meditation practice.

"In the second of those graded paths
is what is called the path of seeing.
It is the path that actualizes timeless awareness
that is untainted by mistaken views.

"The path free of extremes
reveals the integral unity
and enters the great middle way.
Calm abiding, higher insight, and meditative absorptions
increase more and more as the path is refined.
This is taught as the supreme path of mind.

"You have realization similar to mine.
I have received the prophecy of the Victor.
You as well will go from this life
to the buddha realm of Sukhāvatī.

"Don't be discouraged in this age of conflict
by obstinate beings—meditate on awakening mind.
In the land of Cakrasaṃvara's self-appearing mandala,
tens of thousands of disciples will appear." {483}

That was the prediction that Khyungpo Naljor received. He returned to Tibet and did some work for the welfare of migrators. Then he discovered that the gold mine of Gulang was overproducing, so he carried off a lot of gold and went back to Nepal and India. He received many profound teachings there that he had not heard before from Vajrāsana, the Victor Maitrīpa, Dha Bodhisattva, Exalted Ratnadevī, Sumatikīrti, and the Newar Pamtingpa the Great and many other learned and accomplished masters. He received the cycle of the Awareness Protector and innumerable other instructions.

Still not satisfied, Khyungpo Naljor took five hundred pieces of gold and traveled all over India—east, west, south, and north—inquiring after an accomplished guru who had actually met the Buddha face to face. All the paṇḍitas and adepts agreed that there was one awareness ḍākinī known as Niguma, the sister of Nāro Paṇḍita, who had reached the three pure levels [on the bodhisattva path] and who could hear teachings directly from Great Vajradhara. But when he asked where she was, they said:

"If your perception is pure, you can see her anywhere. But if your perception is not pure, you can search everywhere and not find her, because she dwells on the pure stages and has transformed to a rainbow body. Nonetheless, she occasionally shows up in the great charnel ground of Sosadvīpa to preside over the ḍākinīs' communal feasts."

As soon as Khyungpo Naljor heard the Ḍākinī's name, he felt such devotion that tears welled up and his hairs stood on end. Right then and there he set out for the forests of Sosadvīpa Charnel Ground, reciting the *namo buddha* prayer as he went. When he arrived, he saw a brown-skinned ḍākinī in the sky at a height of about seven palmyra trees.[23] She was adorned with bones and held a khaṭvāṅga staff and skull in her hands. She was dancing and displaying multiple images, sometimes singly and sometimes as multiple figures. Khyungpo thought, "This surely is Ḍākinī Niguma." {484} He did many prostrations and circumambulations and then requested authentic instructions.

She said, "I am a flesh-eating ḍākinī. When my entourage arrives, you'll be devoured. Now run along quickly!"

Then again he made prostrations and circumambulations and requested the instructions of Secret Mantra.

Niguma said, "To receive the Mahayana Secret Mantra requires gold. If there's gold, I can do it."

Khyungpo Naljor offered her five hundred gold pieces, but she threw them about the forest. He thought, "Well maybe this is indeed a flesh-eating ḍākinī, as she does not value gold."

When that ḍākinī glanced up into space, her entourage of innumerable ḍākinīs arrived in the sky. Some of them instantly constructed a three-storied celestial palace, some of them made the colored-sand mandala, and some of them collected provisions for a communal feast. That evening of the full moon, the empowerments of Illusory Body and Dream were conferred and Khyungpo received them.

Then she said, "Little Tibetan monk, rise!" Through her miraculous powers, Khyungpo Naljor was transported instantly for three fathoms. He saw a small golden mountain and ḍākinīs in the sky above it who were holding the communal feast and performing the dances. Four rivers of gold flowed down the four sides of the mountain. Khyungpo Naljor asked, "Is this golden mountain in India or is it emanated by the ḍākinīs?" Niguma replied with this:

> The variety of desirous and hateful thoughts
> that strand us in the ocean of cyclic existence,
> once realized to be without intrinsic nature,
> makes everything a golden land, my child.
>
> If you meditate on the illusion-like nature
> of all illusion-like phenomena,
> illusion-like manifest buddhahood
> will arise through the power of devotion. {485}

After saying that, she granted the empowerment of the Five Tantra Classes and countless tantras, sādhanas, and instructions. In particular, she gave him the guidance on the Six Dharmas one time in a dream and three times in actuality, and then sealed it as a single one-to-one lineage for seven generations. Then she promised that she would bless and grant prophecy to that succession.

Once again Khyungpo Naljor took five hundred gold pieces and traveled to the western part of India, asking, "Who is a guru who has met the Buddha in person?" Thirteen adepts, such as Paṇḍita Lalitavajra, Āryadeva, and Ḍākinī Sumati, said, "We will confer empowerment and teach the instructions, and after that we'll tell you the prophecy." So he gave them five hundred gold pieces and received many empowerments and instructions. Then they said, "For we thirteen, the root guru is Ḍākinī of Timeless Awareness Sukhasiddhi. In particular, she taught Paṇḍita Āryadeva [the Brahmin] the Inner Guidance of Nairātmya.[24] After seven months he gained the realization of the eighth stage. She is the one who has heard the dharma directly from Vajradhara and Nairātmya. She will grant you blessings and instructions."

Khyungpo asked where she lived, and they replied, "If your perception is pure, you can see that ḍākinī anywhere. But if your perception is not pure, you can search everywhere and not find her. Sometimes, she goes to the bliss-giving sacred site called the Sandalwood Medicinal Forest on the tenth day of the lunar month and presides over the ḍākinīs' communal feast and teaches the dharma. Or else she just teaches the dharma by speaking. Go there and entreat her to confer the complete four empowerments along with instructions and all the follow-up teachings." {486}

He took another five hundred gold pieces and went to the bliss-giving medicinal forest praying with the *namo buddhaya* supplication along the way. When he arrived, he saw in the sky above the sandalwood forest a white ḍākinī with hair falling down her back, making the mudra that indicates the unborn with her two hands. She was sitting in the midst of rainbow light, surrounded by a host of ḍākinīs. When he saw her, the hairs on his body stood up, tears welled forth, and he had an experience of undissipating bliss like the ecstasy that arises on the first level. He tossed flowers such as utpala, lotus, and kumuta. He did many hundreds of thousands of prostrations and circumambulations and requested instructions. The Ḍākinī said this in response:

Virūpa and Nairātmya
heard this directly from Vajradhara.
The real path of Secret Mantra
is the four ripening empowerments
and the liberating creation and completion.

For that teaching you offered rare jewels and gold dust;
with palms together, you did full prostrations
and placed the bottom of my feet on your head.
At this time I will liberate you;
today you'll discover the best discovery.

You, son of good family—*emaho!*
You, son of good family—*emaho!*
You, son of good family—*emaho!*

I will truly bless your disciples,
the disciples of your disciples,
and all future generations of lineage holders.
They will all go to the pure celestial realm.

First she conferred the complete four empowerments in an emanated mandala. Then she taught him the creation and completion phases of the Secret Sādhana of the Navel Emanation Chakra with all the vital points of practice, leaving nothing out. Khyungpo Naljor said of her:

> The first kindness of this Awareness Ḍākinī Sukhasiddhi was to confer the complete four empowerments in the emanated mandala. The middle kindness was to be my secret consort appearing as a daughter of the gods. {487} The final kindness was to fully grant all the instructions. Then she prophesied that I would attain the fourteenth stage while in Sukhāvatī. She also foretold that she would hold my disciples and all the lineage holders with her compassion and that they too would go to the pure celestial realm of bliss and emptiness. Therefore, all my lineage holders will be the most outstanding and exclusively those with excellent accumulations of merit and wisdom.

Khyungpo Naljor went on to receive countless tantras and instructions from mighty ḍākinīs such as Samantabhadrī and learned and accomplished yogis such as Sukhavajra, Lalitavajra, and Atayavajra. He resolved his misgivings and pleased them with golden flowers. When making great offerings during the holy-day ritual at the Vajra Seat, there were incredible omens. The Indians, both high and low, all praised him with a single voice.

Upon returning to Tibet, he received full ordination from Geshe Langri Tangpa, a magical emanation of Amitābha. Then while he was doing his practice in retreat at Jokpori in Penyul, the adept of immortality Rāhulagupta arrived miraculously and granted him boundless instructions. From those instructions, [Khyungpo Naljor] composed this song of eight esoteric instructions for minor requisites while participating in the subsequent communal feast:[25]

This dualistic conceptual thought is ridiculous.
I hold instructions on the three dissolutions[26]
that will repel the attack of dualism.
Now, dualistic concepts, do what you will!

This great god Pekar is ridiculous.
I hold instructions on the three strings
that will repel attacks of big gods.
Now, all you big gods, do what you will! {488}

This dark nāga devil is ridiculous.
I hold instructions on the joined skulls
that will repel attacks of nāga devils.
Now, all you nāga devils, do what you will!

This bhūta spirit of the night is ridiculous.
I hold instructions on the vital drops of elixir
that will repel attacks of bad spirits.
Now, all you spirits, do what you will!

This evil imprecator is ridiculous.
I hold instructions on using black slabs
that will repel attacks of imprecators.
Now, all you imprecators, do what you will!

This dark death lord is ridiculous.
I hold instructions on skeleton sights
that will repel attacks of death lords.
Now, all you death lords, do what you will!

This dark planet devil is ridiculous.
I hold instructions on the tortoise shell
that will repel attacks of planetary devils.
Now, all you rāhula planets, do what you will!

Previously your speech was not blessed,
so your mantra recitation was ineffective.
I hold instructions on glorious *ālikāli*—
don't worry about not accomplishing mantras.[27]

Then Khyungpo Naljor with his entourage of three thousand went to Shang and within three years established one hundred and eight monasteries, headed by Zhangzhong. When he turned the great wheel of the dharma, fifty thousand monks came together from U, Tsang, and Kham. But most of them were distracted and careless in study and meditation practice, so Khyungpo Naljor took them sightseeing. He manifested many enticing gods and goddesses of the Heaven of the Thirty-Three, and the monks became delighted and desirous. Again he emanated many frightening death-lord minions whose job is to kill and maim, and the disciples became terrified and fainted. At that time, he sang this song to introduce [mind's nature]: {489}

All objects of desire and hatred
come from your own mind.
To the yogin, these appearances
of death-lord forms, like flesh-eaters,
carrying various weapons in their hands
to reap our life force right now,
are liberating if known as illusions.
Even when surrounded by captivating
beautiful goddesses adorned with jewels,
singing songs with sweet melodies,
if you are certain they are self-appearing illusions,
they have no power to ensnare you.

He gave this and other teachings, including teachings on the intermediate state. After that, everyone applied themselves diligently to study and meditation.

One time Geshe Könchok Gyal of Rong presented many offerings to Khyungpo Naljor and made the following request: "It is said that you've gone to India three times and relied on one hundred and fifty learned adepts, including your four root gurus. It is said you are an adept yourself and realize that appearances have no intrinsic nature. So go ahead and pass back and forth through this cliff and sit in vajra position in space." At that, Khyungpo passed through the mountain cliff, sat in vajra posture in space, assumed single and multiple forms, and displayed some other miraculous feats. Rongpo and all the monks were moved to faith. They asked, "What meditation instruction produces such qualities?" He said this in response:

Experience the illusion-like nature
of all illusion-like phenomena
to manifest illusion-like buddhahood.

Phenomena appear but are unreal.
The childish view them as real, causing delusion.
Appearing while nonexistent—*emaho!*

Khyungpo Naljor gave other teachings as well, inspiring Rongpo's faith. After eleven months he had a visionary experience of the yidam and realized that all appearance lacks true reality.

Khyungpo Naljor became aware that his attendant Rinchen Dorje had slightly strayed into mistaken views by holding to the [guru as] an ordinary subjective being. He sent him off to meditate on the hundred syllables and Purifying *A* of Inner Space for seven days. When next he showed up in Khyungpo's room, Rinchen Dorje saw that he had emanated his body as the Thirteen-Deity Hevajra With Weapons. He also saw precisely the Five Tantras' deities arrayed in Khyungpo's five places. When he went outside, he saw Khyungpo Naljor teaching the dharma on one hundred and eight dharma thrones, and made this special verse (*udāna*):

Your awakened body emanated as nine deities,
the Five Tantras' deities in your five places,
one hundred and eight dharma thrones,
your body on each—I can never look enough!

You proclaim the Mahayana beyond extremes,
and display various emanations in ten directions.
Heart emanation of the ocean of victors—
Guru Buddha, I offer you my praise.

Put sentient beings deluded by ignorance
onto the authentic path; I entreat you.

Rinchen Dorje praised him in this way. Never again did wrong view arise for even an instant, and he became a faithful attendant on Khyungpo Naljor's every command.

On one occasion, when Khyungpo was explaining the *Five Treatises of Maitreya*[28] and the *Secret General Tantra*,[29] the monks from U, Tsang, and Kham could not agree on who would serve him food. As they were about to breach their sacred pledge, the gods of the four great kings appeared and gave this warning:

Birth in a land without freedom
and exile from the free places
come from these disagreements—
what need to mention [breaching] sacred pledges.

Those able to bear the hardship of living in harmony
will gain awakening in this life without hardship.
So we gods who are assembled here
will serve during the dharma teaching.

Whether seven palmyra trees high or just one,
please bring the rains of dharma in the sky.
Please sound the great conch of the dharma.
Please raise the banner of the dharma.

He vowed not to eat human-prepared food for seven months, and for those seven months he taught the *Five Treatises of Maitreya* and the *Secret General Tantra* from a height of one palmyra tree. {491} Many there integrated the view of the middle way. The gods said these words with one voice:

Guru Vajrāsana's intention is fulfilled! The gods are satisfied! All humans will be liberated! Great acts for the Buddha's doctrine are done! *Alala!*

They said that three times and a great rain of flowers fell. Then they vanished.

One time Buddha Amitābha displayed the arrays of the realm of Sukhāvatī and spoke these words:

> This is your final rebirth.
> In the pure realm of Sukhāvatī
> you will tame devils of all kinds,
> gain awakening, and turn the dharma wheel.
>
> Whoever follows after you,
> or just hears the name Amitābha
> will be born miraculously
> in the realm of Sukhāvatī.
>
> Your [next] three lineage holders
> will go from pure realm to realm,
> Sukhāvatī and Abhirati,
> and gain manifest awakening there.

He received this and many other prophecies. Then he heard these sounds of dharma from the light rays of the Great Compassionate One and the two other [bodhisattvas]:

> If unrestricted compassion does not arise
> from the unborn innate nature of all phenomena,
> you won't be able to mature and liberate
> your old mothers, the six kinds of beings.
>
> Whether walking, moving, lying down, or sitting,
> hold with the hook of undistracted mindfulness
> the kindness and sufferings of those mothers
> and develop immeasurable great compassion.
>
> The cooling rivers of compassion
> flow from the great snow mountain of love,
> extinguishing the fire of the afflictions.
> I am the form of great compassion.

This and other teachings on the meditative absorption of universal compassion were given. {492} Then Khyungpo Naljor went to Oḍḍiyāna and received empowerment in the mandala of Five-Deity Ḍākinīs.[30] The ḍākinīs of the four classes surrounded Ḍākinī Siṃhamukhā and she sang this vajra song:

> Vajra Ḍākinī guards against obstacles,
> Jewel Ḍākinī increases people and wealth,
> Lotus Ḍākinī gathers consorts,
> Activity Ḍākinī accomplishes all actions.
>
> Once under the influence of craving and clinging
> one has fallen under the power of the ḍākinīs.
> Any unwanted external event can occur;
> recognize the ḍākinī as your own mind.
>
> To recognize that suchness of mind
> and the vajra of conceptual mind itself;
> that is the Vajra Ḍākinī guarding against obstacles.
>
> Contentment with no needs is a precious gift;
> that is the Jewel Ḍākinī accomplishing needs and desires.
>
> The lotus of nonconceptual freedom from attachment;
> that is the Lotus Ḍākinī gathering the mudras.
>
> Karma without arising or ceasing;
> that is the Activity Ḍākinī accomplishing actions.
>
> A yogin who does not recognize that
> will practice for ages without success.
> Therefore, know ḍākinīs as your own mind;
> that is the sublime vital point.

They taught this and other instructions on the three arisings and the three gatherings.[31]

Then, in accordance with the predictions of his gurus, deities, and ḍākinīs, Khyungpo Naljor taught dharma for many years to the ultimate assembly of eighty thousand people. He finished every instruction to his six ultimate disciples. He reached the ultimate age of one hundred and fifty years. He intended to depart for the ultimate pure realm of Sukhāvatī. But the four great kings and the nāga king Anavapta, the gandharvan king Pañcaśikha, and innumerable gods, nāgas, and nonhumans presented unimaginable clouds of offerings and begged him not to enter nirvana. He responded with this and other teachings that satisfied them:

> Now the three ultimates are fulfilled
> that my gurus and yidams had foretold.
> I will go to the realm of Sukhāvatī,
> the ultimate pure realm. {493}
> With limitless pure enjoyment,
> who needs worldly gold and silver?
> If you have faith in me,
> pray to be born in Sukhāvatī
> and you will doubtless be born in that realm.
> On a single atom there appear as many pure realms
> as atoms in the universe, unimaginably perfect.
> Realms, teachers, retinues, and dharma
> are infinite in Amitābha's realm,
> the totally pure realm Sukhāvatī.
> Therefore have no doubt
> and pray to be born there.

Then Khyungpo Naljor attended the assembly on the fourteenth day of the lunar month and displayed many bodily forms in the sky and said these words:

> Alas! All composite things are impermanent.
> They gather and disperse like clouds in the sky.
> To take unreal illusory phenomena
> as real is to be deceived.
>
> My body is the Victor's awakened form;
> do not see it as subject to birth and death.
> My voice is the Victor's awakened speech,
> the innate sound of the inexpressible unborn.

My mind is the Victor's awakened mind
with timeless awareness of inconceivable knowledge.

Thus he spoke and the whole sky was filled with rainbows and the sound of music while a great rain of flowers showered down.

Mokchokpa Rinchen Tsöndru

Khedrup Khyungpo Naljor had six main close disciples who received his perfectly complete instructions. Among them, there was only one, the last, to whom the special legacy of the one-to-one lineage fell: Mokchokpa Rinchen Tsöndru. Mokchokpa held [the status of] a great bodhisattva with a single [remaining] lifetime: right after he passed from this life he attained actual perfect enlightenment in the eastern buddha realm of Radiant Light.[32] He had seen that the conventional explanations of the dharma were hollow and that only the instructions of adept gurus such as Khampa Aseng and Burgom Nakpo hit the mark. {494} Though he took those instructions into his experience, he failed to reach consummation in his spiritual practice. But sometime later, Khedrup Khyungpo Naljor took him as a disciple and gave him all the instructions. First he meditated for two years at Dingma and experienced the culminating realizations of Illusory Body, Dream, and Lucid Clarity. Then, since Lama Shangpa had passed away, he went to see Gampopa, the physician guru of Dakpo, in order to clear up doubts in his spiritual practice. Gampopa was very pleased, telling him that they had been master and student for many lifetimes, and he granted many instructions. There Khyungpo resolved his misgivings about the view of mahāmudrā, and the energy of his experience and realization grew in every respect. During the emanation and transformation of a dream, Mokchokpa sang this vajra song:

The unobstructed flow from the unborn expanse
cannot be encompassed by mere thought.
Illusory body, not distorted by anyone,
arises from the expanse of the yogin's awareness.
Thoughts of this life fade and vanish.
The fully ripened body is the Victor's awakened form—
the venerable precious one introduced me to it.

The mental body is the dharmakāya—
the venerable precious one introduced me to it.
The habitual body is the Victor's awakened form—
the venerable precious one introduced me to it.

He said this and other things, and that henceforth he never experienced the concerns of this life. Then, following the advice of the gurus to never leave the mountains, he decided that he should focus either on death or else on awakening. So he remained in the cliffs of Mokchok for twelve years, sustained by very little food. One time, Sukhasiddhi appeared and thrice repeated:

Until phenomena's nature is actualized,
nourishment by human food obscures experience.
Sever the bonds of food and clothing
and eat the food of meditative absorption.

Thereupon he cut the ties to food and clothing. Unimaginable absorptions arose. {495} During the time of those events, he composed many vajra songs, such as "The Seven Royal Possessions Complete within Oneself":[33]

I acted to defeat enemies and protect friends,
but at no time were the enemies defeated,
and at no time were the friends satisfied.
Now my main act is to live without enemies and friends.

I acted to propitiate gods and exorcise demons,
but at no time were the gods satisfied,
and at no time did the demons leave.
Now my main act is to live without gods and demons.

Though I chased after emptiness,
reaching the view of emptiness is endless.
Now my main act is to cut the one root alone.

In one who is the least of human virtues,
the best of spiritual qualities has arisen.

Without seeing the ultimate meaning,
we err trying to find illusory wealth.
Without seeing what will benefit the mind,
we err following verbal conventions.

Without keeping to a lowly appearance,
we act like a high and mighty lord.
Without begging for alms aimlessly,
we err in empty valleys, ruining anthills.

Without practicing alone,
we act as the leader of many.
This fortunate free and endowed human body
could be lost in constant meaningless activity.

This precious gem of one's mind
could be lost in the swamp of cyclic existence.
This elixir of the guru's instructions
could be lost under the sway of distraction.

This radiant lamp of integral unity
could be lost in the gale winds of thought.
This movement of equal-flavored great bliss
could be quashed by the devil of eight concerns.

This buddha realm of one's own body
could be lost when given ordinary work.
This joy and happiness of a yogin
is aided by appearances of six consciousnesses.

With no fear of samsara and nirvana,
I think, "My own mind is king."
A sovereign who realizes their own mind
also holds the seven royal ornaments. {496}

I did not follow verbal conventions
but preferred the profound meaning

and certainty arose from deep within:
that is the best advice of a minister.

In the presence of the holy guru
the profound instructions were shown:
"Resolve your doubts in the tantras and scriptures
of Lord Nāropa's spiritual descendants."

I gathered all the main esoteric instructions
and severed the root of samsara and nirvana.
Then ignorance vanished in the unborn state:
the supreme horse conveyed five poisons to basic space.

Still, this busyness of big groups was distracting,
so I kept to mountain retreats,
making creation and completion the basis
and training my mind's creative energy.

Like a young garuḍa turning in space,
wherever I go is the precious wheel.
Six sense appearances suddenly blank,
I knew contentment of the present moment.

With no cause for joy over many enjoyments,
I am not disgraced or saddened by praise or insult.
Even the apparitions of the death-lord devil
are my own projections and cause no fear.

Mind itself, free of eternalism and nihilism,
leaves no cause to fear birth or death.
I think, "Isn't this the precious general
who conquers erroneous ideas?"

For the yogin who realizes this,
appearances in the primordially pure mind
arise and exist as the spiritual master.
That's like the elephant that moves armies.

Anger and desire vanish within mindlessness.
A bird flying in the sky has no support;
the six consciousnesses arise momentarily.
Without fixation they arise as allies,
great sights without inhibition,
fitting ornaments worn by the beautiful queen.

For the yogin who realizes this,
like the all-pervading sky,
mind's house has no fixed dimension.
Like space that cannot be identified,
the door of lucid clarity has no fixed dimension.
Since basic space and awareness are inseparable, {497}
the continuum of three kāyas has no fixed dimension.

Just as the sun without effort
shines rays in every direction,
the precious gem fulfills hopes and needs.

This supreme gem of the seven precious ones
is the great ornament of the yogin.
Though we leave the body, we don't lose that.
I think, "Is this not the sacred gem?"

I have no need for royal wealth.
I take no delight in scholarly sophistry.
If this is boasting, then let me die!

"The Song of Six Attitudes of an Experienced Mind":

At first I resolved my false assumptions,
but sometimes doubt still came up.
It's as if even the view tricks the yogin.
Now I ask only to keep a simple mind.

At first I realized the unborn,
but sometimes inflation still came up.

It's as if even meditation tricks the yogin.
Now I ask only to keep an undistracted mind.

At first I acted without fixation,
but sometimes attachment still came up.
It's as if even the conduct tricks the yogin.
Now I ask only to keep an unfixated mind.

At first I rested with one-pointed mind,
but sometimes hopes and fears still came up.
It's as if even the fruition tricks the yogin.
Now I ask only to keep a spontaneous mind.

At first I made surpassing progress,
but sometimes anxiety still came up.
It's as if even the eight concerns trick the yogin.
Now I ask only to keep a crazy mind.

At first I renounced loving relatives,
but sometimes face-saving still came up.
[line missing]
Now I ask only to keep from saving face.

At first faith was born,
but sometimes complacency still came up.
It's as if laziness tricks the yogin.
Now I ask only to keep diligent and yogic.

May I not grow weary of faith and devotion
to the one deity, the Three Jewels.
May my devotion be uninterrupted
to the one parent, the holy guru. {498}

May I not corrupt with extraneous words
the essence of the heart's instructions.
Again, practice is more dear than scholarship.
I will stay by myself and keep practicing.

["Eight Hardships":][34]

It's hard to tire of the faults of cyclic existence
and be devoted to transcendent dharma.
It's hard to believe in the dharma of cause and effect
and then to have faith without sorrow.
It's hard to reject all sickness and pain
and then put this human body to use.
It's hard to find a compassionate guru
who has scripture, reason, and esoteric instruction.
It's hard to find a disciple who rejects distractions
and then cultivates meditative experience.
It's hard to abandon all attachment and aversion
and then compassionately work for others' welfare.
It's hard to meditate single-pointedly,
free of dualistic conceptual thinking.

This instruction on the eight hardships
is valuable to all who practice dharma.
Only a few out of a hundred get them all;
that's why attaining awakening is so hard.

["Eight Great Ornaments":]

Don't they say that the view free of extremes
is to sever assumptions in the mind?
Adding scripture and reason to that is a great ornament.

Don't they say that naturally occurring meditation
is conceptual thought arising as dharmakāya?
Adding experience to that is a great vital point.

Don't they say that conduct without attachment
is the six consciousnesses free in their own ground?
Adding a timely element is a great ornament.

Don't they say that the instruction of the aural lineage
is to connect with the experience of emptiness?
Adding empowerment to that is a great ornament.

Don't they say that the sequence of levels and paths
is the arising of clear appearances of emptiness?
Adding the path signs to that is a great ornament.

Don't they say that buddhahood in one lifetime
is to convey one's mind to the point of exhaustion?
Adding the four kāyas to that is a great ornament.

Don't they say that the lineage-holding gurus
are people endowed with three characteristics?
Adding instructions to that is a great ornament. {499}

Don't they say that a worthy disciple
is one with great faith and wisdom?
Adding devotion to that is a great ornament.

["The Mountain of the Precious Guru":]

On the mountain of the precious guru
there are springs of sacred instructions.
If you can drink from them with unflagging faith,
you will surely be freed from all faults.

Inside the vase of the composite body
there is a lamp of coemergence.
If you are content with meditative absorption,
you will surely illuminate outer and inner dharmakāya.

On the mountain of your own illusory body,
the lion cub of consciousness plays.
If you train the six consciousnesses without attachment,
you will surely outshine existence and transcendence.

Inside the nest of ignorance
is the fledgling garuḍa of consciousness.
If you can engage the wings of method and wisdom,
you will surely fly in the sky of the six migrators.

["Mind! Mind!":]

Mind! Mind! Look at the outer objects.
When you have seen outer objects,
they are like reflections in a mirror,
appearing without intrinsic nature.

Mind! Mind! Look at the inner mind.
When you have seen the inner mind,
it's like a lamp unmoved by wind,
clarity without conceptual thought.

Mind! Mind! Look at the border of outer and inner.
When you have seen the border of outer and inner,
it's like the sun rising in the sky,
characteristics released on their own.

Mind! Mind! Meditate on the profound path of methods.
When you have meditated on the profound path of methods,
it's like being led by an excellent guide,
mind is conveyed to the place of its desires.

Mind! Mind! Meditate on mahāmudrā.
When you have meditated on mahāmudrā,
it's like a flame spreading in the darkness;
everything appears and arises as your ally.

Mind! Mind! Wander aimlessly begging for alms.
When you have wandered aimlessly begging for alms,
it's like snow falling on a lake;
discursive thoughts dissolve instantly. {500}

Thirteen disciples of Gampopa came to see the Venerable One and asked for a mahāmudrā instruction that would prevent harm from discursive thought. He said this:

In the nature of phenomena without birth or cessation,
what is this so-called discursive thought?

> Look upon both thought and nonthought
> as water and water bubbles.

He said that and other teachings, and they all realized that conceptual thought is baseless and rootless. Geshe [Gyal] of Lowo requested a method to actually see whatever deity he practiced, and Rinchen Tsöndru replied with this:

> Mentally forsake worldly deeds,
> and without doubt or indecision
> meditate without concept on the deity's clarity.
> Don't engage in endless idle chatter;
> recite the mantra as empty sound.
> If you do this, there is no doubt
> you will quickly see the deity's form.

The geshe developed deep confidence and after three months of practice saw Tārā. The following story in Rinchen Tsöndru's own words is recounted in his biography:[35]

> One summer, there was a terrible famine. The local people held a council to counteract it and decided to ask the guru's advice. But since [they] carried off my offerings and overpowered the monks, the protector yak set his sights on the village. The monastics all readied themselves to be warrior monks, so one day I insisted on a public hearing and gathered everyone together. But first I put on my cloak and loaded my backpack with my ritual items. Then I spoke these words:
>
> > Consultation with the lord guru as a guide
> > is the measure of skill in traversing the path.
> > A deep sincere focus on the Holy Dharma
> > is the measure of showing initiative.
> > The resolution of hyperbole in your own mind
> > is the measure of your self-assurance.
> > Harmony with the Holy Dharma in whatever you do
> > is the measure of increasing virtuous activity.
> > To give the victory to the other people

is the measure of your mental training.
To control your own mind and not that of others
is the measure of your disregard for saving face. {501}
To behave as a guest wherever you stay
is the measure of your diminished attachment.
To give food and clothes to the defeated
is the measure of peace in body and mind.

After singing that song, Rinchen Tsöndru departed for mountain retreat, the monks gave up their battle plans, and the protector yak came back. The Great Compassionate One made an appearance and said:

With the water of love you've doused
the huge bonfire of anger.
Very well done, yogi!
Anger and desire are the root of samsara and nirvana.
Cast out desire and attachment, yogi!

Then in the month of the horse I entered retreat. I abstained from human food and conferring empowerments. The appearances of lucid clarity increased and I came to know the actions of all the monks and the good or bad acts of the early and later part of their lives. Thus with compassion and affection I was able to offer appropriate advice to each of them. Most of them developed certainty and perfected their virtuous practices. However, there were many that did not listen, such as Ngomshö Lachö. He decided to return home and enter the life of a householder. As this would mean not meeting him again before dying, I asked him not to go. I was pained that he would not listen, so I took his hand and sang this song:

Buddha is the ancestor of sentient beings.
Holy Dharma is the shared wealth of sentient beings.
Once it is apportioned to a person of faith,
to ignore this inheritance is pointless.

The root of the buddhas of the three times
is certainly the guru with a lineage
who fulfills desires in this life and the next;
to be without devotion is pointless.

Not to engage in undistracted diligence
for life's remainder before it runs out,
but to help those who don't want it
and waste life's meaning is pointless.

The small bird of awareness in the branches
will get inspiration from the death-lord devil. {502}
You will go wherever your former actions take you;
to perform negative acts is pointless.

The conditioned body is a vessel of pain,
where dwell birth, old age, sickness, and death.
This body will be discarded like a clay cup;
to hold out hope for its endurance is pointless.

Not to use for your own and others' benefit
food and wealth that is by nature illusory,
but not be able to bear parting with gifts
due to your age-old miserliness is pointless.

Not to hear the call to phenomena's nature
in the spirit escort of discursive thought,
but to fear the separation of body and mind
and become agitated is pointless.

Not to meditate constantly in four sessions
on the Secret Mantra that accomplishes all actions,
but to waste your time in endless talk
while life passes you by is pointless.

Not to meditate on the three kāyas as inseparable
from the wish-fulfilling gem of mind itself
is like a deer chasing a mirage;
pursuing words is pointless.

Without inhabiting the firm land of phenomena's nature,
to constantly keep watch over self-fixation
and grasp at the illusory cities of six classes of beings,
wandering in infinite regress, is pointless.

"The Vajra Song of View, Meditation, Conduct, and Result":

If you realize the meaning of no birth or cessation,
it doesn't matter if your view is the highest or not.
Rest in a state without reference points—
not clinging to duality, it is the view.

If you realize the meaning of ever-present three kāyas,
it doesn't matter if your abiding is stable or not.
Rest in a state without effort—
not wavering from clarity is meditation.

If you are undistracted when walking, moving, lying, or sitting,
it doesn't matter if your behavior is the crudest or not.
Rest in a state without fear—
to be without attachment is the conduct.

If you realize the meaning of insubstantial clarity,
it doesn't matter if your experience shines or not.
Rest in a state that is ineffable—
to have absolute certainty is meditative experience.

If you realize the meaning of no hopes and fears, {503}
it doesn't matter if you attain dharmakāya or not.
Rest in a state without anger or desire—
the primordially existent is the result.

"The Vajra Song of Immortal Mind":

Sutras, tantras, esoteric instructions, and experience
contain the vital point of immortality, buddhahood without
meditation.
Thus this fully ripened body arises by itself
as the body of timeless awareness.

Meditate without grasping to the clarity
of the fully ripened body as the deity's body.

That very body is inseparable from your mind,
and in mind there is no real essence.

So where is the cause of death?
So-called death is just a concept.
Thoughts do not exist, nor do samsara and nirvana.
Transference and the transferred are self-liberated.

Wherever consciousness goes, it goes.
This is the supreme result, boundless immortality.
This is the ḍākinī's vital heart that brings manifest buddhahood
just by recollecting it; hold it as dear as your life.

"The Natural Liberation of One's Mind as Immortal" by Ratnavīrya (Rinchen Tsöndru) is complete. I offered Lama Shangpa fifty gold pieces to request it and have brought it into my own experience. *ithi*

When Rinchen Tsöndru was about to pass away, he gave as his final testament these instructions to the wild tsen spirit Drongbu:[36]

Child, when you resolve misconceptions of verbal designations,
you'll have no need for conventional teachings—
so difficult to learn but so easy to forget.
Though there are eighty-four thousand dharma gates,
they all come down to mind itself.
Whatever dharma you contemplate,
rest in the abiding nature, the uncontrived native state.
Know that appearance is mind,
and that mind's nature is unborn.
If you realize the unborn, it is lucid clarity.
Place all your attention on that.
Since interdependent cause and effect never fails,
practice for this one thing, child.

Öntön Kyergangpa Chökyi Senge

He was nurtured by sublime Exalted Avalokiteśvara in all his lifetimes. In this lifetime he became accomplished through intense discipline and again made that connection, finally attaining the supreme power of inseparability with that Exalted One. {504} The twofold mind of awakening flowed through him effortlessly like a river. From Venerable Mokchokpa he received the Ḍākinī's single lineage and would ultimately attain awakening in the eastern buddha field of Vaiḍūryaprabha as the tathāgata Glory of Immaculate Space. In his final life as a bodhisattva, Öntön Kyergangpa Chökyi Senge was graced with infinite dharma gates opened by the buddhas and their heirs. For example, Exalted Tārā said:

> The vital point of Illusory Body is its lack of reality; destroy reification.
> The vital point of Dream is intentionality; integrate it on the path.
> The vital point of Lucid Clarity is devotion; attain it through prayer.
> The vital point of altruism is compassion; renounce prejudice.

And:

> When dualism is abandoned, desire is calmed within.
> Knowledge [of beings] as parents frees anger on its own.
> In nonconceptual clarity, stupidity dissolves into space.
> This binding of the wanton three poisons in their own ground,
> without fixating there, will surely liberate them in their own ground.
> Watch the afflictions as they self-arise and self-liberate.

Avalokiteśvara said:

> Distraction in busyness is a devilish obstacle.
> Until the variety of love and hate arises as an ally,
> always rely on seclusion, far from adverse conditions.
> It is wise to reflect on life's brevity and think of death.

The Five Tantras' deities said:

Maturation does not happen without the complete four
empowerments.
Liberation is impossible without meditating on creation [and
completion] inseparable.
Since the results won't come through hope and desire to attain
them,
regard self-liberation on arising as inseparable from the three
kāyas.

After Lama Mokchokpa had entered peace, Vajrayoginī said:

Just as there is no birth or death in this sky,
how could the guru be subject to birth and death?
The guru remains constant through your devotion. {505}
Don't grieve, supplicate!

"The Vajra Song Introducing One's Mind as the Guru":

guru bodhicitta namā mi

Homage to all the benevolent gurus,
incomparable teachers who introduce mind itself.
Their own aims achieved, they assume others' welfare
and show unbiased wise compassion equally to all.

Indeed all you gurus demonstrate the way things are,
but the guru who arises as the abiding nature dwells within.
This now is the characteristic guru of one's own mind:

Not arisen from causes but spontaneously present,
unaffected by conditions and without need of antidotes,
not going or coming or changing in the three times,
beyond extremes of being described as real or unreal.

No thing that is perceived by the five senses,
nonexistent and yet the source of everything,
though I look and contrive, I cannot pinpoint "It is this."
But when I give up trying, it is present everywhere.

Not subject to the influence of good or bad actions,
exalted above all but unattached to anything,
separate from everything, yet the actual ground of all,
free of intellect, yet for no reason it is clearly in mind.

In that lack of direction, diversity arises anywhere,
arising but without any definite location.
It is not enough to say, "It's like this."
That is precisely my guru.

If I were to recount the guru's life story, there's this:

That guru is neither near nor far,
yet there is not a single being not pervaded.
That guru, due to pure aspirations,
does not exclude anyone from its family.

That guru, because of great compassion,
does not exclude anyone from original awakening.
That guru, with great powerful deeds,
enters samsara and nirvana with total control. {506}

That guru does not transfer or change,
so even when viewed wrongly, remains the same.
That guru has never been apart for an instant,
but everyone struggles to see this longtime friend.
That guru who is not subject to dying,
watches constantly—what an amazing guru!

This is the guru of one's own mind;
gaze upon its countenance and recognize yourself.
Supplicate without doubt or hesitation,
and cultivate devotion of resting in its uncontrived state.

Serve this guru by always dwelling in its true nature,
bring the food of empty clarity without fixation,
serve the drink of realizing inseparable attention and distraction,
and clothe with the knowledge of appearance and sound as illusion.

Place underneath the soft mat of undissipating bliss,
crown with the hat of what, unsought, was always there,
and present the gifts of whatever arises without fixation.

In the bedroom of omniscience without self-fixation,
surrounded by a retinue of indivisible samsara-nirvana,
the guru dwells continuously in the three times,
always illuminating self-manifesting instructions.

So very wonderful, this guru of my own mind!
Once again kindly nurture me with compassion,
a yogin with karmic propensity from past life training.
Amazing that you have not relinquished compassion.

To rely on the guru in that fashion
elicits the guru's blessings in these ways:
You'll escape without fleeing the swamp of existence.
You'll arrive at awakening without going anywhere.
You'll know there's no good or bad in samsara or nirvana.

The difference between buddhas and beings is realization.
To realize mind's characteristics without error
and to manifest that conviction is called "buddha."
Its qualities are beyond expression.

To rely on another guru will have these results:
You won't realize mind itself as it is
but cling to what it is not and get stuck there. {507}
Following after that, you'll create the karma of suffering.
That is to be designated as "sentient being."

Now, be your own caretaker.
Don't retrace your steps in samsara ad nauseam.
Don't accomplish nirvana with great effort.
Hold mind itself in its own ground and just be.

This mind itself that is not identified by saying "this"
will occur through refining this unknowing.

Now, this knowledge of those characteristics is gratifying.
To rely on this manner of gratification is like this:

You needn't seek the dharmakāya integral to emptiness.
You needn't block the rūpakāyas that self-arise as anything.
You needn't contrive the three kāyas that are mind's own movement.
You needn't discard samsara that is already severed at its root.
You needn't hope for buddhahood that is already one's own mind.
You needn't meditate mentally on what was there since forever.

Wouldn't that be fine if you could do this?

Realized ones who watch the mind without distraction:
What's wrong with being free of the watching mind?
Great meditators who are constantly meditating:
What's wrong with liberation directly on that meditator?
Practitioners who always cultivate the mind of awakening:
What's wrong with knowing spontaneous nonmeditation?
Yogins who stand guard over the uncontrived:
What's wrong with ascertaining your own mind?

Though I attended many qualified gurus,
each guru gave their own words of advice,
but they all came down to one point: the mind.
So with that very guru, my own mind,
I looked at its face, listened to its speech, and took much instruction.
I supplicated before this guru,
offered praises, and requested blessings.

I realized within that my own mind *is* the guru,
so I have written down my understanding.
If you see contradictions or mistakes,
don't look at the words; look at their meaning.

This is the prattle of a madman. {508}
I don't ask for anyone's pardon.
I have nothing to offer by way of apology.

That concludes "One's Mind as the Guru" by precious Kyergangpa. *ithi*

"The Vajra Song of Introducing Immortal Mind":

namo guru
In the daytime, empty appearance is the deity's form.
I realize that it has no sickness or death.
At death, even if only its eyes appear,
death's interruption is self-purified and saṃbhogakāya
attained.
If even one in a hundred does not appear,
the import of previous training will go on unabated,
like ripples of a stone thrown in a deep pond.
The saṃbhogakāya of great bliss will arise of itself.
Until such time as cyclic existence is emptied,
boundless benefit for others will arise spontaneously.

"The Natural Liberation of One's Mind as Immortal" by Venerable Dharmasiṃha is complete. I offered the incomparable Rinchen one hundred gold pieces, thirteen female yaks, and one fur cloak to request it, and have brought it into my own experience.

Rigongpa Sangye [Nyen]tönpa

He received the secret treasury of the one-to-one lineage from Öntön Kyergangpa the Great and reached the culmination of manifest realization in scholarship and practice. He perfected the qualities of the levels and paths, and thereby gained mastery of the domain of great integral unity in a single lifetime. So right after that life, he was born in the eastern buddha field of Avakīrṇakusuma and became enlightened as Victor Padmaśrī, Glorious Lotus. In his last existence as a bodhisattva, he was the great Ringongpa Sangye Tönpa Chökyi Sherap. At a tenth-day communal feast, in response to the entreaty of many disciples, he composed this vajra song:

In the sky of phenomena's realm, Niguma
birthed the Buddha's heirs and bestowed bliss.

Venerable Ratnavīrya (Rinchen Tsöndru),
matured by four empowerments, endowed with three trainings,
attended a supreme guru and realized suchness.

Incomparable Kyergangpa
recognized form and sound as illusion.
Unattached, he helped beings through a deity's form;
a dharma lord, in essence the three kāyas. {509}

I supplicate them with unflagging faith,
not subject to meeting or parting.
All faithful ones gathered here,
please listen a moment to this melody.

The holy guru possessed of lineage
is definitely the buddhas of the three times.
Whoever realizes the guru as dharmakāya
is not ignorant of the meaning of Sutra and Tantra.

Realize the abiding nature of the three bodies like this:
The current body of fully ripened [karma]
was born as a product of the mind.
Based on that, habitual patterns and so forth
create cyclic existence, the mere appearance of joy and sorrow.

As is said, "For the result, look to the past [life];
for the cause, look to the next [life]."[37]

The habits of the daytime saturate
dreams of various faults and qualities.
This is termed the habitual body.

The mental body of the intermediate state
is unhindered and complete in all its senses,
so it is experienced as the previous living body.
It follows after your karma.
If its nature is realized, it is the great-bliss kāya.
If not, you just reenter existence.

This bloody ocean of cyclic existence
is churned by waves of previous anger and desire.
That person with reified attachment,
weary of suffering, has little purpose there.

The fully ripened body is a collection of four elements.
There are many ways to assume a fully ripened body—
without realization, it's in the round of the six kinds of beings.
I assumed the pure illusory body in this way:

The fully ripened body is the Victor's kāya;
it accomplishes all purpose by thought alone.
I am a wanderer in this illusory body with no reference.
The guru of my own mind taught me that.

The mental body is the Victor's kāya;
it accomplishes all purpose by thought alone.
I am a wanderer in this illusory body with no reference.
The guru of my own mind taught me that.

The habitual body is the Victor's kāya;
it accomplishes all purpose by thought alone. {510}
I am a wanderer in this illusory body with no reference.
The guru of my own mind taught me that.

As a result of practicing like that,
the three kāyas arise like this:

Dharmakāya, the unembellished native state,
is unidentifiable as to its essence and
its characteristics are beyond objects of mind.
Indeed *that* is the essence of dharmakāya.

From the dharmakāya, pure as space,
come the two form kāyas,
like a wish-fulfilling tree or gem.
Until cyclic existence is emptied,
they continuously work for others' welfare.

The saṃbhogakāya adorned by marks and signs
appears to bodhisattvas on the ten levels.
The nirmāṇakāya appears to whomever is to be tamed:
to ordinary people and so forth,
and to impure beings, and śrāvakas.
Those three as an inseparable integral unity
are called the sukhakāya, body of bliss.

I have Awareness Ḍākinī Niguma's
maturing and liberating illusory-body instructions.
I'm happy not waiting three incalculable eons.

I have prophecies from the yidam deities—
Hevajra, Cakrasaṃvara, and others—
and every vital point of the instructions.
I'm happy to be without doubts.

I have the Secret Sādhana of the Emanated Navel Chakra,
and the four kinds of generosity to help migrators.
I'm happy not to depend on wrong livelihood.

I have instructions on vase breathing,
the chariot that binds and liberates chakras.
Every instant of meditation on that
makes bliss-heat continually blaze.
I'm happy having that bliss-emptiness.

I have transference through the Skylight of Timeless Awareness.
Even the sinful who recall it at death
go to the celestial realm, so I'm happy too.

I have the dharma protectors: Awareness Protector
and the activity protector Kṣetrapāla.
Since they guard the Buddha's doctrine,
I'm happy that they obey me like servants.

At this special time of the tenth-day waxing moon,
participating in the feast where ḍākinīs gather, {511}

in response to the supplications and requests
of my disciples, who are like my own heart,
I sang this spacious melody of attaining bliss.
It has the blessings of the ḍākinīs.

May all those who hear this melody
realize the guru as dharmakāya,
and may they realize without effort
the mahāmudrā of the deity's form.
All virtue accumulated in the three times
is dedicated to the great awakening of all.

Rigongpa accompanied Yöngom for a short way on his trip to the marketplace and said this in response to his request for teaching:

The precious treasury of the Victor's intent
is the lamplight that dispels the darkness of ignorance.
May there be the auspiciousness of the dharma lord
who spontaneously accomplishes the two pure purposes.

In the fully ripened body, the mind that blends
lucid clarity with the deity's form
knows no cause for sickness or death.
When the breath stops at the time of death,
the suffering of life's interruption is self-purified
and lucid clarity blends with the deity's form.
Meditation object and meditation are liberated in their own ground.
Unborn lucid clarity arises by itself in space
as the two forms of rūpakāya.
Until the ocean of cyclic existence is empty,
they constantly create spontaneous welfare of others.
Such is the instruction for courage at death.

Six-Armed Awareness Protector,
who obeys like a servant, has received my command.
Take him with you on your trip to Tsang, my son.
Apply the four immeasurables and awakening mind

with diligence and go wherever you like.
Please quickly come to see me, your father.
This is my melody of offering auspiciousness.

As recounted at the conclusion of his life story,[38] this vajra testament was granted at the request of the monk Zhönu Senge:

My disciples and their disciples
and all who have connection with me {512}
should abandon misguided thinking
and trust in our ongoing relationship.

My body and the Victor's awakened form
are no different, yogin.
My speech and the Victor's awakened speech
are not separate, yogin.
My mind and the Victor's awakened mind
should be known as one, not two.
The result, the natural arising of a deity's form
inseparable from the three kāyas, is great bliss.

And yet if unlimited devotion does not arise,
you will not see the guru's good qualities.
If ultimate devotion does arise,
the awakened body, speech, and mind
of the guru and buddhas of the three times
is the inexhaustible ornamental wheel
that matures and liberates sentient beings.
Realize this as the excellent awakened activity.

No matter what, hold only a pure view
of that holy guru
and the guru's life story,
without an instant of wrong view.

Until you realize the guru as dharmakāya,
make an effort in excellent practice.
[The guru's] perfect qualities will arise;

this is the ultimate devotion to the liberated life.
Develop pure view, all you students of mine.

"The Vajra Song That Reveals Immortal Mind":

Naturally free unconditioned great bliss;
I bow at the feet of Dharmasiṃha.[39]

In the fully ripened body, the mind that blends
lucid clarity with the deity's form
knows no cause for sickness or death.
Rejecting or accepting samsara and nirvana is freed.

If you know that for even an instant,
then when the breath stops, all the suffering
of transition and so forth will be self-purified
and lucid clarity will merge with the deity's form.

There is neither birth nor death,
neither cessation nor existence.
Freed of something realized or a realizer,
meditation and meditator are self-liberated.

The two form kāyas will last
until the ocean of cyclic existence dries up,
spontaneously accomplishing others' welfare, {513}
appearing constantly without interruption.

These instructions lead to awakening
in a matter of years or months.
By the grace of Guru Kyergangpa,
I realized them for what they were.
The yogin who renounces this life
will be liberated by a week's meditation.

"The Natural Liberation of One's Mind as Immortal" by Venerable Dharmaprajña is complete. I offered the glorious Kyergangpa ten measures (*zho*) of gold and one fur cloak to request it, and I have brought it into my own experience. Three gurus have composed authentic profound esoteric instructions on the Natural Liberation of One's Mind as Immortal. *ithi*

Drogön Sangye Tönpa Tsöndru Senge

He was prophesied by the Ḍākinī of Timeless Awareness as the one who would break the vajra seal of the single lineage of the succession of Seven Jewels that began with Vajradhara. He performed awakened activity throughout all worlds, including that of the gods: Drogön Sangye Tönpa Tsöndru Senge. Here he applies the whip of encouragement for diligence to himself.

I bow at the feet of the Guru Buddha,
the epitome of blessings and compassion.
I have little diligence and great doubt;
I give this advice to my body and mind.

If you just see, without wandering off,
that you made endless plans for this short life,
instead you'll practice meditation for a safe harvest.
Wander into that, great meditator!

If you don't evoke the compassion with devotion
from the clouds of the guru's blessings,
the rain of experiential realization won't fall.
Supplicate the guru, yogin!

If you don't evoke the compassion with approach and attainment
from the yidam's clouds of spiritual powers,
the supreme and common powers won't fall.
Apply yourself to meditation and recitation, yogin!

If you don't evoke compassion with torma and feast
from the dharma protector's clouds of activity,
the rain of actions won't fall.
Apply yourself to torma and feast, yogin! {514}

When practicing supplication, creation, and completion,
don't fall under the influence of discursive thought;

give up hopes and desires for attainment
and meditate without distraction, yogin!

The root of others' welfare is compassion.
Don't think of your own happiness but that of others.
Don't abandon sentient beings in your mind.
Develop a helpful attitude, yogin!

"The Vajra Song of Instruction in Twelve Necessities for Faithful Disciples":

Homage to all the lord gurus.
I supplicate the kind one, whom I need.

I honor those that went before.
Please listen to me for a moment.

Faithful ones who fear birth and death
need a guru possessed of lineage.

For instructions that are beyond doubt,
you need unwavering diligence.

For this short life without leisure,
you need unhurried attention.

To remain in isolated mountain retreat,
you need ever-prolonging patience with hardship.

For anything to arise as meditation,
you need instruction in alchemy.

For self-occurring uncontrived conduct,
you need the eight concerns freed on their own.

For a spontaneous self-arising result,
you need hope and fear freed on its own.

To accomplish awakening in one lifetime,
you need unceasing devotion.

To see the guru as dharmakāya,
you need wrong view freed on its own.

To help migrators by taming their minds,
you need immeasurable great compassion.

This little song of twelve necessities
is a harmonious condition for practice.[40]

When Drogön Sangye Tönpa was intending to demonstrate his departure for the eastern buddha field of Avakīrṇakusuma, he spoke this verse, which captures the essence of his oral instructions, to his disciples:

Guru, yidam, ḍākinīs, and dharma protectors,
protect me as your child with boundless compassion. {515}

The faithful of three places—U, Tsang, and Kham—
and all monks should practice according to this.

Mentally forsake these endless worldly deeds.
Discard your focused fixation on those you can't please.

Spend your time in virtue and defer inexhaustible conversation.
Spurn thoughts of hope and fear that strive after past and future.

There's no leisure in life; sophistry is pointless.
Deer are not quenched by a mirage—drink elixir!

Your own purpose not achieved, you can't help others.
At first, give undivided attention to your own purpose.

Spontaneous welfare of others in this and future lives
occurs through immeasurable compassion for migrators.

Without a moment of entanglement in your own desires,
arouse the spirit of helping beings in whatever you do.

Reflect on death and impermanence constantly;
without any needs, you'll abandon this life.

Your body can accomplish the two purposes in years or months;
meditate constantly on empty appearance without attachment as the deity's form.

With the unsought arising of experience and realization,
constantly pray to the guru with intense longing.

Rely on ḍākinīs and dharma protectors to guard against obstacles
in this life, at death, in the intermediate state, and in the next life.

Outside of your mind there are no buddhas or beings;
therefore know whatever appears as your own mind.

This mind, the empty appearance of the deity's illusory form,
not fixated on illusion, is Lucid Clarity Mahāmudrā.

Beyond ideas of denying or affirming, birth or death, being or not being;
without meditation or mental engagement, samsara and nirvana are freed.

Karma and karmic ripening are released in their own ground.
Free of dualistic clinging, look at great integral unity.

Ema! Everyone has this uncontrived ordinary mind
without knowing it; realize it through [the guru's] kindness.

Now don't question; be decisive and develop certitude.
Actualize the inseparable threefold spontaneous presence.[41]

He gave oral instructions on immortal mind: {516}

I bow to the immortal timeless awareness
of all victorious buddhas of the three times.

Supplicate while endowed with awakening mind
and the practice of guru yoga, then think of your own body
as the empty appearance of the deity's form.

Mind and the deity's form are inseparable:
an empty essence that even buddhas
do not see, did not see, and will not see.

In that there is no cause of sickness or death,
no rejecting and accepting of samsara and nirvana.
If you get that meaning for even an instant,
or recall, hear, or become aware of it,
even during a bad transition where mindfulness falters,
the end-of-life suffering will be self-purified.

Then, in the first intermediate state, lucid clarity
inseparable from saṃbhogakāya and nirmāṇakāya
will always be spontaneously present for others' welfare.

This teaching on immortality, the Victor's intent,
was arranged for the sake of my excellent students.
By that virtue, may sentient beings throughout space
realize the meaning of immortal timeless awareness.

"The Natural Liberation of One's Mind as Immortal" that was written down by Venerable Vīryasiṃha (Tsöndru Senge) for the sake of the most excellent students, the spiritual heirs, is complete. I offered five bags of barley, seven measures of gold, one hybrid yak, and a bolt of fine fabric from Mön to request it, and I have brought it into my own experience.

Khedrup Tsangma Shangtön

The one known as Khedrup Tsangma Shantön was famous throughout the three worlds. He gained the glorious state of one who brings total liberation to anyone when they see, hear, recall, or touch him. He granted these instructions to Khetsun Jakchen Gyaltsen Bum:

Homage to the lord guru,
wise one, unsullied by imperfections,
you dispelled suffering by seeing, hearing, or recalling,
and introduced my mind as dharmakāya.

In order to achieve all welfare for sentient beings
with the desire to attain buddhahood,
one must accumulate all the collections of virtue {517}
and arouse the supreme mind of awakening.

In order to reverse the belief in permanence,
to enter into virtue with diligence,
and be rid of mental attachment and aversion,
meditate again and again on death and impermanence.

Contemplate the unbearable suffering of cyclic existence
and the causes that produce happiness and suffering.
Make the right choices between virtue and nonvirtue.
The corresponding results will inevitably arise.

The way to reverse clinging to the ordinary body
is to meditate without concept on the clarity of the deity's form,
which appears and yet has no intrinsic nature.
The victors' saṃbhogakāya will arise naturally.

The glory that bestows every spiritual power
is the protector who gives refuge from all fears.
Cultivate constant devotion and always supplicate
the glorious protector and holy guru.

Meditate on whatever appears as dream and illusion.
Integrate that through both faith and intention.
Once anger and aversion are liberated in their own ground,
the illusory nature will arise naturally without attachment.

In order to free yourself from clinging to illusion,
rest in the uncontrived native state.
Dualistic concepts will be liberated in their own ground.
Empty clarity without fixation will arise by itself.

The abiding nature of the knowable
is without faults or qualities.
So the yogin who realizes that
engages its meaning without accepting or rejecting.

These appearances of interdependent origin
are complete within the unborn Mother.
Clear empty bliss without fixation arises;
the resulting four kāyas are spontaneously present.

I dedicate the virtue arising from this
to the great unconditioned awakening
of all migrators in common.
That is the special feature of Mahayana.

That completes the teaching that Lama Shangtön Rinpoche gave to Master Gyaltsen Bum.

Tangtong Gyalpo

He was nurtured in person by Niguma, Ḍākinī of Timeless Awareness. {518} He became an unrivaled great adept and received the transmission of the direct lineage of Shangpa teachings. One time when Tangtong Gyalpo was engaging in the secret conduct on the Gyede Plain in Tsang, five awareness ḍākinīs promised to accomplish whatever actions he requested and bestowed [these five] names of suitable meaning on him:

We five girls gathered here
will each give a suitable name
to this most incredible man
staying on the Gyede Plain.

On the great plain of the vast expanse,
the yogin who has realized emptiness
dwells without fear like a king.
Therefore I name you Tangtong Gyalpo,
King of the Empty Plain.

In the valley of unembellished equanimity,
with the view of appearance-emptiness inseparable,
is a madman free of accepting and rejecting.
I name you Madman of the Empty Valley.

Food and drink of a hundred flavors
or bad nauseating filth—whichever comes up,
you extract the nutriment without benefit or harm.
I name you Extractor of Food's Nutriment.

Whatever different conditions arise,
you realize them as like dreams or echoes
with equal taste that overwhelms the eight concerns.
I name you One Who Tastes All Conditions as Equal.

All phenomena of samsara and nirvana appear
and yet they are like water moons;
you fully understand them without offense.
I name you All Things Without Offense.

Yogin beyond compare,
to spread your immeasurable activities
now is the time to lead all migrators
onto the plain of happiness.[42]

The lord himself related this vajra melody of oral instructions on Naturally Free Mahāmudrā to Khetsun Delek Pal:[43]

Listen son, learned monk Delek Pal.
Previously obscured by thick stupidity,
your thoughts to practice dharma

were mixed with the eight worldly concerns. {519}
To accomplish your aims in future lives,
please consider these ideas for practice.

Totally cast out your aims for this life.
Utterly discard clinging to eight concerns.
Thoroughly release fixation and face-saving.
Decisively sever ties to those close and distant.

Extract the stake of existence: self-fixation.
Relax thoughts of hope and fear.
Cut off cravings for food and clothing.
Don't desire status; keep a low profile.

Take on the sufferings of renunciation.
Throw attachment, aversion, and rivalry far away.
Banish evil thoughts of deceit and deception,
and leave hypocritical extortion alone.

Honestly keep the three vows and sacred pledges.
Expel pride, conceit, and anger.
Cultivate patience, though all despise you.
Let loose the ordinary wild enemies
and tame the anger within yourself.

Reject thoughts of miserly hoarding.
Rely on love and compassion in your being.
Establish your own mind as witness
in the dharma of gods and of humans.[44]

If you don't achieve your aims this time,
you'll hope for next time, but hope will be gone.

Relax within the native state.
Cut the taproot of delusion.
Look unwaveringly at your own mind.
Firmly seize mindfulness that never forgets.

If you don't know your own face,
you can try relentlessly but remain afflicted.
If you don't grasp lucid clarity at sleep,
your introduction to mind was not very useful.
If you don't grasp lucid clarity in the intermediate state,
you'll tremble with the suffering of life's interruption.
If you don't gain control over your own mind,
an eon of meditation will just wear you out.

Right after one thought ceases,
before the next one arises, there's a gap.
Within the state of clarity without concept,
without support, free of basis and root,
this fresh awareness of the present moment
is your mind of unembellished dharmakāya. {520}

Whatever arises is all your own mind,
and your mind is unembellished dharmakāya.
So thoughts are dharmakāya's dynamic energy,
unceasing appearance established as empty.

Hold whatever arises and appears with mindfulness,
relax utterly, and let go.
If you recognize yourself, prolong this again and again.
Uncontrived and undistracted, leave everything alone.

Free of going and coming,
or from arising, ceasing, and remaining:
this is mahāmudrā.

It's crucial to integrate this without wavering.
It's crucial to maintain it effortlessly.
Practice like that.

I wander aimlessly through the country.
Both the yogin free of attachment
and the sun that circles the continents
move slowly with no time to linger.

"The Vajra Song of the Natural Liberation of One's Mind as Immortal":

Venerable Guru Buddha,
I respectfully supplicate with body, speech, and mind.

This idea of death is but a semblance
and has no intrinsic nature in its native mode.
Body and mind designated as mortal
are immortal; naturally liberated mahāmudrā.

The fully ripened physical body is deathless,
for how can the habitual dream body die?
Mind's natural radiance is the deity's form,
empty clarity without fixation like a water moon.

The basic condition is empty and unembellished,
without sickness and without death,
without nirvana and without samsara:
all of it is the deluded energy of one's own mind.

The clarity of that energy's display is unceasing;
the unhindered unborn dissolves into basic space.
Without arising, ceasing, or remaining,
this wisdom of immortality is amazing!

Rest within experience without fixation.
Meditate by blending it with all activity.

Whoever becomes accustomed to that
will dissolve into dharmakāya space at death,
achieve the victors' saṃbhogakāya in the intermediate state,
and guide migrators with emanations. {521}

Take this into experience, fortunate ones.

Venerable Great Adept spoke these vajra words on the Natural Liberation of One's Mind as Immortal. *ithi*

Kunga Drolchok

Niguma, Ḍākinī of Timeless Awareness, nurtured him with the transmission of a very direct lineage. Glorious Kunga Drolchok Losal Gyatsoi De was a gentle protector and heroic adept. From his garland of songs spoken in support of Niguma's teachings, these are vajra songs that express the connection with that dharma source.

śrī vajradhara sādhu pāda prāṇamayaṃ

At the zenith of the noble Kagyu's midnight sky,
the adept gurus are as plentiful as the stars.
The brightest sun and moon unhindered by space
must surely be Nāropa and Niguma.

The river flow of practice lineages from those siblings
fully refreshes the fortunate ones even now.
That quenching gift of curative waters
is surely the teachings of Nāropa and Niguma.

The lord protectors of those two traditions
were glorious unrivaled emanated bodies,
single crown jewels of our many realized ones
in the two Kagyu lineages of Dakpo and Shangpa.

Formerly led by Tilo and Nāro,
later preserved by Marpa and Mila,
the profound vital teaching of Nāro's Six Dharmas
produced innumerable adepts with signs of success.

These days, as in the case of [watered-down] market milk,
the words are uncertain, like the babble of a lunatic,
random meanings led by personal ideas,
that left this man's mind somewhat dissatisfied.

Sister Ḍākinī's secret words of innermost potency
were uncorrupted in *The Inventory*, [sealed by] a vajra knot.
The meaning, the true nature of reality, fell into my heart
and gladdened my lowly mind, reviving the path to liberation.

If you have a mind to follow me,
don't think your painful tension is meditation.
Don't present your accomplishments for show.
I put this carefree heartfelt advice to song. {522}

They say the root of spiritual powers is the guru.
They say the guru is the actual Buddha.
They say one must regard the guru's acts as good.
They say beautiful things, but it's just noise.

Whether or not I attain spiritual powers,
whether [the guru] is a buddha or sentient being,
whether good or bad deeds are displayed,
I personally have not an iota of egotistical doubt.

In the upper region, in the Akaniṣṭha palace,
dharmakāya is so-called Great Vajradhara,
deep blue in an effulgence of light rays.
This draws in the small-minded—how incredible!

In the lower region, in Mokchok of Shangpu,
inside the palace of a renunciant's thatched hut,
a human form blazes with light of melting bliss:
Great Vajradhara Gyagom dwells there.

You are inseparable from the primordial ground,
temporarily clothed as a hidden one of deliberate conduct.
But don't the fortunate see you clearly
as a lamp shining within a vase?

My past karmic propensity was not meager:
I understood illusion's own dynamic display from youth
and I saw Mother Ḍākinī's sublime face.
But I was still unsatisfied; it was just illusion's guise.

When I first discovered the visage of Father Lekgyal,[45]
all my mental obsessions freed up by themselves.

A single certitude devoid of doubt was born
which has not changed since that time.

Fixation on equipoise and subsequent attainment faded,
I forgot the distinction of meditation sessions and breaks,
let go of judgment whether "this is it" or "this isn't it,"
and lost the biases of self and other, close and distant.

When the great light of all-pervading empty clarity
arose in the mirror of my intrinsic awareness,
I gained the confidence that the terms of designations,
distinctions, and analyses would show up if needed.

Lord, if you are not possessed of knowledge,
how did you make a stupid fellow like me wise?
If you are not the one endowed with blessings,
how did I show signs of liberation upon arising? {523}

Now, even if the buddhas of the three times arrived,
I would have no further issues to resolve.
Natural thought, like a bird's path in the sky,
travels freely without leaving a trace.

Even meditation is just the guru's natural appearance.
It would be well to rest in clarity and openness,
and to experience yoga and not sporadic practice.
Whether I go high or low, you will know.

Although supplications may be melodious,
if engaged with a hesitant divided mind,
in the long run, wouldn't it just be the song
of a prostitute to seduce the clueless?

Nonsensical words that speak indirectly
agitate the hearts of formless gods and demons.
Fervently recalling the guru and calling from afar;
how could your compassion not stir from basic space?

I, the father, those who have become my children,
and spiritual siblings joined in a single intention
have no other place of hope or reliance than you:
Lord, please prolong your life of liberation.

This was a teaching that supports the guru yoga by means of which one perfects the path through a singular thought of devotion, expressed here in a song. *ithi*

Refuge that I needn't seek elsewhere, Gyagom,
I take refuge in you with mind undivided.
Father, unerring lord guru,
turn your one child's mind to dharma.

In action, I diligently pursued worldly thoughts,
my body disciplined, yet my mind shameful.
In name I'm called religious, but I am a hypocrite.
This you see with your compassion, my chief guru.

The place, samsara, though I seem to know its faults,
my mind is ever wandering in useless activity.
Mentally suspicious, my body is left behind in retreat.
This should be abandoned; please see it with wisdom.

In character, I am decidedly tough.
On the spot, I don't hide from nonsense.
I am betrayed by myself, turning my own head. {524}
Father, doesn't this just stir your tears of love?

In dharma, my fiction of knowledge and awareness
mentally pleases me with my own childish prattle.
Of meditation and the like I take little account.
Father, does this not concern you?

Karma's impressions in my mind are inexhaustible.
My character is not detached from samsara's swamp.
Present-time consciousness has not been recognized.
This song of what I'm missing is getting long!

Hey! This piled-stone illusion of a monk's form,
intelligent or stupid—it's deluded to analyze it.
The venerable image of lovely qualities is a rainbow.
Fixated concepts analyzing its value are vulgar.

Samsara's pit of nasty vomit is ruinous
when touched with the idea that it's delicious.
Mind's indefinite perceptions are pervasive.
To take a tenuous stand on their existence is crazy.

In mindfulness with singular mental consciousness,
witnessing [my own] nondharmic [thoughts] was rough.
Whatever I've done is reflected in illusion's mirror.
By the code of true or false, it was all distraction and deceit.

What I've done has destroyed the crops of emancipation,
scorched by the drought of my conceptual analysis.

I understand but will not leave it at that,
nor ever leave *meditation* as an empty word.
Now if I die it is good; living is also okay.
My aim, I know, is to consummate virtue.

This long-distance [calling] expressed as song was composed spontaneously as a whip to encourage my vigilance. *ithi*

The expanse of dharmakāya, everlasting svāstika,[46]
its radiance, unimpeded appearance, is the actual letter,
a vowel, the invincible natural sound of nāda,
mind's empty movement arising in essence as *A*.

E becomes the source of phenomena, the lion throne,
meaning the great emptiness, the palace of five letters.
Vaṃ is great bliss, unconditioned lucid clarity.
Within, the vital drops of six letters are the gathered deities.

The name *buddha nature* is one that is known, {525}
the one that completely pervades all sentient beings.
I, myself, the yogin, am delighted by this sacred glory.

Timeless unchanging mandala produces
pristine water, a falling rain of elixir.
Mind's latent patterns of conceptual thought,
karma, and afflictions' origins are cleansed.

Mind's own awareness and clarity is a great radiance.
Mentation from afar is the single dharmakāya.
Intellect turning back is the end of analytical process.
Mentation becomes open, spacious, and vivid.[47]

Now the mental patterns fade and vanish.
The body of flesh and blood is pure rainbow-like form.
Speech is beyond word, thought, and expression; mute.
Mind is a state without tracks, like a bird in the sky.

The meaning is the arising of original timeless awareness.
The ground is the collapse of the small dark house of ignorance.
Habitual patterns of impure karma and afflictions are expelled.
The name *ordinary individual* is transcended.
Meditation is met on the great path beyond intellect.

Eighty-four thousand dharmas were contained in *A*,
surely taught by the divine Śākyamuni.
But without understanding this summation of vital points,
repeating the words and letters is just recitation.

This was a song proclaimed for the occasion of practicing the Purifying *A* of Inner Space. *ithi*

Unobscured natural form arises as the deity:
Goddess Yoginī, chief of the glorious ḍākinīs,
the experience of youthful intoxication with empty bliss,
produced in the mind by the essence on the lord's lap.

Outwardly, appearance is the divine celestial palace.
Inwardly, [the body] is a red silk tent, smooth and bright.
To the sides there are four spheres of blazing fire.
Crucially, it is like a fire brand at the navel chakra.

Flames radiating from *raṃ* at the triple junction
shoot lightning up the wide central channel,
passing, white and clear, out the cranial aperture
like shooting stars zooming through space.

Liquid elixir flows from the lord guru's body
and enters fully through your cranial aperture, {526}
setting up connections for four empowerments on the path.
Your mind and the guru's become inseparable.

That was a song for commencing Fierce Inner Heat. *ithi*

Mind's appearances and whatever arises experienced as illusion.
Spontaneous mindfulness is the path of awakening.
The vital point that nails it is the guru's teaching.
Hold the retention of not forgetting this.

Grasping with mindful awareness is beginner's meditation.
The path of analytic meditation is a situational teaching.
A spacious state of inaction in the nature of phenomena
is liberating all things by knowing one thing—it's amazing!

That was a song for the practice of Illusory Body. *ithi*

The perception of dreams is the edge of experience.
Intentionality is joined with speech of mental cognition.
Four movements of vital drops are the vital point of
interdependence.
This is the secret advice of the Mother Ḍākinī of Awareness.

The vagrant mind has no fixed reference point,
so it's not far to go up to Tuṣita heaven.
For example, there's nothing that cannot arise in the mind that
illuminates everything.
Ease of changing instantly into what is needed is the yogin's experience.

Accept all experiences without judgment.
Always guide mindfulness without interruption.

This was a song for the practice of Dream. *ithi*

The ground lucid clarity is unchanging, eternal body.
The path lucid clarity is the unimpeded bliss aspect.
The ultimate result is manifest perfect buddhahood.
This joins the vital points of ground, path, and result.

[This was a song for the practice of Lucid Clarity.]

The path of Transference is buddhahood without meditation.
With intense mental focus [on *A*], the arrow of mindfulness
shoots far out from the path of the cranial aperture
and without mental wavering, remains fully in dharmakāya.

[This was a song for the practice of Transference.]

Whatever karmic appearances are occurring right now
are fundamentally nonexistent, like the moon in water.
When the import of this arises with certainty,
you gain the victors' saṃbhogakāya later in the intermediate state.

This was a song for the practice of the Intermediate State. *ithi*

Jamyang Khyentse Wangchuk[48]

Nesarpa Jampaiyang Khyentsei Wangchuk Tenpai Gyaltsen Palzangpo's song of supplication summarizes the essence of the graded path of the Golden Dharmas of the Glorious Shangpa. {527} It is called "The Heart's Elixir."[49]

namo guruve

1. Lord Vajradhara, embodiment of all victors,
supreme crown jewel of all dharma practice lineages;
Father with whom I have meaningful connection, Kartsipa,[50]
bless me that the son becomes equal to the father.

2. This fresh ordinary mind
not swayed by the four faults[51]
sees its own essence nakedly;
bless me to realize ground mahāmudrā.

3. Below the navel, short *A* blazes with light,
churned by the winds of vital energy,[52]
it burns the fuel of subject-object dualism;
bless my training on the path of Fierce Inner Heat.

4. All dualistic appearance of apparent existence and
samsara-nirvana,
while nonexistent, arises as a multitude.
To realize the hidden nature of intrinsic emptiness,
bless my training on the path of Illusory Body.

5. Strong habitual patterns of double delusion
can be recognized upon arising,
the manifestation of unreality blazes;
bless my training on the path of Dream.

6. When all patterns of ignorant reification
dissolve into the expanse of emptiness,
shining forms of emptiness arise unhindered;
bless my training on the path of Lucid Clarity.

7. Three bodies of deluded appearance are the victors' kāyas.
The recognition of their primordial presence
liberates fear of dualistic appearance in its own ground;
bless my training on the path of the Intermediate State.

8. Not bound by attachment to this life,
not depressed with the fear of death,
I'll transit freely to the realm of reality;
bless my training on the path of Transference.

9. As all apparent existence is the guru's display,
no need to accept or reject, complicate or simplify. {528}

Through my constant intense longing,
bless me to traverse the path by way of the guru.

10. As all samsara and nirvana is the victors' mandala,
I am not bound by fixation on the ordinary.
With awareness of whatever arises as the deity's form;
bless me to traverse the path by way of the yidam.

11. In knowing all appearance as unreal illusion,
I am not bound by reifying fixation.
Untainted by attachment to fixating on illusion;
bless me to traverse the path by way of illusion.

12. This emptiness of my mind is Yoginī,
its dynamic energy is Vārāhī's illusory dance.
I pleased her with feast substances of Secret Mantra;
bless me to achieve the celestial realm of basic nature.

13. Application of the supreme five branches [and] dissolution,[53]
purifies the gate to the impure womb [birth];
I playfully frolic in the bhaga of emptiness.
Bless me with realization of the path of integral unity.

14. The mount of consciousness is karmic winds;
binding them through the application of yogic exercise
brings channels, winds, and drops under control;
bless me to accomplish Immortal Body.

15. Uncontrived consciousness is illusory form,
in a state of great bliss; the dance of father and mother.
Maintaining one's own essence without distraction;
bless me to accomplish Infallible Mind.

16. Glorious Awareness Protector Avalokita,
with outer, inner, and secret offerings I rely on you.
Controlled by the path of creation, completion, and recitation;
bless me to achieve the actions I request.

17. The meaning is the Ḍākinī's heart advice of vajra words,
in the Five Golden Dharmas of profound teaching,
a hundredfold wealth of theory and practice;
bless me to mature into a worthy vessel.

18. From now until I attain buddhahood,
may I never be apart from you, Lord,
and accomplish whatever pleases you;
bless me in this path of meditation. {529}

19. Bless me and those who look to me
with your great compassion.
Bless us with the accomplishment of glorious Cakrasaṃvara,
the lucid clarity of our true nature: dharmakāya.

This was a song of spontaneous aspirations for the Golden Dharmas of Lama Shangpa. *ithi*

Tāranātha

His renunciation and realization were indistinguishable from the mighty adepts of India. He was Great Vajradhara for this age of conflict. At glorious Devīkoṭa, the Awareness Ḍākinī granted him her secret treasury, making him the great champion of the profound path of this very direct transmission. Kunga Nyingpo, or more famously known by the name Jetsun Tamche Khyenpa Tāranātha, ("Venerable All-Knowing Tāranātha") composed many vajra dohas. At the age of twenty-three, while residing at Samding, he gave this counsel to himself as an incentive.[54]

oṃ svasti
I bow to the three precious sources of refuge
and say these words that dawned in my mind.

You tell of meditating in mountain retreats,
which makes a good impression in others' eyes.
But on closer examination, your mind is not joined to dharma.
How can this be the honest Holy Dharma?

Now it's time to practice from the heart.
Discard this life's goals, hollow man!

You hasten to teach, supervising study and contemplation,
but at the slightest adversity abandon the Holy Dharma.
Renowned as a scholar, you're a waste of a human life.
How can someone like you be a good spiritual mentor?
Now it's time to tame your mind.
Point your finger inward, hollow man!

You see the fleeting nature of cyclic existence
but really don't believe it and become negligent.
When it's time to pass on, you will not feel confident,
yet you don't worry about it; a careless madman. {530}
Now it's time to prepare for the next life.
Turn your mind to the dharma, hollow man!

You need nothing more, yet you harbor attachment and aversion.
Your pride in your qualities is as big as Mount Meru.
You conform to social norms, though no one is impressed.
You who have done so little but expect so much:
now it's time to reject the eight worldly concerns.
Whatever happens has the same value, hollow man!

You can't give up even a little sleep for the sake of dharma.
Later this year will do, you think with good-natured forbearance.
You want instant signs of experience, you empty braggart.
You don't control your desire for food, wealth, and fame.
Now it's time to concentrate on a single intention.
Be rid of your deepest hopes and fears, hollow man!

After adolescence, youth fades and deteriorates.
All your followers just repay benefit with harm,
yet you are still open-minded and not sick of it.
You plan for this life as if you don't know better.
Now it's time to wholeheartedly stop activities.
Train your mind to be impartial, hollow man!

All who bear the title of guru don't practice the dharma.
All their disciples are not keepers of sacred pledge.
All the people even lack shame and conscientiousness.
In these hard times of decline of the Buddha's doctrine,
no matter how many ways you try to help others,
mostly it just harms yourself and does not help them.

Once you gain stability in the dharma,
the benefit for others will arise continuously.
Give up the sporadic semblance of helping others
in this life and concentrate on yourself.

This is the time to embrace the Holy Dharma.
Since that is indeed the case, keep it in mind.

The following essential introduction was given to Tāranātha's excellent student from Gangkar, the faithful Nyima Namgyal.[55]

Great Vajradhara in the form of an adept,
just hearing your name is meaningful.
Please turn my disciple's mind to the dharma;
I supplicate you, a treasure of compassion. {531}

At this time, you have obtained a human birth
and met a qualified spiritual master.
If you don't strenuously apply yourself to practice,
you are in jeopardy of a meaningless life.

Devotion is the sovereign of practice.
Renunciation is the sovereign of favorable conditions.
Nonaction is the sovereign of activity.
Self-arising equipoise is the sovereign of equipoise.

This esoteric instruction possessed of four sovereigns
is the speech of the qualified guru.
It is the whole heart's essence of the adepts.
It is Tāranātha's personal experience.

Practice with attributes is insufficient;
a happy dharma of no help in times of suffering.
Sure, it is a skillful way of guidance,
but it can't bring buddhahood within reach.
To see your own face nakedly,
you need devotion to a qualified master.

It is sweet talk to say the guru is buddha,
and loyal to say you must see what the guru does as good.
That devotion is just unproductive thought;
the reverse of the fullness from deep within.

Even an excellent resolve of "I will practice dharma"
is not seeing the meaning beyond the words.

With unbiased assessment of buddhas and beings
by the mind in the single unborn dharmakāya,
even faulty actions can be useful;
the unbiased welfare of migrators is huge.

Whether blessings enter you or not,
whether you attain spiritual powers or not,
supplicate with a decisive mind:
"I have no other place of refuge."
Rest in equipoise of your inseparable minds;
how could you prevent meditation from arising?

The desire for happiness by hoarding food and clothes
is a tremendous distraction from virtuous practice. {532}
To assign it the name "favorable conditions"
is a total distraction that the yogin doesn't need.

Strong renunciation and disillusionment
are your consolers when you live alone
and your nurses when you are sick.
The distraction of obsessing over food and clothes
is the "favorable condition" of reversing your progress.

There is not a single thing you have not done before,
yet all you've done has been food for cyclic existence.
Now, just rest and relax in nonaction.
That is how to reach the permanent safe place.
Even if you strive at mind-made virtue,
you won't reach the changeless safe place.

With that vital point of basic space without change,
if you just let go, you will attain an unchanging state.
Do not seek to fabricate natural arising;
it's extremely important to recognize the uncontrived.

In mind's own clarity, free of discursive thought,
that clarity is lucid and empty.
If you recognize your own nature, it is dharmakāya.
When you know that as your own nature,
no matter how great the apparitions of concept
or how many perceptions of joy and suffering,
they are all the shifting display of dharmakāya.

There's no difference between thought and nonthought.
The faults of abiding or moving [thoughts] are destroyed.
Like ice melting into water,
whatever appears is vividly your own mind.
Object and subject are unhindered perceptions of mere emptiness.

From the buddhas' three kāyas above
down to the hell realms below,
don't act to prevent anything arising.
Let whatever arises be free of embellishment.
Beyond the purview of all verbal expression,
experience the great bliss of your intrinsic awareness.

Again, enhance virtuous practice with attributes;
it's all the shifting display of mahāmudrā.
To perfect the two accumulations of method and wisdom
is to realize the intention of the buddhas. {533}

If you cultivate that experience, it is like elixir,
but if it is just loose talk, it is meaningless.
Seek to practice directly in your mind stream.
I ask you to assimilate this as your practice.

Again Tāranātha granted this personal advice to crack the whip of renunciation.[56]

namo guru bhyaḥ
I pay homage to Father Vajradhara
and express here three words of heartfelt advice.

The appearances of this life are like a rainbow;
please don't chase after them.
These appearances are surely a creation of mind;
please don't fixate on them as separate.

If intrinsic awareness does not arise without attachment,
your successful meditation could be a sham.
If you don't firmly grasp your own mind,
you could squander life on useless activity.
If you don't totally wrap up your own welfare,
you'll fool yourself with the semblance of helping others.

This unique opportunity of a human body
is very difficult to obtain over and over.
Once you are born in the three bad states,
there's no chance to meet the Holy Dharma.

Right now if you take one misstep and slip,
you'll fall like a millstone to the depths of hell.
The results of virtue that benefit the next life
and engaging in practice are just like that.
Unvirtuous acts and violations fall like rain.
Think about that and devote yourself to dharma.

The suffering of old age quickly approaches.
Once sickness and the unwanted occur,

consciousness is pained by suffering
and it's hard to be taken on the path of dharma.
Please pursue dharma while you are still at ease.

During our temporary human life,
the growth and decay of our country,
the circumstances of our gurus and masters,
the fortunes of our fellow monastics and tantric siblings,
and the situations of our parents, friends, and enemies
all expose the inherent flaw of impermanence. {534}

Presently, each passing year, month, and day
is a spiritual master who teaches impermanence
and inspires disillusionment, standing right here beside us.

All acts that we have ever done in this life,
no matter what they are, must be abandoned.
Give up activity, my child, and pursue practice.

Your transient body of flesh and bone seems pleasing,
but no matter how much you cherish it,
in the end it will be a heap of bones.

The wealth you strenuously accumulated by avarice
will be taken and distributed by who knows who.
Even the food and clothing currently in your possession
are death shrouds and dry corpse food.
Even though you amass a mighty army,
when the uncertain time of death comes,
you'll relinquish wealth, power, and enjoyment
and again face roaming in the three bad places.
Still, impermanence is the way of all composite things.
Think on its meaning and devote yourself to dharma.

Train in universal love and compassion
and maintain nonattachment to whatever arises now.
In this life, the next, and the intermediate state,
at all times and circumstances, the most precious

is to maintain confidence in your guru.
Please supplicate the guru from your heart.
Anyway, that would certainly not deceive you.

Maintain renunciation, compassion, devotion,
and nonattachment without distraction—
if you persevere in those four points,
you will reach the summit of your intentions.

Tāranātha said this at Daryul Draknak in response to a request by Rinchen Tashi, the realized one of Gyalzang, for personal instruction.

Homage to all gurus.

Son, appearances are not different in the mind.
Whatever arises, remain without fabrication.
Compassion and emptiness are two sides of the same coin.
Don't lose your hold on compassion
and leave it in nihilistic emptiness:
it's important to practice them in union. {535}

A "great meditator" who narrowly focuses on
the wrong choices concerning actions and their results,
or spurns the renunciation of needing nothing at all,
or secedes from the attitude of universal altruism,
or boasts with highfalutin language of mahāmudrā,
or practices the subtle body yogas of non-Buddhists
may be clever at confusing the gullible
but has strayed from the Buddha's joyful path.

Son, if you do as the Buddha taught,
since that *is* the cause for attaining buddhahood,
your body, speech, and mind will be in harmony with the dharma,
without a lot of frenzied attempts to seem good.

With a view both high and wide,
actions meticulous and appropriate,

and constant meditation without distraction;
these three will mature as the result.

Phonies who wander around the country
using their eloquence to pursue food and drink
won't exude even a whiff of a great meditator.
Please stay in isolation in the mountains.

With attachment and fondness for idle talk,
how can you ever achieve the spoken truth?
Recite the mantras of Secret Mantra if you can.
If not, it is best to remain silent.

If you conform and try to please others with unvirtuous acts,
though you rest the mind, desire and anger will just increase.
It's difficult to give this up even if you want to,
so vigorously cut them off and leave them far behind.

When a little meditative experience arises
but you fixate on its excellence, the devil kidnaps you.
Like falling into a ravine while climbing a mountain,
it's crucial to take great care during the ascent.

Practice all the guru's personal instructions
without letting them go to waste.
Don't become haughty or boastful;
be happy just to meditate with a single intent.

The following was spoken to some yogins of Latö Palung who requested instruction: {536}

namo guru
Sovereign guru, my single sufficient father,
I supplicate you continuously without a break.
Turn my disciples' minds to the dharma
and bless them to realize all-pervasive mind.

At this time, you've accrued all favorable conditions,
you have met a qualified spiritual master
and received many profound instructions.
Now, no matter what, do not render them futile.

This body is a composite heap of flesh and bones,
unbefitting to hold as stable and permanent.
Establish your virtuous practice right away
without postponing it to a later time.

Those without meditative experience make false claims
and mouth on with assertions about emptiness.
They are at risk of succumbing to dark, empty talk.
It's vitally important to scrutinize cause and effect.

With unceasing longing devotion,
fervently engage in supplicating the guru.
But please don't cling to that as real.
Your mind and the guru's are no different.

Not knowing yourself, you wander cyclic existence,
but irresistible compassion is most important.
The delusion of clinging to its reality tricks you.
Regard all joy and sorrow as a dream.

This ordinary consciousness of your mind
need not be modified, for it is dharmakāya.
Whatever arises are the experiences of discursive thought.
Understand them to be like water and waves.

However meticulous your conduct,
please don't be false and hypocritical.
It's crucial to be in harmony with dharma.
Perverse "great meditators": *phaṭ*—be gone!

For continuous meditation day and night,
it's most important to lack action or work.

Effortlessly maintain that with mindfulness.
If you are left in the dark: *te le le*—despair!

The fruition, this buddha of your own mind,
is fundamental, not from baseless delusion.
Do not fall into the abyss of hopes and fears.
You need assurance of knowing this decisively.

All that appears is the dharmakāya. {537}
Sure, it's fine not to make biased distinctions,
but artificial pure view undermines autonomy.
Stick to your guru's lineage.

This one time, when Tāranātha was staying at Yoru in Tsang, all appearances arose to him as teachers to introduce [the nature of mind]. So he sang this vajra song.[57]

oṃ svasti
Here in Yoru where auspiciousness spreads
at the time of flowers in the Ox year,
I, a yogin free from bias,
fondly recall my kind lord guru.

Indeed, I have previously wandered until now
in cyclic existence from beginningless time.
Yet, here in this cycle without bottom or boundary,
the precious one sends beings[58] to buddhahood.

Although the six kinds of migrators are kind parents,
not one has helped me out of cyclic existence;
no guide to prepare me for everlasting [happiness].
For such essential plans I ask my mentor.

This physical composite of flesh and blood
will destruct we know not at all when.
Those who lack confidence in the afterlife,
please focus inward with this knowledge.

Fearing my death, I sought out a guru.
I fully applied all practices, as rock breaks bone.
Since then, I know I'll be perfectly fine when I die.
Don't you need a provision for such a carefree state?

First, these ever-changing four seasons;
second, these pictures of rising and falling prosperity;
third, these grave changes in the land and country:
these are the same teacher showing impermanence of the conditioned.

First, this farming that never ends;
second, these mean, ungrateful responses to care;
third, the salt water that doesn't quench when drunk:
these are the same teacher who shows us futility in action.

First, this seething bustle of the village; {538}
second, this busy-bee activity of insignificant toil;
third, these wispy white clouds that flex and roil:
these are the same introduction showing aimless samsara.

First, this rainbow of formless appearance;
second, this clear echo without locality;
third, this unreal dream that produces joy or pain:
these are the same teacher who shows appearance as mind.

First, the magical machinations of outer appearances;
second, the doors of perception of inner mental awareness;
third, the emptiness of basic space without identity:
these are the same inseparability of pouring water into water.

But when a little meditation experience is born,
any and all appearances demonstrate this.
Any acts of the three doors serve to enhance it.
When you think about this meaning—*a la la!*

Now then, whatever little is left of this life
will be spent in accomplishing the practice,

keeping to remote mountain retreats,
and integrating whatever arises on the path.

Surely my benevolent, precious guru
granted inconceivable blessings in the past.
Now again please grant your blessings;
Dharma Lord, I have no other refuge.

When Tāranātha saw the apparent changes in the country, they seemed to be introducing mind's nature, so he rendered it into song.

While participating in a communal feast in Yardrok Taklung, the natural sound of the vajra nāda resounded:[59]

namo mahāmudrāya
In basic space, the sky of great bliss,
the impartial energy of intrinsic timeless awareness displays
bright stars of knowledge, love, and power.
Lord, glorious guru Vajradhara,
this vagabond respectfully supplicates you:
bless me again, compassionate one.

In the upper regions, the pure realm,
is the unchanging form of the mind of great bliss.
He is known as Vajradhara, {539}
said to be the principal of all mandalas.
But he is not somewhere else—
indeed he is my one father root guru.
Lord, through the kindness of your compassion
this person has gained some stability.

I derive joy from my decisive confidence in the basic ground,
the uncontrived abiding nature of the native state.
In the natural appearances of mind's radiant clarity
there is not a single thing that might not arise.
This liberation at the very moment of arising—
is it not the yoga of self-liberation?

This total recognition of my essence without wavering
is indeed called "meditation of calm abiding."
This rootlessness of not finding an intrinsic nature—
is it not the wisdom of higher insight?

When I knew the lord inseparable from my mind,
it was not hard to meet the face of dharmakāya.
For the yoga of seeing one's own face,
arouse[60] devotion beyond meeting and parting.

I have obtained a free and endowed human form,
encountered the dharma in general,
and found the Secret Mantra in particular.
More specially, this knowledge of profound meaning
is a sign that I previously accumulated a little merit.

My mind has turned somewhat to the dharma,
I was nurtured by a qualified guru, my lord,
I am certain of the dharma, Sutra and Tantra,
and presently I am unbiased by desire or aversion.
Thus, wherever I stay I'll be happy.

I'm not fooled by the delights of this life's sights,
nor taken by the pleasant-sounding flattery.
I don't harbor aspirations for power and influence.
Thus, my mind will be at ease at all times.

Outwardly, a mundane impersonator of a religious person,
inwardly, holding evil within while speaking pleasant words,
ultimately, helping others for winning personal desires—
I renounced these three intentions and turned to the dharma.
This approach was also due to the glorious guru's kindness.

Once again I supplicate you well: {540}
please grant your blessings, compassionate one.
Lord, by your blessings of compassion
may there be abundant auspiciousness
in all places, times, and situations.

The song "Essence of Elixir" is based on the oral instructions relating to the progressive path of the Glorious Shangpa's Golden Dharmas:

namo guruve
In the unborn sky of basic space,
mandalas of unhindered radiance abound
with a hundred lights of compassion—
I bow to Vajradhara, my father guru.

From the rainclouds of your compassion
falls a steady rain of dharma instructions.
It falls on the field of this one's mind,
producing the fruit of experiential realization.
If you [disciples] are lucky, you'll take this from me.

That one called Glorious Great Vajradhara
[taught] infinite tantras, with five essential ones.
A direct path that encompasses many profundities
is called the Six Dharmas of Niguma.

The secret words of all mother ḍākinīs,
the definitive secret, essence of elixir,
is elixir from the mouth of my father guru.

Today, this wandering yogin,
whose conduct is aimless begging
while behaving in indefinite ways,
will sing a vajra song of essential meaning
in this glorious citadel of Rigong.

In the chakra of great bliss in the head,
the symbol *A* signifies the unborn,
emanating a stream of elixir; the vital point of visualization
that ensures our faults, sins, and obscurations are purified.
The name of this is Purifying Inner Space,
the vitally important preliminary practice.

The support is the vajra body, channels, and vital-essence motion;
the basis of vital importance is the four chakras;
now blazing, melting, and four ecstasies move in the body:
this is the vitally important definitive secret of the tantras.

The condition is the meeting of method and wisdom;
the basis is introduction to one's native mind; {541}
the support is the fall and rise of the four ecstasies:
that is the karma[mudrā] of Fierce Inner Heat.
That is to say, instructions on another's body,
the vitally important integration of sense pleasures.

I myself meditated on bliss and emptiness inseparable.
You, assembled here, should practice bliss-emptiness inseparable.
If you want to reach awakening in one lifetime,
there is no other way, fortunate ones.
Try to practice this innate blazing of bliss and heat.

Outward appearance is integrated on the path of illusion,
a body is produced but is just the mind's own appearance.
The self-arising self-appearance of the deity's form
is like an illusion, without intrinsic nature.
This is the essence of Illusory Body instruction.

I myself also practiced this.
Appearances of attraction and aversion were purified in place.
The coiled snake of reification was released.
You, assembled here, should seek the release of reification.

Now, vital points of intentionality and transformation
bring the self-energy of awareness, impartial radiance.
To liberate the bonds of fixating on the reality of things,
it is vitally important to train in unfixed ways.
The designated name is instruction on Dream.
It is required for those who practice Illusory Body.

The basis is to see your own original face;
the condition is intense longing devotion;

the vital point is to make the link of wind-mind united,
by which mind [is known as] vajra nature, great Lucid Clarity.

In time, generating effort repeatedly in the day
brings nighttime's self-arising lucid appearances.
Emptiness arises from mere clarity itself.
This is called lucid clarity of clarity-emptiness inseparable.

By blending the bliss of melting with the native state,
the experience of mere bliss itself is self-purified.
This is the lucid clarity of bliss-emptiness inseparable.

In the mind's nature, which is pure since forever,
the false empty effigy of two obscurations vanishes.
This is the lucid clarity of having two purities. {542}

Regarding that result of the path of Lucid Clarity,
in the presence of my lord Great Vajradhara
I requested instructions, leaving no room for doubt.
And I didn't leave it as a mere request—
I practiced blending them with my own mind.

Impressions of hazy experiences were purified
and I gained a lasting place of unchanging realization.
You, assembled here, should meditate single-mindedly on lucid clarity.

The vital point of amazing wind-mind's magic
is to shoot the focused mind upward and train
with intentionality of the intermediate state, whatever appears.
Integrate on the path whatever arises as pure perception.
Called instructions of Transference and Intermediate State;
they are vitally important for beginners.

In the face of the native state of uncontrived mind,
rest within the vast naked state of whatever arises.
The state with the three doors fresh and uncontrived
is called instructions on relaxed, Naturally Settled State.

Meditate in a state of purity and brilliance;
a relaxed, loose, and open state.
For a yogin who recognizes whatever arises as mind,
it is liberated on its own ground as soon as it arises.
By name, this is called instruction of Self-Liberation.

Clarity, emptiness, and their integral unity, these three,
whether mind abides or moves or whatever,
is recognized as primordially indwelling.
This is called instruction of Self-Arising Three Kāyas.
Movement dissolves within emptiness of movement.
The line between equipoise and postmeditation collapses.

Many possess vast knowledge of Sutra and Tantra,
and certainly there are many masters of instruction.
But few admit "there is no other significance than this."
This yoga of Naturally Free Mahāmudrā
I know is definitely the heart of Sutra and Tantra.
I also brought it into experience in that way.
You, assembled here, should also practice like that.

The self-arising is one with impartial pure perception.
In integrating devotion with whatever appears,
the root of devotion arises as the guru.
In the inseparability of the guru and the yidam, {543}
that yidam is one with the self-arising of illusion.
It is the radiance of relaxed uncontrived self-arising;
the guidance of impartial pure perception.
This is called the Three Integrations on the Path.
I trained in impartial pure perception.
You, assembled here, should also train in impartial pure perception.
The vital point of unceasing method is pure perception.

Mind's clarity-emptiness appearing as the deity's form
and intrinsic awareness within the state of unchanging bliss
were never born in the first place.
What is not born cannot cease.

The unborn, undying intrinsic nature of mind
is introduced at present by the kind guru.
By name, this is called One's Own Mind as Immortal.
It is the heart of creation and completion rolled into one.

The vital point of practice is to bind in basic space
these three: vital winds, thought, and mind.
Mastery of yogic exercises brings energy to practice.
Introduction of the four ecstasies in basic space
comes from the self-liberation of retaining vital drops
in the unobstructed practice based on another's body.
By name, this is called One's Own Body as Immortal.
Yogin, get control of your vital winds and mind!

The vital point of accomplishing the four activities
is both the benevolent root guru
and Swift-Acting Awareness Protector.
With different names, they are not really different.
The yoga practice of this unique devotion
causes an upsurge of the two spiritual powers
that surely arises spontaneously to benefit beings.

I offer this melody to the authentic master.
I offer this melodious song of experience
to all the gurus from Glorious Great Vajradhara
through to my father root guru.

To you, fortunate women and men assembled here,
I give a sublime taste of this secret elixir
in the fine fashion of a celebration.
I, a wanderer without direction or bias,
am a carefree yogin of equal tastes, {544}
a destroyer of the enemy fort of eight concerns,
a resident of the safe place of the native state,
and a seer of the actual face of all things.
Though not ignorant of religious terminology,
my wish for excellence in erudition was lost in space.

Now, with just the appearance of ordinary body-mind,
the name given by my kind preceptor
was Kunga Nyingpo.[61]
The one who introduced the nature of my mind,
the kind one who sends people to buddhahood,
my benevolent father guru
bestowed the name Tāranātha.[62]
Today I have spoken this heartfelt advice.

I composed this song at the age of twenty-five during a communal feast held in the presence of a self-occurring [statue of] the Protector at the sacred site of Glorious Protector in Rigong. *ithi*

The all-knowing Venerable [Tāranātha] actualized the supreme accomplishment and its spontaneously arising conduct with which he tamed innumerable migrators. At that time, he presented this melody of the vajra song of seven auspicious signs:

namo guru
Impartial altruistic compassion arises from great bliss,
the natural experience of dharmakāya.

I bow at the feet of father Vajradhara;
please bless my assembly here.

This growth of impartial altruism
is a sign of mind arising as emptiness and compassion.

This recognition of the abiding nature
is a sign of the full expression of devotion.

This lack of distraction at any time
is a sign of realizing rootless abiding nature.

This resolution of arising thoughts
is a sign of realizing the nature of nonthought.

Continuous felt experiences of bliss-emptiness
are signs of controlling channels, drops, and winds.

This conduct free of reference points
is a sign of calming the gale of eight concerns.

This destruction of hopes and fears for attainment
is a sign of the certainty that my mind is Buddha. {545}

The yogin with all these seven signs
has achieved an innately blissful, happy mind.

I am not unhappy; I'm just fine!
May there be auspiciousness of happiness and well-being.

Lochen Gyurme Dechen[63]

This song called "Rainfall of Great Bliss" is a supplication to the Six Dharmas by Lochen Gyurme Dechen, the nephew of the great adept Tangtong Gyalpo:

namaḥ śrījñāna ḍāki niguptāyai
[Homage to the glorious Awareness Ḍākinī, definitely secret mother.][64]

Compassionate Queen of the Celestial Realm,
Lady of Timeless Awareness, Niguma,
when your child supplicates with longing,
please think of me from unembellished space.

Wise woman who reveals the mandala of great mystery,
bestow now the empowerment of four ecstasies.

Wise woman who opens the door to the unborn,
refine now negativities and obscurations through purifying practice.

Wise woman who radiates the inner heat of the *A*-stroke,
burn now my residual aggregates and elements.

Wise woman who milks great bliss from *haṃ*,
grant now the timeless awareness of coemergence.

Wise woman who shows the natural experience of illusion,
destroy now my fixation on the reality of desire and anger.

Emanating-changing woman at the time of dream,
sever now the bonds of this double delusion.

Illuminating woman who raises spontaneous lucid clarity,
dispel now the darkness of my stupidity.

Guiding woman at the time of passing,
lead me now to the place of the celestial realm.

Vanquishing woman of intermediate state deluded appearances,
grant now the invincible saṃbhogakāya.

This was the supplication of the dharma teacher Gyurme Dechen.

Losal Tenkyong[65]

Nurtured by the Vajra Queen, his channels of experiential realization and highest knowledge were opened. From the songs of Rinchen Losal Tenkyong of Zhalu, this song of experience is a reminder to himself concerning the Amulet Mahāmudrā, called "The Wish-Fulfilling Gem": {546}

The refined elixir of the heart of Niguma,
chief of the mother ḍākinīs, was inscribed
on palm leaves and placed in an amulet
called "Lord Khyungpo's beautiful necklace."

Through the kindness of my spiritual father Tutop,[66]
the dharma lord inseparable from that protector,

I received the guidance in the visualization process
of Amulet Mahāmudrā, here expressed as a reminder.

The preliminary path of Three Naturally Settled States,
the main practice of Liberation from Four Faults,
and the final spontaneous presence of the four kāyas
are the special features of this excellent path.

Aho!
Calm abiding is captured by being (1) uncontrived; (2) thoughts stopped; (3) resolute; (4) tight and relaxed;
[by gazing] (5) high, low; (6) near; and (7) far; [and blending] (8) dharma activities; (9) mantras; (10) sounds; (11) and indefinite activities.

[Insight is] searching for (1) the essence; (2) beginning and end; (3) objective appearance; and (4) thought.
Then for each, searching for the difference between existence and nonexistence—that's [five (5) and] six (6).
Gaining certainty in the natural realm of phenomena is seven (7).
Place that introduction to higher insight in your heart's mandala.

Those are eighteen ways to meditate on Three Naturally Settled States.[67]

Kyeho!
Too close—you don't recognize it.
Too profound—you don't grasp it.
Too easy—you don't believe it.
Too excellent—you don't comprehend it.

Now, dharmakāya, saṃbhogakāya, and nirmāṇakāya
emerge from mind's matrix of clarity, emptiness, and their unity.
Their inseparability is the svabhāvakāya,
complete in intrinsic empty awareness, mind's energy.

The radiance is devotion, compassion, and methods, these three.
The method that blends winds and creation phase as unity

is a device produced by enhancement and holding winds.
If obstructions occur, apply the two methods to remove them.

The wish-fulfilling gem of my father guru's instructions
was in danger of being stolen by the thief of my forgetful mind.
So in the secluded cave of glorious Zhalu,
the Buddhist monk called Losal Tenkyong composed this.

This was the experiential song of remembering Amulet Mahāmudrā. {547}

Jamyang Khyentse Wangpo

In the age of conflict, during extreme degeneration, there is one supreme wondrous emanation as significant and rare as an uḍumbara flower. Master of the seven transmissions (*bka' babs bdun*), Jamyang Khyentse Wangpo and his unrivaled life of freedom is so wonderful that his name is known throughout the surrounding Land of Snows. Profound and vast vajra songs well up spontaneously from the treasury of the timeless awareness of his intentions. The spontaneous vajra song in praise of the inner spiritual biography of the mighty adept Tsöndru Zangpo, called "Flower of the Awareness Holders," is presented for this occasion:[68]

Aho!
In caṇḍālī that consumes the three existences all at once,
the generosity[69] of spreading elixir from the syllable *haṃ*
blazes and drips, dissolves into the central channel, the awareness body.
I bow to the transcendent perfection of Fierce Inner Heat's empty bliss.

Familiarity with the flight and chase of white and red vital drops
creates ethical conduct of satisfaction with the changeless ecstasies,
which is the awakened speech of the nāda of self-purifying double delusion.
I bow to the transcendent perfection of Dream's empty clarity.

Through drinking the elixir waves of unborn total tranquility,
the lotus of patience with the profound meaning

is unrivaled beauty, the perfect vajra awakened mind.
I bow to the transcendent perfection of Lucid Clarity's empty
awareness.

The intelligence of familiarity with phenomena's lack of reality
accompanied closely by the application of diligence[70]
is the delight[71] of spontaneous qualities beyond near and distant.
I bow to the transcendent perfection of Illusory Body's empty
appearance.

Ultimately there is no going or coming, craving or grasping,
but relatively the meditation of applied breath control
is the awakened activity of achieving the unerring celestial realm.
I bow to the transcendent perfection of Transference's empty
sensation.

However much delusion appears in the intermediate existence,
the wisdom that realizes deity and mantra as dharmakāya
is able to raise all of it as the saṃbhogakāya of unity.
I bow to the transcendent perfection of Intermediate State's
empty experience. {548}

In short, the definitive meaning of the six transcendent
perfections
is inseparable from the Six Vajra Dharmas; familiarity breeds
inexhaustible awakened body, speech, mind, qualities, and
activities.
I bow to the transcendent perfection of sublime permanence.

The moving warmth of the rising sun of my devotion
opens the utpala of words that please the awareness holders.
May this smiling display achieve a free life of accomplishment
inseparable from yours, my lord protector.

This song of praise to the foremost of innumerable adepts in the cool region, an emanation of Padma[sambhava], Tangtong [Gyalpo], is a eulogy of his inner spiritual biography in terms of the Six Vajra Dharmas elucidated by Awareness Ḍākinī Niguma. I composed this while praying solely at the sacred site blessed by the lord himself, near the iron bridge of Śrījala Parvata,[72] while crossing the gently flowing Lohita River[73] confluence in the mechanism of a boat decorated with young foot-drinking (i.e., fresh wooden) carvings.

"A Spontaneous Vajra Song That Condenses the Profound Meaning, the Ladder of Definitive Meaning":[74]

Emaho!
Primordial suchness beyond subject-object dualism
is the innate character of unembellished lucid clarity.
Fully enfolded by unchanging great bliss,
the supreme of all aspects dances in my heart.

The secret suchness of the hidden meaning is revealed
in the potency of accomplished awareness-holders' intent.
I have not fully seen it, but this vajra song of whatever occurs
is falling here and now in streams of profound joy.

They fully realized and emphasized the vital points
of the definitive meaning of the vajra body's abiding nature.
[They] saw the birth of timeless awareness of bliss-emptiness
and taught the completion phases of the profound path of
methods.

There is a framework of channels, the movement of winds,
and the supreme bodhicitta of vital drops—these three—
enacting creation, abiding, and destruction; the dance of
completion.
[These three] remain as the support for natural great awareness. {549}

The three channels with their four chakras and all their knots;
the three letters of method, wisdom, and neuter;
the vital winds of vitality, [vitality-]exertion, and [fire-]coinciding,
and the vital drops of emptiness, bliss, and union—
this sequence of sets of three generates
the natures of bliss, emptiness, and nonthought,
and establishes the links for the three kāyas.

The path of channels is to have the vajra features;
the vital points are constraining and yogic exercises.

The path of vital winds is to retain the controlled breath in the vase;
the sublime vital point is fourfold breathing application.[75]

The path of vital drops is the flight and chase of melting bliss of *A-haṃ*;
the vital point is binding in the four chakras.

The path of Illusory Body is to see empty appearance as the deity's form;
the vital point is to manifest as emanation without attachment.

The path of Dream is control through intentionality at sleep;
the vital point is to maintain the unborn when awake.

The path of Lucid Clarity is to gather the environment and inhabitants in luminosity;
the vital point is to bind wind and mind in balance.

The path of Intermediate State is to recall the threefold nature of phenomena;
the vital point is to always see the delusion.

The path of Transference is to eject the essence through the crown aperture;
the vital point is to gather and block the wind-mind.

Thus the sequence of the roots and branches
include the meanings of profound completion.
Moreover, concentrating on the winds
produces the experience of clarity and on vital drops, bliss itself.
Those are distinguished by different results and taught accordingly.

Completion phase without characteristics and concepts
means primordially unborn sky-like lucid clarity.

Not bound by self-identity of persons or phenomena,
it remains wholly within supreme emptiness.

Therefore, mahāmudrā is beyond the intellect,
the essential meaning of mental nonengagement.
For the best,[76] as soon as a holy one introduces it,
naked seeing is born and they are liberated in its nature.
For others, in accord with whatever experience occurs, {550}
taming by the vital points of winds, mind, and drops
supports the arising of unimaginable lucid clarity.

In the words of Venerable Tilopa:

> People of lesser intellect who do not dwell in this actuality
> [should] hold the vital points of the winds and tighten awareness
> with many yogic gazes and concentrations.
> Persevere until you abide within intrinsic awareness.
>
> For example, when you examine the center of the sky,
> fixation on center and circumference ceases.
> Likewise, when you examine the mind with the mind,
> thought patterns cease and are transformed to openness,
> and you see mind's intrinsic nature in unsurpassable awakening.[77]

Therefore, as he said, the intense focus on the vital points,
based on the methods of the profound secret path,
is the supreme essential meaning that liberates in the three times
according to your share of diligence and capability.

I have not personally experienced in my mind stream
the definitive meaning of the Awareness Ḍākinī's advice,
and since I fall to the lowest rank of those who engage devotion
alone,
it is inappropriate for me to be saying these things at all.

In playing the vajra music of whatever arose,
I openly confess all faults before the Three Roots' mandala
and dedicate whatever virtue there is
so that all beings may dwell in mahāmudrā.

"A Spontaneous Vajra Melody of Empty Sound, an Offering Cloud of Illusion":[78]

Aho!
The delusion of eight consciousness groups falls away,
freed on the glorious mountain of primordially pure basic ground.
Lucid clarity is the playful dance of illusion:
I bow to the circle of awareness-holding ḍākinīs.

With an offering of this song of sound and emptiness,
I will sing for the pleasure of heroes and ḍākinīs.

From the throat of infinite pure channels
came the song of creation phase of empty appearance.
My aggregates and constituents of deluded imaginary nature
dissolved into the forms of the deities in the three seats.

From the throat of winds playing in the central channel
came the song of mantra recitation in empty clarity.
All attachment to self-characterized sounds and words
dissolved within the space of scripture and reason.

From the throat of great bliss of the vital drops
came the song of the four ecstasies of empty bliss.
All bonds of ordinary afflictive emotions
dissolved within the integral unity of lucid clarity.

From the throat of inexpressible reflective awareness
came the song of settling in spontaneous vastness.
All concepts of various subject-object dualism
dissolved within simultaneous arising and liberation.

From the throat of the *kati* crystal channel
came the song of drops of rainbow light.
All marks of the corporeal aggregates and elements
dissolved within the unthinkable exhaustion of phenomena.

From the throat of the balanced three doors
came the song of creation, completion, and great completion.
All concepts of the duality of samsara and nirvana
dissolved within the expanse of the effortless result.

From the throat of an unfortunate jaded practitioner
came the song of various empty sounds.
All ideas and desires to practice the Holy Dharma
dissolved within lazy procrastination.

This is my offering of the song of definitive meaning.
It is a melody of searing disappointment with my mind.
By this virtue, may the nature of grandmother migrators
be spontaneously present in the essence of intrinsic awareness.

Jamgön Kongtrul

Praised by all authoritative masters as one who was foretold by the Buddha, Jamgön Vajradhara Karma Ngawang Yönten Gyatso taught the vajra topics of the Glorious Shangpa's Golden Dharmas, such as the profound path of Niguma's Six Dharmas, with the voice of certainty in this "Melodious Song of the Kalaviṅka."[79]

The lineage of Seven Jewels beginning with Great Vajradhara;
the golden rosary of bodhisattvas in their final lives, nonhumans
  assuming human form; {552}
and my glorious root guru who grants naked awakening:
I bow at your lotus feet—increase my experience and realization.

Ema!
My fortune on this essential path is most excellent;
Awareness Ḍākinī's secret words of Vajradhara's oral transmission,
the experiences of the adept lineage, and my root guru's legacy:
all this I hold as the gem of my heart and the focus of my mind.

Through the kindness of dharma kings, translators, and scholars,
the precious dharma of Sutra and Tantra spread widely in Tibet.

Adepts appeared continuously, showing signs of experiential realization.
The Golden Dharmas of the learned adept Khyungpo are better than a wish-fulfilling gem.

Sukhasiddhi and Niguma revealed the five culminating [tantras]
in fivefold mandalas of awareness, illuminating the supreme secret path.
Their system of teaching and practice is held by high-level descendants.
Their blessings are accessible even without practice; what need to mention accomplishment through practice?

Just the mention of the name "Great Garuḍa Soaring in Space"
makes the mind quit pondering the state of other lesser birds.
The brilliant splendor of the title "Khyungpo's [i.e., Garuḍa's] Golden Dharmas"
slackens one's interest in others' writings about their own ideas.

Reciting millions of mantras to accomplish practice from dark letters and dark mouths
doesn't come close to the signs of experience from just a little meditation in this dharma.
Years and months of turning the wheel of theoretical dialectics
doesn't bring a fraction of the wisdom from practicing this subject.

Due to the power of the times, those who can meditate with single focus are rare.
Yet with great certainty in the dharma without hesitant doubt,
and effort in steady practice alone without starting and stopping,
supreme spiritual power won't be far; that was the Awareness Ḍākinī's final promise. {553}

With meager fortitude for practice, the power of my experiential realization is incomplete.
Totally distracted by silly prattle, I am bereft of any actual degree of meditative warmth.

But through residual good karma I have trust and confidence in this dharma;
I cherish it as my heart and life with a devotion that seems innate.

From the precious treasury of Golden Dharmas, the quintessence of the great Five Tantras
is clarified by its title: the roots are the Six Dharmas of Niguma.
A single sitting can germinate the sprout of experiential realization.
This wonder produces the supreme fruits within one life in one body.

The primordially unborn seed syllable is the gate to all phenomena of samsara and nirvana.
Arising in the great-bliss chakra, purifying elixir washes away
negativities, obscurations, sickness, and spirits with an experience of naked empty clarity.
This method, the Purifier of Empty Space, is the preliminary that strikes the vital point.

To achieve buddhahood in a single lifetime, you [must realize] the integral unity of bliss and emptiness.
There is no other way, and its cause is that "one's own body is the means."[80]
To tame wild channels and wild winds, the Wildfire of Fierce Inner Heat is swift:
after three weeks you can endure wearing a white cotton shawl [in the snow].

In the basic support of the vajra body, the empty spaces of three channels and four chakras
are held in the correct vase breath through fourfold breathing applications,
causing the blazing and melting of *A-haṃ*, instantly adorned by the four ecstasies.
This self-igniting bliss-heat in the Path of Methods is the heart jewel of Indian and Tibetan adepts.

Eating the Food of Inner Heat nurtures the youthfulness of bliss and emptiness.
Wearing the Clothes of Inner Heat makes bliss-warmth blaze unbearably.
Spreading the Seat and Riding the Horse are stabilizing, letting you go wherever you wish.
This is the intention of the unsurpassable sovereign tantras that the mere common methods cannot equal.

The path of guru devotion causes the arising of all appearance as unreal. {554}
Empty appearance arises by itself as the deity's form, seen as illusion.
This is the essence of Illusory Body, but those who take it into experience are rare.
The guru, lord of adepts, has tasted the depths of the experience.

Free of four conditions of wakefulness, Make the Six Kinds of Migrators Arise as Illusion.
Apply eight intentions and three sets of three [methods] to understand sickness and spirits as illusion.[81]
A sixfold set of qualities arise and the snake's knot of reification uncoils.
This is elixir of the heart for beginners.

Instruction on the Vital Points of the Four Empowerments of Drops [causes] self-recognition of the appearances of [dream's] double delusion.
If not recognized, Nine Infallible Vital Points will let you recognize delusion when encountered.
Then through the vital points of refining, increasing, and changing [dreams], their natural expression is trained impartially.
In Ascertaining Objective Appearance, the freedom of dreams is further perfected.

The effortless self-arising of the deity's form ultimately dissolves into lucid clarity.
This is the pinnacle of the many profound instructions to sever double delusion by force.
Even simple cowherds can be transported to buddhahood here
with just a minimal connection to Guru Buddha's kindness.

Impermanence, disillusionment, conduct, sacred substances, the path of methods, and supplication
form the root, branches, leaves, flowers, and vines that grow[82]
to produce the light or dense lucid clarity, integrated as three kāyas.
Blend clarity and emptiness, equipoise and postmeditation, day and night, bliss and emptiness.

Thus the lamp of Lucid Clarity vanquishes the darkness of stupid sleep.
Through the connection of gathering wind-mind and the special blessing of the guru,
bliss, clarity, and emptiness become inseparable in the lucid clarity of profound peace and simplicity,
parting the seeming barrier of dualism in the recesses of the surroundings.

Transfer Consciousness to the Suchness of Dharmakāya, to the saṃbhogakāya in Union with the Yidam,
by the force of the Blessings of the Guru, and to the Unerring Celestial Realm above.
Do this according to the level of capability at the moment of passing away. {555}
Now this is the tenet of creation and completion practiced by all tantric practitioners.

Lucid clarity in the Natural Arising of the Dharmakāya, the Victors' Saṃbhogakāya,
the Natural Arising of Unrestricted Nirmāṇakāya, and the General Unerring Vital Points

all liberate in the three intermediate states according to the level
of capability.
By preparing when there's still time, it will work when the time of
death comes.

The preliminary of Three Naturally Settled States gives rise to
absorptions of calm abiding and higher insight.
The main practice is introducing the profound Natural Liberation
of Four Faults.
The concluding realization is to know the unity of clarity and
emptiness as the natural arising of the three kāyas.
This path of mahāmudrā is the trunk of all these doctrines.

In the oral instructions of the two awareness ḍākinīs and
Maitrīpagupta,
the unfabricated settled state in the essence, supported by the
elephant's gaze,
induces the ordinary mind free of all identity, which is fresh
and arises nakedly as three kāyas—buddhahood in the palm of
your hand.

First is impartial devotion of knowing whatever arises as the guru.
Second is impartial pure view of appearance and sound as the
nature of deity and mantra.
Third is the integration of appearance and mind as unreal illusion
and dream.
These three bear the title of the branches, but they are the core of
all Sutra and Mantra.

The absorptions of [two forms of Khecarī] Vajrayoginī, in colors
of the moon and vermilion,
draw their streams of compassion through the power of specially
elevated supplications.
Once you train in the bliss and emptiness of liberated desire
through the light in the four chakras,
the beautiful coemergent goddesses greet you in the flower garden
of the celestial realm.

Since one's mind is not born, it does not cease and die.
The body's nature is inert matter, so even the basis of the term *death* does not exist.
Wind and mind are bound in basic space, as if piloted by yogic exercises, {556}
and the movement of undissipating four ecstasies may be enjoyed as the fruit on display.

Guru-Protector inseparable become five great emanated forms,
granting the supreme spiritual power of four actions in just years or months.
Especially, Swift-Acting Avalokiteśvara gives refuge from fears of the intermediate state.
With devotion, the seal of compassion keeps the abiding gem in the heart.

Buddha Śākyamuni's doctrine is both conventional and definitive, each true in its own context.
The instructions of the adept lineages are each great in their own traditions.
But the great adept Khyungpo's Golden Dharmas are barely even known to others.
Those of us who have drunk of its ambrosial essence don't drool for the likes of beer.

My style of behavior is unpredictable, but my style of thought lands on the ultimate meaning.
My style of appearance seems brainless, but my style of being is confined to a single thing.
The style of my words is contrived, but their style of arising falls in my natural character.
Unable to rest in equanimity, this is the final handwriting of the vagrant Lodrö.

In this and all future lifetimes, may I hold the wish-fulfilling gem of Golden Dharmas
in the brocade cloak of my heart, in the victorious state of vajra unity.

May I see the nonduality of giving liberating refuge to all
migrators throughout space
and quickly achieve this through the compassion of the root and
lineage gurus.

The omniscient mahāguru's great meaning stretched forth from his vajra tongue to nurture the sprout of my devotion. Then the lotus of my speech opened uncontrollably at the isolated grove of Devīkoṭi on the left flank of Tsadra Rinchen Drak. This semblance of a renunciant, a servant of Pema,[83] Yönten Gyatso Lodrö Tayepai De, sang this little song of profound meaning in the voice of a bee. Virtue!

[Conclusion]

At the conclusion of reciting these songs that arouse the strength of devotion and the energy of experiential realization, arrange whatever feast items you have collected. {557} Perform the offering ritual, from the consecration through the offering of leftovers according to the Five-Deity Cakrasaṃvara. Do the confession of faults and request for forbearance to the guests of the feast. If you have a support image, then do the request to remain. Recite the dedication of merit by Khyungpo known as *Sealed Word*:

Lord of dharma with three kāyas and tenfold knowledge,
gurus, yidam deities, ḍākinīs,
dharma protectors, and all others:
remain here with love to witness my dedication.
In this life and in all other lives,
may whatever positive virtue I have made
with my body, speech, and mind
be for the benefit all sentient beings.
May I use afflictive emotions on the path.
May I gain control over appearances.
May I find the three kāyas in myself.
May I accomplish dharmakāya for myself,
and the two rūpakāya for others' sake,
increasing activity for the welfare of migrators
until cyclic existence has become empty.
May I manifest as whatever tames whomever,

and achieve great waves of benefit for others.
May I teach disciples in a timely way.
May I become skilled in the ways of interdependence.
May my relationships be meaningful.
May the ocean of cyclic existence run dry.
May I gain the lucid clarity of dharmakāya.
In whatever way all buddhas of the three times
made their dedications [of merit],
may I accomplish such dedication.
Until I attain buddhahood,
may I have good family, health, and clear senses.
With discipline and alertness in dharma activity,
may I be respected by everyone.
May I fulfill all hopes and desires
until such time as I realize awakening,
may the harm from sickness, spirits, obstructors,
humans, wild animals, sinpo spirits,
the four elements, and so forth
become completely tranquilized.
May longevity and merit increase,
and glory and wealth expand,
so that my renown equals the sky. {558}
May all my thoughts, words, and deeds,
whatever they are, help sentient beings.
May I empty the ocean of cyclic existence
and attain perfect buddhahood.

Recite the *Sealed Word of Auspiciousness*[84] to spread the glory of virtue and well-being to all countries and realms in all directions and times.

[Colophon]

The precious Kagyu tradition considers singing vajra songs extremely important and so the custom has spread widely. But the long tradition of the Shangpa Kagyu has not spread much in this context, so even texts containing the songs of that lineage of adepts have become like daytime stars. I have gathered these mainly from the biographies and similar sources, and supplemented them from the [songs of] the later lineage wherever appropriate.

Whatever sublime quintessence of the elixir of the profound dharma from this lineage was to be found is now contained in this golden receptacle of former virtue. Karma Ngawang Yönten Gyatso Lodrö Tayepai De compiled this at the secluded retreat of Devīkoṭi at Tsadra Rinchen Drak. May this become the cause for the immaculate long tradition of the glorious Shangpa Kagyu to spread and flourish in all directions and times. Let virtue prevail.

[Dedication]

From the pervading lord Vajradhara and ḍākinīs,
and the succession of adepts in the lineage,
the self-occurring self-arising, indestructible sound of nāda
is meaningful to hear and is the source of all blessings.

For yogins who abide in the absorptions of the two phases
or people with single-minded faith and devotion,
reciting these melodies of the vajra dohas
will amass the blessing clouds of the Kagyu gurus,

causing a rain of yidam deities' spiritual powers to fall continuously,
and the ḍākinīs and dharma protectors to accomplish the activity of dispelling obstructions.
It delights benevolent protectors, generates resplendent brilliance,
and discourages malevolent ones by dousing them with the elixir of awakening mind.

The energy of experience is created, and realization enhanced;
the seed of freedom is sown in those with faith. {559}
Since this excellent result ripens in such a meaningful way,
I have prepared this garland of gems in proper order.

Strung with the golden thread of my faithful mind,
a single print [woodblock] that can make many copies,
printed by my, the creator's, pure altruistic intention.
By this virtue, may I and those with whom I'm connected

and all unlimited embodied beings be free of obscuration.
May the two supreme aspirations of awakening arise effortlessly

in their mind streams so that the abiding nature becomes manifest.
Once the spiritual life is perfected like the lineage adepts,

may we be born miraculously in a lotus in Sukhāvatī
and receive the supreme prophecy from Amitābha,
quickly traverse the paths and levels, and with immeasurable activity
place all migrators throughout space in that awakened state.

May we become equal to the supreme victor Amitābha.
May the guru, victors, and their heirs,
with great waves of the awakening mind and the power of aspirations,
grant their blessings to achieve these aspirations.

These words of aspiration for this printing, which have the same number [of verses] as the signs of auspiciousness, were written with good intention by the kusāli Lodrö Taye. Let virtue prevail.

Five Ḍākinīs

Introduction

The five classes or kinds of ḍākinīs correspond to the five buddha families: Buddha, Vajra, Ratna (jewel), Padma (lotus), and Karma (action). These families represent many things, primarily the five kinds of awareness that are the purified state of the five afflictive emotions. Female buddhas or ḍākinīs in particular are associated with the purity of the five elements: space, water, wind, fire, and earth. These five families are represented spatially in the configuration of a mandala, more or less consistently. There are many practices involving the five kinds of ḍākinīs throughout Tibetan Buddhism.

Ḍākinīs of the Five Classes Sādhana and Authorization Ritual in the Shangpa Tradition maintains the same configuration for its visualizations and corresponds to the important Shangpa practice known as Five-Deity Cakrasaṃvara, only without the deity Cakrasaṃvara. In that practice, the central figures are the couple Cakrasaṃvara and Vajravārāhī, who are surrounded by the four ḍākinīs in the four directions. Vajravārāhī in that practice is crowned by the Buddha Vairocana, just as here with the central Buddha Ḍākinī, indicating the buddha family. Likewise, though the ḍākinīs in Cakrasaṃvara have actual names, they belong to the same families as here. The method to accomplish them comes from Tāranātha's collection of sādhanas called *Mine of Jewels: Sādhanas of an Ocean of Yidams* and has been reprinted verbatim. In the section on the torma empowerment, Jamgön Kongtrul has filled in Tāranātha's concise description with the suggested liturgies and directions.

Torma Offering to the Ḍākinīs of the Five Classes Just for Regular Practice is Kongtrul's practical liturgy used primarily as a torma offering to the ḍākinīs in the context of general rituals. It is also based on Tāranātha's text. Tāranātha gives the lineage for the torma empowerment as originating with the lion-faced ḍākinī Siṃhamukhā, the five ḍākinīs themselves, then to Khyungpo Naljor.[1] From there it was transmitted to Geshe Ghapa Chögyal and to Tokden Zhangom Chöseng. Shangom Chökyi Senge (twelfth century) is one of the main early disciples of Khyungpo Naljor. After that it continues through Öntön Kyergangpa and the other familiar names in the lineage. The tale of its origin is found in Khyungpo Naljor's life story:[2]

The scholar Geshe Ghapa Chögyal requested teachings again and again from Khyungpo Naljor but never made any progress on his spiritual path even though he meditated for years. Finally Khyungpo Naljor decided to follow it up through his dreams. He visited various pure buddha realms and collected teachings and empowerments from many of the buddhas. His final dream encounter was in Oḍḍiyāna, where he met Ḍākinī Siṃhamukhā surrounded by four ḍākinīs. She sang him a song that begins:

> Vajra Ḍākinī guards against obstacles,
> Jewel Ḍākinī increases people and wealth,
> Lotus Ḍākinī gathers consorts,
> Activity Ḍākinī accomplishes all actions.
>
> Once under the influence of craving and clinging
> one has fallen under the power of the ḍākinīs.
> There is no external gathering whatsoever.
> Recognize the ḍākinī as your own mind.[3]

After returning from the dream, Khyungpo Naljor transmitted all these teachings to Ghapa Chögyal, who practiced them with great success. But then he asked Khyungpo whether the dream was real or not, to which Khyungpo replied:

> The buddhas' bodies, pure lands,
> entourages, teachings, and so on
> are all of them like illusions;
> real and dream are not different.

31. Ḍākinīs of the Five Classes Sādhana and Authorization Ritual in the Shangpa Tradition[1]

Tāranātha and Jamgön Kongtrul

oṃ svasti
Having bowed to the gurus, yidams, and buddhas,
I will write a concise sādhana
required for proper accomplishment
by all practitioners of the Mantra family.

Visualize yourself as whatever Secret Mantra yidam is appropriate.

> Before me in space, *hūṃ* becomes the protection circle and source of phenomena. In the center of the space element [inside] is the celestial palace with the eight charnel grounds that are the source of spiritual powers. In the middle of the palace is a cluster of five lotus seats. In its center, on a moon, *oṃ* becomes white Buddha Ḍākinī crowned by Vairocana. She has a peaceful expression. On the eastern seat, on a sun, *hūṃ* becomes blue Vajra Ḍākinī crowned by Akṣobhya. She has a wrathful expression. On the southern seat, on a yellow moon, *trāṃ* becomes yellow Jewel Ḍākinī crowned by Ratnasambhava. She has a joyful expression. On the western seat, on a red sun without rays, *hrīḥ* becomes red Lotus Ḍākinī crowned by Amitābha. She has a passionate expression. {563} On the northern seat, on a vajra cross, *āḥ* becomes green Diverse Ḍākinī crowned by Amoghasiddhi. She has shifting expressions, such as wrath and mirth.
>
> All the ḍākinīs are rattling small drums with their right hands

and holding elixir-filled skull cups to their hearts. They have crowns of five dry human skulls, long necklaces of fifty fresh heads, and the five symbolic bone ornaments. Their black hair is partly bound on their heads. On their left sides are khaṭvāṅgas, representing methods (male consort), each adorned by a wheel, vajra, jewel, lotus, and sword, respectively. They stand amid radiating light rays of five colors. Each of the principal ḍākinīs is surrounded by one hundred thousand similar ḍākinīs and innumerable retinue ḍākinīs. At their foreheads is *oṃ*, at their throats *āḥ*, and at their hearts *hūṃ*.

Immeasurable light rays radiate from my heart, invoking the principal five awareness ḍākinīs each with countless worldly and otherworldly ḍākinīs from their natural abodes and all cardinal and intermediate directions—*vajra samājaḥ*. {564}

Flourish the five-pronged vajra mudra.

oṃ śrīheruka mahāvajra ākaḍhaya / ākaḍhaya / praveśaya / praveśaya / bandhaya bandhaya / toṣaya toṣaya / sarva ḍākinīnaṃ / hṛdayaṃ / hūṃ hūṃ phaṭ phaṭ (Repeat three times to invoke them.)

jaḥ hūṃ vaṃ hoḥ (Repeat five times.)

Offer with *arghaṃ* through *śabda*; (the inner offerings with) *oṃ hūṃ trāṃ hrīḥ āḥ / oṃ āḥ hūṃ*, and recite the two verses of praise, "Glorious Vajra Ḍākinī . . . (etc.)" [as in the torma offering].

Repeat the following mantras:

oṃ buddha ḍākinī āḥ hrīḥ oṃ hūṃ phaṭ svāhā / oṃ vajra ḍākinī āḥ hrīḥ hūṃ hūṃ phaṭ svāhā / oṃ ratna ḍākinī āḥ hrīḥ trāṃ hūṃ phaṭ svāhā / oṃ padma ḍākinī āḥ hrīḥ hrīḥ hūṃ phaṭ svāhā / oṃ karma ḍākinī āḥ hrīḥ āḥ hūṃ phaṭ svāhā

The general collective mantra:

oṃ āḥ oṃ hūṃ svā āḥ hā hūṃ phaṭ svāhā

Consecrate the offering torma as in the self-visualization. For the first torma of the select portion, repeat seven times:

> *oṃ śrīheruka mahāvajra pratīccha imaṃ baliṃ hūṃ phaṭ*

Then offer to the ḍākinīs three times or more:

> *oṃ buddha ḍākinī pratīccha imaṃ baliṃ oṃ phaṭ / oṃ vajra ḍākinī pratīccha imaṃ baliṃ hūṃ phaṭ / oṃ ratna ḍākinī pratīccha imaṃ baliṃ trāṃ phaṭ / oṃ padma ḍākinī pratīccha imaṃ baliṃ hrīḥ phaṭ / oṃ viśva ḍākinī pratīccha imaṃ baliṃ hoḥ phaṭ*[2]

For an extensive version, include the [five praise] verses that begin with "Akṣobhya, great timeless awareness . . . (etc.)" [as in the following torma offering], but for a concise version, just use the mantras to present the outer, inner, and secret offerings. Then recite from "All phenomena are like reflections . . . (etc. to) . . . born into the Buddha's family." Supplicate for your desires with "Accept this torma I offer to you . . . (etc.)." Then do the hundred syllables, request for forbearance, request for departure, dissolution of the pledge beings into oneself, self-protection, aspiration prayers, and auspicious verses.

The above torma ritual may be offered one hundred and eight times, or the five sets offered five times in each of four sessions for the one hundred torma offering, or four times in the sixteen [sessions] for the sixty torma offering. Do the mantras for the activities of enriching, pacifying, magnetizing, and destroying. Look elsewhere for those practices and activity manuals. {565}

Torma Empowerment

Now, for the torma empowerment, arrange five heaps in the center of a source of phenomena. Upon that, place five tormas with images of the five classes of ḍākinīs, or with their mantras listed. On a raised platform, place a small select-portion torma. Arrange any nice offerings and recite the liturgies for the self- and front visualizations as before, continuing in the torma offering up to the request for one's desires. [That concludes the ritual master's acts.] Give the disciples the cleansing water, emanate and gather the mandala, and clarify the mind of awakening.[3]

Now, in this profound path of Secret Mantrayāna, there are four classes of tantra. Among them, the most excellent of the higher tantras is Unexcelled Yoga (*anuttarayoga*). This is divided into methods and wisdom or into father tantras and mother tantras. Ultimately, father and mother tantras share a single perspective. However, in terms of how the actual doctrine is presented, all the profound important special features of the father tantras are included in the yoginī [mother] tantras. And there are many profound vital points that do not appear clearly in the father tantras but that are in the mother tantras, so the yoginī tantras are the most profound and efficacious. For that reason, mainly those methods and spiritual accomplishments from the yoginī mother tantras are presented. Therefore, since the vajra emissary (consort) is the primary giver of spiritual powers, it is crucial that those practitioners who have entered the profound path of Mantra should exert themselves in ways of always pleasing the awareness ḍākinīs.

Through their efforts, they will quickly accomplish the knowledge mantras, restore any transgressions and violations, and undoubtedly attain the common spiritual powers, such as the four activities, and the uncommon, supreme accomplishment. So now, offer a mandala in order to request the torma empowerment entrustment of the five classes of awareness ḍākinīs that comes from the esoteric instructions of the great lord of adepts, Khyungpo Lotsāwa.

Have them offer a mandala.

With palms together holding a flower, repeat this supplication three times after me: {566}

"Omniscient one with a heap of wisdom,
purifier of the wheel of existence,
precious giver of today's teachings:
Principal, show me your kindness."[4]

In order to fully purify your mind stream, repeat this regular confession three times after me:

"Whatever negative acts I have done,
[encouraged others to do, or rejoiced in,
I confess every single one
before the eyes of the buddhas.

I rejoice in the accumulated merit
of buddhas and bodhisattvas,
pratyekabuddhas, arhats, and migrators,
in their meditations and recitations.

Gurus and deities of the Five Tantras,
I request you to turn the dharma wheel
by teaching whatever tames beings
according to their particular mind streams.

Gurus and hosts of yidam deities,
I supplicate you to remain
until all sentient beings filling space
are established in pure awakening.

I go for refuge in those who
aroused the awakening mind, attained buddhahood,
and turned the wheel of the dharma,
and in the supreme assembly of bodhisattvas.

Just as the fortunate bodhisattvas
aroused the mind of awakening,
which is the cause of buddhas appearing,
I too will arouse the mind of awakening.

Through this virtuous act of mine,
may I quickly become a buddha in this world
and teach the dharma for the sake of migrators,
liberating them from the torment of suffering.

Guru, yidam, and Buddha,
for the sake of beings, I freely offer
my body, speech, and mind.
May I attain your three kāyas.]"[5]

Now meditate on this visualization: within your hearts, there is a cluster of five lotus seats . . . (etc.).

Follow the visualization description [above]. The awareness beings are invoked and dissolve into you. Continue until the offerings and praises [in the liturgy]. Then refresh and consecrate the tormas and dedicate the torma ritual. Do the supplication for desires. Then hold up the torma and say:

> This torma [carried by] the five classes of awareness ḍākinīs, surrounded by their retinues of innumerable worldly and otherworldly ḍākinīs, arrives at the top of your head. Imagine that you are granted every empowerment, blessing, and spiritual power right where you are. Bhagavatī Siṃhamukha, Khedrup Khyungpo Naljor, and their succession of holy root and lineage gurus, and the five classes of awareness ḍākinīs with their retinues of countless worldly and otherworldly ḍākinīs, please confer empowerment and blessings with your awakened body, speech, and mind on these vajra disciples who hold awareness. Please pacify all their negative actions, obscurations, sickness, spirits, and obstacles. Please increase their life spans, merit, prosperity, experience, realization, and timeless awareness. Please bring under control all winds, mind, and appearance. Please terminate all their self-fixation and afflictions, and hosts of enemies, spirits, and obstructors. In short, please accomplish all their short- and long-term desires, goals, and hopes just as they wish. {567} And please grant them every supreme and common spiritual power.
>
> All the buddhas bless you
> in all awakened body, speech, and mind,
> and give you the torma empowerment conferral,
> the source of the two spiritual powers.

Say the aforementioned mantras and touch [the disciples'] three places with the torma. Afterward, they take the sacred pledges, offer a mandala in gratitude, offer their bodies, and dedicate the merit. Refresh the offerings of the front visualization and do the offerings, praises, request for desires, confession of errors, and request forbearance. If there is a support representation, the awareness beings remain there. The pledge beings gather into you. If there is no support, the deities depart. Dedicate the virtue and do auspicious prayers to widely increase [the benefits].

[Colophon by Tāranātha]

Fully amending transgressions and violations
and practicing the actions is auspicious and joyful.
This requirement for all the practitioners
was written quickly with love from my heart.

[Colophon by Jamgön Kongtrul]

This was taken from [Tāranātha's] *Mine of Jewels*. The authorization ritual was arranged as a liturgical ritual.[6] Let virtue and goodness prevail.

32. Torma Offering to the Ḍākinīs of the Five Classes Just for Regular Practice[1]

Tāranātha and Jamgön Kongtrul

oṃ svasti
To practice just the usual version of the *Torma Offering to the Ḍākinīs of the Five Classes*, put up five round tormas or one torma marked with four dough buttons. Do the consecration as in the yidam practice.

Before me in space, *hūṃ* becomes the protection circle and source of phenomena. In the center of the space element [inside] is the celestial palace with the eight charnel grounds that are the source of spiritual powers. In the middle of the palace is a cluster of five lotus seats. In its center, on a moon, *oṃ* becomes white Buddha Ḍākinī crowned by Vairocana. She has a peaceful expression. On the eastern seat, on a sun, *hūṃ* becomes blue Vajra Ḍākinī crowned by Akṣobhya. She has a wrathful expression. On the southern seat, on a yellow moon, *trāṃ* becomes yellow Jewel Ḍākinī crowned by Ratnasambhava. She has a joyful expression. On the western seat, on a red sun without rays, *hrīḥ* becomes red Lotus Ḍākinī crowned by Amitābha. She has a passionate expression. On the northern seat, on a vajra cross, *āḥ* becomes green Diverse Ḍākinī crowned by Amoghasiddhi. She has shifting expressions, such as wrath and mirth.

All of the ḍākinīs are rattling small drums with their right hands and holding elixir-filled skull cups to their hearts. They have crowns of five dry human skulls, long necklaces of fifty fresh heads, and the five symbolic bone ornaments. Their black hair is partly bound on their heads. On their left sides are khaṭvāṅgas, representing methods, each adorned by a wheel, vajra, jewel, lotus, and sword, respectively. They stand amid radiating light rays of five colors. Each of the principal ḍākinīs is surrounded by one hundred thousand similar ḍākinīs and innumerable retinue ḍākinīs. At their foreheads is *oṃ*, at their throats *āḥ*, and at their hearts *hūṃ*. {570}

Immeasurable light rays radiate from my heart, invoking the principal five awareness ḍākinīs each with countless worldly and otherworldly ḍākinīs from their natural abodes and all cardinal and intermediate directions—*vajra samājaḥ.*

Flourish the five-pronged vajra mudra.

oṃ śrīheruka mahāvajra ākaḍhaya / ākaḍhaya / praveśaya / praveśaya / bandhaya bandhaya / toṣaya toṣaya / sarva vajra ḍākinīnaṃ / hṛdayaṃ / hūṃ hūṃ phaṭ phaṭ (Repeat three times to invoke them.)

jaḥ hūṃ vaṃ hoḥ (Repeat five times.)

Offer with *arghaṃ* through *śabda*. Present the inner offerings:

oṃ hūṃ trāṃ hrīḥ āḥ / oṃ āḥ hūṃ

Glorious Vajra Ḍākinī,
wheel wielder of the ḍākinīs;
five awarenesses and three kāyas—
homage to the protectors of migrators.

Every vajra ḍākinī
severs the bonds of concept
and engages in worldly activity;
I pay homage to every one.[2]

When doing just the torma ritual, the recitation of the mantras is unnecessary, but if you wish, you may do their collective mantra:

oṃ āḥ oṃ hūṃ svā āḥ hā hūṃ phaṭ svāhā

Then to offer the torma, repeat the following mantras three times and so forth.

oṃ buddha ḍākinī pratīccha imaṃ baliṃ oṃ phaṭ / oṃ vajra ḍākinī pratīccha imaṃ baliṃ hūṃ phaṭ / oṃ ratna ḍākinī pratīccha imaṃ baliṃ trāṃ phaṭ / oṃ padma ḍākinī pratīccha imaṃ baliṃ hrīḥ phaṭ / oṃ viśva ḍākinī pratīccha imaṃ baliṃ hoḥ phaṭ

For an extensive version, include the [following five praise] verses, but for a concise version, just use the mantras to present the outer, inner, and secret offerings.

Akṣobhya, great timeless awareness,
vajra expanse, the great space,
three sublime vajras, three mandalas:
Vajra Ḍākinī, I pay homage and praise.

Vairocana, utterly pure,
vajra peace, great joy,
sublime lucid clarity by nature:
Buddha Ḍākinī, I pay homage and praise.

Ratnarāja, utterly profound, {571}
vajra space without defilement,
naturally pure, without covering:
Jewel Ḍākinī, I pay homage and praise.

Amitāvajra, great king,
nonconceptual sky, vajra holder,
the perfection of desire attained:
Lotus Ḍākinī, I pay homage and praise.

Amogharāja, perfect buddha,
bringing fulfillment of all wishes,
the real thing arisen from purity itself:
Diverse Ḍākinī, I pay homage and praise.[3]

Thus praise them with five verses. Then:

> All phenomena are like reflections:
> clear, vivid, and not muddled.
> Ungraspable and inexpressible,
> they arise from causes and actions.
>
> Without real essence or place—
> know phenomena as such
> and create the highest benefit for beings;
> be born in the family of buddhas.[4]

Then recite the supplication for one's desires:

> Accept this torma I offer to you . . . (etc.).

Do the hundred syllables, request for forbearance, request for departure, gathering the pledge beings into oneself, self-protection, aspiration prayers, and auspicious verses.

[Colophon]

This was taken separately from [Tāranātha's] *Mine of Jewels* as a useful supplement by Guṇa.

Six-Armed Mahākāla

Introduction

The Swift-Acting Awareness Protector, Six-Armed Mahākāla, or Chakdrukpa (Phyag drug pa), has been the preeminent dharma protector for the Shangpa Kagyu school since before the beginning. It was Khyungpo Naljor who brought him to Tibet, and though the practice spread into other lineages, all of them explicitly trace back to him.

The origin legends of this protector are different from the other mahākālas described in Indian tantras in that this one is said to be a manifestation of Avalokiteśvara (Chenrezi), the bodhisattva of love and compassion and the special deity of Tibet. In the famous tale, Avalokiteśvara realized that being gentle didn't always work when it came to rescuing all sentient beings, so he created this wrathful and more assertive version of himself, capable of all kinds of activities as needed for their benefit. But since Chakdrukpa's essence is awakened compassion, this mahākāla is a bit more forgiving when it comes to the transmissions and practices. And since his essence is Avalokiteśvara, he is regarded as a yidam deity as much as a protector. What's more, he is an accepted stand-in for the guru in the crucial Vajrayāna practice of guru yoga, as found in the distinctive Shangpa specialty of Guru-Protector Inseparable.

That origin story and others are recounted in Tāranātha's *Brief Account of the Origins of the Dharma Cycle of the Six-Armed Awareness Protector*.[1] It was the Indian mahāsiddha Śavarīpa who first developed the practice after a meditative encounter with the protector in the charnel ground called Cool Grove (bSil ba tshal; Skt. Śītavana). He passed it on to his disciples Maitrīpa and Rāhulagupta. Then Khyungpo Naljor requested a practice from Maitrīpa, saying, "We Tibetans have very little wealth. I request a speedy wealth practice that brings big results." Maitrīpa responded with, "I got this from glorious Śavarīpa," and explains its great efficacy at great length.[2]

In *The Beryl Key*, Jamgön Kongtrul gives a brief overview of the transmissions:

> The great adept Khyungpo received from Maitrīpa, Rāhulagupta, Paṇḍita Rolpai Dorje, and others innumerable transmissions. Master Chökyi Sherap and others granted them as appropriate to most of their disciples. This became the sole dharma protector of all Shangpa lineage holders, so of course there are really countless versions. There are two main ones: the lineage of Latöpa Könchok Khar is called the upper tradition or the Old Place tradition (*gnas rnying lugs*). The lineage that both Mokchokpa Rinchen Tsöndru and Zhangom Chöseng passed to Öntön Kyergangpa is known as the lower tradition or Rigong tradition. The latter passed through Densapa Loppön Ayi Senge and thus spread in the Pakmodru and other schools. From Khedrup Jakpa, the upper, lower, and middle traditions spread especially among the Gelukpa and others. From Khedrup Samdingpa the two lineages of Southern [and] Severance (*gcod*) and so forth developed truly limitless systems. The vast number of teachings, however, can still be summarized into two main types: the wrathful protector to accomplish magical powers and the peaceful protector to accomplish wealth.[3]

As to that division, while explaining the White Mahākāla practice, he states:

> Among all of those, it appears that Khedrup Khyungpo Naljor received the cycle of the wrathful practice mainly from the great master Maitrīpa and the cycle of peaceful practice primarily from the great adept Rāhulaguptavajra.[4]

Despite this long history in the lineage, all eight texts in this section, actually comprising twenty practices, are either authored by Jonang Tāranātha or Jamgön Kongtrul or a combination of both. Tāranātha put great effort into gathering the practices and transmissions of as many sādhanas—the means to accomplish the deities—as he could find in a preservation effort that recalls that of his predecessor Kunga Drolchok. That collection in three volumes is called *Mine of Jewels: Sādhanas of an Ocean of Yidams*.[5] Though it is a large anthology, the individual practices are mostly very concise. In order to create a useful "performing edition," the fourth (or the seventh, counting posthumous recognitions) Paṇchen Lama, Tenpai Nyima (1782–1853), amplified Tāranātha's work in a text called *The Clear Meaning of the Jewel Mine*.[6] That work has been used as a basis for an in-depth study translated by Martin Willson to accompany a set of deity paintings, further amplifying them and creating a truly helpful edition for both actual practice and general deity doxography.[7]

Whether Jamgön Kongtrul had access to Tenpai Nyima's work and others is not known, but it appears that he is basically using a similar methodology. A good example is the first two texts in this section. The first, *Treasure Trove of Awakened Activity*, is Tāranātha's sādhana and torma ritual for Six-Armed Mahākāla. Using that as a basis, Jamgön Kongtrul supplements it with *Spontaneous Accomplishment of the Four Actions*, filling in all the necessary liturgies and doubling the length. As he states at the end, it is only to be used for "extensive holy-day offerings." In direct contradistinction to that, Kongtrul places Tāranātha's two-page *Concise Torma Ritual* next, as if diverting the reader to a convenient alternative.

In *Garland of Cintāmaṇi*, Jamgön Kongtrul gathers the liturgies for performing thirteen major authorizations or empowerments for various versions of Six-Armed Mahākāla. The first five are taken directly from Tāranātha's *Mine of Jewels* and even retain his colophons. The rest seem to be authored by Kongtrul, though he attributes them to other sources and naturally to Jamyang Khyentse Wangpo. Even an empowerment for the Four Deities Combined is included here, as part of the mahākāla series. He follows Tāranātha's general style and often hearkens back to the first and main empowerment, which is called Removing All Obstacles. Kongtrul presents a list of the thirteen from the manual by Kyishö Ngawang Tenzin Trinle,[8] but oddly they are not exactly the same as his thirteen. To clarify, the titles of Kongtrul's thirteen empowerments have been added at the front of his text.

Finally, the last four texts of important Protector practices include two for the cherished practice of Protector Entering the Heart: the authorization *Sealed with Life Force*, and the *Guru Yoga* instruction. Then there is the ritual for investiture of power, called *Clouds of Virtue and Goodness*, and the particular conferral ritual of Kṣetrapāla, one of the retinue of Six-Armed Mahākāla but addressed separately here. All of these are by Jamgön Kongtrul.

At the very end of Tāranātha's *Brief Account of the Origins*, he states that though he wrote this brief account, if one wants to learn more, a holy guru must teach it. This cannot be emphasized enough.

33. Treasure Trove of Awakened Activity

Sādhana and Torma Ritual for Glorious Awareness Protector Six-Armed Mahākāla[1]

Tāranātha

oṃ svasti
I bow and go for refuge to the Guru-Protector inseparable.

Wrathful form of Avalokiteśvara's compassion
who grinds to dust the hordes of nasty devils;
at the lotus feet of the Guru-Protector inseparable
I bow with respect and write this brief sādhana.

A yogin who holds the sacred pledges and has properly received all the stages of blessings for this [practice] should set out unimpaired images, offerings, tormas, and so forth. While you maintain the yoga of yourself as the yidam, consecrate the inner offering[2] as in the yidam's liturgical description, or as described below in the torma consecration. Sprinkle [the liquid inner offering] around the dwelling place, offering substances, and tormas.

Cleanse:

[oṃ vajra] amṛta [kundṇḍali hana hana hūṃ phaṭ]

Purify:

oṃ svabhāva [śuddāḥ sarva dharmaḥ svabhāva 'ham]

> From within emptiness, the dwelling place arises from *bhrūṃ* as a celestial palace. In its center, the syllable *A* becomes a wide and vast kapāla of awareness. Within that, the melting of *hūṃ*s produces drinking water, washing water, flowers, incense, lights, perfume, food, and music—filling the reaches of space.

Say the mantras for consecrating the offerings: *oṃ vajra arghaṃ svāhā / oṃ vajra padyaṃ svāhā / oṃ vajra puṣpe āḥ hūṃ* . . . (etc. through) . . . *śabda*. Play music for the descent of blessings as in general practice. Then the consecration of the torma: {575}

> Wind arises from *yaṃ*, fire from *raṃ*, three skull hearthstones from *kaṃ*, and on them a three-piece kapāla from *A*, white on the outside and red inside. In its center, human meat comes from *na*; in the east, ox meat from *go*; in the south, dog meat from *ku*; in the west, horse meat from *da*; and in the north, elephant meat from *ha*. They are marked by *hūṃ - bhrūṃ - aṃ - jriṃ - khaṃ*. Above them, in the center, urine from *mu*; in the east, feces from *vi*; in the south, blood from *ra*; in the west, semen from *śu*; and in the north, extract of human flesh from *ma*. They are marked by *vāṃ - māṃ - lāṃ - pāṃ - tāṃ*. Above them is an upside-down white *oṃ*, and above that a moon from *A*, and from *hūṃ* a vajra flaying knife marked with *hūṃ*. Light radiates from the *hūṃ*. Wind stirs, fire burns—the contents melt and boil. Steam rises up striking *oṃ* and *hūṃ*; streams of elixir flow down. Light from *hūṃ* invokes the elixir of awareness from the hearts of all the tathāgatas and it dissolves [into the skull]. The *oṃ* letter, moon, and vajra or flaying knife fall. The vajra or flaying knife stirs [the contents] three times. Everything melts and the torma becomes a vast ocean of undissipating elixir.
> *oṃ āḥ hūṃ ha hoḥ hrīḥ* {576}
>
> *oṃ svabhāva śuddha sarva dharma svabhāva śuddho 'haṃ*
>
> From within emptiness, the letter *hūṃ* produces the vajra protection circle. Within it, in the center of the unbearable great charnel ground, a multicolored lotus comes from *paṃ* and a sun from *raṃ*. Upon that, white *gaṃ* melts into light and arises as

white Gaṇapati with a three-eyed elephant's head. In his right hand he holds a leafy radish, the essence of earth, which he feeds to his mouth. In his left hand he holds a mongoose that vomits jewels. He is adorned by silks and jewels. Gems flow out from his orifices—mouth, anus, and pores—as he lies prone. On top of him, *hūṃ* becomes a blazing vajra[-handled] flaying knife marked with a deep-blue *hūṃ*. It radiates light, annihilating all enemies, obstructors, and noxious spirits. The light makes offerings to the noble ones and enacts the welfare of sentient beings, then returns and dissolves [into *hūṃ*].

That completely transforms into Six-Armed Swift-Acting Awareness Protector, fulfiller of the hopes of living beings just as they wish. He is pitch black like the clouds at the end of all time. He has one face and six arms and glares angrily with his three round, red eyes. His gaping mouth reveals bared fangs and a curling tongue that twitches from deep down as he laughs fiercely from his awesome mouth. His tawny eyebrows, whiskers, and hair swirl upward. His forehead is anointed with a drop of vermilion.[3] His head is sealed above by King Akṣobhya. He holds a vajra flaying knife with his first right hand above his heart and a skull cup filled with the flesh and blood of enemies and obstructors with his first left hand, below his heart. He holds a dry skull garland with his middle right hand and violently rattles a ḍamaru with the lower right. He holds a trident with his middle left hand and a black vajra lasso with the lower hand. His two legs, with the strength to completely suppress the three levels of existence, stand in a perfectly straight parallel position pressing down on the obstructor king, Gaṇapati. He wears a tiger-skin skirt tied with a green silk sash. The ornaments of the great nāgas adorn him: {577} blue snakes bind his hair, and he has red snake earrings, striped snake armbands, a white snake collar, yellow snake bracelets, a green snake necklace, and white snake anklets and belt. On all his arms and legs there are strings of large and small bells. He is short and fat, with a protruding belly and thick limbs. He has boundless charisma that is difficult to bear. He has a crown of five dry human skulls and a garland of fifty fresh skulls dripping with blood. He is beautified by the six bone ornaments and a jewel on his crown. His terrifying roars of *ha ha* and *hūṃ*

hūṃ phaṭ phaṭ resound like thunder, annihilating all devils and enemy obstructors. He stands within a bonfire of timeless awareness like the fire at the end of the eon, supported by the trunk of a sandalwood tree.

To his left, in the middle of a turbulent sea of blood and fat, *bhyoḥ* becomes Śrīdevī, mighty queen of the desire realm. She is black, awesome, and wrathful. She waves a devil's black cross-scored stick in her right hand and grasps a bag of diseases with her left. On the front of her mount's harness hang black and white spotted dice and a bundle of red curses (*byad dmar*). On the back is a weaponized ball of yarn. [These are] her five magical weapons.[4] She has three eyes, bared teeth, and her face is gathered into a wrathful grimace. Her hair swirls upward and is adorned by a peacock-feather fan. The sun rises from her navel and the moon from the crown of her head. She rides a three-legged mule. The front part of its saddle is made from the upper jawbone of a bloodthirsty demon (*rākṣasa*), and the back part from the lower jawbone. She wears a hair-felt skirt and black clothing. An elephant hide covers her upper back and an ox hide her lower back. She wears bone ornaments and a crown and garland of human heads. Her right earring is a poisonous snake and the left is a lion. She stands in the midst of a conflagration of fire and dark wind. {578} A retinue of one hundred thousand flesh-eating ḍākinīs and mātṛkās surrounds her.

In front of the principal figures, *kṣiṃ* becomes Yakṣa Kṣetrapāla. He is blue-black with a gaping mouth and bared fangs, bellowing at his enemies. Winds of the end-times rise from his nose. With his right hand he brandishes a flaying knife to the sky, terrifying all the gods and demigods. With his left hand he feeds the principal's mouth from a blood-filled skull cup containing the hearts of enemies and obstructors. He rides a crazed black bear and is surrounded by a retinue of hordes of noxious yakṣas.

To the right, *hūṃ* becomes Īśvara Jinamitra. He is dark red with the body of a wrathful bloodthirsty demon. Poison and blood spews from his mouth. He rattles a ḍamaru violently with his right hand and with his left hand makes the threatening gesture with fire shooting out from his pointing finger. A retinue of planetary spirits and bloodthirsty demons surrounds him.

In back, *ṭaṃ* becomes the death lord, Yamarāja Ṭakkirāja. He is black and ravenous for human flesh and blood. With his right hand he throws a lasso made of intestines at enemies and with his left he shows the threatening gesture to harm-doers. Hordes of death lords surround him. Those three are all adorned by bone ornaments and tiger-skin skirts.

To the left, *hūṃ* becomes the great devil lord, Trakṣad. He is black like the clouds at the end of time. He pierces the enemies' hearts with a red three-pronged ensign spear in his right hand and drinks from a blood-filled skull cup in his left. He bites his lower lip and bares his fangs. He wears a black cloak with maroon svāstika designs, high rawhide boots, and a golden belt. He rides a black devil horse with white fetlocks. He is surrounded by a retinue of countless armies of gods and devils.

All four of them glare at enemies and obstructors with three round red eyes, gnash their terrible four fangs, and appear very agitated, savage, and wrathful. They have stocky, ugly forms and their orange eyebrows, whiskers, and hair blaze like fire. {579} They wear crowns of dry skulls and garlands of human heads dripping with blood. They dwell in the midst of violently swirling fire and wind.

Around them, yellow Śakra is in the east riding an elephant and holding a vajra; red Agni is in the southeast riding a urial goat; blue Yama is in the south riding a water buffalo and holding a club; maroon Rākṣasa is in the southwest riding a zombie and holding a sword; white Varuṇa is in the west riding a makara and holding a snake lasso; green Vāyu is in the northwest riding a stag and holding a banner; yellow Yakṣa is in the north riding a horse and holding a gem-studded club; and white Bhūta is in the northeast riding an ox and holding a trident. Each of them embraces their personal goddess. Above them, yellow Brahmā is riding a swan and holding a vase. Below, black Pārthiva is riding a boar and holding a blazing jewel. They are all completely surrounded by one hundred thousand of their own kind. They pay homage to the principal ones with their left hands.

Further, all around are the seventy-five protectors of the pure abodes: the eight great gods, such as Mahādeva; the eight great nāgas, such as Vāsuki; the eight great planets, such as Sun; the nine great terrifiers (bhairavas), such as Rudra; the twenty-eight constellations, such as Kṛttikā (Pleiades); and the four great kings, such as Dhṛtarāṣṭra. They are each surrounded by a retinue of millions.

Outside of them are the eight classes of gods and rakṣas, the retinue armies of oath-bound [protectors]. They look horrible and ruthless, with gaping mouths, bloodshot eyes, bared fangs, scowling faces, and ferocious demeaners. They carry various lethal weapons in their hands and could suck out the vital breath of all living beings in an instant. {580} They wear the garb of yakṣas, rākṣasas, yamas, māras, and mātṛkās. They completely cover the ground and fill all the sky and space. All are perfectly fulfilling the hopes and desires of practitioners. All are marked with white *oṃ* at the forehead, red *āḥ* at the throat, and blue *hūṃ* at the heart.

Light rays radiate from the *hūṃ* in my heart, invoking Swift-Acting Awareness Protector Six-Armed Mahākāla from in front of the single trunk of a sandalwood tree in the great charnel ground Cool Grove in the southeast.[5] He arrives instantly with the root and lineage gurus above him, strong heroes on his right, smiling heroines on his left, and all the armies of obedient ones, realm protectors, messengers, and an ocean of the oath-bound, accompanied by the sounds of ḍamarus, bells, and small bells: *si li li–khro lo lo–ur ur–chem chem.*

hūṃ
By faith and by sacred pledge,
great Mahākāla, come here.
Glorious Protector with your retinue,
please approach the site of this mandala.

Kṣetrapāla and the others,
retinue of obedient ones, hosts of yakṣas,
you who promised to guard the doctrine,
ocean of the oath-bound, please approach.

When you come to this mandala site,
partake of this decorated torma,

show yourselves in signs and forms,
and accomplish the entrusted activity.

oṃ vajra mahākāla saparivāra kṣiṃ . . . (etc.).

Repeat *kṣiṃ* twenty-one times. Then in place of *kṣiṃ*, insert *e hye hi* [and] *vajra samājaḥ* three times each. Swift Actor and retinue are invoked.

hūṃ
Just as, in the presence of Vajradhara,
you promised and took an oath,
please come to this blessed place
and stay to protect the doctrine.

jaḥ hūṃ vaṃ hoḥ—they dissolve indivisibly.

padma kamalāyastvaṃ

This excellent drinking water, a divine substance {581}
produced through interdependent origination,
I offer to Protector and entourage:
please accept it to guard the doctrine.

oṃ śri mahākālaya sapārivāra arghaṃ pratīccha hūṃ svāhā

Similarly, substitute "washing water" [for drinking water] and *padyaṃ* [for *arghaṃ*]; "flowers" and *puṣpe*; "incense" and *dhūpe*; "light" and *āloke*; "perfume" and *gandhe*; "food" and *naividyā*; and "music" and *śabda.* Present the inner offerings by adding the three seed syllables to the essence mantra.

Without stirring from the realm of reality,
yet your wrathful form to subdue the vicious
vanquishes the rudra of the doctrine;
homage and praise to Great Black One.

Then if you wish to do just the daily practice and torma ritual, it is suitable to only continue from the torma offering below. But if you wish to practice the topics of Guru-Protector Inseparable, Dispelling Defilements, and Getting Down to the Vital Point (*gnad dbab*) to properly receive the precepts, you should know in detail the visualizations and important points according to the esoteric instructions.

Guru-Protector Inseparable

The supplication to the guru and Protector:

> Above Protector's head, my benevolent root guru is yellow and as brilliant as one hundred thousand suns, holds a wish-fulfilling gem to the heart with the right hand, a golden bell at the hip with the left, and sits in vajra posture, adorned by all decorations. The guru is the essence of all the lineage gurus starting with Vajradhara. Light radiates from the guru's body—Protector becomes the nature of light and bliss, dancing with the sounds of *ur ur, sil sil*. Light radiates from Protector and dissolves into the guru's body. Guru becomes the nature of light and bliss, dancing and ringing the bell with the sounds of *sil sil, khrol khrol*. Guru is Protector. Protector is Guru. Guru and Protector are inseparable.
>
> I and all sentient beings throughout the reaches of space
> supplicate Guru-Protector inseparable. {582}
> We supplicate Protector-Guru inseparable.
> We supplicate the benevolent root guru.
> We supplicate the pervading lord Great Vajradhara.
> We supplicate glorious mighty Śavarīpa.
> We supplicate Lord Maitrīpa the Great.
> We supplicate the adept Rāhula the Great.
> We supplicate the learned adept Khyungpo Naljor.
> We supplicate incomparable Rinchen Tsöndru.
> We supplicate the realized Zhangom Chöseng.
> We supplicate the great Öntön Kyergangpa.
> We supplicate Nyentön Bepei Naljor.
> We supplicate Drogön Sangye Tönpa.
> We supplicate Khedrup Shangtön Chöje.
> We supplicate Khyungpo Tsultrim Gönpo.

We supplicate Jadral Ritrö Rechen.
We supplicate Khyenden Shangpa Karpo.
We supplicate Nyame Sangye Palzang.
We supplicate Drupchen Namkha Gyaltsen.
We supplicate Gyagom Lekpa Gyaltsen.
We supplicate Jetsun Kunga Drolchok.
We supplicate Chöku Lhawang Drakpa.
We supplicate Jetsun Tāranātha.[6]
We supplicate Gyaltsap Rinchen Gyatso.
We supplicate Gyaltsap Yeshe Gyatso.
We supplicate Khedrup Lodrö Namgyal.
We supplicate Chöje Ngawang Trinle.
We supplicate Chöje Kunzang Wangpo.
We supplicate Rikzin Tsewang Norbu.
We supplicate Kagyu Trinle Shingta.
We supplicate Tenzin Chökyi Nyima. {583}
We supplicate Kagyu Trinle Namgyal.
We supplicate Pema Nyinje Wangpo.

namo buddhāya / namo guruhe / vajra vīra vīriṇe / śrī ḍāka ḍākinī / joga jogiṇī / sarva buddha bodhisatvaya śarāṇī / gacchāmi

Kyai!
Holy root and lineage gurus dwelling in the ten directions and three times, bless me. Yidam deities of the mandala, bless me. Heroes and heroine yoginīs, bless me. Buddhas and bodhisattvas all, bless me. Glorious Six-Armed Awareness Protector and deities, do not veil your timeless awareness. Do not delay your compassion. Do not block your power and ability. Do not distance your blessings. All of you, bless me through your body, bless me through your speech, bless me through your mind. Bless me through your unlimited awakened body, speech, mind, qualities, and activities. Bless me right now! Bless me quickly! Bless me on this very seat!

Guru-Protector inseparable,
I supplicate you with faith:

remove every affliction
of myself and all sentient beings.
Please grant every spiritual power.

Dispelling Defilements

Above Protector's head, my root guru is white Vajrasattva, his right hand holding a five-pronged crystal vajra at his heart and his left hand in equipoise with an elixir-filled skull cup on top. He sits in vajra cross-legged position, with infinite light radiating from his body. Light rays radiate from his heart and invoke the vajra body, speech, and mind of all buddhas and bodhisattvas in the forms of deities. {584} They are arrayed in the sky above.

Repeat Vajrasattva's hundred syllables twenty-one times. Afterward recite:

Vajradhara and glorious Śavarī,
sovereign Maitrīpa, great adept Rāhula,
Amideva, Lokeśvara,
Hayagrīva, glorious Padmākara,

Khyungpo Yogi, Ratna Vīrya,
Dharma Siṃha, Dharma Prajñā,
Vīrya Siṃha, Shangtön Chöje, and the others,
gurus of the jewel lineage, please think of me.

I did not realize that the guru with a lineage
of perfected qualities that fulfill beings' hopes
was the embodiment of doubly pure buddhas of the three times:
I confess falling under the influence of worldly thought.

All outer, inner, and secret deities with awakened body, speech, mind,
qualities, and activities, please think of me.
Now that I enter the door of supreme Mantra Vehicle,
I confess my transgressions and damages of its root and branch pledges.

With your abundant activity of power and capability,
just recalling you for an instant dispels all obstacles.
Giver of spiritual powers without meeting or parting:
Six-Armed Awareness Protector, please think of me.

In secluded charnel grounds, forests, and islands,
I collected the outer and inner supports and pledge substances,
but did not properly do the recitations, fulfillments, and confessions;
I confess falling under the influence of laziness and distraction.

In particular, I did not realize that the supreme secret support
is the great-bliss kāya of the Guru-Protector inseparable.
Through constant devotion and belief in you,
I confess not realizing you as totally pure dharmakāya.

Whatever I have done under the influence of ignorant delusion
that opposes the body, speech, and mind of Guru-Protector and retinue,
with a mind full of sorrow and regret
I confess before your eyes, sublime deity.

Awareness beings who carry out my commands,
activity messengers Kṣetrapāla, Jinamitra,
Ṭakkirāja, Trakṣad, and Rematī,[7]
protectors of the ten directions and pure regions, please think of me. {585}

True to your word and commitment,
straight away you accomplished my activities,
but sadly I did not offer a flesh-and-blood torma feast;
I confess not giving thanks in a timely way.

With no clairvoyance, I did not realize the faults and mistakes
of the doctrine's destroyers and guru's lethal enemies,
and so I did not destroy them with wrathful activity;
I confess disclosing the secrets and loving them.

Whatever errors, faults, and delusions I have committed,
such as being contaminated by talking or eating with
vow-breakers,
or meager offerings, spoiled select portions, and mixed-up rituals;
I confess with shame and regret.

I confess violating the sacred pledges of awakened body.
I confess violating the sacred pledges of awakened speech.
I confess violating the sacred pledges of awakened mind.
I confess violating the root sacred pledges.
I confess violating the branch sacred pledges.
I confess consciously violating the sacred pledges.
I confess unconsciously violating the sacred pledges.

I have confessed in order to purify the defilement of violation.
Guru and Protector with your entourage,
please be patient with me, as parents with their child,
and now grant me all the spiritual powers.

Though the acts I confess and the act of confession are
nonexistent,
in order to purify the habitual patterns of discursive thought,
I fully confess before the sublime object of my venerable guru.
May I thereby attain great bliss.

Getting Down to the Vital Point

Above Protector's head, my benevolent root guru is red and rattles a skull ḍamaru with the right hand and holds an elixir-filled skull cup to the heart with the left hand. The guru is so brilliant it is hard to bear, youthful and charming with a passionate expression, sitting in cross-legged position. Ḍākinīs and the three existences are brought under control just by the guru's glance. {586} At Protector's forehead there is a triangular spot of vermilion, on which are thirteen red *hrīḥ* letters, the essence of noble Lokeśvara, Lord of the World. They completely transform into thirteen red secret ḍākinīs, youthful, with one face and two arms, holding small drums in their right hands and skull cups filled with elixir in the left. They stand in the posture of right leg bent and left outstretched, gazing with three eyes wide open and dancing; the essence of Tārā. They bring under control all sentient beings in the three realms. All needs and desires fall like rain.

oṃ vajra nara kriṃ kriṃ hūṃ hūṃ phaṭ phaṭ svāhā

Repeat one hundred times or more.

A black mantra garland with red light rays emerges from *hūṃ* in my heart. It appears like rosary beads while the five-colored light rays thread them like a rosary string. It emerges from my mouth and enters Protector's mouth, dissolving into the *hūṃ* in his heart. It arises again from *hūṃ*, emerges from Protector's navel, enters my navel, and dissolves in the *hūṃ* at my heart.

Imagine that it circulates continuously in that way, and say:

oṃ vajra mahākāla saparivāra kṣiṃ kṣetra vighnān vināyaka hūṃ hūṃ phaṭ (say that and add a second) *phaṭ* (and) *svāhā*

It is also appropriate to make it twenty-two letters [by those additions]. Recite the essence mantra however much. Do the visualization for the wrathful recitation:

oṃ śrī mahākāla śāsana / upahāriṇi / eṣo 'paścima kālo ayaṃ idaṃ ratna trayāya / apakāriṇaṃ yadi pratijñāṃ/ smarasi tadā / idaṃ duṣṭaṃ kha kha khāhi khāhi / māra māra / gṛhṇa gṛhṇa / bandha bandha / hana hana / daha daha / paca paca / dinamek-ena māraya hūṃ phaṭ

This wrathful mantra is said to include the three [injunctions to] call, curse, and kill.

Śrīdevī's namesake mantra and essence mantra:

oṃ śrīdevī hūṃ phaṭ
bhyoḥ mamo nakmo vetāli sindha kulu kulu hūṃ phaṭ svāhā

The essence mantras of the four workers:

oṃ kṣetrapāla vighnān hūṃ phaṭ
oṃ jinamitra vāśaṃ kuru hūṃ phaṭ
oṃ ṭakkirāja samaya bhyoḥ du jaḥ hūṃ phaṭ
oṃ du yogja mahākāla trakṣad hūṃ phaṭ {487}

Do as much of those recitations as you can. At the end:

The tongues of the Protector and retinue become tubes of red vajra light arisen from *hūṃ*, through which they suck up the torma and drink it. They are satisfied and delighted by the undissipating bliss in their mind streams.

After the essence mantra, add *idaṃ baliṃta kha kha khāhi khāhi* or

oṃ vajra mahākāla kṣiṃ kṣetra vighanen vināyaka trakrakmo baliṃta māṃsa rakta rudhira kha kha khāhi khāhi

Likewise after the essence mantras of the entourage, add *idam baliṃta kha kha khāhi khāhi* and offer three times each. Then offer with *mahākāla sapārivāra arghaṃ* . . . (etc.) and do the inner offering as before. [The praise:]

hūṃ
Homage to Swift-Acting Avalokita.
Your bangled feet trample Vināyaka.[8]
Great Black One in a tiger-skin skirt,
your six arms are fully adorned by snake ornaments,
top right hand holding flaying knife, the middle a rosary,
and the last fiercely rattling a ḍamaru.
Your left hands hold a skull, a trident,
and a lasso that catches and binds.
Your wrathful gaping mouth fully bares fangs.
You have three eyes, wild hair streaming upward,
and a spot of vermilion anointing your forehead.
King Akṣobhya is the seal above your head.
You wear a garland of fifty blood-dripping human heads
and a crown of five skulls with jewel finials.

Come from your tree to accept the torma.
Glorious Six-Armed One, I pay homage and praise.

Strictly guard the Buddha's doctrine,
strictly honor the sovereignty of the Three Jewels,
and for us, master, disciples, and entourage,
please pacify all adverse conditions and obstacles
and quickly grant whatever spiritual powers we desire.

Thrice you burned Laṅkāpurī to protect
Buddha's doctrine and conquer the devil hordes.
With one face and six arms, Great Black One {589}
with a fearsome form: I pay homage and praise.

bhyoḥ
In a vast lake of seething, boiling blood,
you sit astride a sturdy mule, ablaze with charisma.
Dark blue, with one face and two arms,
you hold a devil's cross-scored stick and a bag of disease.

Emanations of your body guard the Buddha's doctrine.
Emanations of your speech shake the three realms.
Your immutable mind accomplishes beings' welfare.
Sole Mother Rematī: I pay homage to you.

hūṃ
Obedient ones in four directions around glorious Protector,
action messengers who accomplish Awareness's commands,
spreading various emanations to subdue all malevolent forces,
four action messengers; I praise you.

Śakra, Yama, Varuṇa, Yakṣa,
Agni, Rākṣasa, Vāyu, Bhūta,
Brahmā above, and Earth Goddess;
ten emanated direction protectors, I pay homage and praise.

Seventy-five glorious protectors
and armies of an ocean of the oath-bound:

accept this flesh-and-blood torma
and dispel adverse conditions and obstacles,
grant favorable spiritual powers,
and accomplish all entrusted activity
for us yogins and our retinue.

If you have an [end-of-]session torma, attach a flame to it and offer it on top of buildings and other [high] places.

Glorious Protector Mahākāla and Sole Mother Rematī,
mighty one of the desire realm, sister and brother,
and those who do not oppose your command,
Kṣetrapāla, Jinamitra, Ṭakkirāja,
the devil lord Trakṣad and others,
glorious Great Black One and retinue:
come here to accept this decorated torma.
Accept this red torma of flesh and blood.
Accept this Jambudvīpa food.
Accept this beer, the hero's select portion.
I offer it in strict gratitude for previously entrusted action.
Accept it now as strict supplication for entrusted action.
Make your retinue my guards and repel adverse conditions.
Grind into dust all the many forms
of devils and obstacles—
hateful enemies and harmful obstructors. {589}
Quickly accomplish acts that spread the doctrine
and perform the activities that yogins request.

If you do not have the session torma, it is unnecessary to do this general offering during regular practice. Repeat many hundred-syllable mantras. Say, "For whatever has been left out . . ." (*ma 'byor ba dang* . . . etc.) and

Whatever was missing or incomplete,
or anything I was incapable of doing,
for whatever was not done here,
I ask your reasonable forbearance.

Guru-Protector inseparable,
I go for refuge with devotion.
May I dispel every afflictive emotion
of all sentient beings.

oṃ
You enact all benefit for sentient beings
and grant them appropriate spiritual powers.
Though you depart now for the buddha lands,
please be sure to return again.
vajra muḥ

Awareness beings among the torma guests return to their natural abodes. Pledge beings dissolve into my heart.

If there is a support image, do the request [to the awareness beings] to remain immanent. Make aspiration prayers. Recite the *Sealed Word of Auspiciousness*:

Qualities fully perfected like the snow mountains,
from which blessing rivers quench fortunate disciples,
you who reveal my own mind as coemergence:
may there be auspiciousness of the sublime gurus, dharma sovereigns.

You watch over practitioners as your children,
ever together like a body and its shadow,
giver of spiritual powers to those with sacred pledge;
may there be auspiciousness of the yidam deities.

You take care of practitioners holding vows
and properly accomplish various awakened activity,
such as pacifying, enriching, controlling, and subjugating;
may there be auspiciousness of the dharma protectors.

Apparent existence self-liberates like illusion and dream,
that is the experience of uninterrupted great bliss

in the space of empty clarity without mental engagement;
may there be auspiciousness of great-bliss mahāmudrā.

Whether they support and offer to practitioners
or treat them with contempt,
everyone will be placed on the path of awakening; {590}
may there be auspiciousness of the incomparable awakening mind.

However many states of auspiciousness there are
in all of cyclic existence and its transcendence,
like the course of a great river of abundance;
may there be auspiciousness for all beings always.

May merit rise like the sovereign Supreme Mountain,
great acclaim pervade everywhere like the sky,
and long life, health, and others' welfare be spontaneously present;
may there be auspiciousness of an ocean of supreme qualities.[9]

[Variations]

If you would rather do the four-armed goddess, visualize that her right hands hold a sword with a scorpion handle and a flaying knife, and her left hands hold a victory banner of [the skin of] a misbegotten child and a fresh skull. Otherwise, the two-armed version holds a blazing sword in her right hand and a blood-filled skull cup in the left. In both cases, the front part of the saddle is formed from the upper jawbone of a bloodthirsty demon, with the cross-scored stick and the lower jawbone forming the back part with the bag of diseases attached. The mantra for Four-Armed Śrīdevī is *oṃ mama sarva cadur bhakṣa jaḥ / remati urva urva / samatrir / ja hūṃ hūṃ phaṭ phaṭ*. The mantra for this two-armed version is the same as the mantra given in the course of the text and *oṃ trag rakmo rakta rudhira hūṃ phaṭ*.

During the praises for the two-armed goddess, change the line to "holding a flaming sword and blood-filled skull cup." For the four-armed, change the lines to "dark blue, with one face and four arms / holding a sword, flaying knife, banner, and fresh skull."

The activity [protectors] also vary: Kṣetrapāla is dark brown, Jinamitra holds a small hand drum and blood-filled skull cup; Ṭakkirāja holds a small hand drum and makes the threatening gesture; the devil lord Trakṣad has four hands holding a red club, long beam, hammer, and blood-filled skull cup. These versions are also suitable. Moreover, Jinamitra holds a diamond in his right hand and throws a cutting wheel with his left, or else holds a ḍamaru and a wheel. Ṭakkirāja holds a knife and a skull cup with heart inside, or holds Yama's flaying knife and skull cup. Alternatively, keep the hand implements from the main text, except visualize Jinamitra as green and Ṭakkirāja as red. Any of these versions is appropriate.

During the activity application (*las sbyor*), visualize the protectors on mounts. In that case, definitely visualize the goddess and the devil lord with four arms. Jinamitra rides a lion and Ṭakkirāja rides a tiger. Their hand implements are the same as before, or else they ride wolves and hold hooks and lassos. Meditating like that, offer the torma. {591}

If you are unable to do the extensive visualization of the retinue, after the description of the main figure, just say their names or say, "Completely surrounded by an ocean of the oath-bound." Then continue from "At their foreheads is *oṃ* . . . (etc.)."

For a middle-length torma ritual, do not visualize the retinue; just visualize the principal figure alone and continue with the invocation. Make the offerings without the verses. The concise ritual is just an invocation of the awareness beings without visualizing the pledge beings. Recite from "Light rays radiate from the *hūṃ* in my heart, invoking Swift-Acting Awareness Protector Six-Armed Mahākāla from in front of the single trunk of a sandalwood tree in the great charnel ground Cool Grove in the southeast . . . (etc.)." In both the middle-length and abridged versions, skip the visualizations of the three vital topics and just offer the torma and so on. Except for the times of the approach phase of recitation, generally this latter version is the main one for daily practice.

Concerning the self-visualization, in general, any yidam is certainly permissible. It seems that Cakrasaṃvara, Hevajra, Yamāntaka, or Hayagrīva have been the main choices. You can make the self- and front-visualized deity inseparable, or keep them separate, according to this liturgical description of the principal deity alone, or based on such texts as *Adorned Protector Secret Sādhana*.[10] They are all drawn from source esoteric instructions, so there is no contradiction with scripture and reason. Therefore, they are certainly very appropriate. However, a beginner may want to do the practice as described in the course of this text.

[Concluding Verses and Colophon]

This expression of the very short sādhana
of the Guru-Protector Inseparable
was surely well presented by past holy ones.
This was done in response to others' requests.

I have written the lines above,
very clearly and neither too short nor too long,
with the idea to benefit simple folk with various interests,
and divided it into sequences fitting to the individuals.

Through this virtue may obstacles to awakening
be pacified and all conducive conditions attained.
May it become the cause for the immediate attainment
of every common and supreme spiritual power.

May all those with toxic, angry minds
be instantly eliminated;
may pacifying, enriching, controlling, and wrathful
awakened activity spread in the ten directions.

At the request of many excellent spiritual mentors, the vagabond Tāranātha composed this at the age of twenty-seven on the eighth day of the waxing moon under [the constellation] Chitra Nakshatra.

34. Spontaneous Accomplishment of the Four Actions

A Supplement to the Long Torma Ritual of Glorious Swift-Acting Awareness Protector, with a Clearly Arranged Sequence[1]

Jamgön Kongtrul

namo guru jñāna nāthūya

Magical emanation of Avalokiteśvara's compassion,
displaying the form of Great Black Devil Subduer:
Guru-Protector inseparable, bowing to you
I will arrange this supplement to the long torma ritual.

The all-knowing lord Tāranātha created a sādhana and torma ritual for Glorious Awareness Protector Six-Armed Mahākāla called *Treasure Trove of Awakened Activity* at the age of twenty-seven. Everything that is required for practice is complete and explained in detail therein, so it is an indispensable manual for yogins of this protector. A more abbreviated version is now included in *Mine of Jewels: Sādhanas of an Ocean of Yidams*.[2] However, this does not include the full versions of Dispelling Defilements and Getting Down to the Vital Point. So obviously it is somewhat inadequate for those who have received the permissions and wish to do the approach phase of recitation and so on. I see it as convenient for those doing only the simple torma ritual. There is also a text that he wrote at age twenty-three that is all-inclusive but extremely brief, and an even more concise version that he gave to Nyima Namgyal, the attendant at Gangkar (which is chapter 35). These are good as daily yoga practices for those who cannot handle elaboration.

In all of these versions, those who have received the blessings and guidance of the general permission and particularly that of the Guru-Protector

Inseparable Entering the Heart and have previously completed the approach and attainment practices may visualize both themselves and the one in front as the Protector and retinue. Those who have only received the common permission and have not done the approach and attainment stages previously would do well to visualize themselves as the yidam with the Protector and retinue in front. {595} It is said that any appropriate yidam may be used for the self-visualization—for instance, the new Kadampas use the secret sādhana of Hayagrīva as the self-visualization—so it is not restricted. However, in our practice tradition [we should use] the Principal Deities of the Five Families as the [self-visualization of one's] body mandala according to the text of Venerable [Tāranātha] Rinpoche.[3] On occasions like the torma ritual, if you use Tāranātha's own composition of Kyergangpa's Hayagrīva activity manual called *Subduing All Haughty Ones*,[4] it will make a good connection [to our lineage] and turn out very well. I mention this as an aside.

In this case, I took the extensive version of *Treasure Trove of Awakened Activity* as the basic text. Then I added any relevant materials, such as slightly shorter versions for daily practice, the torma rituals for the Great Torma Ritual on the twenty-ninth day [of the lunar month],[5] and additional occasions such as the Flaming [Mouth] offerings. Putting all that together, I wrote this text.

To begin, if you are not able to do the slightly extensive visualization description for situations like daily recitation, then do this:

> *oṃ svabhāva* . . . (etc. purifies).
>
> From within emptiness the letter *hūṃ*
> becomes a protection circle and great charnel ground.
> In its center a lotus comes from *paṃ* and a sun from *raṃ*.
> From *gi* on top comes white Gaṇapati with an elephant's head,
> lying prone and holding a radish and mongoose.
> On him, *hūṃ* becomes a *hūṃ*-marked flaying knife radiating light
> that annihilates enemies, makes offerings to the exalted ones,
> achieves the welfare of beings, and returns, completely transforming
> into Swift-Acting Awareness Protector, blazing blue-black, {596}
> with one face, six arms, and three round, red eyes.
> His curled tongue twitches in his gaping mouth as he laughs fiercely;

his tawny eyebrows, whiskers, and hair swirl upward;
he has a vermilion drop; and is crowned by King Akṣobhya.
He holds a flaying knife and blood-filled skull cup in the upper two hands,
tells a skull garland and waves a trident with his middle hands,
and rattles a ḍamaru and throws a lasso with the lower hands.
His legs in parallel position press on the Obstructor King.
He wears a dry skull crown and wet-head garland,
a tiger-skin skirt, silks, and jewels.
He is adorned by eight great nāgas, six bone ornaments,
and strings of bells that jingle on his wrists and ankles.
He is short with a protruding belly and thick limbs,
unbearably brilliant in an expanse of blazing end-time fire,
his body supported by the trunk of a sandalwood tree.

To his left, in the middle of a turbulent sea of blood and fat,
bhyoḥ becomes Glorious Goddess, black mistress of the desire realm,
with the expression of fury, bearing five magical weapons,
her hair flows upward, adorned by a peacock feather fan.
The sun rises from her navel and the moon from her crown.
Her right earring is a poisonous snake and the left a leaping lion.
Elephant and ox hides cover her upper and lower body,
she wears a thatched felt skirt and black clothing,
is draped with bone ornaments and human-head garland,
and rides a three-legged mule in the midst of fire and wind.
She is surrounded by a hundred thousand flesh-eating mātṛkā ḍākinīs.

In front, from *kṣim*, black Kṣetrapāla appears
holding knife and skull, riding a crazed bear,
surrounded by a host of noxious yakṣas.
To the right, from *hūṃ*, comes red Jinamitra
rattling a small drum, flames blazing from his pointed finger,
surrounded by a retinue of terrifying planets and rākṣasas.
In back, from *ṭāṃ*, comes black Ṭakkirāja,
in his right hand an intestine lasso, the left in pointing gesture,
surrounded by a retinue of wrathful, murderous yamas.

Those three wear bone ornaments and tiger skins.
To the left, from *hūṃ*, is black devil lord Trakṣad,
holding a lance banner and skull cup, riding a white-heeled black horse,
wearing devils' garb, surrounded by an army of gods and devils. {597}
All are fiercely wrathful with skull ornaments
and revel amid conflagrations of fire and wind,
surrounded by hundreds of thousands of their own kind.
Around are the eight gods, eight nāgas, eight planets,
nine bhairavas, twenty-eight constellations,
and the four great kings, each with retinues of millions.
Outside them are the oath-bound, the armies of eight classes,
wearing the garb of yakṣas, rākṣasas, flesh-eaters, yamas,
devils, and mātṛkās; fierce and carrying weapons.
They fill the sky, ground, and intermediate spaces,
looking to fulfill the hopes of practitioners.
All are marked in three places by *oṃ āḥ hūṃ*.
Light radiates from *hūṃ* to the Cool Grove in the southeast,
invoking Great Black from in front of the sandalwood tree
with the guru above, heroes to his right,
heroines to his left, and servants in front.
Instantly with the sounds of drums and bells
they arrive: *sil sil, khrol khrol, ur ur*.

This condensed version of the visualization description is easy to memorize and recite. For extensive activities, once this has been done, apart from doing just these condensed verses of the visualization description, there is no need for other brief [versions]. To begin the invocation, recite this passage by the great adept Khyungpo.

hūṃ
Arise! Arise! Arise from the realm of phenomena.
Without moving from within the pure phenomenal realm,
you display the wrathful form to subdue the wicked.
Great god Mahākāla—you are invoked.

Great Black One, please approach.
Excellent Black One, please approach.
War god of yogins, please approach.
Guardian of awareness holders, please approach.
Black field protector, please approach.
Armies of retinue, please approach.
Attending retinues, hosts of yakṣas,
Kṣetrpāla, please approach.
Ocean of the oath-bound, please approach.

Mahākāla, great mighty one,
with massive body dark blue,
golden-brown hair in dreadlocks, {598}
your topknot locks streaming upward,
sparks darting out from between them,
shooting sparks that burn obstructors.

In an expanse blazing like the final fire of the eon,
on a seat of the enemy vow-breaker,
you stand with feet straight and raised,
three angry eyes darting like lightning.
You snarl at obstructors with sharp, vicious fangs.
You wear a fresh elephant hide on your back
and tiger-skin skirt on the lower body,
draped with a garland of fiery fresh skulls
and adorned by snakes on your ankles and wrists.
You are the great black tamer of nāgas,
with spiders and scorpions shooting out
from your every hair pore.
You disperse emanations to enemy vow-breakers,
filling the three realms by a shake of your topknot
and crushing the spirits of the universe to dust.
Of your six hands, the first right one
wields a blazing meteorite flaying knife
to sever the life of enemies, obstructors, and spirits.
The first left hand holds a blood-filled bhandha
to drink the brain-blood of enemies and obstructors.

The middle right hand tells a rosary
of blazing dry skulls as a sign
of pulling out beings from the six realms.
The middle left hand holds a khaṭvāṅga
with three prongs as a sign
of attaining the resultant three kāyas.
The lower right hand
fiercely rattles a ḍamaru,
taking control of mātṛkās and ḍākinīs.

Mātṛkās and ḍākinīs, please approach!
Come here to accept this flesh-and-blood torma;
perform the action to liberate enemies and obstructors.

The lower left hand
holds a black devil lasso
to snag the necks of doctrine destroyers.

Your retinue—hosts of messengers,
ḍākinīs and powerful movers,
male and female yakṣas,
hosts of Yakṣa Kṣetrapāla—
took vows to act as servants.
Accordingly, come here now.
Take this grain alcohol and rakta blood,
maṃsa flesh and piles of bone, {599}
pledge substances and this torma:
please come here to accomplish the actions.

In the great charnel ground of Cool Grove,
terrifying in the middle of a conflagration
that burns like the fire at the end of the eon,
great mighty Mahākāla
is surrounded by the eight classes, mātṛkās, and ḍākinīs,
unending and inconceivably dark,
and countless white and black goddesses.
In apparent existence, all are your slaves;
in the three existences, all are your retinue;

and all arrogant spirits are your workers.
Quick as lightning, instantly you cover the universe
and reduce hateful enemies and harmful obstructors to dust.

For us practitioners with sacred pledge,
remember the promises you made
before the past and present buddhas:
come here to this place of sacred pledge
with its mountains of torma, lakes of blood,
and elixir swirling like an ocean,
and complete outer, inner, and secret supports.

hūṃ
By faith and by sacred pledge, . . . (etc.).[6]

For a very brief offering, replace "drinking water" and the other specific offerings with "This outer offering of excellent divine substances . . . (etc.)." For the mantras, just recite them together, as in *arghaṃ pādyaṃ* . . . (etc.). For a middle-length offering, follow the main text. For the extensive version, as well as the foregoing, add the offering of five sense pleasures with "This excellent form, a divine substance . . . (etc.)" and insert *rūpa* [in the offering mantra]. Similarly, "music" and *śabda*; "sublime fragrance" and *gandhe*; "sublime taste" and *rasa*; "texture" and *spareśa*. Also, if you wish to do an extensive version of the offering verses, recite the following:

hūṃ
I present actual and imagined offerings, a display of my
absorption:
vajra clouds of outer, inner, and secret offerings
to please in all ways the vajra senses
of my guru, Awareness Protector, and retinue.

I offer libation of pure drinking water with eight qualities,
heaving waves of crimson human blood,
and pristine mahāmudrā devoid of mind-made concepts
to Awareness Protector and retinue.
oṃ śrīvajra mahākāla sapārivara vajra arghaṃ pratīccha svāhā

I offer limpid, smooth, cool washing water: {600}
the water of *A* that purifies all defects in the ocean
that was polluted by the killer Kālakūṭaḥ,[7]
to the feet of Awareness Protector and retinue.
oṃ śrīvajra mahākāla sapārivara vajra padyaṃ pratīccha svāhā

I offer various flowers: utpalas, lilies, hundred-petaled garlands,
the radiant blue lotuses of the five sense organs,
and the open lotus of bliss-emptiness blazing and dripping
to the heads of Awareness Protector and retinue.
oṃ śrīvajra mahākāla sapārivara vajra puṣpe pratīccha svāhā

I offer produced and natural fine aromas pervading everywhere,
smoke clouds of human fat filling space,
and the self-arising incense of illusory false phenomena
to the noses of Awareness Protector and retinue.
oṃ śrīvajra mahākāla sapārivara vajra dhupe pratīccha svāhā

I offer the spreading light of the sun, moon, gems, and lamps,
oil lamps of human fat lit by fires of the hungry ghost realms,
and the lucid clarity of concepts dissolving into the central channel
to the eyes of Awareness Protector and retinue.
oṃ śrīvajra mahākāla sapārivara vajra dīpe pratīccha svāhā

I offer perfumed water of camphor, sandalwood, and saffron,
the five lamps of human blood with congealed fat,
and the sublime salve of dream's delusion arising as the deity
to the bodies of Awareness Protector and retinue.
oṃ śrīvajra mahākāla sapārivara vajra gandhe pratīccha svāhā

I offer food of a hundred flavors and a thousand potencies,
the five special hooks for flesh and bones of enemies and obstructors,
and the quintessence of unhindered awareness to awaken without meditating
to the tongues of Awareness Protector and retinue.
oṃ śrīvajra mahākāla sapārivara vajra naividya pratīccha svāhā

I offer cymbals, horns, flutes, and big drums,
disturbing sounds coming from charnel-ground corpses,
and the natural melody of three bodies refined as three kāyas
to the ears of Awareness Protector and retinue.
oṃ śrīvajra mahākāla sapārivara vajra śabda pratīccha svāhā

Leave it at that or continue with the five sense pleasures:

May the vajra goddess of form, the totally pure object and consciousness
of tangible and intangible appearances of the environment and its contents,
and the merging and radiating of the mudra of self-arising deity's form
satisfy the sublime eyes of Awareness Protector and retinue.
oṃ śrīvajra mahākāla sapārivara rūpa kāma guṇa pratīccha svāhā

May the vajra goddess of sound, the totally pure object and consciousness
of heard and unheard outer and inner expressions,
and the melody of indestructible, self-arising mantra {601}
satisfy the sublime ears of Awareness Protector and retinue.
oṃ śrīvajra mahākāla sapārivara śabda kāma guṇa pratīccha svāhā

May the vajra goddess of smell, the totally pure object and consciousness
of fragrance, whether concocted or natural,
and the aroma of embracing Lucid Clarity Mahāmudrā
satisfy the sublime noses of Awareness Protector and retinue.
oṃ śrīvajra mahākāla sapārivara gandhe kāma guṇa pratīccha svāhā

May the vajra goddess of taste, the totally pure object and consciousness
of food and drink of a hundred excellent flavors,
and the unchanging great bliss of permanent contentment
satisfy the sublime tongues of Awareness Protector and retinue.
oṃ śrīvajra mahākāla sapārivara rasa kāma guṇa pratīccha svāhā

May the vajra goddess of touch, the totally pure object and
consciousness
of flowing clothes and animal furs,
and the caresses of the sixteen ecstasies of union
satisfy the sublime bodies of Awareness Protector and retinue.
oṃ śrīvajra mahākāla sapārivara sparśe kāma guṇa pratīccha svāhā

Then if you would like to do a slightly longer inner offering, do the consecration here, but only if you have not done it earlier. Take [the inner offering] between your thumb and ring finger and sprinkle it as offering successively at the levels of the head, heart, navel, and crotch while reciting:

Vajradhara and mighty Padmākara,
Śavarīpa, Maitrīpa, Rāhula,
Khyungpo, Mokchok, Zhangom Chöseng, and the rest;
root and lineage gurus—into your mouths *oṃ āḥ hūṃ*.

Cakrasaṃvara, glorious Guhyasamāja,
Mahāmāya, Hevajra,
Vajrabhairava, Hayagrīva, and the rest;
yidam deities—into your mouths *oṃ āḥ hūṃ*.

You may also present the inner offering by adding *oṃ āḥ hūṃ* to the mantras of the principal and retinue.

Swift-Acting Mahākāla and Rematī,
four attendant yakṣas and ten direction protectors,
seventy-five protectors of pure domains and the rest;
oceans of the oath-bound—into your mouths *oṃ āḥ hūṃ*.

Heroes and yoginīs of the three places,
virtuous protectors and lords of place and ground,
migrators included in four ways of birth and five paths of being;[8]
appearing as awareness deities—into your mouths *oṃ āḥ hūṃ*.

After that offering, say the three seed syllables and taste the remainder yourself.

(1) [Guru-Protector Inseparable]

Now, of the three uncommon vital topics, the first is the Guru-Protector Inseparable.[9] Imagine that you and all sentient beings supplicate with one voice by saying the *namo buddhāya* mantra seven or more times. {602} Afterward, recite:

> Guru-Protector inseparable,
> I offer flowers and incense outwardly,
> five meats and five elixirs inwardly,
> the timeless awareness of bliss-emptiness secretly,
> and the sacred offering of suchness most secretly.

Do the visualization as taught in the course of the Six Dharmas. After that:

> Please let the blessings of your awakened body enter my body.
> Please let any blessings of awakened body that have not entered my body enter.
> The blessings of awakened body have entered my body.
>
> Please let the blessings of your awakened speech . . . (etc. up to) . . . Please let the blessings of your awakened body, speech, and mind enter . . . (etc.).

Change the recitation by substituting the words as necessary. During the body blessings, visualize white light rays coming from the guru's forehead and, from Protector's forehead, countless miniature protectors with small bodies and thick limbs rattling ḍamarus and bells with sounds of *sil sil*, *khrol khrol* and shouts of *hūṃ phaṭ*. They dissolve into your forehead, purifying your body of all disease, demons, negativities, and obscurations. You receive the vase empowerment and become inseparable from Protector's body.

Apply the same process: red light and bodies come forth, dissolve into your throat, purify your speech of all disease, demons, negativities, and obscurations. You receive the secret empowerment and become inseparable from Protector's speech. Blue light and bodies come forth, dissolve into your heart, purify your mind of all disease, demons, negativities, and obscurations. You receive the wisdom empowerment and become inseparable from Protector's mind. Multicolored light rays and bodies come forth from Protector's three places, dissolve into your three places, and purify the disease, demons, negativities, and obscurations of your three doors equally. You receive the fourth empowerment and become inseparable from Protector's awareness vajra.

Recite the supplication that begins "*Kyai!* Holy root and lineage gurus dwelling in the ten directions and three times, . . . (etc.)." By your developing intense longing, you distinctly hear Protector say, "I will remove all your obstacles. I will create all favorable conditions."

Again, many dark-red light rays break away from all parts of Protector's body; the previous light rays and protector bodies all blend inseparably with your three doors. Think that your whole body and mind are infused with bliss and rest in the equipoise of innate, nonconceptual bliss-emptiness. {603}

Now meditate that within your body those protectors dance and gobble up raw all the disease and demons. Then say, "Please bless me on this very spot." At this point, play intense music. Then repeat the supplication verse as much as you can. ["Guru-Protector inseparable, . . . (*bla ma mgon po dbyer med la* . . . (etc.)."]. When you are doing the attainment practice of Guru-Protector Inseparable, the heart mantra for recitation is *oṃ guru mahākāla siddhi hūṃ*. If you have received the permission, during the fulfillment practice (*skong gso*) it is good to recite it one hundred times as an auxiliary. The visualization is only the one described above. When you are practicing just the main text without these additions, the visualizations must be done with the supplications.

(2) [**Dispelling Defilements**]

In the second vital topic, that of dispelling defilements, there are two versions: extensive and concise. The extensive version is to be done on occasions where it is the main focus, such as the particular attainment practice of Dispelling Defilements.

During the ritual practice of visualizing the guru as Vajrasattva, imagine the Three Roots and all tathāgatas arrive in the space above—their vajra body in the form of white Vairocana, vajra speech as red Amitābha, and vajra mind as blue Akṣobhya. Imagine that they are lined up in three rows from top to bottom, like cloud banks, and generate devotion.

> Vajra body deities, please cleanse and purify any defilements that have touched the guru's body and all violations of the sacred pledges related to awakened body. With this supplication, white hundred-syllable mantras radiate from the deities of vajra body. They touch the guru's forehead, cleansing and purifying the defilements that have stricken the guru's body and all violations of sacred pledges related to awakened body.

Imagine that and recite the hundred syllables. Repeat the process for awakened speech and mind, reciting the hundred syllables each time. Then:

> Precious guru, please cleanse and purify defilements that have touched the Protector's body and all violations in the sacred pledges related to awakened body. With this supplication, white hundred-syllable mantras radiate from the guru's forehead. They dissolve into Protector's forehead . . . (etc.).

Recite the hundred syllables and apply the process to awakened speech and mind, changing them appropriately.

> Guru-Protector inseparable, please cleanse and purify any defilements that have touched the retinue's bodies . . . (etc.). {604}

> White hundred-syllable mantras radiate from the foreheads of both the guru and Protector . . . (etc.).

As before, do the same for awakened speech and mind, along with the hundred syllables.

> Guru-Protector inseparable and retinue, please cleanse and purify all my and sentient beings' negative actions, obscurations, flaws, downfalls, and violations of sacred pledge. With that supplication, white, red, and blue hundred-syllable mantras radiate from the three places of Guru-Protector inseparable and retinue. They touch my three places and those of others and dissolve, cleansing and purifying the defilements that have stricken our body, speech, and mind and all violations of sacred pledges related to awakened body, speech, and mind.

Imagine that and recite the hundred syllables. Regarding this last occasion, the ancient texts state that it may be done with the visualization of taking the four empowerments, as described for the occasion of Guru-Protector Inseparable. Since it is also said that the visualization and recitation may be done separately, do it that way if you are able.

The concise version of Dispelling Defilements is done in the course of the torma ritual for the twenty-ninth day and others. It is a slightly abridged version of the one above.

> Deities of three vajras, please cleanse and purify any defilements that have touched the guru's body, speech, and mind and all violations of the sacred pledges related to awakened body, speech, and mind. With this supplication, white, red, and blue hundred-syllable mantras radiate from the three places of the deities of vajra body, speech, and mind. They touch the guru's three places, cleansing and purifying the defilements that have stricken the guru's body, speech, and mind, and all violations of sacred pledges related to awakened body, speech, and mind.

Recite the hundred syllables. Apply the same formula, making appropriate changes.

> Precious guru, please cleanse and purify defilements that have touched the Protector's body, speech, and mind . . . (etc.) (Afterward, recite the hundred syllables.)

> Guru-Protector inseparable, please cleanse and purify any defilements that have touched the retinue's and my three doors and violations of sacred pledges related to awakened body, speech, and mind. With this supplication, white, red, and blue hundred-syllable mantras radiate from the three places of the Guru-Protector. They dissolve into the retinue's and my three places, {605} cleansing and purifying the defilements that have stricken the retinue's body, speech, and mind, and all violations of sacred pledges related to awakened body, speech, and mind. Within my body, the light rays of the hundred syllables cleanse and purify from the roots all negativities, obscurations, and downfalls.

Imagine that and repeat the hundred syllables seven times. In the normal course of the ritual, without these additions, you must recite the hundred syllables twenty-one times while applying each of these important visualizations. Then do the confession with intense longing.

[Fulfillment]

Consecrate the substances for the fulfillment, and cleanse and purify [*oṃ vajra amṛta . . . oṃ svabhāva . . .* etc.].

> From within emptiness, the residence becomes a terrifying, wrathfully arrayed charnel ground arising from *bhrūṃ*. In its center, countless black *hūṃ*s become the outer, inner, and secret support substances, accomplishment substances, offering substances, fulfillment substances, and other suitably pleasing substances. Nothing is left out of this excellent abundance. Its essence is the nature of timeless awareness. It takes the form of immeasurable offering clouds of sacred-pledge substances that serve to please and fulfill Awareness Protector and his retinue. The offerings expand to fill the realm of space.
>
> *namaḥ sarva tathāgate bhyoḥ viśva mukhebhyaḥ sarvathākhaṃ udgate spharaṇa imaṃ gagana khaṃ svāhā* (Repeat three times.)
>
> *oṃ vajra sparaṇa khaṃ*
>
> *hūṃ*
> Wrathful dancer of Avalokiteśvara's compassion,
> Swift-Acting Protector and your retinue,
> when I invite you with faith to fulfill your sacred pledge,
> by the power of sacred pledge, approach and remain here.
>
> By the truth of the Three Jewels and Three Roots,
> mantras, mudras, and meditative absorptions,
> may these pledge offerings that pervade all realms
> please and appease you, Protector and retinue.
>
> Drinking water, washing water, flowers, incense,
> light, perfume, food, and the sound of music,

parasols, victory banners, fluttering flags—
Awareness Protector and retinue, may sacred pledge be fulfilled.

Mount Meru, four continents, sun, moon, seven royal possessions,
eight substances, auspicious signs, and wish-granting tree, {606}
wish-fulfilling gem, and so on; the prosperity of three existences—
Awareness Protector and retinue, may sacred pledge be fulfilled.

Rainbows, flower showers, jewel clouds,
gem mountains, grains harvested without cultivation,
bathing pools, pleasure gardens, bountiful cows—
Awareness Protector and retinue, may sacred pledge be fulfilled.

Various forms and various melodies,
various fragrances and their pleasurable waters,
nutritious refreshments, soft fabric, and fine clothes—
Awareness Protector and retinue, may sacred pledge be fulfilled.

Terrifying charnel grounds set with wrathful palaces,
animal-skin canopies, wreaths of draped intestines,
human-skin victory banners, and human-hair fans—
Awareness Protector and retinue, may sacred pledge be fulfilled.

Heart-blood *argham*; poisonous washing water;
sense organ flowers; burning-corpse incense;
lamps of human fat; perfume of blood, bile, and fat—
Awareness Protector and retinue, may sacred pledge be fulfilled.

Flesh, bone, and organ baliṃ piled high as mountains,
swirling oceans of elixir made from essential grains,
and towering waves of murderers' blood—
Awareness Protector and retinue, may sacred pledge be fulfilled.

Skull drums, thighbone trumpets, marching bands, majestic melodies;
fumes of burnt frankincense, human flesh, and mustard;
black silk banners and human-skin flags—
Awareness Protector and retinue, may sacred pledge be fulfilled.

Thirteen black birds, black horses, black donkeys, black bears,
black yaks, black sheep, black dogs, and others,
decorated with various ornaments; all outer supports—
Awareness Protector and retinue, may sacred pledge be fulfilled.

Arrows with mirrors, black silk, and mantra texts attached,
embellished with vulture feathers and iron-blade arrowheads,
misbegotten-child victory banners and so on; all inner supports—
Awareness Protector and retinue, may sacred pledge be fulfilled.

The hearts of people killed by knives
filled up with life-force mantras, medicines, grains, jewels, and brocade;
misbegotten-child [skins]; black bear hearts; and so on; all secret supports—
Awareness Protector and retinue, may sacred pledge be fulfilled.

My mind and the guru's are inseparable in the bhaga
of method and wisdom in the celestial woman's dharma cycle,
with strong undivided longing for the body of empty appearance—
Awareness Protector and retinue, may sacred pledge be fulfilled.

Creation-phase deity meditation, paintings, and statues: the awakened body supports; {607}
winds, mantra recitation, life-force chakra: the awakened speech supports;

mudras, absorptions, insignia: the awakened mind supports—
Awareness Protector and retinue, may sacred pledge be fulfilled.

Bhāndha, black hats, cloaks, and skirts,
applied actions of pacifying, enhancing, controlling, and wrath: the awakened activity supports;
wrathful banners, weapons, costumes, and dances—
Awareness Protector and retinue, may sacred pledge be fulfilled.

Ox hide, tiger skin, human skin, and animal hide;
skull necklaces, garlands, and six symbolic ornaments;
clusters of snakes, and vermilion ointment—
Awareness Protector and retinue, may sacred pledge be fulfilled.

Various weapons, assorted ornaments,
unimaginable presents and tribute,
actually present and mentally emanated—
Awareness Protector and retinue, may sacred pledge be fulfilled.

Approach and attainment of unsurpassable awakening,
magic diagrams of four actions, protecting, repelling,
violent direct action, and application of mantras and curses—
Awareness Protector and retinue, may sacred pledge be fulfilled.

The amusement of four ecstasies with sixteen awareness consorts,
and the secret gaṇacakra of union and liberation that severs
the three poisons and three realms at the roots—
Awareness Protector and retinue, may sacred pledge be fulfilled.

Blazing and dripping of great bliss within samsara and nirvana;
the self-arising of unembellished lucid clarity as the deity's form;

supreme mahāmudrā and eight common spiritual powers—
Awareness Protector and retinue, may sacred pledge be fulfilled.

Supports for sādhana rituals, fulfillments, and especially sacred pledges;
the prosperity of existence and peace, and excellent implements
completely filling the far reaches of the realm of phenomena,
and my intense belief, devotion, and single-pointed longing—
Swift-Acting Awareness Protector, may sacred pledge be fulfilled.

Protector [and] Wish-Fulfilling Gem, may sacred pledge be fulfilled.
King of Power [and] Increasing Intelligence, may sacred pledge be fulfilled.
Lord of Life [and] Diverse Ḍāka, may sacred pledge be fulfilled.
One Mother Śrīdevī, may sacred pledge by fulfilled.

Yakṣa Kṣetrapāla, may sacred pledge be fulfilled.
Īśvara Jinamitra, may sacred pledge be fulfilled.
Yama Ṭakkirāja, may sacred pledge be fulfilled.
Devil lord Trakṣad, may sacred pledge be fulfilled.

Seventy protectors of pure regions, may sacred pledge be fulfilled.
Ocean of oath-bound obedient ones, may sacred pledge be fulfilled.
Emanations and further emanations, may sacred pledge be fulfilled.
Messenger and workers, may sacred pledge be fulfilled. {608}

Now that the strict sacred pledge is fulfilled in basic space,
purify and restore my violations, transgressions, and mistakes
of root and branch pledges of awakened body, speech, and mind,
and grant unrestricted actions and spiritual powers.

Protect dharma centers, retreats, yogins, and their retinues;
dispel all outer, inner, and secret adverse conditions;
repel obstacles to the attainment of awakening;
and give refuge from the fears in this life, the next, and in between.

Please increase people, wealth, and food
for teaching and practice gatherings
and expand like the waxing moon the Victor's doctrine in general
and the doctrines of the practice lineage in particular.

Do not forget your sacred pledge of awakening mind,
but always look with compassion after your devoted child.
Please bless my body, speech, and mind
and grant the spontaneous accomplishment of all my desires.

If you want a shorter version that is conducive to accumulating multiple repetitions, then use this one by Chakme Rinpoche:[10]

hūṃ
Swift-Acting Protector and retinue,
I will fulfill our strict sacred pledge
to repair my violations, restore what is damaged,
and purify all my resentment of shame and regret.

Yaks and sheep with meteorite horns, lightning tongues,
and fur like turbulent black clouds,
adorned with various silks—
Awareness Protector and retinue, may sacred pledge be fulfilled.

Bamboo arrows adorned with vulture feathers,
tipped with hard meteorite points,
and fluttering black silk pendants—
Awareness Protector and retinue, may sacred pledge be fulfilled.

Hearts pulled out raw by hand
from enemies who hate the doctrine,

filled with jewels, grain, and medicine—
Awareness Protector and retinue, may sacred pledge be fulfilled.

Guru, the actual Three Jewels,
inseparable from Swift-Acting Protector;
with the certainty of my strong belief in you—
Awareness Protector and retinue, may sacred pledge be fulfilled.

Human-blood tormas stacked like mountains,
alcohol and rakta swirling like oceans,
actually present and mentally emanated without limit—
Awareness Protector and retinue, may sacred pledge be fulfilled.

With your sacred pledge fulfilled by me, {609}
my entrusted actions will be accomplished by you.
When I attend to you, don't be distant.
When I call to you, don't be hard of hearing.
When I meditate on you, don't wander off.
When I beckon you, don't look away.
When I commission you, don't be tardy.

When I rely on you as lord, don't be grand.
When I rely on you as friend, don't be wicked.
When I rely on you like a roommate, don't be bashful.
When I rely on you like a sister, don't be bad-tempered.
When I rely on you like a servant, don't be inattentive.

I give thanks for your past actions.
I bring food for your current actions.
I offer beverage for your future actions.
May our strict sacred pledge be fulfilled.
Accomplish the requested actions.

Then the confession:

hūṃ
Protector and retinue, in your presence

I confess whatever faults I have accrued
through the influence of negligence:
incomplete support substances, meager feast offerings,
unclear visualizations, incorrect mantras,
raw-flour [torma], lacking prepared incense,
harming black birds or dogs, and so forth.
Grant the spiritual power of undefiled purity.

It is also said that you should recite the hundred syllables in the esoteric instructions of this tradition. The fulfillment ritual renowned as the work of Sangye Nyentön does not actually appear in Nyentön's writings. I fear this must come from some uneducated village mantrin who heard a few words from the Nyingma tradition. The one arranged in the torma ritual by Khedrup Je[11] or from any of the writings of Je [Tsongkhapa's] father-son lineage are not from the old texts of the Shangpa tradition and anyway are rather too wordy. Therefore I have written this easy-to-practice version.

After the above [liturgies], according to whether there is a particular need, do the following praise, exhortation, and averting ritual:

hūṃ
Protector, mighty one on the tenth level,
you have no definite residence,
yet to the perception of individual beings
you appear to the south of the Vajra Seat
in the great charnel ground of Cool Grove.

In that terrifying sublime holy site,
death lords roar—*di ri ri*,
mātṛkās whistle tunes—*khyu ru ru*,
oceans of rakta swirl—*chi li li*,
human-fat lamps flicker—*lhap se lhap*,
burning-corpse smoke wafts—*chi li li*, {610}
male devils stamp-dance—*chem se chem*,
female devils twirl-dance—*go ro ro*,
human thighbones blow—*kyu ru ru*,
wild animals roar—*u ru ru*,
blazing lightning flashes—*khyuk se khyuk*,

violent thunder crashes—*chem se chem*,
meteorite hail falls—*sha ra ra*,
and the laughter of devils and
bloodthirsty demons shake the earth.

In such a holy, sublime site
stands your terrifying form with one face and six arms.
In your gaping mouth your tongue curls against your palate
and your three eyes blaze like the fire at time's end.
You are voracious and brilliant with thick limbs,
wrathful sounds of *hūṃ* resounding like thunder;
majestic as Meru, the color of eye medicine.
Laughing with the terrifying sound of *kṣeṃ kṣeṃ*,
you hold flaying knife, skull garland, and rattling ḍamaru,
blood-filled skull cup, trident, and lasso.
You dance to the sound of ringing bells.
One Mother, chief of all the mātṛkās,
four yakṣas, murderous butchers,
direction protectors, hosts of seventy glorious protectors,
with retinues of oceans of the oath-bound:
come here to accept these amenable pledge substances.

hūṃ
Mañjuśrī gave you the name
Powerful Executioner of Misleading Spirits.
Vajrapāṇi gave you the name
Great Black Tamer of Nāgas.
Yamāntaka gave you the name
Vajra Zombie Lord of the Charnel Ground.
Calling you by these secret names—approach!

When I call to you, don't be hard of hearing.
When I beckon you, don't look away.
When I commission you, don't be tardy.
When I incite you, don't use weak magic.
When I appease you, don't be distracted.
When I supplicate you, don't be distant.

By this ocean of pleasing pledge substances,
pure, complete, and undamaged,
this evening, with your retinue, may sacred pledge be fulfilled.
I confess whatever violations I have committed.
I give thanks for previous entrusted actions well done.
I make offerings as support for actions entrusted now.
Accomplish the activities I request!

hūṃ
Regarding my requests for your actions: {611}
there are enemies who threaten the holy guru's body,
enemies who destroy the doctrine and damage vows,
dark creatures who belong to a type of devil,
and obstructing spirits who cause interference.
They violate the sacred mandala,
destroy the Sage's doctrine,
obstruct the yogins' teaching and practice,
and ruin the sacred centers of dharma.
For us yogins and our entourages
of people, wealth, and sangha:
We entrust! We rely! No small magic!
Don't waver during the three watches of the day.
Don't waver during the three watches of the night.
Avert adverse conditions and achieve favorable conditions.

[**Exhortation**]

hūṃ
Weaken the power and magical abilities
of enemies and obstructors who violate vows,
quickly liberating their supportive gods.
Separate them from their companions.
Tear out their hearts and sever their vital channels.
Cut off their family lineage from its roots.

See those criminals—they're getting away!
Quickly bring forth signs and show attributes.
These noxious, hateful enemies

threaten the holy guru's body,
disparage the Vajrayāna,
disturb and suppress the sangha,
insult and condemn monastics,
and harm and threaten all beings.
They insult by saying, "Yogins have no gods."
They condemn by saying, "Your gods are powerless."

Regarding these enemies of the doctrine,
don't delay for months and years—
feed them to the mouth of Yamarāja.
Make winged ones squeeze their extremities,
those with claws hook their hearts,
those with beaks pierce their brains,
karmic winds push their backs,
and black darkness greet them up front.
Ṭakkirāja, squeeze them from the right!
Gaṇapati with your elephant trunk, squeeze from the left.
Cut their cord to the heavens and strand them.
Pull up their stake to the ground and strand them.
Extract their five inner organs.
Make them vomit blood from their mouths.
Send them eighty-four bad omens.
Make devils stomp and dance.
Make tsen spirits throw lassos.
Make mātṛkas send plague on these enemies. {612}
Let those who become enemies of the doctrine
be caught by the fall of the scored stick.
Let their number come up in the dice throw.
To these evil vow-breakers doing bad actions,
quickly display your signs and attributes.
Don't delay for months and years.

If you do not perform these entrusted actions
you break the command of the victors of the three times,
disappoint future generations of mantrins,
dash the hopes of us awareness holders,
damage your former strict sacred pledge,

transgress the sacred pledge of root and lineage gurus,
and become a guardian of the Sage's doctrine in name only.

Better not to contravene your vows!
Accept these amenable sacred substances
and accomplish the entrusted awakened activity.

[**Averting**]

From the vast palace of dharmakāya,
great deity Protector and retinue,
accept these amenable pledge substances,
and for us yogins, master and disciple entourage:

Avert others' bad attitudes and behavior,
thorn weapon magic,[12] and mustard-seed weapon magic.
Bhūtas hurling skull weapon magic—turn it back!
Yamas spinning wheel weapon magic—turn it back!
Māras displaying their scored sticks—turn it back!
Mātṛkās hurling blood weapon magic—turn it back!
Red-metal weapon magic of Zhang Zhung—turn it back!
Hurled-bull weapon magic of Sumpa—turn it back!
Mantra weapon magic sent by Buddhists—turn it back!
Symbol weapon magic sent by Bönpos—turn it back!
Triangular-cup weapon magic sent by mantrins—turn it back!
Arrow weapon magic sent by men—turn it back!
Curse weapon magic cast by women—turn it back!
Obstacles created by heretics—turn it back!
Evil dispatches sent by black magic—turn it back!
Malediction sent by nāgas—turn it back!
Souls stolen by teurang spirits—turn it back!
Insanity sent by gyalpo spirits—turn it back!
Kingkang of ṛṣi planets—turn it back!
Eighty-four evil omens—turn them back!
Three hundred and sixty calamities—turn them back!
Bad dreams and bad signs,
obstacle years, months, or days,
and four hundred and four diseases—turn them back!

Obstacles made by ḍākinīs, zombies,
and gyaltsen spirits—turn them back!

Those and all other malicious thoughts
of all hateful enemies—*bhyoḥ!*
All dangerous obstructors—*bhyoḥ!*

(3) [Getting Down to the Vital Point]

The third vital topic, bringing the ḍākinīs under control, is presented clearly in the source text. Getting Down to the Vital Point is not done in the daily practice. {613} If the need should arise, this and the uncommon esoteric instructions of the second vital topic above can be found elsewhere.

[Mantra Recitation]

For the recitation of the essence mantra, follow the visualization in the source text. When reciting the root mantra, [visualize the following]:

> Light rays like firelight radiate from the *hūṃ* in my heart and strike the *hūṃ* in Protector's heart. Protector becomes wrathfully agitated and ravenous, stamping his feet and roaring with thunderous sounds of *hūṃ hūṃ phaṭ phaṭ*. He violently rattles his ḍamaru and glares at his retinue. Powerless, they also become wrathfully agitated, and each one sends out replicas of themselves with boundless retinues to the ten directions, where they annihilate all obstacles to the successful dharma practice of master and disciples.

Imagine that and recite *śāsana* . . . (etc.).

> Each of the retinue meditates on their respective seed syllables on sun disks in their hearts. As the yidam, red light rays radiate from the seed syllable in my heart, striking all of them and evoking their mind streams.

Imagine that and recite their individual mantras. When finished with the recitation, offer torma.

[Torma Offering]

If you have not already consecrated the torma, begin by sprinkling it successively with alcohol, water, and consecrated inner offering. Then for the consecration:

namo
Swift-Acting Six-Armed Awareness Protector, don't be idle.
Sole Mother Śrīdevī Rematī, don't be idle.
Yakṣa Kṣetrapāla, don't be idle.
Īśvara Jinamitra, don't be idle.
Yama Ṭakkirāja, don't be idle.
Devil lord Trakṣad, don't be idle.
Seventy-five protectors of pure regions, don't be idle.
Ocean of obedient oath-bound ones, don't be idle.
I keep practicing and relying on you, don't be idle.
Guardians of the master's lineage, don't be idle.
The time has come to guard us from obstacles; don't be idle.
The time has come to liberate enemies and obstructors; don't be idle.
The time has come to grant spiritual powers; don't be idle.

From the source text, recite, "The tongues of the Protector and retinue . . . (etc.)." With the visualization, intone the four long *hūṃ*s and offer the tormas with the individual mantras. Offer with *arghaṃ* . . . (etc.) and add *oṃ āḥ hūṃ* to the individual mantras for the inner offering. {614} Then entrust awakened activity:

This clean and cleanly made torma for offering and donating has sacred ornaments, sacred aroma, sacred taste, and sacred texture. The recipients for the offering and dedication are glorious Mahākāla, Excellent Black Protector, devil eradicators, commanders who defeat devils, annihilators of the rākṣasa's three-tiered city of Laṅkāpurī, war gods of yogins, guardians of awareness holders, the guru's command guards, sentries of the doctrine, regulators of good and bad, those with wrathful forms, those with faces of devourers, those with eyes of awareness, chiefs of meat-eaters, kings of blood-drinkers, killers of vow-breakers, and butchers of apostates—surrounded by retinues of one hundred thousand black ones, surrounded by retinues of one million meat-eaters, surrounded by retinues one thousand male protectors on the right, surrounded by one thousand female protectors on the left, attended by Black Goddess with retinue, Yakṣa Kṣetrapāla with retinue, Īśvara Jinamitra with retinue, Yama Ṭakkirāja with retinue, devil lord Trakṣad with retinue, seventy-five protectors of the pure regions, oceans of obedient oath-bound protectors, and retinues of armies:

All of you—accept this torma of sacred substance with ornaments. Guard the Buddha's doctrine, honor the supremacy of the Three Jewels, protect the sangha's dharma centers, and plant the victory banner of everlasting dharma. In particular, for us yogins and our entourage, quickly pacify and prevent all enemies, bad spirits, and obstructors who cause us obstacles. Spread and increase our longevity, merit, prosperity, enjoyments, fame, influence, dharma lineage, experience, realization, and so on. Protect us from all fears in this life, the next, and in between. Quickly grant us all supreme and common spiritual powers without exception.

For occasions such as the Great Torma Ritual: {615}

Please perform actions to totally pacify those who threaten the glorious guru's holy body, discredit the secrets of Vajrayāna, oppose the Buddha's doctrine, degrade the status of the Three Jewels, and destroy the sangha's dharma centers, as well as those who harbor hatred toward us—master, disciples, patrons, and entourage; those with evil thoughts; those with savage thoughts; bhūtas who lead astray; and all evil human and nonhuman bad actors with negative thoughts and violent deeds.

In case you see that they are not subdued by those peaceful methods, finish them off by wrathful action, such as killing, oppressing, banishing, paralyzing, turning them deaf and dumb, intimidating, and threatening them. Reduce them to fine dust.

Guru-Protector and retinue,
I present this offering torma.
Those who degrade the Three Jewels,
discredit the Vajrayāna,
destroy or divide the doctrine,
threaten the guru's body,
or hate us yogins:
Great Black One, liberate them!
amuka māraya phaṭ (Clap hands.)

Now, if you wish to expand on the praise in the source text that begins with "Homage to Swift-Acting Avalokiteśvara . . . (etc.)," or to alternate, use this one by the great brahmin Vararuci, *Resounding Ferocity: Praise to the Great Black One*:[13]

oṃ Let it be done.
In the terrifying great charnel ground,
the dense wilderness[14] of great sandalwood trees,
amid fires blazing like those at the end of time,
on a seat of the twisted body of Great Obstructor, you appear:
magnificent Six-Armed Mahākāla.

The inexhaustible blazing[15] attire of your body
are the attributes of the charnel grounds.
The inexhaustible blazing roars of your speech
are sounds of *hūṃ* and *phaṭ* that fill the universe.
The inexhaustible blazing purity of your mind
is free of elaboration yet displays any characteristic. {616}
I praise you in terms of awakened body, speech, and mind.

You sever the root of affliction and threaten enemies
with the flaying knife in your first right hand.
You account for migrators with the garland you hold.
You bring ḍākinīs under control with your ḍamaru.
I pay homage to the chief of transcendent ones.

You consume the brain-blood of enemies and obstructors
from the blood-filled skull cup in your first left hand.

You bring the three realms under control with the three-pronged
spear.
You bind the bodies of oath-breakers with your lasso.
I pay homage to the giver of blessings and powers.

As a sign of the immutable dharmakāya,
your body color is a radiant dark blue.
You are adorned by fifty-five blood-dripping heads
and beautified by a tiger-skin skirt and snake clusters.
I pay homage and praise you, Mahākāla.

On a seat of twisted Vināyaka,
your stamping feet smash the Great Obstructor to dust.
With voracious gaping mouth and bared fangs
you draw and drink the vital blood of oath-breakers.
I pay homage to the butcher of powerful obstructors.

Your three fiery eyes are opened wide,
taking control and accounting for the three realms.
Above your beautiful, upward-blazing hair,
King Akṣobhya fully adorns you.
I pay homage to you who perfects the four powers.

hūṃ
Arise! Arise! Arise from the realm of phenomena.
Invoke! Invoke! I invoke you to care for migrators.
I invoke your sacred pledge; perform the entrusted activity.
Don't be idle! Don't be idle, Glorious Great Black One!

In the presence of our refuge, Lion of the Śākyas,
you promised to guard the doctrine and took an oath.
Make good on the outcome of those actions.

If a wise and holy person
repeats this praise just once,
like a parent who loves their children,
always support them, Great Black One. {617}

Praise [to Glorious Goddess] by Maitrīpa:

bhyoḥ
Amid a blazing expanse like the fire at the end of the eon,
in a turbulent palace in a tempest of black winds,
appears the one mother, queen of the desire realm, Rematī.
Black as storm clouds, with a crown of dry skulls,
right earring is a leaping lion, left a coiling cobra,
three red agitated eyes, and gaping mouth with bared fangs—
terrifying goddess, I praise you.

You kill enemies with the blazing sword in your right hand
and drink the heart blood of enemies and obstructors from the
fresh skull in your left.
A human skin tied with a black snake belt covers your upper body
and an elephant hide cinched with a buckle on your lower body.
To traverse the threefold universe, you ride a three-legged mule;
the front of the saddle is a rākṣasa's upper jaw with a scored stick
attached,
the saddle straps are black snakes; you shake a bag of disease at
enemies.
Accept this offering torma and liberate enemies and obstructors.
Accomplish all the activities entrusted to you.[16]

bhyoḥ
Amid a blazing expanse like the fire at the end of the eon,
from a turbulent palace in a tempest of black winds,
in an ocean of turbulent waves of horse and human blood,
on a seat of the twisted body of the enemy vow-breaker,
stands the one mother, mistress of the desire realm, Rematī.

Your body is blue-black like storm clouds,
with tawny hair adorned by peacock feathers.
Endowed with awakening mind, the full moon rises from your
head.
You wear a crown of skulls, a leaping lion as your right earring,
the left is jingling bells and a coiling black cobra.

Your three red agitated eyes dart around like lightning
and your mouth emits the fearsome sound of thunder—*chem chem.*
Meteorite hail falls from the center of your forehead
and black winds of disease billow like clouds from your nose.

Your terrifying gaping mouth bares fangs and curled tongue
while your laughter of *a la la* reverberates like thunder,
shaking the hosts of bhūtas in the vast universe.
I pay homage and praise you, terrifying goddess. {618}

You kill enemies with the sword and flaying knife in your right hands,
and hold a victory banner and fresh skull cup in the left hands, drinking their heart blood.
You wear a human skin tied with a black snake on your upper body
and an elephant hide with a black snake belt on the lower body.
To traverse the three-thousandfold universe, you ride a three-legged mule;
the front of the saddle is a rākṣasa's upper jaw with a scored stick attached,
on which there are notches for enemies and obstructors.
A bag of various virulent diseases hangs from the [saddle's] back
with which to annihilate forever the enemy oath-breakers.
The saddle straps are clusters of a thousand black snakes.
Surrounded by a hundred thousand demonesses who guard the doctrine—
great demoness of life force, liberate enemies and obstructors!

Maitrīpa offered that praise when he really saw her.[17] Lama Rāhula's [praise]:

bhyoḥ
You are the self-arisen glory blazing in totally pure space.
Lady who embodies the terrifying form that scares devils.
Lady whose body is adorned with copious charnel-ground garb.
Lady whose hands, the four immeasurables, hold blood-filled skull cup and weapons.

Lady who rides a mule to quickly enact compassion.
Lady who guards the doctrine and protects yogins.
Lady who accomplishes the actions and terminates enemies.
I praise and supplicate you: perform the entrusted activities!

Lama Rāhula took that from the *Tantra Collection* (*rgyud 'bum*). [Another praise by Maitrīpa]:

bhyoḥ
If I undertake hardships to accomplish your practice,
Sole Mother Rematī, don't be idle, don't be idle!
If I put my life on the line to accomplish your practice,
Sole Mother Rematī, don't be distant in your heart.
If the rakta swirls like an ocean to accomplish your practice,
Sole Mother, don't slow your response when I exhort you.
If the tormas are piled like a mountain to accomplish your practice,
Sole Mother, don't be weak when I incite you.
With your rākṣasa-faced servants, unruly and obnoxious,
liberate enemies and obstructors.
With your lion-faced followers behind you,
cut the life force of enemy oath-breakers.

Sole Mother Śrīdevī and your retinue,
accept this red torma of flesh and blood.
Please avert adverse conditions and obstacles,
and grant all suitable spiritual powers. {619}

Then do the praises of the retinue as in the source text. If you wish to do a little more:

hūṃ
Protector's attendants perform actions in the four directions,
with unimaginable strength, miraculous ability, and wrathful energy.
Leaders of all arrogant ones in the three existences—
I praise the great attendants and their retinues.

Yakṣa Kṣetrapāla, the color of gloom,
brandishes a flaying knife, feeds the principal from a blood-filled
skull cup,
and rides a black bear to circle the threefold universe—
I praise you, whose wrath is difficult to bear.

Īśvara Jinamitra blazes like fire,
magic poison and blood hail fall from his mouth,
he rattles a small hand drum, and flings a weapon wheel—
I praise you, terrifying in your rākṣasa's body.

Yama Ṭakkirāja twirls the intestine lasso,
colored like hala poison, frightens obstructors by pointing
and steals the vital hearts just by a glance at enemies and
obstructors—
I praise you, unbearable subduer of all malicious ones.

Devil lord Trakṣad, with a radiance of the gloom at time's end,
pierces with the trident, eats the hearts from a skull cup,
wears a black cape, and rides a black horse with white fetlocks—
I praise you, fierce violent shaker of the three levels.

Armies of yakṣas, gods, yamas, and devils
with terrifying, horrible forms, rain down weapons,
protect keepers of sacred pledge, but execute the violators—
I praise you, each surrounded by a hundred thousand of your own.

Chief actors in glorious Protector's outer circle:
Brahmā rides a swan and lifts a wheel,
Śakra rides on an elephant and holds a vajra,
Agni rides a goat and holds a round-bead rosary,
Yama rides a buffalo and wields a club,
Rākṣasa rides a zombie and brandishes a sword,
Varuṇa sits on a makara and twirls a snake lasso,
Vāyu rides a stag and raises a banner,
Yakṣa rides a horse and squeezes a jewel-vomiting mongoose,
Indra sits on an ox and holds a trident,

Bhūpati rides a pig and holds a golden vase—
I praise you all, with your hundred thousand servant retinues.

Gods, nāgas, planets, twenty-eight constellations, {620}
four great kings, nine terrifying ones,
oceans of the oath-bound, and bhūtas of the three existences—
I praise you, guardians of the doctrine and protectors of
practitioners.

Joyfully accept this offering torma,
spread and enhance the Buddha's doctrine,
prolong the life of the glorious gurus,
and increase yogins' experience, realization, and awareness.

With wrathful actions, annihilate all enemies and obstructors
who threaten the dharma and migrators.
Increase like the waxing moon all conducive conditions
for entourage, prosperity, teaching, and accomplishment.

[Investiture of Power]

At this point, do the investiture of power on special occasions. The extensive liturgy for that is placed elsewhere (chapter 39). For a shorter version, recite this one by the temple attendant Lodrö Senge:[18]

hūṃ
Guru, the real Vajradhara,
inseparable from Protector—power to you.
Since you are the essence of Avalokiteśvara,
supreme yidam—power to you.
Since you manifest the four kāyas,
perfect buddha—power to you.
All Mahayana Holy Dharma's
great master—power to you.
All noble assembly of the sangha's
great chief—power to you.
Since you guard the Buddha's doctrine,
great dharma protector—power to you.

Since you lead the great gods,
great excellent one—power to you.
Since you have the power of wrathful action,
Great Black One—power to you.
All Secret Mantra awareness holders'
great guardian—power to you.
Sacred-pledge-holding yogins'
great war god—power to you.
For all of us with our entourage,
protector and refuge—power to you.

Guard the doctrine of the mighty Sage,
perform awakened activity for me, the yogin;
avert misfortune and accomplish favorable conditions—
make this investiture of power meaningful!

Whether you do a long or short investiture, this is the visualization for generating the brilliant charismatic form [of Protector]. Meditate on a brilliant, radiant dark-blue *hūṃ*, one cubit tall, above Protector's head. {621} Light rays radiate from *hūṃ* and gather all the compassion blessings and abilities of the ten direction buddhas, bodhisattvas, deities, heroes, ḍākinīs, dharma protectors, and guards—and all the luster and splendor of the stable environment and moving inhabitants—in the form of light rays that dissolve into the *hūṃ*. The *hūṃ* grows larger and shines brighter. It enters through the top of Protector's head and reaches his heart. There it becomes wrathful black Yamāntaka Vajrabhairava, with three heads and six arms, standing on a water buffalo and trampling on male and female yamas. That body grows larger and Protector's body also grows larger with magnificent brilliance and splendor. First it fills up the space in front, then fills the whole universe of Endurance. Meditate as far as your mind can encompass. Light rays radiating from Protector strike his retinue and each of them also grows brighter and more magnificent. Imagine that and think, "There is nothing in the world system of Endurance with greater strength and capability than Awareness Protector."

This is primarily a meditation for the self-visualization of the Protector, but former masters also used it for front visualization. In general, these three points—bringing the ḍākinīs under control based on the vermilion spot on the forehead, softening your mind stream based on King Akṣobhya above the head, and developing brilliance based on Yamāntaka—are the three things that are crucial to understand once you begin Protector practice.

The sequence of concluding practices is clear and complete in the source text itself.

This single text containing the supplements to *Awakened Activity* is primarily intended for the Great Torma Ritual and other extensive holy-day offerings. The vital points of most of those visualizations are presented clearly here. If there are mistakes, I beg forgiveness of the Guru-Protector, mighty Compassionate One, and retinue. Please grant me the spiritual power of purity and also be the caretaker of these texts.

The general methods for principally the Secret Sādhana[19] and Guru-Protector Inseparable Entering the Heart, and particularly their vital points and uncommon instructions, must be found in their individual [sources]. Other than that, there is not a single text that could include them all. {622} The application and visualizations of the torma practice and Great Torma Ritual can only be realized from their individual oral instructions. Likewise, in the Great Torma Ritual and others, the wrathful form and so forth required for the wrathful actions are certainly related to this *Awakened Activity* but are not always necessary and so were not written here. If the need arises, take them from the manuals and old texts.

[Concluding Verse and Colophon]

May this faithfully written addendum to *Awakened Activity*
be the excellent precondition for the widespread flourishing
of the practice lineage's ocean of jewels, leading me in this life
to the accomplishment of the Guru-Protector Inseparable.

In the secluded retreat on the slopes of Palpung, Devīkoṭi Tsadra Rinchen Drak, in order to make a needed connection with Awareness Protector's hub of Cool Grove, Karma Ngawang Yönten Gyatso Trinle Kunkhyap Pal Zangpo compiled this on the excellent holy day of the Victor's descent from the gods' realm. May it be the cause for the spreading and flourishing of the precious doctrine. Let virtue prevail.

35. Concise Torma Ritual for Swift-Acting Six-Armed Awareness Protector[1]

Tāranātha

oṃ svāsti
Homage to Guru-Protector inseparable.

Consecrate the inner offering [and] torma as in the yidam ritual.

> Before me, on a lotus and sun, deep-blue Awareness Protector arises from *hūṃ*. He holds a flaying knife and skull cup in his two first hands, a human-skull rosary and trident in the two middle hands, and a ḍamaru and lasso in the last two. He wears a tiger skin and a garland of heads, and is adorned with bones, snakes, and bangles of small bells on his arms and legs. In the position of straight, even legs, he tramples on Gaṇapati. He has three eyes and bared fangs; his beard, eyebrows, and hair stream upward. He is crowned by Akṣobhya and anointed with a spot of vermilion on the forehead. He stands in the midst of a blazing mass of fire, the trunk of a sandalwood tree at his back.
>
> On his left, glorious black Śrīdevī arises from *bhyoḥ* riding a mule and carrying a notched stick and disease bag. In front, dark-brown Yakṣa Kṣetrapāla holds a flaying knife and skull cup, riding on a crazed black bear. To the right, dark-red Jinamitra holds a small hand drum and wheel. Behind, black Ṭakkirāja holds a razor and blood-filled skull cup. On the right, devil lord Trakṣad holds a banner and skull cup containing a heart, riding a black devil horse with white fetlocks, and wearing a black silk cloak

and rawhide boots. All around them are the seventy-five glorious protectors and an ocean of oath-bound hosts.

Light rays radiate from my heart, invoking Six-Armed Awareness Protector from in front of the sandalwood tree in the Cool Grove to the southeast. The root and lineage gurus are above him, grimacing heroes to his right, smiling heroines to his left, with armies of attendants, field protectors, messengers, and an ocean of the oath-bound.

oṃ vajra mahākāla sapārivāra kṣiṃ (Repeat *kṣiṃ* twenty-one times.)
vajra samājaḥ—jaḥ hūṃ vaṃ hoḥ

oṃ vajra mahākāla kṣiṃ kṣetra vighanān vināyaka hūṃ hūṃ phat phaṭ svāhā

Repeat that mantra many times. Then add the following after the mantra and repeat three times:

idaṃ baliṃta kha kha khāhi khāhi {624}

Likewise, add *idaṃ . . .* to each of the following mantras of the retinue and repeat three times:

bhyoḥ mamo nakmo vetāli sindha kulu kulu hūṃ phaṭ
oṃ kṣetrapāla vighnān hūṃ phaṭ
oṃ jinamitra vāśaṃ kuru hūṃ phaṭ
oṃ ṭakkirāja samaya bhyoḥ du jaḥ hūṃ phaṭ
oṃ du yog jaḥ mahākāla trakṣad hūṃ phaṭ

Then repeat the following three times for the general oath-bound protectors, adding *idaṃ . . .* as before:

oṃ śrī mahākāla śāsana / upahāriṇi / eṣo 'paścima kālo ayaṃ idaṃ ratna trayāya / apakāriṇaṃ yadi pratijñāṃ/ smarasi tadā / idaṃ duṣṭaṃ kha kha khāhi khāhi / māra māra / gṛhṇa gṛhṇa /

> *bandha bandha / hana hana / daha daha / paca paca / dinamek-ena māraya hūṃ phaṭ*

Present offerings with *arghaṃ* . . . (etc.). Present the inner offerings with *oṃ āḥ hūṃ*.

> *hūṃ*
> Homage to Swift-Acting Avalokita.
> Your bangled feet trample Vināyaka,
> Great Black One in a tiger-skin skirt,
> six arms well adorned by snake ornaments,
> top right hand holding flaying knife, the middle a rosary,
> and the last fiercely rattling a ḍamaru.
> Your left hands hold a skull, a trident,
> and a lasso that catches and binds.
> Your wrathful gaping mouth fully bares fangs.
> You have three eyes, wild hair streaming upward,
> and a spot of vermilion anoints your forehead.
> King Akṣobhya seals the crown of your head.
> You wear a garland of fifty blood-dripping human heads
> and a crown of five skulls with jewel finials.
> Come from your tree to accept this torma.
>
> Accept this torma I offer to you . . . (*mchod sbyin gtor ma'di bzhes la* . . . etc.).

Continue with this supplication for your desires. It is also fitting to recite the supplications of Guru-Protector Inseparable, Dispelling Defilements, and so forth after this. Do the hundred syllables, request for forbearance, aspirations, and auspicious verses.

[Colophon]

This easy-to-practice *Concise Torma Ritual for Swift-Acting Six-Armed Awareness Protector* was requested by Nyima Namgyal, the caretaker of Gangkar Dorjeden, and written by Tāranātha at the Gangkar Palace.

36. Garland of Cintāmaṇi

Thirteen Major Authorizations for Six-Armed Mahākāla in One Place[1]

Jamgön Kongtrul

[Outline]

I. Removing All Obstacles
II. White Protector
III. Yellow Protector
IV. Red Protector
V. Green Protector
VI. Guru-Protector Inseparable
VII. Protector Dispelling Defilements
VIII. Magnetizing Ḍākinīs and Getting Down to the Vital Point
IX. Liver-Colored Protector
X. Saraha's Tradition of Three-Faced Six-Armed Protector
XI. Adorned Protector Secret Sādhana
XII. Four Deities Combined Practice
XIII. Supplemental Support for Deliberate Conduct

Homage to the guru and Swift-Acting Avalokita.

With eyes of compassion for all migrators,
you watch the wicked with seeming wrath,
creator of all victors, Great Black One:
remove all obstacles now and forever!

Glorious Protector's tantras and sādhanas
are an amazing, secret, profound sky treasury
that came from a line of many sublime adepts,
such as Padmavajra and the Brahmin succession.

Since they did not appear in the minds of great scholars
but like stars filled the masters of the Shangpa long tradition
from the succession of liberators who appeared in the three times,
I will open the door and explain the blessings and permissions.

With the three secrets from the power of wrathful compassion, he uses forceful means to impartially liberate the beings to be tamed in the age of conflict and grants their desires like a wish-fulfilling gem. Unrivaled in awareness and actions, or by any worldly dharma protectors, the one who brings the accomplishment of the supreme state of a buddha is Swift-Acting Protector. That dharma cycle was granted to the learned adept Khyungpo Naljor by two Indian adepts.[2] He gave those instructions to his six main disciples and others.[3] In particular, the lineage from Könchok Khar of Latö is [known as] the upper tradition (*stod lugs*) and the lineage coming from Mokchokpa Rinchen Tsöndru is the lower tradition (*smad lugs*). These two are very well known and are held to be authentic by all schools. Of those, the upper tradition of the Protector was apparently complete with empowerment conferrals, subsequent authorizations, and profound and vast esoteric instructions. {627} However, these days the continuity is very rare, other than the reading transmission of the root text, [*Khedrup's*] *Book* (*be bum*), and a few permissions that are combined into one blessing.[4]

As for the lower tradition, the lineage coming from Muchen Namkhai Naljor, together with the awakened activities of Je Rinpoche [Tsongkhapa] and his successors, have spread throughout the world, and for this one dharma protector that arrived in the Land of Snows, the activity of offering rituals appeared widely. Its permission systems of authorization in the Sakya and Kagyu and other [lineages] only exist for the main deep blue and white [forms] and no others. These are either compatible or incompatible with the main vital points of the practices of our school's own tradition.

The great Jonang Jetsun [Tāranātha asserted that] there did exist some former and later genuine teaching systems. However, they did not continue to the present time, other than the five permissions found in his *Mine of*

Jewels.[5] There is the collection of thirteen major permissions including the supplemental support by Khedrup Gelek Palzang, the three permissions of the single [one-to-one] lineage, along with the special transmissions for the *Book*, which [remain] as a widespread system of virtue. Seeing that it was entirely inappropriate that there was no trustworthy basis for this protector, except for the teachings of the goddess's single lineage, we have obtained all others directly from the mouth of the all-knowing Khyentse Wangpo, through his great kindness. In that system, there is the manual of Kyishöpa Tulku Tenzin Trinle,[6] but here we take as the main source omniscient Venerable One's continual teaching system. Anything not contained in that will be supplemented. {628} This is the list from Kyishö's manual:

1. The root subsequent authorization, Removing All Obstacles
2. The torma empowerment and special visualizations for Removing All Obstacles
3. Protector Dispelling Defilements
4. Guru-Protector Inseparable
5. Getting Down to the Vital Point and Controlling the Ḍākinīs Combined
6. Liver-Colored Protector
7. Saraha's Tradition of Three-Faced Six-Armed Protector
8. Adorned Protector Secret Sādhana with Consort
9. Four Deities Combined Practice
10. King of Power
11. Protector Lord of Life
12. Protector Entering the Heart
13. Wish-Fulfilling Gem

This is the sequence there, which includes general supplemental support and authorization for deliberate conduct. The permission for the Yellow Protector who increases intelligence was not usually included there. Protector Entering the Heart is from the one-to-one lineage, so separating that aside, there are [still] thirteen. He took the sequence mainly from the *Mine of Jewels: Sādhanas of an Ocean of Yidams*; whatever is missing will be added here.

I. Removing All Obstacles

First, the root of all of them is the great permission of Removing All Obstacles borrowed from Venerable Rinpoche's writings[7] and arranged for liturgical recitation.

oṃ svāsti
Well adorned by Avalokiteśvara, Tārā,
and Vajravārāhī: great blessed Protector—
bowing to you, I will explain
the ritual to confer the absorption empowerment.

If you wish to give the permission for Removing All Obstacles, go to a secluded place on the twenty-ninth day of the lunar month or another propitious time. In the center of a circular mandala, draw a deep-blue triangular source of phenomena with a ring of fire, facing toward you. In its center, on six sun seats, arrange heaps [of grain] that correspond in color to the body colors [of the six figures]. The outer corners are red. Outside the circle, make the rings of vajras, fence, and fire. There, upon a mañji, place whatever skull vessel is suitable, filled with the five elixirs; and place each of those great "gem body" (*nor gzugs ma*) tormas. If you put out tormas for the retinue, in that same vessel [put] a three-cornered torma with the tip bent to the right for Yakṣa; a fine three-cornered torma for the action protector (*las mgon*); and for each of the other three retainers, fine round tormas. In the big torma, plant an arrow with a silk scarf and a deity card (*tsa ka li*). Extensive offering tormas are arranged for the Great Torma Ritual, but for a brief version, place one big round torma in front. Arrange the inner offering and other offerings in whatever way is nice.

Then, for the ritual master's acts, put up the preliminary torma. Cleanse it with *sumbha* . . . (etc.) and purify with *svabhāva* . . . (etc.). Consecrate with *oṃ āḥ hūṃ ha hoḥ hriḥ*. {629}

Invoke the guests with

> *pheṃ vajra āralli hoḥ / jaḥ hūṃ vaṃ hoḥ / vajra ḍākinī samaya stvaṃ / ḍriśya hoḥ*

Offer three times with

oṃ kha kha khāhi khāhi / sarva yakṣa rakṣa bhūta preta piśāca unmāda apasmāra ḍāka ḍākinyādaya / idaṃ baliṃ gṛhṇāntu samaya rakṣantu mama sarva siddhi mem pryacchantu yataivaṃ yataiṣṭaṃ bhuñjaṭha jighraṭha pipaṭha mātikramatha / mama sarva kārātaya satsukhaṃ viśuddhaye / sahāyikā bhavantu hūṃ hūṃ phaṭ svāhā

oṃ vajra arghaṃ pratīccha hūṃ svāhā . . . (similarly) . . . *pādyaṃ* . . . (etc.) (Then from) *oṃ vajra puṣpe āḥ hūṃ* . . . (etc. to) . . . *śabda āḥ hūṃ*

Eight great gods with your retinues,
eight great nāgas with your retinues,
the eight world protectors and
hosts of yakṣas without exception,
hosts of rākṣasas without exception,
hosts of bhūtas without exception,
hosts of flesh-eaters without exception,
hosts of crazy-makers without exception,
hosts of forgetful-makers without exception,
hosts of mātṛkas without exception,
those and others—hosts of spirits,
none excluded; however many there are:
come here and pay attention to me.

May we yogins and our retinues . . . (etc. to)
. . . accomplish all that we desire.

You oath-bound ones who guard
the activities of this mandala:
make this area and these patrons
and also these disciples auspicious.

Whatever groups of spirits are here
not empowered to see the secret conduct,
take this leftover torma
and go elsewhere right now.

If somehow you do not leave,
the command of the wrathful great vajra holder
will emanate a cloud of blazing weapons
and reduce your body and mind to dust—beware!

At this juncture, throw the torma outside with wrathful mantras and music. For the consecration of the place and equipment, cleanse and purify as before.

From within emptiness, the protection circle arises from the letter *hūṃ*. Within that, the dwelling place arising from *bhrūṃ* becomes a celestial palace with all characteristics totally perfect. Inside, abundant excellent offering articles made of divine substances arise from *oṃ āḥ hūṃ*—offering water, washing water, flowers, incense, light, perfume, music, and so forth. {630} They completely pervade without interruption of place or time. The unimaginable emanations are in nature the timeless awareness of great bliss. In form they are cloud banks of offering substances that function to satisfy everyone, self and others, through undissipating bliss, filling up everywhere outside and inside the palace.

oṃ vajra arghaṃ svāhā (similarly) . . . *pādyam svāhā*
oṃ vajra puṣpe āḥ hūṃ / . . . āloke . . . gendhe . . . naividya . . . śabda āḥ hūṃ
oṃ sarva vida pūra pūra / sura sura / āvartaya āvartaya hoḥ / oṃ vajra spharaṇa khaṃ

Play music to bring down blessings.

oṃ vajra ghāṇḍeraṇita / praraṇita / sampraraṇita / sarva buddha kṣetra pracālite / prajñāpāramitā nāda sambhavate vajra dharma hṛdaya santoṣani hūṃ hūṃ hūṃ hoḥ hoḥ hoḥ āḥ khaṃ svāhā (Repeat three times.)

Then for the self-visualization, you may follow the Hayagrīva Secret Sādhana or any other suitable practice from the tantra classes. However, the best is to rely solely on the body mandala of the Principal Deities of the Five Tantras.[8] Supplementing from that manual, recite from the consecration of elixir, arousing of awakening mind, and visualizing the protection circle up through the recitation, dissolution, and rearising.

For the front visualization cleanse and purify with *amṛta* . . . and *svabhāva* . . .

> From within emptiness, the letter *hūṃ* in front becomes the protection circle with the unbearable great charnel ground. In its center a lotus arises from *paṃ* and a sun from *raṃ*. Upon that, white *gaṃ* melts into light and becomes glorious Gaṇapati, white, with an elephant head and three eyes, holding in his right hand a leafy daikon radish, the essence of earth, which he is eating. In his left hand is an elixir-filled skull cup. He is lying down, adorned with silks and precious jewels. Upon him, blue-black *hūṃ* becomes a flaying knife marked with *hūṃ*. Light rays radiating from that terminate all enemies, obstructors, and noxious spirits. The light makes offerings to the exalted ones and helps sentient beings. It again returns and dissolves, completely transforming into Swift-Acting Six-Armed Awareness Protector, {631} the perfect fulfiller of the hopes of living beings. He is very black, like the clouds at the end of time. He has one face and six arms. He glares angrily with three round, red eyes. His gaping mouth reveals his bared fangs and curled tongue as he laughs fiercely. His orange beard, eyebrows, and hair stream upward. His forehead is anointed with a drop of vermilion and his head crowned by King Akṣobhya. He holds a vajra[-handled] flaying knife in his top right hand and a blood-filled skull cup with the left, one hand above the other at his heart. In his middle right hand is a rosary of dry skulls, and in the lower one he fiercely rattles a ḍamaru. He holds a trident spear in his second left hand and a vajra lasso in the last left hand. His two legs, with the strength to totally suppress the three existences, stand in a perfectly straight, even position pressing down on the Obstructor King. He wears a tiger-skin skirt tied with a green silk sash. Blue snakes bind his hair, and he has red snake earrings, striped snake armbands, white snake collar, yellow snake bracelets, green snake necklace, and white snake anklets and belt. On all his arms and legs there are strings of large and small bells. He is short and fat, with thick limbs. He has boundless charisma. He has a crown of five dry human skulls topped with jewel finials

and a garland of fifty fresh skulls dripping with blood. The six bone ornaments beautify him. His terrifying roars resound like thunder, annihilating all devils and obstructors. He stands amid a bonfire of timeless awareness like the fire at the end of the eon, supported by the trunk of a sandalwood tree.

To his left, in the middle of an ocean of turbulent blood and fat, *bhyoḥ* becomes Śrīdevī, mighty queen of the desire realm. She is black, waving a devil's black cross-scored board in her right hand and grasping a bag of pestilence with her left. {632} She stands in the midst of a conflagration of fire and wind, riding on a three-legged mule. Her retinue of one hundred thousand flesh-eating ḍākinīs surrounds her.

In front of the principal figure, *hūṃ*[9] becomes Yakṣa Kṣetrapāla, blue-black with a gaping mouth and bared fangs, bellowing at his enemies. Winds of the end-times rise from his nose. With his right hand he brandishes a flaying knife to the sky, terrifying all the gods and demigods. With his left hand he feeds the principal's mouth from a blood-filled skull cup containing the hearts of enemies and obstructors. He rides a crazed black bear.

To the right, *bhyoḥ* becomes dark-red Īśvara Jinamitra fiercely rattling a ḍamaru with his right hand and holding a blood-filled skull cup with the left.

In back, from *jaḥ*, dark-red Yama Ṭakkirāja throws a lasso at enemies with his right hand and points at harm-doers with his left hand in the threatening gesture.

To the left, from *du*, the great devil lord black Trakṣad pierces the enemies' hearts with a red three-pronged ensign spear in his right hand and holds a blood-filled skull cup in this left. He bites his lower lip. He wears a black cloak, high rawhide boots, and a golden belt. He rides a black devil horse with white fetlocks. All four are completely perfect in the garb of wrathful emissaries.

The ten direction protectors are outside of them: Śakra in the east, Agni in the southeast, Yama in the south, Rākṣasa in the southwest, Varuṇa in the west, Vāyu in the northwest, Yakṣa in the north, Bhūta in the northeast, Brahmā above, and Bhūpati below. All around them are the eight great gods, the eight great nāgas, the eight great planets, the nine great terrifiers (bhairavas), the twenty-eight constellations, the four great kings, [and the ten direction protectors]. All these seventy-five protectors of pure clans are each surrounded by a retinue of millions. {633} Outside of them are the armies of an ocean of the oath-bound—loving flesh, reveling in blood, merciless, open-mouthed, bloodshot-eyed, and bearing various lethal weapons in their hands—in an instant they can suck the life force out of all living beings. They wear the garb of yakṣas, rākṣasas, yāmas, māras, and mātṛkās. They completely cover the ground and fill all the sky and space. All are fulfilling the hopes and desires of practitioners.

They all have white *oṃ* at the forehead, red *āḥ* at the throat, and blue *hūṃ* at the heart. Light rays radiate from the *hūṃ* in your own heart, invoking Swift-Acting Six-Armed Awareness Protector from in front of the single trunk of the sandalwood tree in the great charnel ground Cool Grove in the southeast. He arrives instantly with the root and lineage gurus above him, grimacing heroes on his right, smiling heroines on his left, and all the armies of obedient ones, realm protectors, messengers, and an ocean of the oath-bound, accompanied by the sounds of ḍamarus, bells, and small bells: *si li li, khro lo lo, ur ur, chem chem.*

hūṃ
By faith and by sacred pledge,
great Mahākāla, come here.
Glorious Protector with your retinue,
please approach this mandala site.

Kṣetrapāla and the others,
retinue of attendants, hosts of yakṣas,
you who promised to guard the doctrine,
ocean of the oath-bound, please approach.

When you come to this mandala site,
partake of this decorated torma,
show yourselves in signs and forms,
and accomplish the entrusted activity.

oṃ vajra mahākāla saparivāra . . . (etc.).

Add *kṣiṃ* to that twenty-one times. Then in place of *kṣiṃ* insert *e hye hi* and *vajra samājaḥ* three times each. {634} Swift Actor and retinue are invoked.

jaḥ hūṃ vaṃ hoḥ—they dissolve indivisibly.

hūṃ
Great Black One, commander who tames devils,
so magnificent, surrounded by retinues,
in order to subdue every enemy and obstructor,
Great Black One, please remain here.
padma kamalāyastvaṃ

oṃ śri mahākālaya sapārivāra arghaṃ pratīccha hūṃ svāhā

Similarly, add *padyaṃ . . . puṣpe . . . dhūpe . . . āloke . . . gandhe . . . naividyā . . . śabda*. Present the inner offerings by adding the three seed syllables to the essence mantra.

Without stirring from the realm of reality,
yet your wrathful form to subdue the vicious
vanquishes the rudra of the doctrine;
homage and praise to Great Black One.

Then the supplication:

namo buddhāya / namo guruhe / vajra vīra vīreṇī / śrīḍāka ḍākinī / joka jokiṇī / sarva buddha bodhisatvāya śaraṇaṃ gacchāmi
kyai kyai

Holy root and lineage gurus dwelling in the ten directions and three times, bless me! Yidam deities of the mandala, bless me! Heroes and heroines, bless me! Buddhas and bodhisattvas all, bless me! Glorious Six-Armed Awareness Protector and deities, bless me! Do not veil your timeless awareness. Do not delay your compassion. Do not block your power and ability. Do not distance your blessings. All of you, bless me through your body, bless me through your speech, bless me through your mind! Bless me through your unlimited awakened body, speech, mind, qualities, and activities! Bless me right now! Bless me quickly! Bless me on this very seat!

Guru-Protector inseparable,
I supplicate you with faith:
dispel every affliction
of myself and all sentient beings.
Please grant every spiritual power. {635}

Repeat Vajrasattva's hundred syllables twenty-one times. Afterward recite:

Vajradhara and glorious Śavarī,
sovereign Maitrīpa, great adept Rāhula,
Amideva, Lokeśvara,
Hayagrīva, glorious Padmākara,

Khyungpo Yogi, Ratna Vīrya,
Dharma Siṃha, Dharma Prajñā,
Vīrya Siṃha, Khedrup Chöje, and the others,
gurus of the jewel lineage, please think of me.

I did not realize that the guru with a lineage
of perfected qualities that fulfill beings' hopes
was the embodiment of doubly pure buddhas of the three times:
I confess falling under the influence of worldly thought.

All outer, inner, and secret deities with awakened body, speech, mind, qualities, and activities, please think of me.
Once I entered the door of Supreme Vehicle Mantra,
I confess my transgressions and damages of its root and branch pledges.

With your abundant activity of power and capability,
just recalling you for an instant dispels all obstacles.
Giver of spiritual powers without meeting or parting,
Six-Armed Awareness Protector, please think of me.

In secluded charnel grounds, forests, and islands,
I collected the outer and inner supports and pledge substances
but did not properly do the recitations, fulfillments, and
confessions;
I confess falling under the influence of laziness and distraction.

In particular, I did not realize that the supreme secret support
is the great-bliss kāya of Guru-Protector inseparable.
Through constant devotion and belief in you,
I confess not realizing you as totally pure dharmakāya.

Whatever I have done under the influence of ignorant delusion
that opposes the body, speech, and mind of Guru-Protector and
retinue,
with a mind full of sorrow and regret
I confess before your eyes, sublime deity.

Awareness beings who carry out my commands,
activity messengers Kṣetrapāla, Jinamitra,
Ṭakkirāja, Trakṣad, and Rematī,
protectors of the ten directions and pure regions, please think of
me. {636}

True to your word and commitment,
straight away you accomplished my activities,
but sadly I did not offer a flesh-and-blood torma feast;
I confess not giving thanks in a timely way.

With no clairvoyance, I did not realize the faults and mistakes
of the doctrine's destroyers and the guru's lethal enemies,
and so I did not destroy them with wrathful activity;
I confess disclosing the secrets and loving them.

Whatever errors, faults, and delusions I have committed,
such as being contaminated by talking or eating with
vow-breakers,
or meager offerings, spoiled select portions, and confused rituals;
I confess with shame and regret.

I confess violating the sacred pledges of awakened body.
I confess violating the sacred pledges of awakened speech.
I confess violating the sacred pledges of awakened mind.
I confess violating the root sacred pledges.
I confess violating the branch sacred pledges.
I confess consciously violating the sacred pledges.
I confess unconsciously violating the sacred pledges.

I have confessed in order to purify the defilement of violation;
Guru and Protector with your entourage,
please be patient with me, as parents with their child,
and now grant me all the spiritual powers.

Though the acts I confess and the act of confession are
nonexistent,
in order to purify the habitual patterns of discursive thought,
I fully confess before the sublime object of my venerable guru.
May I thereby attain great bliss.

If you don't wish to do the supplication and confession, you may skip them. Then the recitation:

A black mantra garland with red light rays emerges from *hūṃ* in my heart. It appears like rosary beads while the five-colored light rays thread them like a rosary string. It emerges from my mouth and enters Protector's mouth, dissolving into the *hūṃ* in his heart. It arises again from *hūṃ*, emerges from Protector's navel, enters my navel, and dissolves in the *hūṃ* at my heart. It circulates continuously in that way.

oṃ vajra mahākāla saparivāra kṣiṃ kṣetra vighnān vināyaka hūṃ hūṃ phaṭ phaṭ svāhā

Repeat that however many times. Do the visualization for the wrathful recitation: {637}

oṃ śrī mahākāla śāsana / upahāriṇi / eṣo 'paścima kālo ayaṃ idaṃ ratna trayāya / apakāriṇaṃ yadi pratijñāṃ / smarasi tāda /

idaṃ duṣṭaṃ kha kha khāhi khāhi / māra māra / gṛhṇa gṛhṇa / bandha bandha / hana hana / daha daha / paca paca / dinamekena māraya hūṃ phaṭ

This wrathful mantra is held to include the three [injunctions to] call, curse, and kill.

Śrīdevī's namesake mantra:

oṃ śrīdevī hūṃ phaṭ

The essence mantras of the four workers:

oṃ kṣetrapāla vighnān hūṃ phaṭ
oṃ jinamitra vāśaṃ kuru hūṃ phaṭ
oṃ ṭakkirāja samaya bhyoḥ du jaḥ hūṃ phaṭ
oṃ du yog ja mahākāla trakṣad hūṃ phaṭ

From within emptiness, wind comes from *yaṃ*, fire from *raṃ*, three human-head hearthstones from *kaṃ*. Upon that, from *A*, a vast and wide genuine skull cup containing the five meats arisen from *bhrūṃ - āṃ - jiṃ - khaṃ - hūṃ* and five elixirs from *lāṃ - māṃ - pāṃ - tāṃ - vaṃ*. In the space above them is a white *oṃ* [on] a moon from *A* and a vajra from *hūṃ* all stacked up. Wind blows, fire burns—the five meats and five elixirs melt into light. A stream of elixir flows from the three seed syllables. Light from all of that invokes the awareness elixir from the three vajras of all buddhas, which dissolves [into the skull cup]. The *oṃ*, moon, and vajra also melt into light and dissolve into it. It becomes an inexhaustible ocean of elixir with the most excellent color, scent, taste, potency, and power.

oṃ āḥ hūṃ (Repeat three times to consecrate.)

The tongues of the Protector and retinue become tubes of red vajra light arisen from *hūṃ*, through which they suck up the torma and drink it. They are satisfied and delighted by the undissipating bliss in their mind streams.

After the essence mantra, add

> *idaṃ baliṃta kha kha khāhi khāhi*
> *oṃ vajra mahākāla kṣiṃ kṣetra vighanen vināyaka trakrakmo*
> *baliṃta māṃsa rakta rutira kha kha khāhi khāhi*

Similarly, after the retinue's essence mantras, add *idaṃ baliṃta kha kha khāhi khāhi* and offer three times each. Then offer with *mahākāla sapārivāra arghaṃ* . . . (etc.) and do the inner offering as before. {638}

> Glorious Awareness Protector, Excellent Black One, great being who cuts off devils, butcher who cuts the life force, commander who conquers devils, destroyer who thrice burned the rākṣasa city of Laṅkāpuri, war god of yogins, guardian of awareness holders, great devil of oath-breakers' life force and retinue: please accept this sacred substance of decorated torma. Guard the Buddha's doctrine, uplift the status of the Three Jewels, protect the dharma councils of the sangha, and prolong the life of the guru. In particular, pacify those who harm the Three Jewels or harbor evil in thought or deed toward us and our retinues. In case the peaceful methods do not subdue them, then please annihilate them with wrathful awakened activity such as killing, banishing, dividing, paralyzing, tormenting, intimidating, and terrorizing.

> Guru-Protector and retinue,
> since I present this offering torma,
> those who degrade the Three Jewels,
> discredit the Vajrayāna,
> destroy or divide the doctrine,
> threaten the guru's body,
> or hate us yogins:
> Great Black One, liberate them!
> *māraya phaṭ / samaya*

The praise:

> *hūṃ*
> Homage to Swift-Acting Avalokita.

Your bangled feet trample Vināyaka.
Great Black One in a tiger-skin skirt,
six arms well adorned by snake ornaments,
top right hand holding flaying knife, the middle a rosary,
and the last fiercely rattling a ḍamaru.
Your left hands hold a skull, a trident,
and a lasso that catches and binds.
Your wrathful gaping mouth fully bares fangs.
You have three eyes, wild hair streaming upward,
and a spot of vermilion anoints your forehead.
King Akṣobhya is the seal above your head.
You wear a garland of fifty blood-dripping human heads
and a crown of five skulls with jewel finials. {639}
Come from your tree to accept the torma.
Glorious Six-Armed One, I pay homage and praise.

bhyoḥ
In a vast lake of bubbling, boiling blood,
you sit astride a sturdy mule, ablaze with charisma.
Dark blue, with one face and two arms,
you hold a devil's cross-scored board and a bag of pestilence.

Emanations of your body guard the Buddha's doctrine.
Emanations of your speech shake the three realms.
Your immutable mind accomplishes beings' welfare.
Sole Mother Rematī: I pay homage to you.

hūṃ
Attendants in four directions around the glorious Protector,
action messengers who accomplish Awareness's commands,
spreading various emanations to subdue all malevolent forces,
four action messengers, I praise you.

Śakra, Yama, Varuṇa, Yakṣa,
Agni, Rākṣasa, Vāyu, Bhūta,
Brahmā above, and Earth Goddess:
ten emanated direction protectors, I pay homage and praise.

Seventy-five glorious protectors
and armies of an ocean of the oath-bound:
accept this flesh-and-blood torma
and dispel adverse conditions and obstacles,
grant favorable spiritual powers,
and accomplish all entrusted activity
for us yogins and our retinues.

Then, with the visualization for the conferral of the absorption empowerment presented below, perform the self-induction. For the purpose of consecrating the mind streams of the disciples, also do some recitation here. Have the disciples wash and take their seats. Distribute and gather the flowers. The ritual master reads the following:

> You must establish all sentient beings equaling the reaches of space in the state of glorious Heruka. To that end, in the short term, all outer, inner, and secret obstacles of malicious spirits and obstructors must be severed and whatever desired awakened activity of the four kinds must be spontaneously achieved. Ultimately you must actualize the state of Swift-Acting Avalokita. In order to do that, think that you will listen to the stages of the entrustment blessing of glorious Six-Armed Protector without distraction while clearly imagining the higher thought of awakening. {640} So I ask you to pay attention.
>
> Now, in terms of definitive meaning, Exalted Avalokiteśvara is certainly the basis of manifestation of all the victorious ones, and thus the father of all victors. However, to the perceptions of common folk, when manifesting in the manner of an heir of the victors, he gathered the accumulations for many eons and attained the tenth level [of a bodhisattva]. He received the empowerment of the great light rays. One time while remaining in the ranks of the powerful heirs of the victors, he took an oath of awakening mind such as this:
>
>> In this world realm in the manifold universe, I will work for the welfare of sentient beings. I need to liberate all sentient beings from cyclic existence. Moreover, until I establish every single sentient being now in this place of cyclic

> existence in the state of a buddha, I myself will not attain buddhahood. When every sentient being, without a single exception, is placed in the state of a buddha, if I thereafter attain buddhahood, then it is all right. Barring that, I will remain in this cyclic existence and work for the welfare of sentient beings. Should I transgress this oath, may my body shatter into a thousand pieces.

Thus he swore upon his head.

From that time on, he stayed on Mount Potala and with infinite emanations matured and liberated countless sentient beings every second. How could others ever measure up to that? In this way, a number of eons passed. Then one time he believed that now many sentient beings must be free and liberated, so he looked with his supernormal cognition. The number of beings in the realm had neither increased nor decreased. Regarding the fact that they had not diminished, he saw that sentient beings were difficult to train because they were subject to the proliferation of the five degenerations. He thought, "Now I am not capable of enacting the welfare of beings." {641} As previously he had taken a solemn oath of awakening mind and proclaimed that [if transgressed] his body should shatter into a thousand pieces, now Avalokiteśvara's own spiritual master Amitābha arrived in person and spoke: "Son of a good family, your arousal of the mind of awakening was no good. Now for the sake of repairing and restoring that solemn oath, you must generate a mind of awakening even greater than you did before." Then he blessed him by splitting his body into a thousand parts: eleven heads and one thousand arms.

Then again Avalokiteśvara aroused an even more vast mind of awakening: to wrathfully tame the intractable sentient beings during this proliferation of the five degenerations; to give protection from the intermediate state after he saw that even dharma practitioners were not escaping from its terrors; and to fulfill the needs and desires of living beings just by thinking of them as an antidote to the greatest single suffering of the degenerate age: poverty. By means of these three awakened activities, he realized that his arousal of awakening mind could be better than before.

A single *hūṃ* arose from Exalted Avalokita's heart. Then that *hūṃ* became Swift-Acting Awareness Protector, and all the realms quaked six times. Bhagavat Amitābha and all the other tathāgatas in the ten directions sang praises with one voice. They invested him with the power of a great wrathful emanation of the body, speech, mind, qualities, and activities of all buddhas. Indeed, since that time he has remained to guard the doctrine in all the realms of the buddhas.

The manner in which the practice cycle of this great Awareness Protector spread in India and Tibet, and the life stories of great practitioners who displayed manifest wondrous signs [of his practice] are beyond telling. They are clearly described in exhaustive histories in the writings of omniscient Venerable [Tāranātha] and elsewhere. {642}

But in short, about six hundred years after the nirvana of Buddha Śākyamuni, there was a great adept called Śavarīpa who gained accomplishment. He directly perceived this protector in person and was given the life-force mantras and sādhana cycles. He accomplished boundless awakened activity. Glorious Śavarīpa bestowed these on Venerable Maitrīpa. Lord Maitrīpa, while in residence at Vikramaśīla, had attained stability in the creation stages but had not realized the suchness of the abiding nature. He supplicated his special deity, who replied, "Go south to the glorious mountain. The hermit protector will take care of you." In accordance with this prophecy, he went there and the great adept Śavarīpa ["the Hermit"] granted all the instruction of mahāmudrā and gave him the empowerments and sādhana cycles. Then his vision of the abiding nature became as vast as the reaches of space. The dharma protector acted as his servant. Maitrīpa the Great gave all to the great learned adept Khyungpo Lotsāwa.

Khyungpo Lotsāwa was born into the clan Khyung (garuḍa). His birthplace was Nyemo Rama[ng]. At first he adhered to Bön, but then he heard the teachings of the great completion and practiced their fine explications and meditations. Then he attended

Kor Nirupa and received all the cycles of Hevajra and mahāmudrā. At the age of fifty-two he traveled to Nepal and India. Before and after he spent his time in India, Nepal, and Tibet. He attended one hundred and fifty common and extraordinary gurus, primarily Vajrāsana Puṇyākara, Maitrīpa, Hidden Yogi (Abhayākara), Rāhula, and the great Ḍākinīs of Timeless Awareness Niguma and Sukhasiddhi. Those six he adopted as his supreme root gurus. He took the heart essence of those holy gurus and became an unrivaled adept learned in Sutra, Tantra, and all the esoteric instructions of the source traditions. As he was about to return to Tibet, he asked Maitrīpa, "In my country Tibet, there is very little prosperity, therefore please grant me a blessing for the speedy attainment of wealth." {643} Maitrīpa told him the story of this protector, saying that this special precept was like a wish-fulfilling gem. Then he gave him the empowerments and esoteric instructions, as well as making a prophecy.

This great adept Khyungpo could display one hundred and eight emanations of his body at once, pass unhindered through mountain cliffs, and continually meet yidams and protectors in person. He had the ability to dispatch emanated armies and other feats in his amazing life story that is hard to fathom, bringing him the greatest fame as an accomplished adept. In particular, after following this protector's custom of thirteen days of practice, Protector truly revealed himself. From then on, he could be recruited as a servant.

Khyungpo Naljor went before Vajrāsana with eight hundred measures of gold for a great communal feast, which was offered to the adepts for many days. On the occasion of offering the share to the gurus, ḍākinīs, and dharma protectors, all together as one they commended this protector alone with the immutable vajra words of a final testament: "Fortunate son, you and your disciples who hold this lineage should confer empowerment blessings and accomplish the five awakened activities."[10]

Those who take up the practice of the instructions by Awareness Ḍākinī Niguma, who is the main source of the glorious Shangpa Kagyu, even without practicing this dharma protector, will accomplish the four awakened activities without hindrance.

For practitioners, there are greater acts of his patronage, such as his revealing himself and so forth.

Although Khedrup Khyungpo gave whatever minor parts of the Awareness Protector's dharma cycle as appropriate to this or that person, there were three to whom he granted the complete cycle: Latöpa Könchok Khar, Tokden Zhangom Chöseng, and Mokchokpa Rinchen Tsöndru. {644} The lineage of the former [includes the practices of] Nine-Deity Protector, many cycles of Thousand-Armed Thousand-Eyed with Ornaments, and other countless [versions] that were great gates for blessings. This became known as the upper tradition. All the instructions of the latter two [lineages] were collected by Öntön Kyergangpa and passed to Sangye Nyentön, who in turn gave them to Drogön Sangye Tönpa. Then the seal of the one-to-one lineage was released [and the teachings were received] by Khedrup Tsangma Shangtön, Samdingpa Zhönu Drup, Rigong Densawa, Master Ayi Senge, and others. The explicated precepts and so forth that had been granted to these fortunate ones spread widely and became known as the lower tradition.

Of those two primary precept systems, here we are concerned with the lower tradition. That also passed from Densapa to the Pakmo Drupa and the four monastic communities.[11] Thus that lineage spread widely in Central Tibet. The Samding tradition has two sections: South (*lho*) and Severance (*gcod*). From Shangtön's disciple Jakpa came three lineages: upper, lower, and middle. Branching out from those, many cycles of White and Deep-Blue Protectors (*dGon po dkar mthing*) arose, and many sets of teachings proliferated, as exemplified in both Sakya and Kagyu. The father-son line of Venerable Tsongkhapa received [these teachings] from Jakpa's lineage disciples. This protector's awakened activity thus spread widely, including in Tibet, Greater Tibet, China, and other countries, and continues to the present.

In particular, from the Later Seven Jewels [of the Shangpa lineage] it fell as a special legacy to Jonang Jetsun Rinpoche. That Venerable [Tāranātha] himself made this extraordinary dharma protector his main one. Until now, the brilliance of the blessings remains undiminished. Since the time of Khedrup Khyungpo, all the gurus in the lineage of succession have possessed vast knowledge of all there is to know and have been exceedingly learned, righteous, and good. They turned away from the eight worldly concerns, saw all of cyclic existence and its transcendence as illusory, possessed realization of the abiding nature as vast as space, {645} were suffused with unbiased love and compassion, directly saw countless yidams, recruited dharma protectors and guards as if they were servants, and spontaneously accomplished self-arising altruistic benefit for others.

Such holy beings as these practiced an inconceivable variety of sādhanas of this great Awareness Protector. The main ones, however, were certainly the wrathful sādhana for magical power and the peaceful sādhana for wealth. Of those two, the primary one was the wrathful power sādhana, which has many different kinds of permission rituals. However, the root permission empowerment is this very permission of Removing All Obstacles.

In accomplishing this, the ritual master's acts have already been done; now it is the disciples' turn. This has three parts: (1) preparation, (2) main part, and (3) conclusion.

The preparation has six parts: (1) mandala offering, (2) supplication, (3) gathering thoughts, (4) uncommon refuge, (5) uncommon awakening mind, and (6) uncommon supplication.

First, in the presence of the Guru-Protector inseparable, offer a mandala in order to request the conferral of the meditative absorption (*samādhi*) empowerment.

Indicate to the disciples to recite the *Mandala of the Sealed Word* from the Shangpa tradition.[12] If they do not know it, then they can do the general one.

Second, repeat this supplication three times after me:

"Vajra holder, please consider me.
For the sake of benefiting migrators,
I supplicate you, great principal one.
Grant me the Protector's empowerment."

Third, listen to this to gather your thoughts and fully receive it:

> Gather well all of your thoughts,
> and listen with an utterly good attitude.
> Vajrasattva and the other sugatas
> will not bless a forgetful mind.

Thus give up the three faults of a vessel[13] and listen well. {646}

Fourth, the meaning of the special refuge is that it is going for refuge to the guru inseparable from the Protector. Therefore, repeat this three times after me:

> "All buddhas and bodhisattvas dwelling in the ten directions, and the master, please consider me. I, who am called an awareness holder, go for refuge to the gurus who dwell in the ten directions. I go for refuge to the buddhas who dwell in the ten directions. I go for refuge to the dharma that dwells in the ten directions. I go for refuge to the sangha who dwells in the ten directions. I pay homage and go for refuge to the yidam mandala deities and to the deities of Six-Armed Awareness Protector and retinue."

Fifth, repeat this regular confession three times after me:

> "I go for refuge in the Three Jewels . . . (*dkon mchog gsum la bdag skyabs mchi* . . . etc.)."

Sixth, for the uncommon supplication, think that you present mentally emanated offerings and repeat this three times after me:

> "Guru inseparable from the Swift-Acting Awareness Protector, to you I offer sublime outer flowers and incense, inner five meats and five elixirs, secret timeless awareness of bliss-emptiness, and the most secret suchness offering. Please accept and confer the complete four empowerments on me."

This completes the preparation for the empowerments. Second, the main practice of the actual empowerment conferral has four parts: (1) descent of awareness; (2) blessing of awakened body, speech, and mind; (3) blessing of the actual awakened body; and (4) subsequent authorization focused on mantra.

The first of those involves the induction into the mandala and introducing the deities. It has the two parts of (1) visualizing the mandala and (2) the actual descent of the awareness beings.

First, [the descent of awareness] is the visualization of the master as inseparable from the Protector and retinue in front. In the space before you, within a protection circle, is the unbearable great charnel ground. {647} In its center is a lotus and sun upon which is white Gaṇapati with a three-eyed elephant head. In his right hand he holds at his heart a leafy daikon radish, the essence of earth, which he is eating. In his left hand he holds an elixir-filled skull cup. He is adorned with silks and precious jewels and is lying prone. Upon him stands Swift-Acting Six-Armed Awareness Protector, the perfect fulfiller of the hopes of living beings. He is very black, like the clouds at the end of time. He has one face and six arms. He glares angrily with three round, red eyes. His gaping mouth reveals his bared fangs and curled tongue as he laughs ferociously. His orange beard, eyebrows, and hair swirl upward. His forehead is anointed with a drop of vermilion. King Akṣobhya crowns his head. He holds a vajra flaying knife in his top right hand and a blood-filled skull cup with the left; one above the other at his heart. In his middle right hand is a rosary of dry skulls, and in the lower one he fiercely rattles a ḍamaru. He holds a trident spear in his second left hand and a vajra lasso in the last left hand. His two legs, with the strength to totally suppress the three existences, stand in a perfectly straight, even position, pressing down on the Obstructor King. He wears a tiger-skin skirt tied with a green silk sash. Blue snakes bind his hair, and he has red snake earrings, striped snake armbands, white snake collar, yellow snake bracelets, green snake necklace, and white snake anklets and belt. On all his arms and legs are strings of large and small bells. He is short and fat, with thick limbs. He has boundless charisma. He has a crown of five dry human skulls topped with jewel finials and a garland of fifty fresh skulls dripping with blood. The six bone ornaments beautify him. {648} His terrifying roars resound like thunder, annihilating all devils and obstructors. He stands supported by the trunk of a sandalwood tree amid a bonfire of timeless awareness like the fire at the end of the eon.

To his left, in the middle of an ocean of turbulent blood and fat, is Śrīdevī, mighty queen of the desire realm. She is black, waving a devil's black cross-scored board in her right hand and grasping a bag of pestilence with her left. She stands in the midst of a conflagration of fire and wind, riding on a three-legged mule. Her retinue of a hundred thousand flesh-eating mātṛkās and ḍākinīs surrounds her.

In front of the principal, Yakṣa Kṣetrapāla, blue-black with a gaping mouth and bared fangs, bellows at his enemies. Winds of the end-times rise from his nose. With his right hand he brandishes a flaying knife to the sky, terrifying all the gods and demigods. With his left hand he feeds the principal's mouth from a blood-filled skull cup containing the hearts of enemies and obstructors. He rides a crazed black bear.

To the right, dark-red Īśvara Jinamitra fiercely rattles a ḍamaru with his right hand and holds a blood-filled skull cup with the left.

In back, the gray Yama Ṭakkirāja throws a lasso at enemies with his right hand and points at harm-doers with his left hand in the threatening gesture.

To the left, the great devil lord black Trakṣad pierces the enemies' hearts with a red three-pronged ensign spear in his right hand and holds a blood-filled skull cup in this left. He bites his lower lip. He wears a black cloak, high rawhide boots, and a golden belt. He rides a black devil horse with white fetlocks. All four are completely perfect in the garb of wrathful emissaries.

The ten direction protectors are outside of them: Śakra in the east, Agni in the southeast, Yama in the south, Rākṣasa in the southwest, Varuṇa in the west, {649} Vāyu in the northwest, Yakṣa in the north, Bhūta in the northeast, Brahmā above, and Bhūpati below. All around them are the eight great gods, the eight great nāgas, the eight great planets, the nine great terrifiers, the twenty-eight constellations, and the four great kings. All these seventy-five protectors of the pure clans are each surrounded by a retinue of millions. Outside of them are the armies of an ocean of the oath-bound—loving flesh, reveling in blood, merciless, open-mouthed, bloodshot-eyed, and bearing various lethal weapons in their hands—in an instant they can suck the life force out of all living beings. They wear the garb of yakṣas, rākṣasas, yāmas, māras, and mātṛkās. They completely cover the ground and fill all the sky and space. All are fulfilling the hopes and desires of practitioners.

Your yearning devotion to Guru-Protector inseparable causes a haze of light rays to radiate from the heart. It strikes your body and incinerates all negativities and obscurations of your body, speech, and mind. Imagine that all impure appearances are refined and become masses of light. That turns into lucid clarity-emptiness when the master says *oṃ svabhāva* . . . (etc. to) . . . *haṃ*. From within that emptiness, a lotus from *paṃ* and a sun from *raṃ* appear in your stead. Upon that, a white *gaṃ* melts into light and becomes glorious Gaṇapati, white with a three-eyed elephant head, holding in his right hand a leafy daikon radish, the essence of earth, which he is eating. In his left hand is an elixir-filled skull cup. He is adorned with silks and precious jewels and is lying down. Upon him, your mind itself is a blue-black *hūṃ*, from which comes a flaying knife marked with *hūṃ*. {650} Light rays radiate from that and terminate all enemies, obstructors, and noxious spirits. The light makes offerings to the exalted beings and helps sentient beings. It again returns and dissolves, completely transforming you into Swift-Acting Awareness Protector . . . (etc. to) . . . like the fire at the end of the eon.

In that clearly visualized appearance, white *oṃ* is at the forehead, red *āḥ* at the throat, and blue *hūṃ* at the heart. Light rays radiate from the *hūṃ* in the master's heart and invoke Swift-Acting Six-Armed Awareness Protector from in front of the single trunk of the sandalwood tree in the great charnel ground Cool Grove in the southeast. He arrives instantly with the root and lineage gurus above him, grimacing heroes on his right, smiling heroines on his left, and all the armies of obedient ones, realm protectors, messengers, and an ocean of the oath-bound, accompanied by the sounds of ḍamarus, bells, and small bells—*si li li, khro lo lo,ur ur, chem chem*. He dissolves indivisibly into your body.

Play loud music. Circulate the incense smoke of pledge substances.

> *oṃ vajra mahākāla saparivāra kṣiṃ kṣiṃ kṣiṃ* . . . (etc.) (Repeat *kṣiṃ* a total of twenty-one times. In place of *kṣiṃ* insert) *e hye hi* (and) *vajra samājaḥ* (three times each). Swift Actor and retinue are invoked—*jaḥ hūṃ vaṃ hoḥ*—they dissolve indivisibly.

With that, the stage of the descent of awareness beings is done.

> Second, for the blessing of awakened body, speech, and mind, do the following visualization: In Guru inseparable from the Protector in front, white *oṃ* appears clearly in the head, red *āḥ* in the throat, and blue *hūṃ* in the heart. Think, "Please confer the complete four empowerments. Please confer the vase empowerment in particular." Your yearning mental supplication causes light rays to radiate from the *oṃ* in the forehead of the Guru-Protector inseparable. They gather up all the blessings of all buddhas' awakened body in the form of white light rays, which return and dissolve into the *oṃ*. Immeasurable white light rays emerge from the *oṃ* and dissolve into the *oṃ* in your forehead. Imagine that you receive the vase empowerment. {651}

Say that and play music.

> "Now, please confer the secret empowerment" . . . light rays radiate from the *āḥ* in the forehead . . . blessings of all buddhas' awakened speech . . . red light rays emerge from the *āḥ* in the throat and dissolve into the *āḥ* in your throat. Imagine that you receive the secret empowerment.

In this way apply the same pattern:

> "Please confer the wisdom-awareness empowerment". . . light rays radiate from the *hūṃ* in the heart . . . blessings of all buddhas' awakened mind . . . dark-blue light rays emerge from the *hūṃ* in the heart and dissolve into the *hūṃ* in your heart. Imagine that you receive the wisdom empowerment.
>
> Again think, "Please confer the fourth empowerment." Your

yearning devotion to Guru inseparable from the Protector causes [a second set of] the three seed syllables in his three places to break off completely and dissolve into the three seed syllables in your three places. The *hūṃ* in your heart dissolves into the āḥ in your throat. That also dissolves into the *oṃ* in your head. The *oṃ* vanishes like a rainbow in the sky. That purifies the obscuration of fixating on the distinctions of body, speech, and mind, and you receive the fourth empowerment. Rest in mahāmudrā free of mental embellishment.

Play music.

Third is the blessing of the actual awakened body. Visualize that the torma itself is Swift-Acting Awareness Protector with retinue, and through your yearning devotion they arrive above your head with a great rush and rumble. When the guru gives the command to guard against obstacles and achieve favorable conditions, Protector chomps the flesh and chomps the bones, consuming all your sickness, bad spirits, enemies, and obstructors. Meditate that he arrives and loudly declares: "Child of good family, I will guard against your obstacles. I will achieve your favorable conditions."

Hold the torma on the disciples' heads and with music do the exhortation: say the mantras of Protector and entourage, and

Glorious Six-Armed Awareness Protector, {652} One Mother mighty queen of the desire realm, and retinue of the Yakṣa Kṣetrapāla, Īśvara Jinamitra, Yama Ṭakkirāja, black devil-lord Trakṣad, ten direction protectors, and the glorious seventy-five of the pure clans, all with your armies of an ocean of oath-bound protectors, do not contravene the commands and commitments to these glorious gurus: Pervasive Lord Great Vajradhara, mighty glorious Śavarīpa, great adept Maitrīpa, Rāhulagupta, Khedrup Khyungpo Lotsāwa, Mokchokpa Rinchen Tsöndru, Kyergangpa Yeshe Senge, Nyentön Bepe Naljor, Chöje Sangye Tönpa, Shangtön Rinchen Bum, Khyungpo Tsultrim Nyingpo, Drupchen Sangye Senge, Khetsun Shangkarwa Rinchen Gyaltsen,

> Kuklungpa Sangye Palzang, Drupwang Namkha Gyaltsen, Gyagom Lekpa Gyaltsen, Naljor Semkyi Dudrol, Chöku Lhawang Drakpa, Jetsun Drolwai Gönpo, Kunga Tenpai Gyaltsen, Ngawang Kunga Lhundrup, Rwapa Ngawang Trinle, Chöje Kunzang Wangpo, Rikzin Tsewang Norbu, Kagyu Trinle Shingta, Tenzin Chökyi Nyima, Kagyu Trinle Namgyal, up to my root guru Jamgön Dorjechang Pema Nyinje Wangpo—all the glorious holy gurus: do not transgress their commands and vows. Accompany these vajra disciples like a shadow follows the body. Fully pacify all adverse conditions, sickness, spirits obstacles and all that is unharmonious. Increase all favorable conditions, longevity, and merit, entourage, and wealth. Bring under control all migrators, human and otherwise. Annihilate all who would cause harm, such as enemies and obstructors. In short, until we attain awakening, {653} perform the awakened activity of guarding, giving refuge, and concealing. Remove all that is undesirable and accomplish all that is desirable. Perform all activity exactly as requested without restriction.

Fourth, for the mantra transmission, the ritual master should supplicate the front visualization three times:

> Bhagavat, surely grant to these [disciples],
> and please adhere to them.

Now meditate on the essence and root mantras surrounding the *hūṃ* on the sun and lotus in the heart of guru and Protector inseparable. With deep devotion and while tossing flowers, repeat this three times after me:

> "Bhagavat, surely grant to me
> and please adhere to me."

The mantra string in the heart of Guru-Protector inseparable blazes intensely with firelight, radiating dark-red light rays. A second [mantra] breaks away from that, in the way that the light of one candle becomes two, and emerges from his mouth. It enters you, visualized as Protector, through your mouth and settles around the *hūṃ* on the sun in your heart. All the mantras are black and emit dark-red light rays of firelight, which burn up all your sickness, bad spirits, negativities, and obscurations. Imagine the mantra string circulating around and repeat this three times after me:

> "*oṃ vajra mahākāla kṣiṃ kṣetra vighnān vināyaka hūṃ hūṃ phaṭ phaṭ svāhā*
>
> *oṃ śrī mahākāla śāsana / upahāriṇi / eṣo 'paścima kālo ayaṃ idaṃ ratna trayāya / apakāriṇaṃ yadi pratijñāṃ/ smarasi tadā / idaṃ duṣṭaṃ kha kha khāhi khāhi / māra māra / gṛhṇa gṛhṇa / bandha bandha / hana hana / daha daha / paca paca / dinamekena māraya hūṃ phaṭ*
>
> *oṃ śrīdevī hūṃ phaṭ*
> *oṃ kṣetrapāla vighnān hūṃ phaṭ*
> *oṃ jinamitra vāśaṃ kuru hūṃ phaṭ*
> *oṃ ṭakkirāja samaya bhyoḥ du jaḥ hūṃ phaṭ*
> *oṃ du yogja mahākāla trakṣad hūṃ phaṭ*"

Repeat each of those three times.

> In the end, that mantra string in the master's heart breaks away totally and dissolves into the *hūṃ* in your heart. Imagine that your whole being is moistened by all the blessings of Guru-Protector. {654} That concludes the main practice.
>
> Third, the concluding practices have three parts: (1) taking the sacred pledge, (2) offering the gift, and (3) making the aspiration prayer.
>
> First, from now on completely take up all the pure trainings, and especially the training of arousing the awakening mind. It is important not to damage any of the sacred pledges of Mantra. More particularly, keep the sacred pledges of this protector: offer torma of raw black barley, constantly offer incense bundles of pledge substances, do not throw stones at black birds or black dogs, faithfully regard the guru as inseparable [from Protector], do not offer first foods to other elemental spirits, and do not associate with evil, cruel friends. Especially, it is most important to keep this dharma protector secret, to keep the mantras and

esoteric instructions secret, and always be very diligent in offering the daily and special tormas. Thinking that you will guard the sacred pledges and vows that you received on this occasion, repeat this after me:

"I will do all that the master commands."

Second, offer a mandala in gratitude. Repeat this three times after me:

"From now on . . . (*deng nas brtsams te* . . . etc.)."

Third, dedicate the virtue of listening to the dharma to perfect awakening:

"By this merit . . . (*bsod nams 'di yis* . . . etc., or) All my virtuous acts . . . (*bdag gi dge ba'i las rnams* . . . (etc.)."

Recite any appropriate aspiration prayers. At this point, perform a communal feast as in Five-Deity Cakrasaṃvara from the consecration up to the leftovers. Then set out the offerings for the concluding practices. Consecrate them as usual with *arghaṃ* . . . (etc. to) . . . *śabda*. Present the inner offerings with the three syllables. Offer the praise "Without stirring from the realm of reality . . . (*chos dbyings ngang las* . . . etc.)." Say, "For whatever has been left out . . . (*ma 'byor ba dang* . . . etc.)" and

Whatever I did not find or was incomplete,
and anything I was unable to do
of the actions required in this ritual,
it is reasonable that you tolerate them.

Guru-Protector inseparable,
I go for refuge in you with faith:
may I remove every affliction
of myself and all sentient beings. {655}

oṃ You did everything for sentient beings' welfare;
grant the spiritual powers consistent with that.
Though you depart for the land of buddhas,
please return here again.

The awareness beings of the torma dissolve into the painted image's heart.

oṃ vajra muḥ
Torma guests return to their natural abodes.
Pledge beings dissolve into my heart.

Visualize that. Then again consecrate the torma as before. Offer the deity in the painted image as in the torma ritual. Do the request to remain firm in the painted image. Recite aspiration prayers and the *Sealed Word of Auspiciousness*:

Qualities fully perfected like the snow mountains,
from which blessing rivers quench fortunate disciples,
you who reveal my mind as coemergence;
may there be auspiciousness of the sublime gurus, dharma sovereigns.

You watch over practitioners as your children,
ever together like a body and its shadow,
giver of spiritual powers to those with sacred pledge;
may there be auspiciousness of the yidam deities.

You take care of practitioners holding sacred pledge
and properly accomplish various awakened activity,
such as pacifying, enriching, controlling, and subjugating;
may there be auspiciousness of the dharma protectors.

Apparent existence self-liberates like illusion and dream
in the continual experience of great bliss.
Within the space of empty clarity without mental engagement;
may there be auspiciousness of great-bliss mahāmudrā.

Whether they support and offer to practitioners
or treat them with contempt,
everyone will be placed on the path of awakening;
may there be auspiciousness of incomparable awakening mind.

However many states of auspiciousness there are
in all of cyclic existence and its transcendence,

like the course of a great river of abundance;
may there be auspiciousness for all beings always.

May merit rise like the sovereign Supreme Mountain,
great acclaim pervade everywhere like the sky,
and long life, health, and others' welfare be spontaneously present;
may there be auspiciousness of a supreme ocean of qualities. {656}

There are many different special practices associated with this, such as white, red, and blue protectors emanating from the three seed syllables in the guru's three places. There is also a custom of heroes and ḍākinīs emanating from all the upper and lower bodies of all four, [three protectors plus guru]. There is also a version where the three seed syllables radiate and perform the three empowerments. There is the conferral of twenty empowerments of meditative absorptions, so called for the four empowerments of the body [syllable] radiating, four empowerments of the speech seed syllable, four empowerments of the mind by light rays, four empowerments of qualities from the torma, and four empowerments of awakened activity from the hand implements. That is the uncommon tradition of the great Zhangom [Chöseng]. Without understanding that system properly, a version of the ordinary torma empowerment has entered the picture that is merely a subsequent authorization of the six hand implements, and it is pointless. In the upper tradition of the Protector with Nine Deities, some later adherents in the old places added extensive empowerment rituals to any new or old rituals as they found suitable. These were their own creations. Their old texts are mostly in accord with this one, so you only need to practice this ritual of the absorption empowerment.[14]

During the concluding ritual, if you never had a painted, carved, or other image, [do not][15] separate the awareness and pledge beings of the torma deities and raise them into the sky; after offering the torma blessing, [imagine that] the awareness beings depart and the pledge beings dissolve.

[Colophon by Tāranātha (a.k.a. Kunga Nyingpo)]

Higher dharma than all (Kun) other doctrine guards,
to practice the Six-Armed Protector's blessing
is the pinnacle of utter joy (ga).
I have clearly arranged just the essence (Nyingpo).

This ends the chapter of the clear explanation of the practice of the blessing [empowerment] for Six-Armed Awareness Protector's Removing All Obstacles. *maṅgalaṃ*

[Additional Comments]

Having said that, this profound blessing is intended for no one other than extraordinary lineage holders. For the common [version], just perform the regular torma ritual in the tradition that is not profound. Prepare as before. There are two ways to visualize the torma deity: visualizing the Protector on top of the torma or visualizing the torma itself [as the Protector]. There is a big difference in being profound or not profound during the torma empowerment, so it is important to choose correctly. In this instance, the visualization is above [the torma]. In the subsequent authorization, do not do the uncommon supplication. In the main part, other than invoking the awareness being to the front visualization, do not have the visualized Protector dissolve into the disciples. During the empowerment, a second [set of] the three seed syllables that came from the master's three places breaks off and dissolves. {657} But do not do the dissolution in lucid clarity into the disciples' three seed syllables. [During the torma exhortation], do not add "Accompany these vajra disciples like a shadow follows the body . . . (etc. to) . . . Perform all activity exactly as requested without restriction." In the foregoing visualization, do not add the Protector's promise: "Child of good family . . . (etc.)." Do not perform the transmission of the mantra recitation, or if you do, just do it according to the regular version. This is the abbreviated torma empowerment of Removing All Obstacles, or the common regular version.

In particular, to confer the torma empowerment in the profound tradition where there is discord in the dharma lineage or to householders that have not entered the dharma gate will be of no benefit in this life to those who receive it, and you yourself will pay a big price in consequences. So even if you do just the torma empowerment for the sake of wealth and esteem, making this unprofound style seem elaborate with lots of words, it will still be of little import. And, in general, there is not much difference regarding the fault of revealing secrets.

Since the single principal deity is gentle and the retinues are obedient, if you perform the torma empowerment based on the single principal figure, you should know the choices of what to accept and what to reject.

In those statements, Venerable Rinpoche [Tāranātha], apart from just naming the profound and not profound authorizations, did not enumerate them individually. However, Khedrup Je [in *Khedrup's Book*] distinguished the former as *Removing All Obstacles Authorization* and the latter as *Removing All Obstacles Torma Empowerment*, counting them individually. Although it is not necessary to confer the latter as follow-up to receiving the former, it seems best to count it separately [based on] distinguishing the types of recipients. And when enumerating the thirteen major permissions, [the torma empowerment] must be considered separately to calculate the numbers. *maṅgalaṃ*

II. White Protector

oṃ svasti
Guru-Protector inseparable
renowned as King of Power,
I bow to you and the host of ḍākinīs
and write this sādhana of Wish-Fulfilling Gem.

The second major permission of the Protector presents the combined essence of the sādhana and the way to confer the authorization of the White Protector Wish-Fulfilling Gem. On a platform in front of you, make a circular mandala of colored powder with a white circumference. In its center, make a white source of phenomena, a red circular outline (*rekhā*), and green square. In the middle of the source of phenomena, place a white heap [of grain] on a sun seat. {658} Upon that, on a mañji, arrange the support torma decorated with all the ornaments. Make the shape either three-sided or, if the gem shape, then attach three dough balls on the spherical dough torma. Upon that, put something like a Jambu food morsel so that from all angles it will seem fittingly like a three-eyed gem. In any case, make it from the substance of butter flour in which are polished jewels and so forth. In front of the mandala, put the round offering torma adorned with many good edibles. Set out the offerings in the usual way. If you have a deity card, stick it on the support torma, but if not, it is all right. Then consecrate the offerings in the usual way.

In the main practice, there is of course the custom of doing a yidam as the self-visualization, but here the self- and front visualization is mostly inseparable, so the practice is also to make the self- and front inseparable. In that way, having done the preliminaries of going for refuge, arousing awakening mind, and the four immeasurables, purify into emptiness with śūnyata . . . (etc.).

From within emptiness, the letter *hūṃ* in front becomes the protection circle. In its center, a lotus arises from *paṃ* and a sun from *raṃ*. Upon that, *gaṃ* becomes white Gaṇapati[16] with an elephant head, holding a daikon and a mongoose. He has fallen face down, and is adorned with silks and precious jewels. One's own mind, the nature of phenomena, appears as a pink sphere the size of a pea. In its center is *hūṃ*, a color like quicksilver. Light rays radiate from that and dispel the suffering of poverty for all sentient beings. Light rays return again and absorb [into the *hūṃ*], which completely transforms into oneself inseparable from the front creation of Swift-Acting Awareness Protector Wish-Fulfilling Gem, King of Power. His color is brilliant white and his face has an expression of a wrathful smile, laughing ferociously. With three eyes, his tawny eyebrows, beard, and hair swirl upward. His forehead is anointed with a spot of vermilion and his head sealed by King Akṣobhya. His first right hand brandishes skyward a flaying knife, the middle holds the gem Mighty Sovereign to his heart, and the lowest rattles a sandalwood ḍamaru. {659} The first left hand resting against his left thigh holds a jewel-filled vase nestled inside an elixir-filled kapāla, the second one a trident, and the last one holds a lasso. His legs in a dance position stand on the seat of lotus, sun, and Gaṇapati. He wears an elephant skin on his upper body, a crown of five dry skulls, and a garland of fifty fresh heads. He is draped with beautiful precious jewels, bells, and various hanging jewelry. Surrounded by a retinue of one billion magnetizing ḍākinīs, he stands in the midst of a blazing bonfire.

At his forehead is *oṃ*, at his throat *āḥ*, and at his heart is a red magnetizing ḍākinī holding a hook and blood-filled skull cup. In her heart is a vital drop, the nature of phenomena, and in the middle of that is a white *hūṃ*. Light rays radiate from one's heart and invoke from the great charnel ground Cool Grove in the southeast Swift-Acting Awareness Protector Wish-Fulfilling Gem with all the hosts of ḍākinīs—

vajra samājaḥ / padma kamalaye stvaṃ / jaḥ hūṃ vaṃ hoḥ
(Offer with) . . . *arghaṃ* . . . (etc. to) . . . *śabda.*

Compassionate Protector Wish-Fulfilling Gem,
white as a snow mountain, radiating light,
you relieve all the poverty of migrators
and grant the power of fulfilled desires—I bow and praise you.

The mantra circles around the drop in the heart.
guru mahākāla ha ri ni sa siddhi jaḥ

Repeat that as much as you can. Cleanse and purify the torma and consecrate as explained in the visualization description of the Black One.

The tongues of the awareness deities are vajra straws through which they suck up and consume the torma.

After the essence mantra, add *idam baliṃta kha kha khāhi khāhi* and repeat it seven times to offer. Saying . . . *śāsana* . . . (etc.) three times is the practice to offer to the general oath-bound protectors. Then do the offering and praise as above. {660} Supplicate for your desires with "Accept this torma I offer to you . . . (etc.)." If you are just doing the practice for yourself, then at this point do the concluding practices. If you are taking care of disciples, this precedes the concluding ritual. Sprinkle the disciples, distribute and gather flowers, and clarify the arousing of awakening mind. If you want to be more thorough, you can explain the history of the Protector's arousing the awakening mind and other details. More briefly, continue here:

"For the sake of all the many mother sentient beings who equal the reaches of space, I must attain the state of the Guru-Protector inseparable. To that end, I will receive the profound permission of Bhagavat White Protector Wish-Fulfilling Gem, and I will practice its meaning." Arouse the awakening mind with that thought and please pay attention.

In this Land of Snows there are the famed Eight Great Chariots of the practice lineages. Of those long lineages, the most profound and amazing is the glorious Shangpa Kagyu, which possesses the very special singly sufficient dharma protector: Swift-Acting Awareness Protector. Through the power of Exalted Avalokiteśvara's awakening mind and special sacred pledge, a wrathful fierce form was manifested. All the victors of the ten directions empowered and invested him as a mighty one among all the guardians of the doctrine. The great adepts Śavarīpa, Maitrīpa, Rāhulagupta, great adept Khyungpo Naljor, and the succession of holy masters in the Shangpa Kagyu had visionary encounters and became accomplished.

There are many sequences in the Protector's practice cycle, but the main two are the wrathful practices for magical power and the peaceful practices for wealth. In the first of those, there are the sole principal figure, the brother and sister, the three deities, the encirclement by five classes of haughty ones, and so on. Additionally, there are many wrathful practices of the principal with retinue. Among the peaceful wealth practices, there is White Protector, Yellow Protector, Red Protector, Green Protector of Longevity, and others. {661} Among all of those, it appears that Khedrup Khyungpo Naljor received the cycle of the wrathful practice mainly from Master Maitrīpa the Great, and the cycle of peaceful practice primarily from the great adept Rāhulaguptavajra.

One time Khedrup Khyungpo did a retreat at Lönpai Kyilpo Monastery while living alone in Jokpo in Penyul.[17] The great adept Rāhula the Great, who had attained the rainbow vajra body, came to visit him and displayed an array of amazing miracles. He taught the general tantras and instructions, and particularly countless maturing and liberating [empowerments and instructions]; in particular he gave many previously known and unknown [teachings from] the dharma cycle of Swift-Acting Awareness Protector and the cycle of the peaceful practice for wealth.

This especially exalted method of accomplishment of the Protector Wish-Fulfilling Gem is an esoteric instruction requested by all the ḍākinīs from the depths of their hearts; a source of both common and uncommon spiritual powers gained through mere supplication; an attainment of some spiritual powers just through receiving the empowerment; and naturally accumulates

> wealth by just holding the texts. In accomplishing the stages of its authorization blessing, the ritual master's acts are now well completed. Now it is your turn. Please offer a mandala.

At this point, have them offer a mandala.

> Repeat this supplication after me three times:
>
> > "Vajra holder, please consider me . . . (etc.)."

Continue with the gathering of thoughts, uncommon refuge, regular confession in five branches, and the uncommon supplication as in the extensive practice. If you prefer the concise version, have them recite after you three times the regular confession that begins "I go for refuge in the Three Jewels . . . (etc.)." {662}

> Now for the main practice of the authorization, do the following visualization: Since you must clearly imagine the front torma inseparable from the master as the Protector Wish-Fulfilling Gem, I ask you to do this visualization. *oṃ śūnyata jñāna vajra svabhāva atmako 'haṃ*
>
> From within emptiness . . . (etc. as before to) . . . he stands in the midst of a blazing bonfire. With your yearning devotion to this master and front visualization inseparable, on the basis of saying *oṃ śūnya . . . ko 'haṃ*, all phenomena included in relative consciousness disappear and become emptiness. From within emptiness, your mind itself is a vital drop with *hūṃ*. Imagine that completely transforms into the upright body of Glorious Awareness Protector Wish-Fulfilling Gem, King of Power. At your forehead is *oṃ* . . . (etc. to) . . . white *hūṃ*. Light rays radiate from the master's heart and invoke Swift-Acting Awareness Protector Wish-Fulfilling Gem and all the ḍākinī hosts from the great charnel ground Cool Grove in the southeast. At that very instant, they arrive with the sound of ḍamarus and bells—*sil sil, khrol khrol, ur ur, chem chem*. They dissolve indivisibly into you.

Say that and intensely play music. After the essence mantra, add *aveśaya aḥ* and recite intensely. This intense music and mantra recitation should be similarly applied below.

That is the equivalent of the vase empowerment in the authorization of awakened body. Imagine that the mantra circles around the *hūṃ* inside the vital drop of the nature of phenomena in the master's heart. Through your yearning devotion to the master, a second mantra string breaks off from the master's heart mantra string and emerges from the mouth. Imagine that it enters your mouth and settles inside the drop of the nature of phenomena in your heart like a photograph. Repeat [the mantra after me.] {663}

The practice is to repeat the essence mantra thirteen times.

That is the equivalent of the secret empowerment in the authorization of awakened speech. Again, through your yearning devotion, light rays radiate from the master's heart, gather back and dissolve into itself all the compassionate blessings without exception of all buddhas and bodhisattvas. From the *hūṃ* in the heart of the Guru-Protector inseparable boundless hand implements emerge, such as flaying knives, skulls, vases, gems, and hooks. They all melt into light and dissolve into your heart.

Play music.

That is the equivalent of the wisdom-awareness empowerment in the authorization of awakened mind. Again, through your yearning devotion, countless ḍākinīs of the five classes—red colored and carrying ḍamarus and skulls—radiate from the *hūṃ* in the master's heart. They emerge from the left nostril and fill all the realms of worlds in the ten directions. They gather up all the brilliance, potency, refined essence, life force, wealth, and power in all of cyclic existence and transcendence. It all enters your left nostril, descends down through your life-force channel, and dissolves indivisibly into the vital drop of the nature of phenomena at the heart.

Play music.

That is the equivalent of the fourth empowerment in the authorization of awakened qualities. Again, through your yearning devotion in the master, Gaṇapati under the feet of the Guru-Protector inseparable is evoked. From Gaṇapati, countless hosts of identical forms emanate. They bring under control all the human and nonhuman spirits and nine great haughty ones. Imagine that they are offered to you as servants. The Gaṇapati underneath your feet discharges a great rainfall of wish-fulfilling gems from his mouth, anus, and all pores. {664} Your coffers, dwelling places, and the whole country are all filled to the brim with food, money, wealth, and various desires and requisites.

Play music.

That is the equivalent of the follow-up empowerments in the authorization of awakened activity. Imagine the following: this torma is itself the Guru-Protector inseparable. Visualize White Protector Wish-Fulfilling Gem with the host of ḍākinīs. Through your yearning devotion, they arrive at the top of your head—*ur ur, chem chem*—saying, "We will accomplish all your desires just as you wish." Think that they say that distinctly and remain there as if pouring down blessings.

With the sound of music, say:

Glorious Swift-Acting Awareness Protector Wish-Fulfilling Gem, King of Power, and your retinue of hosts of millions of ḍākinīs: Do not forget the series of commands and oaths [you made to] all the mighty adepts of the precept lineage—from the overlord Great Vajradhara, sublime Exalted Avalokiteśvara, great adept Rāhulagupta, and learned adept Khyungpo Naljor down to my root guru Dorje Chang Padma Nyinje Wangpo. Accompany like a shadow to a body these vajra disciples holding sacred pledge. From this time on until they attain awakening, please accomplish without impediment whatever activity is entrusted to you, such as the attainment of all desired supreme and common spiritual powers.

Do this exhortation intensely.

> At the end, imagine that Guru-Protector inseparable melts into light and dissolves into you. Thinking that you will guard the sacred pledges and vows that you received on this occasion . . . (etc. until) . . . please practice. (*gnas skabs su thob pa'i dam tshig dang* . . . (etc. to) . . . *spyad du gsol*).[18]

Follow that formula from the Black Protector's authorization, {665} including the concluding rituals. In its concluding ritual, there is a tradition of practice where the awareness beings of the torma raise up into space and then the torma itself is offered to them. But it seems that it is not done in the normal course of the White Protector.

[Colophon by Tāranātha Kunga Nyingpo]

Greater than all (Kun) other wealth practice,
joyfully (ga) proclaimed as illustrious,
the way drawn from the ḍākinī's heart (Nyingpo)
is clearly spoken here—*emaho!*

This was the chapter on the means of accomplishing White Protector Wish-Fulfilling Gem. *maṅgalaṃ*

III. Yellow Protector

namo guru
The guru of all the victors
manifests as a youthful bodhisattva,
I bow deeply to the world's Protector
and explain Yellow Protector's sādhana.

The third permission is for Three-Faced Six-Armed Yellow Protector. The sequence of taking up the sādhana and authorization is as follows: Make a three-sided yellow torma or the torma with the body of "blazing gem." Above a yellow triangular source of phenomena, place a mañji and so forth; the other arrangements are the same [as before]. The consecration of offerings, going for refuge, arousing the awakening mind, and the four immeasurables are the usual. Purify into emptiness with śūnyata . . . (etc.).

From within emptiness, the letter *hūṃ* becomes the protection circle. In its center on a lotus and sun are male and female Gaṇapatis who have fallen face down. Upon them, yellow *hūṃ* completely transforms into oneself as the glorious Awareness Protector, yellow in color with a slightly red radiance. He has three faces and six arms. His main face is yellow, to its right is white and to the left is red, each with three eyes and bared fangs. His first two right and left hands hold a flaying knife and blood-filled skull cup, one above the other, while embracing the mother consort. The second right hand holds a banner and the third an utpala flower. The second left hand holds a mongoose and the third a lasso. He stands in the position of right leg bent and left straight, pressing on the male and female Gaṇapatis. He has the complete eight charnel-ground accessories. {666} The mother, smoke-colored Wrathful Goddess, embraces him holding a flaying knife and skull cup. The two of them stand within a blazing fire of timeless awareness. At their foreheads is *oṃ*, at their throats *āḥ*, and at their hearts *hūṃ*. Light rays radiate from one's heart and invoke all the buddhas and bodhisattvas, and Swift-Acting One and retinue from the great charnel ground Cool Grove—*vajra samājaḥ. jaḥ hūṃ vaṃ hoḥ*—they dissolve indivisibly into oneself.

Again light rays radiate from the heart invoking the five classes of empowerment deities—*vajra samājaḥ*. (They say) *oṃ vajrī bhava abhiṣiñca hūṃ* and confer empowerment. The [protectors'] bodies are purified of stains, and the excess water rises up and becomes Akṣobhya as the crown.

guru mahākāla kṣiṃ uṣṇiṣaya yakṣa hūṃ / ratna gṛi siddha hūṃ / prajñā vardhani svāhā

Cleanse with *amṛta* . . . purify with *svabhāva* . . . (etc.). As in the self-visualization, say, "From within emptiness . . . (etc. to) . . . Akṣobhya as crown," except omit "one's own mind . . ." and "oneself." Offer with *arghaṃ* . . . (etc. to) . . . *śabda*. Praise with

Averting and guarding against sorcerers,
increasing long life and intelligence,

performer of peaceful and enriching actions:
Guru-Protector, I bow to you.

Focusing on the front visualization, do the mantra recitation however much. The torma consecration is the same as in the liturgical description of the Black One. Then offer [the torma] seven times with *oṃ guru mahākāla idaṃ baliṃta kha kha khāhi khāhi*. Do the offerings and praises as above, and supplicate for your desires with "Accept this torma I offer to you . . . (etc.)." Those were the master's acts.

The disciples do the gift offering [for requesting empowerment] and other preliminary acts in the authorization of both the White and Black Protectors, except during the visualization for the mind of awakening, substitute with "I will receive the profound permission of Bhagavat Three-Faced Six-Armed Yellow Protector" and

> The dharma to receive concerns the Swift-Acting Awareness Protector that the great adept Rāhula the Great granted to the learned adept Khyungpo Naljor. {667} This is the Yellow Protector of qualities from the cycle of peaceful wealth practices. In general, he guards and turns back sorcery and curses, and accomplishes a multitude of peaceful and enriching actions. In particular, he possesses the rapid magical power of immortal vajra life and the profound increase of the strength of intelligence free of desire and obstruction.

Then continue from "the authorization . . . (etc.)," doing the supplication and so forth.

> Now for the main practice of the authorization, do the following visualization: From the mouth of the clearly visualized guru [and] Yellow Protector [comes] *oṃ śūnyata jñāna vajra svabhāva atmako 'haṃ*. On the basis of saying that, all impure appearances are purified in basic space.
>
> From within emptiness, from *hūṃ* . . . (etc. to) . . . "Akṣobhya as crown."

Follow the sādhana, except change the liturgy and instead of one's own mind" say "your minds," and instead of "oneself" say "your." Then say "invokes the awareness beings—*vajra samājaḥ / jaḥ hūṃ vaṃ hoḥ*." Afterward, play grand music, and after the essence mantra, say *aveśaya a*. Make those changes.

> A white *oṃ* letter comes from the guru's forehead and dissolves into your foreheads. You receive the vase empowerment. A red *āḥ* letter comes from the throat and dissolves into your throats. You receive the secret empowerment. A blue *hūṃ* letter comes from the heart and dissolves into your hearts. You receive the wisdom-awareness empowerment. White, red, and blue letters *oṃ*, *āḥ*, and *hūṃ* come from all three places and dissolve into your three places. Imagine that you receive the fourth empowerment.

Here, you do not need the mantra recitation transmission. Now the exhortation for awakened activity.

> Clearly visualize this torma itself as the Guru-Protector inseparable, surrounded by the assemblies of buddhas and bodhisattvas all around. They come to the top of your head. Countless tiny forms of Guru-Protector inseparable come forth. {668} Imagine that they slowly dissolve into your bodies.

> Glorious Swift-Acting Yellow Awareness Protector with the Wrathful Goddess and your emanated retinue of hosts of millions of ḍākinīs: Do not forget the series of commands and oaths you made to all the mighty adepts of the precept lineage—from the overlord Great Vajradhara, sublime Exalted Avalokiteśvara, great adept Rāhulagupta, and learned adept Khyungpo Naljor down to my root guru Dorje Chang Padma Nyinje Wangpo. Accompany like a shadow to the body these vajra disciples holding sacred pledge. From this time on until they attain awakening, please accomplish without impediment whatever activity is entrusted to you. In particular, please turn back and guard against all evil maledictions of magic and curses from adversaries, increase like the waxing moon longevity and intelligence free of desire or obstruction, pacify all adverse conditions of great attachment or fear, and increase the six riches and the qualities of experiential realization more and more.

Do this exhortation intensely accompanied by grand music. The concluding ritual of promising to keep the sacred pledge and other concluding acts were already written down in the authorization of Black Protector, so transpose them here. It is said that there are two permissions for Yellow Protector: this Yellow Protector and Yellow Guru-Protector Inseparable with Eight Faces and Sixteen Arms. But the only real Yellow Protector is this one.

[Colophon by Tāranātha Kunga Nyingpo]

Supreme of all (Kun) guardians who increase wealth,
creator of wisdom and joy (ga),
Yellow Protector's amazing means of accomplishment
so extremely rare, its essence (Nyingpo) is contained.

This was the chapter on the means of accomplishing Yellow Protector Increasing Intelligence.

IV. Red Protector

namo guru
Avalokiteśvara's wrathful form,
magnetizing deity, I respectfully bow.
You radiate the light of rubies.
I write this sādhana of the Protector.

The fourth permission is for Red Protector, King of Power.[19] The sequence of taking up the sādhana and authorization is as follows: On a platform in front of you, make a blue-black triangular mandala with a ring of fire. In its center, draw an eight-petaled red lotus, and in its center draw a vajra marked with *hūṃ* at its center and a flaying knife marked with *āḥ*. If you can't draw that, just place a red heap of grain there. Upon that, put a skull cup full of elixir on a mañji and on that a mirror smeared with vermilion. In the vermilion, inscribe a source of phenomena—two stacked triangles—and in its center a *hūṃ*-marked vajra and *āḥ*-marked flaying knife. In the six corners, write the six letters going clockwise: *ha ri ni sa svā hā*. Above, cover it with a red silk canopy. {669} To the right of that, set out a red glory torma, the "gem form" (*nor gzugs ma*), decorated with all the ornaments made of meat, treacle, and so forth. Arrange the offering torma and general offerings as usual. Perform the consecration of offerings as usual, and, having first recited the refuge, awakening mind, and four immeasurables, purify into emptiness with śūnyatā . . . (etc.).

> From within emptiness, a deep blue source of phenomena arises from an *e* with a red lotus, sun, and face-down obstructor king Gaṇapati all stacked up in its center. A *hūṃ*-marked flaying knife arisen from *hūṃ* radiates and reabsorbs light. That totally transforms into oneself as Red Protector, Mighty King, ruby red with one face and six arms. The first two hands hold a flaying knife and skull cup embracing the mother consort, the middle pair a small hand drum and trident, and the last pair a hook and a lasso.
>
> Three eyes, yellow hair swirling upward,
> wearing a crown of five dry skulls,
> a garland of fifty fresh heads,
> a loose tiger skin, with left leg drawn in,
> adorned by human bones, snakes, bells,
> and all eight charnel-ground accessories.
> Great Mother, Lotus Ḍākinī,
> is red, with an expression of passion,
> naked, with five symbolic ornaments,
> embracing the father holding knife and skull.
> Both stand in an expanse of towering flames.
>
> Black Mahākāla stands in front of the principal couple, holding a flaying knife and skull cup. Red Kṣetrapāla is to their right holding a ḍamaru and making the threatening pointing gesture. Black Jinamitra is in back, holding a flaying knife and skull cup. Yellow Ṭakkirāja is to their left holding a trident and making the threatening gesture. All around are the hosts of an ocean of the oath-bound. In the heart of the principal figure is a vajra marked with a *hūṃ*. In the heart of the mother is a flaying knife marked by *aṃ*. {670} From one's own heart light radiates and invokes the Red Swift-Acting Awareness Protector, King of Power, and his retinue from the great charnel ground Cool Grove in the southeast—*jaḥ hūṃ vaṃ hoḥ*.
>
> At their foreheads is *oṃ*, at their throats *āḥ*, and at their hearts

hūṃ. Again light rays from the heart seed syllables invoke the five classes of empowerment deities with their entourages—*vajra samājaḥ*. (Offer with) *arghaṃ* . . . (etc. to) . . . *śabda*. Supplicate with "All tathāgatas, please confer empowerment on me." Saying *oṃ vajrī bhava abhiṣiñca hūṃ*, they confer empowerment. The [protectors'] bodies are purified of stains, and the excess water rises up and becomes Amitābha as the crown of both father and mother while the retinue is crowned by the principals. Meditate on the mantra string at one's heart:

oṃ vajra mahākāla saparivāra kṣiṃ kṣetra vighnān vināyaka hūṃ hūṃ phaṭ / hūṃ maguye svāhā

Repeat that as much as you can. Then cleanse and purify for the front visualization. From the self-visualization repeat, "From within emptiness a deep-blue source of phenomena arises from an *e* . . . (etc. to) . . . crowned by the principals," except omit the words "one" and "oneself." Offer with

oṃ guru mahākāla saparivāri bhyaḥ / arghaṃ praticcha svāhā . . . (etc. to) . . . *śabda*

Guru-Protector inseparable, great-bliss speech,
the nature of all victors: Amitābha and
dharma lord, migrators' protector, Avalokita,
displayed in the mighty body of Great Black One.

Clearly imagine this according to the front-visualization recitation and repeat however much. Then for the torma consecration, do the same as in the Black Protector. After the essence mantra, add *idaṃ baliṃta gṛhṇa gṛhṇa hūṃ hūṃ phaṭ* and offer it. Do the offerings and praises as above. Supplicate for your desires with "Accept this torma I offer to you . . . (etc.)." Whatever ways the disciples' consecration is done below, you should perform the visualization here in the manner of a self-induction.

All the preliminary acts of the disciples after that are the same as in the Black Protector, except that during the clarification of the mind of awakening, say "the profound permission of the Red Protector, King of Power," {671} and

The dharma to receive concerns Swift-Acting Awareness Protector that the great adept who gained the deathless vajra body, Rāhulaguptavajra, granted to Khedrup Khyungpo Tsultrim Gönpo. This is the Red Protector, King of Power, from the cycle of peaceful wealth practices. With an extremely swift blessing of the essence of Amitābha, the vajra of speech, this powerful one accomplishes longevity and magnetizing actions faster than any others. The practice is similar to the main Black Protector, but it is said that after only seven days of doing it, you will see him, plus other immeasurable qualities.

Then continue from "the authorization for this . . . (etc.)," doing the supplication through the regular confession, and

In your hearts on a white moon, imagine a five-pronged white vajra and repeat this three times after me:

"*oṃ sarva yogacitta utpādayāmi*"

The Secret Mantra is very rare; listen to this teaching and fully receive it.

In this world, omniscient ones
might sometimes arise, or not.
Or like the uḍumbara flowers
appear every few hundred years.
The way of Secret Mantra conduct
occurs even more rarely than that.
This way of conduct of profound nonduality
makes all sentient beings buddhas.

Then light rays radiate from the master's heart and compel the mind stream of the deities in the front visualization, invoking all the buddhas and bodhisattvas in the form of Swift-Acting Awareness Protector. He enters the tops of your heads and dissolves indivisibly.

Play grand music. After the essence mantra, add *āveśaya a a* and repeat seven or twenty-one times.

Through that connection, you instantly become the form of Red Protector, King of Power, {672} red in color, holding a flaying knife, skull cup, ḍamaru, trident, hook, and lasso. Mother Lotus Ḍākinī holds a flaying knife and skull cup, embracing Protector. As for introducing the deities, here they dwell in the mandala of the Swift-Acting Awareness Protector. In the center a deep-blue source of phenomena . . . (etc. to) . . . all stacked up in its center. Upon that is Red Protector, King of Power, ruby red . . . (etc. to) . . . around are all the hosts of an ocean of the oath-bound. Imagine that they are all inseparable from your root guru.

Now for the main part of the empowerment, on the basis of your yearning devotion to the Guru-Protector inseparable, from a white *oṃ* on the crown of his head, countless white protectors with small bodies and thick limbs come to the tops of your heads and dissolve. You receive the vase empowerment.

Play music.

Again from the red *āḥ* in the throat, countless red protectors with small bodies and thick limbs break off and dissolve into your throats. You receive the secret empowerment.

Play music. Apply the same formula:

From the blue *hūṃ* in the heart . . . blue . . . into your hearts . . . (music). Again from the three seed syllables in the places come white, red, and blue . . . into your three places. You receive the precious word empowerment (music). Those were the four outer empowerments.

Then again, on account of your yearning devotion to the Guru-Protector inseparable, the two protectors come to the tops of your heads and melt into light, the essence of bodhicitta. That enters the tops of your heads and fills down to the eyebrow level; you obtain the vase empowerment; down to the throat, the secret empowerment; and down to the breast bone, the wisdom-awareness empowerment. Imagine that as your whole body fills up, you obtain the precious word empowerment, the profound fourth empowerment. {673} Those were the four inner empowerments. Now think of the torma as the Protector.

Place the torma on the disciples' heads:

> *oṃ*
> Blazing glorious charisma, body of Protector father-mother,
> this wondrous, spontaneous torma of pledged substance
> confers empowerment on you, vow-holding noble disciples:
> may you enjoy the unchanging vajra body.
> (Essence mantra plus:) *kāya vajra abhiṣiñca hūṃ*
> Now you have obtained the vase empowerment.

Touch the skull cup filled with elixir at their throats.

> *āḥ*
> Profound Secret Mantra, speech of Protector father-mother,
> this undissipating elixir, the vessel and contents of great bliss,
> confers empowerment on you, vow-holding noble disciples:
> may you enjoy unrestricted divine melodies of speech.
> (Replace *kāya vajra* with) *vāka vajra . . .*
> Now you have obtained the secret empowerment.

Touch the vermilion mandala to their hearts.

> *hūṃ*
> Devoid of dualism, mind of Protector father-mother,
> this awareness mirror, stainless empty appearance,
> confers empowerment on you, vow-holding noble disciples:
> may you enjoy the totally pure awareness mind.
> *citta vajra . . .*
> Now you have obtained the wisdom-awareness empowerment.

At this point, although not elucidated in the ancient texts, there seems to be a practice of giving inner offering to the disciples to drink and anointing them with a drop of vermilion at their hearts.

ho
Limitless realm of phenomena, elaboration fully calmed,
this vast expanse of reflexive awareness in absorption
confers empowerment on you, vow-holding noble disciples:
may you enjoy the utterly pure realm of phenomena.
jñānā vajra . . .

Now you have obtained the word empowerment.

Those were the four secret empowerments of pledge substance.

Sets of mantra strings emerge from the heart of Guru-Protector inseparable. Imagine that they dissolve into your hearts. {674} Repeat this after me three times. (Repeat the essence mantra.)

After tossing flowers at the master, repeat this three times after me:

> "Bhagavat, surely grant to me
> and please adhere to me."

Again, consecrate the flowers as the mantra strings. Tossing them to you, imagine that you have the ability and power of mantra.

> Bhagavat, surely grant to these [disciples],
> and please adhere to them. (Repeat three times.)

The vows that you received on this occasion . . . (etc.).

For the disciples' concluding practices, follow only the description in the Black Protector. The concluding practices of the ritual are the same.

This is the root sādhana of Red Protector; the longevity practice should be understood as an extra deity [practice].

[Colophon by Tāranātha Kunga Nyingpo]

Magnetizing that is most of all joyful (Kunga),
this essence (Nyingpo) of the wonderful means of accomplishment
was written because, apart from the old texts,
the practices that came later are rare.

This was the chapter on the means of accomplishing the Red Protector, King of Power. *maṅgalaṃ*

V. Green Protector

namo guru
Amitāyus and Avalokita,
called Swift-Acting Protector,
I bow to you and explain the sādhana.

The fifth protector permission is for Green Protector, Lord of Longevity. For the sādhana, create a green source of phenomena with a ring of fire arranged on a platform. In its center arrange heaps of grain equal to the number of deities. Upon those, put the glory torma "gem body" adorned with ornaments on a mañji. To the left, put the inner offering of a kapāla full of elixir on a mañji. Upon that, put a vermilion[-smeared mirror] and draw a mandala on it as in the Red Protector practice. Cover it with a green silk canopy. To the right, arrange the vases as usual. Set out the offering torma as usual. After first consecrating the offerings, meditate on going for refuge and the four immeasurables. Purify with *svabhāva* ... (etc.).

> From within emptiness, a protection circle arises from *hūṃ* surrounded by the eight great charnel grounds. Within that is a celestial palace with all characteristics perfectly complete. {675} In its center, in front of a sandalwood tree, a green source of phenomena arises from *e*. In its center, on a seat of a lotus arisen from *paṃ* with a sun at its center and the Obstructor King, one's own mind is a *hūṃ*-marked flaying knife arisen from *hūṃ*. That completely transforms into oneself as Swift-Acting Awareness Protector, green in color, with one face and six arms. The first two hands hold a flaying knife and skull cup embracing the mother consort, the middle pair a small hand drum and trident, and the last pair a rosary and a lasso. He has three eyes and bared fangs, hair swirling upward, a crown and garland of human heads, the six bone ornaments, tiger skin, bells, and strings of small bells, and so on—all adornments completely perfect. Embracing him, Mother Vajra Ḍākinī on his lap is blue, holding a flaying knife and skull cup, with a garland of fifty dry skulls. In front of the

principal figures, white Buddha Ḍākinī holds a wheel and blood-filled skull cup, yellow Ratna Ḍākinī is in the south holding a jewel and blood-filled skull cup, red Padma Ḍākinī is in the west holding a lotus and blood-filled skull cup, and green Karma Ḍākinī is in the north holding a knife and blood-filled skull cup. All of them have bone and human-head garlands and expressions of charm and affection. They stand in the position of left leg extended. One hundred thousand ḍākinīs with an ocean of the oath-bound are situated around them.

At their foreheads is *oṃ*, at their throats *āḥ*, at their hearts *hūṃ*, at their navels *svā*, and at their private parts *hā*. Light rays radiate from my heart and invoke all the buddhas and bodhisattvas with their retinues in the forms of Swift-Acting Awareness Protector. In particular, from the great charnel ground Cool Grove in the southeast {676} comes Protector and ḍākinīs—*vajra samājaḥ*.

Slowly repeat *kṣiṃ* twenty-one times, either with or without a melody. Then invoke them:

From seed syllables *oṃ*, *āḥ*, *hūṃ*, *svā*, and *hā*
in forehead, throat, heart, navel, and private parts,
light radiates and pervades in ten directions,
purifies sins and obscurations of six realms of beings,
makes offerings to all invoked awareness beings
who possess the compassion of three refuges,
and becomes the protectors of longevity activity.
Compelled by the five light rays radiating and returning,
from Cool Grove Charnel Ground,
the nature of Magadha, center of supreme accomplishment,
the glorious ten fortunes, masters of longevity,
Six-Armed Awareness Protector and hosts
in the eight charnel grounds and twenty-four [sites]
with retinues of the oath-bound: gather here
and grant me, the yogin, the supreme [spiritual power].

jaḥ hūṃ vaṃ hoḥ—they dissolve indivisibly into the pledge beings. Again light rays radiate from my heart or from my five places and

> invoke the five families of empowerment deities to the space before me.

Offer with *arghaṃ* . . . (etc. through) . . . *śabda.*

> [The deities] supplicate with "I supplicate all tathāgatas, please confer the empowerment." The [deities] confer empowerment with *oṃ vajri bhāva abhiṣiñca hūṃ*. The [protectors'] bodies are filled, stains purified, and the excess water rises up and becomes Akṣobhya crowning the principal couple, Vairocana on Buddha Ḍākinī, Ratnasambhava on Ratna Ḍākinī, Amitābha on Padma Ḍākinī, and Amoghasiddhi on Karma Ḍākinī.

Consecrate the torma following the liturgical description in the Black Protector practice, then visualize the awareness deities:

> The tongues of the mandala deities become vajra tubes through which they suck up the torma and drink it.

After the essence mantra say *idaṃ baliṃta kha kha khāhi khāhi* seven times to offer the torma. Present offerings with *guru mahākāla viśvadāka saparivara arghaṃ pratīccha svāhā* . . . (etc. through) . . . *śabda*. Praise with

> Guru-Protector inseparable's activity body,
> honored by all buddhas in the three times,
> you show up to whomever is to be trained:
> Six-Armed Diverse Ḍāka—homage to you. {677}

Clearly keep in mind the recitation visualization, and recite the mantra however much:

> *oṃ vajra mahākāla ha ri ni sa sarva āyur jñāna siddhi jaḥ*

Here one [normally] meditates separately on the self- and front visualizations. However, since the creation ritual joins them, the [preceding liturgy] accomplishes both the self- and front visualizations. Within the vase:

> Swift-Acting Protector and the five ḍākinīs are instantly present. The mantra string with light rays radiate from my heart and evoke the mind streams of the deities created in front. The mantra's light rays coil into a dhāraṇī cord and dissolve into the contents inside the vase. Light rays radiate from the five places of the deities in front, drawing in the brilliance, radiance, and refined essence of all the environment and its inhabitants in the form of elixir, which also dissolves [into the vase].

Visualize the vase and do some hundred repetitions of the essence mantra. All of the rituals done in the following [actions for] the disciples are practiced by means of this visualization in the manner of a self-induction. The preliminary acts of the disciples are prostrating, cleansing, and distributing and collecting the flowers. During the refuge and awakening mind, say "the profound permission of the Green Protector, Lord of Longevity." Then for the main practice:

> The dharma to receive came from the mouth of the mighty adept Rāhulagupta in India and was received by Khedrup Khyungpo Naljor as a direct lineage. From the cycle of peaceful wealth practices of the Swift-Acting Awareness Protector, this is the particular practice of Green Protector, Lord of Longevity, also known as Six-Armed Diverse Ḍāka. It states in the Indian source text:
>
> > Practice this for seven days without break—
> > you will see him, attain both spiritual powers,
> > extend your life, and grow more youthful;
> > the prophesied three gatherings will occur.
>
> That is how it was praised. This protector is accomplished in an uncommon way. The general supreme and common spiritual powers, and particularly the extension of the life span is supremely extolled. The authorization for this . . . (etc.).

Add the rest, as far as offering the mandala. The supplications are the same as the general protector permissions. If you prefer the extensive version, then do refuge, awakening mind, granting permission, gathering thoughts, the five branches, and taking the vows of the five families. For short, recite only the seven-branch practice from the *[Vajra] Tent [Tantra]*: "I go for refuge in the Three Jewels . . . (etc.)." {678} Say, "In this world, omniscient ones . . . (etc.)," from the Red Protector practice.

For the visualization of the mandala of the ritual master inseparable from the front visualization [of the protectors], (recite from the liturgical description starting with) "*oṃ svabhāva* . . . (etc. to) . . . situated around them." That is the equivalent of introducing the deities.

In a mere instant, you all clearly appear as the Green Protector couple, lords of longevity, with *oṃ* at the forehead, *āḥ* at the throat, *hūṃ* at the heart, *svā* at the navel, and *hā* at the private parts. Light rays radiate from the master's five places. Imagine that from the great charnel ground Cool Grove in the southeast, Swift-Acting Awareness Protector with hosts of ḍākinīs arrives—*ur ur, chem chem*—and dissolves slowly into you.

Accompanied by grand music, repeat the essence mantra and add *aveśaya āḥ āḥ āḥ*, reciting intensely.

That is the equivalent of the descent of the awareness beings. Then offer a mandala for the sake of the main part, and repeat this supplication three times after me:

"Guru-Protector inseparable, please confer the four
empowerments on me."

A white stream of elixir emerges from the foreheads of the vase deities. Imagine that it washes away all your outer and inner sickness, spirits, negativities, and obscurations.

In the excellent all-victorious vase of auspicious steadfast life,
the deity of the awareness of the purified affliction of
stupidity
dwells as the Victor's body of light, unobscured
saṃbhogakāya.
Six-Armed Amitāyus Protector confers empowerment
with radiating and gathering light rays of mirror awareness.
You obtain the empowerment of indestructible vajra body.

As you repeat the mantra, touch the vase to their foreheads and pour them some vase water. Follow the same pattern in the following sections.

A red stream of elixir emerges from the throats . . . (etc.).

In the excellent all-victorious vase of auspicious steadfast life,
the deity of the awareness of the purified affliction of desire
dwells as the Victor's eighty-four thousand sets of dharma
and confers the empowerment of essence mantras, heart of emptiness,
with radiating and gathering light rays of discriminating awareness.
You obtain the empowerment of melodious speech with sixty branches.

Touch the vase to their throats.

A blue stream of elixir emerges from the heart . . . (etc.).

In the excellent all-victorious vase of auspicious steadfast life,
the deity of the awareness of the purified affliction of hatred
dwells as the Victor's supreme mind, glorious timeless awareness, {679}
and confers the empowerment of unchanging coemergent purity
with radiating and gathering light rays of the realm-of-phenomena awareness.
You obtain the empowerment of knowing everything in all aspects.

Touch the vase to their hearts.

A yellow stream of elixir emerges from the navel . . . (etc.).

In the excellent all-victorious vase of auspicious steadfast life,
the deity of the awareness of the purified affliction of pride
dwells as the Victor's qualities, granting supreme welfare,
the realm of phenomena inseparable from intrinsic awareness,

[conferred] with radiating and gathering light rays of equality awareness.
May you quickly attain awakening by seeing, hearing, recalling, and touching.

Touch the vase to their navels.

A green stream of elixir emerges from the private parts . . . (etc.).

In the excellent all-victorious vase of auspicious steadfast life,
the deity of the awareness of the purified affliction of jealousy
dwells as the Victor's unceasing awakened activity,
the master of fivefold secret knowledge dhāraṇīs,
and confers the empowerment of great all-accomplishing awareness.
May you obtain infinite buddha realms spontaneously.

As you repeat the essence mantra, gesture in the direction of their groin and pour the vase water. It seems there is also a practice of sprinkling the vase water later on.

Those were the vase empowerments.

Place the mirror mandala of vermilion to their heads. Touch their hearts with the elixir-filled skull cup.

With the authentic skull cup filled with elixir
from the lineage of an infinite ocean realm of victors
and the ḍākinīs' palace of the vermilion source of phenomena
on the dust-free mirror of form-emptiness inseparable,
the deities of root mantras, hand implements, and seed syllables of bliss-emptiness
confer empowerment on the fortunate children of good family.

Recite the root mantras while marking the disciples' foreheads with a spot of vermilion. Give the inner offering elixir.

This was the secret empowerment.

Then repeat this:

> The secret mother Vajra Ḍākinī
> emanates a consort to give to the disciples.
> They enter into union and fill with bliss;
> method and wisdom become inseparable.
> With infinite deity forms to train whomever,
> may you enact the welfare of sentient beings.

Repeat the root mantra and have them meditate on its meaning.

> This was the wisdom-awareness empowerment.

Have them meditate on the meaning of mahāmudrā. {680}

> Free of elaboration's limits, this intrinsic awareness with naked perception
> in union with the space realm of phenomena
> confers empowerment on the fortunate children of good family,
> severing the roots of ignorance, the cyclic suffering of the six realms,
> and the delusional concepts of five toxic afflictive emotions.
> May you attain the supreme state of the unified three refuges.
> *oṃ dhare dhare dharaṇa bhate svāhā*

Toss flowers. If you are interested in more, recite the *Sealed Word of Auspiciousness*. For a brief version, recite the single verse, "May the day be auspicious . . . (*nyin mo bde legs* . . . etc.)." Now for the torma exhortation, hold the torma on their heads.

> Clearly visualize this torma itself as the Guru-Protector inseparable, surrounded by the assemblies of buddhas and bodhisattvas all around. They come to the top of your head. Countless tiny forms of Guru-Protector inseparable come forth. Imagine that they slowly dissolve into your bodies. Glorious Swift-Acting Awareness Protector, Green Lord of Longevity, Diverse Ḍāka, with retinue of millions of ḍākinī hosts . . . (etc., as in the White

> Protector) . . . accomplish without impediment whatever activity is entrusted to you. In particular, guard against and avert all harmful interruptions in the life span. Please grant the spiritual power of undying vajra longevity.

Give this command exhortation accompanied by music. Then the transmission of the mantra recitation:

> The mantra strings emerge from the heart of Guru-Protector inseparable. Imagine that they dissolve into your hearts and repeat this after me. (Say the essence mantra three times.) As the master scatters flowers, repeat this after me:
>
> > "Bhagavat, surely grant to me
> > and please adhere to me."
>
> Again, the flowers . . . (consecrate them as the mantra strings). Tossing them to you, imagine that you have the ability and power of mantra. {681}
>
> > Bhagavat, surely grant to these [disciples],
> > and please adhere to them. (Repeat three times.)
>
> The vows that you received on this occasion . . . (etc.).

For the disciples' concluding practices and the concluding ritual of the mandala, follow what has already been described for the Black Protector.

[Colophon by Tāranātha Kunga Nyingpo]

More profound than all (Kun) longevity practices,
pinnacle of joyful (ga) methods to guard against obstacles,
this essence (Nyingpo) of Green Protector's sādhana
was added to share with others.

This was the chapter on the means of accomplishing the Green Protector, Lord of Longevity. *maṅgalaṃ*

VI. Permission for Guru-Protector Inseparable

oṃ svasti
Vajra root and lineage gurus appearing
in the form of the Awareness Protector;
I prostrate to your lotus feet and write
the permission of Guru-Protector Inseparable.

In a secluded place, sprinkle and sweep the ground. Make a nice arrangement of supports for the Three Jewels and particularly for the Protector, such as a picture of his form. Anoint the ground with a suitable number of drops of saffron water and make a square. Make it black between the two, and draw one charnel ground. Make two circles within that. Between the circles and square, make the east white, the south yellow, the west red, and the north green. Make one circle area blue and the inner circle green. In its center make a blue-black source of phenomena, with three corners and a ring of fire. In its center, draw a *hūṃ* or a flaying knife marked with *hūṃ* at its hub. Upon that, on the opening of a mañji, place a three-cornered glorious-food torma made from raw black barley, adorned with dough buttons (*mtheb kyus*) around the edges. Then stick in an arrow with attached silk, mirror, and a card drawing (*tsak li*) of Protector. Around that, place the offerings, tormas, and various protector offerings.[20] Consecrate the preliminary torma, dwelling place, and implements. Begin with the yidam's meditation, recitation, and so forth. The way to generate the front visualization is the same as described for the root practice of Removing All Obstacles. Particularly, before the supplication, say:

> Above Protector's head, my benevolent root guru is yellow and as brilliant as one hundred thousand suns; he holds a wish-fulfilling gem to the heart with the right hand, a golden bell at the hip with the left, sitting in vajra posture, adorned by all decorations. {682} The guru is the essence of all the lineage gurus starting with Vajradhara. Light radiates from the guru's body—Protector becomes the nature of light and bliss, dancing with the sounds of *ur ur, sil sil*. Light radiates from Protector and dissolves into the guru's body. Guru becomes the nature of light and bliss, dancing and ringing the bell with the sounds of *sil sil, khrol khrol*. Guru is Protector. Protector is Guru. Guru and Protector are inseparable.

I and all sentient beings throughout the reaches of space
supplicate the Guru-Protector inseparable.
We supplicate Protector-Guru inseparable.
We supplicate the benevolent root guru.

Repeat an appropriate number of times. Then repeat the *namo buddha* supplication no less than one hundred times. Repeat the five lines of supplication to the Guru-Protector inseparable many times. After briefly doing the approach [recitation] from the source text, recite the prose words of the torma offering without the supplication for desires, finish up through the praises, and perform the self-induction. Do the cleansing of the disciples, who offer the mandala of gold in front. Then the ritual master says:

Now then, for the sake of all mother sentient beings equal to the reaches of space, you absolutely must attain the state of Avalokiteśvara, Lord of the World. In order to do that, cultivate the special motivation and think that you will receive the profound permission of Guru-Protector Inseparable. Please pay attention.

All of us now have obtained the excellent support of a human body, which is so difficult to find. We have encountered the precious doctrine of the Buddha, so difficult to encounter. At this time, while we have [the opportunity to] practice the essence of the doctrine—the Secret Mantra Vajrayāna—you must strive from the bottom of your heart to practice the dharma. In these days of degeneration, there are few favorable conditions for the practice of the dharma, but many adverse conditions. {683} It states in the Mother [*Perfection of Wisdom*]: "The precious dharma is rare, while constant dangers are many."[21] To counteract that, you need to rely on a special dharma protector. This is the spiritual practice of the incomparable Shangpa Kagyu, which is not the same as systems that "rely on neither Tibetan gods nor demons" (i.e., haphazard). The protector of the customs of the pure adepts' lineage was Khyungpo Naljor. He was the one who invited this Six-Armed Protector to Tibet from India.

Khyungpo went to India and offered seven measures of gold to the guru Maitrīpa, who was living in the beggar's (*bhikṣu*) charnel ground in Kośala. He said, "We Tibetans have very little wealth. I request a speedy wealth practice that has big results."

Maitrīpa said, "Called Wish-Fulfilling Gem, also called Tree-Dwelling Protector, also called Sandalwood Protector, also called Black Compassionate One, also called Six-Armed Protector—it guards from the fears of this life and the intermediate state. It brings gods, demons, and humans under control. It naturally attracts people, riches, and food. It destroys all enemies and repels invasions. It establishes all supreme and common powers in a matter of years and months. The attainment of supreme powers automatically entails the common ones. The attainment of common powers automatically entails the supreme ones. I'll give you that one!"

"From which guru did you receive that?" asked Khyungpo.

"I got it from glorious Śavarīpa. The one called glorious Śavarīpa was [once] born into the brahmin caste and became a talented musician known as Tripala who lived in the center of the thirty-two great cities near glorious Dhānyakaṭaka. He delighted the previous buddha with his singing and playing. Once when [in his later life as Śavarīpa] he was doing his practice in a grass hut in the great charnel ground Cool Grove, {684} a great pounding sound of ḍamarus and bells reverberated from the sky. He looked up and saw this Awareness Protector arrive and say, 'Son of good family, receive my sādhana!'

"So Śavarīpa wrote the text for this sādhana. Also Exalted Yoginī, Avalokiteśvara, and Tārā arrived and transmitted their sādhanas with praises.[22] At the time that this guru was living at the Śrīparvata mountain in the south, I received the mahāmudrā tantra and instructions. It was then that he granted the Six-Armed Mahākāla. After practicing it for twenty-one days, I saw the Protector face to face. Now, Khyungpo Naljor, you too must offer a torma of raw black barley dough and continuously burn incense for this Six-Armed One. And do not throw rocks at black dogs. Believe, and regard [the Protector] as inseparable from the guru. If you do this, all the spiritual powers will be duly granted."

He made this prediction and then granted the permission blessing three times. Furthermore, in an early account of a time past, in the great charnel ground of Intolerable Darkness,[23] there was a great master ācārya named Dhanasaṃskṛta who had actually seen this Awareness Protector. He brought under his control an entourage and accomplished all activities. That guru appeared in a vision to Rāhulaguptavajra and bestowed a direct lineage. Rāhula left from India at dawn and arrived in Tibet at sunrise one morning when Khyungpo Naljor was staying at Jokpori in Penyul and transferred the instruction to him.

There are many different kinds of permissions for authorization blessings of this Swift-Acting Awareness Protector's instruction cycle in the lineages coming from those two adepts. However, the profound vital points of all the peaceful and wrathful means of accomplishment that are like an indispensable life force are the three branch permissions. {685}

The first of those is this Guru-Protector Inseparable, about which the great adept Śavarīpa said that if one offers a torma of buttered flour with mantras and supplications, the Protector would quickly reveal himself. Furthermore, if you supplicate him in the common way of all sentient beings and think that you bow repeatedly with devotion, immeasurable benefit for others will arise. If you hold in your mind the forms of the guru and Protector, however clearly, you will gain enlightenment as saṃbhogakāya and nirmāṇakāya. If the degree of your realization is decisive, like cutting down a tree at the roots, you will gain the three pure levels. If, after supplicating or whenever you are moving about, you regard whatever appears clearly without fixation, resting with the elephant's yogic gaze, then you will attain enlightenment as dharmakāya. If, with mandalas and torma, you supplicate with belief free of doubt, you will be given the common spiritual powers. If you meditate for seven months without distraction, you will be awakened in that suchness. If you meditate for every session at dawn, at death you will attain the rūpakāyas and dharmakāya. If you once obtain the empowerment and make a connection, even if you have committed the five acts with immediate retribution, it is impossible that you will not be enlightened in the intermediate state.

Guru-Protector inseparable,
I go for refuge with devotion.

May I dispel every afflictive emotion
of all sentient beings.

If you hear that [prayer] just once or if you write it in gold letters and wear it, you will see them at death.

> "Awareness Protector arrived in front,
> and to one such as myself, Śavarīpa,
> spoke thrice and sealed his command
> then departed into the sky.
> *Ema!* this wonderful, amazing dharma:
> do no spread it beyond the single lineage."

As it was extolled purposefully in that way, it is a golden dharma sealed by command. {686} In general, although other dharma protectors sometimes have a mere proverbial guru and protector inseparable, those dharma protectors are practiced as awareness beings, and the guru must be understood as the union of all Three Roots through logic alone. This one here is the special manner of practice with authentic origins in Indian scripture, and it is endowed with the exclusive permission blessings. So by practicing in this way, it becomes a special kind of guru yoga that generates experiential realization. Not only that, this protector has what is called "four supports and three vital points." Thus this practice of Guru-Protector Inseparable is "the support of suchness" (*de kho na nyid kyi rten*), also making it an indispensable branch on which to depend.

Please offer a mandala and visualize it as a gift to request such a profound permission.

Have them offer the mandala.

Hold a flower between your joined palms and repeat this three times after me:

> "Once your lotus feet are abandoned,
> there is no other lord of refuge.

Great mighty hero of migrators,
please grant me the sublime mind."

Then the introduction to the deities:

This mandala in front of you has the protection circle with the unbearable great charnel ground. In its center . . . (etc., as in the authorization of the main Black Protector). Do the fulfillment ritual properly. Above [the front visualization], the benevolent root guru and all the lineage gurus dwell like a dense mass of clouds. In their presence, think that you arouse the sublime mind of awakening that begins with the regular confession and repeat this three times after me:

"I go for refuge in the Three Jewels . . . (etc.)."

In particular, think that you will fully undertake the Vajrayāna sacred pledges and vows and will keep them properly, and repeat this three times after me:

"All buddhas and bodhisattvas,
however many in all times—
all of you, please heed me.

I, named *so-and-so*,
from this time forward
until such time as I fully abide
in the heart of awakening,
will arouse every aspect {687}
of the mind of supreme awakening.

Just as the lords of the three times
roused the unsurpassable awakening mind
that definitely leads to awakening,
I too will produce that holy thought.

I resolutely take the vows of the buddha yoga
of the three ethical behaviors:
the training [of controlling malpractices],
gathering virtuous dharmas, and helping sentient beings.

From now on I resolutely take the vows
to [honor] the Buddha, dharma, and sangha,
the unsurpassable Three Jewels,
and never to reject them.

I take as the true state
vajra, bell, [and] mudra
of the great, sublime vajra family.
I also accept the [vajra] master.

The pleasant sacred pledge
of the great, sublime jewel family
is to always give the four gifts
at the six times of every day.

I uphold every Holy Dharma
of the outer, inner, and secret three vehicles
of the pure great lotus family
that arises from great awakening.

The great, sublime action family
possesses all the vows.
I take them as the genuine state
and will make all possible offerings.

Awakening mind is most sublime;
I will arouse that holy aspiration
and maintain all vows without exception
for the sake of all sentient beings.

I shall free those not freed.
I shall liberate those not liberated.
I shall relieve those not relieved
and place all sentient beings beyond misery."

Repeat three times.

After completing those brief practices of induction, in order to bring down blessings in the main practice, your yearning devotion to the Guru-Protector inseparable . . . (etc., as in Black Protector practice). Meditate that the heart is marked with blue *hūṃ*. {688} Then, on the crown of Protector inseparable from the torma visualized in front, my benevolent root guru is yellow . . . (etc., as in the section on accomplishing the empowerment). Arouse strong devotion to that embodiment of Guru-Protector inseparable and repeat this supplication after me to receive the blessing of awakened body:

> "*namo buddhāya / namo guruve / vajra vīra vīreṇe / śrī ḍāka ḍākinī / joka jokinī / sarva buddha bodhisatvāya śaraṇaṃ / gacchāmi kyai*" (Repeat three times.)
>
> "I and all sentient beings throughout the reaches of space supplicate the Guru-Protector inseparable.
> We supplicate Protector-Guru inseparable." (Repeat three times.)

By your supplicating like that, white light rays emerge from between the eyebrows of the guru atop Protector's head and from Protector's midbrow many miniature protectors with small white bodies and thick limbs arise. They come across to the point between your eyebrows and slowly dissolve. Think that you have obtained the blessing of the awakened body of Guru-Protector inseparable.

The guru powerfully recites the *namo buddha* and *vajra mahākāla* mantras and plays intense music.

With that, you have obtained the blessing of the guru's and Protector's awakened body. All negative actions and obscurations accumulated through your body are purified. Think that you have obtained the vase empowerment.

Supplicate as before to request the blessing of awakened speech.

Red light rays emerge from the throat of the guru atop Protector's head and from Protector's throat many miniature protectors with small red bodies and thick limbs arise. They come across to your throat and slowly dissolve. Think that you have obtained the blessing of the awakened speech of Guru-Protector inseparable.

Repeat the mantra and play music. {689}

With that, you have obtained the blessing of the guru's and Protector's awakened speech. All negative actions and obscurations accumulated through your speech are purified. Think that you have obtained the secret empowerment.

Supplicate as before to request the blessing of awakened mind.

Blue light rays emerge from the heart of the guru atop Protector's head, and from Protector's heart many miniature protectors with small blue bodies and thick limbs arise. They come across to your heart and slowly dissolve. Think that you have obtained the blessing of the awakened mind of Guru-Protector inseparable.

Repeat the mantra accompanied by music.

With that, you have obtained the blessing of the guru's and Protector's awakened mind. All negative actions and obscurations accumulated through your mind are purified. Think that you have obtained the wisdom-awareness empowerment.

Again, repeat this supplication after me to request the blessings of Guru-Protector inseparable's awakened body, speech, mind, qualities, and activities:

> "I and all sentient beings throughout the reaches of space . . . (etc.)."

Repeat that supplication twenty-one times and *namo buddhā* . . . three times.

By your supplicating like that, countless multicolored light rays emerge from all physical aspects of the guru atop Protector's head and from Protector's physical aspects countless miniature protectors with small bodies in different colors and thick limbs arise with the sounds of ḍamarus and bells and shouts of *hūṃ hūṃ phaṭ phaṭ*. They come across and dissolve slowly into your body's upper, lower, and in-between parts, filling your body and mind with bliss. Inside your body, the protectors dance and devour all your sickness, spirits, negativities, and obscurations. As they arrive they loudly declare, "I will remove all your obstacles. I will create all favorable conditions." {690} Think that as your whole body is filled, you obtain the blessings of the awakened body, speech, mind, qualities, and activities of Guru-Protector inseparable.

Repeat the mantra accompanied by music.

Holy root and lineage gurus dwelling in the ten directions and three times, bless me! Yidam deities of the mandala, bless me! Heroes and heroine yoginīs, bless me! Buddhas and bodhisattvas all, bless me! Glorious Six-Armed Awareness Protector and deities, do not veil your timeless awareness. Do not delay your compassion. Do not block your power and ability. Do not distance your blessings. All of you, bless me through your body, bless me through your speech, bless me through your mind! Bless me through your unlimited awakened body, speech, mind, qualities, and activities! Bless me right now! Bless me quickly! Bless me on this very seat!

With that, you have obtained the blessing of the guru's and Protector's awakened body, speech, mind, qualities, and activities. All negative actions and obscurations accumulated through your body, speech, and mind are purified. Think that you have obtained the fourth empowerment.

Repeat this supplication after me to receive the supplemental support of the torma empowerment:

"Guru-Protector inseparable . . . (etc.)."

Say the five lines three times.

Through your supplicating in that way, light rays from the *hūṃ* in the guru's heart invoke the torma appearing clearly as Protector to the top of your head. Arouse yearning devotion, and when the guru exhorts [Protector], {691} from his body comes elixir in the form of light rays and countless wrathful miniatures with fireweapons. They enter your body and vanquish all negativities, obscurations, sickness, spirits, and adverse conditions, like sunrays striking frost. They increase and expand your life span, merit, experience, realization, and so forth. Imagine that you are blessed by the three secrets of Guru-Protector with retinue.

Glorious Awareness Protector, Swift-Acting Avalokiteśvara; root and lineage gurus; buddhas and bodhisattvas; heroes and ḍākinīs; ocean of the oath-bound; emanations and further emanations with retinues: do not forget your strict sacred pledge of awakening mind just as you promised. Please quickly grant your blessings to these vajra disciples. Please constantly consider and accompany them, never apart, and be their lord protector and champion. Please remove all adverse conditions that interfere with their attainment of awakening and increase like the waxing moon their prosperity of the necessities conducive to practicing the Holy Dharma. Accomplish peaceful, enriching, magnetizing, and wrathful awakened activity without restriction just as it is desired. In short, please quickly and easily obtain [for them] every common and supreme spiritual power.

Say the mantras of the principals and retinue. At the end:

jaḥ hūṃ vaṃ hoḥ

By saying that, the root and lineage gurus in the space above melt into light and dissolve into the torma visualized as Protector. From that, a second identical form radiates and dissolves into you. Imagine that you are blessed with Protector's awakened body, speech, and mind inseparable from your own body, speech, and mind.

If you wish, distribute parts of the torma. Recite verses of auspiciousness. {692}

It is said of this that if you once obtain the empowerment and make a connection, even if you have committed the five acts

> with immediate retribution, it is impossible that you will not be enlightened in the intermediate state. The profound permission of Guru-Protector Inseparable is well achieved . . . (etc.).

Make the connection with that, and continue up through taking the sacred pledges. The concluding rituals of the mandala are the same as in the main protector practice.

[Colophon by Jamgön Kongtrul Yönten Gyatso]

The source of all qualities (Yönten)
is the supplication of Guru-Protector inseparable.
If you can enter the ocean (Gyatso) of blessings,
it will surely yield the gems of two purposes.

This was the chapter on the authorization for Guru-Protector Inseparable.

VII. Protector Dispelling Defilements

oṃ svasti
Mighty compassionate one, great hero,
in wrathful form to conquer negativities and obscurations;
I bow to your lotus feet
and arrange the authorization of Dispelling Defilements.

Lay out the mandala, offerings, and torma as in Removing All Obstacles. The same for the activities of the sādhana. After the invocation, offerings, and praises, begin:

> Above Protector's head, the root guru is white Vajrasattva, his right hand holding a five-pronged crystal vajra at his heart and his left hand in equipoise with an elixir-filled skull cup. He sits in vajra cross-legged position, with infinite light radiating from his body. Light rays radiate from his heart and invoke the vajra body, speech, and mind of all buddhas and bodhisattvas in the form of deities. They are arrayed in the sky above.
>
> Deities of three vajras, please cleanse and purify any defilement that has touched the guru's body, speech, and mind and all

> violations of the sacred pledges related to awakened body, speech, and mind. With this supplication, white, red, and blue hundred-syllable mantras radiate from the three places of the deities of vajra body, speech, and mind. They dissolve into the guru's three places, cleansing and purifying the defilements that have stricken the guru's body, speech, and mind, and all violations of sacred pledges related to awakened body, speech, and mind.

Repeat the hundred syllables seven times. Then apply the same formula: {693}

> Precious guru, please cleanse and purify defilements that have touched Protector's body, speech, and mind . . . (etc., and) . . . hundred-syllable mantras radiate from the guru's three places . . . (etc.).

At the end, repeat the hundred syllables seven times.

> Guru-Protector inseparable, please cleanse and purify any defilement that has touched the retinue's and my three doors and violations of sacred pledges related to awakened body, speech, and mind. With this supplication, white, red, and blue hundred-syllable mantras radiate from the three places of the Guru and Protector. They dissolve into the retinue's and my three places, cleansing and purifying the defilements that have stricken the retinue's body, speech, and mind, and all violations of sacred pledges related to awakened body, speech, and mind. My body inside is filled with the light rays of the hundred syllables, which cleanse and purify from the roots all negativities, obscurations, and downfalls.

Imagine that and repeat the hundred syllables seven or twenty-one times or, to accomplish it, recite many times for each [visualization]. Afterward, do the confession and a cursory approach from the source. After practicing the torma offering, praises, and self-induction, the disciples wash and the mind of awakening is clarified as before, except change to:

"To that end, I will receive the permission for Awareness Protector who purifies negative acts and obscurations."

In that, this is the indispensable branch, the second permission, [which forms part of] the general peaceful and wrathful sādhanas of Swift-Acting Awareness Protector—that is, the Protector Dispelling Defilements. An Indian source text states:

If sacred pledge is transgressed and defiles
the guru [and] Awareness Protector,
confess and amend the sacred pledge;
by fulfilling the pledge, spiritual powers are attained.

For instance, just as someone of the pure kṣatriya or brahmin caste cannot visit the impure dwelling of a caṇḍāla person, Guru-Protector's compassion and blessings will not enter a person with the obscuration of an impure mind stream. Especially if they have gone astray by transgressing and damaging the root and branch sacred pledges, not only will they not obtain spiritual powers, various obstacles will occur as well. {694} But if they purify the obscurations, blessings will enter unbidden. If violations are amended, spiritual powers will easily accrue. And there is no more profound method to do that than the meditation-recitation of Vajrasattva. There is not one instance from the Sarma or Nyingma traditions that does not concur. Of all the suitable versions, this occasion is for the purification of the obscuration of violations, the extremely profound practice of the permission for Dispelling Defilements . . . (etc.).

Continue with the mandala, supplication, introducing the deities, regular confession, taking vows, and up to the disciple's visualization as the deity. Then:

Visualize the Protector in front inseparable from the [support] torma. Above Protector's head, the benevolent root guru is white Vajrasattva, his right hand holding a five-pronged crystal vajra at his heart and his left hand in equipoise with an elixir-filled skull cup. He sits in vajra cross-legged position, with infinite light radiating from his body. A mass of light rays radiate from his heart and invoke from all the buddhas and bodhisattvas in the ten directions, their vajra bodies in the forms of Vairocana, vajra speech as Amitābha, and vajra mind as Akṣobhya. Imagine that they come before you in the sky like dense cloud banks. Then with intense devotion to all of them, repeat this supplication after me:

> "Guru, yidams, buddhas, bodhisattvas, and deities of the three vajras, please bless me with cleansing and purifying all violations of sacred pledge related to the awakened body, speech, and mind of my holy root and lineage gurus."

Have them say that.

By your supplicating in that way, a white letter *oṃ* along with white light rays of the hundred syllables emerge from the hearts of the body vajras. {695} From the point between the eyebrows of the guru atop the head of Protector and torma inseparable, they come over and dissolve. The inside of the guru's midbrow is all filled with white *oṃ* letters and white light rays of the hundred syllables. Think that all the violations of sacred pledge relating to the guru's body are purified. Imagine that and repeat the hundred syllables three times.

Have them recite the hundred syllables. Apply that pattern to the following:

A red letter *āḥ* along with red light rays of the hundred syllables emerge from the hearts of the speech vajras . . . (etc., as before). The inside of the guru's throat is all filled. Think that all the violations of sacred pledge relating to the guru's speech are purified.

Recite the hundred syllables three times.

A blue letter *hūṃ* along with blue light rays of the hundred syllables emerge from the hearts of the mind vajras . . . (etc., as before). The inside of the guru's heart is all filled. Think that all the violations of sacred pledge relating to the guru's mind are purified.

Recite the hundred syllables three times.

Again repeat this supplication after me:

"Guru, deities of the three vajras, please bless me and all sentient beings with purifying all violations of sacred pledge related to the awakened body, speech, and mind of the Swift-Acting Awareness Protector."

By your supplicating in that way, a white letter *oṃ* along with white light rays of the hundred syllables emerge from the guru's head. They come over and dissolve at the point between the eyebrows of the Protector and torma indivisible. The coiled hair between the eyebrows of the Protector is filled with white *oṃ* letters and white light rays of the hundred syllables. Think that all the violations of sacred pledge relating to Protector's body are purified.

Say that and have them repeat the hundred syllables three times. Similarly:

A red letter *āḥ* along with red light rays of the hundred syllables emerge from the guru's throat. Protector's throat inside is all filled. {696} Think that all the violations of sacred pledge relating to Protector's speech are purified.

Say the hundred syllables three times.

A blue letter *hūṃ* along with blue light rays of the hundred syllables emerge from the guru's heart. Protector's heart inside is all filled. Think that all the violations of sacred pledge relating to Protector's mind are purified.

Say the hundred syllables three times.

Again repeat this supplication after me:

"Guru-Protector inseparable, please bless me and all sentient beings with purifying all violations of sacred pledge

> related to the awakened body, speech, and mind of the retinue."

By your supplicating in that way, a white letter *oṃ* along with white light rays of the hundred syllables emerge from the Protector's head. They come over and dissolve at the point between the eyebrows of the retinue, such as the four yakṣas and goddesses. The coiled hairs between the eyebrows of the retinue are filled with white *oṃ* letters and white light rays of the hundred syllables. Think all the violations of sacred pledge of the body are purified.

Say that and have them say the hundred syllables three times. Similarly:

A red letter *āḥ* along with red light rays of the hundred syllables emerge from Protector's throat. [The retinue's] throats inside are all filled. Think that all the violations of sacred pledge of speech are purified.

Say the hundred syllables three times.

A blue letter *hūṃ* along with blue light rays of the hundred syllables emerge from Protector's heart. [The retinue's] hearts inside are all filled. Think that all the violations of sacred pledge of the mind are purified.

Say the hundred syllables three times.

Again repeat this supplication after me:

> "Guru-Protector inseparable with retinue, please bless me and all sentient beings with cleansing and purifying all negative actions, obscurations, faults, downfalls, outer and inner defilements, and dangerous impurities accumulated through body, speech, and mind since beginningless time."

By your supplicating in that way, a white letter *oṃ* along with white light rays of the hundred syllables emerge from between the eyebrows of the guru atop the head of Protector inseparable from the torma and from between Protector's eyebrows. They come over and dissolve at the point between your own eyebrows. Between your eyebrows inside is all filled with white *oṃ* letters and white light rays of the hundred syllables. Think that all the violations of sacred pledge of the body are purified. {697} Think that you have obtained the body blessing of both the guru and Protector. Imagine that and repeat the hundred syllables three times after me.

Have them repeat the hundred syllables three times. The guru also says the hundred syllables while music plays.

That purifies all physical sickness, spirits, negativities, obscurations, and violations of sacred pledge accumulated in your lives of beginningless cycle existence. You become inseparable from the awakened body of the guru and Protector.

Again, a red letter *āḥ* along with red light rays of the hundred syllables emerge from the guru's and Protector's throats. They come over and dissolve from your throat. Your throat inside is all filled with red *āḥ* letters and red light rays of the hundred syllables. Think that you have obtained the speech blessing of both the guru and Protector.

Say that and do the hundred syllables with music, and so on.

That purifies all verbal sickness, spirits, negativities, obscurations, and violations of sacred pledge accumulated in your lives of beginningless cycle existence. You become inseparable from the awakened speech of the guru and Protector.

Again, a blue letter *hūṃ* along with blue light rays of the hundred syllables emerge from the guru's and Protector's hearts. They come over and dissolve into your heart. Your heart inside is all filled with blue *hūṃ* letters and blue light rays of the hundred syllables. Think that you have obtained the mind blessing of both the guru and Protector. {698}

Say that and do the hundred syllables with music, and so on.

> That purifies all mental sickness, spirits, negativities, obscurations, and violations of sacred pledge accumulated in your lives of beginningless cycle existence. You become inseparable from the awakened mind of the guru and Protector.
>
> Again, *oṃ*, *āḥ*, and *hūṃ* along with white, red, and blue light rays of the hundred syllables emerge from the guru's and Protector's three places. They dissolve into all your upper and lower body. Your whole body inside is filled with *oṃ*, *āḥ*, and *hūṃ* letters and white, red, and blue light rays of the hundred syllables. Think that you have obtained the blessings of the awakened body, speech, mind, qualities, and activities of the guru and Protector.

Say that and do the hundred syllables with music, and so on.

> That purifies all physical, verbal, and mental sickness, spirits, negativities, and obscurations accumulated in your lives of beginningless cycle existence. You become inseparable from the awakened body, speech, mind, qualities, and activities of the guru and Protector. Therefore, be joyful and arouse certitude.

Then do the [remaining] stages from the torma empowerment to auspicious verses that you can apply from the previous descriptions.

[Colophon by Jamgön Kongtrul Lodrö Taye]

As this is the essence of what to practice
for those with merit and intelligence (Lodrö),
rightly have they sought it with great effort
throughout all the boundless (Taye) worlds.

This was the chapter on the authorization for Protector Dispelling Defilements. *maṅgalaṃ*

VIII. Authorization for Both Magnetizing Ḍākinīs and Getting Down to the Vital Point

oṃ svasti
Lord of the hosts of heroes and ḍākinīs,
overpowering cyclic existence and transcendence,
to you I bow and write the wonderful instructions
to open the door to magnetizing ḍākinīs.

The ritual preparation of the mandala is the same as before, except in the absence of a support torma, [use] an arrow with attached silk and mirror along with the secret support [i.e., vermilion]. If you don't have that, use [just] the mirror with thirteen *hrīḥ* syllables drawn in the vermilion. As in the basic activity sādhana of Removing All Obstacles, before the recitation, say:

> Above Protector's head, the benevolent root guru is red and rattles a skull ḍamaru with the right hand {699} and holds an elixir-filled skull cup to the heart with the left hand. The guru is so brilliant it is hard to bear, youthful and charming with a passionate expression, sitting in cross-legged position. Ḍākinīs and the three existences are brought under control just by the guru's glance. At Protector's forehead there is a triangular spot of vermillion, on which are thirteen red *hrīḥ* letters, the essence of Exalted Lokeśvara, Lord of the World. Those completely transform into thirteen red secret ḍākinīs, youthful, with one face and two arms, holding small drums in their right hands and skull cups filled with elixir in the left. They stand in the posture of right leg bent and left outstretched, gazing with three eyes wide-open and dancing; the essence of Tārā. They bring under control all sentient beings in the three realms. All needs and desires fall like rain.
>
> *oṃ vajra nara kriṃ kriṃ hūṃ hūṃ phaṭ phaṭ svāhā*

Repeat one hundred times or more. Then from the source text [*Treasure Trove of Awakened Activity*], do the mantra recitation, torma offering, praise, and self-induction. Cleanse the disciples, and during the clarification of awakening mind, change to:

> "To that end, I will receive the permission of Awareness Protector Magnetizing Ḍākinīs."

Now, from the general peaceful and wrathful sādhanas of Swift-Acting Awareness Protector, the extremely important branch of the third permission is Magnetizing Ḍākinīs.[24] It states in the vajra speech of the Indian source:

> Guru-Protector's vermilion mantras
> with the color of overpowering
> protectors, heroes, and ḍākinīs;
> this supreme vital point of magnetizing
> will bring supreme attainment now and in the future.
> Keep this single lineage as if it were your life. {700}

The natural emanated embodiment of this Awareness Protector is constantly present in the charnel ground Cool Grove. He acts as chief and dominates all the hosts of heroes and ḍākinīs in the eight great charnel grounds and twenty-four great sacred sites. Therefore, based on this profound yoga, you can get down to the vital point and bring under control all ḍākas, ḍākinīs, awareness actors, and worldly protectors, and thereby achieve all supreme and common spiritual powers in a matter of months or years. It presents the vital point of accomplishing the four awakened activities without restriction just by thinking of them. Since this single lineage of extraordinary instructions is as precious as one's life force, you will practice this profound permission of blessings . . . (etc.).

Continue at this juncture with mandala, supplication, and so on up through the generation of the disciples as deities as before.

Then, on the crown of Protector inseparable from the torma visualized in front, the benevolent root guru . . . (etc. to) . . . the essence of Tārā. Visualize that and repeat this supplication three times after me:

> "Precious guru, please grant your blessing to magnetize all heroes and ḍākinīs of the three places."

> Through supplicating in that way, infinite light rays like hooks radiate from the body of the guru on Protector's head. They strike all the heroes and ḍākinīs dwelling in the ten directions and invoke them all in the form of the nature of radiant light rays. Those dissolve into the guru and Protector with the ḍākinīs. The guru shines with the nature of light and bliss. The red ḍākinīs dance in circles. The Protector plays the ḍamaru and small drum with sounds of *ur ur, sil sil* while countless ḍākinīs emanate from his body. {701} The bodies of the disciples, visualized as protectors, and especially the vermilion at their foreheads, become the thirteen ḍākinīs who shake the billionfold universe. Imagine that from their bodies, light rays like hooks radiate to the ten directions and gather up all the needs and desires of the world and beyond, and blessings ensue.

Say that and *nara kriṃ kriṃ* . . . (etc.), accompanied by the ḍamaru and bell.

> That concludes the practice of the blessing of Magnetizing Ḍākinīs. Now for Getting Down to the Vital Point, repeat this supplication three times after me:

> "Precious guru, please grant me your blessing for Protector and retinue's Getting Down to the Vital Point."

> By your supplicating like that, light rays radiate from the body of the guru on Protector's head. They invoke all the buddhas and bodhisattvas in the ten directions in extremely wrathful forms, which dissolve into the guru. The guru appears in the form of a maroon body with radiating red light rays, the very nature of extreme wrath, dancing on the Protector's head with thundering and roaring—*chem chem, ur ur*. Maroon light radiates and strikes the Protector with retinue, particularly striking the Protector's body with utter redness, and [inciting] Protector and retinue to get down to the vital point. Protector dances—*mer mer, sil sil*—upon the enemies and obstructors and fiercely stamps his feet on the ground. He roars with sounds of *hūṃ phaṭ* reverberating

> from his mouth and glares with his three eyes at his retinue. The retinue becomes uncontrollably enraged and wrathful. Those who would cause harmful obstacles to the accomplishment of the Holy Dharma and evil enemies of the doctrine are caught by hooks in their hearts, tied by lassos around their throats, bound by chains on their limbs, and slaughtered, cut up, and chopped. {702} Their organs are fed to the principal. The retinue finish off the flesh and bones without remainder. Imagine that blessing occurs by means of smashing to fine dust all harm-doers and enemy obstructors.

Burn incense prepared with human flesh and so on, accompanied by the sound of music.

> *oṃ vajra mahākāla kṣiṃ kṣetra vighanen vināyaka trakrakmo rakṣa rudhira citta la a dun be hūṃ hūṃ phaṭ phaṭ svāhā / oṃ vajra mahākāla kṣiṃ kṣetra vighanen citta la a dun dun vi vi nāya hūṃ phaṭ*

Recite that life-force mantra.

> That completes the blessing of Getting Down to the Vital Point of the Protector. As supplemental support, visualize the subsequent authorization blessing of awakened body, speech, and mind, and practice like this. The torma appears clearly as the Awareness Protector, with *oṃ* at the head emitting white light rays. They touch the *oṃ* in the disciples' heads, which makes the *oṃ* letters brilliant and clear, the nature of light. A stream of elixir emerges from them, fills the insides of the body, and purifies physical obscurations. Imagine that the blessing of Protector's body has entered you.

Say that and subdue with music and incense.

> Again, the torma appears clearly as the Awareness Protector, with *āḥ* at the throat emitting red light rays. They touch the *āḥ* in the disciples' throats, which makes the *āḥ* letters brilliant and clear,

> the nature of light. A stream of elixir emerges from them, fills the insides of the body, and purifies verbal obscurations. Imagine that the blessing of Protector's speech has entered you.

Offer incense and music.

> Again, the torma appears clearly as the Awareness Protector, with *hūṃ* at the heart emitting blue light rays. They touch the *hūṃ* in the disciples' hearts, which makes the *hūṃ* letters brilliant and clear, the nature of light. A stream of elixir emerges from them, fills the insides of the body, and purifies mental obscurations. {703} Imagine that the blessing of Protector's mind has entered you.

Offer incense and music.

> Then from Protector's three places, white *oṃ*, red *āḥ*, and blue *hūṃ* suddenly break off and sequentially dissolve into the three letters in your three places. Then *oṃ* and *āḥ* dissolve into *hūṃ*. The vowel sign (*zhabs kyu*) dissolves into the small *a-chung*. That into the *ha* letter, that into the head stroke, that into the crescent moon, that into the drop, and the drop into the nāda. That becomes subtler and subtler until it vanishes in emptiness. Please rest in the nature of Lucid Clarity Mahāmudrā.

Thus rest in equipoise for a while. Then do the torma empowerment and other parts of the concluding rituals as before.

[Colophon by Jamgön Kongtrul Yönten Gyatso]

This dharma clothed in immeasurable qualities (Yönten)
an ocean (Gyatso) that pervades everything,
has access to blessings faster than others,
a suitable support for those who desire powers.

This was the chapter on the authorization for both Magnetizing Ḍākinīs and Getting Down to the Vital Point combined. *maṅgalaṃ*

IX. Liver-Colored Protector

oṃ svasti
Protector Amitābha's body of compassion
displaying the wrathful manner of a heruka,
I bow to you and write the blessing permission
of the Secret Sādhana of Liver-Colored Protector.

Draw the mandala as a triangular, dark-blue source of phenomena with a fire ring and in its center an eight-petaled lotus marked with *hūṃ* at its center. Do the support torma, offering torma, and other ritual preparations as in Removing All Obstacles. The way to practice the self-visualization and so forth is no different, but for the front visualization, after cleansing and purifying, say:

> From within emptiness appears a vast and wide triangular source of phenomena. In its center, a lotus appears from *paṃ* and a sun from *raṃ*. Upon that, from *gaṃ*, white Gaṇapati appears with the head of an elephant. In his right hand he holds leaves of the essence of earth (daikon radish) that he feeds to his mouth, and in his left hand a mongoose that is vomiting various jewels. He has three eyes and is adorned with various jewels and ornaments. He is fallen on his back with a maroon *hūṃ* on him, which becomes a *hūṃ*-marked flaying knife. That radiates light that terminates all evil ones. {704} The light returns and completely transforms into Swift-Acting Awareness Protector, fulfiller of the hopes of living beings just as they wish. He is liver-colored, black with a red hue. He has one face and six arms and glares angrily with his three round, red eyes. His gaping mouth reveals bared fangs and a curling tongue as he laughs loudly. His orange eyebrows, whiskers, and hair swirl upward. His forehead is anointed with a drop of vermilion. His head is sealed above by King Akṣobhya. He holds a vajra flaying knife with his upper right hand above his heart and a skull cup filled with the flesh and blood of enemies and obstructors with his upper left hand, below his heart. He holds a dry skull garland with his middle right hand and violently rattles a ḍamaru with the lower right. He holds a trident with his middle left hand and a black vajra lasso with the lower hand.

His two legs, with the strength to completely suppress the three levels of existence, stand in a perfectly straight parallel position pressing down on the Obstructor King. He wears a tiger-skin skirt tied with a green silk sash. The ornaments of the great nāgas adorn him: blue snakes bind his hair, and he has red snake earrings, striped snake armbands, white snake collar, yellow snake bracelets, green snake necklace, and white snake anklets and belt. On all his arms and legs there are strings of large and small bells. He is short and fat, with a protruding belly and thick limbs. He has boundless charisma. He has a crown of five dry human skulls with golden finials and a garland of fifty fresh skulls dripping with blood. He is beautified by the six bone ornaments and a jewel on his crown. His terrifying roars resound like thunder, annihilating all devils and enemy obstructors. He stands within a bonfire of timeless awareness like the fire at the end of the eon. {705}

To his left, in a great ocean of pure red rakta, stands a yellow dun mule with a blaze [on its forehead]. Upon it, *bhyoḥ* becomes the One Mother, mighty queen of the desire realm. She is black as storm clouds, with one face and four arms. She holds a sword in her first right hand, and a flaying knife in the second, with a misbegotten-child victory banner in the first left hand and a fresh hair-attached skull filled with blood in the second. She bares her teeth in her open mouth. Her tawny hair streams upward, decorated in between [the locks] with a peacock feather fan and crescent moon. Her right earring is a lion, and the left is a black coiling snake.[25] She has a crown of five dry skulls and a garland of fifty fresh heads. She wears a human-skin cloak and a yellow hair-felt skirt cinched with a snake belt. The sun rises from the middle of her navel. She sits in half-lotus position on top of the mule, her face looking back. In front of her are the makara-faced, behind are the lion-faced, and all around she is surrounded by a retinue of mātṛkās.

In front of the principal couple, *hūṃ* (or *kṣiṃ*) becomes Yakṣa Kṣetrapāla, dark maroon with one face and two arms, brandishing a flaying knife to cut the enemy's life force with the right hand, and with his left hand he feeds the principal's mouth from a blood-filled skull cup. He rides a crazed black bear.

To the right, green *tri* (or *traṃ*) becomes Jinamitra. He is dark green with one face and two arms. He rattles a ḍamaru violently with his right hand, and with his left hand points to the sky with the threatening gesture. He rides a tiger.

In back, *jaḥ* becomes the death lord Ṭakkirāja. He is dark maroon, with one face and two arms. With his right hand he throws a lasso made of intestines, and with his left he points to the sky with the threatening gesture. He rides a wolf.

To the left of the goddess, *hūṃ* becomes the devil lord Trakṣad. He is black, with one face and four arms. The first right hand holds a blood-filled skull cup and the left brandishes a red ensign spear. {706} His first left hand holds an iron-ball hammer (*tho lum*) and the second a sandalwood club (*bing chen*). He wears a brocade cloak with blue designs and high boots with black design. He rides on a black horse with white fetlocks.

All of them are ravenous and bare their fangs. Their orange eyebrows, whiskers, and hair bristles upward. Their three round, red eyes rove around intimidating enemies and obstructors. They are draped with dry and wet human-head garlands.

Around them, yellow Śakra is in the east . . . (etc.).

Follow the liturgy in the root text, [*Treasure Trove of*] *Awakened Activity*. It is also suitable to do the supplication and hundred-syllable practice. Add the recitation and visualization from the section on Getting Down to the Vital Point clarified above. The main recitation practice is the *śāsana* mantra. Continue with the torma offering, praise, self-induction, up to the washing of the disciples and the section of clarifying the awakening mind, except change to

> "To that end, I will receive the permission of Swift-Acting Awareness Protector's Secret Sādhana, the Liver-Colored."

Buddha Amitābha himself manifested the form of a vajra dharma protector called Vajradhara's Protector, through which the supreme and common [spiritual powers] can be accomplished in a matter of months or years. In this, the outer practice is Lokeśvara, the inner practice is wrathful Hayagrīva, and the secret practice is the Awareness Protector. In this practice cycle, there are countless systems that come from the tantras and individual adepts. From among those, the most excellent is this special transmission system that fell to the great chariots of the practice lineages and the glorious Shangpa Kagyu. In this also there is not just one means of accomplishment. Of the many that exist, now the approach is that of the secret sādhana of the Liver-Colored [Protector]. To practice the authorization for this . . . (etc.).

Continue with the mandala, supplication, and introduction to the deities as before. Then:

[The kind root guru and all the lineage gurus] dwell like a dense mass of clouds. In their presence, think that you and all other sentient beings throughout the reaches of space go for refuge until reaching enlightenment {707} and will take the common vows. Repeat three times after me:

"I go for refuge to the buddhas who dwell in the ten directions. I go for refuge to the dharma that dwells in the ten directions. I go for refuge to the sangha who dwell in the ten directions. I pay homage and go for refuge to the yidam mandala deities and to the deities of Six-Armed Awareness Protector and retinue. Please grant me your blessings."

Apply the previous way of visualizing the disciples as deities, and visualize the three seed syllables in their three places.

Now repeat this supplication after me:

"Precious guru, please grant me the authorization of Glorious Awareness Protector's awakened body. Please make the body blessings enter my body. Please confer the vase empowerment."

By your supplicating in that way, light rays radiate from the *hūṃ* in the guru's heart. They strike the heart of the torma appearing as Protector and evoke his mind stream, so that light rays radiate from the *oṃ* in his head. Those invoke all the blessings of awakened body from all the buddhas and bodhisattvas in the ten directions, particularly from Protector, in the form of light rays, which dissolve into the *oṃ*. A stream of liver-colored elixir falls from there and enters the point between the eyebrows of the disciples. It fills precisely the great-bliss chakra in the head, cleansing and purifying all physical sickness, spirits, negativities, and obscurations. You obtain the vase empowerment. Imagine that you have obtained the blessing of Awareness Protector's awakened body.

Say the mantra accompanied by the ḍamaru and bell.

Again repeat this supplication after me:

"Precious guru, please grant me the authorization of Glorious Awareness Protector's awakened speech. Please make the speech blessings enter my speech. Please confer the secret empowerment." {708}

By your supplicating in that way, light rays radiate from the *hūṃ* in the guru's heart. They strike the heart of the torma appearing as Protector and evoke his mind stream, so that light rays radiate from the *āḥ* in his throat. Those invoke all the blessings of awakened speech from all the buddhas and bodhisattvas in the ten directions, particularly from Protector, in the form of light rays, which dissolve into the *āḥ*. A stream of liver-colored elixir falls from there and enters the throats of the disciples. It fills precisely the enjoyment chakra in the throat, cleansing and purifying all verbal sickness, spirits, negativities, and obscurations. You obtain the secret empowerment. Imagine that you have obtained the blessings of Awareness Protector's awakened speech.

Say the mantra accompanied by the ḍamaru and bell.

Again repeat this supplication after me:

"Precious guru, please grant me the authorization of Glorious Awareness Protector's awakened mind. Please make the mind blessings enter my mind. Please confer the wisdom-awareness empowerment."

By your supplicating in that way, light rays radiate from the *hūṃ* in the guru's heart. They strike the heart of the torma appearing as Protector and evoke his mind stream, so that light rays radiate from the *hūṃ* in his heart. Those invoke all the blessings of awakened mind from all the buddhas and bodhisattvas in the ten directions, particularly from Protector, in the form of light rays, which dissolve into the *hūṃ*. A stream of liver-colored elixir falls from there and enters the hearts of the disciples. It fills precisely the dharma chakra in the heart, cleansing and purifying all mental sickness, spirits, negativities, and obscurations. You obtain the wisdom-awareness empowerment. Imagine that you have obtained the blessings of Awareness Protector's awakened mind. {709}

Say the mantra accompanied by the ḍamaru and bell.

Again repeat this supplication after me:

"Precious guru, please grant me the authorization of Glorious Awareness Protector's awakened body, speech, mind, qualities, and activities. Please make the body, speech, mind, qualities, and activities blessings enter my body, speech, and mind. Please confer the fourth empowerment, the precious word empowerment."

By your supplicating in that way, light rays radiate from the *hūṃ* in the guru's heart. They strike the heart of the torma appearing as Protector and evoke his mind stream, so that light rays radiate from the three seed syllables in his three places. Those invoke all the blessings of awakened body, speech, mind, qualities, and activities from all the buddhas and bodhisattvas in the ten directions, particularly from Protector, in the form of light rays, which dissolve into the three letters in Protector's three places. A stream of elixir falls from there and enters the heads of the disciples. It fills from there to the soles of their feet, cleansing and purifying all physical, verbal, and mental sickness, spirits, negativities, and obscurations. You obtain the precious word empowerment.

Imagine that you have obtained the blessings of Awareness Protector's awakened body, speech, mind, qualities, and activities.

Say the mantra.

Then in order to request the mantra empowerment, toss flowers and repeat this three times after me:

"Bhagavat, take hold of me (*bcom ldan bdag gi bzung lags kyi*),
please fully bestow on me" (*bdag la nye bar mdzad du gsol*)."

By your supplicating in that way, a second mantra string emerges from the mantra string in the heart of the front visualization. It enters the disciples' mouths and moves down to the *hūṃ* on sun seats in their hearts, settling around it in a clockwise direction. Imagine that and repeat after me.

Say the essence mantra and the root mantra śāsana three times. Put the disciples' flowers on their heads. {710}

Bhagavat, surely grant to these [disciples],
and please adhere to them. (Repeat three times.)

Then do the torma empowerment and concluding acts as before.

[Colophon by Jamgön Kongtrul Lodrö Taye]

Endowed with vast and very profound intelligence (Lodrö)
from Khyungpo's infinite (Taye) instructions,
this that equals a wish-fulfilling gem
and achieves all one's wishes spontaneously.

This was the chapter on the authorization for the Secret Sādhana of Liver-Colored. *maṅgalaṃ*

X. Saraha's Tradition of Three-Faced Six-Armed Protector

oṃ svasti
After placing an indestructible vital drop,
blessings in Protector's heart center,
I will explain the great sharp arrow system
of the chief of all Indian adepts.

The ritual preparations of the mandala, torma, and such are the same as the section in the authorization of Removing All Obstacles, and the ritual master's consecration of the place, articles, inner offering, and the self-visualization and so forth are the same as before. Cleanse and purify the mandala torma in front.

> From within emptiness, appears a source of phenomena, white outside and red inside, vast and wide. Within it, on a vajra rock of various colors, *hūṃ* becomes a *hūṃ*-marked flaying knife radiating light rays that make offerings to all the exalted assembly and purify all sentient beings of negativities, obscurations, sickness, and spirits. The light rays gather back in and completely transform into glorious Wrathful Awareness Protector, blue-black in color with three heads and six arms. His first two hands hold a flaying knife and blood-filled skull cup, one above the other. In the rest, he holds a skull rosary and a ḍamaru in the two right hands, and a khaṭvāṅga and lasso in the left. His middle face is deep blue, the right one white, and the left one red. Those extremely wrathful three gaping mouths bare his fangs. Three red, round eyes look glaringly in the ten directions. He scowls with shifting wrinkles. His orange eyebrows and whiskers quiver like lightning and his tawny hair bristles upward. {711} Five dry skulls adorn his head, and he wears a garland of fifty blood-dripping heads. His earrings, collar, anklets, belt, and so on are precious jewels, bones, bells, and small bells. A variety of snakes adorn him. He wears a tiger-skin skirt and an elephant-skin upper garment. With his thick limbs, he is unbearably charismatic. At his forehead is a vermilion svāstika swirl. His right leg is contracted, and his left is

straight. He stands in the midst of intensely blazing fire of timeless awareness arisen from his body.

In the four directions, upon lotus, sun, and enemy obstructors, in front from *jā* appears black Jālima with one face and two hands holding a flaying knife in her right hand and a blood-filled skull cup in the left. To the right, smoke-colored Kṣetrapālama appears from *kṣe*, with one face and two hands holding a ḍamaru in her right hand and pointing with the threatening gesture with the left. In back, maroon Mahākālīma arises from *ma*, with one face and two hands, holding a flaying knife in her right and blood-filled skull cup in the left. To the left, yellow Ṭakkirājama comes from *ṭā*, holding a trident in her right hand and a lasso in the left. Those four are very wrathful, each with three eyes, tawny eyebrows, whiskers, and hair swirling upward, and adorned by bones and other scary ornaments. They stand in the midst of blazing fire arisen from their bodies. Around them are immeasurable hosts of attendants and an ocean of the oath-bound. The principals and all retinues have white *oṃ* at the head, red *āḥ* at the throat, and blue *hūṃ* at the heart, from which light rays radiate and invoke the Protector and retinue from the sacred sites, such as Potala and Cool Grove. {712}

oṃ śrī mahākāla sapariwāra ehyahi khriṃ khriṃ . . . (etc., invokes). *jaḥ hūṃ vaṃ hoḥ*—they become indivisible with the pledge beings.

Again, light radiates from the *hūṃ* in their hearts and invokes the empowerment deities. The [protectors] say, "Please confer empowerment." [The deities] say, "*oṃ sarva tathāgata abhiṣekate samaya śrī hūṃ*" and confer empowerment. Their bodies are filled, stains purified, and they taste great bliss. The excess water rises up to the place on their heads and completely transforms into Akṣobhya crowning the principal figures and Awareness Protector crowning all the retinue.

oṃ śrī mahākāla sapariwāra arghaṃ praticcha hūṃ svāhā (similarly) *pādyaṃ* . . . (etc. through) . . . *śabda*

Present the inner offerings by adding the three seed syllables to the essence mantra. Then the praise:

> Your body, terrifying form with three heads and six arms,
> your speech, resounding roars of *hūṃ* and *phaṭ*,
> your mind, blazing with inexhaustible compassion:
> tamer of all outer and inner obstacles, I praise you.
>
> Four goddesses in the four directions,
> you follow the commands of glorious Heruka,
> in such actions as peaceful, enriching, magnetizing, wrathful:
> accomplish them right now without wavering.
>
> Protector and retinue of attendants,
> accept these outer, inner, and secret offerings
> consecrated by absorptions, mantras, and mudras,
> and perform the acts that I, the yogin, charge you with.

For the mantra recitation:

> Light rays radiate from the *hūṃ* in the heart of oneself as yidam, evoking the mind streams of the Protector, principals, and retinue. Think that they accomplish infinite actions.
>
> *oṃ śrī mahākāla kṣiṃ kṣetra* . . . (etc.).

Recite that quintessence mantra and śāsana. {713} If you would like to recite the retinues' mantras:

> *oṃ mahākālī hūṃ hūṃ phaṭ / oṃ mahākālī kṣetrapāla hūṃ phaṭ / oṃ rāja ṭakkirāja hūṃ phaṭ / oṃ mahākālī niśa trūṃ māraya hūṃ phaṭ*

Recite the offerings and praises again, and the self-induction. The disciples wash. During the clarification of the mind of awakening, change to

> "To that end, I will receive the authorization of Three-Faced Six-Armed Swift-Acting Awareness Protector."

Formerly, the great upāsaka known as Śāntivarman with iron armor visited Mount Potala three times and saw Exalted Avalokita face to face. Before and after, he traveled around and saw all the other celestial palaces. He made prostrations and offerings to all the images. At one place, there was a very big fine mansion with a door that never opened. He politely requested the heroes and ḍākinīs to open the door. They replied, "If we open this door, all the [inhabitants of] the entire three worlds will be frightened and die or come close to death." So then he supplicated and again requested it from Exalted Avalokita, who requisitioned one emanated messenger who, due to the strength of being commanded by the Exalted One, opened the door that no living being could open without harm. Inside there, Śāntivarman encountered this very Awareness Protector. He prayed and received blessing. He supplicated, saying, "I have come to request protection of the Buddha's doctrine for the sake of all sentient beings in the world." Protector swore to it, and accordingly one emanated form remains forever in the great charnel ground of Cool Grove, in the hollow of a nyagroda (banyan) tree. Based on that, glorious Saraha and others are known to have created means for accomplishment. Meanwhile, it is said that one form of the Awareness Protector resided at the stupa of glorious Dhānyakaṭaka and was invited from there by Master Nāgārjuna and Brahmin Vararuci.[26] {714} Based on these, all kinds of instruction systems arose in the exalted land of India. In Tibet, Gyijo [Lotsāwa] Dawai Özer[27] translated the cycle of the Single Protector. Tengpa Lotsāwa[28] translated the instructions of [Protector] Surrounded by Six Ḍākinīs. Gar Chözang[29] translated the source texts of Saraha, Śavarīpa, and others. From among those, the particular precept system from exalted Khedrup Khyungpo's Swift-Acting Awareness Protector's dharma cycle, now is the authorization for the great brahmin Saraha's tradition of Three-Faced Six-Armed Protector . . . (etc.).

Continue as before to the mandala offering.

Repeat this supplication three times after me:

"Awareness form of powerful activities
of all buddhas in the three times—
glorious Protector with retinue,
grant the authorization of body, speech, and mind."

Then do the introduction to the deities, the taking of common and uncommon vows, and the visualization of the disciples as deities as in Guru-Protector Inseparable. Continue as far as "Meditate that the heart is marked with blue *hūṃ*."

> Now, in order to request the authorization for Glorious Awareness Protector's awakened body, speech, and mind, repeat this after me:
>
> "Guru Awareness Protector,
> please confer the complete four empowerments.
> Please purify the four obscurations.
> Please help me accomplish the four actions
> and attain the four kāyas."
>
> By your supplicating in that way, light rays radiate from the *hūṃ* in the heart of the guru as the yidam. They strike the hearts of the Protector and retinue dwelling in front of the single trunk of the sandalwood tree in the Cool Grove Charnel Ground in the southeast and evoke their mind streams. Immeasurable large and small bodies of Protector and retinue arise from all aspects of awakened body. {715} Also from the forehead of the torma visualized as Protector and retinue immeasurable large and small bodies arise. Their bodies are voracious and brilliant. Their speech resounds with wrathful *hūṃ phaṭ* and *ha ha*. They arrive and loudly declare, "Children of good family, I will remove all your obstacles. I will create all favorable conditions." These unimaginable miniatures enter the disciples' foreheads. Their whole bodies are filled inside with redness. Imagine that all physical sickness, spirits, and obstacles in the form of flesh and blood of enemy obstructors are consumed red and raw, and annihilated.

Accompanied by the ḍamaru, bell, and incense smoke, repeat the essence and quintessence mantras. Do the same for the following:

Through that, the blessings of the Protector and retinue's awakened body enter your body. All physical negativities, obscurations, and obstacles are purified. You obtain the vase empowerment. Especially, think that your body becomes inseparable from Protector's awakened body.

Again, light rays radiate from the *hūṃ* in the heart of the guru as the yidam . . . (etc., as before). From the throat of the torma visualized as Protector . . . (etc., and) . . . enter the disciples' throats . . . (etc. to) Imagine that all verbal sickness, spirits . . . (etc.). Blessings of the Protector and retinue's awakened speech enter your speech. All verbal negativities, obscurations . . . (etc.) . . . the vase empowerment . . . (etc.) . . . speech becomes inseparable from Protector's awakened speech.

Again, light rays radiate from the *hūṃ* in the heart of the guru as the yidam . . . (etc., as before). From the heart of the torma visualized as Protector . . . (etc.) . . . enter the disciples' hearts . . . (etc.). Imagine that all mental sickness, spirits . . . (etc.). Blessings of the Protector and retinue's awakened mind enters your mind. All mental negativities, obscurations . . . (etc.) . . . the wisdom-awareness empowerment . . . (etc.) . . . mind becomes inseparable from Protector's awakened mind.

Again, light rays radiate from the *hūṃ* in the heart of the guru as the yidam . . . (etc., as before). From the five places of the torma visualized as Protector . . . (etc.) . . . enter the disciples' five places . . . (etc.). {716} Imagine that all three doors' sickness, spirits . . . (etc.). Blessings of the Protector and retinue's complete awakened body, speech, and mind enter your three doors all at once. All physical, verbal, and mental negativities, obscurations . . . (etc.). You obtain the fourth the empowerment. Your three doors become inseparable from Protector's awakened body, speech, and mind.

Then to request the transmission of the mantra recitation, repeat this supplication three times after me:

> "Bhagavat, take hold of me,
> please fully bestow it on me."

By your supplicating in that way, the black mantra string radiating red light rays situated around the *hūṃ* letter on the sun seat in Protector's heart splits off a second mantra string in the way that the light from one candle lights a second one. It enters your mouth and moves down to the *hūṃ* on a sun mandala in your hearts, settling around it in a clockwise direction. Intense light rays fiercely blazing with firelight radiate from that. All sickness, spirits, negativities, and obscurations are singed like chicken feathers in a fire and burned up, completely eliminated. Imagine that and repeat this after me:

Have them repeat all the mantras of the principal and retinue three times each. Place flowers on the disciples' heads and say three times:

> Bhagavat, surely grant to these [disciples],
> and please adhere to them.

Then for the completely perfect blessings, do this visualization of the torma's exhortation: This torma itself is Swift-Acting Awareness Protector . . . (etc.).

Continue as in Removing All Obstacles, except that during the guru lineage supplication, change to:

Pervasive Lord Great Vajradhara, great brahmin Saraha, mighty glorious Śavarīpa . . . (etc. to) . . . Chöje Sangye Tönpa . . . (etc. to) . . . up to my root guru—all these glorious holy gurus . . . (etc.). {717}

Similarly, follow [that liturgy] for the concluding practices.

[Colophon by Jamgön Kongtrul Yönten Gyatso]

Of all the accomplished adepts of India,
the especially exalted qualities (Yönten) of the brahmin's tradition,

known for its retinue of four ḍākinīs,
is indeed the essence of the ocean (Gyatso) of sādhanas.

This was the chapter on the authorization for Saraha's Tradition of Three-Faced Six-Armed Protector. *maṅgalaṃ*

XI. Adorned Protector Secret Sādhana

oṃ svasti
Guardian of all buddhas' doctrines,
inseparable from all buddhas;
I bow to Swift-Acting Avalokiteśvara
and write the permission for Adorned Protector.

Draw a *hūṃ* and an *A* in the center of the blue-black source-of-phenomena mandala with its ring of fire. Place the support torma in its center and the offering torma in front as before. To the right, place a vase filled with elixir and saffron water with an ornament at its opening and [silk ribbon] tied around its neck. To the left, put up a skull cup full of elixir. Begin with the consecrations and the self-visualization, then cleanse and purify the mandala in front.

> From within emptiness, the letter *E* becomes a blue-black source of phenomena with a ring of fiercely blazing fire. Within that is a seat of a multicolored lotus, sun, and Gaṇapati. Upon that, a *hūṃ*-marked flaying knife arises from *hūṃ*, and an *A*-marked vajra from *A*. Light rays radiate from both and accomplish the two purposes. They gather back and transform into Glorious Awareness Protector, pitch black, with one face and six arms. Of his six hands, in the first two he holds a vajra flaying knife in his top right hand and a blood-filled skull cup in the left, one above the other at his heart, and embraces the mother. In his two lower right hands he holds a skull rosary and a ḍamaru, and in his two lower left hands a khaṭvāṅga and vajra lasso. His gaping mouth reveals his bared fangs. He glares angrily with three round, red eyes. He grimaces with wrathful frowns and his black beard, eyebrows, and hair swirl upward. He has a crown of five dry human

skulls and a garland of fifty fresh heads. His forehead is anointed with a drop of vermilion. {718} White mottled snakes bind his hair, and he has red mottled snake earrings, yellow snake collar, green snake armbands, and black mottled snake anklets and belt. He is draped with bone ornaments and strings of large and small bells. He wears a tiger-skin skirt and an elephant skin over his torso. With right leg contracted and left leg straight, he stands in the midst of a bonfire arisen from his body.

In his lap is the mother Vajra Knows One (rDo rje gcig shes ma), black, with one face and two arms. Her left hand holds a blood-filled skull cup feeding the father and the right holds a flaying knife and embraces the father. She wears a crown of five dry skulls and a garland of fifty fresh heads, and is adorned by the five symbolic ornaments.

In the four directions around them: in front on a lotus and sun seat, black Jālima appears from *jaḥ* with one face and two hands holding flaying knife in the right and blood-filled skull cup in the left. To the right, upon a lotus and sun, smoke-colored Kṣetrapālama from *kṣe* holds a ḍamaru in her right hand and points with the threatening gesture with the left. In back, upon a lotus and sun, maroon Mahākālīma arises from *ma*, holding a flaying knife in her right and a blood-filled skull cup in the left. To the left, upon a lotus and sun, yellow Ṭakkirājama comes from *ṭā*, holding a trident in her right hand and a lasso in the left. They all have one face, three eyes, and bared fangs. Their eyebrows and whiskers flash and hair flows upward. They are adorned by bones, with very wrathful forms. Around them are immeasurable hosts of attendants and an ocean of the oath-bound. The principals and all retinues have white *oṃ* at the head, red *āḥ* at the throat, and blue *hūṃ* at the heart. Light rays radiate from their hearts and instantly invoke the Protector and retinue from Cool Grove and other [charnel grounds]. {719}

oṃ śrī mahākāla saparivāra e hye hi khriṃ khriṃ . . . (etc., say that and)
jaḥ hūṃ vaṃ hoḥ—the awareness beings and pledge beings become indivisible.

> Again light rays radiate from *hūṃ* in the heart and invoke the empowerment deities. [Protector and retinue] say, "Please confer the empowerment." They all say "*oṃ sarva tathāgata abhiṣekate samaya śrīye hūṃ*" and confer empowerment. [Protector's and retinue's] bodies are filled and the excess water overflows to the tops of their heads, becoming Akṣobhya crowning the principals and the principals crowning the retinue.

Make the offerings with just the mantra *oṃ śrī mahākāla* . . . (etc.). Present the inner offering. Recite the praises from "Without stirring from the realm of phenomena . . . (etc.)." Clarify the visualization of the mantra recitation and repeat the essence mantra and *oṃ a svāhā* for the mother. Perfectly perform a brief torma offering with offerings and praise. Then cleanse and purify the vase.

> From within emptiness, from *paṃ* appears a precious vase with all characteristics perfectly complete. Within that, from *E*, appears a blue-black source of phenomena . . . (etc.).

Continue until the recitation as before. In the recitation section, say:

> Light rays from *hūṃ* in my heart radiate and evoke the mind streams of the deities inside the vase. A stream of elixir falls and fills the vase.

Imagine that and recite the two mantras. Do the offering and praise as before.

> The principal protectors and retinue melt and become elixir.

Imagine that and practice the self-induction. Then the disciples are cleansed. During the clarification of the mind of awakening, change to:

> "To that end, I will receive the profound permission of Adorned Awareness Protector Secret Sādhana."

> In general, it is important for all sentient beings that the precious doctrine of the Buddha abides and flourishes. For that, a

special dharma protector who guards the doctrine is a definite requirement. There has never ever been a better one than this Awareness Protector, who is the power of Exalted Avalokita's mind of awakening. {720} So for all those who have entered the Buddha's doctrine, if they occasionally offer [this protector] a torma and charge him with guarding the doctrine, then the precious doctrine will spread and flourish for a long time, one's own and others' obstacles will be removed, and all one's wishes will be accomplished. So it is said. In particular, for those who teach, listen to, or practice the instructions of Niguma, Ḍākinī of Timeless Awareness, even if they don't personally practice this protector, he will stand by them and automatically accomplish awakened activity. From all the infinite instructions on this protector that were held in Khedrup Khyungpo's tradition, the present occasion is the practice of the profound permission known as Adorned [Protector] Secret Sādhana . . . (etc.).

After this juncture, have the disciples offer a mandala.

Repeat this supplication three times after me:

"*namo buddhāya / namo dharmāya / namo saṃghaya*
With the heart of omniscient timeless awareness,
completely purifying the wheel of existence,
principal one, kindly grant me today
the explanation of this precious gift."

Do the introduction to the deities, the taking of common and uncommon vows, the visualization of disciples as deities, and up through the blessing of the three places, as in Guru-Protector Inseparable.

Light rays radiate from the *hūṃ* in the master's heart. They strike the torma appearing as Protector and evoke his mind stream. From his heart infinite light rays radiate and invoke all the body blessings of all tathāgatas and victors' heirs from the ten directions in the forms of countless big and small bodies of the principals and retinue. They dissolve into the disciples' heads and fill their whole bodies with deity bodies and light rays. Based on that, all physical negativities, obscurations, and obstacles are purified. Imagine that you have obtained Protector's blessings of awakened body.

Recite the root mantra and offer incense and music. Apply [to this the following]: {721}

That was the authorization of awakened body. Again light rays radiate from *hūṃ* in the guru's heart. They strike the torma appearing as Protector and evoke his mind stream. From his heart, infinite light rays radiate and invoke all the speech blessings of all tathāgatas and victors' heirs from the ten directions in the forms of countless big and small bodies of the principals and retinue. They dissolve into the disciples' throats and fill their whole bodies with deity bodies and light rays. Based on that, all verbal negativities, obscurations, and obstacles are purified. Imagine that you have obtained the Protector's blessings of awakened speech.

Say the root mantra while offering incense and music.

That was the authorization of awakened speech. Again light rays radiate from *hūṃ* in the guru's heart. They strike the torma appearing as Protector and evoke his mind stream. From his heart infinite light rays radiate and invoke all the mind blessings of all tathāgatas and victors' heirs from the ten directions in the forms of countless big and small bodies of the principals and retinue. They dissolve into the disciples' hearts and fill their whole bodies with deity bodies and light rays. Based on that, all mental negativities, obscurations, and obstacles are purified. Imagine that you have obtained the Protector's blessings of awakened mind.

Say the root mantra while offering incense and music.

That was the authorization of awakened mind. Then to request the four empowerments, repeat this three times after me:

"Guru Awareness Protector,
please confer the complete four empowerments.
Please purify the four obscurations.

Please let me accomplish the four awakened actions
and obtain the four kāyas." {722}

For the vase empowerment, imagine that the whole sky is filled with the victors and their heirs who arrive holding vases full of elixir water and confer the empowerment.

Place the vase on their heads.

Just as the tathāgatas bathed him
as soon as he was born,
just so I confer empowerment
with pure water of the gods.
oṃ sarva tathagata abhiṣiñca mi

Say that and give them the vase water.

That conferral of the vase empowerment purifies physical obscurations. You obtain the vase empowerment and are empowered to meditate on the deity's body. It establishes the ability to attain nirmāṇakāya.

Then visualize this for the secret empowerment: Light rays radiate from *hūṃ* in the master's heart and invoke the father and mother victors in the ten directions. They enter the mouth of the Protector visualized in front and melt in the fire of great passion. They emerge from his vajra and arrive in the mother's lotus, generating bliss. The support of that bliss is the bodhicitta, which is placed upon your tongues. Imagine that it confers the secret empowerment.

Give them the inner offering or elixir from the skull cup.

Arisen from the place of the three secrets
of all victors in the ten directions,
venerated by all in the three realms,
I bestow the great vajra empowerment.
oṃ sarva tathāgata guhya abhiṣiñca mi

Based on your tasting of the bodhicitta, the experiences of bliss, clarity, and nonthought arise. Rest in the equipoise of that very state. Imagine that the timeless awareness of undivided clarity-emptiness is actualized. That conferral of the secret empowerment purifies verbal obscurations. You obtain the secret empowerment and are empowered to recite mantra. It establishes the ability to attain saṃbhogakāya.

Then visualize like this for the wisdom-awareness empowerment: {723} The torma appears clearly as Awareness Protector father and mother. A second mother consort resembling the first emanates and enters into union with you, who appear as the Protector. The sounds of your ecstasy invoke the victor couples from the ten directions. They enter the disciples' bodies. They melt in the fire of great bliss, inducing the sequence of the four ecstasies. Based on the coemergent ecstasy at the tip of the vajra gem, great bliss without center or boundary arises. Rest in the equipoise of that very state. Imagine that the timeless awareness of integral unity of bliss-emptiness is actualized.

The secret mother, awareness ḍākinī,
emanates a ḍākinī to give to the child.
They join in union and fill with bliss:
great coemergent awareness is obtained.
oṃ sarva tathāgata prajñājñāna abhiṣeñca māṃ

That conferral of the third empowerment purifies mental obscurations. You obtain the wisdom-awareness empowerment and are empowered to rely on a real or imagined awareness consort. It establishes the ability to attain dharmakāya.

Then visualize like this for the fourth empowerment: Instantly visualize yourself as Awareness Protector, principals and retinue, radiating light from the *hūṃ*s in your hearts that strike all of the environment and its inhabitants. The environment all becomes a celestial palace and the inhabitants all become Awareness Protector. All of that in the form of light is drawn in and dissolves into the retinue. The retinue dissolves into Awareness Protector.

The disciples' bodies appearing as Protector melt into light from the top and bottom and dissolve into the *hūṃ* letter in the heart. That also gradually shrinks from the vowel sign up and vanishes into basic space. Please rest in equipoise within a state of lucid clarity and emptiness.

Say that and have them rest in equipoise for a moment.

As the sky illustrates the unborn, {724}
the sky has no characteristics.
By joining equanimity to the sky,
one's mind is empty dharmakāya.
Show the essence of the word.

All phenomena are free of all extremes of embellishment—that is the essence of the fourth empowerment.

Say that to introduce [mind's nature].

That conferral of the precious word empowerment purifies obscurations of the three doors in equal measure. You obtain the fourth empowerment and are empowered to meditate on the path of integral unity. It establishes the ability to attain the fruition of svabhāvakāya.

Thus engender realization. Do the mantra recitation transmission, torma empowerment, and concluding acts as they were described in Removing All Obstacles.

[Colophon by Jamgön Kongtrul Lodrö Taye]

In the sky of previously cultivated pure intelligence (Lodrö)
the moon's reflection of profound dharma rises,
soothing the mental pain
of infinite (Taye) living beings.

This was the chapter on the authorization for Adorned Protector Secret Sādhana. *maṅgalaṃ*

XII. Four Deities Combined Practice

oṃ svasti
Avalokiteśvara, Yoginī,
Tārā, and Swift-Acting Protector,
inseparable from Guru Vajradhara,
I place you on my head and compose the authorization.

On a four-petaled lotus mandala, place a blue heap [of grain] on a sun-moon seat in the center, a black heap on a sun seat on the lotus petal in the east, red on the lotus petal in the south, white in the west, and green in the north, making five heaps. Then place offering tormas around it and do the refuge and awakening mind as usual.

> *oṃ vajra rakṣa rakṣa hūṃ phaṭ*
>
> Outside appears the protection circle with a ring of blazing fire, a vajra enclosure, and tent. Within that, one appears clearly in the form of the yidam [Cakrasaṃvara] with a source of phenomena on the head, white outside and red inside. It arises as bliss and expands in the nature of light. In its center is a four- petaled lotus with stamens that rise a cubit in height. Upon them, on a stacked seat of the sun and moon, *hūṃ* becomes a blue vajra marked by *hūṃ*. That becomes the root guru in the form of Great Vajradhara, blue, with one face and two arms. He holds a vajra in his right hand and a bell in the left, embracing Vajradhātviśvarī, who holds a flaying knife and skull cup. {725} They are both adorned by bones and precious jewels, and clothed in silks. They sit in vajra posture and lotus posture [respectively], radiating light.
>
> On the lotus petal in front, on a sun seat, *hūṃ* becomes a flaying knife marked by *hūṃ*. That transforms into Awareness Protector. He is as black as storm clouds, with one face and six arms, standing in the position of straight legs. He holds a flaying knife in his top right hand, a skull rosary in the middle hand, and fiercely rattles a ḍamaru in the lower right hand. He holds a blood-filled skull in his upper left hand, a trident in the middle hand, and a vajra lasso in the lower left hand. He has three round, red eyes, and fangs bared in his open mouth. His eyebrows,

whiskers, and goatee are resplendent; and orange hair streams upward. He wears a crown of five dry skulls and a garland of fifty wet skulls dripping with blood. He is adorned by the six bone ornaments and snakes, and wears a tiger-skin skirt cinched by a green silk sash. He is short and stocky, with thick limbs and protruding belly. His forehead is smeared with vermilion. Large and small bells adorn his arms and legs. His upper body is cloaked in a wet elephant skin. He stands in the midst of blazing fire on a seat of white Gaṇapati fallen on his back.

On the lotus petal to the right, on a sun seat, *hrīḥ* becomes a *hrīḥ*-marked flaying knife. That becomes Exalted Vajrayoginī, red, with one face and two arms, youthful as a sixteen-year-old. As she smiles, her eyeteeth protrude slightly. Her three eyes glance to the left. Her right hand holds a flaying knife downward, {726} and her left holds up a skull cup full of elixir for her to drink. She has a khaṭvāṅga in the crook of her left elbow and is adorned by the five symbolic ornaments. She stands with right leg extended, trampling on Bhairava, and the left bent, pressing on Kālarātri.

On the lotus petal in the back, a white *hrīḥ* on a moon seat becomes a white lotus marked by *hrīḥ*. That transforms into Avalokita, white, with one face and two arms. He is peaceful and smiling, adorned by all the silks and precious ornaments. His right hand holds a vase with the mudra of supreme generosity; his left hand grasps the stem of a white lotus flower at his heart, the full blossom near his left ear. His hair is piled on top with locks falling loosely, and a crown of Amitābha. He sits in the position of right leg extended and left contracted.

On the lotus petal to the left, upon a moon seat, *tāṃ* becomes an utpala flower marked by *tāṃ*. That becomes Exalted Tārā. She is green and in the prime of youth, in a form like a sixteen-year-old. Her right hand is in the mudra of supreme generosity, and her left hand holds the stem of a green utpala flower. She is crowned by Amoghasiddhi. She sits in the position of right leg slightly extended and the left drawn in.

All are marked with white *oṃ* at their foreheads, red *āḥ* at their throats, and blue *hūṃ* at their hearts. Light rays radiate from the *hūṃ*s, invoking the gurus, yidams, buddhas, bodhisattvas, heroes, ḍākinīs, and hosts of dharma protectors and guards, all in the forms of Vajradhara and the four deities—*jaḥ hūṃ vaṃ hoḥ*. They dissolve indivisibly [into the respective deities above your head]. They become the unified essence of every source of refuge.

Guru and group of four deities: Outwardly I offer flowers and incense; inwardly five meats and five elixirs; secretly the bliss of union; and the offering of suchness is the timeless awareness of nondual bliss and emptiness. These and other special unimaginable offerings I present for your pleasure. Please partake of them and grant your blessings. {727}

namo buddhāya / namo guruhe / vajra vīra vīriṇī / śrī ḍāka ḍākinī / joka jokinī / sarva buddha bodhisatvāya śaraṇa gacchāmi kyai (Repeat three times.)

A stream of elixir falls from the guru's body and enters the crown of my head. It fills the body and purifies sickness, spirits, negativities, and obscurations. I obtain the blessings of the guru's awakened body, speech, and mind. Likewise, visualize each of the deities (and say their mantras in order):

oṃ vajra mahākāla kṣiṃ kṣetra vighanāṃ vināyaka hūṃ hūṃ phaṭ phaṭ svāhā (Repeat three times.)
A stream of elixir falls from Protector's body . . . (etc. to) . . . obtain the blessings of the Protector's awakened body, speech, and mind.

oṃ vajra nara kriṃ kriṃ hūṃ hūṃ phaṭ phaṭ svāhā (Repeat three times.)
A stream of elixir falls from Yoginī's body . . . (etc.)

oṃ maṇi padme hūṃ / oṃ vajra rakṣa namaḥ samanta hūṃ phaṭ (Repeat three times.)
A stream of elixir falls from Avalokita's body . . . (etc.)

oṃ tāre tuttāre ture svāhā (Repeat three times.)
A stream of elixir falls from Tārā's body and enters the crown of my head. It fills the body and purifies sickness, spirits, negativi-

ties, and obscurations. I obtain the blessings of the Tārā's awakened body, speech, and mind.

Light rays radiate from *hūṃ* in Guru Vajradhara's heart and invoke the four deities. Avalokita comes to dwell on guru's head, Tārā at the throat, Protector at the heart, and Yoginī at the navel.

Connect the set of five mantras and repeat them three times.

Wind stirs in my perineum, the fierce inner heat of awareness fire blazes at the navel. It strikes the guru's body and great bliss melts the four deities into elixir, which fills the [guru's] body. It emerges from the secret path and enters through the head. It fills down to the throat, purifying physical negativities and obscurations. I obtain the vase empowerment and the blessing of awakened body enters. {728} It fills down to the heart, purifying verbal negativities and obscurations. I obtain the secret empowerment and the blessing of awakened speech enters. It fills down to the navel, purifying mental negativities and obscurations. I obtain the wisdom-awareness empowerment and the blessing of awakened mind enters. It fills the whole body, purifying negativities and obscurations of the three doors. I obtain the word empowerment and the blessing of awakened body, speech, and mind enter. The guru melts into light and dissolves into me. My body disappears in light. Mind rests in equipoise without contrivance.

Then cleanse and purify the mandala.

From within emptiness, appears a four-petaled lotus with stamens that rise a cubit in height. Upon them, on a stacked seat of the sun and moon, *hūṃ* becomes a blue vajra marked by *hūṃ*. That becomes the root guru in the form of Great Vajradhara . . . (etc. to) . . . They become the unified essence of every source of refuge.

Recite that as above. Then for the consecration of offerings, say *guru deva catura saparivāra argham* . . . (etc.) for the outer offerings; *oṃ āḥ hūṃ* for the inner offering; and present the secret and suchness offerings mentally.

Then the praises with the one quatrain that begins "The benevolent one . . ." (*gang gi drin gyis* . . . etc.) and

> Door to the source of every blessing,
> place to attain every spiritual power,
> deities who remove every obstacle:
> I bow to the guru and group of four deities.

If you have a torma, then consecrate as in general yidam practice.

> The tongues of the deities are vajra straws through which they suck up and consume the torma.
> *oṃ guru vajradhara idaṃ baliṃta kha kha khahi* (Repeat three times.)

Say the personal mantras of each of the deities, adding that torma mantra and repeating three times to offer it. Make offerings, praises, and the request for desires with "Accept this torma I offer to you . . ." (*mchod sbyin gtor ma* . . . etc.).

Now cleanse the disciples. During the clarification of the mind of awakening, change to:

> "To that end, I will receive the profound permission of the guru and Four Deities Combined Practice."

> This one time, when the great adept Śavarīpa was doing his practice in the charnel ground Cool Grove, {729} first Glorious Awareness Protector himself arrived and said, "Receive my sādhana . . ." and so forth. Then Exalted Vajrayoginī, Avalokita, and Tārā all came and taught their own sādhanas. Since it is said of this, "The four blessing deities are never apart," any one of these four practices will achieve all of them in terms of the essence and awakened activity. Therefore, there is never any distinction between them. However, in appearance, it was made into a sādhana that combines the four separate [deities] into one and was given [in that form] to Maitrīpa. Rāhula, the great adept from the south, had a visionary experience of the four deities as soon as his mother gave birth to him. Later, Vajra Khecarī

granted him all the sādhanas. Khedrup Khyungpo received them from those two holy gurus and especially from the Awareness Ḍākinī Sukhasiddhi. As spoken:

> Accomplished in three months without distraction,
> meditating without fail in each session at dawn
> accomplishes supreme and common spiritual powers.

In offering you the permission of the four deities with this kind of blessing, the ritual master's acts were completed previously. Now it is your turn. As a gift to request entrance into this teaching, now offer a mandala. Now repeat this supplication after me:

> "Great joy, you, my teacher,
> you, Master, please consider me.
> You teach the way to great awakening;
> I pay homage to you, great lord.
> Grant me the actual sacred pledge.
> Grant me the mind of awakening.
> Grant me the triple refuge
> in Buddha, dharma, and sangha.
> Protector, please usher me into
> the supreme city of emancipation."
> (Repeat three times.) {730}

In the presence of the guru and four deities in the front visualization, repeat this confession and taking of the vows after me:

> "I go for refuge to the Three Jewels . . ." (*dkon mchog sum la* . . . etc.)

Then on account of your intense devotion to the ritual master who dwells as the essence of the guru and four deities, light rays radiate from the heart and evoke the mind streams of the guru and four deities visualized in front. Boundless light rays come from their hearts, and by merely touching your bodies, they purify impure perceptions and attachments. Imagine that your body is Cakrasaṃvara. On the head of your body as the yidam is a source of phenomena, white on the outside and red on the inside . . . (etc. to) . . . *hūṃ* at their hearts. Imagine that.

Thus recite the words of the creation ritual above and create the deities in the manner of pledge beings.

> Through your supplicating with intense devotion to Guru Vajradhara who sits in the center of the mandala visualized in front, he comes quickly and dissolves into the Vajradhara above your head. A stream of elixir falls from the body and enters in the crown of your head, filling your body and purifying sickness, spirits, negativities, and obscurations. Imagine that you have obtained the blessing of the guru's awakened body, speech, and mind.

Offer incense and play the ḍamaru and bell. Supplicate three times with *namo buddhāya* ... (etc.).

> Again by supplicating the Protector visualized in front, he comes quickly and dissolves into the Protector above your head. Boundless replicas break off from his body and enter in the crown of your head. They fill your body and ravenously consume raw all the sickness, spirits, negativities, and obscurations. Imagine that Protector's awakened body, speech, and mind merge inseparably with your three doors.

Offer incense, play the ḍamaru and bell, and say the mantra three times for the descent of blessings. Apply that to the following. {731}

> Again by your supplicating Vajrayoginī, she comes quickly and dissolves into Vajrayoginī above your head. A stream of red elixir falls from her vagina and enters your head. It fills your body, purifying sickness, spirits, negativities, and obscurations. Imagine that you obtain the blessings of Yoginī's awakened body, speech, and mind.

Offer incense, play the ḍamaru and bell, and say the mantra three times.

> Again by your supplicating Avalokita, he comes quickly and dissolves into Avalokiteśvara above your head. A stream of white elixir falls from the vase and body, and enters your head. It fills your body, purifying sickness, spirits, negativities, and obscura-

tions. Imagine that you obtain the blessings of Great Compassionate One's awakened body, speech, and mind.

Offer incense, play the ḍamaru and bell, and say the mantra three times.

Again by your supplicating Tārā, she comes quickly and dissolves into Exalted Tārā above your head. A stream of white elixir falls from her right big toe and enters your head. It fills your body, purifying sickness, spirits, negativities, and obscurations. Imagine that you obtain the blessings of Tārā's awakened body, speech, and mind.

Repeat the mantra, offer incense, and play the ḍamaru and bell.

Now as a gift to request the main [empowerment], offer the mandala and repeat this supplication three times after me:

"Just as Awakened Vajra granted
[the great offering to the Buddha,
grant me this today, Vajra Space,
in order to protect me.]"

Light rays from the heart of Guru Vajradhara on your heads invoke the four deities—Avalokita to the guru's crown, Tārā to the throat, Protector to the heart, and Yoginī to the navel. With devotion to those deities dwelling there, repeat this after me:

"*namo buddhāya* . . . (etc. to) . . . *ture svāhā*"

Repeat the set of five mantras three times. {732}

Then, beneath your feet, the wind stirs and light rays from the blazing fire of awareness in the fierce inner heat at your navel strikes the guru's body. The four deities melt into light. A stream of awareness elixir falls from all aspects of [the guru's] body and enters the top of your head. As it fills up above the throat, physical negativities and obscurations are purified. You obtain the vase empowerment. Imagine that the blessing of awakened body has entered. (Play ḍamaru and bell.)

As the stream of elixir fills up above the heart, verbal negativities and obscurations are purified. You obtain the secret empowerment. Imagine that the blessing of awakened speech has entered. (Play ḍamaru and bell.)

As the stream of elixir fills up above the navel, mental negativities and obscurations are purified. You obtain the wisdom-awareness empowerment. Imagine that the blessing of awakened mind has entered. (Play ḍamaru and bell.)

As the stream of elixir fills your whole body, negativities and obscurations of the three doors are purified. You obtain the fourth empowerment. Imagine that the blessings of awakened body, speech, mind, qualities, and activities have entered.

In the end, the guru melts into light and dissolves into you. Imagine that the three vajras become inseparable from your three doors and rest in that equipoise without mental fixation for as long as you can.

Other than the occasional brief playing of the ḍamaru and bell, anything else is unnecessary.

That accomplishes the permission of the four blessing deities. Think that you will take this as your yidam [practice] and will not transgress the sacred pledges, and repeat this:

"I will do all that the master commands."

Also do the general practices for concluding empowerments. Once the deities have dissolved, say the hundred syllables and request for forbearance. Other than the verses of auspiciousness, other concluding rituals are not necessary.

[Colophon by Jamgön Kongtrul Yönten Gyatso]

Praise of its qualities (Yönten) are infinite.
This combined practice is the heart's Spring

for those with unembellished yoga;
it is the essence of an ocean (Gyatso) of instructions.

That was the chapter describing the authorization for Four Deities Combined Practice. *maṅgalaṃ*

XIII. Supplemental Support for Deliberate Conduct

oṃ svasti
Unrestricted awakened activity defeating evil, {733}
great Blood Drinker, here today
make auspicious the accomplishment of all actions
and the spread of the essential doctrine.

For those who like embellishment and wish to do an extensive practice, there is the custom of giving the authorization for deliberate conduct at the end of the thirteen great permissions of the Protector. The general explanation in the manuals suggests doing it in connection with White Protector Wish-Fulfilling Gem, at the end of that authorization. However, here, doing it in connection with the Adorned Protector Secret Sādhana is a convenient way to proceed. In that case, right after the torma empowerment, commence with the consecration of this [practice]. It is not necessary to do the generation of the guru as deity or the invocation. Nevertheless, at the completion of just the permission of the main practice of Deep-Blue Protector, it is suitable to perform just this authorization. The difference is that, if done in connection with the white, red, or other protectors, then it is required to follow the course of the descriptions and generate the disciples as the deity.

Whichever authorization it is connected with, at the same time as arranging its shrine, do the prelude for the individual six hand implements, such as the flaying knife, and the crown ornament, skull garland, snake ornaments, elephant skin, tiger skin, six bone ornaments, and vermilion [mirror]. For that, cleanse and purify.

> From within emptiness, one's own name's initials adorned by vital drops completely transforms into, in essence, the embodiment of glorious Protector's body, speech, mind, qualities, and activities—in form, the individual hand implements and adornments.

Say that and repeat the essence mantras three times each to consecrate. Then the disciples cleanse and purify. Then recite "From within emptiness appears a lotus from *paṃ* and a sun mandala from *raṃ* . . . (etc.)" according to the liturgical description, visualizing the complete Protector with retinue and invoking them.

> *jaḥ hūṃ vaṃ hoḥ*—they become indivisible with the respective pledge beings . . . (etc.). You clearly manifest as Swift-Acting Awareness Protector with vajra weapons in your hands and all the great charnel-ground accessories on all parts of your body, head, and so forth. Imagine that you are thus invested with power. {734}

At this juncture, present the flaying knife in each disciple's right hand [and say]:

> Fortunate child of good family, I confer on you
> the empowerment of the flaying-knife hand implement:
> split open the bodies of enemy obstructors
> and [perform] unrestricted actions of slaughter.

Present the skull rosary:

> Fortunate child of good family, I give you
> this skull rosary dripping with blood:
> extract the inner organs of enemy obstructors
> and satisfy the guardians by your actions.

Small hand drum:

> Fortunate child of good family, I give you
> this small hand drum made of skulls:
> bring the heroes and ḍākinīs under control
> and act to drive the enemy obstructors crazy.

Skull cup:

> Fortunate child of good family, I confer on you
> this empowerment of the skull hand implement:

revel in the heart blood of enemy obstructors
and perform unrestricted actions of paralyzing.

Trident:

Fortunate child of good family, I give you
this three-pronged khaṭvāṅga:
impale the three places of enemy instructors
and complete actions of liberating and exorcising.

Vajra lasso:

Fortunate child of good family, I give you
this vajra lasso:
rope in every enemy obstructor
and complete the actions of binding.

Crown of five dry skulls:

Swift-Acting Awareness Protector's
ornaments and accessories are ablaze:
fortunate child of good family,
take the five dry skulls as five timeless awarenesses.

Skull garland:

Swift-Acting Awareness Protector's
ornaments and accessories are ablaze:
fortunate child of good family,
take this skull garland that liberates evil types.

Snake ornaments:

Swift-Acting Awareness Protector's
ornaments and accessories are ablaze:
fortunate child of good family,
take these snake ornaments, the five poisons purified.

Elephant skin:

> Swift-Acting Awareness Protector's
> ornaments and accessories are ablaze: {735}
> fortunate child of good family,
> take the elephant skin, stupidity purified.

Tiger-skin skirt:

> Swift-Acting Awareness Protector's
> ornaments and accessories are ablaze:
> fortunate child of good family,
> wear this tiger skin, pride purified.

Six ornaments:

> Swift-Acting Awareness Protector's
> ornaments and accessories are ablaze:
> fortunate child of good family,
> take the pure ornaments of the six perfections.

Then put a spot of vermilion on their foreheads:

> Swift-Acting Awareness Protector's
> ornaments and accessories are ablaze.
> I confer empowerment on the fortunate child
> with this secret substance, excellent vermilion:
> bring heroes and ḍākinīs under control.

Visualize clearly on this spot of vermilion the thirteen red *hrīḥ* letters, each long and with final aspiration marks (*visarga*).

> Great glorious Protector, guide of the six migrators,
> epitome of Avalokiteśvara's compassion,
> with this great compassion letter *hrīḥ*
> I confer empowerment on you, fortunate child.

> Having been given the authorization for deliberate conduct, you are imbued with power and charisma beyond compare in all the three existences. You are invested as the lord of the hosts of an ocean of the oath-bound. Think that they make various and sundry offerings to you and offer you praise with vajra songs.

Put up fresh offerings on the shrine, consecrate them, and offer them with verses or just mantras. Do long or short praises of the principal figures, as appropriate.

> Again, imagine that all the victors and their heirs who dwell throughout space, as well as the ritual master and mandala deities, all together say auspicious verses and congratulate you on the great investiture of increasing and stabilizing awareness. {736}

Say that and the *Sealed Word of Auspiciousness*, and toss flowers.

> Thus, with all of these, the root and branch permission blessings of Swift-Acting Awareness Protector that continue today have been well accomplished. Therefore, keep all the sacred pledges of Vajrayāna in general and in particular all the especially vital points of this protector's sacred pledges without damaging them. Devote yourself with diligence to the stages of approach and activity. Know that the guru and yidam are none other than the totally pure dharmakāya by nature and think that you will uphold them as your own life force, and repeat this three times after me:
>
> "I will do all that the master commands."

In gratitude, the disciples offer a golden mandala and their bodies and possessions. Dedicate the virtue to perfect awakening. Afterward, hold a delightful communal feast that the master and disciples enjoy. The ritual master performs extensive thanksgiving, offerings, praises, and requests forbearance.

[Colophon by Jamgön Kongtrul Lodrö Taye]

Attaining the power of mind (Lo) regarding the doctrine,
and aims (drö) tending toward definite goodness,

I did this to accomplish infinite (Taye) welfare,
not just for myself but for others' sake.

That was the chapter on the authorization of the Supplemental Support for Deliberate Conduct.

[General Concluding Words]

I should say something about how I received this permission tradition of authorizations for the Awareness Protector, who is the indispensable superior dharma protector. The permission for the main Deep-Blue Protector, Removing All Obstacles, came down from the great Venerable One of Jonang in three distinct lineages. White and Deep-Blue [Protectors] include various special practices—I received them from both the Kagyu Kamtsang and Sakya traditions. All the others came with those two lineage systems. From [the time of] Khedrup Khyungpo until now, the existence of permissions is definite, and they are totally pure, without corruption.

For the benefit of all, now and later,
this convenient supplication is granted;
the blessing permission of Guru Mahākāla,
clearly arranged and then revised.

May obstacles on the path to awakening subside,
spiritual powers and prosperity expand,
and may Awareness Protector guide those with connection
to the pure land of long-life Amitābha. {737}

With great effort and interest, I became a pure vessel to obtain a small portion of the contained blessings of Guru-Protector Inseparable. So that others whose fortune equals mine could easily be given their share, this was written by the vagabond who is looked after by Guru Awareness Protector, Karma Ngawang Yönten Gyatso Lodrö Tayepai De, at the sacred site protected by the appearance of the Swift-Acting Protector's blessings, the practice site at Tsadra Rinchen Drak, Kunzang Dechen Ösal Ling. Let virtue prevail.

37. Sealed with Life Force

The Extraordinary Authorization of Swift-Acting Protector Entering the Heart[1]

Jamgön Kongtrul

Guru Vajradhara, pervading lord of existence and quiescence,
inseparable from Swift-Acting Avalokiteśvara,
always present within the sphere of my heart;
this is especially distinct from all others.

Grant this permission to select disciples who have never transgressed the general and particular sacred pledges; who hold this protector as their main dharma practice and are able to pursue its approach and accomplishment, and the torma offering; and who definitely hold this dharma lineage. On that occasion, the preparation, mandala, supports, and offerings are the same as in the main practice of Removing All Obstacles. Begin with the consecration of the place, articles, offerings, and tormas. Continue with the self-visualization, meditation, recitation, and front visualization, which are all accomplished in the same manner. Then do the torma offering, praise, and self-induction, continuing in the main practice with the cleansing of the disciples. During the clarification of the awakening mind, change the line to:

> "To that end, I will receive the profound permission of Swift-Acting Awareness Protector Entering the Heart."

The one who possesses the especially exalted Five [Golden] Dharmas, superior to all other dharma protectors who guard the Buddha's doctrine, is this Six-Armed Awareness Protector. He is the self-embodiment arising from the power of the highest awakening mind of Avalokiteśvara, who is always present for the living beings of the world. By the accomplishment of the supreme [spiritual powers through his practice,] the common are accomplished automatically; and by accomplishing the common, the supreme is automatically accomplished. By your obtaining the permission of his blessing, even if you don't practice this path, the blessing will be granted. Just by supplicating him, obstacles will be removed. Just through offering and praising, prosperity that is in harmony with the dharma will increase and will not become the cause of obscuring the supreme. He protects from the terrors of the intermediate state and guides you on the path to the pure realm of Sukhāvatī. Such a one as this wish-granting gem of a protector has many different kinds of blessing permissions. {741} From among those, the one that is distinct from all the others, and possesses the vital point of support like a shadow that follows the body or like a companion who is constantly present as one's life force, is this Entering the Heart. To accomplish this profound permission . . . (etc.).

At this point, have [the disciples] definitely offer a golden mandala.

With flowers in your hands, repeat these supplications three times after me:

"The benevolent one . . ." (*gang gi drin gyis* . . . etc., one quatrain)

"Once your lotus feet are abandoned,
there is no other lord of refuge.
Great mighty hero of migrators,
please grant me the sublime mind."

Then proceed with revealing the deities, taking the common and uncommon vows, generating the disciples as deities, up to the consecration of the three places as was described in the section on Guru-Protector Inseparable.

Then repeat this special supplication three times after me:

"Guru-Protector and deities,
please descend to me."

Place the vajra on the disciples' heads.

Child, I proclaim to you
the sacred pledge of Great Black One.
Refined by that unimaginable one,
and his excellent characteristics, with nine dance expressions,
do meditation, visualization, recitation, and offerings.
Always recite continuous mantras
and hold the wrathful hand implements, and so on.
Whatever actions you undertake,
offer them to the guru and supplicate.
Give up the love of procrastination
in the methods and actions of practice.
Possess the mind of awakening.

Thus bind them under oath.

Main Practice

To establish the foundation of this special blessing, do the following visualization without being distracted by anything else. The central channel is situated from the cranial aperture in the crown of your head straight down the middle to the perineum. It is white outside and red inside. From the top of your head to the heart it is wide, and the cranial aperture is suitably big. {742} At the level of the heart, inside the central channel, your heart is reversed upward and has become an eight-petaled lotus. At its center, on a sun disk, imagine that your own mind has become a blue letter *hūṃ*. Upon the cranial aperture on your head, on a seat of lotus, sun, and Gaṇapati, Swift-Acting Awareness Protector . . . (etc., as in the torma ritual) . . . stands in the midst of an expanse of fiercely blazing fire.

Upon his head, the benevolent root guru is yellow in color, with one face and two hands, holding a wish-fulfilling gem at the heart with the right hand and a golden bell with the left, so brilliant it is hard to bear. Just bringing the guru to mind makes you attain the level of a nonreturner. If you supplicate, the guru will grant the felicitous attainment of supreme and common spiritual powers. Once you have imagined the presence of such a one, repeat this supplication three times:

> "Deities indistinguishable from the guru and Protector, do not veil your timeless awareness. Do not block your power and magical ability. Do not delay your compassion. Do not distance your blessings. All of you, bless me through your inexhaustible awakened body, speech, mind, qualities, and activities. Bless me right now! Bless me quickly! Bless me on this very seat!"

Through supplicating in that way, light rays like hooks radiate from the guru's heart and strike the Protector dwelling in the Cool Grove and, like catching a fish with an iron hook, he is helplessly invoked. He arrives in the space above your head amid the sounds of the ḍamaru and bell, loudly declaring, "I will remove all your obstacles. I will create all favorable conditions." {743} He then dissolves into the pledge-being Protector on your head. Imagine that has become the real Awareness Protector of Cool Grove.

Again, by your arousing intense devotion, the guru sitting on the Protector's head melts into light and dissolves into Protector. The Protector himself enters the cranial aperture on your head and travels down inside the central channel and dissolves into your mind visualized as *hūṃ*, merging inseparably like quicksilver merging with quicksilver. That becomes the form of the Awareness Protector. He is pitch black like the clouds at the end of all time . . . (etc. to) . . . standing in the midst of the expanse, marked with a white *oṃ* at the head, red *āḥ* at the throat, and blue *hūṃ* on a sun disk at the heart.

Gain the heightened clarity of your main body also as the Awareness Protector; appearance and emptiness like an illusion. Swift-Acting Awareness Protector, fulfiller of the hopes of living beings just as they wish, with the intrinsic nature of totally pure dharmakāya—that's me! Hold that thought of pride [of being Protector], and rest for a moment in that equipoise.

Have them rest in equipoise.

Now light rays come from the guru's heart and move down inside the central channel. They strike the lotus with the Protector at the heart. The lotus is gathered up like a vase body, and at its tip, in the manner of a top ornament, is a black five-pronged vajra marked by *hūṃ* in its hub. A mantra string emerges from the guru's mouth and enters down through the central channel. It comes to the Protector at the heart with the lotus like a vase body and [settles] around its circular opening. The letters of the essence mantra sparkle with light in the form of latticework, its filigrees bonding like a child. Think that in all your lifetimes, until such time as you attain awakening, [the Protector] remains there constantly nurturing and blessing you. {744}

In order to stabilize that, place the vajra on their hearts and say, "*vajra mahākāla tiṣṭha vajra*."

Now that the main practice of Entering the Heart is done, the supplemental support is the blessing by the totally complete awakened body, speech, and mind based on the torma. For that, do the following visualization. Clearly visualize the torma as Awareness Protector. White light rays emerge from the *oṃ* letter on his head. They dissolve into the *oṃ* letters on the head of the disciple as Protector and on the Protector in the heart. Physical obscurations are purified. Imagine that and you receive the vase empowerment and blessings of awakened body.

Say the mantra and play music.

Again visualize the torma as Awareness Protector. Red light rays emerge from the *āḥ* letter in his throat. They dissolve into the *āḥ* letter in the throat of the disciple as Protector and in the Protector in the heart. Verbal obscurations are purified. Imagine that

> and you receive the secret empowerment and blessings of awakened speech.

Say the mantra and play music.

> Again visualize the torma as Awareness Protector. Blue light rays emerge from the *hūṃ* letter in his heart. They dissolve into the *hūṃ* letter in the heart of the disciple as Protector and in the Protector in the heart. Mental obscurations are purified. Imagine that and you receive the wisdom empowerment and blessings of awakened mind.

Say the mantra and play music.

> Again visualize the torma as Awareness Protector. The three seed syllables abruptly separate off from the three places. They dissolve into the three seed syllables in the three places of the disciple as Protector and in the Protector in the heart. Physical, verbal, and mental obscurations, and their functions, are purified. Imagine that you receive the word empowerment and blessings of awakened qualities and activities.

Then, when placing [the torma] upon the head:

> Guru-Protector gladly comes to the top of your head. They slowly dissolve into you visualized as Protector and, particularly, into your mind as Protector in your heart. Guru-Protector's blessing enters. Guru-Protector inseparable and your very subtle wind-mind—think that these three become inseparable in essence. {745}

Place the torma on their heads and play the bell.

> From Vajradhara down to my root guru.
> recall the commands just as they were given.
> Please remove all fortunate ones' adverse conditions,
> grant favorable conditions, and supreme and common powers.
> *jāḥ hūṃ vaṃ hoḥ*

That fully completes the permission of Protector Entering the Heart, from the extraordinary word lineage of the Golden Dharmas. Never transgress for a moment all the sacred pledges contained in the general and particular root and branches. Properly hold these outer, inner, and secret supports, and strive to make offerings without break during the times of approach and accomplishment practices. In particular, do not forget to do the yoga of hidden life force, the secret support, every twenty-four-hour day. From the time of receiving this, at all times think that the Protector dissolved into the center of your heart and does not dissolve outside it. These are the vital sacred pledges. So it is taught. Think that you will follow these practices without contradicting how they were explained, and mentally repeat this:

"I will do all that the master commands."

Offer a mandala in gratitude and the other concluding acts of the [deity] mandala. Resolutely do the feast offering, thanks giving, request for forbearance, and so forth as described on the occasion of the main [empowerment] blessing—do all that properly to complete it.

[Concluding Verse and Colophon]

Guru-Awareness Protector's three secrets,
dwell in the center of my faithful heart,
never apart until my awakening, and bless me
with the ability of this supreme state for all beings.

The preservation of this material is extremely tenuous. This is an attempt to clarify the old manuals by Yönten Gyatso Lodrö Tayepai De, who holds the Guru-Protector inseparable constantly in the sphere of my heart. Written during the time and place that delights the Protector. Let virtue prevail.

38. Guru Yoga Connected with Six-Armed Protector Entering the Heart[1]

The Sealed One

Jamgön Kongtrul

Guru-Protector, great treasure of compassion,
I bow with respect until the heart of awakening.
I will write briefly on that extraordinary yoga
from the profound aural lineage.

Those individuals who have received the authorization for this uncommon practice and abide in the sacred pledges and vows, begin with going for refuge, arousing awakening mind, and meditating on the four immeasurables.

> In the center of my body, (Note: it is taught to meditate either as one's yidam or as the Protector, which is also appropriate.) the central channel is the thickness of a cane. The upper end reaches the cranial aperture and the lower end just at the heart. A red eight-petaled lotus at the heart is compressed at the opening like a vase body. At its tip it is marked with a top ornament of a blue five-pronged vajra. In the center of the lotus is a very subtle pink vital sphere, within which is one's mind. That completely transforms into Swift-Acting Awareness Protector, blue-black in color, with one face and six arms. He is greatly ablaze and extremely wrathful and very voracious. His facial expression moves, and his four sharp fangs are bared. {749} His three eyes are red and round, darting around like lightning. His frowning wrinkles are drawn into a

scowl. His tawny hair flows upward, and his eyebrows and whiskers blaze like fire at the end of time. His tongue is curled up as he roars with the laughter of *ha ha*, resounding like thunder. He holds a flaying knife in his first right hand, a skull rosary in the second, and is rattling a skull ḍamaru with the third. He holds a blood-filled skull cup in his first left hand, a trident in the second, and a vajra lasso in the third. Blue snakes bind his hair, and he has red snake earrings, striped snake armbands, white snake collar, yellow snake bracelets, green snake necklace, and white snake anklets and belt. He wears a fresh tiger-skin skirt tied with a green silk belt. He has a very protruding belly and thick limbs, with charisma that is difficult to bear. He has a crown of five dry human skulls and a garland of fifty fresh skulls dripping with blood. His forehead is well anointed with a drop of vermilion. Akṣobhya crowns his head. On all his arms and legs there are strings of large and small bells. He wears an elephant-skin cape. He stands in the dance posture of right foot contracted and the left straight, standing in the midst of intensely blazing fire of timeless awareness.

Upon Protector's head, the benevolent root guru is yellow with the radiance of one hundred thousand suns, holding a wish-fulfilling gem at the heart with the right hand and a golden bell with the left. The guru sits in vajra posture, adorned with countless precious ornaments. {750} Both the guru and Protector are marked with *oṃ* at their heads, *āḥ* at their throats, and *hūṃ* at their hearts. Light rays radiate from the *hūṃ* in the guru's heart, invoking all the benevolent root and lineage gurus.

namo buddhāya / namo guruhe / vajra vīra vīreṇe śrīye / ḍāka ḍākinī / joka jokinī / sarva buddhāya / bodhisatvā śaraṇaṃ gacchāmi / kye kye
(Repeat three times.)

jaḥ hūṃ vaṃ hoḥ—the guru becomes the united essence of all gurus.

Light rays radiate from all three—the guru and Protector on the head and the Protector in the heart—and joins into one, invoking Mahākāla instantly from in front of the single trunk of the sandalwood tree in the Cool Grove Charnel Ground in the southeast.

By faith and by sacred pledge,
from Cool Grove Charnel Ground,
great Mahākāla, come here:
please approach this site of the mandala.

oṃ śrī mahākāla e hye hi kṣiṃ kṣiṃ

Repeat [*kṣiṃ*] twenty-one times, and

jaḥ hūṃ vaṃ hoḥ—he becomes indivisible with the pledge being.

Through saying that, the actual Protector of Cool Grove arrives to the sound of ḍamarus and bells, and loudly declares, "Child of good family, I will remove all your obstacles. I will create all favorable conditions." He dissolves into the Guru-Protector on my head, which becomes the real Protector. From his mouth the sounds of *hūṃ phaṭ* reverberate like thunder. All my sickness and spirits in general, and in particular, all harm done to me by planetary and constellation spirits above, tsen and gyalgong spirits in between, and nāgas and earth lord spirits below, are singed like chicken feathers in a fire and burned up. [Protector] chops them up with the blade of his flaying knife and gobbles them down raw in the form of flesh, blood, and bones. Then offering goddesses emanate from my heart and make the offerings: {751}

oṃ guru mahākāla arghaṃ . . . (etc. to) . . . *śabda*, (and from) *rūpa* . . . (etc. to) . . . *spareśa*. (Present the inner offerings with) *oṃ guru mahākāla oṃ āḥ hūṃ*

He enters into union with the emanated goddesses and delights in great bliss.

Benevolent one who abides in great bliss
and who instantly attains it,

guru, with vajra like a precious jewel:
I bow at your lotus feet.

Praise:

Without stirring from the realm of reality,
yet your wrathful form to subdue the vicious
vanquishes the rudra of the doctrine;
homage and praise to Great Black One.

Offer the mandala with "The ground is anointed with perfume . . . (etc.)." Then with intense yearning, supplicate:

Guru-Protector inseparable, I supplicate you. Grant your blessings to accomplish Guru-Protector Inseparable.

Through supplicating three times, light rays radiate from [the guru's] body, which has become the essence of Vajradhara and all the lineage gurus. They strike Protector (Note: it is said to meditate that his color becomes dark green), who blazes with the nature of light and bliss, dancing with the sounds of *ur ur, sil sil*. Light rays radiate from Protector and strike the guru's body. Guru (Note: meditate on the guru's color as yellow-green) becomes the nature of shimmering light and rings the bell. Guru is Protector. Protector is Guru. Guru and Protector are inseparable.

I and all sentient beings throughout the reaches of space
supplicate the precious kind root guru, epitome of the four kāyas.
We supplicate the mighty victor Vajradhara.
We supplicate mighty glorious Śavarīpa.
We supplicate great Venerable Maitrīpa.
We supplicate the great adept Rāhula.
We supplicate the learned adept Khyungpo Naljor. {752}
We supplicate the incomparable Rinchen Tsöndru.
We supplicate the great Öntön Kyergangpa.
We supplicate Nyentön Bepai Naljor.
We supplicate Chöje Sangye Tönpa.

We supplicate great Khedrup Shangtön.
We supplicate Muchen Gyaltsen Palzangpo.
We supplicate Ngakchang Dorje Zhönu.
We supplicate the great Nyame Namkhai Naljor.
We supplicate the great Chöje Tsongkhapa.
We supplicate Khedrup Gelek Palzangpo.
We supplicate Paṇchen Chökyi Gyaltsen.
We supplicate Drupchen Chökyi Dorje.
We supplicate Gyalwa Lozang Döndrup.
We supplicate Khedrup Sangye Yeshe.
We supplicate Paṇchen Lozang Chökyi Gyaltsen.
We supplicate Dorje Dzinpa Könchok Gyaltsen.
We supplicate Kyishö Ngawang Tenzin Trinle.
We supplicate Je Lozang Chöpel.
We supplicate Je Lozang Dargye.
We supplicate Je Lozang Jinpa.
We supplicate Ngawang Chokden.
(Supplement:)
We supplicate Omniscient Rolpai Dorje.
We supplicate Venerable Könchok Dechen.
We supplicate Jamyang Tupten Nyima.
We supplicate Jamgön Döndrup Gyaltsen.
(And:)
We supplicate the benevolent root guru.
We supplicate Six-Armed Awareness Protector.
We supplicate Protector Wish-Fulfilling Gem.
We supplicate Protector Swift-Acting Compassion.
We supplicate Guru-Protector inseparable.
We supplicate Protector-Guru inseparable.

Through supplicating with intense yearning, think that the Protector loudly says, "I will remove all your obstacles. I will create all favorable conditions."

namo buddhāya / namo guruhe / vajra vīra vīriṇe śrīye / ḍāka ḍākinī / joga jogiṇī / sarva buddhāya / bodhisatva śarāṇī / gacchāmi / kyai
(Repeat however many times.)

From the body of Guru-Protector on my head emerge {753} boundless elixir and light rays of the five colors and short, thick-limbed replicas of Protector. (Note: It is said to meditate on this occasion that elixir and multicolored light rays from the body of the guru on the head, and boundless white, red, and blue forms from the Protector's three places arise and dissolve into oneself.) They completely fill my body, and all obstacles of sickness, spirits, negativities, and obscurations are burned away and cleansed. Protector consumes them and they are purified. All qualities of longevity, merit, prosperity, scripture, and realization increase. (Thinking that, say:)

> Holy root and lineage gurus dwelling in the ten directions and three times, bless me! Buddhas and bodhisattvas all, bless me! Yidam deities of the mandala, bless me! Heroes and heroine yoginīs, bless me! Glorious Six-Armed Awareness Protector and deities, do not veil your timeless awareness. Do not block your power and ability. Do not delay your compassion. Do not distance your blessings. All of you, bless me through your unlimited awakened body, speech, mind, qualities, and activities. Bless me right now! Bless me quickly! Bless me on this very seat!
>
> White light rays and countless white bodies of the Protector emerge from the *oṃ* in Protector's head. They enter my forehead. All physical obstacles of sickness, spirits, negativities, and obscurations are purified. I obtain the vase empowerment, which instills the ability to achieve nirmāṇakāya. {754}
>
> Red light rays and countless red bodies of the Protector emerge from the *āḥ* in Protector's throat. They enter my throat. All verbal obstacles of sickness, spirits, negativities, and obscurations are purified. I obtain the secret empowerment, which instills the ability to achieve saṃbhogakāya.
>
> Blue light rays and countless blue bodies of the Protector emerge from the *hūṃ* in Protector's heart. They enter my heart. All mental obstacles of sickness, spirits, negativities, and obscurations are purified. I obtain the wisdom-

awareness empowerment, which instills the ability to achieve dharmakāya.

Again, light rays of five colors and countless Protector's bodies of five colors emerge from his five places. They enter my five places and fill my whole body inside. All physical, verbal, and mental obstacles of sickness, spirits, negativities, and obscurations are purified. I obtain the fourth empowerment, which instills the ability to achieve svabhāvakāya.

Holy root and lineage gurus dwelling in the ten directions and three times, bless me! Buddhas and bodhisattvas all, bless me! Yidam deities of the mandala, bless me! Heroes and heroine yoginīs, bless me! Glorious Six-Armed Awareness Protector and deities, do not veil your timeless awareness. Do not block your power and ability. Do not delay your compassion. Do not distance your blessings. All of you, bless me through your unlimited awakened body, speech, mind, qualities, and activities. Bless me right now! Bless me quickly! Bless me on this very seat!

Especially, come to the center of the eight-petaled lotus in my heart and remain there steadily without leaving until I attain awakening. Please protect me from all terrors of this life, the next, and the intermediate state. {755} Please grant all the supreme and common spiritual powers.

Guru-Protector on my head eradicates Gaṇapati underfoot and says loudly, "Child of a good family, until you attain awakening, I will remove all adverse conditions. I will create all favorable conditions." He enters the cranial aperture to the sound of the mantra while swaying in dance, coming down the central channel and dissolving into the Protector in my heart and into the vajra top ornament of the vase body of the guru. Imagine that the hub of the blue vajra is marked with a yellow letter. From that, light rays like the firelight at the end of time radiate from the mantra string around the letter *hūṃ* upon the sun mandala in Protector's heart. They fill my whole body. All sickness, spirits, negativities, and obscurations are ignited and burned up. My corporeal

> form of flesh and bones suddenly becomes the awakened body of Swift-Acting Six-Armed Awareness Protector.

Say that and stabilize the pride.

> Then the firelight of awareness radiates throughout all the billionfold universe. All sentient beings change into the form of the Awareness Protector. The sound of the mantra resounds:
>
> *oṃ śrī mahākāla śāsana / upahāriṇi / eṣo 'paścima kālo ayaṃ / idaṃ ratna trayāya / apakāriṇaṃ / yadi pratijñā/ smarasi tadā / idaṃ duṣṭaṃ kha kha khāhi khāhi / māra māra / gṛhṇa gṛhṇa / bandha bandha / hana hana / daha daha / paca paca / dīnamekena / māraya hūṃ hūṃ phaṭ phaṭ svāhā*

Recite that as much as you can. {756} Afterward, repeat this three or seven or more times:

> Guru-Protector inseparable,
> I go for refuge in you with faith:
> may I dispel every affliction
> of myself and all sentient beings.
>
> Protector-Guru inseparable,
> I go for refuge in you with faith:
> may I remove every obstacle
> of myself and all sentient beings.

During the regular mantra recitation (Note: including the śāsana mantra), it is good to focus the visualization on the mantra circling in the heart of Protector at your heart while reciting (and to do the vajra recitation as usual). And it is said to be excellent to present torma and offerings and so forth to the Protector in the heart.

If you do this practice diligently, the immediate results are that any sickness, spirit, or obstacle will not take hold and longevity, merit, prosperity, Holy Dharma teachings and practice, and so on will increase. Since this is the most sublime method of keeping the protection of Guru-Protector inseparable constantly present in this life, the next, and in the intermediate state, it is important to do the practice while keeping it secret from others. The details should be learned directly from the guru, (as is clarified in these notes).

Concluding Words

Through meditating with single focus and supplicating with belief
that the sublime deity will spontaneously achieve the two purposes,
one who sincerely trusts in that is a fortunate one.
By whatever virtue was attained from striving at this,
the pure white excellence like moonbeams without clouds,
may I be held by Guru-Protector inseparable in life after life
and may the Victor's doctrine flourish.

This extremely profound uncommon yoga of Guru-Protector Inseparable [was written] exactly as it was understood from the mouth of my guru. Since it was arranged in an easily read and understood format by the awareness holder Changkya Rolpai Dorje,[2] {757} keep it secret from those who have not received authorization and from unsuitable recipients. May this increase the doctrine. *maṅgalaṃ*

In addition to this manual, the continuous guidance with the reading transmission was received by Khyentse Wangpo at the great monastic center of Tashi Lhunpo from Kachen Lozang Gelek.[3]

39. Clouds of Virtue and Goodness

The Investiture of Power for Deep-Blue and White Swift-Acting Awareness Protectors[1]

Jamgön Kongtrul

oṃ svasti siddhaṃ

[Deep-Blue Protector]

To offer the investiture of power to Vajra Six-Armed Awareness Protector, arrange a big ornamented torma and whatever offering items you have gathered, such as medicine, first offerings, and so on. To consecrate them, cleanse with *vajra amṛta* . . . (etc.) and purify with *svabhāva* . . . (etc.).

> From within emptiness, *yaṃ* becomes wind, *raṃ* becomes fire, and *kaṃ* becomes three hearth skulls. Upon that, from *A*, the vast and wide perfect skull cup contains the five meats arising from *brūṃ*, *āṃ*, *jriṃ*, *kha*, and *hūṃ*, and the five elixirs from *lāṃ*, *māṃ*, *bāṃ*, *tāṃ*, and *pāṃ*. In the space above them is stacked a white *oṃ*, a moon from *A*, and a vajra from *hūṃ*. Wind stirs, fire blazes, and the five meats and five elixirs melt into light. A stream of elixir flows from the three seed syllables. Their light invokes the three vajras of all buddhas to dissolve into them. The *oṃ*, moon, and vajra also melt into light and dissolve [into the skull cup]. Its contents become an ocean of elixir imbued with inexhaustible color, smell, taste, power, and potency, and the supports fulfilling all requirements. The unimaginable sacred substances expand and fill all the realms of all worlds.

oṃ āḥ hūṃ (Repeat three times.)

Recite the following with melody and music.

Arise! Arise! Arise from the realm of phenomena.
Without moving from within the pure phenomenal realm,
you display the wrathful form to subdue the wicked: {761}
Swift-Acting Protector, come here to accept offerings.

Amid an expanse of awareness fire like that of the end-times,
with skillful means you display a wrathful form,
great warrior who vanquishes unruly devil hordes:
Swift-Acting Avalokiteśvara—power to you!

With constant all-encompassing compassion for migrators,
in total serenity yet your form is sublimely fierce,
dark as clouds of the end-times or blue eye tincture:
terrifying lord of blood drinkers—power to you!

In mirth, your loud vajra laughter bursts the hearts
and confounds the brains of devils and death lords;
vicious gods and demigods with claws are brought down:
chief of the unbearably savage—power to you!

All victors' great love filling the ten directions of space
is subsumed in Avalokiteśvara
as supremely blessed Protector who grants all powers:
swift accomplisher of activity—power to you!

Gaping mouth, bared teeth, and three eyes blazing like fire,
beard, eyebrows, and hair blazing upward,
adorned by eight great nāgas and strings of bells:
Six-Armed Awareness Protector—power to you! {762}

With jeweled crown and garland of bleeding heads,
right hands holding a flaying knife, skull rosary, and rattling a drum;
left hands holding a skull, trident, and lasso:
beautiful in a tiger-skin robe—power to you!

Reveling upon the errant one with various dance postures
such as even-footed, left extended, or a champion's pose,
standing on a lotus-sun seat before the sandalwood tree support:
Mahākāla—power to you!

Tapping your toenail on the ground, the earth quakes;
uttering *hūṃ*, the mountains crack and the oceans heave;
a wink of your eye banishes all obstacles:
powerful one of unrestrained might—power to you!

Precious guru, all buddhas in actuality, takes the form
of an obedient protector to guard against obstacles,
watching over practitioners as your own child:
Guru-Protector inseparable—power to you!

Essence of Vajrasattva, purifying all obscurations,
on your brow, the shape of a source of phenomena
in a vermilion drop is the One Mother Yoginī:
birth mother of all things in existence and transcendence—power to you!

In the drop's center, *hrīḥ* is glorious World Protector,
commanding the three realms, emanating ḍākinīs
who magnetize with the sublime secret mantra of thirteen letters:
essence of Exalted Tārā—power to you!

Mighty Akṣobhya sits as lord of the family,
conqueror Yamāntaka bestows strength and power:
I pay homage and go for refuge with all my heart,
and I always supplicate you—grant your blessings.

Outer, inner, and secret substances of support, fulfillment, and accomplishment,
offerings of medicine, rakta, torma, and feasts,
real and mentally emanated, filling the realms of the world:
Awareness Protector and retinue—power to you!

Bless me to be free of obstacles to practice.
Bless me to realize all things as illusion.
Bless me with the arising of self-liberating dreams.
Bless me with the arising of inner heat's great bliss.
Bless me to realize the lucid clarity of mahāmudrā.
Bless me to attain buddhahood in this lifetime.
Bless me to dispel fears of the intermediate state. {763}
Bless me to attain saṃbhogakāya in the intermediate state.
Bless me with pacification of all adverse conditions.
Bless me with attainment of all favorable conditions.
Bless me so that our minds become one.
Grant your blessings to spread the Buddha's teaching.

hūṃ
Power to the guru, the real Vajradhara,
inseparable from the Protector.
Power to the sublime yidam,
the essence of Avalokiteśvara.
Power to the perfect Buddha
who manifests the four kāyas.
Power to the great masters
of all Mahayana Holy Dharma.
Power to the great leaders
of the noble assembly of sangha.
Power to the great dharma protectors
who guard the mighty Sage's doctrine.
Power to the Great Excellent One,
chief of the great gods.
Power to the Great Black One,
who controls wrathful actions.
Power to the great guardians
of all Secret Mantra awareness holders.
Power to the great warrior gods
of yogins who hold sacred pledges.
Power to the protectors and refuges
of all of us and our entourages.

Guard the doctrine of the mighty Sage!
Perform activity for me, the yogin!
Avert misfortune, accomplish favorable conditions.
Perform the purpose of your power investiture!

Glorious Swift-Acting Awareness Protector and retinue—I supplicate you! I offer to you! Great Black Vajra, one with glorious Heruka within the nature of phenomena—identical in timeless awareness. In characteristics, you are equal in impartial awakened activity. You are the warrior who vanquishes adverse conditions everywhere, lord over all gods and demons in apparent existence, commander over obedient wrathful field protectors, king of invincible vajra charisma, parental guardian of mighty awareness holders, watcher over the meditation success of avowed practitioners. You are endowed with the countenance of peace, the resplendence of enrichment, the masterful energy of magnetizing, and the fast actions of wrathfully liberating enemies and obstructors. You display the dynamic energy of a doctrine guard. {764}

Mighty one of power and strength, field protector, Vajra Black Six-Armed One; Glorious Goddess Rematī, Yakṣa Kṣetrapāla, Yama Ṭakkirāja, Īśvara Jinamitra, devil lord Black Trakṣad, ten great direction protectors, seventy-five protectors of the pure regions, armies of an ocean of the obedient oath-bound, and your retinues—I supplicate you! I offer to you! I invest you with power!

Accept this donation of vast offering torma. For this yogin, be my sacred guide to eliminate all obstacles and fears of the four devils as I travel the path to awakening and the Sukhāvatī pure land. Be my escort who welcomes me with meditative absorption when meeting the genuine path. Until I attain awakening, do not let me go down the wrong path in my body, speech, or mind, but guide my thoughts toward the path of awakening and emancipation. Once I have obtained all the supreme and common spiritual powers, may I become the protector and glory of all migrators. At all times and circumstances, please perform all the actions of the four awakened activities exactly according to the intent of my requests. Please pacify my sicknesses, bad spirits, negative actions, obscurations, and the eight fears. Please increase the six kinds of fortune[2] and longevity, merit, prosperity, renown, enjoyments, and so forth. Please bring gods, demons, and humans of the three realms under control through the four admirations.[3] Please quell and terminate all kinds of calamities—such as curses, ritual daggers, inciting sorcery—and the hosts of enemies, spirits, and obstructors. In short, do not abandon your compassion for me for a moment in all my lives and bless me to spontaneously accomplish the two purposes.

[White Protector Wish-Fulfilling Gem]

To offer the investiture of power to White Protector Wish-Fulfilling Gem, prepare clean and pure torma, first offerings, and abundant offerings. Cleanse and purify [with the mantras]. {765}

From within emptiness, *yaṃ* becomes wind and *raṃ* becomes fire. Above that, from *A*, the vast and wide perfect skull cup contains the five meats marked with *brūṃ*, *āṃ*, *jriṃ*, *kha*, and *hūṃ*, and the five elixirs [marked with *lāṃ*, *māṃ*, *bāṃ*, *tāṃ*, and *pāṃ*]. Wind stirs, fire blazes, and the ten ingredients with their letters melt. Elixir from the hearts of all buddhas is invoked and dissolves [into the skull cup], filling it with a great ocean of the elixir of awareness.

oṃ āḥ hūṃ ha ho hrīḥ (Repeat three times to consecrate.)

hūṃ
Compassionate Protector Wish-Fulfilling Gem,
white as a snow mountain, radiating light,
you relieve all the poverty of migrators,
and grant the power of fulfilled desires—approach and accept offerings.

Like Mount Kailash, you are massive and dense,
wreathed by particles of a million light rays,

master of a thousand magnetizing ḍākinīs:
Swift-Acting Avalokiteśvara—power to you!

Your smiling resplendent facade is slightly wrathful,
you bring rains of desires and needs, king of power,
your original mind in the vital drop of phenomenal nature
manifests as the form of timeless awareness—power to you!

Born from a *hūṃ* letter with the luster of quicksilver,
you fulfill the hopes of living beings and relieve poverty's pain.
King Akṣobhya above your bristling hair
seals and confers great empowerment—power to you!

Like dawn on the freshly snowed mountain,
your brow is beautified by a drop of vermilion,
your six arms jingling with jeweled bracelets and armlets,
essence of supreme transcendent perfections—power to you!

You hold flaying knife, wish-fulfilling gem, ḍamaru,
gem-filled vase in a skull cup, trident, and hook
for capturing the spiritual powers:
Six-Armed Awareness Protector—power to you!

With flowing silks and tiger-skin clothes,
radiant lights and precious ornaments tinkling,
beautified by draped clusters of many gems,
blazing with resplendent brilliance—power to you! {766}

You stand playing upon Vināyaka,
who rains down a wealth of desirables,
joyful in your grove of verdant sandalwood trees:
master of ḍākinīs of three regions—power to you!

Youthful goddess of power at your heart,
like new light rays at dawn or lightning garlands,
gorgeous and moving, holding the hook of spiritual powers,
she magnetizes the three existences—power to you!

With this investiture, praise, supplication,
and heartfelt devotion to you, sublime deity,
I offer this investiture; now grant me supreme powers
and accomplishment of all desired goals and glory.

The rainfall of virtue and goodness from your compassionate activity
swells the rolling sets of waves of desires and needs.
May the ocean of prosperity forever increase,
bringing food, wealth, virtue, and goodness.

I supplicate you. I offer to you.
Wish-Fulfilling Gem of Swift-Acting Awareness: just recalling you protects me from the sufferings of this life, the next, and the intermediate state. Just supplicating you causes a rainfall of the powers of desires and needs. With your hosts of billions of ḍākinīs of the three places, I supplicate you. I offer to you. Power to you!

I offer special offerings of actual and mentally emanated gifts that fill the earth and sky and space to the Guru-Protector inseparable, and meditate with undivided trust and devotion in that great bliss of phenomena's nature. May these unsurpassable offering clouds delight and please you. With great affection for me, the practitioner, like a mother's for her only child, watch over me constantly until I attain awakening. In the immediate situation, please accomplish the conducive conditions for dharma practice, such as longevity, merit, glory, power, food, wealth, possessions, fame, and influence—always expanding and flourishing without diminishing. Please grant me the supreme gift of unhindered control of the three realms, the three existences, and all the vital essence of the animate and inanimate. {767} Ultimately, be my guide on the path to the Sukhāvatī pure land and carry me to liberation from cyclic existence. Please bless me to readily attain the state of Protector Lokeśvara, the Lord of Compassion.

Offer the torma to the sky accompanied by the sound of music.

[Colophon]

Seeing that this was suitable to add during offering rituals, such as the Great Burnt Offering Ritual for Encampment, I used the teachings of the great Venerable Jonang Tāranātha and others endowed with blessings, changing section endings of the lines to those for investiture of power and making them easy to recite. I, Karma Ngawang Yönten Gyatso, wrote this at Palpung's remote retreat of Vajra Devīkoṭi, the pleasure grove where the Awareness Protector enjoys himself in play.

sarva maṅgalaṃ bhavantu

40. Ritual for Conferring the Uncommon Authorization of the Great Field Protector Kṣetrapāla Father-Mother[1]

Jamgön Kongtrul

namo mahākālaye

This is the uncommon authorization for the great protector of the fields, Kṣetrapāla father-mother, the very wrathful emanation of Swift-Acting Awareness Protector. To proceed, on a platform make a triangular source of phenomena that is black outside and red inside. Within that, place two black heaps. On that, put a mañji; at its opening, place two three-cornered tormas filled with flesh and blood and decorated with black silk. In front of that, carefully arrange two three-cornered offering tormas and offering substances made serviceable by the smoke of frankincense and human flesh.[2] Visualize yourself as sole Protector and perform the recitation, offerings, and praises. After that, consecrate the offerings and tormas in front with cleansing and purifying. Cleanse and purify the two tormas.

> From within emptiness, in the midst of countless yakṣas, *kṣeṃ* becomes Kṣetrapāla, dark as storm clouds with a touch of red. With his right hand he brandishes a flaying knife to the sky, terrifying all the eight classes of gods and spirits. With his left hand he holds at his heart a skull cup filled with the hearts of enemies, from which he drinks. His two legs are spread apart as he rides a crazed black bear. He wears a black silk loin cloth. He glares at enemy obstructors with his three red, round eyes. His frowning wrinkles and eyebrows are intensely contorted and his mouth is wide open, his tongue darting like lightning, his four-plus-

four sharp fangs bared, and blood frothing from his mouth. The great wind of the end-times blows from his nose. He is fat and short with thick limbs. He has a big household escort. His tawny dreadlocks blaze upward like fire.

To his left, in the midst of boundless mātṛkās and ḍākinīs, *bhyoḥ* becomes the black goddess Kālarātri with a raven's head. {771} She wears a long black cloak. With her copper-clawed hands she holds a bag of pestilence in the right and waves a lance with the left. She is wholly wrathful, laughing with terrifying sounds, and moving around naked. Her bloodshot eyes dart like lightning. In an instant she reduces enemies and obstructors to dust.

These two have white *oṃ* at their heads, red *āḥ* at their throats, and blue *hūṃ* at their hearts. Light rays radiate from the [*hūṃ*s] and instantly invoke Yakṣa Kṣetrapāla father-mother and their retinues from the Cool Grove Charnel Ground in the southeast.

e hye hi ja jaḥ hūṃ vaṃ hoḥ—they become indivisible with the pledge beings.

Offer with *oṃ kṣetrapāla saparivara arghaṃ* . . . (etc. to) . . . *śabda*. Present the inner offering. To the end of the essence mantra add *balimta kha kha khāhi khāhi* and offer the torma. Praise with "You are the chief of Protector's attendants . . ." (*mgon po'i bka' nyan kun gyi gtso bo khyod* . . . etc.). Think that both father and mother Kṣetrapāla look up to you, appearing as the protector, and obey. Visualize that with the recitation.

oṃ kṣetrapāla vighnān hūṃ phaṭ / oṃ mahākāla yakṣa dam nyams dgra bgegs kyi citta la dun dun rbad[3]

For the mother:

rakmo nakmo dam nyams kyi citta la rbad kha la phur ya svāhā

Recite however much, then do the offerings and praises. Supplicate for the sake of the disciples. For the main part of the authorization, the disciples prostrate and offer a mandala. Then they supplicate three times:

Guru, great Awareness Protector,
at this time please consider me.
Please grant me the permission entrustment
by the wrathful field protector, father-mother.

In the space before you, visualize the Guru-Protector with retinue. Do the regular confession. Then the special supplication three times:

> Precious guru, in order to guard the Buddha's doctrine, please grant me all the authorizations of Kṣetrapāla father-mother—yakṣa wealth lord, {772} chief of all butchers, captain of all cannibals.

Visualize the disciples as [sole] protectors and the Kṣetrapāla couple in front.

> Light radiates from the guru's heart and evokes the mind stream of the front visualization. From their hearts, countless yakṣas arise and dissolve into the zhapkyu of the *hūṃ* in the disciples' hearts.

Circulate smoke of human flesh and frankincense. Accompanied by music, say *avēśya jaḥ hūṃ vaṃ hoḥ* at the end of the essence mantra. Repeating that again and again is the authorization of awakened body.

> Again, from the master's heart light rays arise (as before except) unimaginable mantra strings arise from the Kṣetrapāla couple's mouths and dissolve into the zhapkyu of the *hūṃ* . . . (etc. as before) . . . the authorization for awakened speech.
>
> Again, from the master's heart light rays radiate . . . (etc. as in the body authorization except that) the Kṣetrapāla couple comes above the disciples' heads. From the master's heart the big brilliant form of the protector arrives. He plants his feet on the heads of the disciples and the Yakṣa couple and remains there. Your strong respect and devotion causes infinite light rays to emerge from their bodies and pervade everywhere, removing all

> obstacles. You obtain all magical abilities. At the end, they melt into light and dissolve into the disciples.

Light incense and play music as before. Give the flaying knife, blood-filled skull cup, and lance standard while reciting the essence mantra.

> This is the authorization of awakened mind. Imagine that the guru visualized as this protector takes [the implements] from the two hands of the Yakṣa mother and places them in the disciples' hands. {774}

Place two tormas in the disciples' hands and repeat the exhortation three times:

> Without contradicting the gurus' names and Awareness Protector's commands and vows, accompany these vajra disciples until their awakening! Dispel all adverse conditions! Accomplish all awakened activities!

Recite verses of auspiciousness. Perform the usual offerings and praises in gratitude.

These three authorizations [of awakened body, speech, and mind] exist only as word lineages from Omniscient Khedrup to my own root guru. Due to the fact that the words of the authorization have not remained very clear other than in a few places, I supplicated the Guru-Protector and wrote this based on what my guru gave me, adding just a little from others, in order to arrange a clear version. Guru-Protector, please forbear.

sarvadā maṅgalaṃ

Abbreviations

BA	George N. Roerich, *The Blue Annals.* 1949. 2nd ed. Delhi: Motilal Banarsidass, 1976/1988.
BDRC	Buddhist Digital Resource Center. Online catalog at www.bdrc.io.
Catalog	Jamgön Kongtrul Lodrö Taye, *The Catalog of The Treasury of Precious Instructions. DNZ*, vol. 18. Delhi: Shechen Publications, 1999. Translated by Richard Barron. New York: Tsadra Foundation, 2013.
CT	Collated Tengyur (bsTan 'gyur dpe bsdur ma). 120 vols. Beijing: Krung go'i bod rig pa'i dpe skrun khang, 1994–2008. Available at www.bdrc.io.
Dg.K.	Derge Kangyur (sDe dge bka' 'gyur): xylograph edition. 103 vols. Edited by Situ Chökyi Jungne.
Dg.T.	Derge Tengyur (sDe dge bstan 'gyur): xylograph edition. 213 vols. Edited by Zhuchen Tsultrim Rinchen.
DNZ	Jamgön Kongtrul Lodrö Taye, *gDams ngag rin po che'i mdzod* (*The Treasury of Precious Instructions*). 18 vols. Shechen printing. Delhi: Shechen Publications, 1999.
Skt.	Sanskrit
ST	*Shangpa Texts: Indian Source Texts of the Dharma Cycle of Five Golden Dharmas of the Glorious Shangpa.* Edited by Karma Rangjung Kunkhyap (Kalu Rinpoche). 11 vols. Sonada, India: Samdrup Darje Ling Monastery, n.d. Based on the Palpung edition. Reprinted by Lama Tsengyur Rinpoche. Vancouver: Kagyu Kunkhyab Chuling, 1982.
Tib.	Tibetan
Toh.	*A Complete Catalogue of the Tibetan Buddhist Canons*, edited by Hakuju Ui et al. Sendai, Japan: Tohoku University, 1934.
TOK	Jamgön Kongtrul Lodrö Taye, *Shes bya kun khyab* (*The Treasury of Knowledge*). 3 vols. Lhasa: Mi rigs dpe skrun khang, 1982.
TTG-S.	*Supplemental Text to the Collected Works of Thang-stong-rgyal po. Grub chen thang stong bka' 'bum gyi rgyab chos ni gu chos drug pod dang pa.* 1 vol. Thimphu: Royal Government of Bhutan Publishing House. dPal ldan 'brug gzhung dpe mdzod khang, 1984.

ch.	chapter
f., ff.	(Tibetan) folio, folios
n	note
p., pp.	page, pages
vol., vols.	volume, volumes

Notes

Series Introduction

1. 'Jam dbyangs mkhyen brtse dbang po (1820–1892), mChog 'gyur bDe chen gling pa (1829–1870), Mi pham rgya mtsho (1846–1912), and many more masters were involved in this movement, including Kongtrul's guru Si tu Pad ma nyin byed (1774–1853). See E. Gene Smith, "'Jam mgon Kong sprul and His Friends," in *Among Tibetan Texts*, pp. 247–50; Jamgön Kongtrul, *Treasury of Knowledge, Book 8, Part 4: Esoteric Instructions*, pp. 25–48; Ringu Tulku, *Ri-me Philosophy of Jamgön Kongtrul the Great*, etc.
2. The specific text by Shes rab 'od zer that expounds the eight chariots is *Meditation's Ambrosia of Immortality* (*sGom pa 'chi med kyi bdud rtsi*). A study of this has been done by Marc-Henri Deroche: "'Phreng po gter ston Shes rab 'od zer (1518–1584) on the Eight Lineages of Attainment." According to Deroche, "This text may be considered as an (if not the) original source of the '*ris med* paradigm' of the eight lineages of attainment" (p. 17). It is interesting to note that the eight lineages are arranged in a different sequence in that text—Nyingma, Kadampa, Shangpa Kagyu, Lamdre, Marpa Kagyu, Zhije, Jordruk, Dorje Sumgyi Nyendrup—which may have been more chronological than Kongtrul's preferred order.
3. One finds this idea developed in the volume on esoteric instructions in *The Treasury of Knowledge*, where Kongtrul describes in incredibly condensed detail the basic principles and sources of these eight lineages. It is expounded in the catalog of *The Treasury of Precious Instructions* (*DNZ*, vol. 18), published in English as *The Catalog of The Treasury of Precious Instructions*, trans. Richard Barron (Chökyi Nyima). Also see Stearns, *Luminous Lives*, pp. 3–8.
4. Jamgön Kongtrul Lodrö Taye, *Catalog*, p. 21. Translation by Richard Barron.
5. *The Treasury of Precious Instructions. gDams ngag rin po che'i mdzod* (*DNZ*), 12 vols. (Delhi: N. Lungtok and N. Gyaltsan, 1971–1972). Known as the Kundeling printing.

6. *The Treasury of Precious Instructions. gDams ngag rin po che'i mdzod* (*DNZ*), 18 vols. (Delhi: Shechen Publications, 1998). Known as the Shechen printing.

Translator's Introduction

1. From his biography, we know only that he was born in a Tiger year, which occurs every twelve years. This is traditionally put at the years 978 or 990 (Kapstein, "Chronological Conundrums," 1). The tradition maintains that he lived for 150 years, a feat easy for Tibetans to accept. However, this birth date is too early to account for some of the events in his life. Matthew Kapstein has carefully calculated various scraps of information to come to 1050–1140 as viable dates. However, this still does not explain certain crucial events, such as his meeting with Atiśa at Toling Monastery. See Kapstein, "Chronological Conundrums in the Life of Khyung po rnal 'byor: Hagiography and Historical Time."
2. *ST*, vol. 9, pp. 44–46. Aside from the regular biography in the *Golden Rosary of Shangpa Biographies*, Kongtrul also mentions (p. 51) a possible biography known as *The Paper Scroll* (*Shog ril ma*), which would be a fabulous find.
3. "Supplementary Historical Anecdotes," in Jamgön Kongtrul, *The Treasury of Precious Instructions, Volume 18: Jonang*, p. 192. Translated by Gyurme Dorje, and retaining his style.
4. For Jamgön Kongtrul's brief summary of his received teachings, see *The Treasury of Knowledge, Books 2–4: Buddhism's Journey to Tibet*, pp. 351–52 (in Tibetan, *TOK*, vol. 1, pp. 533–34), or find them listed in his biography.
5. In present-day China, Zhang Zhong is Nanmuling xian, just east of the county seat, along the Shang River. The nearest big town is Shigatze.
6. Smith, *Among Tibetan Texts*, p. 54. These names transliterated are rMe'u ston, G.yor po rGya mo che, rNgul ston Rin dbang, La stod pa dKon mchog mkhar, Zhang sgom Chos seng, and rMog lcog pa Rin chen brtson 'grus.
7. Ibid., p. 54.
8. See note 1 above.
9. *[Questions Concerning] the Instructions of Glorious Niguma, Mighty Khecarī*, in *Collected Works*, vol. 2, pp. 612–14.
10. For instance, in the lineage of the Navel Emanation Chakra, a teaching that is found in this volume. See *The Treasury of Precious Instructions, Volume 18: Jonang*, 88–89.
11. *TOK*, vol. 1, p. 536.
12. *The Treasury of Precious Instructions, Volume 18: Jonang*, 192. *The Inventory Clarifying the Six Dharmas* by Khyungpo Naljor is translated in ch. 1 of *The Treasury of Precious Instructions, Volume 11: Shangpa Kagyu.*
13. Smith, *Among Tibetan Texts*, pp. 54–55.
14. Kunga Drolchok, "An Autobiographical Record," in *The Treasury of Precious Instructions, Volume 18: Jonang*, p. 148.
15. Texts by Tangtong Gyalpo are in the second section of this volume. Also there

is good information about his encounters with Niguma in Stearns, *King of the Empty Plain*.

16. Kongtrul, *Catalog*, pp. 149–50. In *DNZ*, vol. 18, p. 512 (f. 66b).
17. *De nyid 'dus pa*, published as *Encyclopedia Tibetica* by Tibet House in 137 volumes. The Shangpa sections can be found in vols. 57, 93, and 103.
18. In addition to minor inclusions in several scholarly publications, some of the practice texts contained herein were recently translated by Ngawang Zangpo for three-year retreat in the Shangpa tradition. Those remain unpublished and restricted. Bits of translation by Sherap Drime and much accessible information can be learned from the Shangpa Foundation website: www.shangpafoundation.org.
19. Sarah Harding, trans., *Four Tibetan Lineages: Core Teachings of Pacification, Severance, Shangpa Kagyü, and Bodongpa* (Boston: Wisdom, 2021).
20. This was previously translated by Ngawang Zangpo in the book *Timeless Rapture: Inspired Verse of the Shangpa Masters* (Ithaca, NY: Snow Lion, 2003), pp. 37–217.

Tāranātha's Commentaries on the Six Dharmas of Niguma: Introduction

1. Information on Tāranātha's life is taken mainly from Cyrus Stearns in The Treasury of Lives, https://treasuryoflives.org/biographies/view/Taranata/2712, accessed 12/7/21.
2. See Losal Tenkyong's compositions of the Shangpa empowerment liturgies and my introduction to them in *The Treasury of Precious Instructions, Volume 11: Shangpa Kagyu*, pp. 455–627.
3. *Autobiography of Jamgön Kongtrul*, p. 144.
4. All the source texts attributed to Niguma in the Peking and Narthang Tengyurs are translated in Harding, *Niguma, Lady of Illusion*.
5. *sKyes bu gsum gyi man ngag gi khrid yig bdud rtsi'i nying khu*, *DNZ*, vol. 3, pp. 181–273. Translated by Willa Baker as *Essence of Ambrosia: A Guide to Buddhist Contemplations*. It will appear in *The Treasury of Precious Instructions, Volume 3*, translated by Artemis Engle, forthcoming from Shambhala Publications.
6. *Channel Chakras of One's Body* (P 4649); *Meditation on Channels, Winds, and Such* (P 4646); *Opening the Channels* (P 4645); *Inner Heat in the Path of Methods* (P 4647); *Yoga of Meditation in the Path of Methods* (P 4646). See Harding, *Niguma, Lady of Illusion*, pp. 183–92, for translations, introduction, and annotations.
7. *The Beryl Key*, *ST*, vol. 6, p. 118.

1. *Tangdalma*: Displaying the Profound Meaning

1. *Zab lam ni gu chos drug gi khrid yig zab don thang mar brdal ba zhes bya ba bklags chog ma*, *DNZ*, vol. 12, pp. 1–101; *ST*, vol. 3, pp. 335–512; *Tāranātha's Collected Works*, vol. 12, pp. 825–955. Previously translated in Harding, *Four Tibetan Lineages*, pp. 343–423. The title is sometimes translated literally as *Profound Meaning That Covers the Plains* or something similar.
2. The first line is in Mokchokpa et al., *A Brief Life Story of Lama Khyungpo Naljor*, *ST*, vol. 1, p. 92. The second line appears previous to that on p. 91.
3. Amogavajra's entire prophecy concerning Khyungpo Naljor is in Mokchokpa et al., *A Brief Life Story of Lama Khyungpo Naljor*, *ST*, vol. 1, pp. 61–62. However, there are the following differences: Khyungpo's body is Cakrasaṃvara, speech is Mahāmāya, mind is Hevajra, emanation site (chakra) is Guhyasamāja, and bliss-holding secret site is Vajrabhairava. Amoga further states that even his disciples will be able to see this manifestation of his form.
4. Tāranātha, *Essence of Ambrosia: A Guidance Manual of Instructions for the Three Types of Person*. *DNZ*, vol. 3, pp. 181–273; *ST*, vol. 6, pp. 437–703. Known for short as *Kyebu Sumkyi Lamrim*. Translated by Willa Baker in *Essence of Ambrosia*, 2005.
5. In most editions of this and other texts in *DNZ*, *ST*, and *TTG-S*, the name of this visualization is written as *me rgod* and has been known as "wildfire visualization." However, it sometimes appears as *me rgong* or *me gong*, "fireball." Considering the details of the actual visualization, that name seems to make more sense.
6. *me thab drug chings*. In this stabilizing position, the legs form two triangles and the arms form another four triangles. See Roberts, *Mahāmudrā and Related Instructions*, p. 617.
7. These are five yogic exercises, or *trulkhor* (*'khrul 'khor*), for cleansing the channels (*rtsa khrus yan lag lnga sbyongs*) as preparation for the main exercises in Niguma's Six Dharmas.
8. *gtsubs shing dang gtsubs stan ma*: the example of making fire with flint is used as a name for a particular yogic exercise involving rotation of the torso.
9. Jakpa Gyaltsen Bum (1261–1334) was a disciple of Khedrup Shangtön (1234–1309). They coauthored *Collection of Essential Directives on the Six Dharmas of Niguma*, *ST*, vol. 8, pp. 311–68. But other commentaries on Niguma's Six Dharmas are attributed to him in the *Drepung Catalog* that may be the source reference here.
10. *The Vajra Lines of the Six Dharmas*, *DNZ*, vol. 11, p. 3.
11. *mkhal khung*: the "kidney beds," which lie about an inch (*tshon gang*) to the right and to the left of the fourteenth vertebra and are visible as small depressions when standing, according to the *Great Dictionary of Tibetan Medicine*.
12. See Khyungpo Naljor's *Clarification of the Six Dharmas* in *DNZ*, vol. 11, for his early list of five main and two concluding practices of Inner Heat.
13. rDo rje bdan pa in Tibetan. Although at least four people had this title of "the

one at the Vajra Seat" (or abbot of Bodhgaya), this would seem to be Khyungpo Naljor's guru Puṇyākaragupta. Another option would be Abhayākaragupta. See Harding, *Niguma, Lady of Illusion*, pp. 268–69n120.

14. Sangye Langripa, a.k.a. Langri Tangpa Dorje Senge (1054–1123), an exemplary Kadampa teacher most famous for his instructions on mind training.
15. This quotation was not found in the collected works of Zhönu Drup.
16. Mokchokpa Rinchen Tsöndru (1110–1170), the principal lineage holder after Khyungpo Naljor.
17. *'dun pa gsum*: explained below as meditating with intentionality on death and impermanence, devotion to the guru, and the unreal, illusory-like nature of whatever arises.
18. *Thems yig*. This is the common name for Khyungpo Naljor's *The Inventory Clarifying the Six Dharmas* (*DNZ*, vol. 11, pp. 6–10). *The Inventory* is an outline of the number of supplications in each practice, but unlike here, there are only two supplications for those of lesser capability.
19. Dharmakīrti, *Commentary on Valid Cognition*, Toh. 4210, *tshad grub*, v. 254, f. 117a5.
20. The way the stages of this visualization are correlated with the four empowerments is described later in Tangtong Gyalpo, *Collection of Essentials*, or an alternative interpretation in the following section on the nine infallible vital points.
21. Samdingpa, or Khetsun Zhönu Drup (d. 1319), was seated at Samding Monastery and authored *Guidance on Nigu's Six Dharmas*, *ST*, vol. 7, pp. 545–59.
22. "Jak" is Jakpa Gyaltsen Bum and "Sam" is Khetsun Zhönu Drup (see previous note). "Serlingpa" was his student Tashi Pal (1292–1365), who was born at Serling (gSer gling) in Yolphu. (Not to be confused with the Indian Dharmakīrti.) His relevant text not yet located.
23. *'Byams gcod nyer mkho zhal shes ma*. Apparently by Gyaltsen Bum, but not located. An outline on the teachings on severing excessive diffusion is in *ST*, vol. 8, pp. 722–24.
24. The order of the outline has been adjusted to match the actual order of the instructions here. Tāranātha explains in the last paragraph of the section that the order of the second and third instructions were reversed in the old books, and so apparently he left that order in the outline.
25. *gSang 'dus rim lnga*. There are numerous commentaries on the five stages of completion-phase practice of the *Secret Assembly Tantra* (*Guhyasamāja*), including by Nāgārjuna, Nāropa, Jñānapada, Serdingpa, and Tsongkhapa, to name a few. See, for instance, Jamgön Kongtrul, *The Treasury of Knowledge, Book 8, Part 3: The Elements of Tantric Practice*, pp. 137–52.
26. For example, Marpa's presentation of the "three cycles of blending" (*bsre ba'i skor gsum*) in *Esoteric Instructions on Blending* (*bSre ba'i man ngag*) in Mar pa'i bKa' 'bum, *kha*, in *'Bri gung bka' brgyud chos mdzod chen mo*, vol. 6, f. 131a–136b.
27. This refers to the third of the Five Golden Dharmas of the Glorious Shangpa: concerning the Three Integrations on the Path. The exact quotation was not located.

28. The first one, (1) Dispelling Sickness and Spirits, is already session 4. The last two in Illusory Body (2) would be the Sixfold Set of Qualities That Develop and (3) the Natural Arising of Illusion Free of Attachment, follow session 18. (4) Ultimate Lucid Clarity follows session 50. The five concluding parts of Lucid Clarity are (5) general and specific sacred pledges, (6) Removing Obstructions, the Self-Purification of Faults and Mistakes, (7) Enhancement Practices That Resolve Doubt, (8) Identifying Special Perceptions, and (9) Divisions of Daytime and Nighttime, Experiences and Realizations. These follow session 50. The Transference practices in the first intermediate state are (10) Transference in the Suchness of Dharmakāya (in the Transference section) and (11) the Natural Arising of Dharmakāya in the Lucid Clarity of the First Intermediate State (in the Intermediate State section.) These last must be counted as two, if we are to reach a total of sixty-seven (despite the first, which already is a session).
29. *bka' bcu*: These permission empowerments organized by Losal Tenkyong in 1849 and apparently based on teachings of Ngawang Chödrak (1572–1641) are in *DNZ*, vol. 11, pp. 373–449, translated in *The Treasury of Precious Instructions, Volume 11: Shangpa Kagyu*, ch. 23. The two permissions that open the door to blessings are (1) the empowerment of Five-Deity Cakrasaṃvara (which is not presented) and (2) Five-Deity Cakrasaṃvara absorption. The two permissions that establish the blessings are (3) the Great Empowerment of Illusory Body and (4) Five Tantras' Deities absorption. The six particular permissions are for (5) Fierce Inner Heat, (6) Illusory Body, (7) Dream, (8) Lucid Clarity, (9) Transference, and (10) Intermediate State.
30. Possibly a reference to *Garland of Offerings for Five-Deity Cakrasaṃvara* by Khedrup Tsangma Shangtön found in *Shangpa Dharma Cycle Etcetera*.
31. *rGyud sde lnga gtso bsdus kyi dbang*, an empowerment for the practice of the Principal Deities of the Five Tantras that consists of only the five principal deity couples of the Five Tantras practiced together.
32. The remaining source permissions can be found in another text by Losal Tenkyong in *DNZ*, vol. 11, pp. 373–449. Translated in *The Treasury of Precious Instructions, Volume 11: Shangpa Kagyu*, ch. 24.
33. See the following chapter and Kongtrul, *The Single Sitting*, in ch. 9 of this volume.

2. A Supplement to the Source Guide on the Profound Path of Niguma's Six Dharmas

1. *Zab lam ni gu chos drug gi gzhung khrid ma mo'i lhan thabs kha skong*. *DNZ*, vol. 12, pp. 103–35; *ST*, vol. 3, pp. 579–654; *Tāranātha's Collected Works*, vol. 12, pp. 973–1011.
2. Written more clearly by Kunga Drolchok: "Understand as that the gem (glans) is inverted upward into the intestine and a radiant red letter *hūṃ* draws it up through the central channel and reaches the cranial aperture" (*nor bu rgyu ma*

nang bzlog tu gyen la byung bas hūṃ yig dmar la dwangs pa gcig dbu ma'i lam nas tshangs bug bar du byon pa la shes pa gtad). *DNZ*, vol. 18, p. 284. Translated by Gyurme Dorje as "the penis (*nor bu*) appears to be inverted upward into the small intestine" (p. 416).

3. From Niguma's *Vajra Lines of the Six Dharmas*, in the section on Dream practice, it says, "Excessive delusion is not recognizing dreams, excessive insomnia is waking from sleep again and again, excessive bliss is losing bodhicitta, and excessive emptiness is not wanting to dream." Another translation for *'byams gcod* is "losing focus." A summary of these practices is *Meaningful Summary of Severing Excess*, in *ST*, vol. 8, pp. 722–23, by one Mokchokpa (not sure which one).
4. *thod pa mtshan ldan dum bu gcig pa*. This means a skull with all specified qualifications, or well formed, and consisting of a single bone rather than the normal skull with the four bones that are joined by sutures. Or perhaps just a singular parietal plate, a rare condition known as craniosynostosis.
5. *[gSang 'dus] rim lnga gdan rdzogs*. An explication of the Guhyasamāja practice by Serdingpa (gSer sding pa gZhon nu 'od, 12th century) or its many commentaries, such as Tsongkhapa, *Vital Guide*, on the subject (*rGyud kyi rgyal po dpal gsang ba 'dus pa'i rdzogs rim lnga gdan rdzogs kyi dmar khrid*). In vol. 8 (*nya*) of his *Collected Works*, pp. 201–315. See Tsong Khapa, *Brilliant Illumination of the Lamp of the Five Stages*, p. 153.
6. *lan brdugs 'byams*, but in the Tāranātha edition it is *lan brtul 'byams*. Tentative translation.
7. *'Chug* [or *'phyug*] *med mkha' spyod kyi 'pho ba*. Tāranātha included it in the outline of *Tangdalma*, but commented on its secret nature and so did not explain it there. Obviously he is concerned about what he regards as inauthentic versions, perhaps like that of the second Dalai Lama, Gendun Gyatso, *How to Practice Transference to the Unerring Celestial Realm*, in his *Collected Works*, vol. 2, ff. 58–60. See Tāranātha's explicit comments about this author in this chapter or in *DNZ*, vol. 12, pp. 132–33.
8. *rDo rje rnal 'byor ma'i phyag mtshan gyi 'pho ba*. Not located.
9. *Rin po che 'od kyi phreng ba mnyam med rin chen brtson 'grus mdzad*, *ST*, vol. 8, pp. 275–310. Mokchokpa Rinchen Tsöndru (1110–1170) signs with a Sanskrit rendition "Ratnavīrya." Also found as text #17 in the handwritten collection of forty-nine texts called *Shangpa Dharma Cycle Etcetera: Mahāmudrā Empowerment Permission; Five-Deity Cakrasaṃvara Direct Realization and Offerings; Hevajra Empowerment Conferral* (BDRC MW8LS32723), pp. 221–40.
10. Though our texts say *der rmi lam dam du ma zin 'ong*, the text that is being summarized here has *dam dum kram krim 'byung bar 'gyur*: "various scattered dreams will occur." *Jeweled Light Garland*, *ST*, vol. 8, p. 280.
11. These subjects are all explained in some detail in Mokchokpa's text, *Jeweled Light Garland*.
12. Tāranātha's reference only makes sense if we know that Burgom's lineage is that of the Rechung Aural Transmission (*Ras chung snyan rgyud*), which traces to

Tilopa. In Mokchokpa's biography, Lama Burgom Nakpo (Bur sgom nag po: "black meditator in the sugarcane [grove]") is a yogi with whom he studied for five years. The teachings of Rechungpa (1084–1161) that Mokchokpa received from Burgom are listed in the biography (although not in the translation by Riggs). These are different from the Niguma lineage but, as Tāranātha suggests, "not unrelated." Mokchokpa Kunga Ö, *Life Story of Mokchokpa Rinchen Tsöndru*, *ST*, vol. 1, pp. 157–59.

13. *Lam dri med 'od phreng* by Sangye Tönpa. In *Shangpa Dharma Cycle Etcetera: Mahāmudrā Empowerment Permission*; *Five-Deity Cakrasaṃvara Direct Realization and Offerings*; *Hevajra Empowerment Conferral*, text #27, titled *Lam mchog dri ma med pa* but identified as *Lam dri med 'od phreng* in the colophon.
14. The source text says, "After offering guru devotion and intentionality a hundred times, illusion will arise by itself" (*bla ma'i mos gus dang 'dun pa brgya phul nas / sgyu ma rang du 'byung ste*), f. 3b3. In our text, *brgya phul* seems to be misprinted as *rgyab phul*, which isn't really a word.
15. "Revealed secret" is translating *gab bsgyur*, which is perhaps a misprint of *gab phyung* (*gab pa mngon phyung*), meaning the disclosure of hidden meaning. The particular permission for Illusory Body is in Losal Tenkyong, *A Garland of Grain Ears of Great Bliss: A Liturgical Ritual for the Practice of the Ten Permissions in the Profound Path of Niguma's Six Dharmas*, in *DNZ*, vol. 11, pp. 424–29, translated in *The Treasury of Precious Instructions, Volume 11: Shangpa Kagyu*, pp. 519–23. This statement is not in the original.
16. *Nyams myong yon tan rgya mtsho*. Two slightly different handwritten versions in headless script can be found in *Shangpa Dharma Cycle Etcetera*. I have depended on the second one (#29) that stands as an autonomous text. It is attributed to an aural transmission but does not provide an author. According to Tāranātha, the author is Sangye Tönpa Tsöndru Senge (1207–1278), but according to Amye Zhab Ngawang Kunga Sönam, it is Khyungpo Naljor.
17. *shes rab bzhi*: In the source text of *Ocean of Experiential Qualities*: (1) knowing that a dream is a dream is the wisdom of dreaming (blending and transference of day, night, and dream); (2) knowing that as untrue illusion is the wisdom of knowing illusion (blending dream and illusion); (3) without fixating on the illusion of those two, realizing lucid clarity is the wisdom of realizing the ultimate (blending transference of illusion and lucid clarity); and (4) the deity's form, illusory body, and lucid clarity [blended] is the wisdom of meditation (ff. 5b7–6a3). For Tāranātha's version, see *Tangdalma*, *DNZ*, vol. 12, p. 84; this volume, ch. 1, pp. 80–81.
18. I do not see such an interlinear note in the editions available.
19. Niguma's command was to transmit the entire corpus of the Six Dharmas to only one person for seven generations, counting from Buddha Vajradhara. Sangye Tönpa was the seventh, so the seal was lifted and he could spread the complete teachings.
20. A reference to *The Words of the Ḍākinī of Timeless Awareness: A Guidebook on the Profound Path of Niguma's Six Dharmas* by Gendun Gyatso (1476–1542). Though

he was recognized as the second Dalai Lama, he came from a family holding a lineage of a Shangpa subsect and received the teachings from his father. His text is largely based on Tsongkhapa's teachings on the Six Dharmas of Nāropa: *Endowed with Threefold Confidence*. For my translation of Gendun Gyatso's text, see Harding, *Four Tibetan Lineages*, pp. 449–96.

21. *sGyus lus stan thog gcig ma.*
22. Khyungpo Naljor, *The Inventory Clarifying the Six Dharmas* (*Them[s] yig chos drug gi tshig gsal*), *DNZ*, vol. 11, pp. 9–10. Translated in *The Treasury of Precious Instructions, Volume 11: Shangpa Kagyu*, pp. 17–18. However there, in all editions, the last line reads "eight supplications and eight intentions."
23. Jakpa Gyaltsen Bum (1261–1334) was a disciple of Khedrup Shangtön (1234–1309). They coauthored *Collection of Essential Directives on the Six Dharmas of Niguma*, *ST*, vol. 8, pp. 311–68. But other commentaries on the Six Dharmas are attributed to him in the *Drepung Catalog* that may be the source reference here.

3. Niguma's Yogic Exercises, Root and Commentary

1. *Ni gu'i 'khrul 'khor rtsa 'grel*, *DNZ*, vol. 12, pp. 137–45; *ST*, vol. 6, pp. 143–60. Also in *Tāranātha's Collected Works*, vol. 12, pp. 1013–26.
2. *dbyug mchongs byed par brgyad.* But *brgyad* here ("eight") should be *bshad* ("explained") as in the Tāranātha edition. See the following note as well.
3. *gtum mo'i stangs.* Since this comes before the Fireball and main practices, it seems to refer to the outer and inner visualizations of oneself as Vajravārāhī. See *Tangdalma*, session 6.
4. This can be seen in a very different form in Niguma's source text, *Channel Chakras of One's Body*: "To raise oneself up by the palms, grasp a staff with two hands. Put the heel of the right [foot] on the thigh of the left [leg], move back the right knee, and lift up the body. . . . After that [exercise], set aside the staff." Harding, *Niguma, Lady of Illusion*, pp. 191–92. Originally it seems the staff was only used to hold oneself up.
5. *rdo rje gar gyi 'khrul 'khor.* In the Tengyur editions of *Niguma's Yogic Exercises*, only the text called *Meditation on Inner Heat in the Path of Methods* that contains only these last three is labeled as vajra dance. Harding, *Niguma, Lady of Illusion*, pp. 187–88.
6. In Niguma's *Yoga of Meditation in the Path of Methods*, this is clearly described as the physical sitting posture of Vairocana (*rnam par snang mdzad 'dug stangs*). Vairocana generally is shown with the wheel of dharma mudra, which is different from the mudra of supreme awakening. For illustrations, see Willson and Brauen, *Deities of Tibetan Buddhism*, pp. 580–81.
7. *DNZ*, *khra tshag* ("variegated yak") is clearly a mistake for *khro tshig* ("reproach") as in *ST* and Tāranātha, or else for *'khro 'tshig* ("fury") as in Niguma's text, where it says *yi dwags stobs kyis 'khro 'tshig* ("infuriated by the force of hungry ghosts"). Harding, *Niguma, Lady of Illusion*, p. 189.

Tangtong Gyalpo and the Direct Lineage: Introduction

1. Stearns, *King of the Empty Plain*, p. 1.
2. Ibid., pp. 18–19.
3. *'Gro don mkha' khyab ma*. This has been translated countless times and is possibly the most widespread of all Tibetan Buddhist practices in the West thanks to the efforts of the sixteenth Karmapa and Kyapje Kalu Rinpoche. Also see interesting research by Janet Gyatso on this and other of Tangtong Gyalpo's compositions that question their visionary sources: "Genre, Authorship, and Transmission in Visionary Buddhism," in Goodman and Davidson, *Tibetan Buddhism: Reason and Revelation*, pp. 102–3. See also Gyatso's PhD dissertation, "The Literary Traditions of Thang-stong rGyalpo: A Study of Visionary Buddhism in Tibet."
4. Stearns, *King of the Empty Plain*, p. 19.
5. *Ye shes mkha' 'gro ma'i chos drug rdo rje'i tshig rkang*, *DNZ*, vol. 11, pp. 2–6; translated in *The Treasury of Precious Instructions, Volume 11: Shangpa Kagyu*, pp. 7–12.
6. Stearns, *King of the Empty Plain*, p. 508n443.

4. Collection of Essentials

1. *Ye shes mkha' 'gro ni gu ma'i chos drug gi khrid kyi gnad yig snying po kun 'dus*, *DNZ*, vol. 12, pp. 147–79; *ST*, vol. 3, pp. 773–840. Also in *Supplemental Text to the Collected Works of Thang-stong-rgyal-po* (*TTG-S*), vol. 1, pp. 241–336. Previously translated in Harding, *Four Tibetan Lineages*, pp. 299–328.
2. The opening lines of Niguma's *Vajra Lines of the Six Dharmas*, *DNZ*, vol. 11, p. 2; translated in *The Treasury of Precious Instructions, Volume 11, Shangpa Kagyu*, p. 7.
3. *Vajra Lines of the Six Dharmas*, *DNZ*, vol. 11, p. 2; *The Treasury of Precious Instructions, Volume 11: Shangpa Kagyu*, p. 7.
4. There is an interlinear note in the text that reads "check if this is in a text." This note is not in the edition of Tangtong Gyalpo's *Collected Works*, and was probably left in by accident.
5. *DNZ*, vol. 11, p. 3; *The Treasury of Precious Instructions, Volume 11: Shangpa Kagyu*, p. 8. The descending sequence of four ecstasies is dissipating or defiled (*zag bcas*), while the ascending sequence is undefiled (*zag med*). Tangtong Gyalpo also describes the sequence of experience as first heat, then bliss, then the absorption of bliss-emptiness (*Collection of the Essentials*, p. 260, f. 10b4). For third empowerment practices, see Gray, *The Chakrasamvara Tantra*, p. 113, and Jamgön Kongtrul, *The Treasury of Knowledge: Esoteric Instructions*, p. 252.
6. Regarding this, an interlinear note in *DNZ* but not in the *TTG-S* reads: *rtags gnyis par dpe gcig la mi snang*. Assuming *rtags* is a mistake for *brtags*, this would be a reference to the *Two-Part Hevajra Explanatory Tantra* (Toh. 417–18). The note

would indicate that this "single example does not occur in the *Two-Part* [*Hevajra Tantra*]."

7. *DNZ*, vol. 11, p. 3; *The Treasury of Precious Instructions, Volume 11: Shangpa Kagyu*, p. 8. Note that "nondual" (*gnyis med*) is not in the original *Vajra Lines*.
8. *Ye shes mngon byung* (*Ye shes mngon par 'byung ba'i rgyud rgyas pa*); Skt. *Jñānābhyudaya*. Not located and possibly not extant. However, this tantra is often cited and is attested in the lineage by the record of its transmission by Khyungpo Naljor, who received it from the Ḍākinī Kanakaśrī of Devīkoṭi.
9. From *Stages in the Path of Illusion* (*sGyu ma lam rim;* Skt. *Māyādhanakrama*), Collated Tengyur, vol. 42, verse 9. Translation in Harding, *Niguma, Lady of Illusion*, p. 55.
10. *Khye'u rab snang gis zhus pa'i mdo*; reconstructed Sanskrit: *Kumāraprabha*. This sutra is often cited in Niguma's *Stages of the Path of Illusion* (*sGyu ma lam rim*), as well as in Longchenpa's *Finding Rest in Illusion*.
11. *DNZ*, vol. 11, pp. 3–4; *The Treasury of Precious Instructions, Volume 11: Shangpa Kagyu*, pp. 8–9.
12. *DNZ*, vol. 11, p. 4; *The Treasury of Precious Instructions, Volume 11: Shangpa Kagyu*, p. 9.
13. *'Byams gcod*. A summary of these practices is *Meaningful Summary of Severing Excess* (*'Byams gcod kyi bsdus don yod*) in *ST*, vol. 8, pp. 722–23. Mokchokpa may be Mokchokpa Rinchen Tsöndru (1110–1170), the main disciple of Khyungpo Naljor, but might also be the second Mokchokpa, Kunga Ö (a.k.a., Jatang Kunga Yeshe).
14. According to Tāranātha's *Tangdalma*, this should be Recognizing Lucid Clarity Based on the Guru.
15. *bsdus don*. This may refer to *Clarification of the Root Verses of the Six Dharmas*, *DNZ*, vol. 11, pp. 6–9; *The Treasury of Precious Instructions, Volume 11: Shangpa*, pp. 13–16, which, however, only provides names of the practices.
16. *DNZ*, vol. 11, p. 4; *The Treasury of Precious Instructions, Volume 11: Shangpa Kagyu*, pp. 9–10.
17. *DNZ*, vol. 11, p. 5; *The Treasury of Precious Instructions, Volume 11: Shangpa Kagyu*, p. 10.
18. *DNZ*, vol. 11, p. 5; *The Treasury of Precious Instructions, Volume 11: Shangpa Kagyu*, pp. 10–11.
19. *Ye shes rol pa'i rgyud*, not located, but quoted elsewhere in the Shangpa corpus.
20. *DNZ*, vol. 11, pp. 5–6; *The Treasury of Precious Instructions, Volume 11: Shangpa Kagyu*, p. 11.

5. Niguma's Auxiliary Practice, Guidance in Amulet Mahāmudrā

1. *Ni gu'i yan lag phyag chen ga'u ma'i khrid*, *DNZ*, vol. 12, pp. 181–87; *ST*, vol. 3, pp. 683–94; *TTG-S*, pp. 337–52. Previously translated in Harding, *Four Tibetan Lineages*, pp. 329–42.

2. *rkun po'i ngo sprod*, or sometimes *rkun bur ngo sprad*. This practice is described in Tāranātha's *Amulet Mahāmudrā*, *ST*, vol. 3, pp. 667–71. See the preliminary of Naturally Free of Four Faults in ch. 10 of this volume. In the *Catalog*, Kongtrul says, "In the main practice, the descent of vajra timeless awareness points out [mind's nature] in a sneaky way . . ." (*rku thabs su ngo sprad*). *DNZ*, vol. 18, p. 433.

6. Niguma's Auxiliary Practice, Guidance in the Three Integrations

1. *Ni gu'i yan lag lam khyer gsum gyi khrid*, *DNZ*, vol. 12, pp. 187–92; *ST*, vol. 3, pp. 694–703; *TTG-S*, pp. 353–67.

7. Niguma's Auxiliary Practices, Guidance in Immortal Body and Mind

1. *Ni gu'i yan lag lus sems 'chi med kyi khrid*, *DNZ*, vol. 12, pp. 192–98. *ST*, vol. 3, pp. 703–13; *TTG-S*, pp. 369–86.
2. These are thirty-two exercises associated with Immortal Body (*lus 'chi med*). See, for instance, Sangye Tönpa Tsöndru Senge, *Sun That Illuminates the Practice of the Thirty-Two Yogic Exercises of Attaining Immortality*, *ST*, vol. 7, pp. 267–97. For the source text by Virūpa, see *Attaining Immortality of the Body Root Text*, in *The Treasury of Precious Instructions, Volume 11: Shangpa Kagyu*, pp. 51–59.
3. *Rang sems 'chi med rang grol*. The root text by Niguma, titled *Śri Amāramahājñāna* (*dPal 'chi med ye shes chen po*) but with this title in the colophon, can be found in *DNZ*, vol. 11, pp. 25–27. It is translated as *Immortal Mind Root Text* in *The Treasury of Precious Instructions, Volume 11: Shangpa Kagyu*, pp. 61–64, and in Harding, *Niguma, Lady of Illusion* (pp. 161–66) from a version in the Tengyur with interlinear notes. There are commentaries with the same name by Sangye Tönpa, Gyaltsen Bum, and perhaps others with different titles in the *Shangpa Texts*.

8. Niguma's Auxiliary Quintessential Practice, Guidance in the Six-Armed Awareness Protector

1. *Nying khu'i yan lag phyag drug ye shes mgon po'i khrid*, *DNZ*, vol. 12, pp. 198–205; *DNZ*, Kundeling edition, vol. 8, pp. 325–32; *ST*, vol. 3, pp. 713–27. Not included in *TTG-S*.
2. This section may be used as a liturgy in the practice, though I have translated it as instruction.
3. For the story of how Maitrīpa received the Six-Armed Mahākāla practice from Śavarīpa and thence gave it to Khyungpo Naljor, see Losal Tenkyong, "Five Permissions for the Protector" in *DNZ*, vol. 11, pp. 514–17; *The Treasury of Precious*

Instructions, Volume 11: Shangpa Kagyu, pp. 614–27. For a description of Tangtong Gyalpo's meeting with Śavarīpa, see Stearns, *King of the Empty Plain*, pp. 142–43.

9. The Single Sitting, Words of the Ḍākinī of Timeless Awareness

1. *dPal ldan shangs pa'i gser chos las rtsa ba ni gu chos drug gi khrid bsdus stan thog gcig ma'i nyams len ye shes ḍāki'i zhal lung*, *DNZ*, vol. 12, pp. 207–35; *ST*, vol. 3, pp. 513–77; *GK*, vol. 8, pp. 303–37. Previously translated in Harding, *Four Tibetan Lineages*, pp. 425–48.
2. *mthar thug ston pa rnam lnga*: the principal deities of the Five Tantras that Khyungpo Naljor mastered—Hevajra, Cakrasaṃvara, Guhyasamāja, Mahāmāya, and Yamāntaka.
3. Tāranātha's much shorter version of the Six Dharmas in a Single Sitting can be found in ch. 2 of this volume.
4. Sometimes called the Inner Heat of Fireballs. See ch. 1, note 5.
5. See *Tangdalma*, *DNZ*, pp. 27–29; this volume, ch. 1, session 12, pp. 34–35.
6. Since there is no visualization of the right and left channels, as in the longer version, it seems the winds travel within the central channel then come together to fan the *raṃ* syllable. According to Ngawang Zangpo, Bokar Rinpoche believed that the word *right* was missing in the text.
7. Tāranātha, *A Supplement to the Source Guide on the Profound Path of Niguma's Six Dharmas*, *DNZ*, vol. 12, p. 109; in this volume, ch. 2, p. 101.
8. The Jonang master Kunga Drolchok (Kun dga' grol mchog, 1507–1566) received the direct or short lineage (*nye brgyud*) twice from Niguma in visionary encounters, as well as receiving the teachings from the lineage gurus.
9. A reference to Tāranātha's *Tangdalma* (ch. 1), which consists of sixty-seven visualizations, though it only describes fifty-six of them. The enumeration is explained in this volume on p. 90 and the "concise" style of seventeen visualizations on pp. 93–94.
10. Mokchokpa Rinchen Tsöndrü (rMog lcog pa Rin chen brtson 'grus), main lineage holder and disciple of Khyungpo Naljor. Quotation not located.
11. Not located.
12. Öntön Kyergangpa Chökyi Senge (sKyer sgang pa Chos kyi seng ge, 1154/1143–1217, later called Tshul khrims seng ge) was a student of Mokchokpa in the Shangpa lineage. His biography appears under the name Kyergangpa Dharma Senge in Roerich, *The Blue Annals*, pp. 737–41. This quote from the songs of realization of the Shangpa masters is attributed to words spoken to him by Tārā. Jamgön Kongtrul, *An Ocean of Blessings Meaningful to Hear*, *DNZ*, vol. 12, p. 504; ch. 30, p. 564 in this volume.
13. *log lta*; note that in *Tangdalma*, this fourth "frost" is *log gtam*: perverse talk or discussion.

14. The statement "There will never be someone better than I, or even someone equal" is recorded in *A Brief Life Story of Lama Khyungpo Naljor*, just before he passes away. *ST*, vol. 1, p. 141.
15. Karma gZhan phan 'od zer, successor of Karma Lhaktong (Karma Lhag mthong) in the Jonang tradition.
16. Mokchokpa et al., *A Brief Life Story of Lama Khyungpo Naljor*, *ST*, vol. 1, p. 135.

10. Amulet Mahāmudrā or Three Naturally Settled States Guidance Manual

1. *Phyag chen ga'u ma'am rang babs rnam gsum zhes bya ba'i khrid yig*, *DNZ*, vol. 12, pp. 237–49; *ST*, vol. 3, pp. 655–82; *Tāranātha's Collected Works*, vol. 20, pp. 563–78. In the Tāranātha edition, *ma'am* ("or") has been manually changed to *ma'i* ("of") in this title, thus rendering it as *Three Naturally Settled States of Amulet Mahāmudrā*.
2. These are shortened versions of what is found in Niguma's *Vajra Lines of the Amulet Mahāmudrā*, *DNZ*, vol. 11, p. 14; *The Treasury of Precious Instructions, Volume 11: Shangpa Kagyu*, p. 29. The complete section reads, "Though the dharmakāya is beyond inclusion or separation [from mind], it is so close that it is not recognized. Though it arises to oneself, it is so profound that it is not grasped. So easy, without believing in it one departs from nondistraction. So excellent that it is not comprehended by the intellect; without conviction one wanders in cyclic existence."
3. *rang lus thabs ldan*: a reference to Niguma's *Vajra Lines* on the subject of Fierce Inner Heat.

Two Celestial Goddesses: Introduction

1. *DNZ*, vol. 18, pp. 433–34. Translated as *The Catalog of The Treasury of Precious Instructions* by Richard Barron (Chökyi Nyima) (p. 71).
2. *Radiant Blessings of the Vajra Lines*, *DNZ*, vol. 11, p. 39; *The Treasury of Precious Instructions, Volume 11: Shangpa Kagyu*, p. 81.
3. *DNZ*, vol. 11, p. 58; *The Treasury of Precious Instructions, Volume 11: Shangpa Kagyu*, pp. 105–7.
4. Translated in Stearns, *King of the Empty Plain*, pp. 81–439.

11. Releasing the Knots of the Central Channel

1. *Me tog mkha' spyod dkar dmar gyi nyams len dbu ma'i mdud 'grol*, *DNZ*, vol. 12, 251–69; *ST*, vol. 3, pp. 191–235; *GK*, vol. 8, pp. 339–63.
2. See Kongtrul's *Radiant Blessings of the Vajra Lines* in *DNZ*, vol. 11, p. 33, for the whole recitation. The last line should be changed to ". . . profound path of Khecarī yoga."

3. This would presumably be the lineage of Tangtong Gyalpo. See the following text by Lochen Gyurme Dechen, *White Khecarī Transference.*
4. See above for the liturgies of White Khecarī and Red Khecarī. In *DNZ*, pp. 252–53.
5. An interlinear note says to change the white to red (*dkar mos dmar sgyur*), presumably for Red Khecarī.
6. Sangye Tönpa, *Red Khecarī's Sadhāna, Empowerment Ritual, and Hand Offering or Defilement Removal*, *ST*, vol. 8, pp. 407–41. Note that even that text suggests learning the visualizations elsewhere.
7. More details on the tenth-day offerings are in Jamgön Kongtrul's *Tenth-Day Offerings for White Khecarī in the Shangpa Tradition*, *ST*, vol. 3, pp. 237–67; *GK*, vol. 8, pp. 385–404; and *Tenth-Day Offerings for Red Khecarī in the Shangpa Tradition*, *ST*, vol. 3, pp. 269–96; *GK*, vol. 8, pp. 405–21.
8. The five products from a cow are dung, urine, milk, yogurt, and butter.
9. *chos 'byung gnyis brtsegs*; when drawn in two dimensions, this appears as one triangle on top and at angles from a lower triangle, similar to the Star of David.
10. The *DNZ* edition mistakenly has *suṃ vaṃ* here, appearing to be two seed syllables, but in *ST* and *GK* editions, it is *dbu su vaṃ* ("*vaṃ* in the center").
11. See Tāranātha, *Five-Deity Cakrasaṃvara Mandala Ritual in the Tradition of Niguma*, *DNZ*, vol. 11, pp. 264–67 for the full offerings. Translated in *The Treasury of Precious Instructions, Volume 11: Shangpa Kagyu*, pp. 336–42.
12. *grub pa brgyad*, eight siddhi: spiritual powers based on (or power over) celestial land, sword, pill, swift feet, vase, yakṣa, and eye lotion. Variations occur in some lists.
13. Jamgön Kongtrul, based on Mokchokpa Ngakgi Wangchuk, *Increasing Awakened Activity: Five-Deity Cakrasaṃvara Ritual for Communal Feast in the Tradition of Niguma*, *DNZ*, vol. 11, pp. 287–95. Translated in *The Treasury of Precious Instructions, Volume 11: Shangpa Kagyu*, pp. 369–78.
14. *Increasing Awakened Activity*, *DNZ*, vol. 11, p. 291; *The Treasury of Precious Instructions, Volume 11: Shangpa Kagyu*, p. 372.
15. Khyungpo Naljor, *bKra shis bka' brgya ma*, in *The Eight Songs and Four Sealed Words of the Great Adept Khyungpo*. In *Compendium of Sādhanas*, vol. 11, p. 192.
16. These three are the permission empowerments for White Khecarī, Red Khecarī, and Threefold Khecara. See Losal Tenkyong, *A Sheaf of Grain Ears of Great Bliss: Collected Ritual Practices of the Latter Source Permissions of the Glorious Shangpa Kagyu* in *DNZ*, vol. 11, pp. 475–87; *The Treasury of Precious Instructions, Volume 11: Shangpa Kagyu*, pp. 574–86.

12. In Praise of Vajrayoginī, the Especially Exalted Praise

1. *Vajrayoginīstotra*. *rDo rje rnal 'byor ma la bstod pa*. *DNZ*, vol. 12, pp. 271–72. Dg.T. rgyud, *ha*, f. 103a–b. (Toh. 1587); *ST*, vol. 3, pp. 331–34, as *In Praise of White Khecarī* (*mKha' spyod dkar mo'i bstod pa*). This is also referred to as

"Especially Exalted Praise" (*Khyad 'phags gi bstod pa*) or "Especially Exalted Supplication" (*Khyad 'phags gi gsol 'debs*) in the Shangpa literature. (A different version with the same title *Vajrayoginīstotra* is in *Atiśa's Collected Works* (BDRC W1GS66286), which corresponds to Tengyur, Toh. 1594.

2. *Ga shal* is specifically a garland that goes from the shoulders to under the arms.
3. The Tengyur edition shows *thugs su drang* rather than *DNZ gnas su drang*.

13. White Khecarī Transference

1. *mKha' spyod dkar mo'i 'pho ba*, *DNZ*, vol. 12, pp. 273–74; *ST*, vol. 3, pp. 315–25. In *Collected Works of Lochen Gyurme Dechen*, vol. 2, pp. 605–6. The same text, called *Siddhi mka' spyod dkar mo'i 'pho ba*, is also in Tangtong Gyalpo, *Supplemental Texts*, pp. 169–77; and in Ngawang Chodrak, *Volume of Miscellaneous Texts of Shangpa Kagyu and Others*, vol. 1, pp. 203–7. Transference to Khecara is mentioned as one of the methods in the notes (probably added by Gyurme Dechen) in Niguma's *Vajra Lines*: "Transference to the Unerring Celestial Realm." *DNZ*, vol. 11, p. 5.
2. *Naiguptā* (Tib: *sbas pa*, "hidden"), with no explanation for the "*nai*" here, but in the other editions it is just *guhyā* (Tib. *gsang ba*), which means "secret."
3. *sNying po kun 'dus*. See chapters 4 through 8 in this volume.
4. This same exact narrative until here is found in Lochen Gyurme Dechen's biography of Tangtong Gyalpo, *A Jewel Mirror in Which All Is Clear*, translated in Stearns, *King of the Empty Plain*, pp. 150–51. There, this section ends by saying that he taught these practices "with the tune of the indestructible nāda," meaning that he taught them orally without writing them down.
5. Ngag gi dbang po (1439–1491) was a Pakmodru ruler, enthroned as the abbot of Densatel Monastery in 1454, but he did not rule the dynasty until 1481. He supported Tangtong Gyalpo's bridge building (Stearns, p. 471n55). However, according to the available dates, he would have passed away long before Gyurme Dechen's time (1540–1615). Note that both other versions of the text have Ngakgi Wangmo, with a feminine ending, perhaps a royal female patron. Kunga Drolchok (1507–1566) gave Gyurme Dechen the instructions of Niguma. His main heir for Niguma's teachings was Ngawang Chödrak (1572–1641).

14. Red Khecarī Transference

1. *mKha' spyod dmar mo'i 'pho ba*, *DNZ*, vol. 12, pp. 277–78; *ST*, vol. 3, pp. 325–30. A text by the same name and similar content by Kunga Drolchok is in Tangtong Gyalpo, *Supplemental Texts*, pp. 179–83.
2. The amusing story of Lama Rāhula's miraculous appearance in Tibet, where he granted all the instructions to Khyungpo Naljor, is recounted in two places with slight variations in the *Golden Rosary of Shangpa Biographies*: Mokchokpa et al., *Brief Life Story of Lama Khyungpo Naljor*, *ST*, vol. 1, pp. 108–13 (Riggs,

pp. 71–73); and in the history of Six-Armed Mahākāla by Tāranātha, *Rainfall of Spiritual Power Elixir*, *ST*, vol. 1, pp. 732–34.

3. *sgog sgra*. This is clarified in Kunga Drolchok's text: *thugs khar slebs pa tsam la tog sgra dang bcas* ("Just arriving at the heart with a snapping sound"), p. 182.

Sukhasiddhi, Ḍākinī of Timeless Awareness: Introduction

1. See Āryadeva the Brahmin, "Esoteric Instructions on the Noble Perfection of Wisdom," in *The Treasury of Precious Instructions, Volume 14: Chöd*, pp. 3–11.
2. For example, *DNZ*, vol. 13, p. 370; Jamgön Kongtrul, *The Treasury of Precious Instructions, Volume 13: Zhije*, p. 469.
3. "The Pure Stainless Egg of the Stainless Path," *DNZ*, vol. 13, p. 21. Translation in Jamgön Kongtrul, *The Treasury of Precious Instructions, Volume 13: Zhije*, p. 40.
4. "The Pure Golden Egg of the Stainless Path," *DNZ*, vol. 13, p. 25. Translation in ibid., p. 48.
5. Tāranātha states, "The great adept Khyungpo did not receive from Awareness Ḍākinī Sukhasiddhi the great word transmission (*tshig brgyud*) associated with the classic [Sanskrit] source tantras. However, he did receive three unsurpassable boons through her kindness: instructions on the essential meaning, the profound empowerment conferral, and the blessing of the great adept himself and all his lineage holders." He says this, and some rather confusing things about the various texts. *DNZ*, vol. 18, p. 105. See translation in "Supplementary Historical Anecdotes," in Jamgön Kongtrul, *The Treasury of Precious Instructions, Volume 18: Jonang*, p. 194.

15. Sukhasiddhi's Story, Indian Source Text, Secret Sādhana of the Navel Emanation Chakra, and Empowerment Ritual

1. *Su kha siddhi'i lo rgyus / rgya gzhung / gsang sgrub lte ba sprul 'khor / dbang chog rnams*, *DNZ*, vol. 12, pp. 279–96.
2. This version follows Sukhasiddhi's life story closely from other versions, such as in the *Golden Rosary of Shangpa Biographies* in *ST*, vol. 1, pp. 49–58, but with noticeable variations that seem more intentional than mistakes. It is also distinguished by its colophon, indicating Jampa Rinchen Zangpo as the author.
3. In the translation of Kalu Rinpoche's oral retelling of this story, the beggar is actually a mahāsiddha, a great adept. One might think that would explain the event as a test of faith, but according to Rinpoche, it explains how he knew where to find food! *Luminous Mind*, p. 175.
4. According to the spelling here, *'du ba rnam gsum*, this would be the ability to gather or attract people in the daytime, ḍākinīs at night, and food and wealth all the time, part of the third kind of awakened activity, that of magnetizing or controlling (*dbang gi phrin las*).
5. In the life story elsewhere (*ST*, vol. 1, p. 54), this is fifty-nine.

6. *dus drug* can be the six watches of the day and night or the six seasons of the year.
7. This narrative is also found in Khyungpo Naljor's biography, except there it is related to him by Āryadeva. Mokchokpa et al., *Brief Life Story of Lama Khyungpo Naljor*, *ST*, vol. 1, pp. 94–97; Riggs, *Like an Illusion*, pp. 64–66.
8. Kun dga' bkra shis rgyal mtshan dpal bzang po, named in the *Drepung Catalog* on the same page as author of *Ni gu chos drug gi dbang gi zin bris*. Martin, Tibskrit2019.
9. *sgrub bya* or *bsgrub bya'i yul*: the object of what is to be achieved. In this context, it is always the female consort, whether real or imagined, so will be translated henceforth as "practice consort" rather than, literally, "object."
10. *sdom pa rgya mtsho'i rgyud phyi ma las . . .*" Added from *Khyungpo's Collected Works*, missing in *DNZ*.
11. A variant of Sukhasiddhi used by Tibetans, adding the feminine ending "*ma*" to Sukha, something like "bliss woman." In the handwritten edition from *Khyungpo's Collected Works*, it is spelled out as *ḍākima suka matra siddhi*.
12. Kongtrul identifies this text as authored by Sangye Nyentön [Chökyi Sherap] in Tashi Chöpel, *Record of Teachings Received*, p. 752. A different text with nearly the same name: *Oral Instruction of the Secret Sādhana of the Navel Emanation Chakra* is in *ST*, vol. 3, pp. 841–65, and is said in the colophon to be Lama Shangpa's (i.e., Khyungpo Naljor's). It includes several subtexts, including a section entitled just "Navel Emanation Chakra." This practice is similar to the one entitled *The Inner Guidance of Nairātmya*, the eighty-second guidebook of *The One Hundred and Eight Teaching Manuals of Jonang*. See translation in *The Treasury of Precious Instructions, Volume 18: Jonang*, p. 427. There (p. 697n847) the author is identified as Rinchen Chokdrub Palzang (1436–1497). I believe this is probably a different source text.
13. The homage to Kyergangpa Chökyi Senge (1154–1217) confirms the author here was his disciple, Rigongpa Sangye Nyentön Chökyi Sherap (1175–1255), who had direct visionary experiences of Sukhasiddhi and authored a following text.
14. *dran pa bsgrub pa* here should be *nye bar bsgrub pa* ("close attainment"), as in *Khyungpo's Collected Works*.
15. *Su kha siddhi'i dbang chog*. Confirmed in Tashi Chöpel, *Record of Teachings Received*, p. 752, and known as the *zin bri*.
16. It seems from the context here and further down that this represents a Tibetan form of the Sanskrit *puṣpe*, meaning the flower offering. See following note.
17. If *putsa* are flowers, then the five *me tog lnga* are *ug chos* (*Incarvillea compacta maxim*), *lug ru smug po* (*Pedicularis muscicola Maxim*, "brown sheep's horn"), *sran ma* (bean or pea flowers), *rgya lcam* (Chinese malve), and *ram bu* (*Roundel polygonum viviparum*). These are all native to the Himalayan region.
18. The following two short parts are listed as separate texts in the cycle of Navel Emanated Chakra in Jamgön Kongtrul, *The Beryl Key* (*ST*, vol. 6, p. 101), and Tashi Chöpel, *Record of Teachings Received*, p. 752.
19. In this edition, *yum pha* must be a mistake for *yul pha*, as seen in this passage

from Khyungpo Naljor's edition: *khaṭvāṅga yul pha dar bskyed rang de'i byang sems de yul pha da la sib sib thim song ba dang / bde phril li song bar bsgom / yul pha de'i byub sems dmar po rang gi lus la tshug la lus dmar yer gyis song par bsgom.*

16. Bringing Down the Rain of Great Bliss

1. *Zab lam su kha chos drug gi brgyud pa'i gsol 'debs bde chen char 'bebs*, *DNZ*, vol. 12, pp. 297–99; *ST*, vol. 3, pp. 729–33.
2. Up to here corresponds to the lineage for *The Six Doctrines of Sukhasiddhi*, the eighty-first guidebook in Kunga Drolchok's *One Hundred and Eight Teaching Manuals* (*DNZ*, vol. 18, p. 26), and in Kongtrul's *Catalog* (*DNZ*, vol. 18, p. 513). Changlungpa Zhönu Chödrup taught Kunga Drolchok, pp. 87–88.

17. Fast Path of Integral Unity

1. *Ye shes mkha' 'gro su kha siddhi'i bskyed pa'i lam zab dang / chos drug gi khrid yig zung 'jug myur lam*, *DNZ*, vol. 12, pp. 299–313; *ST*, vol. 3, pp. 733–72. In the Shechen edition, this text is continuous with the previous supplication.
2. *mi gnas pa rnam pa gsum*. From *Sukhasiddhi's Six Dharmas*: nonabiding body is the shaking/moving (*sgul bskyod*), nonabiding speech is the recitation, and nonabiding mind is resting in the equipoise of phenomena's nature (*dharmatā*) and loving passion (*byams chags*) (or mentally think it is illusion, for Illusory Body practice, and so on). *ST*, vol. 7, p. 265.
3. The verse attributed to Sukhasiddhi often used as the pointing-out instruction in the fourth empowerment.
4. mKhyen rab chos rje. In Losal Tenkyong's Sukhasiddhi empowerment (*DNZ*, vol. 11, p. 504) he is called Zha lu sku zhang rDo rje 'chang mKhyen rab chos rje, also known as sKu zhang mKhyen rab or Rin chen mKhyen rab mchog grub (1436–1497) of Zhalu Monastery and the first Chöje Trichen. This current text does not seem to be his writing but rather descriptive of it.
5. *sbyor ba bzhi ldan [gyi rlung sbyor]*, the four applications of vital-wind practice are inhalation (*rngub pa*), filling (*dgang*), crushing (*gzhil ba*), and elevation or ejection (*'phangs*).
6. According to Tāranātha, there are sixteen categories of Lucid Clarity. *DNZ*, vol. 12, p. 83. In this volume, see ch. 1, *Tangdalma*.
7. See previous note. There is a brief version of this text in *ST*, vol. 7, pp. 565–68, which is also said to be extracted from his guidebook (*mkhyen rab rje'i khrid*).
8. *ming bzhi 'dus pa'i phung po*, the four aggregates under the heading of "name": feeling, perception, formation, and consciousness. This excludes form.
9. *bsNgo ba bka' rgya ma*. This can be found in the present volume, at the end of chapter 30, *An Ocean of Blessings Meaningful to Hear*; *DNZ*, vol. 12, pp. 557–58.
10. Bodong Chokle Namgyal (Bo dong Phyogs las rnam rgyal, 1375/1376–1451). According to Kongtrul, "The profound long-life empowerment of Ni and Dhi

(Niguma and Sukhasiddhi) was bestowed by the two ḍākinīs of timeless awareness on the one known as Bodong Jikme at the age of sixteen." See Kongtrul, *Catalog*, *DNZ*, vol. 18, p. 512. This would be the direct lineage mentioned. The Shangpa-related texts in Bodong's huge collection *Compendium of Suchness* are in volumes 57, 93, and 103.

18. Sukhasiddhi's Cycle of Oral Instructions and Instructions on Three Nails

1. *Su kha siddhi'i zhal gdams kyi skor dang / gzer gsum gdams pa rnams*. Another title, *Blazing Light of Bliss-Clarity* (*bde gsal 'od 'bar*) is found only in the *Shangpa Texts*, where the title is *Su kha siddhi'i zhal gdams gsang sgrub lte ba sprul 'kor bde gsal 'od 'bar*. *DNZ*, vol. 12, pp. 315–28; *ST*, vol. 3, pp. 841–65.
2. *gSang sgrub lte ba sprul 'khor*. The phrase "secret sādhana" (*gsang sgrub*) has an interlinear note that states "oral instruction of four empowerments," which seems to clarify their equivalence.
3. Here, spelled *pañca li ka*, seems to be a reference to the female residents of a kingdom in a northern region of ancient India called Pāñcāla, who must have had beautiful, godly clothes.
4. *mas brtan gyi dga' ba bzhi*: ecstasy (*dga' ba*), supreme ecstasy (*mchog tu dga' ba*), special ecstasy (*khyad par gyi dga' ba*), and coemergent ecstasy (*lhan skyes kyi dga' ba*).
5. A guru with three qualities is one who confers empowerment (*dbang bskur*), explains Tantra (*rgyud bshad*), and grants esoteric instructions (*man ngag gnang ba*).
6. Sangye Tönpa Tsöndru Senge (1207–1278) transmitted the teachings to Khedrup Tsangma Shangtön, also known as Shangtönpa (1234–1309).
7. *Ngo sprod kyi zhal gdams*, *DNZ*, vol. 12, pp. 318–18; *ST*, vol. 3, pp. 846–48.
8. These phrases are also found in the following text, *Sukhasiddhi's Introduction to Mahāmudrā*. There are a few spelling differences that alter the meaning. Here *spyod pa skyung* is *spyod pa dkrug* ("shake up activity"); and *'tshangs yul nas 'don* there is *mtshang yul nas 'don* ("leave the flawed country").
9. Again, phrases similar in *Sukhasiddhi's Introduction to Mahāmudrā*, this time it seems two phrases here have been combined. Here *dbang po la khrog dbyung / rig pa la gsal gdab* in the following text is *rig pa khrog phyung* ("awareness quickly? drawn out").
10. *sgrub pa'i zhal gdams*. The opening verse clarifies this as the Secret Practice (*gsang sgrub*) or Secret Sādhana, if *sgrub* is short for *sgrub thabs* ("means of accomplishment"). Generally the secret practice seems to be part of the name of the Navel Emanation Chakra, which is presented separately below.
11. Seed syllables in *DNZ* are misplaced here, and they do not appear in *Khyungpo Naljor's Collected Works*. BDRC W3CN18508.
12. These are specific practices from the Six Dharmas.

13. *lTe ba sprul 'khor*, *DNZ*, vol. 12, pp. 321–23; *ST*, vol. 3, pp. 852–56. Jamgön Kongtrul, *The Treasury of Precious Instructions, Volume 18: Jonang*, p. 194 (81st and 82nd guidebooks).
14. *nor*, a mistake for *nor bu* in this context.
15. Nyentön Chökyi Sherap, *gZer gsum gyi man ngag*, *DNZ*, vol. 12, pp. 323–28; *ST*, vol. 3, pp. 856–65.
16. The Sanskrit translation of the name Chökyi Sherap, the sixth of the Seven Jewels of the Glorious Shangpa from the early one-to-one lineage.
17. With oneself visualized as the female form of Vajrayoginī, it is hard to understand this interlinear note that references the penis glans (*nor bu*).
18. The interlinear notes here include three different names for the same person: Rigongpa Sangye Nyentön, Chökyi Sherap (Skt: Dharmaprajña).

19. Sukhasiddhi's Introduction to Mahāmudrā

1. *Su kha ma siddhi'i phyag rgya chen po'i ngo sprod*, *DNZ*, vol. 12, pp. 329–30; *ST*, vol. 3, pp. 867–68.

Lineage Supplications for the Six Dharmas of Niguma: Introduction

1. *DNZ*, vol. 18, p. 454.
2. Byang sems sbyin pa bzang po and 'Jag chung pa gTsang ma shangs ston (1234–1309), the main lineage-holding disciple of Sangye Tönpa. See an interesting narrative on this transmission in Stearns, *King of the Empty Plain*, p. 51n462.
3. Smith, *Among Tibetan Texts*, p. 284n131.
4. *Collection of Liturgical Texts in Use in the Shangpa Kagyu Lineage*, vol. 1.

20. Supplication to Niguma's Lineage

1. *Ni gu'i brgyud 'debs*, *DNZ*, vol. 12, pp. 331–32; *ST*, vol. 4, pp. 1–6. In Kongtrul's *Catalog*, this is identified as "supplications with attached locations for the long lineage and the direct lineage." *DNZ*, vol. 18, p. 454. Tāranātha lineage supplication is called *Naiguma's Supplication: The Syllable A, Source of Phenomena* in his *Collected Works*, vol. 20, pp. 595–604.
2. These two verses added by Kyapje Kalu Rinpoche or his editor.

21. Clouds of Blessing

1. *Zab lam ni gu chos drug gi bla ma brgyud pa'i gsol 'debs byin rlabs sprin phung*, *DNZ*, vol. 12, pp. 333–34; *ST*, vol. 4, pp. 7–13. In the Kundeling printing, these two lineage supplications plus another to the long lineage (*Shower of Great Bliss*, a supplication to the Sukhasiddhi lineage that comes later in this volume) are

placed at the end of the section under the Direct Lineage of the Tangtong Tradition with the footnote that they were misplaced. *DNZ*, Kundeling edition, vol. 8, pp. 595–98.

22. Shower of Great Bliss

1. *Zab chos ni gu chos drug gi brgyud 'debs nyung 'dus bde chen 'bebs pa*, *DNZ*, vol. 12, pp. 457–58; *GK*, vol. 8, pp. 461–64. Signed as Dewai Dorje (bDe ba'i rdo rje), one of many aliases Kongtrul employed. In the *Catalog* (*DNZ*, vol. 18, p. 454), the prayer of the same abbreviated title (*bDe chen char 'bebs*) to the Sukhasiddhi lineage is found above in ch. 16, *Bringing Down the Rain of Great Bliss*.

Four Deities Combined: Introduction

1. Rāhulaguptavajra (?), *Lha bzhi'i lo rgyus gnyis*, *ST*, vol. 9, pp. 697–710. This text is attested in Kongtrul, *The Beryl Key*, *ST*, vol. 6, p. 103, where he adds that other than this, neither text nor transmission exist.
2. Ibid., p. 709. In another version, the *Brief Life Story of Lama Khyungpo Naljor*, which contains considerable detail on their meeting, Rāhula's departing words to Khyungpo Naljor are only slightly less harsh. *ST*, vol. 1, pp. 113. Riggs, *Like an Illusion*, pp. 73–74.

23. Naturally Luminous Timeless Awareness

1. *dPal ldan shangs pa bka' brgyud kyi zab chos lha bzhi dril sgrub kyi nyams len ye shes rang gsal*, *DNZ*, vol. 12, pp. 335–41; *ST*, vol. 4, pp. 93–107; *GK*, vol. 8, pp. 453–60.
2. It is unusual for Avalokita (here, sPyan ras gzigs, "Chenrezik"), or the long appellation Avalokiteśvara (sPyan ras gzigs dbang phyug), to be portrayed with a vase in his two-armed form in Tibetan art. It is reminiscent of Chinese images of Guanyin after her transition.
3. The mantra as written here would be *oṃ vajra nara kraṃ kraṃ* (or *kriṃ kriṃ*) *hūṃ hūṃ phaṭ phaṭ svāhā*. Though I haven't located this exact mantra in other texts, the similar-looking letter *hrīṃ* is a seed syllable for Vajrayoginī or her source of phenomena (*dharmodaya*) and can form part of her mantras, such as in the heart mantra *oṃ vajra ḍākinīye hrīṃ hūṃ phaṭ svāhā* (English, *Vajrayoginī*, p. 411n130). The more common "three-*oṃ* mantra" is *oṃ oṃ oṃ sarvabuddhaḍākinīye vajra varṇanīye vajra vairocanīye hūṃ hūṃ hūṃ phaṭ phaṭ phaṭ svāhā*.
4. As explained by Tāranātha in *Clarifying the Profound Meaning*, "'Awakened Vajra' refers to Vajradhara, who lauded and praised two kinds of conduct: whatever conduct is done for the sake of attaining perfect awakening for oneself and whatever conduct benefits others after one has attained perfect buddhahood.

'May I practice those two conducts.'" *DNZ*, vol. 11, p. 324; *The Treasury of Precious Instructions, Volume 11: Shangpa Kagyu*, p. 402.

24. Radiant Light of Timeless Awareness

1. *dPal ldan shangs pa bka' brgyud kyi zab chos lha bzhi dril sgrub kyi khrid yig ye shes 'od 'phro*, *DNZ*, vol. 12, pp. 343–56; *ST*, vol. 3, pp. 163–89; *GK*, vol. 9, pp. 3–19.
2. Here, *shing lung rta can* is a mistake for *rlung shing rta can*, as in Khyungpo's life story. The vital winds are often described as *rlung rta*, the energetic "wind horse" and here a literal translation might be "vital winds with a horse-drawn chariot." Apparently the name of a particular practice.
3. *gan rkyal du bsgyel ba*. In some tangkha paintings, he is depicted face down.
4. *gang gis drin gyi bde chen nyid / skad cig nyid la 'char ba gang / bla ma rin chen lta bu'i sku / rdo rje can zhabs pad mor 'dud.*
5. *srin po'i gzugs kyi gdug pa can / tshar gcod byang chub sems dpa' ste / grong khyer sum brtsegs 'jig byed pa / gtum po khyod la bdag phyag'tsal.* The three-tiered cities represent the desire realm, the form realm, and the formless realm (*khams gsum*).
6. *dpal ldan rdo rje mkha' 'gro ma / mkha' 'gro ma'i 'khor lo bsgyur / ye shes lnga dang sku gsum nyid / 'gro ba skyob la phyag 'tshal lo.*
7. *skyon gyi ma gos sku mdog dkar / rdzogs sangs rgyas kyis dbu la brgyan / thugs rje spyan gyis 'gro la gzigs / spyan ras gzigs la phyag 'tshal lo.*
8. *lha dang lha min cod pan gyis / zhabs gnyis padmo la btud cing / 'phongs pa kun las sgrol mdzad ma / sgrol ma yum la phyag 'tshal lo.*
9. Khyungpo Naljor, *bLa ma shangs pa'i maṇḍala mkha' rgya ma*. In *Compendium of Sādhanas*, vol. 11, pp. 187–88.

Liturgical Practices and Supplications: Introduction

1. Losel Tenkyong, *A Garland of Grain Ears of Great Bliss*, *DNZ*, vol. 11, p. 402; *The Treasury of Precious Instructions, Volume 11: Shangpa Kagyu*, p. 494.

25. A Wish-Fulfilling Gem

1. *'Gro mgon shangs pa bka' brgyud kyi bla ma mchod pa'i cho ga yid bzhin nor bu*, *DNZ*, vol. 12, pp. 357–87; *ST*, vol. 5, pp. 7–78; *GK*, vol. 2, pp. 207–43. Also in *Collection of Liturgical Texts in Use in the Shangpa Kagyu Lineage*, pp. 99–170.
2. *lus gsum*. Generally, the three bodies refer to the fully ripened karmic body, the body of habitual patterns, and the mental body.
3. Also spelled Gaṅgādharā, a daughter of the king of Malabar, said to be the wife or teacher (*jo mo*) of Maitrīpa. Roerich, *The Blue Annals*, p. 731. She also gave instructions to Khyungpo Naljor.
4. *sbrul snying* (same as *srad ser*), an herb with yellow flowers, *Astragalus chrysopterus Bunge*.

5. *mnom pa'i dri* should be *mnon pa'i dri*, as in *GK* edition.
6. From Tāranātha's *Guru Offering, Spreading Happiness and Well-Being*, *bLa ma mchod pa bde legs rab rgyas*, Dzamthang edition, vol. 14, pp. 283–85.
7. Khyungpo Naljor, *bLa ma shangs pa'i maṇḍala bka' rgya ma*, in *The Eight Songs and Four Sealed Words of the Great Adept Khyungpo*, in *Compendium of Sādhanas*, vol. 11, pp. 187–88.
8. The Sanskrit names that were used here, with adjusted diacritics, are *utpala* (blue or green lotus or water lily); *jāti* (nutmeg); *karṇikāra* (muchakunda or karnikar tree, or golden shower, purging cassia, Indian laburnum, or pudding-pipe tree); *mālaka* (chinaberry tree, pride of India, bead tree, Cape lilac, syringa berrytree, Persian lilac, Indian lilac, or white cedar, or hibiscus); *yuthika* (ornamental jasmine or A'knadi, or Nemuka); *kāravīra* (a species of soma, oleander). It's hard to know which choice is right, and probably the Tibetans were not sure of these foreign tropical plants. Thanks to L. S. Summer for the research.
9. *gser las byas pa'i mchod phyir thogs*. This refers to the sash or scarf worn over the shoulder and used to hold offerings as they are presented. Possibly *gser las byas pa* here is a mistake for *se ral kha* ("shoulder sash"), according to the description by Tāranātha, in *Clarifying the Profound Meaning*, in *DNZ*, vol. 11, pp. 311–12; *The Treasury of Precious Instructions, Volume 11: Shangpa Kagyu*, p. 392.
10. The verses up to here appear in Nāgārjuna's *Five Stages* (*Pañcakrama*; *Rim lnga pa*. Toh. 1802), the first five on page 52a, and the last four on p. 54a. It seems Kongtrul may have taken them from a Guhyasamāja empowerment ritual where they appear in the same continuous order as here. Nāgārjuna, *Glorious Guhyasamāja Mandala Ritual* (Toh. 1798), pp. 29b–30a.
11. From *Saṃvarodaya Tantra*, *Mahāsaṃvarodayatantra* (Toh. 373), p. 310b. Translation from the Sanskrit in Tsuda, *The Saṃvarodaya Tantra*, p. 332. The one notable difference in the tantra is in the second-to-last line, where it is "unimaginable form" rather than "unimaginable mind."
12. *gnas sbyar ma* refers to a common style of prayer that includes locations for each figure—for instance, "I supplicate Buddha Great Vajradhara / in the palace of Dharmadhātu Akaniṣṭha . . ." and so forth. In this volume, there are two such prayers in chapters 20 and 21.
13. *kha sbyor bdun ldan*: complete enjoyment, union, great bliss, no intrinsic nature, completely filled with compassion, uninterrupted, and unceasing.
14. *sa gsum = srid pa gsum*: the three existences above, upon, and below the earth—that is, gods, humans, and nāgas.
15. Matibhadra is back-translated from Lodrö Zangpo. He is in the lineage of Cakrasaṃvara in Tāranātha's *Five Tantras' Deities Lineage Supplication in the Shangpa Tradition*. See *The Treasury of Precious Instructions, Volume 11: Shangpa Kagyu*, pp. 117–19.
16. *dbang bcu*: power over life, seeds, necessities, devotion, aspiration, miraculous abilities, birth, dharma, mind, and timeless awareness.
17. *[sngags kyi] de nyid bcu*: mandala; mantra; mudra; protection of self, place, and so

forth; ritual invocation of deities; mantra recitation; meditation; outer and inner master's burnt offerings; final dissolution; and request for departure.

18. Karma Rangjung Kunkhyab, also known as Kalu Rinpoche (1905–1989), added these three masters who came after Jamgön Kongtrul. They are found in the *Shangpa Text* edition, though obviously not in the *DNZ* or *GK* editions.
19. *rgyun bshags*. This is generally the seven-branch service that begins "I go for refuge to the Three Jewels . . . (*dkon mchog gsum la bdag skyabs mchi . . .*) from the *Ḍākinī Vajra Tent Tantra* (*Ḍākinīvajrapañjara*), f. 53b4–5. (Toh. 419).
20. For Kongtrul's adjusted liturgy based on Kunga Drolchok, see *Increasing Awakened Activity*, in *DNZ*, vol. 11, pp. 287–95; *The Treasury of Precious Instructions, Volume 11: Shangpa Kagyu*, pp. 369–78.
21. *gdan gsum tshang ba*: the [deities of] the three seats complete in the body are the aggregates (*skandha*) and elements (*dhātu*) as the seat of the male and female tathāgatas, the sense fields (*āyatana*) as the seat of the male and female bodhisattvas, and the body and sense faculties (*indriya*) as the seat of the male and female wrathful gatekeepers. "Complete" refers to being fully contained within the body.
22. *gTor chog bsdus pa*. Tāranātha, *Concise Torma Ritual for Swift-Acting Six-Armed Awareness Protector*, *DNZ*, vol. 12, pp. 623–24. Translated later in this volume in ch. 35.
23. *Torma Offering to the Ḍākinīs of the Five Classes Just for Regular Practice*, *DNZ*, vol. 12, pp. 569–71. Translated later in this volume in ch. 32.
24. *'phrog pa* in *DNZ* and *ST* should be *mchod pa*, as in *GK* and *Compendium of Sādhanas* cited below.
25. Khyungpo Naljor, *Sealed Word of Auspiciousness*, in *The Eight Songs and Four Sealed Words of the Great Adept Khyungpo*, in *Compendium of Sādhanas*, vol. 11, p. 192.
26. Much of this compilation seems to come from Tāranātha's general guru puja: *Guru Offering, Spreading Happiness and Well-Being*, in *Collected Works*, vol. 14, pp. 279–96.

26. Garland of Uḍumbara Flowers

1. *dPal ldan shangs pa bka' brgyud kyi ngo mtshar rin chen brgyud pa'i rnam thar la gsol ba 'debs pa u dum ba ra'i phreng ba*, *DNZ*, vol. 12, pp. 389–447; *ST*, vol. 5, pp. 87–233. Also in *Collection of Liturgical Texts for Use in the Shangpa Kagyu Lineage*. The uḍumbara is a fig tree (*Ficus glomerata*). It is unknown in Tibet, and in fact does not have perceptible flowers. So it is used as a simile for extreme rarity, a huge lotus-like flower that only blooms once in an era when a Buddha appears.
2. The eight metaphors of illusion (*sgyu ma'i dpe brgyad*) vary but are often dreams (*rmi lam*), echoes (*brag ca*), city of gandharvas (*dri za'i grong khyer*), optical illusions (*mig tor*), mirages (*smig rgyu*), illusion (*sgyu ma*), emanated cities (*sprul

pa'i gron khyer), and mirror reflections (*gzugs brnyan gyi snang ba*), or, as here, the appearances that arise in a divination mirror (*pra phab*) seen by a skilled diviner.

3. *khams drug nyi zla dag pa'i yon tan brgyad*: The purity of the six elements plus the sun (red element) and moon (white element) results in eight qualities of limitless power (earth), being forever without faults such as sickness (water), light pervading all buddha realms (fire), swift movement like magic (wind), arriving anywhere (space), displaying various emanations (sun), mind filled with bliss (moon), and never moving from the timeless awareness of bliss-emptiness and remaining in desireless and unhindered awareness in all three times (consciousness). Dungkar Lobzang Trinle, *Big Dictionary of Dungkar*.
4. *yan lag bdun*: seven aspects or branches conducive to enlightenment are mindfulness (*dran pa*), fully distinguishing all phenomena (*chos rab tu rnam par 'byed pa*), diligence (*brtson 'grus*), joy (*dga' ba*), very intelligent (*shin tu spyangs pa*), meditative absorption (*ting nge 'dzin*), and equanimity (*btang snyoms*).
5. For the story of Madhyāntika (Nyi ma gung pa) and his clever creation of the land of Kashmir and the city Anupama ("incomparable"), see the translation in Chattopadhyaya, *Tāranātha's History of Buddhism in India*, ch. 3, pp. 29–33. For a discussion, see Harding, *Niguma, Lady of Illusion*, p. 3, and pp. 3–6 for discussion of her family.
6. Here, *mun can*, "the dark one," a name for Rāhula, the planet causing eclipses in ancient cosmology; and also the life-force wind (*srog rtsol*), which is said to be the nature of Rāhula. See Rangjung Dorje, *The Profound Inner Principles*, p. 144.
7. The last two and following two verses refer to the four branches (or stages) of approach and attainment (*bsnyen sgrub yan lag bzhi*). These usually apply to creation-phase practice, but here to the yogic practices of completion phase. The usual list is approach (*bsnyen pa*), close approach (*nye bsnyen*), attainment (*sgrub pa*), and great attainment (*sgrub chen*). In this verse, "near attainment" (*nyer sgrub*) is likely a mistake for close approach.
8. Another name for Virūpa, as attested in Sukhasiddhi's life story in the *Golden Rosary of Shangpa Biographies*, *ST*, vol. 1, p. 53. However, it is a name applied to many masters.
9. *Byams pa'i sgra dbyangs*. The details of Maitrīpa's life that are referenced in this prayer can be explored in Mathes, *Maitrīpa: India's Yogi of Nondual Bliss*, pp. 17–36.
10. Those were the two women that had accompanied him earlier.
11. According to Tāranātha's *Mine of Jewels*, these are Sahajavajra (Lhan skyes rdo rje), Śunyatāsamādhi (sTong nyid ting 'dzin), Rāmapāla (Rā ma pā la), and Vajrapāṇi (Badzra pā ṇi). *Collected Works*, vol. 15, p. 24. Also Roerich, *The Blue Annals*, p. 842.
12. *Rang byung sgra dbyangs*.
13. Puṇyākaragupta (bSod nams 'byung gnas) is probably the first or "senior" Vajrāsana (rDo rje gdan pa), or abbot of Bodhgaya, the Vajra Seat (the location

is also called Vajrāsana or Dorjeden). The others are Ratnākaragupta, Abhayākaragupta, and Tsami Lotsāwa, according to Katok Rikdzin Tsewang Norbu (1698–1755), who tried to sort it all out. *Biographies of Some Holy Ones* in *Selected Writings*, vol. 1, pp. 669–705. Abhayākaragupta also appears in Shangpa lineages, and in the supplication that follows.

14. Malabar district in India, now Madras state, and parts of Kerala state.
15. *klu dbang kun las bsdus pa*. Nāga King is an epithet of the Buddha, but nāgas are also the holders of great wealth, so there is double imagery here.
16. *rig grol spobs can*. Knowledge or awareness (*rig*) and liberation (*grol*) is an epithet for the sangha or assembly of monastics, so this is another double meaning.
17. Dza ri khaṇḍa. Various sources online give Abhayākara's birthplace as the city of Gaur, West Bengal, in eastern India, but according to Tāranātha, this was rather the birthplace of the middle Vajrāsana, Ratnākaragupta. Again according to Tāranātha, Abhayākara was born in southern India in Jārikhaṇḍa near Oḍiviśa. *Mine of Jewels*, pp. 110–11.
18. In Tāranātha, this is specified as the non-Buddhist tantras and classics. Ibid., p. 111.
19. Sauripa (which means someone from Sauri Monastery) is another name for Ratnākaragupta, or the middle Vajrāsana[pāda], who is considered the root guru of Abhayākara. Ibid., p. 112.
20. That would be *Moonlight of Vital Points: A Commentary on the Eight-Thousand-Line Perfection of Wisdom*, Toh. 3805.
21. The *Vajrāvali*, or *Vajra Garland Mandala Ritual*, may be his most famous work, among many dozens of compositions and translations. Toh. 3140.
22. Āmnāyamañjarī ("*Ears of Grain Esoteric Instructions*"), Toh. 1198.
23. sGra gcan 'dzin sbas pa'i rdo rje (10th–11th centuries), an Indian mahāsiddha also known as Rāhulagupta or Rāhulabhadra. See the introduction to ch. 23.
24. *tshogs gsum*: There are many possible definitions of the three collections. It seems the most likely here is the accumulation of merit, wisdom, and timeless awareness.
25. *sā la*, *Shorea robusta*, also known as shua or shala tree (Skt. *śāla*); it is the tree under which the Buddha was born.
26. De ba sa tva (Tib. Lha'i sems dpa') is the name he was given by his parents, according to *Two Histories of the Four Deities*, *ST*, vol. 9, p. 699. Devasatva was also the name of a buddha under whom Śākyamuni acquired merit during his journey through the first nine bodhisattva levels (Skt. *bhūmi*).
27. *a ba dhū ti'i spyod pa*: the conduct of practice based on the central channel, which supports all the tantric or subtle-body practices. This is also called *kun 'dar ma'i spyod pa*, "conduct of the all-vibrating one," *kun 'dar ma* being a synonym for the central channel. However, in Tāranātha's *Mine of Jewels*, in the version of what seems to be the same incident, the unidentified guru says, "Be a renunciate" or "Give up everything" (*kun spangs gyis shig*). *Collected Works*, vol. 15, p. 38.
28. mKhas grub Khyung po rnal 'byor. He is also known as Tsultrim Gönpo (Tshul

khrim mgon po), Shangpa Dugupa (Shangs pa gDu gu pa), Lama Shangpa (bLa ma Shangs pa), Lama Zhangzhong (bLa ma Zhang zhong), and others.

29. gNyis [su] med [pa'i] rdo rje (11th or early 12th century). Author of nearly fifty short pieces in the Tengyur and elsewhere. Usually identified as Maitrīpa (Maitrīpāda, also Avadhūtipāda), as apparently in this verse. The phrase "in the mandala" refers to an empowerment ritual.

30. An explanation of these three bodies is found in an important text by Khyungpo Naljor: *Infallible Instructions on the Three Intermediate States*, *ST*, vol. 8, pp. 187–207.

31. In the description of his death, the disciples specifically ask to where they should direct their prayers, and Khyungpo repeats three times: "From here, I will be awakened in Sukhāvatī, so supplicate me there and have no doubts or hesitations." Mokchokpa et al., *Brief Life Story of Lama Khyungpo Naljor*, *ST*, vol. 1, p. 141.

32. mNyam med rMog lcog pa Rin chen brtson 'grus (1110–1170). Also known as Jetsun Ratnavīrya.He was Khyungpo Naljor's main disciple to whom he passed the lineage, and the fourth of the initial Seven Jewels.

33. Khams pa (or 'Khams pa) A seng rDo rje brtan pa (12th century), well known as the first disciple to receive one of Sachen Kunga Nyingpo's commentaries on Virūpa's *Vajra Lines* in 1141, which was called after him the *Asengma*. See Stearns, *Luminous Lives*, pp. 18–19 and 153. Also said to be a teacher of the first Karmapa.

34. Bur sgom nag po, a disciple of Rechungpa. Mokchokpa studied with him for five years. His name could be translated as "the black meditator of Bur."

35. Abhirati (mngon dga'; "wondrous joy") is the pure realm of Buddha Akṣobhya, which seems to be preferred here over Sukhāvatī (bde ba can, "blissful"), the pure realm of Buddha Amitābha in the west. "Radiant light" (*'od 'phro can*; Skt. *arciṣmatī*) is also the fourth of the ten bodhisattva levels (*bhūmi*), or a buddha of that level who radiates light.

36. This confusing verse makes it seem as if Mokchokpa almost forgot this important act of ensuring the two lineages of dharma and family. In his biography, Mokchokpa is very clear: "This dharma lineage of Lama Shangpa [will pass to] Önton Kyergangpa, an emanation of the Great Compassionate One; then to his renowned student Sangye Nyentön; and on to his student and the lineage students, who will ultimately protect and spread it." *ST*, vol. 1, p. 220. Although "protector of migrators" (Drogön) can be any master, in this lineage it is most often used for Sangye Tönpa Tsöndru Senge (a.k.a. Drogön Chöje Tönpa), the student of Sangye Nyentön (a.k.a. Rigongpa Nyentön Chökyi Sherap).
But Kongtrul apparently followed a verse on the next page that reads: "Miraculously, he returned on a path of light, / and to Lopön Drogön Jotsun / he invested with empowerment for unbroken lineage; / to Önpo Sherap Repa / he entrusted the status of unbroken family lineage." Ibid., p. 221. Sherap Repa was Mokchokpa's nephew (*dbon po*).

37. dBon ston skyer sgang pa Chos kyi seng ge (1154–1217). Also known as Dharma-

siṃha. The title of Öntön means "nephew," indicating his early connection to his uncle, Bal Tamche Khyenpa ('Bal thams cad mkhyen pa), *The Blue Annals*, pp. 737–38.

38. These events from his previous lives are recounted in *Kyergangpa's Sealed Life Story*, sometimes called his secret biography, as told to his student Sangye Nyentön. In the story of his previous Chinese birth, he emanated as a harm-doer (*rākṣasa*) to tame the cannibal (*piśāca*) who was eating one human a day, and as a monkey to tame the monkeys and their king who had overrun and desecrated a jungle temple, like a page from Kipling's *Jungle Book*. *ST*, vol. 1, pp. 284–86.

39. 'Bal Thams cad mkhyen pa, or 'Bal tshad ma ba was Kyergangpa's uncle, from whom he received ordination as well as teachings. Roerich, *The Blue Annals*, pp. 735–36.

40. sNye mo [g]Zhu yas. Snye mo is a place name, as is gZhu. This person has not been identified.

41. Zhang sgom chos seng: One of the main disciples of Khyungpo Naljor.

42. [Ri gong pa] Sangs rgyas gnyan ston (1175–1255). He was also known as Chökyi Sherap (Chos kyi shes rab), Nyentön Bepe Naljor (gNyan ston sBas pa'i rnal 'byor), and Nyentön Chöje (gNyan ston chos rje.) He is the sixth lineage holder of the initial Seven Jewels. Sometimes there is confusion with the seventh Jewel, Sangye Tönpa, due to their similar names.

43. This important event deserves some comment. Dur khrod nag po ("black one of the charnel ground") is the later Virūpa, or Kāla Virūpa. According to Jo Nang Tāranātha, *The Seven Instruction Lineages* (*mKa' babs bdun ldan*), he was prophesied to commit four inexpiable sins and hence called "black." Virūpa's teachings of physical immortality are in the Tengyur, and apparently entered the Shangpa lineage at this event. Rigongpa's channel knots were released through these yogic exercises, which cleared up the "handicap of the secret [place]." Virūpa's *Attaining Immortality of the Body Root Text* is included in *DNZ*, volume 11, ch. 11. The original is in the Tengyur (Toh. 2285 and P 3133). Latöpa (la stod pa) is apparently a lama from Latö Monastery (la stod mgon pa), as mentioned in Ringongpa's *Life Story* (*ST*, vol. 1, p. 314.) See the story recounted more clearly in Roerich, *The Blue Annals*, p. 743.

44. 'Gro mgon Chos rje Sangs rgyas ston pa (1207–1278). Also known as brTson 'grus seng ge, and Chos rje ston pa. He was the final master in the initial Seven Jewels of the one-to-one lineage commanded by Niguma and therefore the one who opened it up.

45. *gcod kyi chos dbang sems la bskur*. The dharma empowerment conferred on the mind, which Machik Lapdrön received from her guru Kyotön Sönam Lama, is distinguished from the mere "deity empowerment conferred on the body" (*lha dbang lus la bskur ba*). See Kongtrul, *The Treasury of Precious Instructions, Volume 14: Chöd*, p. 231, and Harding, *Machik's Complete Explanation*, pp. 69–72.

46. [Ma cig] Grub pa'i rgyal mo, a teacher of Rechungpa, source of many texts in the Tengyur. It seems Sangye Tönpa was the seventh in both these lineages, as

clarified in the *Inner Life Story of Sangye Tönpa*, *ST*, vol. 1, p. 396, and Riggs, *Like an Illusion*, p. 157.

47. *lus gsum*. The fully ripened body, habitual body, and mental body.
48. mKhas grub gtsang ma Shangs ston (1234–1309). Also known as Samdingpa Khedrup Chöje (bSam sding pa mKhas grub chos rje), or Samdingpa, or just "Sam" for short. He is the first of the Later Seven Jewels of the Shangpa lineage. Tāranātha added the epithet sTan pa'i srog shing, "life-pillar of the doctrine," to his name.
49. mKhas grub bSam sdings pa gZhon nu grub (d. 1319). A disciple of Sangye Tönpa, he founded the Samding Monastery and established the Nyangme Samding transmission.
50. mKhas btsun 'Jag chen rGyal mtshan 'bum (1261–1334). Also known as mKhas btsun pa. A disciple of Tsangma Shangtön and also the third Karmapa Rangjung Dorje (1284–1339). He was an important master in the Jak transmission.
51. Khyung po Tshul khrims mgon po (fl. 13th century). Also known as Khyung po gnyis pa ("the second Khyungpo"). The name Khyungpo is said to be given to him in a dream of Khyungpo Naljor. Tāranātha, *Clearing Up the Darkness of Mind*, in *Collected Works*, vol. 17, p. 490. He is the second of the Later Seven Jewels.
52. *rdul [ba rnam par] bzhi*. The four kinds of instruction of the supreme nirmāṇakāya: by the great merit of the kāya, by the direct perception of awakened mind, by inconceivable miraculous abilities, and by knowledge conveyed by speech.
53. Tsultrim Gönpo was widely known as the "second Khyungpo." But since the "third Khyungpo" is used here and again in the following supplication, it has been retained with the far-fetched idea that it might refer to his place as the third of the second set of seven precious ones.
54. Bya bral Ri khrod ras chen (fl. 14th century), also known as Ri khrod ras chen Sangs rgyas seng ge and Chos rje Khams pa. Associated with Zhangzhong Monastery. Tāranātha, *Clearing Up the Darkness of Mind*, in *Collected Works*, vol. 17, p. 492.
55. *gdong lnga'i dbang po*. A reference to the lion, because the four paws resemble its face, making five faces. Both Ritrö ("mountain fastness") and Senge ("lion") are part of Jadral's name.
56. *ltos med bzhi*. The four things to be disregarded are the resources of mundane body, speech, and mind, along with consciousness transference. *DNZ*, vol. 15, p. 150, lines 4–5. Cited in *The Treasury of Precious Instructions, Volume 18: Jonang*, p. 671n295.
57. mKhyen ldan Shangs pa dkar po (1353–1434). Also known as Shangs dkar ba Rin chen rgyal mtshan, or just Shankarwa. He was the fourth of the Later Seven Jewels of the Shangpa lineage. Tāranātha, *Clearing Up the Darkness of Mind*, in *Collected Works*, vol. 17, p. 494.
58. mNyam med Sangs rgyas dpal bzang (1398–1465). He was the fifth of the Later Seven Jewels of the Shangpa.

59. The monastery of Kuklung (lha phu lkugs lung gi dgon pa) was established in the twelfth century in northern Shang by Mokchokpa. Sangye Palzang found it in disrepair and set about restoring it over ten years. Therefore he is called Kuklungpa, "he of Kuklung." Riggs, *Like an Illusion*, p. 239.
60. This is a confusing statement to make here, and I believe something is amiss. For one thing, all of these supplications are "just general praises." Moreover, the previous four masters—Khyungpo Tsultrim Gönpo, Jadral Ritrö Rechen, Shangpa Karpo, and Nyame Sangye Palzang—are all members of the Seven Later Jewels of whom there is as much information as for any of the line. Possibly this was misplaced from the *Golden Rosary*, where there is a section called "Brief Life Stories of Four Lamas" (*ST*, vol. 1, pp. 657–67), which are indeed very brief. Those four are Khedrup Tsangma Shangtön, Muchen Gyaltsen Palzang, Khedrup Dorje Zhönu, and Muchen Namkhai Naljor. At the end of those four short accounts, it states, "For longer biographies of these [four], see the work of Kachupa Rinchen Dargye, and the supplement written after his eighty-fourth year" (pp. 666–67). That has not been located.
61. rTogs ldan (or Grub chen) Nam mkha' rgyal mtshan (fl. 14th–15th centuries). Perhaps the same as Kun spangs chen po, who also got the name Namkha Gyaltsen at ordination.
62. Shangs phu'i dgon gsar could be Sang phu ne'u thog dgon pa, first built in 1072. Tāranātha calls it "Mi shangs dgon gsar."
63. Nags kyi rin chen (1384–1468), born in Bengal, translator of many texts in the Tengyur. He traveled to Tibet three times, and was one of the last Indian masters to do so; called "the last paṇḍita" in *The Blue Annals*.
64. Mu chen rgyal mtshan dpal bzang (d. 1347). Also known as gNags ston chos rje rGyal mtshan dpal bzang.
65. Chu dbar sprul pa'i gnas, in Tsang, the site where Milarepa passed away.
66. mKhas grub rDo rje gzhon nu (fl. 14th century). One of Tangtong Gyalpo's teachers.
67. Mus chen Nam mkha'i rnal 'byor. Also known as Grub thog Bya 'phur ba or mTsan ldan Nam mkha'i rnal 'byor or Nam mkha' rgyal mtshan. He received Niguma's teachings from Muchen Gyaltsen Palzangpo. See Stearns, *King of the Empty Plain*, p. 473n74.
68. It is confusing to have his name in all copies the same as Tokden Namkha Gyaltsen above, but in the "brief biography" in the *Golden Rosary*, it is given as his ordination name (*ST*, vol. 1, p. 665).
69. Grub chen Thang stong rgyal po (1361?–1485). Also known as Lung ston smyon pa, lCags zam pa, brTson 'grus bzang po, etc. See following notes, and introduction to the section on "Tangtong Gyalpo and the Direct Lineage" above.
70. His "unique" or overriding name bestowed in song by the ḍākinīs was Tangtong Gyalpo, "King of the Empty Plain." The others are Madman of the Empty Valley, Extractor of Food's Nutriment, One Who Tastes All Conditions as

Equal, and All Things Without Offense. See ch. 30 in the present volume and Stearns, *King of the Empty Plain*, pp. 160–61.

71. brTson 'grus bzang po was the name he received at full ordination (Ibid., p. 128). His novice ordination name was Tsöndru Senge (brTson 'grus seng ge).
72. Angaja or Aṅgara (Yan lag 'byung) was one of the sixteen arhats and is said to reside on Mount Kailash. On this occasion he taught Tangtong Gyalpo the *Perfection of Wisdom in Eight Thousand Lines*. Stearns, *King of the Empty Plain*, p. 164.
73. Zangs gling yul ("Copper Island") is probably ancient Ceylon.
74. Vararuci (Bram ze mChog sred) was a master from eastern India, a disciple of the master Kāṇha, and a practitioner of the dharma protector Mahākāla Pañjaranātha (Gur gyi mgon po), the particular protector of the Sakya tradition. In other sources, this event took place in a charnel ground called Grove of Terrifying Darkness ('Jigs byed mun pa tshal) rather than Blazing Rock (rDo la me 'bar). Stearns, *King of the Empty Plain*, p. 182.
75. Kalinga is an ancient area of India generally defined as the eastern coastal region between the Mahanadi and Godavari rivers, including present-day Orissa. The other names—zla ba, nas gling, pri yangku—in this line have not been identified.
76. Kra shis sgo mang mchod rten, the most famous and magnificent of the 111 stupas built on focal points by Tangtong Gyalpo to repel negative forces. This one is at Riwoche in Latö Jang in western Tsang.
77. rGya sgom Legs pa rgyal mtshan (b. 1484?). Also known as rGya sgom Legs rgyal Bas pa'i rnal 'byor and rGya sgom Ri khrod pa chen po. A short biography is in Tāranātha, *Clearing Up the Darkness of Mind*, in *Collected Works*, vol. 17, p. 501–3. Lekpa Gyaltsen is the source of Shangpa teachings for Kunga Drolchok and therefore important in the Jonang lineage of the Shangpa.
78. 'Jam mgon grub pa'i dpa' bo is a descriptive epithet for Kunga Drolchok (kun dga' grol mchog, 1507–1566), the great master of Jonang. (See following note.) Mañjunātha is another name for the bodhisattva Mañjuśrī.
79. Kun dga' grol mchog (1507–1566) was the great master who compiled the *One Hundred and Eight Teaching Manuals of Jonang*. He was the twenty-fourth throne holder of Jonang Monastery, and the lineage holder for the Jonang sublineage of the Shangpa Kagyu, which was passed on in his incarnations of Tāranātha and Jamgön Kongtrul.
80. gLo bo sman thang (not smon thang, as here), the capital of Mustang, Kunga Drolchok's birthplace. It has been part of northwestern Nepal since 1795.
81. Probably Lochen Ratnabhadra (1489–1563) and Paṇchen Jampa Lingpa (d. 1528).
82. *sNying po don gsum* by Mitrayogin, who is also known as Mitra Dzoki as here, or Ajitamitragupta. In Roerich, *The Blue Annals*, pp. 1031–34. Several commentaries on it were penned by the first Paṇchen Lama, Lozang Chökyi Gyaltsen.
83. [Zhing skyong] sTobs 'phrog dbang po (or "Mighty Strength-Sapping Field Protector") is a name for Four-Faced Mahākāla (mGon po zhal bzhi pa). There are

several versions with differing functions; this case is probably the yellow, wealth-increasing one (*nor 'phel*) since Vaiśravaṇa (rNam thos sras) is also associated with wealth. Willson and Brauen, *Deities of Tibetan Buddhism*, p. 364.

84. Chos sku Lha dbang grags pa (fl. 16th century). Also known as Brag stod pa Lha dbang grags pa and rDo rje 'chang Lha dbang grags pa. The student of Kunga Drolchok who passed the Shangpa teachings and others to Tāranātha, who called him his root lama.

85. An interlinear note here states, "This verse was written by Jetsun Rinpoche [Tāranātha]."

86. *pho nya gsum* (Skt. *Kingkara*, transliterated in Tibetan as "ging"): the ging who captures the objects to be delivered and holds a hook, the ging who delivers and holds a weapon, and the ging who proffers and holds a *homsar*, pit ladle.

87. This will be found in the following text by Tāranātha, *Verdant Tree of Faith*, in *DNZ*, pp. 449–52. In the *Shangpa Texts*, the editors have added it directly in at this point, along with Kongtrul's addition to it, *Flowers of Faith* (*DNZ*, pp. 453–56). This order makes sense chronologically, since it is a supplication to Tāranātha himself, but here we keep to the order of the *DNZ*. *Verdant Tree of Faith* is also in *Tāranātha's Collected Works*, vol. 1, pp. 999–1005.

88. Karma gZhan phan 'od zer (fl. 18th century) transmitted the Shangpa teachings of the Jonang tradition to Jamgön Kongtrul. Disciple of Karma Lhaktong. Strangely this name is not mentioned in Kongtrul's *Autobiography*, although his Shangpa transmission is identified as coming from a certain Karma Norbu, possibly the same. "A Gem of Many Colors," p. 41 and p. 317n317.

89. 'Jam dbyangs mkhyen brtse'i dbang po (1820–1892). Also known as Kun dga' bstan pa'i rgyal mtshan dPal bzang po, Thar rtse sprul sku, mDo sngags gling pa, among many other names. An incredible master who was Kongtrul's mentor and colleague.

90. Four kinds (*sde bzhi*) are the four kinds of magnificence: instruction, wealth, pleasure, and freedom. Zangpo, *Timeless Rapture*, p. 405n56. Ten virtues (*dge bcu*) here refer to virtues of a place. The region of Amdo in eastern Tibet is here called Domey (mdo smad).

91. *mchog gi gzigs pa lnga*: the five predeterminations of Buddha Śākyamuni before taking birth in this realm: observation of time, family, caste, mother, and land.

92. *gter chen brgyad*. The eight great treasures are recollection, intelligence, realization, form, confidence, dharma, awakening mind, and accomplishment. Twofold knowledge (*mkhyen gnyis*) is of the nature of things as they truly are (*ji lta ba*) and their full extent of manifestation (*ji rnyed pa*), as occurred in the first stanza.

93. *'bar ba gsum*: the blazing of warmth in the body, the blazing of potency in speech, and the blazing of realization in the mind.

94. Pad ma nor bu, the one who requested this supplication and the father of Kalu Rinpoche. Zangpo, *Timeless Rapture*, p. 363.

95. *'du ba gsum*: eating, sleeping, and elimination.

27. Verdant Tree of Faith

1. *dPal ldan bla ma dam pa'i rnam par thar pa dad pa'i ljon shing*, *DNZ*, vol. 12, pp. 449–52. Also in *Tāranātha's Collected Works*, Dzamtang edition, as *dPal ldan bla ma dam pa'i rnam thar bstod pa dad pa'i ljon shing*, vol. 1, pp. 999–1005.

28. Flowers of Faith

1. *rJe btsun rin po che'i rnam thar gsol 'debs kha skong dad pa'i me tog*, *DNZ*, vol. 12, pp. 453–56.
2. rNam gzigs. The bodhisattva who would become the Buddha Śākyamuni.
3. *chos drug thang mar brdal*. Probably a reference to Tāranātha's major commentary on the Six Dharmas of Niguma, known as *Tangdalma* (*DNZ*, vol. 12, pp. 1–101). Translated as the first chapter of the present volume. Also in Harding, *Four Tibetan Lineages*, pp. 343–423.
4. *mdo sgyu sems*. The main source texts of creation, completion, and great completion of the Nyingma tradition: specifically, the *Sutra That Gathers All Intentions* (*mDo dgongs pa 'dus pa*); the *Tantra of the Net of Magical Emanation* or *Guhyagarbha* (*rGyud sgyu 'phrul drwa ba* ste *dpal gsang ba snying po*); and the *Mind Marvels: Eighteen Mother and Children* (*sems smad ma bu bcho brgyad*) of the Ati mind class of dzogchen. *sMon lam tshig mdzod chen mo* (*Monlam Grand Dictionary*), s.v. "mdo sgyu sems," http://monlamit.com.

29. Niguma's Aspiration Prayer of the Sealed Word

1. *Ni gu ma'i smon lam bka' rgya ma*, also called *'Phags pa smon lam gyi rgyal po* ("The Sovereign of Noble Aspirations"), *DNZ*, vol. 12, pp. 459–62. Under the latter title, it is also found in the Peking Tengyur (rgyud 'grel, *pu*, ff. 201a7–203a8). This prayer is popularly known simply as "Kagyama."
2. Following the reading in the Tengyur: *rnam dag lus dang longs spyod* rather than the edition in the *Shangpa Texts* and *DNZ*, which reads *rnam dag lus ngag longs spyod* ("pure body, speech, [and] enjoyments").
3. The four gifts or kinds of generosity are the gifts of possessions, dharma, fearlessness, and love. Generosity is the first of the ten transcendent perfections.
4. *['thab] rtsod [dang] bral [ba'i] lha*: those gods living above Mount Meru who are free of fighting with the demigods. The third of the six kinds of gods of the desire realm (*'dod lha*).
5. There are six excellent qualities (*legs pa'i yon tan drug*): excellence in physical form, power, glory, renown, awareness, and diligence.
6. This is the intermediate state of the ceasing of the vital elements at the moment of death (*'chi kha gnad gcod kyi bar do*). In other words, one could skip straight to dharmakāya without going through the stages of normal death and thus manifest form bodies for the benefit of beings.

7. These verses referencing the bodhisattva Samantabhadra recall his vows and prayers in the famous aspiration at the end of the *Sutra of the Arrayed Trees* (*Gaṇḍavyūha*).

Songs of Experience: Introduction

1. *Thos pa don ldan byin rlabs rgya mtsho*. Previously translated by Ngawang Zangpo as "A Sea of Blessings" in *Timeless Rapture: Inspired Verse of the Shangpa Masters*, pp. 37–217.
2. For examples of Apabhraṃśa dohas and their translations, see Roger R. Jackson, *Tantric Treasures: Three Collections of Mystical Verse from Buddhist India*.
3. See Kurtis R. Schaeffer, *Dreaming the Great Brahmin*. Also, for Dampa Sangye, see Kongtrul, *The Treasury of Precious Instructions, Volume 13: Zhije*.
4. Milarepa's dates are usually given as 1052–1135. See the perennial classic, Chang, *One Hundred Thousand Songs of Milarepa*.

30. An Ocean of Blessings Meaningful to Hear

1. *dPal ldan shangs pa bka' brgyud kyi do ha rdo rje'i tshig rkang dang mgur dbyangs phyogs gcig tu bsgrigs pa thos pa don ldan byin rlabs rgya mtsho*, *DNZ*, vol. 12, pp. 463–559; *ST*, vol. 5, pp. 225–438. Also in *Collection of Liturgical Texts in Use in the Shangpa Kagyu Lineage*, pp. 317–530. Previously translated by Ngawang Zangpo in *Timeless Rapture: Inspired Verse of the Shangpa Masters*. Also see *Garland of Uḍumbara Flowers* in ch. 26 for more information on most of these authors.
2. *Nāda* in Sanskrit means a subtle sound or vibration. In this context it means that the teaching has been transmitted in a nonverbal way, certainly not by writing. It is said that Vajradhara even taught the *Jewel Ocean Tantra*, the elusive source of many Shangpa instructions, "through the sounds of nāda." *DNZ*, vol. 11, p. 207; *The Treasury of Precious Instructions, Volume 11: Shangpa Kagyu*, p. 264.
3. See ch. 25, *A Wish-Fulfilling Gem*; *DNZ*, vol. 12, pp. 366–67.
4. *rgyun bshags*. From the *Ḍākinī Vajra Tent Tantra* (*Ḍākinīvajrapañjara*), Toh. 419, rgyud, *nga*, 53b4–5.
5. Found also in *DNZ*, vol. 11, pp. 13–15, as *Vajra Lines of the Amulet Mahāmudrā* (*sDong po phyag rgya chen po gwa'u ma'i rdo rje tshig rkang*), and with interlinear comments in the Peking Tengyur, rgyud 'grel, *pu*, ff. 163a8–164b8 (4642). See my previous translations in Kongtrul, *The Treasury of Precious Instructions, Volume 11: Shangpa Kagyu*, pp. 29–33; and in Harding, *Niguma, Lady of Illusion*, pp. 145–47.
6. *Rang grol phyag rgya chen po*. Previously translated in Harding, *Niguma, Lady of Illusion*, pp. 150–52.
7. This archetypical expulsion story, not found in the Sanskrit source of Maitrīpa's life, is examined by Klaus-Dieter Mathes in *Maitrīpa, India's Yogi of Nondual Bliss*, pp. 31–34, and Brunnhölzl, *Straight from the Heart*, p. 511n448.

8. Added from the Tengyur version. See note below.
9. *sgom pa'i snyan brgyud*, but in the Tengyur *dgon pa'i snyan rgyud*, which is probably a mistake but could mean "the aural transmission of the hermitage."
10. *de nyid kyi ni 'phro 'du las*, added from the Tengyur version, where it seems to replace the next line.
11. *lha bzhi*, but the Tengyur has *lha mo bzhi*, "four goddesses." Either could be correct, since the only deity mentioned is the goddess Vajrayoginī. However, since the Shangpa practice of the Four Deities Combined is relevant to Rāhula, who was the main source of its transmission to Khyungpo Naljor, the current version makes sense.
12. This line is also different: "Some rely on the meaning of purity" (*dag gi don la*).
13. In the Tengyur as *Meditation on the Inconceivable* [*Four Immeasurables*], *Acintya-parībhāvana; bSam gyi mi khyab pa bsgom pa*, Dg.T. rgyud, *zi*, 25b–26a (Toh. 2399). The colophon there reads, "This concludes the Meditation on the Inconceivable Four Immeasurables by Ācārya Rāhula."
14. *rDo rje'i tshigs drug ma*. See a longer version of Rāhula's story and this incident in ch. 23.
15. This brief versified autobiographical account by Khyungpo Naljor and all the following narratives can be found as part of his biography in *Shangpa Texts*, vol. 1, pp. 60–63.
16. Shangs pa gDu gu pa, "Shangpa Bracelet," a name for Khyungpo Naljor. Sometimes spelled Shangs pa bsDu bu pa.
17. Gu lang was a huge gold field in Central Tibet, now mined by the Chinese.
18. gLang ri 'od ldan, the same as Langri Tangpa (gLang ri thang pa rDor rje seng ge, 1054–1123).
19. From Mokchokpa et al., *Brief Life Story of Lama Khyungpo Naljor*, *ST*, vol. 1, pp. 69–72, as is most of the following.
20. *'Dul ba'i mdo*, on rules of Buddhist monastic discipline by Ācārya Guṇaprabha (Tib. Yon tan 'od, ninth century), Toh. 4117, 'dul ba, *wu*, ff. 1b1–100a7.
21. There is brief mention of this Harikela in Tāranātha's history of the sixth instruction lineage, a disciple of Lūhipa, who turned his consort into a cat named Bhirḍipa. *Mine of Jewels*, p. 105.
22. The thirty-seven factors of enlightenment, faculties that the practitioner must develop for progress on the path, were basically present in the Nikāyas and throughout the Abhidharma. The five paths, including the ten levels, were developed by early Mahayana, as revealed in the *Stages of Yogic Practice* (*Yogācārabhūmi*). The thirty-seven factors are often overlaid onto the Mahayana path system to emphasize their correspondences. After all, there must be just one path to enlightenment. See translation and discussion of Niguma's *Stages in the Path of Illusion* in Harding, *Niguma, Lady of Illusion*, pp. 37–142 and appendix 2, pp. 201–55, for the Tibetan. Also Kapstein's summary in "The Illusion of Spiritual Progress," pp. 203–4.
23. The Asian palmyra palm, or tāla palm (*Borassus flabellifer*), grows to a height of twenty meters.

24. This corresponds to the Navel Emanation Chakra, described in chapters 15 and 18. It can be found as guidebook 82 of the one hundred and eight guidebooks in Kongtrul, *The Treasury of Precious Instructions, Volume 18: Jonang*. Also see note there on p. 697n847.
25. This song is usually referred to as Khyungpo's *Eight Songs* (*mgur brgyad*), though it is really eight verses. There is a brief commentary (*mGur brgyad rtsa 'grel*) that explains those strange esoteric practices in *The Eight Songs and Four Sealed Words of the Great Adept Khyungpo*, in the *Compendium of Sādhanas*, vol. 11, pp. 181–84. The *Eight Songs* as well as the commentary are both mentioned in Kongtrul, *Blue Beryl Key* (p. 108).
26. *thim pa rnam gsum*. According to the commentary (see above note), the three dissolutions are all thoughts of attachment to outer objects dissolve into dreamlike illusion, subjective mental thoughts that cling to them dissolve into mere appearance that has no intrinsic nature, and the consciousness that meditates in such a way also dissolves in the realm of phenomena (p. 181).
27. This last verse seems to be the origin of the widely used practice called Voice Blessing (*Ngag gi byin rlabs*) attributed to Khyungpo Naljor. That this is so is indicated in a commentary by Lozang Tenpa Rabgye (1647–1726): *Swift Advance of Blessings: How to Put into Practice the Instructions on Ālikāli from the Teachings of Khedrup Khyungpo Naljor Known as the Eight Songs.*
28. *Byams chos sde lnga*, made up of the five individual works of Maitreya, Toh. 3786, 4020–22, and 4024.
29. *Secret Tantra of the General Ritual of All Mandalas* (Toh. 806), Dg.K. rgyud, *ka*, ff. 141a–167b.
30. Here *rJe btsun ma lha lnga*, elsewhere *mKha' 'gro sde lnga* (Ḍākinīs of the Five Classes) as in chs. 31–32, which was transmitted to Khyungpo Naljor by Siṃhamukhā.
31. According to the interlinear notes in ch. 15, the three gatherings (*'du ba rnam gsum*) are of humans or ḍākinīs, food, and wealth; and the three arisings (*'char ba rnam pa gsum*) are of physical well-being, verbal ability, and mental realization.
32. *Shar phyogs 'od 'phro can gyi shing khams*. A bit confusing here, as the eastern buddha realm is that of Akṣobhya, called Abhirati (*mngon dga'*), where in other accounts Mokchokpa is born after his life and attains a state of the Radiant One (Arcimat). Also, it is the name of the fourth of the ten bodhisattva levels (*bhūmi*), or a buddha of that level who radiates light (*'od 'phro can gyis sa*, Skt. *arciṣmatī*). See ch. 26, *Garland of Uḍumbara Flowers.*
33. *rgyal srid sna bdun*, the seven possessions or attributes or treasures of a ruler or universal monarch are the precious wheel, gem, queen, minister, elephant, horse, and general.
34. Although this and the following three song sections are continuous with "The Song of Six Attitudes of an Experienced Mind," without separate headings, I've taken the liberty of adding headings taken from the contents as the style

changes. These particular songs are not included in Mokchokpa's biography and must have a different source.

35. *Life Story of Precious Guru Mokchokpa*, *ST*, vol. 1, pp. 206–7. Missing here is how the yak swung his head back and forth with flames shooting out of his horns.
36. 'Brong bu'i btsan rgod [dregs pa can]. The story of this deathbed encounter with a fierce but faithful demon and the rest of Mokchokpa's song, as well as the spirit's own verses, are in *Life Story of Precious Guru Mokchokpa*, *ST*, vol. 1, pp. 213–19. *'Brong bu* means "wild yak."
37. This is the well-known adage that to know why you are the way you are now, look at the deeds of the last life; and if you want to know how you will be, look at your causal actions now.
38. Rigongpa, *Life Story of Lama Rigongpa*, *ST*, vol. 1, pp. 331–33.
39. A Sanskrit translation of Chökyi Senge (Chos kyi seng ge, "Lion of Dharma"), the name of his guru, Kyergangpa.
40. The reader may notice that this doesn't add up to twelve. If we count the first "need" in the author's homage, there are still only eleven. The Tibetans often calculate the total number to include one final count of all the preceding as an additional number in itself.
41. *lhun grub rnam [pa] gsum*: the ground, path, and result of spontaneous presence.
42. This song and its circumstances were previously translated in Stearns, *King of the Empty Plain*, pp. 160–61; also in Brunnhölzl, *Straight from the Heart*, pp. 287–88. It is from Gyurme Dechen, *Life Story of Tangtong Gyalpo*, pp. 73–75 (BDRC W21690).
43. mKhas btsun bDe legs dpal, a geshe from Kham. This song and its circumstances are also in Stearns, *King of the Empty Plain*, pp. 326–31, and Brunnhölzl, *Straight from the Heart*, pp. 298–300. From Gyurme Dechen, *Life Story of Tangtong Gyalpo*, pp. 236–39.
44. The "dharma of the gods" or "divine religion" (*lha chos*) is an ancient term originally applied to the Bön and later to Buddhism. The dharma of humans (*mi chos*) specifically was a sixteen-point moral code established by King Songtsen Gampo in the seventh century. Stearns, *King of the Empty Plain*, p. 558n879. Generally, it refers to the customs of human society, literally the "ways of men."
45. Gyagom Lekpa Gyaltsen (rGya sgom Legs pa rgyal mtshan; fl. 15th–16th centuries) was Kunga Drolchok's teacher from whom he received the Shangpa teachings. Lekpa Gyaltsen here is shortened to Lekgyal.
46. *g.yung drung*: an equilateral cross with arms bent at right angles, all in the same rotary direction. It was an ancient symbol of permanence and well-being. Though co-opted by the Nazis and therefore bearing negative connotations, it is kept here to help restore its original meaning of immutability.
47. Three terms for "mind" are used here in this verse: *sems*, *blo*, and *yid*. Different translations are used here to reflect that.
48. gNas gsar pa 'Jam dbyangs mkhyen tse'i dbang phyug bsTan pa'i rgyal mtshan dPal bzang po, 1524–1568. Also known as Zhalu Khenchen Khyentse Wang-

chuk. Tsis gnas gsar is a place in Upper Nyang. Jamyang Khyentse Wangchuk was an important Sakya treasure revealer and teacher, and the fourteenth abbot of Zhalu Monastery in Tsang. He received the Shangpa lineage from his teacher, Tsarchen Losal Gyatso (1502–1566), who received them from his teacher Doringpa (d. 1524), who had been a student of Tangtong Gyalpo. Stearns, *Song of the Road*, p. 2.

49. *sNying gi bdud rtsi*. Each quatrain refers to a specific practice. I've taken the liberty of numbering and listing them here for clarification: (1) author's homage; (2) Amulet Mahāmudrā; (3) [Six Dharmas:] Fierce Inner Heat, (4) Illusory Body, (5) Dream, (6) Lucid Clarity, (7) Intermediate State, (8) Transference; (9) [Three Integrations:] Integration of the Guru, (10) Integration of the Yidam, (11) Integration of Illusion; (12) [Khecarīs:] White Khecarī, (13) Red Khecarī; (14) [Immortal and Infallible:] Immortal Body, (15) Infallible Mind; (16) Six-Armed Mahākāla; (17) reference to Niguma's *Vajra Lines*; (18–19) final aspirations.
50. *dkar rtsi pa*, described as someone who takes care of only their cup during a big celebration. *sMon lam tshig mdzod chen mo* (*Monlam Grand Dictionary*), s.v. "*dkar rtsi pa*," http://monlamit.com. As this verse is about his teacher Tsarchen Losal Gyatso, perhaps it is a reference to Tsarchen's long travels on the road without much luggage. See Stearns, *Song of the Road*.
51. *skyon bzhi*: the four faults of not realizing mahāmudrā or the nature of mind found in the earliest Shangpa teachings. They are that it is too close to recognize, too profound to grasp, too easy believe, and too excellent to comprehend. See Niguma, *Vajra Lines of the Amulet Mahāmudrā*, in *DNZ*, vol. 11, pp. 13–15; *The Treasury of Precious Instructions, Volume 11: Shangpa Kagyu*, pp. 29–30.
52. *srog rtsol rlung*. Vital energy can translate *srog rtsol* in general, though it is also a specific name, while *rlung* is the circulating or vital energy winds. Together, the Sanskrit is *prāṇāyāma*, meaning to control those energies.
53. *mchog yan lag lnga bsdu'i sbyor ba*. There are several possibilities for "five branches," but with the next line it seems to refer to the five manifest awakenings (*mngon byang lnga*), a creation-phase practice that specifically purifies womb birth.
54. Also in *Songs of the Oral Instructions of Venerable Tāranātha*, *Collected Works*, vol. 1, pp. 783–85. All of the following songs are also found in that collection.
55. In *Songs of the Oral Instructions of Venerable Tāranātha*, this note refers rather to the following song. *Collected Works*, vol. 1, p. 844.
56. *Songs of the Oral Instructions of Venerable Tāranātha*, in *Collected Works*, vol. 1, pp. 842–44.
57. *Collected Works*, vol. 1, pp. 976–78.
58. *sems can*, but in the Tāranātha edition it is just "mind" (*sems*). Ibid., p. 976.
59. *Collected Works*, vol. 1, pp. 978–80.
60. Here *mos gus skyes*, but in Tāranātha, the transitive form: *mos gus bskyed*.
61. Kun dga' snying po (Skt. Ānandagarbha), given by Jampa Lhundrup.
62. The Sanskrit name (Tib. sGrol ba'i mgon po) was given him by his Indian guru Buddhaguptanātha, whom he met at the age of fourteen.

63. Lo chen ("great translator") 'Gyur med bde chen (1540–1615), a maternal descendant ("nephew") of Tangtong Gyalpo (1361?–1485) and considered a master of his tradition of the Shangpa Kagyu (*thang lugs*). He received the instructions of Niguma from Kunga Drolchok (1507–1566). Among his contributions to the Shangpa doctrines, see ch. 13, *White Khecarī Transference*. This song, but without the title, is found in illuminated texts of the *Collected Works of Lochen Gyurme Dechen*, vol. 2, pp. 605–6.
64. This translation of the Sanskrit homage is added from the edition in the *Collected Works of Lochen Gyurme Dechen*, vol. 2.
65. bLo gsal bstan skyong (1804–1865?) was abbot of Zhalu Monastery in Tsang, and his primary residence was Ribuk Ritrö, "Mountain Cave Hermitage," in the caves above Zhalu. Hence he was also known as Ribuk Tulku, and he often signed as Losal Ritröpa, "the hermit Losel." Kongtrul also called him Zhalu Choktrul after his recognition as the incarnation of Tsechokling Yeshe Gyaltsen (1727–1802). See *The Treasury of Precious Instructions, Volume 11: Shangpa Kagyu*, pp. 455–57, for an introduction to his contributions to the Shangpa corpus.
66. bLo bzang mthu stobs (fl. late 18th–early 19th centuries), also called Avadhūtipa by Losal Tenkyong, was his direct source for the Shangpa teachings. See ch. 5, "Guidance in Amulet Mahāmudrā" for Tangtong Gyalpo's description of the meditation, and ch. 10 for Tāranātha's. Also, *The Treasury of Precious Instructions, Volume 11: Shangpa Kagyu*, pp. 29–33, for Niguma's root text, *Vajra Lines of the Amulet Mahāmudrā*.
67. These are the eighteen visualization rounds clearly described in Tāranātha's *Amulet Mahāmudrā or Three Naturally Settled States Guidance Manual* in ch. 10.
68. *Flower of the Awareness Holders: A Vajra Song of Praise to the Inner Life Story of the Mighty Adept Tsöndru Zangpo*, in mKhyen brtse'i bka' 'bum, vol. 2, pp. 203–4.
69. The underline here and in the following instances indicate the circular marks below certain words in the Shechen edition, which are apparently meant to bring attention to those words.
70. Here, *gcig tu 'dza' ba'i brtson 'grus brtsams pa yis*. Since *'dza'* ("waste") didn't make sense to me, I've taken from Khyentse's version, where it is *mdza' ba*. In *Khyentse's Collected Works*, vol. 2, p. 203.
71. Using *dbyid* from ibid. (p. 203) rather than *dbyings* ("space") here in *DNZ*.
72. *shrī dza la parva* (misspelled here as *sarva*) *ta'i lcags zam* (Tib. *dpal chu bo ri*). That is, Mount Chuwori on the south bank of the Yarlung Tsangpo River above its confluence with the Kyichu River, south of Lhasa. It is a sacred site of Padmasambhava. Jamgön Kongtrul, *The Life of Jamyang Khyentsé Wangpo*, p. 212n224. Chakzam Monastery was built on that hill by Tangtong Gyalpo, and established as his main seat and of the Chaksam lineage. It was named after the nearby iron suspension bridge that he built in 1444. But neither structure remains: "The monastery of lCags-zam has been totally destroyed, without a brick remaining in place." The bridge had also been destroyed in 1950, "with just a pile of stones in

the middle of the river that once served as the support for the northern end of the bridge." Donald S. Lopez Jr. and Cyrus Stearns, "A Report on Religious Activity in Central Tibet, October, 1984," pp. 101–07. Thank you to Gregory Forgues for his help sorting this.

73. Lohita or Lohit is a name for the "the upper waters of the gTsangpo" or else the Brahmaputra.
74. *Zab don bsdus pa'i rdo rje'i thol glu nges don them skas*, in *Khyentse's Collected Works*, vol. 2, pp. 205–8.
75. *sbyor ba gzhi ldan*: *rngub* ("inhaling"), *dgang ba* ("filling"), *gzhil ba* ("dispersing"), and *mda' ltar 'phang ba* ("shooting like an arrow").
76. *rab* refers to the practitioners of highest acumen. Khyentse's version has *rab kyis dam pas* (p. 206), but in *DNZ* the "*sa*" has clearly been scratched out, making it *rab kyi dam pas*, and losing the intent.
77. Two separate verses from *Pith Instructions on Mahāmudrā* (Skt. *Mahāmudropadeśa*), also known as the *Ganges Mahāmudrā* in the Tibetan tradition because it was taught to Nāropa on the shores of the Ganges by Tilopa (988–1069). These two verses appear in separate locations, the second verse here is the third verse in the original, while the first verse here is verse 27, near the end. The version here seems to accord mostly with that in the Peking edition of the Tengyur (Toh. 2303).
78. *Grags stong rdo rje'i thol glu sgyu ma'i mchod sprin*, in *Khyentse's Collected Works*, vol. 2, pp. 209–10.
79. A red finch belonging to the *Amandava* genus, renowned as songbirds. Outside India, they evolved into a mythical half-human bird.
80. This phrase is originally from *Niguma's Vajra Lines of the Six Dharmas* (*DNZ*, vol. 11, pp. 7–12).
81. See Tāranātha's *Tangdalma*, ch. 1, session 18, "Integrating Sickness and Spirits as Illusion," where these enumerations are explained.
82. "The roots are impermanence and disillusionment, the branches are conduct and pledge substances, the leaves are the innate radiance of the path of methods, and the flowers grow from supplications." *Tangdalma*, *DNZ*, pp. 66–69; this volume, ch. 1, pp. 66–68.
83. Si tu pad ma nyin byed dbang po (1774–1853), the ninth Situ incarnation at Palpung Monastery (dPal spungs dgon), the location of Kongtrul's retreat of Tsadra Rinchen Drak.
84. *bKra shis bka' rgya ma*, in Khyungpo Naljor, *The Eight Songs and Four Sealed Words of the Great Adept Khyungpo*, in *Compendium of Sādhanas*, vol. 11, p. 192. See ch. 25, pp. 413–14 in this volume for the translation.

Five Ḍākinīs: Introduction

1. *Mine of Jewels [2]: Sādhanas of an Ocean of Yidams Taught in the Four Tantra Classes*, in *Tāranātha's Collected Works*, vol. 15, p. 1235.

2. Mokchokpa et al., *Brief Life Story of Lama Khyungpo Naljor*, *ST*, vol. 1, pp. 126–30. See Riggs, *Like an Illusion*, pp. 82–85. Ghapa (Gha pa) in the life story is spelled 'Ga' pa.
3. *ST*, vol. 1, pp. 129–130; *DNZ*, p. 492. The whole song can be found in ch. 30, *An Ocean of Blessings Meaningful to Hear*, p. 548. There is a slight difference in the third line there, reflected in that translation.

31. Ḍākinīs of the Five Classes Sādhana and Authorization Ritual in the Shangpa Tradition

1. *Shangs lugs mkha' 'gro sde lnga'i sgrub thabs rjes gnang dang bcas pa*, *DNZ*, vol. 12, pp. 561–67; *ST*, vol. 2, pp. 755–68. Original from *Mine of Jewels: Sādhanas of an Ocean of Yidams* (*Yi dam rgya mtsho'i sgrub thabs rin chen 'byung gnas*) (in a section entitled *rgyud sde bzhi las gsungs pa'i* . . .), in *Tāranātha's Collected Works*, vol. 15, pp. 1148–51.
2. In Kongtrul's torma offering in *Treasury of Vast Precepts*, the offering mantra for the diverse ḍākinī is *oṃ viśva ḍākinī pratīccha imaṃ baliṃ a phaṭ*, which is followed by the mantra for all ḍākinīs: *oṃ sarva ḍākinī pratīccha imaṃ baliṃ ho phaṭ*. *GK*, vol. 8, p. 467.
3. Here ends the sādhana composed by Tāranātha in *Mine of Jewels*. The empowerment is filled in by Jamgön Kongtrul.
4. Standard verse for requesting empowerment, found in *All Tathāgatas' Secret Great Yoga* (Toh. 453), p. 299b.
5. This standard confession appears throughout the liturgies of empowerment. Filled in here from Tāranātha's *Five Tantras' Mandala Sādhana*, in *DNZ*, vol. 11, pp. 79–80.
6. In Tāranātha's *Mine of Jewels: Sādhanas of an Ocean of Yidams*, after the sādhana, there are brief instructions on how to perform the torma empowerment. Kongtrul has basically filled in the blanks by writing out the suggested prayers and expanding the instructions.

32. Torma Offering to the Ḍākinīs of the Five Classes Just for Regular Practice

1. *Shangs lugs mkha' 'gro sde lnga'i mchod gtor 'bul ba dkyus ma tsam gyi lag len*, *DNZ*, vol. 12, pp. 569–71; *ST*, vol. 5, pp. 79–86; *GK*, vol. 8, pp. 465–68.
2. In the Kangyur, these verses appear only in the *Mahāmāya Tantra*, a mother tantra. Toh. 425, f. 167.
3. This supplication to the five buddha families seems to originate in *All Tathāgatas' Great Secret Body, Speech, and Mind Guhyasamāja Tantra*. Toh. 442, f. 138a–b. It varies widely for each liturgy.
4. *All Tathāgatas' Secret Great Yoga*, Toh. 453, f. 296a.

Six-Armed Mahākāla: Introduction

1. *Ye shes kyi mgon po phyag drug pa'i chos skor gyi byung tshul mdo tsam brjod pa,* in *Collected Works*, vol. 21, pp. 875–99. It was included in the *Golden Rosary of Shangpa Biographies* with the added title of *Rain of Elixir of Spiritual Powers* (*dNgos grub bdud rtsi'i char 'bebs*) and a short colophon by Kyapje Kalu Rinpoche. *ST*, vol. 1, pp. 717–49.
2. See versions of the story in the permissions for Removing All Obstacles and for Guru-Protector Inseparable in ch. 36, *Garland of Cintāmaṇi.*
3. *The Beryl Key*, *ST*, vol. 6, pp. 124–25.
4. *DNZ*, vol. 12, p. 661; in this volume, ch. 36, *Garland of Cintāmaṇi.*
5. In *Tāranātha's Collected Works*, filling volume 15. Known simply as the *Rinjung*.
6. *Yi dam rgya mtsho'i sgrub thabs rin chen 'byung gnas kyi lhan thabs rin 'byung don gsal*, reproduced by Lokesh Chandra from the collections of Raghu Vira. BDRC MW1KG10237.
7. Martin Willson and Martin Brauen, *Deities of Tibetan Buddhism: The Zürich Paintings of the Icons Worthwhile to See (Bris sku mthong ba don ldan).*
8. sKyid shod [mchog sprul] Ngag dbang bstan 'dzin 'phrin las (1639–1682), the second Zhabs drung. In his *Collected Works*, BDRC: W22116.

33. Treasure Trove of Awakened Activity

1. *dPal ye shes kyi mgon po phyag drug pa'i sgrub thabs gtor ma'i cho ga dang bcas pa phrin las gter mdzod*, *DNZ*, vol. 12, pp. 573–91. Also in *Tāranātha's Collected Works*, vol. 14, pp. 515–42, and another version with the same title on pp. 543–57. The version in *Shangpa Texts* (vol. 4, pp. 211–71) is quite different from this one and has been rendered into metered verse, apparently by Kalu Rinpoche. It is the shorter, chantable verse version that is used in monasteries and dharma centers and has been translated many times.
2. *nang mchod*. In this case, it is a small kapāla or vessel in front of the officiant containing liquid representing *amṛta* (*bdud rtsi*) which is used to consecrate the rest of the ritual articles after it has been itself consecrated.
3. Skt. sindhura, a brilliant red (vermilion) pigment made from mercury sulfide (cinnabar), commonly seen between the eyebrows of Indian people, called "bindi" (from *bindu*, spot or sphere).
4. For descriptions and illustrations of Śrīdevī's five magical weapons, see Willson and Brauen, *Deities of Tibetan Buddhism*, pp. 566–67.
5. bSil ba'i tshal; Skt. Śītavana. There are generally eight great charnel grounds in a wrathful mandala visualization, though the actual list varies with the tantra source. However, Cool Grove is not among them, but apparently belongs to the peaceful mandala. The geographical location is in the east, near Bodhgaya, India.
6. In the version in *Tāranātha's Collected Works*, Tāranātha names himself as Jamyang Kunga Nyingpo and ends there. All the following masters are not mentioned,

since obviously they come after Tāranātha. No doubt they were added here by Kongtrul.

7. Rematī (Tib. dMag zor ma) is being used as a name for Śrīdevī (dPal ldan lha mo), "Glorious Goddess," a form of Mahākalī.
8. Vināyaka is another name for Gaṇeśa. Also Gaṇapati, Obstructor King, and Lord of the Assembly.
9. Khyungpo Naljor, *bKra shis bka' brgya ma*. In *The Eight Songs and Four Sealed Words of the Great Adept Khyungpo*, in *Compenium of Sādhanas*, vol. 11, p. 192.
10. *gSang sgrub rgyan can*, the practice of Six-Armed Protector with a consort. See the empowerment below in *Garland of Cintāmaṇi* or that of Kyishö Ngawang Tenzin Trinle, which carries the clarifying title of *The Authorization for Adorned Awareness Protector; or, The Secret Sādhana*. In his *Collected Works*, pp. 480–86, ff. 21b–24b.

34. Spontaneous Accomplishment of the Four Actions

1. *dPal myur mdzad ye shes kyi mgon po'i gtor chog rgyas pa'i kha skong dmigs rim dang bcas pa gsal bar bkod pa las bzhi lhun grub*, *DNZ*, vol. 12, pp. 593–622; *ST*, vol. 4, pp. 274–339.
2. This shorter text with the same title as the long one, *Treasure Trove of Awakened Activity*, is in *Tāranātha's Collected Works*, vol. 15, pp. 745–65. It is the first of a set of texts, or "chapters" (*le tshan*), concerning Mahākāla that follows directly after the first section of the *Mine of Jewels*.
3. See Tāranātha's *The Practice of Past Gurus: Esoteric Instructions on the Principal Five Deities of the Five Tantras*, *DNZ*, vol. 11, pp. 333–39; *The Treasury of Precious Instructions, Volume 11: Shangpa Kagyu*, pp. 415–21.
4. *Dregs pa kun 'dul*, in *Tāranātha's Collected Works*, vol. 13, pp. 249–73.
5. Jamgön Kongtrul, *Pool of Spiritual Powers: Practicing the Great Torma Ritual*, *GK*, vol. 13, pp. 29–53.
6. See the previous text in ch. 33, *Treasure Trove of Awakened Activity* (*DNZ*, p. 580).
7. gSod byed Nag po brtsegs pa. From a creation story recounted in the Abhidharma.
8. The four ways of birth (*skyes bzhi*) are from a womb, from an egg, from warmth, and miraculous. The five paths of being (*lam rgyud lnga*) are the gods and demigods, humans, and the beings of the three lower states.
9. The three, described in Tāranātha's text, are Guru-Protector Inseparable, Dispelling Defilements, and Getting Down to the Vital Point to bring ḍākinīs under control. The third, where the guru is visualized as red in color, according to Tāranātha, is not elaborated further in this commentary.
10. Not located in the *Collected Works of Karma Chakme*. It appears to be a general fulfillment for a dharma protector, not specifically Six-Armed Mahākāla.
11. Khedrup Je Gelek Palzang (mKhas grub rje dGe legs dpal bzang, 1385–1438), one of the main disciples of Je Tsongkhapa, who had brought Shangpa teachings into the Gelukpa sect.

12. According to Nebesky-Wojkowitz in *Oracles and Demons of Tibet* (p. 357), this should read *mtshe zor* rather than here, *'tshe zor* ("harmful *zor*"). The *zor* are magical weapons or spells, used primarily by Bönpo priests (according to Buddhists), in which an object or pyramid-shaped torma resembling it is imbued with magical abilities or spells and then cast or flung (*'phen pa*) in the direction of the adversary, thus releasing its lethal powers. The example here, according to Nebesky-Wojkowitz, is described as a torma in the likeness of a thorny weed (*mtshe*) made of barley dough with thorns inserted into the tips of the leaves (cluster-bomb torma). After the formula to imbue it with magic, it is cast out. Similar descriptions of almost all of the following *zor* and more are found in Nebesky-Wojkowitz, *Oracles and Demons of Tibet*, pp. 355–58. Thanks to Gregory Forgues for tracking sources in English and Polish.
13. *Mahākālastotrākṣepa; Nag po chen po'i bstod pa rngam pa sgra sgrogs*, Peking Tengyur, rgyud 'grel, *'u*, f. 11a4–11b8 (vol. 86, p. 176). There are some thirteen texts by Brahmin Vararuci (Bram se mchog sred) in the Tengyur, many of them concerning Mahākāla. For an episode where he gives Six-Armed Mahākāla as a protector to Tangtong Gyalpo, see Stearns, *King of the Empty Plain*, pp. 182, 519n523.
14. Tshang tshing 'khrigs; Skt. Gahvara. This is the actual name of one of the traditional eight great charnel grounds of India (*dur khrod chen po brgyad; mahāśmaśānāni*), but it may be just descriptive here, since usually Six-Armed Mahākāla is associated with the Cool Grove Charnel Ground (Skt. Śītavana).
15. In the Tengyur edition, the phrase "inexhaustible blazing" is *mi zad 'bar ba* rather than *DNZ*, "unbearable blazing" (*mi bzad 'bar ba*).
16. Śrīdevīkālīstotra; dPal lha mo la bstod pa. Peking Tengyur, rgyud 'grel, *zu*, ff. 270b–271a (vol. 86, p. 160). The colophon states that it was composed by Maitrīpa when he saw the goddess face to face. Translated by Lalitavajra and Lotsāwa Gyi ljang dbu dkar (BDRC W1KG13126).
17. This second praise attributed here to Maitrīpa does not appear in the Peking Tengyur.
18. According to Barron, *The Autobiography of Jamgön Kongtrul* (p. 403n27), this is probably Jamyang Lodrö Senge, Kongtrul's grandnephew.
19. "Secret Sādhana" in the context here probably refers to the *Adorned Protector Secret Sādhana*, but it could also be the Liver-Colored Protector, which is also called a "secret sādhana," although not in the title. Or it could refer to something outside of this collection.

35. Concise Torma Ritual for Swift-Acting Six-Armed Awareness Protector

1. *Myur mdzad ye shes kyi mgon po phyag drug pa'i gtor chog nyer bsdus*, *DNZ*, vol. 12, pp. 623–24; *ST*, vol. 4, pp. 381–93. Also in *Tāranātha's Collected Works*, vol. 21, pp. 957–61.

36. Garland of Cintāmaṇi

1. *Phyag drug pa'i rjes gnang gi bka' chen bcu gsum phyogs bsdebs tsintā maṇi'i phreng ba*, *DNZ*, vol. 12, pp. 625–737; *ST*, vol. 2, pp. 387–693. Not in *GK*. Cintāmaṇi (Tib. *yid bzhin nor bu*) is the wish-fullfilling gem. It is said to be one of four relics in a chest that fell from the sky during the reign of King Lhatotori Nyentsen (5th century).
2. The two Indian sources for Khyungpo Naljor's transmission were Maitrīpa, who himself received it from Śavarīpa, and Rāhulagupta, who received it from Atayavajra and Śavarīpa. Maitrīpa's own detailed account of the transmission is recorded in Mokchokpa et al., *Brief Life Story of Lama Khyungpo Naljor*, *ST*, vol. 1, pp. 82–88.
3. Khyungpo Naljor's six main disciples were rMe'u ston, G.yor po or rGya mo che, rNgul ston ring dbang or dNgul btsun ri dbang, La stod pa dKon mchog mkhar, Zhang sgom Chos seng, and rMog lcog pa Rin chen brtson 'grus. Smith, *Among Tibetan Texts*, p. 54. Also in Tāranātha, *Clearing Up the Darkness of Mind*, p. 466 (with spelling variations).
4. *[mKhas grub] be bum*. That is, *Khedrup's Book of Awareness Protector Six-Armed Mahākāla's Eight-Chapter Tantra and So On*, arranged by Khedrup Je Gelek Palzang (1385–1438), the third Ganden Tripa and a disciple of Tsongkhapa. In *The Beryl Key*, Kongtrul states that *Khedrup's Book* in the lower tradition is so widespread that he needn't even comment on it (*ST*, vol. 6, p 126). *Khedrup's Book* and excerpted texts are in *ST*, vol. 11, filling the whole volume.
5. *Mine of Jewels: Sādhanas of an Ocean of Yidams*. *Tāranātha's Collected Works*, vol. 15, pp. 765–804. These five are Removing All Obstacles, Guru-Protector Inseparable, Yellow Protector, Red Protector, and Green Protector.
6. Kyishö Zhabdrung Tulku Ngawang Tenzin Trinle (sKyi shod Zhabs drung Ngag dbang bstan 'dzin 'phrin las, 1639–1682), a Gelukpa master, student of the fourth Paṇchen Lama and fifth Dalai Lama. He received the transmission from Könchok Gyaltsen and others. His manual is called *Lucky Necklace: How to Practice the Thirteen Authorizations of Glorious Swift-Acting Protector* in his *Collected Works*, vol. 1, pp. 439–527 (BDRC: W22116). The liturgies there closely resemble Kongtrul's. The lineages for each of the empowerments are given in the colophon.
7. In *Tāranātha's Collected Works*, vol. 15, pp. 765–75. It appears that mainly what has been added by Kongtrul is the history of Mahākāla as part of the introduction to the empowerment.
8. See Tāranātha's *The Practice of Past Gurus*, *DNZ*, vol. 11 pp. 333–39; and Kongtrul's commentary on it, *Essence of Maturing and Liberating*, *DNZ*, vol. 11, pp. 341–53. Translations in *The Treasury of Precious Instructions, Volume 11: Shangpa Kagyu*, pp. 415–39.
9. In other places, the retinue's seed syllables are *kṣim* for Kṣetrapāla, *hūṃ* for Jina-

mitra, *ṭāṃ* for Ṭakkirāja, and *hūṃ* for Trakṣad, rather than *hūṃ*, *byo*[*ḥ*?], *jaḥ*, and *du* here in *DNZ*.

10. *phrin las rnam pa lnga*: pacification of suffering and its causes, enrichment of excellent provisions, overpowering those who require training, wrathfully uprooting those who are difficult to train, and spontaneously accomplishing whatever emerges without effort. Dudjom Rinpoche, *The Nyingma School of Tibetan Buddhism*, vol. 2, p. 143.
11. *tshogs sde bzhi*, four monastic communities founded in Tibet by Paṇchen Śakyaśrī. *The Treasury of Precious Instructions, Volume 18: Jonang*, p. 638n20.
12. *Maṇḍala bka' rgya ma*, in *Compendium of Sādhanas*, vol. 11, pp. 187–88. See ch. 25, *A Wish-Fulfilling Gem*, in this volume, pp. 388–89.
13. *snod kyi skyon gsum*: to listen to the dharma like an upside-down vessel, like a vessel with a hole in it, or like a vessel with poison in it.
14. Many more variations of the practice and warnings of the malpractice may be found in the original Tāranātha composition, *Collected Works*, vol. 15, pp. 773–75. Kongtrul has rearranged them in a way that is, admittedly, much more sensible.
15. Important omission added from Tāranātha, ibid., p. 775.
16. Unlike this case, in most descriptions and depictions there are two identical Gaṇapatis (*tshogs kyi bdag po*), one each under the Protector's two feet.
17. Lon pa'i skyil po dgon pa seems an odd name for a monastery and is not mentioned in a list of monasteries in Penyul ('Phan yul). There is one Langtang Monastery (gLang thang dgon) established in 1093 by the Kadampa Langri Tangpa, from whom Khyungpo Naljor received ordination, which was indicated previously in regard to the Four Deities Combined Practice. See Batchelor, *The Tibet Guide*, p. 142. The specific area Jokpo in Penyul (an area north of Lhasa, also known as the region of Penbo) is spelled here as *skyog po* but later as *jog po*. There was also a monastery founded by Khyungpo Naljor in Penyul called Penyul Chekha ('Phan yul 'chad kha dgon) which might be indicated here. The "ri" in Jokpori may be short for *ri khrod* ("hermitage") and not necessarily mean mountain.
18. Although there is no actual phrase "please practice" (*spyad du gsol*) in the preceding Black Protector authorization, the direction indicates finishing with all the concluding practices that are there.
19. King of Power (dBang gi rgyal po) refers to the third of the four kinds of actions or "karmas" (*las bzhi*), variously translated as magnetizing, controlling, overpowering, or bringing under control. *Dbang* here is short for *dbang du 'dus*.
20. *spyan gzigs*: mostly, the stuffed animal skins suspended in protector chapels (*mgon khang*).
21. *chos kyang dkon la rtag tu 'tshe ba 'ang mang*. *Perfection of Wisdom Verse Summary*, Dg.K., shes phyin, *ka*, f. 8a (Toh. 13).
22. Thus initiating at the same time the important Shangpa practice of Four Deities Combined Practice, which includes Six-Armed Mahākāla.

23. *mun pa mi bzad pa*, though if it is spelled *mun pa bzad pa*, as it is elsewhere, it could be "Interminable Darkness." It is also called *mun pa nag po*, "Black Darkness," and *mun pa drag po*, "Intense Darkness," one of the eight great charnel grounds of the Cakrasaṃvara mandala (*dur khrod chen po brgyad*; Skt. *aṣṭa mahāśmaśānāni*).
24. Third permission: after the first five permissions based on Tāranātha's sources, this is the third one created by Jamgön Kongtrul.
25. In most other sources, the earrings are the reverse of here.
26. Vararuci (mChog sred) authored several Mahākāla texts located in the Tengyur: Toh. 1761, 1763, 1774, 3386, and others.
27. Gyi jo/co Lo tsā ba Zla ba'i 'od zer, early eleventh century. Known mainly for the first translation of the *Kālacakra Tantra* in 1027.
28. sTengs pa Lo tsā ba (also known as Ga rod) Tshul khrims 'byung gnas sbas pa (1107–1190), Roerich, *The Blue Annals*, pp. 1052–54.
29. Lo tsā ba mGar Chos kyi bzang po. A list of his translations are in *Bibliography of Works of Many Translators of the Himalayan Region*, pp. 99–103 (BDRC W24697).

37. Sealed with Life Force

1. *Myur mdzad ye shes mgon po snying zhugs kyi rjes gnang thun mong ma yin pa srog gi rgya chen*, *DNZ*, vol. 12, pp. 739–45; *ST*, vol. 2, pp. 723–41.

38. Guru Yoga Connected with Six-Armed Protector Entering the Heart

1. *mGon po phyag drug pa snying zhugs dang 'brel ba'i bla ma'i rnal 'byor*, *DNZ*, vol. 12, pp. 747–57; *ST*, vol. 2, pp. 695–721.
2. lCang skya rol pa'i rdo rje (1717–1786; the third Changkya). The text referenced is *How to Practice the Yoga of Guru-Protector Inseparable. Collected Works of Rolpai Dorje*, vol. 2, pp. 523–28 (BDRC W29035). Rolpai Dorje spent most of his time in the Manchu court in Beijing, and though he influenced the court to the benefit of the Lhasa government, that benevolence did not extend to Derge. (See van Schaik, *Tibet: A History*, pp. 160–64.) My sense of the statement is that since that easy-to-do Gelukpa version is available, the profound Shangpa tradition should not be disseminated widely.
3. Ka chen blo bzang dge legs, listed in lineages directly before Jamyang Khyentse Wangpo.

39. Clouds of Virtue and Goodness

1. *Myur mdzad ye shes kyi mgon po mthing dkar gnyis kyi mnga' gsol dge legs sprin phung*, *DNZ*, vol. 12, pp. 759–67; *ST*, vol. 4, pp. 341–63. Also in *GK*, vol. 13, pp. 227–39.

2. *'byor pa drug*: long life, power, auspiciousness, majesty, many attendants, and great prosperity.
3. *mos bzhi* or *mos pa rnam bzhi*: the four ways one can be admired by others—as a parent, as a teacher, as a sovereign, or as a friend or lord.

40. Ritual for Conferring the Uncommon Authorization of the Great Field Protector Kṣetrapāla Father-Mother

1. *Zhing skyong chen po kṣetrpāla yab yum gyi thun mong ma yin pa'i rjes gnang bskur chog*, *DNZ*, vol. 12, pp. 769–73; *ST*, vol. 2, pp. 743–53. A different text on Kṣetrapāla by Jamgön Kongtrul is in *GK*, vol. 13, pp. 241–43. Note that this text is not distinguished according to instructions or liturgy in large or small font. Therefore the translator has had to create the formatting.
2. *bying sha chen*, though *sha chen* ("great meat") is normally human flesh, I am not sure about *bying*.
3. These mantras are Sanskrit and Tibetan combined. I have kept the Tibetan in Wylie transliteration style.

Bibliography

This bibliography is presented in five alphabetically arranged sections: (1) the texts that are translated in this volume, (2) sutras and tantras cited in the texts or consulted by the translator, (3) treatises of Indic origin cited in the texts or consulted by the translator, (4) Tibetan works cited in the texts or consulted by the translator, and (5) translations and other works in English.

1. The Present Texts

Source Volumes

Jamgön Kongtrul Lodrö Taye, comp. *The Treasury of Precious Instructions. gDams ngag rin po che'i mdzod.* Vol. 12 (*na*). Delhi: Shechen Publications, 1999. dnz.tsadra.org.

Jamgön Kongtrul Lodrö Taye, comp. *The Treasury of Precious Instructions. gDams ngag rin po che'i mdzod.* Vol. 8. Delhi: N. Lungtok and N. Gyaltsan, 1971–72 (Kundeling printing).

Translated Texts

Atiśa Dīpaṃkara. *In Praise of Vajrayoginī, the Especially Exalted Praise. Vajrayoginīstotra. rDo rje rnal 'byor ma la bstod pa. DNZ*, pp. 271–72; *ST*, vol. 3, pp. 331–34. Also in Tengyur, rgyud, *ha*, ff. 113a5–114a1 (Toh. 1594).

Khyungpo Naljor and Sangye Nyentön Chökyi Sherap. *Sukhasiddhi's Story, Indian Source Text, Navel Emanation Chakra Secret Sādhana, and Empowerment Ritual. Su kha siddhi'i lo rgyus / rgya gzhung / gsang sgrub lte ba sprul 'khor / dbang chog rnams. DNZ*, pp. 279–96.

Jamgön Kongtrul Lodrö Taye. *Bringing Down the Rain of Great Bliss: A Lineage Supplication for the Profound Path of Sukha's Six Dharmas. Zab lam su kha chos drug gi brgyud pa'i gsol 'debs bde chen char 'bebs. DNZ*, pp. 297–99; *ST*, vol. 3, pp. 729–33.

———. *Clouds of Virtue and Goodness: The Investiture of Power for Deep-Blue and

White Swift-Acting Awareness Protectors. Myur mdzad ye shes kyi mgon po mthing dkar gnyis kyi mnga' gsol dge legs sprin phung. DNZ, pp. 759–67; *ST*, vol. 4, pp. 341–63; *GK*, vol. 3, pp. 227–39.

———. *Fast Path of Integral Unity: Awareness Ḍākinī Sukhasiddhi's Profound Path of Creation and Guidance on the Six Dharmas. Ye shes mkha' 'gro su kha siddhi'i bskyed pa'i lam zab dang / chos drug gi khrid yig zung 'jug nyur lam. DNZ*, pp. 299–313; *ST*, vol. 3, pp. 733–72.

———. *Flowers of Faith: A Supplement to Venerable Tāranātha Rinpoche's Biographical Supplication. rJe btsun rin po che'i rnam thar gsol 'debs kha skong dad pa'i me tog. DNZ*, pp. 453–56.

———. *Garland of Cintāmaṇi: Thirteen Major Authorization Permissions for Six-Armed Mahākāla in One Place: Phyag drug pa'i rjes gnang gi bka' chen bcu gsum phyogs bsdebs tsintā maṇi'i phreng ba. DNZ*, pp. 625–737; *ST*, vol. 2, pp. 387–693.

———. *Garland of Uḍumbara Flowers: Supplications to the Lives of the Amazing Jewel Lineage of the Glorious Shangpa Kagyu. dPal ldan shangs pa bka' brgyud kyi ngo mtshar rin chen brgyud pa'i rnam thar la gsol ba 'debs pa udumbara'i phreng ba. DNZ*, pp. 389–447; *ST*, vol. 5, pp. 87–233.

———. *Guru Yoga Connected with Six-Armed Protector Entering the Heart. mGon po phyag drug pa snying zhugs dang 'brel ba'i bla ma'i rnal 'byor. DNZ*, pp. 747–57; *ST*, vol. 2, pp. 695–721.

———. *Naturally Luminous Timeless Awareness: Four Deities Combined Practice, a Profound Dharma of the Glorious Shangpa Kagyu. dPal ldan shangs pa bka' brgyud kyi zab chos lha bzhi dril sgrub kyi nyams len ye shes rang gsal. DNZ*, pp. 335–41; *ST*, vol. 4, pp. 93–107; *GK*, vol. 8, pp. 453–60.

———. *Radiant Light of Timeless Awareness: A Guidebook on the Four Deities Combined Practice, a Profound Dharma of the Glorious Shangpa Kagyu. dPal ldan shangs pa bka' brgyud kyi zab chos lha bzhi dril sgrub kyi khrid yig ye shes 'od 'phro. DNZ*, pp. 343–56; *ST*, vol. 3, pp. 163–89; *GK*, vol. 9, pp. 3–19.

———. *Releasing the Knots of the Central Channel: A Practice of White and Red Khecarīs. Me tog mkha' spyod dkar dmar gyi nyams len dbu ma'i mdud grol. DNZ*, pp. 251–69; *ST*, vol. 3, pp. 191–235; *GK*, vol. 8, pp. 339–63.

———. *Ritual for Conferring the Uncommon Authorization of the Great Field Protector Kṣetrapāla Father-Mother. Shing skyong chen po kṣetrpāla yab yum gyi thun mong ma yin pa'i rjes gnang bskur chog. DNZ*, pp. 769–73; *ST*, vol. 2, pp. 743–53.

———. *Sealed with Life Force: The Extraordinary Authorization of Swift-Acting Protector Entering the Heart. Myur mdzad ye shes mgon po snying zhugs kyi rje gnang thun mong ma yin pa srog gi rgya chen. DNZ*, pp. 739–45; *ST*, vol. 2, pp. 723–41.

———. *Shower of Great Bliss: A Concise Supplication to the Lineage of Profound Teaching of Niguma's Six Dharmas. Zab chos ni gu chos drug gi brgyud 'debs nyung 'dus bde chen 'bebs pa. DNZ*, pp. 457–58; *GK*, vol. 8, pp. 461–64.

———. *The Single Sitting Practice: Words of the Ḍākinī of Timeless Awareness, a Concise Guide to Niguma's Six Dharmas, the Root of the Golden Dharmas of the Glorious Shangpa. dPal ldan shangs pa'i gser chos las rtsa ba ni gu chos drug gi khrid *bsdus stan thog gcig ma'i nyams len ye shes ḍākī'i zhal lung. DNZ*, pp. 207–35; *ST*, vol. 3, pp. 513–77; *GK*, vol. 8, pp. 303–37.

———. *Spontaneous Accomplishment of the Four Actions: A Supplement to the Long Torma Ritual of Glorious Swift-Acting Awareness Protector, with a Clearly Arranged Sequence. dPal myur mdzad ye shes kyi mgon po'i gtor chog rgyas pa'i kha skong dmigs rim dang bcas pa gsal bar bkod pa las bzhi lhun grub. DNZ*, pp. 593–622; *ST*, vol. 4, pp. 274–339.

———. *Supplication to Niguma's Lineage. Ni gu'i brgyud 'debs. DNZ*, pp. 331–32; *ST*, vol. 4, pp. 1–6.

———. *A Wish-Fulfilling Gem: Offering Ritual for the Lineage Gurus of the Shangpa Kagyu, Protectors of Beings. 'Gro mgon shangs pa bka' brgyud kyi bla ma mchod pa'i cho ga yid bzhin nor bu. DNZ*, pp. 357–87; *ST*, vol. 5, pp. 7–78; *GK*, vol. 2, pp. 207–43.

Jamgön Kongtrul Lodrö Taye, comp. *An Ocean of Blessings Meaningful to Hear: Collected Vajra Lines, Dohas, and Melodious Songs of the Glorious Shangpa Kagyu. dPal ldan shangs pa bka' brgyud kyi do ha rdo rje'i tshig rkang dang mgur dbyangs phyogs gcig tu bsgrigs pa thos pa don ldan byin rlabs rgya mtsho. DNZ*, pp. 464–559; *ST*, vol. 5, pp. 225–438.

Jamgön Kongtrul and Kagyu Trinle Shingta. *Clouds of Blessing: Supplication to the Guru of the Profound Path of Niguma's Six Dharmas. Zab lam ni gu chos drug gi bla ma brgyud pa'i gsol 'debs byin rlabs sprin phung. DNZ*, pp. 333–34; *ST*, vol. 4, pp. 7–13.

Lochen Gyurme Dechen. *White Khecarī Transference. mKha' spyod dkar mo'i 'pho ba. DNZ*, pp. 273–74; *ST*, vol. 3, pp. 315–25. Also in *Collected Works of Lochen Gyurme Dechen*, vol. 2, pp. 605–6.

Niguma. *Niguma's Aspiration Prayer of the Sealed Word. Ni gu ma'i smon lam bka' rgya ma. DNZ*, pp. 459–62. Also in Peking Tengyur as *The Sovereign of Noble Aspirations* (*'Phags pa smon lam gyi rgyal po*), rgyud 'grel, *pu*, ff. 201a–203a (P. 4650); CT, vol. 42, pp. 959–63 (2530).

Rāhulagupta. *Red Khecarī Transference. mKha spyod dmar mo'i 'pho ba. DNZ*, pp. 277–78; *ST*, vol. 3, pp. 325–30.

Sangye Nyentön Chökyi Sherap. *Blazing Light of Bliss-Clarity: Sukhasiddhi's Cycle of Oral Instructions and Instructions on Three Nails. Su kha siddhi'i zhal gdams kyi skor dang / gzer gsum gdams pa rnam [bde gsal 'od 'bar]. DNZ*, pp. 315–28; *ST*, vol. 3, pp. 841–65.

———. *Sukhasiddhi's Introduction to Mahāmudrā. Su kha ma siddhi'i phyag rgya chen po'i ngo sprod. DNZ*, pp. 329–30; *ST*, vol. 3, pp. 867–68.

Tangtong Gyalpo. *Collection of Essentials: Vital Words of Instruction on the Six Dharmas of Niguma, Ḍākinī of Timeless Awareness. Ye shes mkha' 'gro ni gu ma'i chos drug gi khrid kyi gnad yig snying po kun 'dus. DNZ*, pp. 147–79; *ST*, vol. 3, pp. 773–840. Also in *Supplemental Text to the Collected Works of Thang-stong-rgyal po* (*TTG-S*), pp. 241–336.

———. *Niguma's Auxiliary Practices: Guidance in Amulet Mahāmudrā. Ni gu'i yan lag phyag chen ga'u ma'i khrid. DNZ*, pp. 181–87; *ST*, vol. 3, pp. 683–94; *TTG-S*, pp. 337–52.

———. *Niguma's Auxiliary Practices: Guidance in Immortal Body and Mind. Ni gu'i yan lag lus sems 'chi med kyi khrid. DNZ*, pp. 192–98; *ST*, vol. 3, pp. 703–13; *TTG-S*, pp. 369–86.

———. *Niguma's Auxiliary Practices: Guidance in the Three Integrations. Ni gu'i yan lag lam khyer gsum gyi khrid. DNZ*, pp. 187–92; *ST*, vol. 3, pp. 694–703; *TTG-S*, pp. 353–67.

———. *Niguma's Auxiliary Quintessential Practice: Guidance in the Six-Armed Awareness Protector. Nying khu'i yan lag phyag drug ye shes mgon po'i khrid. DNZ*, pp. 198–205; *ST*, vol 3, pp. 713–27.

Tāranātha. *Amulet Mahāmudrā or Three Naturally Settled States Guidance Manual. Phyag chen ga'u ma'am rang babs rnam gsum zhes bya ba'i khrid yig. DNZ*, pp. 237–49: *ST*, vol. 3, pp. 655–82; *Tāranātha's Collected Works*, vol. 20, pp. 563–78.

———. *Concise Torma Ritual for Swift-Acting Six-Armed Awareness Protector. Myur mdzad ye shes kyi mgon po phyag drug pa'i gtor chog nyer bsdus. DNZ*, pp. 623–24; *ST*, vol. 4, pp. 381–93; *Tāranātha's Collected Works*, vol. 21, pp. 957–61.

———. *Niguma's Yogic Exercises, Root and Commentary. Ni gu'i 'khrul 'khor rtsa 'grel. DNZ*, pp. 137–45; *ST*, vol. 6, pp. 143–60; *Tāranātha's Collected Works*, vol. 12, pp. 1013–26.

———. *A Supplement Added to the Source Guide on the Profound Path of Niguma's Six Dharmas. Zab lam ni gu chos drug gi gzhung khrid ma mo'i lhan thabs kha skong. DNZ*, pp 103–35; *ST*, vol. 3, pp. 579–654; *Tāranātha's Collected Works*, vol. 12, pp. 973–1011.

———. *Tangdalma, Displaying the Profound Meaning: A Guidebook on the Profound Path of Niguma's Six Dharmas, the One Sufficient Reading. Zab lam ni gu chos drug gi khrid yig zab don thang mar brdal ba zhes bya ba bklags chog ma. DNZ*, pp. 1–101; *ST*, vol. 6, pp. 335–512; *Tāranātha's Collected Works*, vol. 12, pp. 825–955.

———. *Treasure Trove of Awakened Activity: Sādhana and Torma Ritual of Glorious Protector Six-Armed Mahākāla. dPal ye shes kyi mgon po phyag drug pa'i sgrub thabs gtor ma'i chog phrin las gter mdzod. DNZ*, pp. 573–91; *Tāranātha's Collected Works*, vol. 14, pp. 515–42.

———. *Verdant Tree of Faith: The Life Story of the Glorious Holy Guru. dPal ldan bla ma dam pa'i rnam par thar pa dad pa'i ljon shing. DNZ*, pp. 449–52; *Tāranātha's Collected Works*, vol. 1, pp. 999–1005.

Tāranātha and Jamgön Kongtrul. *Ḍākinīs of the Five Classes Sādhana and Authorization Ritual in the Shangpa Tradition. Shangs lugs mkha' 'gro sde lnga'i sgrub thabs rjes gnang dang bcas pa. DNZ*, pp. 561–67; *ST*, vol. 2, pp. 755–68; *Tāranātha's Collected Works*, vol. 15, pp. 1148–68.

———. *Torma Offering to the Ḍākinīs of the Five Classes Just for Regular Practice. Shangs lugs mkha' 'gro sde lnga'i mchod gtor 'bul ba dkyus ma tsam gyi lag len. DNZ*, pp. 569–71; *ST*, vol. 5, pp. 79–86; *GK*, vol. 8, pp. 465–68.

2. Sutra and Tantra (*Kangyur*)

All Tathāgatas' Great Secret Body, Speech, and Mind Guhyasamāja Tantra. Sarvatathāgatakāyacāacittarahasyaguhyasamāja. De bzhin gshegs pa thams cad kyi sku gsung thugs kyi gsang chen gsang ba 'dus pa. Dg.K. rgyud 'bum, *ca*, ff. 90a–148a (Toh. 442).

All Tathāgatas' Secret Great Yoga. Sarvatathāgataguhyatantrayoga. dPal de bzhin gshegs pa thams cad kyi gsang ba rnal 'byor chen po. Dg.K. rgyud 'bum, *cha*, ff. 103a–331a. (Toh. 453).

Collated Kangyur. bKa' 'gyur: dpe bsdur ma. 109 vols. Beijing: Krung go'i bod rig pa'i dpe skrun khang, 2006–2009. BDRC W1PD96682.

Ḍākinī Vajra Tent Tantra. Ḍākinīvajrapañjaramahātantra. mKha' 'gro ma rdo rje gur. Dg.K. rgyud 'bum, *nga*, ff. 30a–65b (Toh. 419).

Display of Timeless Awareness Tantra. Ye shes rol pa'i rgyud. Not located.

Drop of Timeless Awareness. Dg.K. rgyud 'bum, *nga*, ff. 96b–136b (Toh. 422).

Flower Ornament Sutra. Avataṃsaka Sūtra / Buddhaāvataṃsakanāmamahāvaipulyasūtra. Sangs rgyas phal po che shes bya ba shin tu rgyas pa chen po'i mdo. Dg.K. phal chen, *ka*, ff. 1b–393a (Toh. 44).

Jewel Ocean Tantra. Rin chen rgya mtsho'i rgyud. Not translated into Tibetan.

Mahāmāya Tantra. Mahāmāyātantrarāja. dPal sgyu 'phrul chen po'i rgyud kyi rgyal po. Dg.K. rgyud 'bum, *nga*, ff. 167a–171a (Toh. 425).

Perfection of Wisdom in Eight Thousand Lines. Aṣṭasāhasrikāprajñāpāramitā. Shes rab kyi pha rol tu phyin pa brgyad stong pa. Dg.K. shes byin, *ka*, ff. 1b–286a (Toh. 12).

Perfection of Wisdom Verse Summary. Prajñāpāramitāsañcayagāthā. Shes rab kyi pha rol tu phyin pa sdud pa tshigs su bcad pa. Dg.K. shes byin, *ka*, ff. 1b–19b (Toh. 13).

Saṃvarodaya Tantra. Mahāsaṃvarodayatantra. bDe mchog 'byung ba'i rgyud. Dg.K. rgyud 'bum, *kha*, ff. 265a–311a (Toh. 373).

Secret Tantra of the General Ritual of All Mandalas. Sarvamaṇḍalasāmānyavidhiguhyatantra. dKyil 'khor thams cad kyi spyi'i cho ga gsang ba'i rgyud. Dg.K. rgyud 'bum, *wa*, ff. 141a–167b (Toh. 806).

Sutra of the Arrayed Trees. Gaṇḍhavyūhasūtra. sDong po bkod pa'i mdo. Dg.K. phal chen, *kha*, ff. 1b–396.

*Sutra of the Questions of *Kumāraprabha. Khye'u rab snang gis zhus pa'i mdo.* Not located.

Two-Part Hevajra Explanatory Tantra. Hevajratantrarāja. brTag gnyis bshad rgyud. Dg.K. rgyud 'bum, *nga*, ff. 1b–30a (Toh. 417/18).

3. Treatises of Indic Origin (*Tengyur*)

Abhayākaragupta. *Ears of Grain Esoteric Instructions.* Āmnāyamañjarī. *Man ngag gi snye ma.* Dg.T. rgyud, *cha*, ff. 1b–316a (Toh. 1198).

———. *Moonlight of Vital Points: A Commentary on the Eight-Thousand-Line Perfection of Wisdom. Aṣṭasāhasrikāprajñāpāramitāvṛttimarmakaumundī. Shes rab kyi pha rol tu phyin pa brgyad stong pa'i 'grel pa gnad kyi zla ba'i 'od*. Dg.T. shes spyin, *da*, ff. 1b–228a (Toh. 3805).

———. *Vajra Garland Mandala Ritual. Vajrāvali. dKyil 'khor gyi cho ga rdo rje phreng ba*. Dg.T. rgyud, *phu*, ff. 1b–94b (Toh. 3140).

Asaṅga. *Stages of Yogic Practice. Yogācarābhūmi. rNal 'byor spyod pa'i sa*. Dg.T. sems tsam, *tshi*, ff. 1b–283a (Toh. 4035).

Collated Tengyur. bsTan 'gyur: dpe bsdur ma. Beijing: Krung go'i bod kyi shes rig dpe skrun khang, 1995–2005.

Dharmakīrti. *Commentary on Valid Cognition. Pramāṇavārttikakārikā. Tshad ma rnam 'grel gyi tshig le'ur byas pa*. Dg.T. tshad ma, *ce*, ff. 94b–151a.

Guṇaprabha. *Vinayasūtra. 'Dul ba'i mdo*. Dg.T. 'dul ba, *wu*, ff. 1b–100a (Toh. 4117).

Maitreya. *Five Treatises of Maitreya. Byams chos sde lnga*. Comprising the five individual works of Maitreya. Dg.T. Toh. 378, 4020, 4021, 4022, 4024.

Maitrīpa. *Praise to Glorious Goddess. Śrīdevīkālīstrota. dPal lha mo la bstod pa*. Peking Tengyur, rgyud 'grel, *zu*, ff. 270b–71a. Vol. 86, p. 160. BDRC W1KG13126.

Nāgārjuna. *Five Stages. Pañcakrama. Rim lnga pa*. Dg.T. rgyud, *nyi*, ff. 45b–57a (Toh. 1802).

———. *Glorious Guhyasamāja Mandala Ritual. Śrīsuhyasamājamaṇḍalvidhi. dPal gsang ba 'dus pa'i dkyil 'khor gyi cho ga*. Dg.T. rgyud, *nyi*, ff. 15b–35a (Toh. 1798).

Tilopa. *Pith Instructions on Mahāmudrā / Ganges Mahāmudrā. Mahāmudropadeśa. Phyag rgya chen po'i man ngag*. Dg.T. rgyud, *zhi*, ff. 242b–244a (Toh. 2303).

Vararuci. *Resounding Ferocity: Praise to the Great Black One. Mahākālastotrākṣepa. Nag po chen po'i bstod pa rngam pa sgra sgrogs*. Peking Tengyur, rgyud 'grel, *'u* (vol. 85), pp. 25–26. Pe cing pho brang, 1724.

4. Tibetan Texts

Auspicious Verses. bKra shis brjod pa. In *Old Texts at Palpung Monastery (dPal yul dgon du bzhugs pa'i dpe rnying)*. Vol. 21, pp. 1049–54.

Bibliography of Works of Many Translators of the Himalayan Region. Gangs ljongs skad gnyis smra ba du ma'i 'gyur byang blos gsal dga' skyed. 1 vol. Mtsho ngon, Tibet: Kan Lho Bod Rigs Rang Skyong Khul Rtsom Sgyur Cu'u, 1983. BDRC W24697.

Big Dictionary of Tibetan Medicine. Bod lugs gso rig tshig mdzod chen mo. Bod rang skyong ljongs snam rtsis khang. Beijing: Mi rigs dpe skrun khang, 2006.

Big Tibetan-Chinese Dictionary. Bod rgya tshig mdzod chen mo. Edited by Zhang Yisun et al. 2 vols. Beijing: Mi rigs dpe skrun khang, 1985, 1987.

Biographical Dictionary of Tibet and Tibetan Buddhism. Compiled by Khetsun Sangpo. Dharamsala: Library of Tibetan Works and Archives, 1973.

Bodong Chokle Namgyal (Bo dong Phyogs las rnam rgyal). *The Compendium of Suchness. De nyid 'dus pa. Encyclopedia Tibetica*, or *Collected Works of Bodong Chokle Namgyal*. 137 vols. New Delhi: Tibet House, 1969–1981. BDRC W22103.

Changkya Rolpai Dorje (lCang skya Rol pa'i rdo rje). *How to Practice the Yoga of Guru -Protector Inseparable. bLa mgon dbyer med kyi rnal 'byor nyams su len tshul.*

In *Collected Works of Rolpai Dorje*. Vol. 2 (*kha*), pp. 523–28. Dharamsala: Library of Tibetan Works and Archives, 2003. BDRC W29035.

Collection of Liturgical Texts in Use in the Shangpa Kagyu Lineage. dPal ldan shangs pa bka' brgyud kyi 'don cha nyer mkho. 3 vols. Delhi: Konchog Lhadrepa, 1996.

Compendium of Sādhanas. sGrub thabs kun btus. Compiled and edited by Jamyang Khyentse Wangpo and Jamyang Loter Wangpo. Kangra, HP, India: Indo-Tibetan Buddhist Literature Publisher and Dzongsar Institute for Advanced Studies, 1902. BDRC W23681.

Dorje Tsewang (rDo rje tshe dbang). *A History of the Glorious Shangpa Kagyu. dPal ldan shangs pa bka' brgyud kyi chos 'byung*. Lhasa: Bod ljongs mi dmangs dpe skrun khang, 2014. BDRC W1KG26279.

Dungkar Lobzang Trinle (Dung dkar bLo bzang phrin las). *Big Dictionary of Dungkar. Dung dkar tshig mdzod chen mo*. Beijing: Krung go'i bod rig pa dpe skrun khang, 2002.

Gendun Gyatso (dGe 'dun rgya mtsho), the second Dalai Lama. *Collected Works of Gendun Gyatso. gSung 'bum dge 'dun rgya mtsho*. 6 vols. Dharamsala: Library of Tibetan Works and Archives, 2006.

———. *The Words of the Ḍākinī of Timeless Awareness: A Guidebook on the Profound Path of Niguma's Six Dharmas. Zab lam ni gu'i chos drug gi 'khrid yig ye shes mkha' 'gro'i zhal gyi lung*. In *Collected Works of Gendun Gyatso*. Vol. 2, pp. 43–96. Dharamsala: Library of Tibetan Works and Archives, 2006.

Gö Lotsāwa Zhönu Pal ('Gos lo tsā ba gZhon nu dpal). *The Blue Annals. Deb ther sngon po*. 2 vols. Chengdu: Si khron mi rigs dpe skrun khang, 1984.

Great Dictionary of Tibetan Medicine. Bod lugs gso rig tshig mdzod chen mo. Beijing: Mi rigs dpe skrun khang, 2006.

Jakpa Gyaltsen Bum ('Jag pa rGyal mtshan 'bum). *Direct Advice on the Required Severing of Diffusion. 'Byams gcod nyer mkho zhal shes ma*. Not located.

Jakpa Gyaltsen Bum and Khedrup Shangtön ('Jag pa rGyal mtshan 'bum and mKhas grub Shangs ston). *Collection of Essential Directives on the Six Dharmas of Niguma. Ni gu chos drug gi zhal shes dgos rnams kyis lhan thabs*. In *Shangpa Texts*. Vol. 8, pp. 311–68.

Jamgön Kongtrul Lodrö Taye ('Jam mgon kong sprul bLo gros mtha' yas). *The Beryl Key: A Detailed Account of the Contents of the Precious Golden Dharmas of the Glorious Shangpa Kagyu. dPal ldan shangs pa bka' brgyud kyi gser chos rin po che'i mdzod yongs su phye dkar chag baiḍūrya'i lde'u mig*. In *The Treasury of Extensive Teachings* (*rGya chen bka' mdzod*). Paro, Bhutan: Ngodrup, 1976. Vol. 10, pp. 459–509. Also in *Shangpa Texts*. Vol. 6, pp. 51–141.

———. *The Catalog of The Treasury of Precious Instructions, Ocean of Auspicious Renown: A Collection of the Ripening and Liberation Essence of the Eight Great Chariots of the Practice Lineages. sGrub brgyud shing rta chen po brgyad kyi smin grol snying po phyogs gcig bsdus pa gdams ngag rin po che'i mdzod kyi dkar chag bkra shis grags pa'i rgya mtsho*. In *DNZ*. Vol. 18, pp. 381–547. Delhi: Shechen Publications, 1999.

———. *Essence of Maturing and Liberating: An Offering Ritual and Self-Induction into the Mandala Based on the Principal Deities of the Five Tantras. rGyud sde lnga gtso bsdus la brten pa'i dkyil 'khor mchod chog bdag 'jug dang bcas pa smin grol snying po*. In *DNZ*. Vol. 11, pp. 341–53; *Shangpa Texts*. Vol. 5, pp. 823–58. Also in *The Treasury of Extensive Teachings*. Vol. 8, pp. 285–302.

———. *Increasing Awakened Activity: Five-Deity Cakrasaṃvara Ritual for Communal Feast in the Tradition of Niguma. Ni gu lugs kyi bde mchog lha lnga'i tshogs kyi 'khor lo'i cho ga phrin las yar 'phel*. In *DNZ*. Vol. 11, pp. 287–95; *Shangpa Texts*. Vol. 3, pp. 81–97.

———. *Pool of Spiritual Powers: Practicing the Great Torma Ritual. dPal myur mdzad ye shes kyi mgon po'i gtor sgrub chen mo'i lag len bltas chog tu bkod pa dngos grub rdzing bu*. In *The Treasury of Extensive Teachings*. Vol. 13, pp. 29–53.

———. *Shangpa Dharma Directory: A Key to Open the Door of the Vast and Profound Teachings. Shangs chos dkar chag zab rgyas chos kyi sgo 'byed lde mig*. In *Shangpa Texts*. Vol. 9, pp. 43–70.

———. *Tenth-Day Offerings for Red Khecarī in the Shangpa Tradition. Shangs lugs mkha' spyod dmar mo'i tshes bcu'i mchod pa 'don 'grigs bltas mchog tu mkod pa*. In *Shangpa Texts*. Vol. 3, pp. 269–96. And in *The Treasury of Extensive Teachings*. Vol. 8, pp. 405–21.

———. *The Treasury of Extensive Teachings. rGya chen bka' mdzod*. 13 vols. Paro, Bhutan: Ngodrup, 1976–1977.

Jamyang Khyentse Wangpo ('Jam dbyangs mkhyen brtse'i dbang po). *Flower of the Awareness Holders: A Vajra Song of Praise to the Inner Life Story of the Mighty Adept Tsöndru Zangpo. Grub pa'i dbang phyug brtson 'grus bzang po'i nang gi rnam par thar pa la bsngags pa rdo rje'i thol glu rig pa 'dzin pa'i me tog*. In *Khyentse's Collected Works* (*mKhyen brtse'i bka' 'bum*). Vol. 2, pp. 203–4.

———. *Khyentse's Collected Works. mKhyen brtse'i bka' 'bum*. Rdzong sar 'jam dbyangs mkhyen brtse'i dbang po'i bka' babs. Dkar mdzes bod rigs rang skyong khul sde dge rdzong: Rdzong sar khams bye'i slob gling, 2013.

Katok Rikzin Tsewang Norbu (Ka thog rig 'dzin Tshe dbang nor bu). *Biographies of Some Holy Ones, Such as Marpa, Mila, Gampopa, Atiśa, and Sons. Mar mi dwags po jo bo rje yab sras sogs dam pa 'ga' zhig gi rnam thar sa bon dus kyi nges pa brjod pa dag ldan nyung gsal*. In *Selected Writings of Ka-thog rig-'dzin Tshe-dbang nor bu*. Vol. 1, pp. 669–705. Darjeeling: Kargyud Sungrab Nyamso Khang, 1973.

Khedrup Je Gelek Palzang (mKhas grub rje dGe legs dpal bzang), comp. *Khedrup's Book of Awareness Protector Six-Armed Mahākāla's Eight-Chapter Tantra and so on. Nag po chen po ye shes kyi mgon po phyag drug pa'i rgyud le'u brgyad pa sogs mkhas grub be bum* ("Khedrup Bebum"). 1 vol. New Delhi: Don 'grub rdo rje, 1973.

Khyungpo Naljor (Khyung po rnal 'byor). *Clarification of the Root Verses of the Six Dharmas. rTsa ba chos drug gi tshig gsal*. In *DNZ*. Vol. 11, pp. 6–9; *Shangpa Texts*. Vol. 6, pp. 173–80, and vol. 7, pp. 525–33.

———. *Five-Deity Cakrasaṃvara Direct Realization Manual in Nigu's Tradition.*

Khyung po rnal 'byor lugs kyi bde mchog lha lnga'i mgon rtogs. In *Shangpa Texts*. Vol. 7, pp. 377–404.

———. *Infallible Instructions on the Three Intermediate States. 'Chugs med bar do gsum gyi gdams pa*. In *Shangpa Texts*. Vol. 8, pp. 187–207.

———. *The Inventory Clarifying the Six Dharmas. Them yig chos drug gi tshig gsal*. In *DNZ*. Vol. 11, pp. 9–10; *Shangpa Texts*. Vol. 7, pp. 533–35.

———. *Khyungpo Naljor's Collected Works. gSung'bum / khyung po rnal 'byor*. Three volumes. BDRC W3CN18508.

———. *Mandala of the Sealed Word. bLa ma shangs pa'i maṇḍala bka' rgya ma*. In *The Eight Songs and Four Sealed Words of the Great Adept Khyungpo* (*Grub chen khyung po'i mgur brgyad dang bka' rgya ma bzhi bcas*). In *Compendium of Sādhanas*. Vol. 11, pp. 187–88.

———. *Oral Instruction of the Secret Sādhana of the Navel Emanation Chakra. Zhal gdams gsang sgrub lte ba sprul 'khor bde gsal 'od 'bar*. In *Shangpa Texts*. Vol. 3, pp. 841–65.

———. *Sealed Word of Auspiciousness. bKra shis bka' brgya ma*. In *The Eight Songs and Four Sealed Words of the Great Adept Khyungpo. Grub chen khyung po'i mgur brgyad dang bka' rgya ma bzhi bcas*. In *Compendium of Sādhanas*. Vol. 11, pp. 179–92. BDRC W23681.

Kinnaur Shangpa Texts. Śaṅs-pa Bka'-brgyud-pa Texts: A Collection of Rare Manuscripts of Doctrinal, Ritual, and Biographical Works of Scholars of the Śaṅs-pa Bka'-brgyud-pa Tradition from the Monastery of Gsaṅ-sngags-chos-gliṅ in Kinnaur. Sumra, HP, India: Urgyan Dorje, 1977. BDRC W23708.

Kyishö Ngawang Tenzin Trinle (sKyi shod Ngag dbang bstan 'dzin 'phrin las). *Lucky Necklace: How to Practice the Thirteen Authorizations of Glorious Swift-Acting Protector. dPal myur mdzad ye shes kyi mgon po'i rjes gnang bcu gsum ji ltar bya tshul skal bzang mgul rgyan*. In *Collected Works of Ngawang Tenzin Trinle*. Vol. 1, pp. 439–527. Lhasa: Zhol par khang gsar pa, 2000. BDRC MW22116

Lochen Gyurme Dechen (Lo chen 'Gyur med bde chen). *Collected Works of Lochen Gyurme Dechen. gsung 'bum / 'gyur med bde chen*. BDRC W2DB16431.

———. *Glorious Gift of Liberation: The Complete Explanation of the Vajra Lines of the Six Dharmas. Chos drug rdo rje'i tshig rkang gi rnam bshad grol ba'i dpal ster*. In *Collected Works of Lochen Gyurme Dechen*. Vol. 2, pp. 453–574. Also in *Shangpa Texts*. Vol. 8, pp. 469–615.

———. *Life Story of Tangtong Gyalpo. Thang stong rgyal po'i rnam thar*. 1 vol. Khreng tu'u: Si khron mi rigs dpe skrun khang, 1982. BDRC W21690.

———. *[Questions Concerning] the Instructions of Glorious Niguma, Mighty Khecarī. mKha' spyod dbang mo dpal ldan ni gu ma'i zhes pa*. In *Collected Works of Lochen Gyurme Dechen*. Vol. 2, pp. 612–14. BDRC W2DB16431.

Losal Tenkyong (bLo gsal bstan skyong). *A Garland of Grain Ears of Great Bliss: A Liturgical Ritual for the Practice of the Ten Permissions in the Profound Path of Niguma's Six Dharmas. Zab lam ni gu chos drug gi bka' bcu'i phyag len bklags chog tu bkod pa bde chen myu gu'i phreng ba. DNZ.* Vol. 11, pp. 373–449. Also in *Shangpa Texts*. Vol. 2, pp. 1–203.

———. *A Sheaf of Grain Ears of Great Bliss: Collected Ritual Practices of the Latter Source Permissions of the Glorious Shangpa Kagyu. dPal ldan shangs pa bka' brgyud kyi gzhung bka' phyi ma rnams phyogs gcig tu bsgril ba'i phyag len bde chen snye ma'i chun po. DNZ.* Vol. 11, pp. 451–529; *Shangpa Texts*. Vol. 2, pp. 205–385.

Lozang Tenpa Rabgye (bLo bzang bstan pa rab rgyas). *Swift Advance of Blessings: How to Put into Practice the Instructions on Ālikāli from the Teachings of Khedrup Khyungpo Naljor Known as the Eight Songs. mKhas grub khyung po rnal 'byor gyi zhal gdams mgur brgyad du grags pa'i nang tshan ālikāli'i gdams pa nyams su len tshul byin rlabs nyer 'jug.* In Gsung 'bum blo bzang bstan pa rab rgyas. Vol. 2, pp. 7–12. Rong bo Dgon Chen, Quinghai: 1990–1999. BDRC W28897.

Marpa Chökyi Lodrö (Mar pa Chos kyi blo grus). *Esoteric Instructions on Blending. bSre ba'i man ngag.* In Mar pa'i bKa' 'bum, vol. 2 (*kha*). In *'Bri gung bka' brgyud chos mdzod chen mo*. Vol. 6, ff. 131a–136b. Lhasa, 2004. BDRC W00J501203.

Mokchokpa et al. *Brief Life Story of Lama Khyungpo Naljor. bLa ma khyung po rnal 'byor gyi rnam thar zur tsam.* In *Golden Rosary of Shangpa Biographies*. In *Shangpa Texts*. Vol. 1, pp. 59–143. Sonada, India: Samdrup Darje Ling Monastery, n.d.

Mokchokpa Kunga Ö (rMog lcog pa Kun dga' 'od). *Life Story of Precious Guru Mokchokpa. bLa ma rin po che rmog lcog pa'i rnam par thar pa.* In *Shangpa Texts*. Vol. 1, pp. 145–222.

Mokchokpa Rinchen Tsöndru (rMog lcog pa Rin chen brtson 'gros). *Jeweled Light Garland by the Incomparable Rinchen Tsöndru. Rin po che 'od kyi phreng ba mnyam med rin chen brtson 'grus mdzad.* In *Shangpa Texts*. Vol. 8, pp. 275–310.

———. *Meaningful Summary of Severing Excess. 'Byams gcod kyi bsdus don yod.* In *Shangpa Texts*. Vol. 8, pp. 722–23.

Ngawang Chödrak (Ngag dbang chos grags). *Blessings for the Secret Sādhana Trilogy of Glorious Shangpa Kagyu. dPal ldan shangs pa bka' brgyud pa'i gsang sgrub skor gsum gyi byin rlabs.* In *Volume of Miscellaneous Texts of Shangpa Kagyu and Others* (*Shangs pa bka' brgyud sogs pa'i sna tshogs glegs bam*). Vol. 1, pp. 121–32. BDRC W1KG4284.

Niguma. *Channel Chakras of One's Body. Svaśarīranāḍīcakra. Rang lus rtsa yi 'khor lo.* P. rgyud 'grel, *pu*, f. 201 (P 4649). Also in *Shangpa Texts* as *Extending and Contracting the Channels. rTsa bkyang bskum.* Vol. 8, pp. 745–46.

———. *Esoteric Instructions on Opening the Channel. rTsa kha 'byed pa'i man ngag. Nāḍīvikāsanopadeśa.* Peking Tengyur, rgyud 'grel, *pu*, f. 199 (4645). Also in *Shangpa Texts*. Vol. 8, pp. 746–47.

———. *Immortal Mind Root Text. Śrī Amāramahājñānanāma. Sems 'chi med kyi rtsa ba.* Peking Tengyur, rgyud 'grel, *pu*, ff. 324–26. *DNZ*. Vol. 11, pp. 24–28. *Shangpa Texts*. Vol. 6, pp. 224–31.

———. *Meditation on Channels, Winds, and Such. Nāḍyādibhāvanā. rTsa rlung la sogs sgom pa.* Peking Tengyur, rgyud 'grel, *pu*, f. 199 (4646). Also in *Shangpa Texts*. Vol. 8, pp. 742–44.

———. *Meditation on Inner Heat in the Path of Methods. Upāyamārgacaṇḍālikābhāvanā. Thabs lam gtum mo sgom pa.* Peking Tengyur, rgyud 'grel, *pu*, f. 199–200 (4647). Also in *Shangpa Texts*, vol. 8, pp. 747–49.

———. *Stages in the Path of Illusion. Māyādhanakrama. sGyu ma lam gyi rim pa.* Peking Tengyur, rgyud 'grel, *pu*, ff 165a–176a (4643). Also in *Shangpa Texts*. Vol. 6, pp. 705–33.

———. *Vajra Lines of the Six Dharmas of Niguma. Ye shes mkha' 'gro ma'i chos drug rdo rje'i tshig rkang.* Peking Tengyur, rgyud, *pu*, ff. 142b–144a (4633). *DNZ*. Vol. 11, pp. 2–6; *Shangpa Texts*. Vol. 6, pp. 161–73. Also in *Collected Works of Lochen Gyurme Dechen*. Vol. 2, pp. 439–448.

———. *Yoga of Meditation in the Path of Methods. Upāyamārgabhāvavāyoga. Thabs lam sgom pa'i rnal 'byor.* Peking Tengyur, rgyud 'grel, *pu*, f. 200 (4646). Also in *Shangpa Texts*. Vol. 8, pp. 749–52.

Old Texts at Palpung Monastery. dPal yul dgon du bzhugs pa'i dpe rnying. 63 vols. s.l.: s.n., n.d. BDRC W4PD294.

Rāhulagupta. *Two Histories of the Four Deities. Lha bzhi'i lo rgyus gnyis.* In *Shangpa Texts*. Vol. 9, pp. 687–710.

Samdingpa Zhönu Drup (bSam dings pa gZhon nu grub). *Guidance on Nigu's Six Dharmas. Ni gu chos drug gi khrid.* In *Shangpa Texts*. Vol. 7, pp. 545–59.

Sangye Nyentön Chökyi Sherap (Sangs rgyas gnyan ston Chos kyi shes rab). *Kyergangpa's Sealed Life Story. sKyer sgang pa'i rnam thar bka' rgya ma.* In *Shangpa Texts*. Vol. 1, pp. 275–95.

———. *Life Story of Lama Rigongpa. bLa ma ri gong pa'i rnam par thar pa.* In *Shangpa Texts*. Vol. 1, pp. 297–333.

Sangye Tönpa Tsöndru Senge (Sangs rgyas ston pa brTson 'brus seng ge) Also known as Chöje Tönpa. *Collection of Necessary Oral Advice on Niguma's Six Dharmas. Ni gu chos drug gi zhal shes dgos rnams kyis lhan thabs.* In *Shangpa Texts*. Vol. 8, pp. 311–68.

———. *Inner Life Story of Sangye Tönpa. Sangs rgyas ston pa'i rnam thar.* In *Shangpa Texts*. Vol. 1, pp. 393–400.

———. *Ocean of Experiential Qualities. Nyams myong yon tan rgya mtsho.* In *Shangpa Dharma Cycle Etcetera: Mahāmudrā Empowerment Permission; Five-Deity Cakrasaṃvara Direct Realization and Offerings; Hevajra Empowerment Conferral.* Text #29. BDRC W8LS32723.

———. *Red Khecarī's Sādhana, Empowerment Ritual, and Hand Offering or Defilement Removal. mKha' spyod dmar mo'i sgrub thabs dbang mchog phyag mchod dam grib bsel ba.* In *Shangpa Texts*. Vol. 8, pp. 407–41, and vol. 9, pp. 761–73.

———. *Stainless Light Garland of the Path. Lam dri med 'od phreng.* In *Shangpa Dharma Cycle Etcetera.* Text #27, titled *Lam mchog dri ma med pa*, but identified as *Lam dri med 'od phreng* in the colophon. BDRC W8LS32723.

———. *Sun That Illuminates the Practice of the Thirty-Two Yogic Exercises of Attaining Immortality. 'Chi med grub pa'i 'khrul 'khor sum cu rtsa gnyis kyi lag len gsal byed nyi ma.* In *Shangpa Texts*. Vol. 7, pp. 267–97. Signed as Vīryasiṃha.

Shangpa Dharma Cycle Etcetera: Mahāmudrā Empowerment Permission; Five-Deity Cakrasaṃvara Direct Realization and Offerings; Hevajra Empowerment Conferral. Phag rgya chen po'i dbang bka' bde mchog lha lnga'i mngon rtogs dang mchod phreng kyai rdor dbang bskur shangs pa'i chos skor sogs. 1 vol. BDRC W8LS32723.

Shangpa Texts / Indian Source Texts of the Five Dharma Cycles of Glorious Shangpa. dPal ldan shangs pa'i chos skor rnam lnga'i rgya gzhung. Edited by Karma Rangjung Kunkhyab (Kalu Rinpoche, based on the Palpung edition). 11 vols. Sonada, India: Samdrup Darje Ling Monastery, 199?. Reprinted by Lama Tsengyur Rinpoche. Vancouver: Kagyu Kunkhyab Chuling, 1982.

Tangtong Gyalpo (Thang stong rgyal po). *Gateway to the Source of All Qualities. [Ni gu chos drug gi] 'jug sgo yon tan kun 'byung.* In *Supplemental Texts to the Collected Works of Thang-stong-rgyal po*, pp. 1–67.

———. *Supplemental Texts to the Collected Works of Thaṅ-stoṅ-rgyal-po Series, Volume 1. Grub chen thang stong bka' 'bum gyi rgyab chos ni gu chos drug pod dang pa.* Thimphu: Royal Government of Bhutan Publishing House (dPal ldan 'brug gzhung dpe mdzod khang), 1984.

———. *White Khecarī and the Threefold Blessing. mKha' spyod dkar mo dang sum phrugs kyi byin rlabs.* In *Supplemental Texts to the Collected Works of Thaṅ-stoṅ-rgyal-po*, pp. 145–55.

Tāranātha. *Brief Account of the Origins of the Dharma Cycle of the Six-Armed Awareness Protector. Ye shes kyi mgon po phyag drug pa'i chos skor gyi byung tshul mdo tsam brjod pa.* In *Tāranātha's Collected Works.* Vol. 21, pp. 875–99. Also in *Shangpa Texts.* Vol. 1, pp. 717–49.

———. *Clarifying the Profound Meaning: A Complete Explanation of the Five-Deity Cakrasaṃvara Sādhana in the Shangpa Tradition. Shangs lugs bde mchog lha lnga'i sgrub thabs kyi rnam par bshad pa zab don gsal byed.* In *DNZ.* Vol. 11, pp. 297–331. In *Shangpa Texts.* Vol. 3, pp. 99–161.

———. *Clearing Up the Darkness of Mind. rGyal ba'i bstan pa rin po che spyi'i rnam bzhag las 'phros pa'i dpal ldan shangs pa'i chos skor gyi 'byung khung yid kyi mun sel pa.* In *Tāranātha's Collected Works.* Dzamtang edition. Vol. 17, pp. 417–535.

———. *Entrance to Good Fortune: A Guru Offering Ritual. bLa ma mchod pa'i cho ga skal pa bzang po'i 'jug ngogs.* In *Tāranātha's Collected Works.* Dzamtang edition. Vol. 7, pp. 5–41.

———. *Essence of Ambrosia: A Guidance Manual of Instructions for the Three Types of Person. sKyes bu gsum gyi man ngag gi khrid yig bdud rtsi'i nying khu.* In *DNZ.* Vol. 3, pp. 181–273.

———. *The Essence of the Last Four of the Golden Dharmas Taken from Tāranātha's Teachings. gSer chos phyi ma bzhi'i snying po rje btsun tā ra nā tha'i gsung las byung ba'o.* In *Shangpa Texts.* Vol. 7, pp. 109–24.

———. *Five-Deity Cakrasaṃvara Mandala Ritual in the Tradition of Niguma. Ni gu lugs kyi bde mchog lha lnga'i dkyil chog.* In *DNZ.* Vol. 11, pp. 255–85. In *Shangpa Texts.* Vol. 3, pp. 21–79. Also in *Tāranātha's Collected Works*, as *Ni gu lugs kyi bde mchog lha lnga'i dbang chog.* Vol. 12, pp. 769–808.

———. *Five Tantras' Deities Lineage Supplication in the Shangpa Tradition. Shangs lugs rgyud sde lnga'i brgyud pa'i gsol 'debs*. In *DNZ*. Vol. 11, pp. 62–64. In *Shangpa Texts*. Vol. 5, pp. 439–44.

———. *Guru Offering: Spreading Happiness and Well-Being. bLa ma mchod pa bde legs rab rgyas*. In *Tāranātha's Collected Works*. Dzamtang edition. Vol. 14, pp. 279–96.

———. *Mine of Jewels: Sādhanas of an Ocean of Yidams. Yi dam rgya mtsho'i sgrub thabs rin chen 'byung gnas*. In *Tāranātha's Collected Works*. Dzamtang edition. Vol. 15, pp. 3–744.

———. *Mine of Jewels [2]: Sādhanas of an Ocean of Yidams Taught in the Four Tantra Classes. rGyud sde bzhi las gsungs pa'i yi dam rgya mtsho'i sgrub thabs rin chen 'byung gnas*. In *Tāranātha's Collected Works*. Dzamtang edition. Vol. 15, pp. 1141–1238.

———. *Naiguma's Supplication: The Syllable A, Source of Phenomena. Nai gus brgyud 'debs a yig chos 'byung ma*. In *Tāranātha's Collected Works*. Dzamtang edition. Vol. 20, pp. 595–604.

———. *The Practice of Past Gurus: Esoteric Instructions on the Principal Five Deities of the Five Tantras. rGyud sde lnga'i lha lnga gtso bor bsdus pa'i man ngag bla ma gong ma'i phyag len*. In *DNZ*. Vol. 11, pp. 333–39. In *Shangpa Texts*. Vol. 4, pp. 115–31.

———. *Rainfall of Spiritual Power Elixir: Sources of the Dharma Cycle of Glorious Six-Armed Awareness Protector. dPal ye shes kyi mgon po phyag drug pa'i chos skor byung tshul dngos grub bdud rtsi'i char 'bebs*. In *Shangpa Texts*. Vol. 1, pp. 717–49.

———. *Songs of the Oral Instructions of Venerable Tāranātha. rJe btsun tā ra nā tha'i zhal gdams mgur 'bum gyi skor*. In *Tāranātha's Collected Works*. Dzamtang edition. Vol. 1, pp. 723–997.

———. *Subduing All Haughty Ones: An Activity Manual to Engage Hāyagriva, the Glorious King of Wrath. dPal khro bo'i rgyal po rta mchog rol pa'i las byang dregs pa kun 'dul*. In *Tāranātha's Collected Works*. Dzamtang edition. Vol. 13, pp. 249–21.

———. *Supplement to the Lineage Stories of One Hundred Guides. Khrid brgya'i brgyud pa'i lo rgyus kha skong*. In *DNZ*. Vol. 18, pp. 99–118.

———. *Tāranātha's Collected Works. rJe btsun Tā-ra-nā-tha'i gsung 'bum*. jonangfoundation.org/sites/default/files/catalogue-taranatha-dzamthang.pdf.

Tashi Chöpel (bKra shis chos 'phel). *Record of Teachings Received* ("*Record of How Jamgön Kongtrul Yönten Gyatso Received the Precious Teachings of Sutra, Tantra, and Classical Studies with Their Source Lineages*"). *'Jam mgon kong sprul yon tan rgya mtshos dam pa'i chos rin po che mdo sngags rig gnas dang bcas pa ji ltar thos shing de dag gang las brgyud pa'i yi ge dgos 'dod kun 'byung nor bu'i bang mdzod*. Beijing: Mi rigs dpe skrun khang, 2008.

Tenpai Nyima (bsTan pa'i nyi ma). *The Clear Meaning of the Jewel Mine. Yi dam rgya mthso'i sgrub thabs rin chen 'byung gnas kyi lhan thabs rin 'byung don gsal*. 2 vols. New Delhi: International Academy of Indian Culture, 1974.

Tsongkhapa, Je (rJe Tsong kha pa bLo bzang grags pa). *Endowed with Threefold Confidence: Guided Stages by Means of the Profound Path of Nāropa's Six Dharmas.*

Zab lam na ro'i chos drug gi sgo nas 'khrid pa'i rim pa yid ches gsum ldan. In *Collected Works of Rje Tsoṅ Kha pa Blo bzaṅ Grags pa*. Vol. 9 (*ta*). New Delhi: Ngawang Gelek Demo, 1975.

———. *Vital Guide on the Five Stages Complete in One Sitting of the Sovereign Tantra Guhyasamāja. rGyud kyi rgyal po dpal gsang ba 'dus pa'i rdzogs rim lnga gdan rdzogs kyi dmar khrid*. In *Collected Works of Rje Tsoṅ Kha pa Blo bzaṅ Grags pa*. Vol. 8, pp. 201–315. New Delhi: Ngawang Gelek Demo, 1975.

Virūpa. *Attaining Immortality of the Body Root Text. Amārasiddhimūla. 'Chi med grub pa zhes bya ba'i rtsa ba / 'Bras bu lus 'chi med kyi rtsa ba*. In *DNZ*. Vol. 11, pp. 19–24. In *Shangpa Texts*. Vol. 6, pp. 210–25. Also as *Amṛtasiddhimūla. bDud rtsi grub pa'i rtsa ba* in CT rgyud, vol. 26, pp. 1333–39.

5. Translations and Other Works in English

Batchelor, Stephen. *The Tibet Guide*. London: Wisdom, 1987.

Brunnhölzl, Karl. *Straight from the Heart: Buddhist Pith Instructions*. Ithaca, NY: Snow Lion, 2007.

Callahan, Elizabeth M., trans. "The Two-Part Hevajra Tantra" (*brtags gnyis*). Selected chapters, with commentary from *Revealing the Indestructible Vajra Secrets* by Jamgön Kongtrul Lodrö Taye. Unpublished manuscript, 2012.

Chang, Garma C. C., trans. *The Hundred Thousand Songs of Milarepa*. 2 vols. New Hyde Park, NY: University Books, 1962.

Chattopadhyaya, Alaka, and Lama Chinpa, trans. *Tāranātha's History of Buddhism in India*. Delhi: Motilal Banarsidass, 1970/1990.

Deroche, Marc-Henri. "'Phreng po gter ston Shes rab 'od zer (1518–1584) on the Eight Lineages of Attainment: Research on a Ris med Paradigm." In *Contemporary Visions in Tibetan Studies. Proceedings of the First International Seminar of Young Tibetologists*, 319–42. Chicago: Serindia, 2009.

English, Elizabeth. *Vajrayoginī: Her Visualizations, Rituals, and Forms*. Boston: Wisdom, 2002.

Gray, David B. *The Cakrasaṃvara Tantra (The Discourse of Śrī Heruka)*. New York: American Institute of Buddhist Studies at Columbia University in New York and Columbia University's Center for Buddhist Studies and Tibet House US, 2007.

Gyatso, Janet. "Genre, Authorship, and Transmission in Visionary Buddhism: The Literary Traditions of Thang-stong rGyalpo." In *Tibetan Buddhism: Reason and Revelation*, edited by Steven D. Goodman and Ronald M. Davidson, 5–106. Albany: State University of New York Press, 1992.

———. "The Literary Traditions of Thang-stong rGyalpo: A Study of Visionary Buddhism in Tibet." PhD diss., University of California at Berkeley, 1981.

Harding, Sarah, trans. *Four Tibetan Lineages: Core Teachings of Pacification, Severance, Shangpa Kagyü, and Bodongpa*. Institute of Tibetan Classics. Boston: Wisdom, 2021.

———. *Machik's Complete Explanation: Clarifying the Meaning of Chöd.* Boston: Snow Lion, 2013.

———. *Niguma, Lady of Illusion.* Ithaca, NY: Snow Lion, 2013.

Jackson, Roger R. *Tantric Treasures: Three Collections of Mystical Verse from Buddhist India.* New York: Oxford University Press, 2004.

Jamgön Kongtrul Lodrö Taye. *The Autobiography of Jamgön Kongtrul: A Gem of Many Colors.* Translated by Richard Barron. Ithaca, NY: Snow Lion, 2003.

———. *The Catalog of The Treasury of Precious Instructions.* Translated by Richard Barron (Chökyi Nyima). New York: Tsadra Foundation, 2013.

———. *Creation and Completion: Essential Points of Tantric Meditation.* Translated by Sarah Harding. Boston: Wisdom, 2002.

———. *The Life of Jamyang Khyentse Wangpo.* Translated by Matthew Akester. New Delhi: Shechen Publications, 2012.

———. *The Treasury of Knowledge, Books 2–4: Buddhism's Journey to Tibet.* Translated by the Kalu Rinpoché Translation Group (Ngawang Zangpo). Ithaca, NY: Snow Lion, 2010.

———. *The Treasury of Knowledge, Book 6, Parts 1 and 2: Indo-Tibetan Classical Learning and Buddhist Phenomenology.* Translated by the Kalu Rinpoché Translation Group (Gyurme Dorje). Boston: Snow Lion, 2012.

———. *The Treasury of Knowledge, Book 6, Part 4: Systems of Buddhist Tantra.* Translated by the Kalu Rinpoché Translation Group (Elio Guarisco and Ingrid McLeod). Ithaca, NY: Snow Lion, 2005.

———. *The Treasury of Knowledge, Book 8, Part 3: The Elements of Tantric Practice.* Translated by the Kalu Rinpoché Translation Group (Elio Guarisco and Ingrid McLeod). Ithaca, NY: Snow Lion, 2008.

———. *The Treasury of Knowledge, Book 8, Part 4: Esoteric Instructions.* Translated by the Kalu Rinpoché Translation Group (Sarah Harding). Ithaca, NY: Snow Lion, 2007.

Jamgön Kongtrul Lodrö Taye, comp. *The Treasury of Precious Instructions: Essential Teachings of the Eight Practice Lineages of Tibet. Volume 11: Shangpa Kagyu.* Translated by Sarah Harding. Boulder: Snow Lion, 2022.

———. *The Treasury of Precious Instructions: Essential Teachings of the Eight Practice Lineages of Tibet. Volume 13: Zhije.* Translated by Sarah Harding. Boulder: Snow Lion, 2019.

———. *The Treasury of Precious Instructions: Essential Teachings of the Eight Practice Lineages of Tibet. Volume 14: Chöd.* Translated by Sarah Harding. Boulder: Snow Lion, 2016.

———. *The Treasury of Precious Instructions: Essential Teachings of the Eight Practice Lineages of Tibet. Volume 18: Jonang.* Translated by Gyurme Dorje. Boulder: Snow Lion, 2020.

Jo Nang Tāranātha. *The Seven Instruction Lineages.* Translated and edited by David Templeman. Dharamsala: Library of Tibetan Works and Archives, 1983/1990.

Kalu Rinpoche. *Luminous Mind: The Way of the Buddha*. Boston: Wisdom, 1997.

Kapstein, Matthew T. "Chronological Conundrums in the Life of Khyung po rnal 'byor: Hagiography and Historical Time." *Journal of the International Association of Tibetan Studies* 1 (October 2005): pp. 1–14. http://www.thlib.org?tid=T1221

———. "The Illusion of Spiritual Progress: Remarks on Indo-Tibetan Buddhist Soteriology." In *Paths to Liberation: The Mārga and Its Transformations in Buddhist Thought*, edited by Robert E. Buswell Jr. and Robert M Gimello, pp. 193–224. Honolulu: University of Hawaii Press, 1992.

Lopez, Donald S., Jr., and Cyrus Stearns. "A Report on Religious Activity in Central Tibet, October, 1984." *Journal of the International Association of Buddhist Studies* 9, no. 2 (1986): pp. 101–7.

Martin, Dan. *Tibskrit: A Bibliography of Tibetan Philology*. Edited by Alexander Cherniak. Jerusalem, 2019. Available widely in electronic version only.

Mathes, Klaus-Dieter. *Maitrīpa: India's Yogi of Nondual Bliss*. Boulder: Shambhala, 2021.

Nebesky-Wojkowitz, René de. *Oracles and Demons of Tibet: The Cult and Iconography of the Tibetan Protective Deities*. The Hague: Mouton, 1956.

Rangjung Dorje. *The Profound Inner Principles*. Translated by Elizabeth M. Callahan. Boston: Snow Lion, 2014.

Riggs, Nicole. *Like an Illusion: Lives of the Shangpa Masters*. Eugene, OR: Dharma Cloud, 2001.

Ringu Tulku. *The Ri-me Philosophy of Jamgön Kongtrul the Great: A Study of the Buddhist Lineages of Tibet*. Edited by Ann Helm. Boston: Shambhala, 2006.

Roberts, Peter Alan. *Mahāmudrā and Related Instructions: Core Teachings of the Kagyü Schools*. Library of Tibetan Classics, edited by Thubten Jinpa, vol. 5. Boston: Wisdom, 2011.

Roerich, George N., trans. *The Blue Annals*. 2nd ed. Delhi: Motilal Banarsidass, 1976/1988.

Schaeffer, Kurtis R. *Dreaming the Great Brahmin: Tibetan Traditions of the Poet-Saint Saraha*. New York: Oxford University Press, 2005.

Smith, E. Gene. *Among Tibetan Texts: History and Literature of the Himalayan Plateau*. Boston: Wisdom, 2001.

Stearns, Cyrus. *King of the Empty Plain: The Tibetan Iron-Bridge Builder Tangtong Gyalpo*. Ithaca, NY: Snow Lion, 2007.

———. *Luminous Lives: The Story of the Early Masters of the Lam 'Bras Tradition in Tibet*. Boston: Wisdom, 2001.

———. *Song of the Road: The Poetic Travel Journal of Tsarchen Losal Gyatso*. Boston: Wisdom, 2012.

———. "Tāranātha." In *Treasury of Lives*. August, 2008. https://treasuryoflives.org/biographies/view/Taranata/2712.

Taranatha. *Essence of Ambrosia: A Guide to Buddhist Contemplations*. Translated by Willa Baker. Dharamsala: Library of Tibetan Works and Archives, 2005.

Tsong Khapa Losang Drakpa. *Brilliant Illumination of the Lamp of the Five Stages:*

Practical Instructions in the King of Tantras, The Glorious Esoteric Community. Translated by Robert A. F. Thurman. New York: American Institute of Buddhist Studies, 2011.

Tsuda, Shiníchi, ed. and trans. *The Saṃvarodaya Tantra, Selected Chapters.* Tokyo: Hokuseido Press, 1974.

van Schaik, Sam. *Tibet: A History.* New Haven, CT: Yale University Press, 2011.

Willson, Martin, and Martin Brauen, trans. and eds. *Deities of Tibetan Buddhism: The Zürich Paintings of the Icons Worthwhile to See* (*Bris sku mthoṅ ba don ldan*). Boston: Wisdom, 2000.

Zangpo, Ngawang, trans. *Timeless Rapture: Inspired Verse of the Shangpa Masters.* Ithaca, NY: Snow Lion, 2003.

Index